Cages of Reason

BERNARD S. SILBERMAN

Cages of Reason

THE RISE OF THE RATIONAL STATE IN FRANCE, JAPAN, THE UNITED STATES, AND GREAT BRITAIN

THE UNIVERSITY OF CHICAGO PRESS
CHICAGO AND LONDON

Bernard S. Silberman is professor of political science and chair of the Department of Political Science at the University of Chicago.

The University of Chicago Press, Chicago 60637
The University of Chicago Press, Ltd., London
© 1993 by The University of Chicago
All rights reserved. Published 1993
Printed in the United States of America

02 01 00 99 98 97 96 95 94 93   5 4 3 2 1

ISBN (cloth): 0–226–75736–6
ISBN (paper): 0–226–75737–4

Library of Congress Cataloging-in-Publication Data
Silberman, Bernard S., 1930–
    Cages of reason: The rise of the rational state in France, Japan, the United States, and Great Britain/Bernard S. Silberman.
        p. cm.
    Includes bibliographical references and index.
    1. Public administration—History. 2. Bureaucracy—History.
3. Rationalism—History. 4. Public administration—United States—History. 5. Public administration—Europe—History. 6. Public administration—Japan—History. I. Title.
JF1341.S55 1993
351′.0009—dc20   92–31653
                                                                              CIP

⊗ The paper used in this publication meets the minimum requirements
of the American National Standard for Information Sciences—Permanence
of Paper for Printed Library Materials, ANSI Z39.48–1984.

This book is dedicated to my beloved wife
Pauline Lea Lipschitz Silberman

Contents

Preface

This work attempts to provide explanations for several blank spaces in the study of comparative administration and bureaucratic organization. One of the major problems for students of comparative public administration and comparative bureaucracy has been the inability to provide a general explanation for the absence of convergence in state bureaucratic rationalization. Max Weber clearly felt that the administration of all modern nation-states was proceeding toward a generally similar institutional structure characterized by the norms and values of rationality and legal authority. Within the terms of Weber's definition, rationality and legal authority resulted everywhere in the emergence of similar organizational characteristics—the famous formula which included specialization, differentiation, achievement, careerism, hierarchy, hierarchical authority, secularism, and nonownership of the means of administration. Weber's expectations with regard to the convergence of bureaucratic structure throughout modern industrial societies, however, have been disappointed.

Nowhere is this more glaringly true than in the United States, where bureaucratic rationalization is usually regarded as having stalled somewhere between feudal patrimonial society and modern legal-rational society.[1] The failure of the American system to follow the continental European or British path of bureaucratic rationalization has been a puzzle for students of public administration. Some form of American exceptionalism has generally been the answer supplied. The problem is finding the variable which produced this exceptional response and explaining how it is part of some more general explanatory structure.

Some degree of puzzlement is also exhibited when the British pattern of rationalization is compared with those of France, Germany, or Japan. While there are some similarities of structure, the differences are far more glaring. In Britain, the senior civil service role was constructed around an

---

1. See, for example, the characterizations of the development of the U.S. national civil bureaucracy in the following: Richard J. Stillman II, *Preface to Public Administration: A Search for Themes and Direction* (New York: St. Martin's Press, [1990] 1991); Stephen Skowronek, *Building a New American State: The Expansion of National Administrative Capacities, 1877–1920* (New York: Cambridge University Press, 1982); Samuel P. Huntington, *Political Order in Changing Societies* (New Haven, CT: Yale University Press, 1968).

educational experience stressing character formation and classical education. Since this training was basic to all of the higher professions—barrister, physician, and clergy—it allowed individuals to forestall final career decisions until leaving university and to learn the substance of their profession through in-service training. The continental pattern was constructed around an elite education culminating in either technical and/or legal training, which was viewed as the basis for only one profession—civil servant. Why then did rationalization seem to take, in contravention to Weber, at least three different courses?

Essentially, I argue in the Introduction that rationalization took only two courses. One of these was characterized by the location of skills, information, and their regulation in the individual per se through the process of professional training. Entrance into the highest levels of state bureaucracies was mediated by this professional educational experience. The educational career successfully excluded a very large proportion of the adult population while securing a relatively homogenous body of eligibles.

The social structure of these eligibles effectively constrained the manner in which the bureaucratic role would be structured. Since individuals had professional training, they would not be forced to pay opportunity costs by foregoing a career in a senior civil service. Consequently, political leaders acting within a set of institutional constraints were forced, I argue, to create a new kind of bureaucratic role. This role emphasized individual control of information and relied on training and commitment to professional ethics to keep individuals from using information on their own behalf. The necessity for providing incentives for those with professional credentials to give up other professional careers produced an organizational structure that stressed individual career tracks, mobility within the bureaucracy, and less emphasis on hierarchy and seniority. The rationality of this role was reflected in the manner in which educational careers were directly related to predictable patterns of life chances. I term this type "professionally oriented rationalization."

The second basic type of rationalization is characterized by organizational control and allocation of information and skills as well as by organizational surveillance and control of information usage. Because of its emphasis on the control of information, the organization creates a "firm-specific" role with organizationally specific or firm-specific skills. Recruitment stresses a relatively uniform educational experience characterized by early commitment to a bureaucratic career. This is partly because early commitment coincides with the desire of political leaders to exclude officials from alternative careers or organizational loyalties.

To make up for the opportunity costs inherent in early commitment to a bureaucratic career, the bureaucratic role stresses the predictability of career through the creation of highly visible career tracks. These career patterns stress seniority, hierarchy, and departmental specialization as the means of exhibiting predictable career paths and rewards. Here rationalization of the role is once again reflected in the direct relationship between educational career and the predictability of occupational career.

But, how do we account for the development of these two patterns of rationalization? What was, or is, the force that generates the process of rationalization? That is, to what problem of state organization was rationalization a response and why did it occur in two forms? Chapter 1 examines the literature on bureaucratic structure and its independent variables in the attempt to find suitable clues. I conclude that the literature is overdetermining in its supply of independent variables. Nevertheless, the literature provides clues when it is reduced to its common themes: uncertainty, bounded rationality, and internalization.

Chapter 2 examines the question of how these basic themes are related to the historical occurrence of state bureaucratic rationalization in the late nineteenth and early twentieth centuries. Here, I ask how these themes might be related to problems of state organization and argue that these three themes are problems raised in state development by the problems of political succession. This leads to the conclusion that rational bureaucratization is a consequence of strategic choices made by those holding political power in environments of greater or lesser uncertainty.

Chapter 3 is devoted to the explication of how the strategies of high uncertainty and low uncertainty with regard to political succession might be conceived to have occurred if political leaders acted within the constraints of bounded rationality. From this deductive exercise, I posit two independent variables—political succession (high uncertainty/low uncertainty) and political leadership accountability as indicated by the nature of leadership organization (social network/party structure). These two variables determine types of rationalization. The predominance of: social networks and high uncertainty produces rationalization dominated by bureaucratic autonomy; social networks and low uncertainty produces bureaucratic consensus; party structure and high uncertainty produces single-party domination; party structure and low uncertainty produces pluralist-party domination. In short, bureaucratic rationalization was, in the immediate sense, primarily a response to persisting political, rather than economic or social, crises or problems. Bureaucratic rationalization was a function of the problems raised by the redefinition of the public and political in the late eighteenth and early nineteenth centuries.

On the basis of these distinctions I select four cases to explicate these types respectively: Japan, Great Britain, France, and the United States. Chapters 4 and 5 deal with France; chapters 6 and 7 with Japan; chapters 8 and 9 with the United States; and chapters 10, 11, and 12 with Great Britain.

This Preface would be sadly incomplete without acknowledging the help provided by a number of institutions and individuals. The Social Science Research Council provided the means for time off at the early stages of this project. The Spencer Foundation provided research funds at a critical time. Most important, the Committee on Japanese Studies has provided research support over a number of years; this project would have had difficulty in reaching completion without their generosity. My colleagues in the Center for East Asian Studies and the Department of Political Science were greatly supportive. My thanks go especially to Harry Harootunian, Chris Ansell, Suzanne Ryan, and Daniel Verdier who read the manuscript and made significant suggestions. Arif Dirlik of Duke University also read the manuscript with his usual critical grace and support. Mark Hansen, Gerald Rosenberg, Daniel Verdier, and Gary Herrigel allowed me to present various chapters to their unsuspecting workshop students. Their criticisms and assessments were extremely helpful. Natalie Silberman-Wainwright and Andrea Silberman need to be thanked for their considerable help in the research at varying times. Throughout much of the work, Suzanne Ryan acted as my research assistant, and her assistance was indispensable. She was unfailingly responsible, helpful, and even-tempered despite my frequent lapses into irascibility. I owe her a great deal and I hope to repay it someday. My wife, Pauline Lea Lipschitz Silberman, stuck it out with me as I agonized my way through the research and writing of this book. It is to my great sorrow that the only visible means of repaying her for her loyalty and support is by dedicating this book to her.

Introduction

The study of bureaucracy has been a central concern of social scientists since Weber first sought to define types of legitimate authority and their organizational concomitants. His work has given birth to an entire industry concerned with examining the patterns of social relations within organizations, especially so-called formal bureaucratic ones, and with the articulation of organizations with each other and their environments. Interestingly enough, however, relatively little interest has been taken in analyzing the sources of bureaucratization; or, to put it more broadly, why complex organizations in the modern period have taken on the form Weber described (Markoff 1975:479–80; Meyer and Brown 1977:365; Meyer 1979; Williamson 1981). This neglect has been especially notable in the study of state bureaucracies (Sheriff 1976b:38–40). The primary emphasis in this area has been on how either central or local bureaucracies and bureaucrats work, with special concern for decision making and makers (Allison 1971; Downs 1967; Lowi 1969, 1978; Heady 1979; Borcherding 1977; Blanc 1971; Crozier 1964; Debbasch 1969; Isomura and Kuronuma 1974; Ide et al. 1974). The question of why bureaucracies take on a particular form has been addressed only in the most general terms or is implicit in historical descriptions (DiMaggio and Powell 1983).

The lack of interest in the question of why state bureaucracies take on particular forms is rather puzzling. The problem is, at least theoretically, if not instrumentally, important for political scientists, sociologists, and economists. In terms of theory, the problem is related to general questions of state formation and organizational change within the state and its political structure. The literature on modern state formation and development appears to view the process of bureaucratization along the lines described by Weber as a central feature of the evolution of the rational state (Tilly 1975:29; Bendix 1964:136–37; Skocpol 1979:47–48, 286; Skocpol 1985:14–18; Poggi 1978:86–116; Huntington 1968:157–58; MIT Study Group 1967:32–33; Ward 1968:7–8; Organski 1965 [1967]; Almond and Powell 1966:36–46; Marx and Engels 1971; Anderson 1979:19–20). Agreement exists that bureaucratization is one of the identifying characteristics of the emergence and development of the modern state. Nevertheless, there have been few attempts to construct an appropriate explanation, on the basis of comparative analysis, of the process by which the rationalization of state bureaucracies was originally institutionalized.

The literature on state development appears to take for granted that ra-

1

tionalization of state authority *must* take on the particular structural characteristics Weber so acutely observed in Western European societies. Hierarchy, hierarchical authority, career, specialization, differentiation, expertise, and contractual possession of office have been viewed as necessary because they seem to constitute the only functionally efficient way of reducing the social and private costs of uncoordinated activities. From this point of view, as societies became more complex the problem of coordination worsened. Bureaucratic or rationalized administration came to be viewed as the response to the high costs of uncoordinated activities. While there is a logical ring to this deduction, there is not much more substance to it than that provided by Weber. We are left with the questions of whether this was in fact the case and, if so, of how bureaucratic organization uniquely meets the demands of uncoordinated activity.

The question, then, of the relationship of the state to the bureaucratic administrative structure is also raised. Clearly no one assumes that the former is the equivalent of the latter—state and administration are not usually seen as synonymous. There is good reason not to make this assumption. Since the end of the eighteenth century, states have acquired seemingly similar rational bureaucratic administrative structures even though they took on different political forms. The resultant paradox has been well and often noted by a broad range of nineteenth- and twentieth-century observers, of whom Tocqueville, Weber, and Durkheim are the best known. On the one hand, the seemingly convergent process of bureaucratization seems to imply that the state is in some way autonomous; else why the ubiquitous nature of rational administration? On the other hand, the differences in political structure seem to suggest that the state is informed and subsumed by society; else how to explain the variety of political forms?

What is striking about the observation of this seeming paradox is the lack of attention paid to the idea of the state as an autonomous organization until quite recently. A considerable body of theory and opinion stresses the illusory nature of the state's autonomy and, therefore, of the paradox as well (Dahl 1956; Huntington 1968; Parsons and Shils 1951:162; Binder, Coleman et al. 1971; Almond, Flanagan, and Mundt 1973; Marx and Engels 1971; Poulantzas 1978; Anderson 1979; Miliband 1969; Therborn 1978). Such arguments are largely functional ones that have not produced much in the way of an empirical base. The argument is that modern society, however defined, requires the rational-legal bureaucratic state and therefore it is assumed to be a reflection of or epiphenomenal to social dynamics. Recently, a number of writers have argued that states, as collective actors in both domestic and international arenas, are autonomous (Skocpol 1979 and 1985; Trimberger 1978; Krasner 1984; Evans, Rueschmeyer, and Skocpol 1985).

These ideas suggest that the organizational characteristics of the state have emergent properties which make it possible for policies to appear which are not the expected consequences of any single interest or class pressure. Rather, policies in this view are seen sometimes, if not always, as functional responses to long-term problems. In this respect, the solutions are beneficial in the long run but not necessarily in the short run. This is the characteristic sometimes described as "rational."

Which view is substantially correct is not clear. But it seems both rather odd and extremely difficult to pursue either argument for very long without examining theoretically and substantively the question of why state organization takes on the form it does despite wide variations in class structure, economic development, and political form from state to state. The question is critical primarily because the question of state autonomy centers precisely on the problem of the institutionalization of bureaucratic organization. How and under what circumstances state bureaucracies take on the characteristics that render them "rational" and thus putatively autonomous—that is, possessing the capacity to make policies and decisions free from constraints which we might normally expect to operate—is thus of central importance in assessing the whole problem of the relation of state to society. Substantively, the problem is important because it bears directly on the formation and implementation of public policy. Clearly, it makes a difference for evaluating public policy outcomes if we have different explanations as to why administrative organization and roles take on a particular form. Suspending disbelief for the moment and assuming, for example, that bureaucratic organization is indeed the "efficient" and "rational" response to political or economic problems provides a structural approach to overcoming the oft-noted gap between stated policy goals and their implementation. This view is likely to lead to attempts to specify the nature of the failure and thereby create the appropriate public or private structure for dealing with the problem. In short, this view tends to assume that the rational norms of efficient organizations will provide efficient responses to implementation problems. Suspending disbelief in another direction, however, and assuming that organizational characteristics are not functional responses to political or economic market failures but responses to individual fears over uncertain futures produces quite different prescriptions. If bureaucrats are committed to organizational roles out of concern for individual and institutional futures, then we can conclude that some policies will never be implemented. Attempts will then be made to reduce the discretion of bureaucrats and to hold them strictly accountable. One view might thus lead to increasing state autonomy while the other to decreasing state autonomy. At the same time, one leads to the increasing bureaucratization of policy-making while the other leads to increasing decentralization.

The Problem: The Nature of Rationalization

By 1920, the institutionalization of rational-legal bureaucracy had become the predominant mode of organizing the authoritative distribution of resources in many states. Weber's observation about the ubiquity of bureaucratic administration was not only a prophecy about the course of state development but also an assertion about secular trends. The nineteenth century had seen every major state transform the means by which public goods and benefits were distributed. In the process, the structures of power were profoundly reshaped. Several things appear to be characteristic of these transformations. First, Weber noted, there was a convergence toward uniformity of organizational characteristics. What he termed "rational-legal" organizational structure seemed everywhere to be organized around the transformation of the administrative *role,* which, in turn, produced structural change. The transformation of two aspects of this role was crucial—the relationship of the individual to the office and the criteria for acquiring, holding, and advancing in office.

The relationship of the individual to the office focused on the question of whether office-holding was a matter of public or private law. Certainly, by the end of the century all the major states had removed office-holding from the domain of private property and private law. Individuals no longer had property rights to offices. The public character of the role was established by removing the officeholder from ownership of the "means of administration" and by creating uniform rules that qualitatively and quantitatively defined the function and discretion of office. The officeholder now became accountable to a set of formal organizational rules that could be observed and regulated rather than to the informal and unregulated rules governing patron-client relations.

This shift in the definition of role immediately created, wherever it occurred, the problem of selection. If the holding of administrative office was not the gift of an individual who conveyed it on the basis of rules which assumed that private and public interest were synonymous, then what mechanism of selection could be put in its place? Furthermore, how would one be assured that such a mechanism would not produce an equally private pursuit of interest? The solution that emerged entailed the utilization of a system of knowledge, the possession of which could be measured. The acquisition of knowledge was established as the basis for appointment to office. Notably, the required knowledge was not necessarily technical or expert in character. Instead, it was the length and nature of the educational career that came to be valued, and tests were devised to measure the degree to which individuals possessed this experience. A corollary of this rule developed: the more exclusive and the higher the cost of the knowledge acquired, the greater the capacity to hold office.

The problems of continuity and succession posed by removing offices from the private sphere were resolved by relating offices to levels of knowledge in an hierarchical manner. This made it possible to move individuals through a series of offices on the basis of some easily observable and measurable criterion. Seniority became the measure for determining knowledge acquired by experience. By extension, seniority then became a standard minimal means for determining a systematic movement through offices. This resolution transformed office-holding into a career.

This metamorphosis of the administrative role produced an organizational structure that was relatively autonomous by virtue of possessing an internal labor market. The administrative structure now possessed a distinct set of rules for allocating both labor and resources. These rules were internal to the organization and thus considerably, if not completely, removed from market forces. Moreover, these rules distanced the official from direct external sources of influence and control. Crucial to the autonomy of this market was that access to it was limited not by private interest but by "objectively" determined merit. The use of objective criteria—examinations and seniority—was seen to reflect the public character of the role. In sum, the rationalization of the administrative role focused on the separation of office-holding from the "ownership" of the means of administration; explicit public rules defining eligibility, recruitment, and advancement in office; and the predictability of career and career status.

The seeming autonomy of the rationalized administrative structures that emerged provides further perplexities. From the end of the eighteenth century on there seems to have been a correlation between the rationalization and autonomy of state administration and the erosion and dissolution of stratified castelike relations of individuals to the state. Equality before the law became singularly characteristic of nineteenth-century regimes, regardless of how this was translated into political power and rights. This seems contradictory. We might expect ideas of equality to produce state administrations that were more, rather than less, accountable to society. That it is a practical and not just a theoretical contradiction is reflected in the problem of integrating the executive and legislative structures to the structure of administration which has been a major focus of political energies since the end of the eighteenth century. At the heart of this problem was the self-conscious transformation of the administrative role from the easily accountable but private, informal patron-client base to the protected but public, contractual administrative role that was, paradoxically, much less accountable in a direct fashion.

This transformation of the administrative role was institutionalized in such a manner in the nineteenth and early twentieth centuries that it has not only endured great political and economic upheavals but has become the basic building block of organizational life. The process of institutionalization enlisted the values of "publicness," or accountability and merit. These values were vested primarily in the institutions of education, law, and lawmaking. As a result, the institutionalization of the "rational" administrative role came to rest on a complex structure of relationships between schools, universities, legal systems, and lawmakers. This body of relationships sustained and continue to sustain the status and legitimacy of the rational bureaucratic role in so interdependent a fashion that failure to continue this support would call into question the legitimacy and social value of these institutions.

Variations in Organizational Rationality

Most perplexing about the transformation of the administrative role, perhaps, is that there appear to be quite different organizational outcomes in this process. Despite the similarities in the definition of the rationalized administrative role as it emerged in the late nineteenth and early twentieth centuries, all bureaucratic roles and organizational structures did not end up alike. Students of comparative public administration have long noted this anomaly (Heady 1979; Chapman 1959; Ridley 1979; Armstrong 1973; Barker 1944; Peters 1978; Crozier 1964; Crozier 1970; Morstein Marx 1957). They have, however, provided very little in the way of convincing arguments as to why a seemingly universal process results in such different forms. In large part, this weakness is the consequence of a failure to provide an adequate set of analytical categories (Heady 1979).

At the heart of this failure to provide an adequate taxonomy of administrative bureaucratic organization is the reliance over the past several decades on Weber's ideal types as the basis for analysis. This arises, I believe, from a basic flaw in the Weberian approach. The flaw arises from the temptation to transform Weber's ideal types of authority—charismatic, traditional, and the legal-rational (Weber 1978, 1:215)—into a continuum with charismatic as a transitional category. This has been produced by taking Weber's laundry-list of characteristics that supposedly typify legal-rational structures and converting them into scalar indices. In this process, the traditional type becomes one anchor of the scale. The logical conclusion of this transformation of categories is that the other end of the scale becomes the most rational and, at the same time, the least traditional.

The resultant categorization of real-world administrative structures turns out to be somewhat odd, to say the least. At one end of the scale are the state administrations most closely approximating the Weberian ideal type:[1] these include France, Germany, Japan, and, to a lesser extent, Italy and Spain (Heady 1979; Morstein Marx 1957). At the other end of the scale are those that closely approach traditional authority and its associated patrimonial organizational structure:[2] these have been identified by various names and acronyms, such as LDC's (less-developed countries) and developing societies (Heady 1979; Riggs 1964). On this scaling system, the United States and Great Britain, for example, seem to fall somewhere in the middle. The inference that one must draw from this evaluation and categorization produces no small difficulties. This placement does violence to our intuitive feeling that these two countries are as well developed as those at the most legal-rational/least-traditional end.

How can we satisfactorily explain the placement of these two countries as somewhere between less-developed countries and Germany, France, or Japan? The obvious correlation and explanation—the extent of the division of labor and its correlation with legal-rational characteristics—doesn't really work very well. First, if there is a strong correlation between the division of labor and organizational rationality, then we could expect the United States and Great Britain to be well up on the scale along with the others. Second, if this is generally the right correlation, then how do we explain that historically, France, Japan, and Germany experienced the institutionalization of rationalized administration at the very early stages of industrialization in their societies? Furthermore, given the developmental experience of France, Japan, and Germany, how do we explain the now irritating fact that whatever rationalization occurred in the United States and Great Britain (and for that matter in Canada, Australia, and Switzerland) did so at quite late stages of industrialization? Any division-of-labor\rationalized-bureaucracy argument cannot explain both sets of developmental experience.

Somewhat similar things might be said regarding an argument stressing the role of increasing general economic complexity and differentiation. It is difficult, however, to think of a division-of-labor argument that would satisfactorily explain the development of the variations in state bureaucratic organization. One might argue, as Weber has done, that capitalism produces

---

1. These characteristics are usually described as follows: hierarchy, hierarchical responsibility, discipline, achievement orientation, the utilization of rules to qualitatively and quantitatively define office, specialization, differentiation, contractual participation, secular fixed compensation and career (see Weber 1978).

2. The patrimonial structure is generally characterized in the following fashion: patronage, status hierarchy, ascriptive orientation, diffusion, custom as the basis of defining office, ownership of the means of administration, randomness in the terms of office (Weber 1978:I, 228–41 and 217–23).

the urge toward convergence in this area of behavior. But, whatever state organizational rationalization took place in the United States and Great Britain did so in a way that seems epiphenomenal to an advanced industrial capitalism. The opposite seems to be the case in France, Japan, and Germany—rationalized capitalism appears to be in many ways epiphenomenal to rationalized state bureaucracy. This suggests that, unless one is prepared to make a vigorous and rigorous argument about the existence of systematically different forms of capitalism and how these have different organizational outcomes, we cannot rely on macrofunctionalist explanations of the variations in bureaucratic organizational development. The problem cannot be solved by lumping the United States', the English, and similar administrative structures with those of Western continental Europe and Japan on a set of scalar indices. Nevertheless, it seems clear that we are right to think of these as dissimilar in structure.

The strong-state/weak-state distinction suggested by Nettl and others (Nettl 1968; Barker 1944) as basic categories that explain the variation in the structure of state bureaucracies does not, upon close examination, help us very much. It is, first of all, a tautology if a "strong state" is one possessing a state administration closely resembling the Weberian legal-rational ideal type. If, however, the strong state is defined as the capacity of a central government to determine policy over the possible or putative resistance of the periphery, then a different objection arises. The argument then is that, historically, we should expect strong states to produce highly rationalized state administrative structures. In this situation, the historical correlation between a strong state and the extent of bureaucratic rationalization and/or centralization does not turn out to be all that great. Witness the strong state in England and the weak state in Japan in the early modern period. On the Weberian legal-rational organizational scale of characteristics, Japan ended with a more rationalized bureaucratic structure than did England at the beginning of the twentieth century, even though they started from quite different levels of "strength."

One result of facing these anomalies has been that some analysts have sought to assign differences in administrative organizational structure to differences in culture, especially political culture (Heady 1979; Morstein Marx 1957; Crozier 1964; Berger 1957; Tsuji 1952; Nakane 1970; Krislov 1974). This approach leads to a difficult position in which neither the extent of the division of labor nor political culture appear to be necessary conditions for the emergence and shaping of rational bureaucratic organization. In the latter case, even if we suspend disbelief about the ability to define political culture and the warrants for its underlying assumptions of isomorphism, we are still faced with the problem of how to explain that such widely differing societies as Japan, France, and Germany end up possessing similar state admin istrative structures. The problem becomes even more difficult when we note that Spain, Italy, Norway, and Denmark, for example, have state administrative organizations and structures that resemble those of France, Japan, and Germany far more than they do those of the United States and Great Britain. The idea that these societies share or shared a sufficient number of cultural constructs so that the process of political development could be shaped by isomorphic transference from social structure in such a way so as to produce similar outcomes places considerable strain on our credulity.

One might argue that political culture is in good part the inheritance of history. Institutions get created and, for a variety of reasons, get to be sufficiently valued that they persist even though social values and behavior change. Thus, some behaviors seem at odds with others, but both are sufficiently valued that interested groups make strenuous efforts to explain away or legitimize such anomalies. In this way, it might well be argued that in Japan, to take one case, there was a proto-legal-rational bureaucratic organization in existence prior to the modern period. This proto-bureaucratic organization and its values came to be valued so that even in the absence of a complex division of labor it persisted and enabled the emergence of a fully rationalized structure prior to an advanced division of labor (Najita 1974:16–42).

The major problem with such proto-bureaucratic explanations is that the notion of bureaucratic legacy is derived primarily from chronological sequence rather than from an argument that spells out the dynamics of how proto- moves to mature rationalization. Such arguments commit the scalar fallacy. As we move toward the low end of the continuum of rationalization, there are points at which it is possible to say that they are proto-rational. Reading backward along the Weberian scalar indices is, however, not an explanation but an argument about the present being the function of the past. Such a view leads to infinite regression with no explanation in sight as to what fuels the drive toward rationalization.

The problem of categorization can be resolved to a large extent if we view the Weberian characteristics not as a series of scalar indices of structure but rather as a description or definition of role characteristics.[3] The question then is no longer whether an administrative structure is more or less rational

3. This seems to be what Weber had in mind with his notion of ideal type. It does not seem to have been meant to provide scalar structural characteristics: "For purposes of the causal *imputation* of empirical events, we need the rational, empirical-technical and logical constructions, which help us to answer the question as to what *a behavior pattern or thought pattern (e.g., a philosophical system)* [my emphasis added] would be like if it possessed completely rational, empirical and logical 'correctness' and 'consistency.' From the logical viewpoint, the construction of such a rationally 'correct utopia' or 'ideal' is, however, only one of the various forms of the 'ideal-type'—as I have called such logical constructs" (Weber 1949:42).

but whether an essential constellation of role characteristics is present. This allows us to ask whether or not there are different ways of arriving at this constellation of role characteristics described as "rational" (Stinchcombe 1959; Meyer 1968; Child 1973a). This focuses attention on the following aspects: the quantified and qualified definitions of eligibility, recruitment, appointment, promotion, career, and discretion, primarily of upper-level civil servants. Indeed, the literature on organizations, especially state administrative organizations, suggests there are two basic ways the bureaucratic role may be organized. Despite the particular historical forms that state bureaucratization has taken, at least two varieties of role systems govern the form and structure of the rationalized administrative organization.

① Organizational Orientation

This pattern is characterized by the presence of rules governing the criteria for higher offices that stress entry into the organizational career prior to appointment to office. In this pattern, early commitment to the bureaucratic role is critical. The high value placed on early commitment by the individual is reflected in the establishment of severe restrictions on eligibility and recruitment. These take the form of limiting eligibility to those who have passed through highly specific courses of university training (such as, and usually, law); and/or attended specific schools designed to train upper-level civil servants; and/or served in some form of apprenticeship program before being appointed to office. Whatever the particular form of the requirement, the general result is that individuals are asked to forego other alternatives and give themselves over to the idea of a bureaucratic career relatively early in their educational careers. As Armstrong has acutely noted:

Future European elite administrators (even, as we shall see, in the U.S.S.R.) almost invariably become aware of their career prospects at least a few years in advance. In fact, . . . the higher educational experience of most young men who eventually enter the administrative elites is structured to create awareness. The Oxbridge experience is least structured, for at graduation a young man is just as well equipped to continue toward any other elite profession as to enter the Administrative Class. (Armstrong 1973:201)

Such early commitment requires incentives, since other career possibilities become closed off. These incentives take the form of career predictability—or reducing uncertainty about one's future. There are two aspects to this predictability: one is a more general concern, and the other relates to specific personal status. The former takes the shape of limiting entry into higher office only to those who have made the prescribed early commitment.

Appointment to this level of office by other means, such as promotion from lower ranks or lateral entry from another organization, is rare. Early commitment assures the individual of eligibility for a high-status office. The aspect related to personal status takes the form of highly predictable patterns of promotion, usually based on seniority. This provides a minimal assurance of career advancement. In combination, these two status incentives ensure eligibility for high office and, if one is appointed, promotion to a minimally high level of office within the upper levels of the civil service.

Incentive systems of this kind have produced, or are at least highly correlated with, significant consequences for the organization of roles. Departmental specialization is one major outcome. Movement across ministries is likely to be viewed with disfavor by both superiors and subordinates since it introduces a discordant note of career unpredictability. Furthermore, knowledge acquired in one department or ministry is not always easily transferable. Nor is a transfer with promotion easily translated into advancement by its recipient and his or her new colleagues. New superiors must now expand or reorganize their structures of advancement. Equals or subordinates are uneasy about how to integrate the newcomer and uncertain as to how his or her presence affects the patterns of promotion—that is, *their* expectations.

This stress on hierarchy as predictability is also evident in personal terms. Monopoly or near monopoly of higher offices by those who committed themselves to the bureaucratic role while still pursuing their education produces a distinct segment of the administrative organization and provides predictable boundaries that cannot be crossed. This produces a condition in which the entry level is highly uniform. Individuals here possess pretty much the same skills and experience. Without some highly visible means of predicting early career movement, incentives to give up other alternatives would have to be relatively high. This appears to be resolved by resorting to seniority to sustain the career structure and to predictability as an incentive. Because its variability is based on nonevaluative grounds, seniority provides predictability without negative overtones and consequences for later promotion. Distinctions in rank, authority, and status in the early career are thus seen as the products of impersonal, fortuitous conditions. Early commitment and its associated incentive structure thus produces a homogeneous corps of upper-level administrators whose careers are highly predictable and offer high rewards for early career commitment. The specification of the career role is, or appears to be, very consciously dominated by the organization.

Restricted entry into the highest offices, high organizational boundaries formed by early commitment, departmental specialization, and career structure all contribute to the definition of the rational bureaucratic role as one in which organizational commitment is crucial and the reward for this commitment is high levels of predictability about status and career. When such restrictions on entry, appointment, and promotion exist, the organization has considerable capacity to resist outside intervention. Its lack of permeability renders it difficult to manipulate. The autonomy this condition implies makes the higher civil servant an admired figure. To be called a bureaucrat in these systems is no insult. Major examples of this type are: Japan,[4] France,[5] Germany,[6] Spain,[7] Italy,[8] and the Soviet Union.[9]

2 . Professional Orientation

This mode is characterized by the rule that professional or preprofessional training (not necessarily directly related to assuming bureaucratic roles) is the primary criterion for holding higher administrative office.[10] Rather than orientation toward organizational roles and norms, the assumption of the professional role and its accompanying status is considered sufficient and, indeed, superior in this mode of administrative organization. The professionally oriented bureaucratic role stresses the acquisition of a body of knowledge and techniques by the individual. This expertise is accompanied by a public service orientation with a distinctive ethic that justifies the privilege of self-regulation and a status that underscores autonomy and prestige

4. See: Silberman 1973, 1978, and 1982; Spaulding 1967; Kubota 1969; Ide 1974; Tsuji 1976; Johnson 1978 and 1982; Tsuji 1952; Taniuchi 1974.

5. See: Suleiman 1974 and 1978; Kessler 1978; Darbel and Schnapper 1969 and 1972; Lalumière and Demichel 1969; Thoenig 1973; Chapman 1959; P. Grémion 1976; C. Grémion 1979; Dupuy and Thoenig 1983; Crozier 1964 and 1970; Ridley and Blondel 1964; Siwek-Pouydesseau 1969a, 1969b, and 1975; Grégoire 1943; Debbasch 1969; Bourdieu and Passeron 1964; Armstrong 1972; Silvera and Salon 1969.

6. See: Mayntz and Scharpf 1975; Luhmann and Mayntz 1973; Studienkommission für die Reform des öffentlichen Dienstrechts 1973; Bleek 1972; Sontheimer and Bleek 1973; Steinkemper 1974; Dyson 1977; Hattenhauer 1980; Beyme 1971; Battis 1980; Putnam 1975; Armstrong 1972; Ellwein and Zoll 1973; Friedrich 1939; Ule 1961; Chapman 1959; Lotz [1909] 1914.

7. See: Chapman 1959; Carrasco Canals 1975; Carr 1980; Gunther 1980; Linz and de Miguel 1968; Medhurst 1973; Arango 1978.

8. See: Treves 1964; Juso 1970; Passigli 1975; Italy, Consiglio dei Ministri 1953; Spinetti 1964.

9. See: Hough 1969 and 1973; Churchward 1968; Armstrong 1959, 1965, and 1972; DeWitt 1961; Fleron 1970; Farrell 1970; Granick 1960 and 1973; Lebed 1965; Rigby 1971 and 1977; Scott 1969; Moore 1965; Hough and Fainsod 1979; Bialer 1989 and 1986.

10. By preprofessional training I mean the existence of a formal or informal rule that the individual acquire a specific kind of higher education in order to undertake professional training. Thus, for example, an education at a leading university in England seemed to be a requirement for passing on to the higher status professions of barrister as opposed to solicitor, physician as opposed to surgeon, and high-level administrator as opposed to lower-level ones.

(Larson 1977:x–xii, 187–207; Freidson 1986:20–38; Millerson 1964:5; Barber 1963; Collins 1979; Greenwood 1957; Roth 1974; Cogan 1953).

Where professional orientation is stressed, the bureaucratic organization, very often private as well as public, takes advantage of the existing high social and economic incentives for individuals to take on professional training and roles. By recruiting professionals or those with preprofessional training, the organization need not offer high incentives for early commitment to the bureaucratic career. The promised rewards of a professional career already provide such incentives. Instead, incentives are directed toward recognizing the status of the professional role through salary, flexibility of entry (lateral entry and/or promotion through the ranks—the latter indicating that professional status has been achieved), flexibility of assignment, and greater discretion and autonomy (Hammond and Miller 1985:6). In this arrangement, career structures are less systematic and predictable. Seniority plays a lesser role in determining promotion. So-called "fast-tracks" exist; these take advantage of and offer incentives for higher levels of professional capacity. As one might expect, organizational specialization and hierarchy tend to suffer in this context.

In this kind of organizational environment, professional training and some forms of preprofessional training result in the acquisition of a body of knowledge and techniques defined by an association of practitioners. The profession has defined the individual as the means by which information is transmitted and as the source for the decision about the conditions under which it can be used. The internalization of skills and the norms of their use by the individual makes organizational definition of these aspects through career experience and formal rules less necessary. Moreover, the individual's internalization of the criteria for the appropriate use of his or her's skills produces high predictability of role behavior. Since predictability of individual behavior is high, organizational definition of hierarchy as a means of delimiting discretion need not be heavily emphasized (Perrow 1986:22–23; Freidson and Rhea 1965). This kind of role structure can produce considerable homogeneity among senior officials, but it is a uniformity of outlook fashioned by the professional rather than the organizational role.

Precisely because the professionally oriented bureaucratic role is governed by norms derived from extra-organizational sources to a greater or lesser degree, the organization is likely to be more permeable than is the case in the organizationally oriented mode. The emphasis on professional training makes public and private bureaucratic roles relatively interchangeable. This capacity for interchangeability has the consequence of encouraging or allowing both vertical and horizontal mobility between organizations. Organizational boundaries are lower, making them more permeable. In this organizational mode, the term bureaucrat unaccompanied by professional status is often used as a pejorative term. The United States,[11] Great Britain,[12] Canada,[13] and Switzerland[14] are examples of this mode.

In sum, then, we can distinguish between two general patterns of the institutionalization of the rationalized administrative role. Each has quite different structural characteristics attendant on the definition of the role. In one mode, stress is placed on the role of organizations in determining tasks. Rules, especially those that quantify and qualify bureaucratic office, operate to define tasks and the conditions of whatever skills the individual possesses. In the absence of internalized norms of discretion and praxis, organizational rules perform these duties. In the other mode, the role is characterized by the individual acquisition and control of a task. In societies where this mode is dominant the task is usually defined as a complex one entrusted by training to the individual who views himself or herself as better suited to determine the conditions of its use than any organizational structure. In a sense, task and skill make up the central notion that defines occupation and, at a longer distance, role as well. The existence of these two patterns suggests two tentative conclusions regarding the structural relationships between professionalization and bureaucratization. First, it is sometimes argued that the mutual incompatibility of professional and bureaucratic roles makes relatively little sense in the case of national state bureaucracies. As a number of studies have shown, the two elements are not incompatible in a wide range of organizational settings (Blau 1968 and 1970; Blau, Heydebrand, and Stauffer 1973; Meyer 1968; Katz and Kahn 1966; Montagna 1973; Hall 1968). The second possibility is that Stinchcombe is correct in suggesting bureaucracy and professionalism as two types of rational administration (Stinchcombe 1959:183–86; also, Litwak 1959–60). To explain, then, the course of the institutionalization of rational state bureaucracy, the operational problem is to explain why rational bureaucratic organization developed in these two

11. See: Mosher 1982 and 1978; Heady 1979; Bendix 1949; Warner 1963; Van Riper 1958a and 1958b; Corson and Paul 1966; Stanley 1964; Stanley, Mann, and Doig 1967; Heclo 1977; Niskanen 1971; Cayer 1987; Nelson 1975; Seidman 1980; Macy, Adams, Walters, and MacKenzie 1983; Murphy, Neuchterlein, and Stupak 1978; Plumlee 1981.

12. See: Great Britain 1968; Sheriff 1976b; Kelsall 1955; Chapman 1970 and 1982; Harris and Garcia 1966; Kingsley 1944; Cohen 1941; Baker 1972; Parris 1969; Atkinson Report 1983; Civil Service Commission 1979; Kellner and Crowther-Hunt 1980; Rhodes 1977; Robson 1956; Bridges 1950; Brown 1970; Dale 1942; Fry 1969; Finer 1937.

13. See: Porter 1968; Cole 1949; Dawson 1936; Chartrand and Pond 1969; Presthus 1973; Canada 1979; Hodgetts 1955 [1956] and 1973; Kernaghan 1969; Campbell and Szablowski 1979; Collins 1964.

14. See: Chapman 1959; Friedrich and Cole 1932; Ruffieux 1975; Morstein Marx 1957; Décosterd 1959.

modes across quite different polities at different stages in their social and economic development. This work describes how two types of strategies evolved—in France and Japan on the one hand, and in the United States and Great Britain on the other—and led to the institutionalization of these two modes of legal-rational state bureaucratization.

PART ONE

Bureaucratic Structure as a Contingent Problem

1

Organization Theory and Bureaucratic Structure

Categories of Explanations

When we examine the extensive literature on complex organizations in the fields of economics, sociology, political science, and history, there appears to be no adequate explanation of why different modes of bureaucratic rationalization occur. The explanations that do exist appear to be of three basic types: system needs/coordination, bounded rationality/uncertainty, and natural selection/ecological.

① System Needs or Coordination Explanations

In this type of explanation, rational bureaucratization and its structural form (viewed primarily in terms of Weber's description of legal-rational bureaucracy) is seen as emerging as a response to problems of coordination. Failures in coordination are seen as arising from a variety of sources: (1) *size*—large numbers of actors and/or transactions without any systematic rules for sharing information (Dahl and Lindblom 1963; Blau 1970; Blau and Schoenherr 1971; Hickson et al. 1969; Goldman 1973; Child 1973a; Hage 1980; Weber 1947:334–38); (2) *social and economic complexity*—specialization and differentiation of roles and organizations (Parsons 1964:507–8; Cutright 1965:548; Tilly 1975:72–73); (3) *interdependence*—complexity of systemic relations (Thompson 1967; Boulding 1964); (4) *technology and technological innovation*—economies of size and scale (Woodward 1965; Lorsch 1965; Aldrich 1972; Lawrence and Lorsch 1967a; Perrow 1968, 1986; Hickson et al. 1979; Mohr 1971; Leatt and Schneck 1982; Chandler 1977; Chandler and Daems 1979; Finer 1975; Hage 1980; Jones 1982); (5) *internalization of cost externalities*—public provision of social welfare, education, health care, etc. and internalization of various functions with high transaction costs (Barker 1944; Baumol 1967; Buchanan and Tullock 1962; Coase 1960; Williamson 1975, 1985); and (6) *war or external threat* as the source of state organizational structure (Hintze 1968; Skocpol 1979; Dorn 1963; Tilly 1975, 1990; Schmitt 1984 [1963]; Brewer 1989).

Whatever variable is emphasized, the development of the large-scale bureaucratic organization along legal-rational lines is seen as a response by decision-makers to the need of the organization or of society to avoid the costly consequences of uncoordinated activity. In this view, state bureaucratization

19

and, indeed, sometimes the modern state itself, is seen as emerging from demands by elites and/or various social and economic interest groups for coordination of critical elements of the social-economic system or organizational system. The demands are seen as emerging "naturally" in increasingly complex systems where maximization of utility is viewed as the basic goal of individuals and groups. Rational organizations are thus sometimes seen as responses to system needs for stability and survival. In this regard, individual actors are seen as "black boxes" for system needs. The desire to coordinate arises out of the individual's conflation of his or her interest with that of the system or organization.

Bureaucratization is seen here as a systemic response (Astley and Van de Ven 1983). It is functionally efficient in doing what the market does inefficiently in the case of private organizations—it provides greater information, more efficient allocation of resources, and reduces opportunism. Or, as in the case of the state, bureaucratization of administration does what voluntary association or social organization cannot or will not do: enforce the distribution of social costs and/or services over a wider number of actors. Systemic conflict and instability in the society are avoided by the expansion of social and/or private values through the allocational efficiency provided by the bureaucratic structure. In this approach, bureaucracy's structural characteristics are seen as possessing a kind of allocative and relatively frictionless efficiency, especially in the areas of decision making, organizational control, information and communication (Arrow 1974; Williamson 1975, 1981; Perrow 1986:46–48). As one sociologist put it, "Nevertheless, the vast majority of large organizations are fairly bureaucratic, and, for all but a few, the rational-legal form of bureaucracy is the most efficient form of administration known" (Perrow 1986 [1972]:5). Efficiency is seen as a function only of organizations possessing the Weberian rational-legal characteristics. These characteristics are viewed as emerging from a logic of systemic structural demands.

Bounded Rationality-Uncertainty Explanations

This approach combines the bounded rationality of the decision-maker with environmental uncertainty (although sometimes the latter is confusingly seen as a function of the former) as the starting point for general explanations of the emergence and variation of bureaucratic organization.[1] Simply put, bureaucratic organization is seen as the means for overcoming both of

1. Bounded rationality may be defined as those limitations on an individual's capacity to make the most efficient decisions and actions. These limitations are: (1) skills, habits, and reflexes; (2) values and goals; and (3) extent of the individual's knowledge. Of these, the third limitation is perhaps the most important (see H. Simon 1976:40–41; 1972 [1982]:410).

these conditions. There are two distinct strands in this literature. One of these, primarily sociological in character, emphasizes the problems of structuring and allocating power as the focus of decision-makers' concerns. The other, dominated largely by economists but including sociologists and political scientists as well, stresses the problem of profit or efficiency maximization as the goal of decision-makers. Both strands tend to view bureaucratization as a function of conscious choice about pursuing maximizing strategies.

The first of these sees challenges to decision-makers' power and their legitimacy as being most likely to occur under conditions of continued environmental uncertainty. It is not always clear what is meant by uncertainty here, but it usually seems to mean the inability to predict the kind of decisions that will arise and/or the degree of acceptance of decisions. This condition most often arises at those times when there has been a change in leadership in organizations that do not have highly specified rules governing leadership succession or when such rules have been abrogated (Gouldner 1954; Grusky 1964). Under these conditions, the bounded rationality of individuals leads them to seek to maintain their power and status by resorting to the utilization of rules of decision making that are presented as being objective—that is, as stemming from organizational and not personal necessity. These rules require hierarchy of authority, obedience, well-defined roles, and what constitutes appropriate knowledge for decision making (Gouldner 1954; Selznick 1957:105; Grusky 1961, 1964; Zald 1970; Crozier 1964; Palumbo 1975:357–58; Dreyfuss 1938; Warner and Low 1947:78–80, 174; Selznick 1949:252; Clegg and Dunkerley 1980; Pfeffer 1981; Pfeffer and Salancik 1978).

Here the concept of expertise is seen almost as an ideology in which decision-makers claim obedience because of their possession of systematic knowledge about the organization and/or the means for achieving its goals (Wolin 1960:352–434; Urban 1982; Braverman 1974; Clawson 1980; Meyer and Rowan 1978; Habermas 1975; Dunn and Fozouni 1976; Denhardt 1981; Marglin 1974; Goldman and Van Houten 1977). Expertise thus becomes the basis of legitimate authority, and rules of bureaucratic organization become legitimate because they appear to be based on scientific observation and analysis of large populations of organizations or analogous systems. Bureaucratization, in this view, is seen as the product of elites or managers seeking to maintain or hold power in the face of uncertainty by transforming the structure of authority and legitimacy into both an object of systematic analysis and an "objectively" rational organization.

In sum, the warrant for authority in such organizations is no longer manifestly the quest for or possession of individual power, status, and material rewards. It stems, rather, from the emergence of a science of organizations or social behavior that "reveals" the necessity for rules, hierarchy, and other characteristics of rational-legal organization. In this explanation, bureaucratization is constrained by the desire of decision-makers to maximize the security of their position. They seek to achieve this by emphasizing the necessity for hierarchical discretion and obedience to organizational rules as the most efficient means for arriving at decisions and achieving goals (Crozier 1964; Reder 1947; Barnard 1938; Papandreou 1952; Gordon 1961; Monsen and Downs 1965; Gouldner 1954; Williamson 1964; Marris 1964; Marris and Mueller 1980).

② The second strand in the bounded rationality/uncertainty literature views rational bureaucratization primarily as the solution imposed by the nature of environmental uncertainty, given the bounded rationality of decision-makers and the ubiquitous character of opportunism. Under these conditions, it is assumed that organizational utility maximization (sometimes fused with the idea of organizational survival when there is the assumption of large numbers and low entry costs) is the aim of decision-makers. On the economics side of this literature, rational bureaucratic structure—described in terms of the organizational structure and behavior of the firm—is seen as the direct consequence of internalizing external functions. When faced with market uncertainty or market failure, decision-makers seek to overcome the high transaction costs generated by imperfect information, the inability to write contracts covering all contingencies, and the tendency of some individuals to use guile in pursuing self-interest. The most efficient way of overcoming the costs generated by these problems, it is argued, is by internalizing a number of functions previously performed outside of the organization. Internalization provides greater information, control over opportunism, greater predictability, and the capacity to stretch decisions out over time, thereby avoiding the worst aspects of failed contracts (Williamson 1975:1–40; 1981, 1983, 1984, 1985:15–130; Coase 1937, 1972; Alchian and Demsetz 1972:779–81; H. Simon 1957, 1973:183–95; Carlton 1979; Ouchi 1980; Francis 1983; Cheung 1983; Teece 1982). The following bureaucratic characteristics result from this internalization process: specialization and differentiation, managerial control in the form of rules regarding allocation of resources and utilization of resources for individual goals, and hierarchy as an efficient means of allocating decision making. Bureaucratization is seen as the result of adjustment to change in which the individual interests of the decision-maker about security are synonymous with the survival of the organization. As a distinguished economist has put it:

[I]n the economics of adjustment to change the issues of security, survival and maximum profit are merged . . . If a change in conditions calls for a certain reaction in the name of maximum profits, the very same reaction is called for also in the name of security or survival. (Machlup 1967:13)

More recently, some of the economics literature has focused on the opportunism aspect as one, or the sole, major constraint on the emergence of firm or organization structure. This literature suggests that hierarchy and division of labor are the means by which the free-rider or shirking problem in any group contractual arrangement is overcome (Jensen 1983; Alchian and Demsetz 1972; Fama 1980; Jensen and Meckling 1976; Williamson 1981:1,545). The political science version of this approach stresses the agency problem (all organizational arrangements are contractual between a principal and his or her agent) as the source of developing governmental structure (Moe 1984; Miller and Moe 1983; Hammond and Miller 1985). A range of functions, such as hierarchy, hierarchical responsibility, financial and decisional rules of accountability, are developed and internalized to overcome the negative externalities of unenforced and/or unmonitored contracts. Organizational structure is the outcome, then, of the problems inherent in those forms of economic or social contract where there are strong incentives to shirk or withhold information.

The sociological side of the bounded rationality/uncertainty literature goes under two names: "open system" (Katz and Kahn 1966; Baker 1973; Cyert and March 1963; Emery and Trist 1965; Terreberry 1968; Lawrence and Lorsch 1967a, 1967b; Rice 1963; Burns and Stalker 1961; Weick 1969; Dill 1958; Duncan 1972; Thompson 1967; Hickson et al. 1971) and "dependence exchange" (Jacobs 1974; Hasenfeld 1972; Aldrich and Pfeffer 1976; Aldrich 1979). Here, as in the bounded rationality discourse generally, the environment is seen as contingent but it is not well specified. Sometimes contingency is defined as lack of information, sometimes as unpredictability arising from organizational or system complexity, sometimes as uncertainty about resources, and sometimes as the unpredictability about the consequences of any set of decisions (Simon 1972; Luce and Raiffa 1957; Terreberry 1968). Organizational structure is viewed as variable and the result of constant adaptation to uncertainty by decision-makers who make relatively unconstrained strategic choices. A major concern in this part of the literature is with the structural variations that occur within organizational populations. In this aspect, the open systems/dependence exchange literature is closely related to the evolutionary and ecological concepts of organizational formation. Like the ecological view, the open systems outlook concludes that structural outcomes are survival-functional for specific environments. Where attention is paid to general bureaucratic characteristics, such as hierarchy, specialization and differentiation, and hierarchical authority (Katz and Kahn 1966; Pugh et al. 1968; Child 1972a, 1972b; Lawrence and Lorsch 1967a, 1967b; Hage 1980), variations in these aspects of bureaucratization are seen as a consequence of environmental contingency (Leibenstein 1966, 1969, 1976, 1987). On the whole, however, the implication of this literature is that while rational-legal characteristics may be dysfunctional in some ways, they are, for the most part, functionally efficient in overcoming internal "transaction costs" stemming from conflict, opportunism, or inability to predict behavior. At the same time, they are efficient in reducing environmental uncertainty by internalizing functions and providing the capacity to restructure relationships to the market to capture externalities. In short, like the economics view, this one takes the position that bureaucratic structure is functionally determined and therefore efficient in a context of uncertainty and bounded rationality. Rational-legal characteristics are the response to both internal and external (inter- and intra-organizational) uncertainty about behavior and outcomes. In this sense, much of the literature constituting this view seems to agree with Machlup's statement about the identity of reactions called for by changes in conditions.

3 Natural Selection-Evolution-Ecological Explanations

This view includes several strands of literature: one that has implicit evolutionary explanations, a second that is explicit in its use of a natural selection model, and a third that seeks to construct an ecosystem as the engine of evolutionary change.

The first view suggests that bureaucratization grows out of historical conditions of cultural and structural conduciveness. Some environments have evolved to a point where they possess values and social structural characteristics which make it possible for rational-legal bureaucracy to emerge (Weber 1958; Bellah 1957; Eisenstadt 1969; Bendix 1964; Riggs 1964; Stinchcombe 1965; Huntington 1968; Huntington and Dominguez 1975; Jaguaribe 1973; Skocpol 1979). "[C]ertain kinds of organizations . . . could not be invented before the social structure was appropriate to them" (Stinchcombe 1965:160).

The conditions said to reflect conduciveness for rational bureaucratic organization are the existence of free-floating resources, manpower, and a value system that is not completely tied to ascriptive or particularistic groups (Eisenstadt 1969; Stinchcombe 1965). Elites, rulers, or entrepreneurs are in the position to take advantage of these resources by virtue of their smaller numbers, their access to information and symbols, and their wealth. Bureaucratic characteristics are functional in these environments but not in others. Inherent in this argument is a notion of selection that provides for survival functional outcomes. Thus, environments that provide high levels of uncertainty produce variant solutions, some of which are successful in constraining the centrifugal forces inherent in these conditions. Uncertainty is indicated by unallocated resources, undifferentiated or nonallocated resources, undifferentiated or nonallocated human resources, and values that allow unpredictable choices. Success in gaining access to these resources produces widespread imitation and thus institutionalization.

The second strand in this literature, that of explicit natural selection, is difficult to separate clearly from the ecological view; thus, they will be treated together here. The basic premise is that bureaucratic organization is seen as the consequence of a process of natural selection occurring within a population or ecosystem of organizations (Granovetter 1979; Hannan and Freeman 1977, 1984, 1986; Freeman 1982; Aldrich and Mueller 1982; Aldrich 1971; Campbell 1969; McKelvey 1982; McKelvey and Aldrich 1983; Kaufman 1991; Blute 1979; Carroll 1984; Nelson and Winter 1982; Langton 1984; Bidwell and Kasarda 1984, 1985; Astley 1985). The Marxian version of environmental dominance over selection is well-stated (Heydebrand 1977; Goldman 1973; Clegg and Dunkerley 1980). Bureaucratization occurs as the result of the environment differentially selecting either of the organizational variations for survival on the basis of the functional fit between organizational structure and environment. "Those organizations that have appropriate social structure, for whatever reasons, are selected over those that do not" (Aldrich and Pfeffer 1976:81). With the exception of the recent work by Bidwell and Kasarda (1985), the literature does not provide much in the way of specifying the criteria for selection or retention of variants. Implicit in much of this work, however, is the view that retention of functional random variations occurs through their contribution to organizational stability or survival under conditions of competition with large numbers (Weick 1969; Aldrich and Pfeffer 1976; Astley and Van de Ven 1983; Langton 1984; Perrow 1986 [1972]:208–18; Nelson and Winter 1982; Hannan and Freeman 1989). This approach is similar to the coordination explanation in that both stress the determination of organizational characteristics primarily by external market or environmental constraints. They differ, however, in that the natural selection explanation does not specify maximization of profits as the primary criterion for selecting out organizational form. Rather, the emphasis on appropriateness of fit between environmental demands and organizational structure allows the inference that criteria for selection and retention may vary over time, place, and goals. An approach intermediate between macrostructural and individual determinants of organizational structure is represented by Hrebiniak and Joyce (1985), who argue, with considerable cogency, that adaptation is a function of the interdependent relations between individual choice, strategic choice, and external constraints.

One example of how this view has spurred new thoughts on environmental variables is the isomorphic-legitimization approach to structural change in organizational populations. This view argues that once structural changes are adopted by significant organizations, they become legitimized. Once changes are adopted by some organizations, other organizations also adopt the changes in order to acquire the benefits of organizational legitimacy—even though such changes may bring no other organizational benefits (Meyer and Rowan 1977; Rowan 1982; Tolbert and Zucker 1983; DiMaggio and Powell 1983; Meyer and Scott 1983).

Finally, in recent years, the concern with environmental constraints and the ambiguity of the concept has led to attempts to specify variables that make up the environment. This specification has emerged out of the population-community concepts of ecology (Hawley 1950, 1968; Duncan and Hauser 1959; O. D. Duncan 1964). One strand of this relatively new literature tries to follow the dynamic process (Bidwell and Kasarda 1985). Another strand stresses the texture, density, and interdependence of the environmental population and community (Evan 1960; Weick 1979; Laumann, Verbrugge, and Pappi 1974; Laumann and Pappi 1976; Aldrich and Whetten 1981). Network analysis as utilized by organizational theorists is an attempt to put some empirical bite into propositions about natural selection. By tracing networks and organizational changes over time, the hope is that relationships between environmental changes and organizational structure can be specified. Presently, the literature in this area stresses the degree to which the environment is constructed by organizations as they seek rules of cooperation for organizational populations (Emery and Trist 1973; Cook 1977; Van de Ven, Delbecq, and Koenig 1968) or seek rules which allow certain organizational types and goals to dominate (Benson 1975; Clegg 1981; Jackson 1983; Perrow 1984).

Problems Arising from the Literature

At first glance the literature seems both overdetermined and overdetermining. The state of the literature seems analogous to the situation of the man who has lent his lawn mower to his next-door neighbor. On seeking its return after several weeks, his neighbor explains his failure to return it by saying, "In the first place it wasn't working; in the second place, I haven't finished using it; in the third place, you didn't lend it to me." Like the lender, we seem to be confronted with explanations, each one of which would be, on the face of it, sufficient to explain the behavior but when taken together seem at times to be mutually exclusive or contradictory. All of them can't be right, thus the possibility arises that none of them are.

Part of this apparent overdetermination is illusory. Like the neighbor's response, these explanations are aimed at different possible questions. Coordination explanations seem to be directed primarily at explaining and predicting changes in observed levels of coordination. That is to say, it seems to be the attempt to work out systematically the way in which coordination levels will vary with particular changes in conditions such as system size, technology, war, interest-group formation, system complexity, etc. In this sense, the explanation is not aimed at explaining or predicting the behavior of any particular real set of organizations but only the reactions of numerous actors to the existence of changes in the environment affecting coordination. The bureaucratic organization is the theoretical link or "black box" that helps explain how one gets from cause to effect. Indeed, this appears to be the deductive mode utilized by Weber in constructing his ideal type of legal-rational bureaucracy—it is a mental device that explains the capacity of individuals and groups in Western society to grasp positive externalities, to maximize profits or utility. Just as in the marginalist or equilibrium theory of the firm (Machlup 1967; Loasby 1968, 1971; Horowitz 1970:154–248; Williamson 1981:1,539), a set of organizational characteristics is posited that is assumed to be functional to profit or utility maximization on the part of decision-makers.

Although the assumption about maximization is logically necessary, it must be combined with the concept of effective competition in order to produce a conclusion about the identical nature of individual and organizational goals. The efficiency of bureaucratic organization does not rest solely on its allocative capacities but also on both organizational competition and individual competition to induce persistent attempts to grasp externalities (Leibenstein 1966, 1973, 1975; Jackson 1983:178–84). Characteristics such as hierarchy, hierarchy of authority, specialization, differentiation, decision-making rules based on the accumulation of information, expertise, careerism, and secularity are all deduced as efficient responses to *ceteris paribus* conditions of effective competition and maximization of utility. In short, bureaucratic organization or the firm, in the theory of the firm, is a heuristic device adopted as the simplest and most efficient way to explain the relationship between variations in levels of coordination and variations or changes in conditions. By inference, bureaucratic organization in this kind of explanation is not meant to be a concept by which to examine any real organization either in processual or normative terms. This explanation uses price theory as a model of explanation.

Precisely because of the heuristic character assigned to the organization, this explanation is poorly equipped to examine the process of bureaucratization and thus to provide an understanding of why it takes on different modes. The weakness of the explanation in this regard stems from assumptions utilized to create the link between cause and effect. There are two such assumptions: (1) decision-makers seek to maximize profit, and (2) there is effective competition. The two must be joined since either one by itself clearly is not sufficient to explain why changes in coordination should occur. The explanation thus assumes a uniform set of constraints over time. It is not at all clear that these constraints *require* any narrowly specific form of organization. They require only that decision-makers pursue profit-maximization as their goal. Presumably, they can use any means that existing rules allow and they will make the most of those means if there are large numbers competing. The point is, it is not necessary for this explanation to specify any particular form, so long as the aim is *not* to explain bureaucratic organization but rather the change in coordination levels. It is merely sufficient, in a logical sense, to say that the organization is rational or utility maximizing.

Due to its heuristic "black box" approach to organizations, this view suffers from the defects of its advantages. It appears to be an entirely appropriate approach, if the idea is to provide a set of variables governing the relationship between environment and levels of coordination in the manner of price theory. It faces severe problems, however, because it views rational bureaucratic organization as a category that emerges unmediated from a specific environment of the division of labor—that is, the greater the division of labor, the greater the number of actors; the greater the need for coordination, the greater the rationality (utility maximization) of the organization. Other concerns of social or collective choice do not enter into the equation.

When it comes to the question of explaining concrete examples, this explication runs contrary to our knowledge and understanding of contemporary and recent history. Even a brief glance at the historical development of three major cases of state bureaucratic rationalization in the late nineteenth century, France, Japan and Prussia-Germany, indicates that rationalization did not arise unmediated from problems of coordination. In the 1870s and 1880s, when state bureaucratic rationalization became institutionalized in these countries, problems of economic coordination (or resource allocation) arising from an expanding division of labor were considerably fewer and less intense than in the United States and Great Britain, where the process of industrialization was farther along (Mathias and Postan 1978; Ohkawa and Rosovsky 1973; Landes 1965, 1969; Chandler and Daems 1980). Indeed it was the rationalized state administration in Japan and Prussia-Germany that undertook to subsidize and encourage the economic transformation of society. This developmental pattern forcefully suggests that problems of governmental coordination may not arise simply out of the failure of the market or politics to coordinate. Rather, such problems may be the result of self-con-

scious decisions arrived at by rationalized bureaucratic organizations aiming
to achieve politically determined goals. In this situation, coordination problems are not the cause of bureaucratization so much as the symptom of the
bureaucratization process itself (Silberman 1982; O'Donnell 1973; Collier
1979).

The natural selection explanation raises problems in a somewhat different
direction. It fails to specify in any but the broadest terms the criteria for selection and retention of bureaucratic structures. This view recognizes that
different modes of bureaucratization occur, but it doesn't tell us why there
are systematic variations. Nor does it specify any process or mechanism to
help us understand why some rulers, elites, or entrepreneurs are capable of
seizing opportunities presented by the environment while others in similar
situations are not. The implication seems to be that those who are successful
operate not only on short-term maximization of utility as everyone might
but also have specific opportunistic advantages—more information and resources. Bureaucratization is thus seen as arising out of the attempt to institutionalize or stabilize organizational success. Weber's routinization of charisma is an example of this approach. The problem lies, however, in
specifying the mechanism or process and the conditions which lead strategic
choosers to the same or similar choices. The systematic character of similarities and variations in the history of bureaucratic evolution in the late nineteenth and early twentieth centuries clearly suggests nonrandom constraints
on the selection process.

One inference we might draw is that varying bureaucratic modes are selected as a result of variations in uncertainty about organizational authority,
power, and stability (Aldrich and Pfeffer 1976). This suggests there are close
similarities between this approach and the bounded rationality/uncertainty
explanation. This latter approach has been largely confined to analysis
within the framework of the theory of the firm (Coase 1937; Williamson
1975, 1985; Marris 1964); organizational behavior theory (Simon 1976;
Cyert and March 1963; Zald 1970a; Thompson 1967; Hickson et al. 1971;
Allison 1971); and complex organizations (Gouldner 1954). Only in some
recent studies has uncertainty as a variable been utilized in attempting to explain systematic differences in public bureaucratic organization (Meyer and
Brown 1977; Meyer 1975, 1979; Meyer, Stevenson, and Webster 1985).

Of course, bounded rationality and uncertainty about authority, power,
and control is a recurrent theme in much of the historical literature on the
emergence and development of the modern state. However, uncertainty is
not viewed in a systematic way by historians. It is usually seen as a background constant against which is played out the virtuosity of historical actors. That is, historical explanations or descriptions often fail to define the

constraints within which individuals make choices in a systematic way. Thus, for example, where war is seen as the major dynamic driving state bureaucratization, no explanation is provided as to why *rationalization* of bureaucracy occurs the way it does. Tilly is instructive in this regard. His discussion of the emergence of "direct rule" as an aspect of rational administration following the French Revolution emphasizes the uncertainty of political leaders as the driving force rather than war itself (Tilly 1990:109). Brewer, in his analysis of English development, describes the eighteenth century as a period of bureaucratic rationalization. Even if we suspend disbelief on this issue, Brewer provides us with no explanation as to why rationalization took on the particular forms he describes (Brewer 1989:64–87). In both cases, which are in many ways typical of historically oriented analyses, the assumption appears to be that war and its demand on finances automatically produces rationalization of bureaucracy with no mediation. This is essentially a systemic functionalist account in which the agents are passive objects of systemic requirements. However, there is no inherent logic in the demands stemming from war that requires the production of a specific organizational structure except the argument that war creates problems of coordination. But this does not, for example, answer the question of why the English in the eighteenth century choose to create bureaus in the form of collegial boards (Brewer 1989:83). Coordination, while it might constrain organizational behavior in some directions, does not provide any logic for the production of the kind of structures described by Tilly or Brewer.

In more traditional Marxist analysis, however, there is the assumption of rationality that is almost completely constrained and, therefore, unable to explain the variation (Marx and Engels 1965:59; Lenin 1947). More recently, there have been attempts to explain the variation in organizational structure in terms of variations in capitalist structure and the path of capitalist accumulation (Johnson 1977; Carchedi 1977:127–34). This provides no clear explanation about how specific paths of capitalist development and capitalist organization produce the variation in organizational forms that exists in a systematic way across capitalist countries. Nor does it explain why some noncapitalist societies like the traditional Soviet regime underwent bureaucratic rationalization similar to those of noncapitalist societies.

In the nonhistorical literature, analysis is rather narrowly limited to contemporaneous private organizations within single societies. The results are generalizations largely deduced from static analysis within the framework of market or general environmental uncertainty. These shed little light on public bureaucracies precisely because the latter do not have to face conditions of market competition. Thus, if generalizations are to be deduced, an analog of economic market competition must be well specified (Niskanen 1971). Furthermore, the static character of the analysis assumes a *ceteris paribus* condition of uncertainty—uncertainty is seen as constant. But, as historians are fond of pointing out, uncertainty varies over time and place as well as over a cross section of societies, markets, or what have you (Meyer 1979:2, 5–10).

If variation occurs, then the problem is to explain how *systematic* variations in bureaucratic organization occur over time in a variety of settings. Historical case studies and descriptions of the development of the modern state system aim to do this but err in the opposite direction. The historical literature by and large, as I have argued, fails to provide us with any systematic generalizations of process because of its inevitable emphasis on the uniqueness of organizational development and change. There have been, as a consequence, almost no attempts to conceptualize which elements of uncertainty in the environment are critical to producing those outcomes we characterize as legal-rational bureaucratic.

In sum, the existing literature suffers from both overdetermination and underdetermination. On the one hand, it cites many conditions to which rational bureaucratization is a functional response, but it does not specify any particular set of conditions to which rational bureaucratization is *always* the response. On the other hand, these explanations fail to provide any adequate proposition for why systematic differences occur across historical, cultural, and national boundaries.

Common Themes

Some of the reasons for this continuing confusion and ambiguity with regard to state bureaucratization are partly revealed when we look at the major themes running through the literature. Despite the considerable differences between explanations, there appear to be three common themes. First, all of them stress some aspect of uncertainty—uncertainty about availability or proper allocation of resources, about legitimate authority, transaction costs, organizational environment, organizational stability or managerial power or status. Second, there seems to be common agreement that limited or bounded rationality—that is, limitations on the availability of information and the limited capacity to search for the best solution—of decision-makers is a major factor in rational bureaucratization. Bureaucratic organizations are seen as the response to the continuing problem of imperfections of individual decisions in situations where neither perfect information nor a perfect market exist. Third, all of the explanations appear to agree that internalization is the processual means by which bureaucratization occurs. It is either a process of internalizing positive externalities or of internalizing transaction costs, or it is the internalization of information and resources generally. The internalization process is seen as the primary mechanism of response. "Adaptation" is the most commonly used word to describe this process. Whatever the wording, agreement is widespread that internalization accounts for the emergence of hierarchy, specialization and differentiation, career structures, and the utilization of formal rules. This process, depending on the point of view, produces different organizational shapes: unitary or multidivisional (Williamson 1975; Chandler 1962, 1977); loose-rigid (Lawrence and Lorsch 1967a, 1967b); centralized-decentralized (Pugh et al. 1968); tall-short [hierarchies] (Woodward 1958, 1965). Whatever the shape, they all appear to exhibit the structured role characteristics implied by Weber's description (Mansfield 1973; Aldrich and Pfeffer 1976; Perrow 1986 [1972]).

The presence of these themes over a wide variety of explanations reveals the long-standing debate in organizational theory about what it is that constrains organizational emergence and change. The debate revolves around whether (1) rational strategic choices of decision-makers seeking to maximize their and their organization's interests; or, (2) environmental factors to which organizations respond in the systemic pursuit of survival and growth, are chiefly responsible for molding the shape of organizations (Astley and Van de Ven 1983). In terms of the paired notions of bounded rationality/uncertainty, the debate is focused on the question of what constrains decisions—the role and nature of the decision-maker or the environment. From the point of view of internalization, the debate centers on what shapes process—the maximization of the decision-makers's utility or environmental demands which enforce systemic maximization of utility. Thus, while there seems to be agreement on the central factors in the emergence of organizational rationality, wide differences remain in explanation, depending upon which side of the debate one stands.

The problem is, however, that a commitment to either side makes it impossible to explain the existence of the two major modes of state bureaucratization. To depend only on rational choice arguments without specifying different environmental states is to ignore differences in the institutionalization of rational bureaucratic modes and to seek explanations only at the most general level. Environmental states provide a powerful variable in the search for explanations as to variations in modes of bureaucratization. At the other extreme, to depend solely on macro constraints invites the criticism that all one has said is that different environments produce different modes of institutionalization. This does not tell us what factors in the environment vary systematically so as to produce different modes. Such an approach must rely on some notion of organizational or emergent rationality distinct from those who make and organize its decisions. This would have strong appeal, had we some clearer understanding of how such emergent properties worked, so as to allow us to distinguish between more or less structured rationality. In the last analysis, macro explanations centering on environmental forces lead only to rather gross distinctions between more or less complex or uncertain environments and thus help explain, as Weber did, the differences between patrimonial and rational bureaucratic administrations. Reliance on either one or the other explanatory approach, therefore, leaves us in the dark about the whole process of rational bureaucratization in the state and why it should take on the general and specific forms we observe.

2

Political Uncertainty, Leadership Succession, and the Modes of Administration

Although the literature presents some problems, it does, at the same time, provide us with tools to explain why state bureaucratization has had at least two modes of rationalization. Bounded rationality and uncertainty are central elements in the literature. This agreement suggests that they are really paired aspects (Williamson 1975:23, 39) of rational choice and environment; that is to say, boundedness of rationality does not arise as a problem unless there are persistent uncertainties in the environment which call attention to the limits of existing decision-making rules. Here we must be careful to understand that uncertainty does not refer to either psychological or cognitive states of the actors. Rather, it refers to the presence or absence of rules governing role behavior which have the capacity to predict, to a greater or lesser extent, the outcome of choices made by the actors. Uncertainty in this sense does not reside in the general incapacity to know anything for certain but rather in the observable absence of predictability about what outcomes follow from actions or choices. This is akin to the concept of risk economists sometimes use—a state in which complete information is not available, but sufficient information is present to assign probabilities and then select the best outcome (Luce and Raiffa 1957; Coase 1937).

In this context, rational bureaucratization may be seen to occur as the consequence of persistent uncertainty or risk in the environment, thus revealing the unsuitability of old rules for making decisions and provoking attempts to provide new rules which produce greater predictability. Or, to put it in a different way, rational bureaucratization emerges as the result of rational choices made within a context of persistent decision-making problems. The solutions to these problems are constrained by the existence of other structures or role aggregates having rules governing choices and possible outcomes—in short, the environment. Structural change in organizations is shaped by the interaction between individual decision making and environmental constraints in the form of a relatively homogeneous population of rules governing decisions or choices. From this perspective, we might argue that the two different forms of state bureaucratization represent different strategies of choice for dealing with the same specific recurring problem within different environments.

34

Approaching the Problem

The emphasis in this approach on both strategic choices and the environment as embodied in "ruleful" systems of decision making requires us to engage in a deductive exercise aimed at doing two things. First, we want to arrive at some idea or propositions as to what might have been the recurring problem of state administration and organization in the nineteenth century. Second, having arrived at some such notions, we need to provide an outline of how such solutions could have been reached by individuals making strategic choices within varying kinds of decision-making environments. In so doing, it should be clear that the descriptions of the patterns of strategic choices, characterizing what I have called "professionally" and "organizationally" oriented bureaucracies, are not of any actual historical events. Rather, the descriptions that follow are attempts to provide a deductive account of what choices would be available under certain circumstances and which would be viewed as the most reasonable strategically for individuals making choices.

This, of course, raises the problems of who makes the significant choices and on what basis. In answer to the first question—the agents are no mystery. They are those in a position to make choices about allocating scarce resources. Our interest is not, however, in those who are in a position to make any choice or set of choices. We are interested in those who make choices in similar ways, especially with regard to the development of institutions and roles centering on the structure of decision making. Thus this analysis is focused on the upper-level civil servant.

The concern here is with the way in which decision-makers came to create structures for the perpetuation of decision-making roles. This suggests to us that the standard for reasonableness about choices must at least coincide with the desire to sustain or enhance the status, power, and material well-being of those making choices. To do otherwise would subvert the legitimacy of choices made. After all, if you don't think well enough of your own capacities and attributes to want to sustain them in the process of decision making, then who is likely to think well of your decisions? Therefore, in this account of what might have occurred, we take the position that significant social choices are made on a day-to-day basis within the framework of reasonable self-interest. That is to say, individuals who claim positions of leadership and decision making and who seek to make decisions that have allocative consequences will try to dedicate considerable resources to maintaining themselves in such offices. Furthermore, we also assume that individuals will not make eccentric choices. Individuals similarly placed are likely to make similar choices when faced with similar circumstances. This is to say that the range of choices is always limited to some degree by the institutional structure and its norms. But where these constraints are similar, we should expect similarly placed individuals to make similar choices. Here, what we want to do is see just how reasonable a set of propositions and descriptions can be derived from the assumption of individual agency acting in reasonable self-interest within specific kinds of institutional constraints or environments.

We also need, then, to specify the environments—the structure of, or rather, the rulefulness of decision making. In this account, we want to specify at least two kinds of environments which would provide an independent variable to account for the two types of organizational resolution to the problem faced by decision-makers. Following from this abstraction or typification of historical conditions surrounding strategic decision-makers, we want to find and select historically concrete environments that fit the two categories. We should expect to find the historical examples of these two different conditions of decision making are correlated with the appropriate type of bureaucratic orientation. Finally, having elicited this correlation, we should be able to examine each of the historical cases and show how the process of strategic choice in each type of environment worked to produce similar outcomes in each environment.

To do the above analysis, I have chosen four cases of institutionalization of state bureaucracies: the United States, Great Britain, France, and Japan. This selection was motivated by a number of considerations. First, these are major instances of state administrative rationalization. All four states played major roles in international relations in the nineteenth and/or twentieth centuries. Second, this group covers the spectrum of administrative types. France has often been seen as one of the "classic" continental bureaucratic administrative systems (Heady 1979; Barker 1944; F. Morstein Marx 1957). The United States and Great Britain have usually been considered as the classic cases of "representative" or politically dominated rational bureaucracies (Ripley and Franklin 1976; Kingsley 1944; Krislov and Rosenbloom 1981). Japan was the first non-Western nation to institutionalize a rational state bureaucracy—one similar to the classic continental European mode, and it was the first case of a non-European so-called developing society producing a highly rationalized state administration (Silberman 1970, 1967; Spaulding 1967). These four cases are "classic" in the sense that the basic forms of bureaucratic role and structure they now bear were institutionalized by the end of the nineteenth or in the early twentieth century and have served as models for latecomers. They are also classic in the sense that this institutionalization is relatively well-documented and widely recognized. They are the best-known and most often-cited examples of the emergence of the basic patterns of rational state bureaucratization, as well as being examples of the two modes of bureaucratization I suggested earlier.

There is a third important reason for the selection of these cases. While they seem to be representative of the patterns of institutionalization described in the literature, these cases are representative of processual development as well. That is, while these cases represent several categories, they also represent varying paths to similar modes of organizational structure. France and Japan seem to have quite different histories of bureaucratic rationalization. France did not reach the classic Weberian mode until the late nineteenth century after almost a hundred years of resolving the problems of centralization and the relationship of political parties to public institutions of decision making. Japan achieved its classic bureaucratic condition with great rapidity, after only thirty-odd years in which centralization and the differentiation of social, political, and economic structures occurred. The United States came to its particular form of bureaucratic rationalization after a process of political reform centering on intense political contestation in the period between approximately 1870 and 1900. Finally, Great Britain arrived at the professionalization of its civil service at exactly the same time, following some forty years of franchise and parliamentary reform centering on the question of parliamentary control and the nature of political leadership.

Different economic environments also graced each of these cases of bureaucratic change. Bureaucratization occurred in France in the early stages of industrialization. In Japan, bureaucratic rationalization predated industrialization. Additionally, the argument has often been made that bureaucratization was an essential step in the success of Japan's rapid industrialization. In the United States and Great Britain, bureaucratic rationalization came at the height of industrialization. This suggests that the industrialization stage of economic development was neither a necessary nor a sufficient cause for bureaucratization, unless one wishes to argue that there is an inverse relationship between bureaucratization and industrialization. This line of reasoning implies that for those countries which had early industrialization, state bureaucratic rationalization came as the result of bitter lessons about complexity and coordination. On the other hand, for late industrializers, bureaucratization came as a result of observing the experiences of the early industrializers.

There are two basic reasons for thinking the relationship to be a false one. For the inverse relationship between organizational orientation and late industrialization to provide a clue to explaining the variation, we have to assume that rationalization of the bureaucratic role occurred because either there was a powerful systemic push and/or political leaders in these countries were prescient. In the latter case, we would have to assume that political leaders knew, through their observation of European historical experience, that a particular structure of the bureaucratic role—the organizationally oriented role structure—was the best means for catching up with Great Britain or the United States.

The former possibility, as we have noted, does not seem possible. While increased complexity or industrialization might be viewed as a systemic force, it is difficult to know how less complexity provides systemic demand for a certain kind of rationalization. That is to say, what kind of systemic demand could one envision, outside of increased complexity, that would require rationalization as a response? Nor does it seem possible that political leaders were able to know that the organizationally oriented pattern of bureaucratic role structure was the appropriate mechanism to bring about rapid industrialization. This was clearly not the case. The two most prominent examples of industrial development, Great Britain and the United States, were anything but organizationally oriented. Furthermore, there appears to be little evidence, if any, to indicate that Japanese and French political leaders thought seriously of these two countries as possible models. In the French case, the commitment to the organizationally oriented mode was made at the beginning of the nineteenth century when neither the British or American solution had yet emerged. Nor were there any clearly successful models of organizational orientation. In fact, there were no models for this approach, with the possible exception of Prussia/Germany, and this one came late for the French and for the Japanese was an ambiguous example. Nor was there any theory of appropriate bureaucratic role structure. Such theories would not be coherently presented until the next century.

It is difficult to conceive of how bureaucratization and industrialization are related, unless one is willing to concede that political and economic elites are prescient about the administrative forms necessary to carry out industrialization within their societies and have the capacity to enforce those functional changes. While this is not an impossible scenario for the twentieth century, it does seem an improbable one for the nineteenth. Latecomers, it is true, have more than one mode of bureaucratic rationalization to choose from. Thus, the Japanese faced the quandary of choosing between the relatively successful form of bureaucratic rationalization in Great Britain, a considerably less successful one in France, and one in Prussia which had won wars but had not yet reached the high levels of industrialization. Furthermore, this puzzle leaves us dangling with a new question: How is it that some political elites are better able to transform their administrative structures than others? At any rate, the functional explanation of the relationship between industrialization and its requirements and the growth of rational bureaucratic forms seems to require some suspension of disbelief. These four cases present a broad variation in a number of aspects that produced what I have suggested are the two types of bureaucratic rationalization. They vary significantly in culture, economic development, political development, and political institutions.

Within the two categories of rationalization I have outlined, each path to bureaucratic rationalization seems to vary to a considerable extent. In the category of professionally oriented rationalization, however, political contestation and reform are the central features of the process. Within the organizationally oriented category, institutional differentiation, the contest for administrative specialization and autonomy, seems to have been central to the rationalization process. This suggests that, despite the historical variation distinguishing each case, there are systematic differences within the two categories. The question is whether these differences are linked by one or more constraining variables or whether they are the product of two distinct sets of variables.

The Problem of Leadership Succession

What is the common recurring problem in a large number of nineteenth-century states which appears to have produced the institutionalization of the rationalized administrative role as the solution? It is extremely doubtful, in the case of state bureaucracies, that allocational efficiency was the central problem, especially since there was no market to test efficiency in price terms. Although attempts have been made to apply cost-benefit analysis (Zeckhauser and Schaefer 1968; Wildavsky 1968; Weisbrod 1968; Foster 1966; Prest and Turvey 1972; Layard 1972; Borcherding 1977, 45–70; Abouchar 1984), the difficulty is that no reasons are given as to why redistribution decisions made by government officials should be considered as efficient even when goals are specified (Foster 1966; Palumbo 1975; Loasby 1976; Jackson 1983:176–210). Indeed, public choice analysis seems to show that no clear or consistent criteria of weighting exists nor what criteria of weighting ought to be used in organizing or distributing any benefits or services (Palumbo 1975; Elkin 1974; Contini 1969: chapter 4).

Precisely because the state is a monopoly and the state administration has no competition (except, perhaps, intramurally), efficiency of its operations cannot be a recurring problem (except, of course, to members of the political opposition) to which the response is rationalization. This is reflected in several aspects of the role structure often associated with rational bureaucracy. Role hierarchy and hierarchical responsibility are not by any means always highly or positively correlated with other aspects of role structure (Udy 1959; Pugh et al. 1963, 1968, 1969a, 1969b). Nor is it clear from the wide variations in criteria for recruitment and advancement in so-called rational bureaucracies that these are directly related to questions of efficiency in the distribution of the state's resources. Indeed, there is a considerable literature anxious to show us instead that rational-legal role characteristics produce inefficiency and conflict (Gouldner 1954; Olson 1968:62; Michels 1966:71; Boulding 1966:8; Williamson 1975:125; Monsen and Downs 1965; Mirlees 1976; Braverman 1974; Marglin 1974; Clawson 1980). Such criticism is also widespread in the literature evaluating the performance of public bureaucracies (Kaufman 1977; Pressman and Wildavsky 1979; Sheriff 1975).

As Perrow points out, a major reason for conflicts is that while bureaucratic rules spell out the limits of subordinate roles they also provide the means by which subordinates may resist incursions or demands by superiors (Perrow 1986 [1972]:28–30; also Crozier 1964). The two-edged character of rules gives rise to informal structures of behavior in which the rules are utilized for individual as against organizational interests. In this sense, rules in and of themselves are by no means consistently efficient from the standpoint of the price of services or goods. Finally, arguments about operational or X-efficiency as the main recurring problem do not explain why distinct patterns of rational organizational roles should emerge (Leibenstein 1973, 1975). If operational efficiency were the recurring problem, it seems reasonable to expect that the limited variables related to operational efficiency would result in very similar structural outcomes for organizational roles.

If the central recurring problem of state organizational life is neither general allocative efficiency nor operational efficiency, what then remains? One clue is provided by the historical conditions under which the two modes of bureaucratic rationality were institutionalized. I have already noted earlier that the cases in the organizationally oriented category seem to share a similar road to bureaucratic rationalization—one centered on the problem of differentiation. What is noticeable is that the problems of institutional differentiation in these countries all seemed to have emanated from total or partial successions of leadership. Organizationally oriented bureaucracies emerged following, in the cases of France after 1789 and Japan after 1868, total successions of leadership.[1]

What was the connection between crises of leadership succession and a process of differentiation that led to a specific mode of bureaucratic role rationalization? Part of the connection lies in the understanding that leadership succession (when it is total or partial) is not simply some mechanical rotation of elites. It implies the substitution of one means of, and criteria for, selecting leaders by another. When such substitutions are made, there must

---

1. For descriptions of state development following these crises of leadership succession, see: *France*: Suleiman 1974; Godechot 1968; Church 1970; Thuillier 1980; *Japan*: Silberman 1967, 1973, 1976; Spaulding 1967; Beasley 1972; Yamanaka 1974; Norman [1940] 1975; *Germany*: Gillis 1971; Delbrück 1917; Engelsing 1968; Kehr 1965; Koselleck 1967; Lotz 1909.

be new institutional arrangements for the selection process as well as new arrangements for acquiring the criteria for selection. To replace one process of leadership selection with another is to change the whole basis on which decision-makers are selected and decisions are made.

Weber sought to make the point that the rules by which decision-makers were selected were intimately tied to the kinds of information thought to be appropriate for making decisions. The relationship between patrimonial authority and custom as the basis for traditional decision making was not arbitrary. Past decisions with "satisficing" outcomes became the standard criterion for appropriateness in the absence of any other system for determining what information was appropriate for producing decisions with relatively predictable outcomes. Where this was the case, custom as a body of knowledge could not be entrusted to anyone or everyone. It could only be entrusted to those who had acted out the custom and who had been trained to do so. Birth became one of the means by which customary practice as a body of information was not corrupted by open contestation. How nice it was that this arrangement worked out so well for those who held power and status.

In the same way, Weber's conception of rational-legal authority did not combine certain structural characteristics of decision making and role characteristics of decision-makers coincidentally. With the shattering of custom as the means for arriving at decisions in the late eighteenth and early nineteenth centuries, some systematic constraint had to be placed on information used for this purpose. Those constraints had to provide decision making with the capacity for producing relatively high levels of predictability with regard to outcomes. What was available was science or rather, perhaps, scientism. In scientism, information was ordered not on past trial and error performance but on some notion of the discreteness of cause and effect. Physical and supposedly social facts were seen as functions of theoretically holistic and discrete ideas of physical and social nature. The correct application of information to specific problems became a function of education and not primarily of birth; of knowledge publicly displayed and not of esoteric private knowledge. The result was that leadership succession was processually related to a totally new criterion for leadership eligibility.

In this sense then, total or partial successions of leadership are not descriptions of individual replacement but rather of a systematic structure of replacement. Thus, for example, the Meiji Restoration of 1868 in Japan led to a complete restructuring of the criteria for leadership and, as a consequence, leadership succession and decision making. Similarly, the French Revolution led to a century-long struggle over the criteria for determining political leadership and power, resulting in an equally transformed structure of leadership succession and decision making.

Yet, this transformation in Japan did not result in the elimination of all those who were members of the traditional elite, in which entrance had been almost completely restricted by birth. Indeed, the majority of those who came to govern after 1868 were members of the pre-1868 ascriptive elites—although they were drawn mostly from the lower end of the hierarchy of birth and social rank (Silberman 1964). Again, the same phenomenon can be noted in France. The change in the criteria of leadership after the Revolution of 1789 did not eliminate the nobility from entrance to leadership roles in subsequent decades (Baecque et al. 1976). Napoleon was notorious for resurrecting the nobility but provided them with no essential claims to power or status (Tulard 1976:8–13).

At the same time, the transformation of the structure of leadership presents powerful pressures for the reconstruction of decision making. The existence of new leadership criteria implies the necessity of new kinds of information for decision making. New kinds of information require new rules or customs of usage and application. Where such restructuring occurs in a formal manner, accompanied by the appearance of new rules for decision making, we have strong reason to believe that a crisis in leadership succession has occurred. We may call this a revolutionary condition. While such a crisis may not be sufficient for a definition of revolution, it seems necessary for one. Total successions of leadership or crises in leadership succession which bring new decision-making rules into existence offer clear opportunities for the reconstruction of administrative systems and for the reconstruction of the relationship between state and civil society.

Professionally oriented bureaucracies, such as the United States and Great Britain, emerged under conditions in which there were relatively well-defined and well-regulated rules governing the succession of political leadership.[2] While the task of leadership succession in these two countries came to be organized around well-specified rules of voting and well-governed access to candidacy, these rules did not provide certainty about the outcomes of elections. Hard as candidates might try—through such ploys as organizing political parties, careful surveillance of voter rights and voter lists, and reducing the number of contested offices—they nevertheless could not fix voters in easily predicted outcomes. Despite several hundred years of historical experience, candidates still find voters to be volatile. Indeed, it seems that this volatility was one of the prime if not *the* prime incentive to engage in reforms that would reduce voting instability. Not only may such reforms include at-

2. On the United States, see: Van Riper 1958a; Hoogenboom 1961; White 1958; Fish 1904 [1963]; Wiebe 1967; for Great Britain, see: Parris 1969; Kingsley 1944; Cohen 1941; Great Britain 1968; MacDonagh 1961.

tempts to regulate voters' choices, but also they may include attempts to re-move some choices from the public arena and place them in the hands of ad-ministrators, thereby reducing the sources of contestation. Party contest-ation then also provides opportunities or conditions, although not in anywhere near the dramatic and disconcerting fashion of cases of total lead-ership succession, for restructuring decision-making rules and thus the cri-teria for selecting decision-makers.

Both sets of cases had conditions under which political leadership succes-sion crises have occurred and which were followed by the restructuring of decision-making rules and administrative structure. This suggests that the continuing problem facing many nineteenth- and early twentieth-century states was the dilemma of the succession of political leaders and the level of uncertainty regarding their possession of power. *Rational bureaucratization may thus be construed as a consequence of strategic choices by those holding po-litical power in environments of greater or lesser uncertainty.*

Greater or high uncertainty in this context is a situation in which there is relatively little information about the possible forms of rules concerning de-cision making, but sufficient is available to assign probabilities to the out-comes of some but not all choices. This condition exists certainly, but not exclusively, in situations where existing rules for selecting political leaders have been suspended or dissolved. One of these situations is where there has been a total or partial succession of political leaders. Lesser or low uncer-tainty is where there is considerable information available in the form of op-erating rules about the probabilities of the outcomes of choices. This situ-ation applies to conditions where there are well-articulated and regulated systems of leadership selection. One of these conditions is that of elective systems where the process is highly predictive although the winner is not. There is a general well-understood rule about how to decide a winner which helps to determine the predictability of the processual outcome, that is, we can predict with great certainty that a winner will emerge from any specific election and that nearly everybody will accept the outcome. Utilizing these two aspects of uncertainty, we can construct two quite distinct strategies—the strategy of political leaders in low uncertainty situations produces the professionally oriented bureaucracy, while the high uncertainty situations produce organizationally oriented bureaucracies.

Uncertainty and Equality

One might argue, however, that political leadership succession entails risk at almost any time in any society. Rarely is there absolute certainty about the outcomes of political leadership succession. No set of rules governing leadership selection can forestall every possible contingency. Thus, each succession must produce some uncertainty, if not anxiety, as to the outcome of rules which govern the role behavior of political leadership. Low-risk situations abound in history in the forms of dynastic, oligarchic, and chieftainship rules. The problem (at least in terms of this argument) is that such situations did not produce rational bureaucratization. Bureaucratic rationalization is peculiar, for the most part, to the post-1800 world. What then was distinctive about the environment of the nineteenth century so that uncertainty about rules governing political leadership was sufficiently high that it produced a transformation of the administrative role and organizational structure? Here I would like to suggest that the emergence in the late eighteenth and especially in the early part of the nineteenth centuries of institutionalized patterns reflecting some condition of equality raised the threshold of uncertainty about outcomes of choice (that is, the odds on assigned possibilities rose significantly).

For political leadership, the problem of risk as a function of the way in which equality was institutionalized took on two forms in the nineteenth century. In the cases of the United States and Great Britain (and to a considerable degree Switzerland as well), risk for political leaders grew as a consequence of the expansion of franchise and/or the expansion in the number of elective offices. The development presented increasingly complex problems for determining outcomes of elective processes. In this sense, as many politicians have found, elective processes may not always be low-risk situations. Since the low level of risk in electoral situations is not a result of electoral predictability (except in one-party systems), it seems likely that it stems, at least in large part, from the acceptance or legitimacy of the electoral process.

By the beginning of the nineteenth century, in both the United States and Great Britain, the basic processes of franchise were firmly established on the basis of a civil law that assured the equality of individuals in their civil and economic, if not their political, relations. The development of contract in English, and subsequently American, common law rested on the assumption that everyday forms of exchange were based on the equal capacity of individuals to enter into contracts (Atiyah 1979:261–62, 342–54). This civil equality made political participation in the form of the franchise subject to purely nonascriptive criteria. One might be barred from voting by not paying a sufficient amount of taxes, since this was applied equally to all regardless of birth. One, however, could not be barred from voting simply because he was not a gentleman (Atiyah 1979: 76–77). If birth were a distinguishing criterion, then civil relations would, of necessity, be carried out among unequals with vast consequences for the way in which contracts could be entered into and enforced.

The emergence of contract might be seen as a means by which individuals seeking to exercise choices and lacking a centralized state administrative structure could try to overcome some of the consequent risks and contingencies of economic life (Atiyah 1979: 94, 102). In the same way, the franchise emerged as a similar means to overcome the risks and contingencies of political life. The franchise was not simply analogous to the equality of civil transactions and liberties but was a direct outgrowth of this form of equality. So long as political liberties were merely a function of the possession of wealth (rather than of *both* status and wealth) seen as the measure of the capacity to serve the public interest, then political liberties would always be viewed as merely arbitrary. After all, if wealth were the sole criterion, how could one determine the exact amount of wealth necessary to act rationally for oneself and the public interest? The expansion of the franchise was, thus, inevitable insofar as it was in anyone's interest (regardless of whether that person was enfranchised or not) to show just how arbitrary such a criterion was when it was compared to the conception of equality (that is, economic enfranchisement) in civil law. In civil law, there came to be no monetary limitations placed on the individual's capacity to act rationally—even the poorest man (women were excluded from this capacity) was viewed as capable of entering into a contract.

The fact that political liberties—the right to vote, the right of association, and the right to seek elective office—stemmed from well-ordered and well-understood rules of civil relations meant that elective procedures would not, indeed could not, result in suspension of contract and other civil liberties. Political leaders accordingly knew beforehand that loss of an election was not the equivalent of losing one's head or even completely losing power. Hence, on at least two distinct but closely related accounts, the existence of civil and political equality reduced risks for leadership. While outcomes of elections might not be specifically predictable, the processes were and this provided a stable political structure.

In situations where there was a total or partial succession of leadership coinciding with a structural crisis of leadership, the problem of equality had quite different origins and organizational problems. In the cases of what might be called a "revolutionary condition," such as Japan in 1868 and France in 1789, the suspension of the old rules governing the selection of leadership produced a "revolutionary moment." One of the characteristics of this "moment" was the rejection of birth or estate as the primary criterion for determining either leadership ability or leadership status. The French Revolution, once and for all, turned our collective backs on the past precisely on this issue. When the Estates-General selected themselves to create a constitutional monarchy rather than serve under the rules of the "absolute" monarchy, they created a condition of political participation which could end only in some notion of equality. At the revolutionary moment when self-selected putative leaders ended the claims of birth and estate, the road was left open to a number of possible alternative claims to the right to lead. Neither birth nor estate as criteria for leadership could be resurrected since their demise was characterized almost everywhere it occurred as the direct result of class selfishness, self-interest, or the pursuit of private ends. Now only some standard which could incorporate equality could be used. What that standard would be was not easily predictable by the participants. The revolutionary moment was the moment of greatest risk since it imposed no predictable patterns on leadership or decision making.

To those would-be leaders facing such situations, no less than two forms of equality presented themselves. First, claims could be made by putative political leaders that leadership was based on the representation of public interest. Such representation then required a notion of political liberties in which, ultimately, individuals had equality of chance and choice to pursue their interests or to be selected as representing interests. The other form in which claims could be made was that which argued that representation of public interest must be based on merit as determined by some objective standard of evaluation or judgment—the idea that the public interest was simply too important to be left to the public. Here individuals had to have equality of chances as well as choice to achieve a standard which could be defined as meritorious. Equality in the sense of the absence of ascriptive obstacles to chances and choices were common to both situations. The first, however, saw equality as essentially a positive statement of the worth of individual choice and interest. The second saw equality as the necessary condition for providing the means by which merit might be utilized and judged. The first saw the transformation of a private right (choice) into a public one. The second saw the transformation of the idea of merit as residing in birth to that of merit as resident in educational certification and achievement.

In neither the Japanese nor the French case were these notions of equality well set in structures of civil law where the relations between individuals were regulated and ordered on the basis of equal capacity to enter into contracts. Equality did not stem from civil liberties and the attempt to minimize the role of the state as a definer and participant in the contractual process. Equality stemmed from strategic considerations regarding what claims putative leaders might make to establish their right to make decisions. It is precisely for this reason that the idea of equality had such difficult sledding under revolutionary conditions in these two countries. Since equality as an organizational property was unregulated, it could produce the highest levels of uncertainty for those laying claim to power—much higher than in those situations where equality was mediated and kept within well-charted channels by the entire edifice of civil law and civil liberties.

In short, the emergence in the nineteenth century of institutional patterns associated with role equality created an environment where levels of uncertainty about political leadership succession were significantly higher than they had been in the past when role behaviors associated with general equality were absent. The appearance of equality as an institutional norm occurred in two ways, under revolutionary conditions or under the expansion of economic equality to the realm of politics. These two conditions created the environments of high and low uncertainty examined in the next chapter.

3

The Strategies of Uncertainty

This chapter is concerned with delineating the problems of political leaders under conditions of high and low uncertainty and the strategies they might employ to retain or stabilize their power and status. This chapter also takes up the problem of how such strategies create dilemmas for political leaders over how to hold rationalized bureaucracies accountable. The analysis of this problem provides another variable which, when combined with uncertainty, provides a somewhat finer way to distinguish the outcomes of high and low uncertainty alone.

The Strategy of High Uncertainty

Under conditions of high uncertainty brought about by total or partial successions of leadership, a number of problems face those who have seized power or those who would like to do so. In the broadest sense, these may be termed the problems of legitimacy, equality, community, and history. The problem of legitimacy is raised since it is not clear in revolutionary conditions on what grounds or by whom decisions are made. This ambiguity makes it extremely difficult to predict the outcomes of choices made by any set of putative leaders or by individuals in general. Putative leaders must reject past rules for determining what information is appropriate for use in decision making. Historically, the revolutionary moment meant the abandonment of custom and tradition as the primary constraint on utilizing information for decision making. At the revolutionary moment, presumptive leaders are self-selected or at least not selected by the former rules of leadership succession. In this condition, would-be leaders are bound to reject both the traditional criteria for leadership selection and the structure of rules governing how and on what basis decisions are made. To do otherwise subverts any claims that new leaders may have. Why should new leaders be selected outside the traditional formal structure if the old structure of decision making is seen as perfectly valid? For those who would take power there appears to be little choice but to reject the traditional basis of decision making as well as the traditional structure of leadership selection.

This creates conditions in which there is uncertainty about what information is appropriate, what rules are to be used to determine appropriateness, and how predictable the consequences of decisions stemming from new rules about decision making will be. Bounded rationality on the part of would-be leaders makes it impossible to assign very high probabilities as to the outcomes of their decisions, since they are presumably operating under quite different rules of decision making than those which obtained under the old regime. The major problem for leaders seeking to hold on to their precarious power during and immediately after the revolutionary moment is clear. They must find a decision-making rule system that, when combined with a new and systematic structure of leadership selection, will produce the capacity to make decisions with relatively predictable outcomes. If power stems from the barrels of guns, legitimacy must surely sprout from the more mundane but equally important books of rules which keep daily life from being an exercise in arbitrariness.

The total or partial suspension of rules governing leadership selection and succession also immediately raises the question of equality. Where birth or some such ascriptive criterion is the basis for determining eligibility for leadership or leadership selection—as was the case in pre–nineteenth-century Europe and almost everywhere else—then the revolutionary moment produces the idea of equality immediately. This arises simply because the replacement of old-regime leaders by self-selected, would-be leaders promptly destroys the ascriptive criteria. Any structure of self-selection must subvert existing organizational rules. Under these circumstances, any claim to power may have equal weight. After all, where no rules exist except those of self-selection the contest for power is anarchic and without exception destructive. Would-be leaders must provide a non-narcissistic answer to the uncomfortable question: why should you run things rather than us? What way is there out of this dilemma? What qualities can putative leaders claim give them the right to wield power other than their own selfish desires? Clearly birth cannot be a criterion. The only strategy putative leaders seem to have here is to establish some criterion for which they can claim social equality as a base. No ascriptive or self-seeking criteria can be used.

As we have seen, the claims of equality may take at least two forms: claims for equality of representation or claims for equality to exhibit capacity or merit. The former produces criteria for leadership associated with capacity for rational choice. Everyone has equality of choice and their desires have equality of weight so long as they meet some general standard of rationality. Accordingly, age, sex, race, and economic condition have all been used to exclude individuals from participation in forms of representation. Individuals falling into these categories are not excluded on the basis of birth but on the claim that they do not possess the capacity for making rational choices. Equality, thus, would be constrained only by those elements thought to keep individuals from attaining a mental capacity to make rational choices about their preferences. This kind of claim, of course, may be, and often is, purely ideological in the sense that it seeks to provide a rational discourse for existing customary systems of exclusion.

Claims of equality to exhibit merit without regard to ascriptive criteria tend to produce criteria for leadership based on the ability to achieve high standards of some measurable characteristic. Achievement in this sense might be measured by economic wealth. There, leadership selection and succession would be based on a hierarchy of wealth. Instrumental capacity might be used to narrow claims to the right to govern. The problem is, except in the most extreme cases, how to measure instrumental capacity with any accuracy. Capacity in revolutionary or crisis conditions seems relatively easy to determine—those who come out on top in a free-for-all are, it can be argued, those with the greatest capacity to lead. Despite Jefferson's dictum about watering the tree of liberty with blood every generation, this is an extremely costly test of ability, as the failure to follow this advice indicates. This difficulty inevitably leads to claims of substitutability in predicting ability. The claim is often made that future instrumental capacity is relatively well predicted by the ability to acquire objectively testable knowledge of some kind—classical education or legal training, for example. The claims of equality are met by imposing no obstacles of an ascriptive nature on individuals seeking to acquire the appropriate knowledge.

In any situation of social equality, leaders must provide some rationale as to why they should govern. The two dominant strategies for doing so, representation of individual "subjective" rational choices or the possession of knowledge enabling one to make "objective" rational choices, are responses to the greater uncertainty produced by the emergence of social equality. One emerged through the evolution of contract under common law, while the other appeared as the result of "revolutionary moments" or major successions of leadership.

Would-be leaders, in those moments following the suspension of the rules of leadership succession, are also inevitably faced with the problem of community. Not only are they confronted with the general problem of the possible breakdown of rules governing social and economic relationships, but they are also confronted with the problem of community as reflected in the capacity to have relatively well defined notions of leadership. If the existence of community is dependent on the widespread agreement on the rules governing behavior and their meaning, then agreement on who is to interpret and enforce the rules is essential to the continuity of the community. In essence, the inability to define leadership is the inability to define community. However, the absence of rules about what constitutes political leadership and its continuity and selection means that claimant leaders cannot predict the consequences of their choices or of anyone else's. More important, perhaps, in the absence of rules governing leadership, claims as to who will represent the community remain unresolved and open. Without any agreed-upon criteria for leadership, the sense of community is fractionated. Without systematic rules governing leadership succession, there can hardly be any legitimate system of decision making—that is, one that produces relatively predictable outcomes. Lacking such a structure, there cannot be a uniform or homogeneous representation of the public or social good or of public interest. Presumptive leaders will thus face a multitude of claimants who assert their right to represent the community. Thus, leaders must solve the problem of community. One powerful strategy for doing so is the creation of new systematic structures of leadership selection and succession which promise both stability and continuity of community life.

Finally, claimant leaders in high uncertainty or revolutionary conditions face the problem of history. The total or critical succession of political leadership has clearly shown that history is not the history of a "natural" social order. Once the old regime is overthrown or has itself thrown in the towel, history appears as subject to will or, perhaps more accurately, the object of will. Leaders have to deal with the dilemma, so neatly and elegantly put by Marx, that men make their own history, but they do not make it just as they please, rather than to Hegel's conclusion that history makes men pretty much as it pleases. By overthrowing and bringing to naught preceding systems of leadership, decision making, and community, new leadership seems to have shown that history is secular and given over to will. Order, it would appear, is as contingent as disorder. The latter is not seen as a lapse, moral or otherwise, of a natural stable order. Inherently this must pose a powerful problem for would-be leaders. If the past order is not morally superior or essential, then the future one *must* be so.

But on what basis can the claim be made that the future order—that which the new leaders will construct—is superior? How will they sustain the claim when faced by others who may, and no doubt will, argue that history is really theirs? The problem is twofold: on the one hand, the structure of order must be seen to be the necessary product of the revolutionary condition; on the other hand, the new leadership must be seen as the rightful purveyors of this superior and necessary social order. In short, the problem is to put history back in its cage. Any new leadership must stuff it back in or face powerful contesting stories of how history can proceed only in the hands of very different actors. History cannot be seen as contingent on human preference and will.

The Organizational Resolution of High Uncertainty Problems

To resolve these problems would-be leaders must construct or reconstruct a system of rules that covers a broad range of social and political behavior. The reconstruction of these rules also implies the reordering of rules governing economic relations. Thus, critical incidents of leadership succession bring in their wake the suspension of a broad spectrum of rules. How will aspiring leaders, confronted with such conditions, decide to act in order to secure their status, power, and material resources? What possible choices are there? One choice that might well resolve the general problems raised by the collapse of leadership succession rules is to depend on some collective choice mechanism that incorporates individual preferences. The problems of equality, legitimacy, community, and history are rather easily resolved by this choice. Equality in the determination of the public interest could plausibly be assured by giving each vote an equal weight. While outcomes in this mode might not always be happy ones, they will be public. Legitimacy can also be assured through the process of voting. Rules governing franchise and the selection and election of candidates produce high levels of predictability about the nature of leadership succession and decision making. The community problem is solved by resorting to procedures determining majorities and protecting minorities. The community of shared experience is the community of shared procedures. Community integrity comes to be based on agreement about the inviolability of selection procedures and the protection of the losers from arbitrary acts. History as a problem is resolved by the notion of progress. The revolutionary condition is defined not as the product of arbitrary will but as part of some greater urge toward civility, humanity, and justice. Or, to put it another way, the historical revolutionary condition is redefined as ideology. The revolutionary condition is now seen as a consequence of some inherent structural flaw, which is cured by political leaders possessing an understanding of a universally applicable solution.

The one problem not resolved by recourse to voting is the specific uncertainty of those laying claim to leadership. Any group of self-selected leaders emerging from the thickets of a revolutionary condition is not likely to find comfort in a system based on individual subjective rational choice. Reliance on such a system might lead to completely unanticipated or uncomfortable consequences. Voters, left free to choose, are notoriously fickle. Would-be leaders are thus likely to want to avoid, as much as possible, any reliance on mechanisms that utilize and allow voting as the means for selecting political leaders unless choice is carefully constrained as in plebiscites. This is a somewhat windy way of saying that leaders who appear after critical events of leadership succession are not likely to endanger their claims to status and power by resorting to open elections.

Strategies and Tactics to Reduce Uncertainty

What choices are left if claimants to leadership wish to secure and maintain their positions? Only two broad possibilities appear: (1) to maintain their power and positions by the use of force alone to eliminate challengers or (2) to seek a leadership structure that excludes solipsistic challenges on the one side and reliance on voting on the other side.

The first option does not resolve matters well since it allows a broad range of solipsistic or opportunistic appeals to moral or other authority. Some sort of civil war is thus a likely possibility and these are well known to have unpredictable outcomes. They nevertheless occur with considerable frequency in early stages of total or critical political successions when either or both sides feel they have everything to gain and nothing to lose or when sufficient time to utilize other solutions is not available. At any rate, victory does not resolve matters in a sufficiently suitable manner. The problem of allocating power and position among the victors is now pushed to the fore. Once again, leadership among the victors cannot resort to open elections lest they be voted out of office. Nor can offices and accompanying benefits be allocated on the basis of loyalty since presumably all those on the winning side may sensibly argue that degrees of loyalty are difficult to determine in any satisfying way. The problem for victors becomes the same as in the second option.

When the second choice is made, the resolution to this problem appears to be the pursuit of two strategies. First, a short-term strategy, with the aim of replacing those in the secondary and tertiary levels of the decision-making structure with those who are seen to be loyal (the criterion in this case is usually some direct knowledge of the individual), is implemented. Second, a long-term strategy emerges from the tactics employed in the short-term strategy. This long-term strategy is based on the development of a qualitatively and quantitatively defined career structure. The aim of this career structure is to create a cadre of decision-makers that is homogeneous and committed to the organization above all personal obligations. The resort to rules reduces ambiguity and conflict engendered by the lack of homogeneity among this first-generation group of leaders over definition of goals and how they should be implemented (Gouldner 1954; Selznick 1957).

The short-term strategy relies on what Gouldner called "strategic replacement" (Gouldner 1954). This action implies more profound consequences than just the replacement of one set of individuals or officials by another set.

The strategy of replacement as opposed to simply getting one's friends in positions of power as often and as best one can emphasizes the attempt to create an interdependent structure of leadership positions. Such a structure seeks to cover as many layers of decision making as possible. In the first instance, the strategy emanates from the well-understood desire to have those you do not or cannot trust out of offices that have discretion over important resources. The greater the capacity to remove potential obstacles to the implementation of decisions, the greater the ability to reduce uncertainty and all of its attendant evils.

Three types of tactics can be seen to follow from this strategy of replacement. First, and certainly the most easily arrived at by leaders, is to replace all members (or as many as possible) of the preceding regime. This seems simple and to a considerable extent it is, albeit with several important exceptions. Second is the perceived necessity of gaining control over as many offices as possible. Officials who hold offices based on independent access to, and control of, resources are not easily removed. So long as they remain in office they represent alternative sources of power. At the same time, they control resources for which new leaders have a generally voracious appetite. The tactical choice in this strategy of replacement is to try to internalize these positions, that is, to incorporate them within the structure of decision making over which the new or would-be leaders lay claim. This internalization poses several organizational problems. The most significant of these is the problem of "managerial control" or how to get everyone to execute decisions in a more or less uniform manner. From this also follows another important problem—*how* to internalize positions. For leaders facing the problem of control, the way in which new offices are incorporated into the administrative organization is more than just a trivial technical adjustment. Failure to internalize offices in identifiable systematic categories within a realistic structure of oversight leads to administrative anarchy. The short-term strategy of "strategic replacement" thus leads to attempts to create loyal cadres, to internalization of offices and general organizational centralization, and finally to the creation of systems of internal control and management in order to maintain centralized power and authority.

The third tactic, the creation of loyal cadres within the framework of the revolutionary condition, does not provide much in the way of alternatives for leaders. Unless, as with Lenin, the leaders foresee this problem and create cadres prior to the revolutionary condition, would-be leaders are forced to fall back on contingent tests of loyalty as the sole criterion for entry into the cadre. The criterion for loyalty will most likely be based on personal knowledge of the leaders regarding who can be trusted. The test of trust in this situation will surely be the degree to which individuals supported the putative leaders in bringing about the crisis and the rapidity with which they joined the leaders in their action. In this regard, loyalty may well be sufficient to overcome the problem posed by leaving officials of the former regime in possession of their offices. Regardless of their mixed backgrounds, the newly appointed officials will at least not intend to oppose the leaders to whom they are indebted. Nevertheless, the very criterion used to select them may pose serious problems for the implementation of decisions made by their patrons.

Loyalty as a criterion for decision making and administration is, at best, indifferent and, at worst, a source of disruption and disorder. The most glaring weakness of loyalty as a test for administrative capacity is its inability to provide any guidelines for decision making or implementation except self-interest or patron interest. These are insufficient since the desire to please or to support one's patrons is not in itself any assurance that any particular act will be helpful or what is desired by the patron. Certainly, self-interest as a guide will not work either, since there can be no assurance that what is good for me will be good for my patron or anyone else. Perhaps a more pressing problem presented by loyalty is the question of how to differentiate between loyal individuals. How can one judge the intensity of loyalty? The inability of loyalty to be subject to a fine test of discrimination must produce a range of problems for the development of any kind of internal labor market or organization.

Only slightly less important is that loyalty, as determined by highly contingent criteria, does not provide any means for organizational continuity. What is to be done about replacements once there are no longer any survivors of the original event that served as the measure of loyalty? Surely a new revolution cannot be created every twenty years or so to produce a new set of leaders—the Cultural Revolution in China has shown us just how futile that can be. Resorting to replacement by personal patronage presents the problem of trying to distinguish between public and private. The continued use of loyalty as a means of selecting and replacing officials is not likely to survive the accusation that leaders are, in fact, pursuing their private interests rather than those of the public. Replacement of officials on the basis of loyalty may solve the short-term problem of administrative opposition, but it does not solve the long-term problems of uniformity of decision making and implementation, organizational continuity, leadership selection and appointment, and the publicness and predictability of leadership.

In the same way, the wholesale internalization of offices, especially local ones as opposed to the central offices claimed by the leaders themselves, solves some of the problems related to institutional sources of opposition, but mere transformation from autonomy or partial autonomy without also transforming the relationship of the offices within the administrative organization is to invite a return to autonomy. Put another way, centralization or internalization without uniform categories of offices defined by the new leaders may only be a reaffirmation of localism or of the autonomy of the functional division of offices. This internalization creates the long-term problem of defining categories of offices with reference to a center or a central set of decision-making capacities and resources. The long-term problem here, as with the case of loyalty, is the problem of defining roles.

Problems of "managerial control"—keeping everyone from acting in terms of their own subjective rationality—have a short-term solution. Control of subordinates sufficient to provide a half-way reasonable approximation of consensus on decision making and implementation can be arrived at in several ways. One of these is the age-old recourse to cliques or factions. Structures of personal relations, such as patron-client ones, can provide constraints on excessive opportunism or eccentricity precisely because of their high level of personal interaction and short span of control. They can thus create a minimal level of uniform behavior. Under conditions of critical occurrences of leadership succession, however, this pragmatic solution has all the defects of its advantages. The persistence of clique or factional structures seems inevitably to produce challengers who argue that such personalized structures serve private rather than public interest.

There are several other ways to achieve reasonable levels of uniformity in decision making and implementation when faced with the problem of officials with heterogeneous backgrounds. One of these is to define each position extensively, create categories of positions, define or draw from these categories a set of job descriptions, designate appropriate skills, and train or appoint people possessing those skills. "The right person for the right job" allows heterogeneity to exist so long as the individual's actions are constrained by the skill aspect of his or her training. The problem here is that there is no powerful pressure for individuals to be loyal, except, perhaps, to their skills. The use of specific skills as the criterion for office-holding in order to overcome the problem of differing backgrounds gives the possessor a considerable degree of autonomy. The individual can practice his skills anywhere since they are not organization specific. Thus leadership may face the problem of being unable to get subordinates to implement decisions because they represent "unskilled" (or "unprofessional") solutions. In political terms, then, leaders in this type of situation may find themselves in difficulty. They now lead organizations in which there is agreement on the structure of decision making and implementation but in which decision-makers have great autonomy.

Finally, there is the situation noted by Gouldner (1954): the resort to rules to specify the boundaries of decision making as well as the procedures and the appropriate information to be used in arriving at decisions. This has clear advantages over the preceding solutions. It does not preclude the reliance on contingent tests of loyalty as the criterion for appointment. Nor does it preclude the reliance on external or independently held bodies of information or ethical rules on utilization of information since they are constrained by organizational rules. The resort to rules emphasizes the organizational source of information and procedures as against individual and private sources.

Employing rules as a tactic to impose uniformity of decision making and implementation does not solve everything. This tactic has serious defects. While rule-making gives new leaders the capacity to hedge in and restrain individuals from pursuing their own beliefs or interests, the rules can also be subversive if they appear to be arbitrary. In this regard then, the rules defining administrative roles and their boundaries must be related in a systematic way to achieving the public interest since this is the only ground on which the seizure of power can be legitimately claimed. The real problem for leaders is how to indicate that the decision-making process is not arbitrary or for private purposes. How can decision making be made to appear to be public in character without resorting to one person, one vote? Rationalization of administrative roles in the Weberian sense—the quantitative and qualitative definition of role—seems to provide the only organizational solution to the problems of uniformity and legitimacy created by the dissolution of preceding rules governing leadership roles.

The problem of defining roles so that they are not private and individual possessions can only be fully resolved by eliminating office as a private and individual good. The former is accomplished by separating payment from the possession of office. The latter can only be accomplished through reliance on two tactics. The first is the use of uniformly applied formal rules defining roles. By relying on rules, political leaders create a uniformity that makes administrative leadership and its status an *organizational* rather than an individual characteristic. Second, the problem of the public character of such rules is assured by positing the existence of an objective reality—a body of rules that exists in nature and is capable of being and has been in fact discovered. That is, there is the claim that systems of knowledge exist, the possession of which allows the appropriate ordering of priorities and their implementation. The reliance on expertise as a means of ordering priorities and implementing them seemingly removes issues from politics; and, in effect, science or scientism is substituted for personal interest, and administration is substituted for politics (Wolin 1960:407–34).

Transforming political leadership into an organizational role centered on expertise and competence resolves the problems of authority and community faced by political leaders under these conditions. On the one hand, it vitiates the grounds on which challengers stand. Unless they accept these "objective" criteria, challengers to leadership may be accused of pursuing only personal desires rather than society's interests. On the other hand, the resort to "scientifically" derived rules resolves the question of why leadership should rest in a self-selected rather than a publicly selected group. Revolutionary leadership holds power or has seized it in the name of society in order to achieve society's wants or needs. These wants and needs can only be known and organized rationally, they argue, by possessing and utilizing a science or sciences of society. This tactic not only reveals the public spiritedness of leaders, it also resolves the problem of community raised by the rejection of preceding rules. As a consequence of this rejection of custom or tradition, the community must find another means for arriving at a society's interest. By substituting rules derived from a "scientific" understanding of how to achieve society's wants or needs, the new political leaders reconstitute community while sustaining their own status and power.

Emphasizing the acquisition of knowledge as a major test of leadership capability results in the reliance on merit or achievement as a general value. This goes a long way toward resolving the problem of equality. Rather than defining equality as a direct political or economic characteristic, merit defines it as the uniform application of "objective" standards of intelligence and instrumental ability. From this point of view, anyone, regardless of social station or birth, who meets a uniform test of educational competence may be eligible for entrance into the ranks of political leadership. For those who come to power through self-selection, the problem of reducing uncertainty about their positions is resolved by elevating administration to a systematic science. Only through a science of administration and the elimination of politics can the public interest be achieved.

Administrative Ideology

Under these conditions of uncertainty, leaders are led willy-nilly into assuming an organic utilitarian posture regarding the question of determining public policy. In this posture leaders are unwilling to rely on individual or subjective rational choices regarding wants or needs and are forced instead to argue that society may be conflated to the position of an individual. If they wish to reduce uncertainty about their authority, political leaders must take the view Utilitarians have taken, that "just as it is rational for man to maximize the fulfillment of his system of desires it is right for a society to maximize the net balance of satisfaction over all its members" (Rawls 1971:20). The acceptance of this principle of rational choice for one person would seem to require a conception of the policymaker as an impartial spectator who is capable of predicting appropriate priorities that would maximize the net balance of satisfaction taken over all its members. Rawls describes this position neatly:

[It is this impartial spectator] who is conceived of as carrying out the required organization of desires of all persons into one coherent system of desire; it is by this construction that many persons are fused into one. Endowed with ideal powers of sympathy and imagination, the impartial spectator is the perfectly rational individual who identifies with the experiences and the desires of others as if these desires were his own. In this way he ascertains the intensity of these desires and assigns them their appropriate weight in the one system of desire. . . . On this conception of society separate individuals are thought of as so many different lines along which rights and duties are to be assigned and scarce means of satisfaction allocated in accordance with rules so as to give the greatest fulfillment of wants. . . . The correct decision is essentially a question of efficient administration. (Rawls 1971:26–27)

From this point of view, administration not only substitutes for politics, it also becomes the representative of the public interest. Political cum administrative leaders under the condition of total or critical leadership succession thus become committed to the restructuring of leadership not only because they wish to retain their power, status, and material goods but also because they have come to believe in the superior capacity of these new organizations to determine the public interest. It appears to them that the public interest is simply too important to be left to the public. In this construction or reconstruction of the idea of public interest, political\administrative leaders have also transformed the boundaries of discussion about the public interest. Once they have come to view public interest as a matter of "efficient administration," political leaders come to value administrative reform as the means to achieve the public interest.

Organizational Closure

The problem for political leaders is how to make sure that this reordering of leadership will be able to maintain its integrity as an organization—the problem of insulating the role from external interest and influences. This requires a strategy aimed at successfully masking the self-interest aspects of reform and, at the same time, convincing the public that their interest is best served by this redefinition of administrative role. This can only be done by seeking homogeneity of leadership and high levels of organizational commitment. The constraints of role autonomy, publicness, and equality must lead to the elimination of class as a means of seeking homogeneity or organizational commitment.

The only apparent solution is to narrow entry into policy-making administrative roles by creating high standards for eligibility and entry. Limiting the number of schools that provide access to appropriate education and narrowly specifying the contents of appropriate education tends to resolve this problem. High standards for entry lengthen the time required for sufficient training to meet eligibility requirements. Limiting the number of schools available for this training not only encourages and sustains homogeneity of socialization, it also reduces the number of trained individuals available to private organizations. Narrowly specifying the contents of appropriate education reinforces the elements of uniformity and scarcity. The stress on merit and ability fends off possible criticism of self-interest. The insistence on an educational career helps to resolve the problem of convincing the public that policy-making is a function of utilitarian criteria for decision making. In short, if administration is to dominate policy-making and implementation, then it must seek to depoliticize the idea of public interest. This is achieved by making the understanding of public interest a function of educational standards. To this end, the education and the training of future civil servants must be directly controlled by the administrative structure.

The result, however, is a situation in which the critical structural element that emerges is the necessarily early commitment to bureaucratic careers by those who wish to become leaders. This follows inevitably from the narrowness of access to training. In order to get into the limited number of schools that formally or informally monopolize correct training, commitments by individuals to such careers must often be made long before entry into the university. Early commitment has high costs for the individual since it means rejecting alternative careers. Two types of incentives might be offered to offset these costs. First are social incentives—encouraging and subsidizing specific occupations requiring well-defined training, such as law. Such encouragement might take the form of legal requirements that individuals and groups must always be represented by lawyers with proper certification as to their training when contracts are entered into or when engaged in litigation. In other words, social incentives can be provided by giving a monopoly over certain general social or economic functions to a group of people who have invested early and heavily in certain kinds of training.

The danger of encouraging professionalism as the means of providing incentives for administrators or any other "professional" entering organizational careers is quite clear. Monopoly of this kind places the control of role definition in the hands of the practitioners—the recipients of the training. Commitment to an organization is thus likely to be undercut by commitments to the professional role and its organization. In the case of administrators, this kind of situation deprives political leaders of the monopoly or near monopoly over that expertise defined as necessary to determine public policy and, at the same time, provides private interests with the capacity to provide definitions of public policy. This kind of incentive will not provide the kind of organizational commitment that political leaders seek in the condition of high uncertainty.

The alternative to this incentive is to provide purely organizational inducement. To provide such an inducement, one basic constraint must be considered—the organizational consequences of remuneration by salary. If office-holding as a private good is eliminated, the problem of job security immediately becomes a problem. Separation of the holding of the office from its material benefits implies that that officeholder has no rights to the office or any office. Payment by salary is thus seen as implying the possibility of arbitrary dismissal. Thus in any system in which the officeholder no longer owns the means of administration, incentives for early commitment to an organizational career must be addressed to the problems of job security; high investment in time, effort, and money to acquire the appropriate training; and the forgoing of other possibly profitable occupations.

These problems are resolved and can probably only be resolved by structuring the role in the following specific ways. First, the problem of security from arbitrary dismissal must be met by a commitment, formally or informally, to tenure or to a very well defined structure for determining dismissal. Second, the payoff for the high investment and possible losses by the individual must be a highly predictable pattern of movement through a series of offices that are hierarchically ordered in terms of status, prestige, and reward (Williamson 1975:77–78). The assurance of a lifetime career so long as one does not violate explicit codes of action and behavior provides both opportunities for security and increases in wealth and status. Third, the beginning stage of the career must be sufficiently prestigious so as to reduce risks about advancement and ensure a minimal movement upward—the great expenditure on education and lost alternatives must be offset in the short-term by creating a distinct category of offices distinguished from run-of-the-mill administrative positions.

From these structural features other elements of bureaucratization emerge. The necessity for providing a highly predictable and special career structure creates great pressure for the development of single departmental-ministerial specialization. This results from the fact that interdepartmental transfers are likely to increase uncertainty about career—they simply create too many possible career tracks. This undermines predictability. At the same time, some transfers may be primarily horizontal and thus are demoralizing also in terms of upsetting the career predictability of those who are the new colleagues of the transferee. Uncertainty about the future clearly reduces the incentive to make an early commitment to enter the organization and, for those already in the organization, it reduces organizational commitment. Recognition of, or experience with, this fact thus tends to produce careers bounded by departments or ministries and, hence, ones that are relatively predictable. This outcome creates a career official who is likely to have broad experience within his department and is therefore oriented toward the department's structure as a whole rather than to any specific program of the department. Further specialization occurs not through the horizontal admittance of trained specialists but rather through the completion of career promotion. Individuals will not always rise to the very top and the place where their promotion possibilities end becomes the individual's specialty. This career pattern specialization also, unfortunately, has the consequence of producing a sectionalism within the bureaucratic structure that is difficult to mitigate.

The creation of a highly regular, systematic, and predictable career structure also produces an organizational structure that dominates the allocation of information. In a system where the individual is moved through a series of roles for which he or she has not been specifically trained, information about decision making is attached to the role structure. The individual acquires the appropriate information through serving in the role. Here the individual does not bring with him or her a body of information acquired outside of the organization and maintained over time by an occupationally or professionally set body of standards. The individual thus acquires a body of information that is highly organizationally and, often, ministerially or departmentally specific. This specificity makes it extremely difficult for the individual to transfer skills to another organization or ministry. This arrangement of information allocation thus reduces the opportunistic capacities of individuals to withhold information for the purposes of bargaining for promotion, higher wages, or other benefits (Williamson 1975:31–33). When information or skills of the individual are organizationally or departmentally specific, there are fewer chances of mobility outside of his or her venue. This situation tends to make organizational loyalty a necessity and not just a virtue.

The pressure to provide a highly predictable career produces other consequences for role definition. At the early stages of the career, seniority must be the major criterion for advancement. If this is not the case, then, once again, a higher level of career risk is introduced with its attendant effects on incentives. Some criterion other than experience, as reflected in seniority, must be applied at the higher levels of the hierarchy where fewer and fewer offices are available. Nevertheless, seniority is the primary constraint on determining advancement to that point. As a consequence, seniority is likely to emerge as a high value and in itself is likely to reinforce hierarchy and help define its character.

A second problem arising from the emergent career structure is that of providing sufficient offices throughout the hierarchy to maintain the organizationally oriented incentive. Since there is no way to predict the number of offices that will become available over time in a "natural" fashion (that is, as the result of illnesses, resignations, deaths, etc.), some means must be found to maintain incentives to enter while at the same time ensuring the existence of sufficient offices to sustain careers. Two alternative solutions to this problem are available: rapid succession within the career combined with relatively early and well-defined retirement; or expansion of the number of offices on a sufficiently predictable basis. The first is risky since it reduces incentives to enter unless there is high retirement pay or the organizational career is extended by a second career in the private or semipublic sectors. In either case, there is strong pressure for internal growth (Marris 1964; Williamson 1975:120; Marshall 1932:321–22), which entails further specialization and differentiation driven by career demand pressures.

In sum, the organizationally oriented pattern of bureaucratic organization derives and owes its character to the condition of high uncertainty that surrounds political leadership following a total or critical succession of leadership. The necessity for newly emergent leaders to organize their status and power in a ruleful fashion leads them to engage in a strategy that eventually results in a rationalization of political and administrative roles.

The aim of the strategy is not the rationalization of role. Rather the strategy seems to center on the autonomy of the administrative role. The aim of establishing this autonomy is to safeguard political leadership from the volatility of public opinion and choice. The goal of this strategy is achieved through the creation of the organizationally dominated and protected administrative role. This organizational orientation resolves many of the problems facing new political leaders by providing an institutional arrangement that isolates them from environmental risks—it provides them with continuity of power, authority, and legitimacy without serious challenges from other sources. From the point of view of the organizational members, the role structure provides high incentives for early organizational career commitment—direct entry into the higher levels of administration, highly predictable careers, and a minimal upward mobility.

Bureaucratic Autonomy, Accountability, and Integration Under Conditions of High Uncertainty

This strategy, however, has certain defects. Not the least of these is the blurring of the line between administration and politics—or rather the attempt to substitute the former for the latter. This must, over time, create serious problems for political succession at the highest levels. The rationalization of the administrative role provides for orderly succession at all levels of political leadership except the very highest. The absence of other institutions that might play a mediating role in selecting the highest levels of policymakers can only produce *ad hoc* succession arrangements. Who will select the selectors? The bureaucratic role structure that has emerged under these conditions is clearly loath to hand this privilege over to outsiders. Yet, by its very nature, bureaucratic structure is incapable of providing adequate rules for determining its ultimate leaders. This condition arises because at the penultimate level of bureaucratic hierarchy there can be no internal bureaucratic criteria for distinguishing between possible ultimate leaders. Presumably, everyone at the penultimate level shares the same characteristics. Any selection from among them by themselves would appear to be arbitrary and based upon nonbureaucratic role characteristics. This kind of system must lead to the creation of factionalism within the bureaucracy as the system for selecting leaders. Selections will be made on the basis of the number of followers who can be organized to support a particular individual.

If factionalism within the bureaucracy is the system for selection of leaders, then the penultimate leaders who do not get selected must somehow be rewarded or consoled. If not, they may join together to eliminate the victor. The nature of the consolation is powerfully constrained by the factional system. The ones who get to the top must maintain the group that was responsible for getting them there or else they risk being eliminated by other factions. The reward for those left behind must be to continue to hold high office and thus maintain factional offices. All of this clearly subverts the basic incentive system within the bureaucracy. If factional membership is determinant, career structure predictability declines. Furthermore, as factionalism comes to dominate, the resulting lower levels of predictability produce a decline in the legitimacy of the organization. Advancement comes to have less and less of a public character. Soon, bureaucratic office is seen as the means for fulfilling private rather than public interests.

There are several solutions to the above problem. One solution is to create or encourage the creation of a single authority, external to the bureaucracy, who selects the ultimate leaders—an emperor or an imperial president. This clearly has dangers since a single authority with such power must have support from sources outside the bureaucracy or else he or she will be perceived as pursuing a self- or bureaucratic interest at the expense of the public interest. To reduce the single authority to no more than a symbol is to recreate the problem. The result may thus be that a single authority will represent external interests and constantly seek to reform the bureaucratic structure. Furthermore, this solution is notoriously unstable since an individual with such power cannot afford to make big mistakes as this undermines the charismatic authority that renders such positions tenable.

A second solution is to allow an outside institution, which itself is organized around limited access to eligibility and leadership and utilizes or shares bureaucratic values, to make the selections. The problem here, of course, is how to create such an institution in an environment in which equality of standards or educational/expertise merit is the means used to select leadership in all organizations. The same problem of ultimate leadership selection would emerge here as in the case of an administrative bureaucratic organization—there would have to be some mechanism for selecting leaders external to the organization. Only by gaining a monopoly over the representation and organization of private interests can such an organization avoid being held accountable to external authority, if not power. Under these conditions, the public bureaucracy becomes subsumed by the outside organization. The bureaucratic role maintains autonomy only in the sense that membership in both organizations is acquired.

Another solution, not quite so disastrous from the point of view of bureaucrats who seek to dominate political leadership institutionally, is to have outside organizations that do not have a monopoly over private interest make the selection of ultimate leaders. Since the absence of monopoly produces competitive organizations, such organizations should only be periodic visitors to positions where they make the selections of ultimate bureaucratic leaders. Thus, while they may make selections and perhaps politicize the highest levels of officials to some degree, episodic possession of power by such organizations leaves the bureaucratic organization largely in control of itself. The bureaucracy and bureaucratic leaders become indispensable as parties or other organizations go in and out of the revolving door of power.

The main problem for organizations such as political parties is that arriving at a position of power is coincident with attempting to structure the means to remain in power. Attempts will be made to bend the bureaucracy to the will of the organization. One of the means for doing so is to hold out the promise of promotion to individual bureaucrats. But this has only limited effect since political leaders have no stick to go along with the carrot. Any attempt to change the bureaucratic structure drastically is not only likely to create resistance among bureaucratic leaders, it is also likely to open a Pandora's box for those who seek to make the change since such attempts appear to be incited by self-interest. The result is likely to be an uneasy standoff unless one of the parties or organizations can gain sufficient support from private actors for a long period of time—sufficiently long enough, that is, to produce a pattern of cooperation between this external organization and the public bureaucracy. If this occurs, then bureaucratic role autonomy will be maintained in return for bureaucratic cooperation in implementing choices made by leaders of the external organization.

Any or all of the above resolutions, it is reasonable to assume, can occur over time after the institutionalization of the organizationally oriented bureaucratic structure. In the most general sense, which outcome occurs would seem to depend on the degree to which, at any point in time, the bureaucracy or external parties or organizations are the primary means for organizing and defining leadership and of creating monopolies or near monopolies over private interest. When the bureaucracy has such a monopoly, whether by intent or default, imperial solutions to the problem of external accountability seem most likely. When a single external institution holds a monopoly, the party/bureaucracy solution appears to be the most likely result. Where no single organization has a monopoly, a co-optive solution seems the most likely to emerge.

The Strategy of Low Uncertainty

At the other end of the spectrum of uncertainty are those conditions in which there are clear and systematic rules for determining the succession of political leaders and decision-makers. There are a number of systems governing decision-making roles which do so with a clear and systematic body of rules: dynastic, oligarchic, chieftainship, elective, as well as bureaucratic. None of these eliminates uncertainty about succession altogether, although some dynastic or chieftainship rules have probably come quite close. Here, however, we are concerned with open elective systems because events and developments since the nineteenth century have tended to limit low uncertainty situations to well-defined electoral systems. Furthermore, elective systems, even under limited suffrage, have greater uncertainty than other rule-bound systems for selecting leadership. Where voters have choices, the rules may carefully prescribe the process of selecting eligibles and the winners but they do not provide certainty of outcomes. In this situation, the rules provide legitimacy. What is primarily at stake for political leaders is acquiring and/or retaining their elective official roles and the accompanying status and power.

Prior to rationalization, political leadership and official roles in elective systems tend to be structured around the capacity to organize votes pure and simple. This would seem to make it inevitable that parties of some kind will emerge if only as a means by which candidates seek to reduce uncertainties about voter choices. Among other things, parties play an important role in attempting to reduce the possible volatility of voters when they are left to their own devices. In a sense, parties are partly a response to a "market failure." Lacking sufficient information about voters' preferences, candidates seek to overcome this failure by organizing. Information thus acquired is used to reduce the number of candidates and to write "contracts" with groups of voters rather than have each candidate attempt to write contracts on every issue with individual constituents.

While the organized parties may help significantly to reduce voter volatility, they cannot eliminate it completely. Party organizations may come to exercise powerful constraints on who gets to be a candidate and thereby reduce voter choices. They cannot, however, create binding "contracts" with voters. Platforms, party principles, and candidates' promises are simply incapable of covering all or even most of the contingencies arising in relation to the issues in the public domain. This creates uncertainties for aspirants and incumbents since failure to satisfy what constituents perceive as a contract is likely to result in losing office the next time voters have a choice.

Several problems arise from this highly contingent situation. First, since party contests center on the capacity to stabilize a sufficient number and range of groups of voters (or interests) to ensure victory, the contracts with voters are likely to be concerned primarily with the distribution or allocation of public goods. This stems, in good part, from the difficulty in predicting the aggregate outcome of individual systems of subjective rational choices. One way to reduce this uncertainty is to enter into contracts with voters over the distribution of a broad range of goods. This narrows the area over which contests for voters take place, while at the same time providing a criterion by which voters and officeholders and candidates may judge performance. Victory for a candidate raises further problems related to the fulfillment of contract. The most significant of these problems is loyalty.

Victory for candidates presents a collective problem—how to ensure that officeholders in the same party get their promises carried out by an administrative organization. While there may be several resolutions to this problem, most certainly an autonomous bureaucratic role does not seem to be one of them. An autonomous bureaucracy operating on scientific or scientistic expertise would result in situations where individuals and parties might well be unable to carry out their electoral promises. The most obvious strategy for elected officeholders and their parties is to seek to insure the implementation of their policies through the creation of an administrative structure in which offices are held by virtue of party and officeholder loyalty. In this sense, patronage serves not only as a distributive good by which to organize voters but also as a means by which the party reduces uncertainty about delivering on its promises.

Party loyalty as the primary criterion for holding administrative office poses a number of problems for participants. As a criterion, it provides no means for either participants or observers to decide whether distributive decisions are made on the basis of private (individual and party) or public interest. As a result of this ambiguity, the decisions of those in power, whether elected or appointed, are seen as somehow fulfilling the requirements of all three interests. Failure to make such distinctions or to have criteria by which to distinguish these areas allows those out of power to pose challenges on the basis of legitimacy. Individuals or parties out of power may well argue that choices made on the basis of loyalty ignore the possibility and probability of these three levels of interest being in conflict. The fuzziness of the boundaries between these three levels of interest makes it difficult to predict outcomes of policy choices as they are implemented by individuals. At the same time, administrative officials are open to the charge that since they came by their positions through personal and party loyalty, it is not unreasonable to assume that their decisions will be heavily influenced by patron and party goals, to the detriment of the public interest. Those in power are thus open to the charge of using public resources to corrupt the rules governing political leadership succession.

Role ambiguity is not the only problem arising from the utilization of loyalty as the criterion for administrative leadership. As the determinant of eligibility, loyalty does little to provide a basis for general agreement as to how decisions made by elective leaders ought to be implemented. Party or individual loyalty provides little homogeneity with regard to administrative practice. This is a sure way to create conflict and uncertainty over how policy decisions are to be carried out. This kind of uncertainty is crucial for elected leaders since failure to fulfill their promises may have unhappy consequences for their incumbency. In short, the absence of assurance that appropriate distribution of public goods will take place raises the question of accountability of administrative officials to elected public leaders—another stick with which opponents may beat incumbents.

A final problem arising from the dependence on loyalty and patronage is the difficulty of distinguishing between degrees of loyalty. This difficulty creates the problem of allocating positions. Not only does this problem make it difficult to allocate offices in hierarchical terms, but it also creates the equally difficult problem of trying to decide who should get a position and who should not. There will always be more claimants for rewards than available offices. Any set of choices by a patron or a party must produce some discontent and competition, which in turn produces intraparty conflict. Electoral victory produces intraparty tensions wherever patronage is the means for determining eligibility for administrative leadership.

The uncertainties of party stem from the unhappy fact that voter contracts also produce the inability to predict whether voters will fulfill their part of the bargain. Unpredictability of voter behavior is raised by at least two situations: major shifts in voters' preferences or major expansion of the electorate. For those who come to power as a consequence of one or the other kind of major shift, the unpredictability of their victory can only be disquieting. Once exhibited, voter volatility must be viewed with as much concern by the victors as by the vanquished since it portends the possibility of their own arbitrary dismissal from power. The victors face a real dilemma. They cannot know whether the major shift in voters' preferences is relatively long term or merely a short-term deviation from preceding patterns. How to reduce this particular form of uncertainty is crucial. Political leaders cannot rely on the tried and true patterns of patronage politics and distribution since they seem, in part at least, to be discredited or rendered obsolete by the major shift of votes. The whole structure of administrative office-holding comes under powerful scrutiny as it no longer seems to perform the function for which it was intended.

The resolution of these problems would seem to be a resort to bureaucratization or, rather, the rationalization of the administrative structure. In the first instance, the problems raised by the utilization of loyalty as the criterion for appointment to administrative positions would seem to lead to bureaucratic resolutions. In terms of goal conflicts between personal, party, and public interests that raise the question of legitimacy, the only alternative would seem to be to resort to rules governing decision making and implementation that clearly draw a line between public and private goals. What kind of rules and criteria for office-holding would not only provide for such a distinction but also serve given problems of being unable to distinguish clearly between degrees of loyalty, of homogeneity of training, and the allocation of offices? The difficulty is that this body of rules must also have the capacity of maintaining an open and flexible role structure. That is, the rule system cannot result in the creation of an autonomous bureaucratic role capable of resisting the demands of political leaders.

The only solution appears to be a set of rules governing the selection of officials which requires that they possess: (1) a systematic capacity to distinguish between subjective and objective rationality—some sort of internal accounting mechanism that provides criteria for making the distinction; (2) an expertise based on the possession of knowledge about the relationship of specific actions to specific consequences; and, (3) a set of rules governing the accountability of administrative officials to elected ones. These rule systems seem to solve all of the problems mentioned above. The rules governing eligibility for office reduce the problem of too many claimants by introducing discriminatory criteria; they eliminate or reduce the problem of goal conflicts by specifying what kinds of information may be used in making decisions and by specifying the procedures for reducing opportunism; these rules also reduce the problem of administrative conflict by specifying or implying a uniform pre-entrance training.

Not surprisingly, this strategy helps to resolve the problem of voter volatility. It does so by establishing the grounds for internalizing functions. Utilizing a system of objective knowledge that is public in character as the basis for decision making makes it possible for elective leaders to shift the ground on how to achieve their constituents' satisfaction without doing violence to the public interest. They do so by arguing that objective knowledge provides a superior, more efficient way of relating actions to consequences. From this position they must proceed to the conflation of society to the single individual. Just as individuals have the right to order preferences that maximize their utility, so do societies have the same right, indeed, the obligation to do so.

Once this shift occurs, political leaders move to internalize functions on the grounds that the public interest cannot otherwise be achieved. This internalization process reduces the number of issues over which voters have a chance to make choices. An increasing number of choices are viewed as technical and administrative in character. In this process, voter choices become increasingly choices about leaders rather than about issues. This narrows the range of choices over which voters may exhibit volatility. By making more issues subject to objective rules and a system of objective knowledge, party leadership at once legitimizes its claim to act in the public interest and at the same time reduces the number of issues over which voter realignment or the attraction of first-time voters may take place. Moving major issues from the realm of politics and debate to that of "scientific" administration and expertise becomes the hallmark of political reform.

What occasions these reforms? Under well-defined rule systems there do not seem to be great incentives for political leaders to leave the well-charted waters of patronage for the impersonal and unknown ones of rational bureaucratization. Two possible answers are suggested by the conditions of administration under elective systems. The first is the challenge and charge of corruption. Corruption becomes an engine of rationalization under those circumstances where political parties contest relatively evenly for political power and rights to patronage. Where party loyalty dominates in the appointment of administrative leaders, the "outs" have a ready-made issue with which to appeal to voters. The problem is especially acute when there are few other issues around which the outs can organize. Party contestation, then, may drive elective leaders gradually toward attempts to distinguish clearly between individual, party, and public interests, even though rationalizing the administrative role may be the last thing they desire.

A second driving force is the problem of providing sufficient offices for patronage. The success of patronage organizations may carry within it the seeds of subversion. Success attracts more and more demands and the very ambiguity of the criterion for selection makes it extraordinarily difficult to make clear-cut distinctions about who does and does not deserve an appointment. The highly personal character of the criterion (the evidence for party loyalty is the evocation of support from party leaders) makes it very difficult to find a rational system of patronage allocation. Over time, especially in a system with a growing electorate and a growing number of patronage positions, the demands must become increasingly importunate and a source of divisiveness among party leaders.

Party contestation and patronage are incremental and developmental forces arising out of the very nature of political parties. A third driving force toward rationalization, however, arises out of specific contingent historical moments that are related to the structural properties of parties but do not arise directly from their structural characteristics. This factor is the well-articulated rule system's approximation of the "revolutionary moment." The wholesale addition of voters to the rolls either by group or individual enfranchisement or the wholesale shift in preferences of voters produces major moments of leadership uncertainty. As I have suggested earlier, such major shifts or large additions to the electorate are as worrisome to the winners as to the losers since they must now seek to understand the sources of the shift and the means to maintain its orientation. This would seem to suggest a strategy to further rationalization of the administrative role. Removing controversial issues from the public arena and removing offices from the elective and patronage arena and placing them within the administrative structure are strategies that seem to arise logically from such situations. Thus major moments of electoral change would seem to be followed almost always by attempts to reform administration.

In this tactic, elected political leaders are led to a distributive conception of utilitarianism. Elected leaders who are unable to rely on the party mechanism, especially patronage, to distribute public goods and unable to gain a monopoly or near monopoly over private interests are forced to argue that the social means of distribution may be conflated to the position of the individual. If they wish to reduce uncertainty about incumbency, and they lack the other alternatives, they must take the view that just as it is rational for individuals to organize means of maximizing the fulfillment of their desires, so it is right for society to organize means of maximizing the net balance of satisfaction over all members of society. Accepting this conflationary principle would seem to require: (1) a conception of the public policymaker as one who is capable of translating revealed choices into a system of priorities and; (2) a public policy implementor who is capable of predicting the appropriate means by which such priorities can be implemented to maximize the net balance of satisfaction taken over all of society's members. The latter must be an impartial spectator who possesses the capacity of determining the one best way of organizing the distribution of public goods so as to meet the system of desires organized by elected officials.

Endowed with ideal powers of rational instrumentality, this individual is one who selects the best way to achieve the distribution of public goods. The impartial spectator would thus seem to be required to possess a body of organized knowledge that has the capacity to predict the outcomes of specific courses of action. In this conception of society, to paraphrase our earlier Rawls quote (1971:26–27), separate individuals are thought of as so many different lines along which rights and duties have been acquired (rather than assigned by the administrator) and scarce means of satisfaction allocated in accordance with rules so as to give the greatest fulfillment. Here the correct decision is essentially a question of efficient administration of the *allocation* rather than the priority process. *In effect, administration comes to be substituted for the politics of distribution rather than the politics of preferences.* Delegating the administration of distribution completely to a corp of homogeneous officials whose roles are autonomous and committed to the organizational structure would deprive elected politicians of the means to organize voters in any significant fashion. Loss of discretion with regard to policies of distribution of public goods would tend to undermine the structure of party roles. Yet, when faced with the continuing problems of leadership homogeneity, publicness, and accountability of the administrative role, the party or elected leader must move to some form of rationalization of the administrative role.

The central problem as seen from the point of view of elected officials is how to devise an administrative role that is not anchored in an organization over which administrators themselves have control. The only strategy available for elected leaders here is to utilize some existing social roles that already possess the basic elements of publicness and expertise but are not rooted in organizational structures directly related to the public bureaucracy. The professional role in low-uncertainty societies like the United States and Great Britain met these criteria. In the late nineteenth and early twentieth centuries, the role came to be organized around: (1) a conception of public service; (2) the possession of a body of specialized knowledge and training that is "scientifically" based; (3) the possession of a distinctive ethic of role behavior, especially with regard to the way in which knowledge and information may be used to arrive at decisions; (4) the capacity for self-regulation arising out of the internalization of codes of behavior; and (5) the creation, within a community of professionals, of an organization that produces a monopoly or near monopoly over the supply of trained service (Larson 1977; Millerson 1964; Cogan 1953; Goode 1957; Freidson 1970:78; Elliot and Kuhn 1978).

The distinctiveness of the professions appears to be founded on the combination of these general dimensions. These uncommon occupations tend to become 'real' communities, whose members share a relatively permanent affiliation, an identity, personal commitment, specific interests, and general loyalties. (Larson 1977:x)

The commitment is to a loosely organized community of status and identity centered on the professional organization, the professional school, and a self-administered code of ethics. Professionalism is broadly defined since it is never stated with precision and evidence how long, how theoretical, or how specialized training must be in order to qualify (Freidson 1970:78). The breadth of this definition allows the elected political leader leeway to change the criteria of the administrative role depending on the conditions or problems that arise.

The major difference between this strategy and the one adopted in the high uncertainty case is that the professional role rather than the bureaucratic administrative organization comes to represent the public interest. By emphasizing or encouraging the acquisition of expertise by individuals rather than by organization, political leaders undermine the capacity of bureaucratic organizations and their leaders to lay claim to a monopoly of expertise. Where expertise is structured by individual possession of the appropriate skills and knowledge to make decisions, organizations are less central to the process of ordering information. Expertise often exists outside of organizations. Thus, insofar as elected leaders can claim professional status they appear to have the capacity and legitimacy to intervene in or govern the administrative process. Or, to the extent that elected and administrative leaders share professional status, they may come to share the same views about policy and policy-making. In either case, resorting to the structure of professional autonomy makes it possible for the elected leader to retain considerable discretion over the administrative role.

The problem for elected leaders in this situation is one of incentives. Professional status has a built-in incentive structure that is oriented toward individual autonomy. The most important elements of the incentive structure are: self-regulation, the ability to practice the profession in a self-determined way (in the sense that practitioners collectively determine the nature of their practice); the ability to select a specialized area of competency; and the ability to gain high individual rewards. Any incentive structure aimed at attracting people to administrative roles must stress most of the elements that make up individual occupational autonomy and professional practice. If the individual is to be allowed to retain the basic elements of the professional role, then the administrative structure must take on a very different look than is the case under high-uncertainty strategies.

With this emphasis on individual capacity and discretion, career flexibility becomes a central attribute of administrative structures emerging out of low-uncertainty situations. This flexibility may be reflected in a number of structural characteristics: lateral entry, interdepartmental mobility, greater range of vertical mobility, and mobility across public and private organizations. These characteristics reflect the greater leeway that may be given individuals entering the upper levels of civil bureaucracies. The flexibility of career that these characteristics indicate is a recognition of the professional status—the capacity of the individual to utilize his training and expertise in a variety of settings. It is recognition that the individual is not a mere "clerk" or "employee" serving as a cog in a large organization.

Building incentives around an individually acquired status has great consequences for the structure of higher administrative roles. There is less emphasis on career predictability since the career is tied to the professional role rather than to any organizational one. People have careers as doctors, lawyers, engineers, etc., and these can take place in a number of settings. The professional status assures the individual of a social and often an economic place. The result must be that there is less emphasis on the necessity for insuring high payoffs through a highly specified career structure. Professional skills that are not narrowly oriented toward one specific organization but are generalizable throughout the society means alternatives are available to individuals at varying stages of their careers. This means, in effect, that the bureaucratic administration need not be overly concerned with maintaining rigid hierarchical structures of offices.

At the same time the desire on the part of elected officials to avoid creating a bureaucratic structure that controls the definition of eligibility and appointment leads them to encourage professionalism. Elected political leaders will provide direct and indirect subsidies for universities and professional schools, for professional associations, and, perhaps most important, will grant the power of self-regulation and monopoly over the provision of services. It is in this manner that they provide the institutional basis for professional careers. The payoff for the individual is admission to a professional role and only secondarily to an organizational role. The administrative structure confirms this by emphasizing the characteristics of the professional role. In other words, elected officials seek to avoid creating a powerful autonomous administrative role by turning to and encouraging the professional role with its characteristics of built-in incentives and individual autonomy.

The recognition of professional status does appear to require the incentive of entry directly into a relatively high level of administrative office. This is a function not only of providing an incentive to overcome the cost of training but also of recognizing the status of the professional. It follows from this that distinctions in entry level will be oriented toward the possession of professional credentials. Indeed, the logical outcome of stressing professional certification is to specify the qualifications required for specific positions. This has a number of likely consequences. First, it would make lateral entry—entry at a number of points instead of only one—an acceptable characteristic. People enter to take positions for which they are qualified as professionals. Under these conditions, individuals may or may not move to other offices. They may stay put, they may advance, they may move laterally to other similar offices, they may simply leave and never return, or they may leave and return after acquiring more skills and hold a higher office; a large number of alternatives are possible under this kind of professional incentive system.

A second likely consequence of the emphasis on professional credentials is that less attention will be paid to seniority and hierarchy. Because high levels of predictability about career are of less importance than possession of professional credentials, seniority is likely to be important but not crucial. It is the varying levels of professional expertise and certification that are crucial. Since these levels may vary considerably from individual to individual, they provide a means of differentiating between people when promotions are at stake. Hierarchy is also likely to take on less importance since professional roles have referent points outside of the organization that are more important in determining status. Organizational hierarchy will therefore play a lesser role in determining status—it may help confirm it but that is about all. What is more probable is that hierarchy in this mode of bureaucratization will reflect the social hierarchy of status accorded to the various professions, and within the profession it will reflect the criteria (publications, for example) used to establish professional standing.

Hierarchy will also suffer because of the difficulty in imposing power over people with specialized training. Specialized knowledge and training gives its holder the opportunity to withhold it when placed under pressure—information impactedness is difficult to overcome under conditions where the knowledge may be somewhat arcane. To put it the other way around, the internalized ethic and specialized training of the professional requires less in the way of rules for defining their discretion; at least this would seem so from the professional's point of view. Heavy dependence on rules to define role behavior would seem to be a real disincentive given the individual autonomy orientation of professionals.

The professionally oriented pattern of bureaucratization outlined here emerges, I have argued, out of the problems that elected leaders face in seeking to secure their incumbency in the face of equally legitimate challengers. Over time, especially within the context of modern economic development and change, the primary mechanism of party organization—patronage—creates severe problems of publicness as well as rulefulness in the distribution of patronage and public goods. At different times, these problems are greatly exacerbated by major shifts in voters' preferences or the number of voters. These problems lead elected political leaders to engage in strategies of rationalization of patronage appointments. This overall strategy has as its aim limiting the autonomy of the administrative role. To do so allows elected leaders to continue to have discretion over the allocation of resources that will ensure their reelection. Their aim is to continue to dominate the administrative structure and bend it to political will. This is achieved by creating an administrative role organized around existing professional roles or which incorporates major aspects of these roles.

The professional orientation resolves the problem faced by elected leaders by providing an institutional arrangement that insulates them from charges of corruption and at the same time provides them with a well-defined means of distributing public goods. Equally important, this resolution produces a bureaucratic structure that, on the face of it, seems to have little capacity to assert its own will or interests. The professional role with its lack of organizational commitment, its emphasis on individual autonomy, and its roots in external (private) social and economic organization seems to provide a nice foil for elected officials seeking to avoid loss of control over administrative structure. Recruiting professionals seems to provide a corps of administrators and a structure of administration which would be highly instrumentally oriented but which would lack an organizational ethos or monopoly of expertise that might serve to challenge the power and legitimacy of elected leaders. From the point of view of the organization's members, the administrative structure provides incentives by recognizing and rewarding professional status or by conferring professional status on those who have not completely followed the social and educational canons of professionalism. In short, low uncertainty for political leaders produces, over time, an organization with low boundaries and high permeability. The organization is easily penetrable because it shares a role structure readily found in society at large. The bureaucratic administrative structure in itself has no distinctive character that would allow it to make special claims about representing and formulating the public interest. This capacity is shared with all those organizations which systematically use professionals to staff the highest levels of their bureaucracies.

Bureaucratic Autonomy, Accountability, and Integration
under Conditions of Low Uncertainty

The solution described above is not without its drawbacks. The central problem is accountability. How can elected officials be sure that administrators will organize the distribution of public resources in ways that will help, or at least not threaten, their incumbencies? Control over budget does not seem to have much leverage since failure to allocate funds will surely hurt elected officials as much or almost as much as administrators. Budget manipulation seems to be too gross an instrument. Specifying by legislation the way in which distribution should be carried out seems to have equally great dangers. First, there is no possible way to stipulate every contingency. Administrators will thus continue to have discretion. Furthermore, attempts to specify the contingencies may lead to intensification of conflicts among elected officials. The problem for officials arises from the absence of agreement as to which contingencies ought to be spelled out and how they are to be met. There does not seem to be a way in which formal rules can resolve the problem of close oversight and accountability.

If we turn to informal solutions, the only strategy that seems available is to attempt to make administrative officials share the same distributive aims as elected officials. There are several ways this might be achieved. One solution would be to select the very senior civil servants on the basis of their party membership. In effect, party leaders have a veto power over administrative appointments. The problem with this solution is that party turnover, if frequent, results in the turnover of senior civil servants. This has the effect of pushing real power in the administrative structure down to those middle-level officials whose stay in office is relatively unaffected by party turnover. The problem of accountability is thus not resolved. Even if party turnover is infrequent, lack of tenure for those at the very top produces lower incentives for people to want such offices except as a step to a postservice career. Lower incentives will produce high administrative turnover even if party turnover is not rapid. This allows administrative power to descend to middle-level officials as in the first strategy. In this sense, party can no longer serve to bridge the gap between elected and appointed officials. Where party once helped to guarantee a minimal homogeneity of policy aims and implementation among elected and appointed officials, expertise and the resort to professional criteria remove that constraint. Elected officials are condemned to use *ad hoc* measures to enforce accountability if party continues to be the reference point for appointment of officials.

A second solution to the accountability problem is to select higher administrative officials using criteria similar to that which emerges for elected officials, excepting party identification. The most evident and significant criterion is education. If elected officials have acquired advanced education and/or specialized training, this could be the basis for requiring similar criteria from civil officials. Creating accountability through consensus based on homogeneity of education requires a fairly narrow definition of appropriate preprofessional and/or professional training. Broad definitions are likely to fail to bring about agreement. One way to narrow the criteria is to require, formally or informally, that professional training of some kind be the criterion for elected and administrative offices. The problem is how to arrive at this condition for elected leaders. Unless such training has very high status and political careers offer high incentives, it is difficult to see how professional education can become the basis of accountability. These are contingent characteristics which may obtain in some conditions but not others.

What is not contingent is the reliance on advanced education generally to reduce the number of eligibles. Surely this is a strategy likely to be available under a wide range of circumstances. If advanced education is easily available, then its usefulness as a means of reducing the number of eligibles is diminished. Professionalism is one solution, but there are others. For example, one solution is to make advanced preprofessional education a scarce commodity. Scarcity may provide high status for those who acquire advanced education. It can then be used as a criterion for elective political leadership and for administrative leadership. The problem once again is how to arrive at the condition in which political leaders are selected from a group of individuals who have acquired advanced education where it is scarce. Here, as in the case of professional training, there is no general social constraint that would lead to this condition. The most one can argue is that where the state does not control the structure of advanced education and professional training, these characteristics will emerge as criteria for elected leadership only where these kinds of training form the basis of occupational opportunity and status. Where advanced preprofessional and/or professional training provide the basis for high social status, then it is possible that they will become the criteria for a number of leadership positions—economic and social as well as political. In this way, leadership will come to have considerable homogeneity. It then follows that formal structures of accountability are not so necessary since there is a consensus on implementation if not the content of policy. This is a consensus arrived at through a common educational experience that produces a common set of norms concerning the occupational experience and practice.

At the heart of the accountability problem lies the difficulty for elected leaders in finding an institutional mechanism of administration that can substitute for party in providing for consensus. Education and/or professional training are one solution. However, it is only a solution where elected leaders are themselves selected by this criterion. In the long run, this must create some ambiguity about the role of political parties as the structures for selecting political leadership. If education is the primary sifting mechanism for eligibles, then parties become increasingly secondary devices for reducing the number of eligibles. They become secondary to the occupational and status structures determined by advanced education.

Conclusion: High and Low Uncertainty Strategies

The two modes in which the administrative role has been institutionalized may be viewed, then, as the result of strategies of response to two central problems of politics in the nineteenth century. In both strategies of response, equality played a catalytic role. The two problems were leadership succession and leadership organization. The different outcomes with regard to administrative structure and role are the result of variation in the level of uncertainty about leadership succession. Within these two categories, variation in the nature of political leadership organization at the beginning of the process accounts for the differences in the way the administrative role is integrated into the political structure. Where rules concerning leadership selection and succession are in the process of being transformed—as is the case following total or critical successions of political leadership—*high uncertainty over holding power, characterized by the absence of rules of succession and the absence or presence of formal leadership organization and role definition, is the major constraint on putative leaders as they seek to reduce the uncertainties these aspects produce.*

Where the uncertainty is high and is combined with the absence of formal leadership role organization or definition, the strategies are carried out by individuals held together by social networks. Such groups attempt to remove similarly organized groups by pursuing a strategy of establishing a set of formal rules governing leadership roles and succession over which they alone have dominion. Autonomy and insulation of the leaders is the central goal, and this produces a set of choices leading to the organizationally oriented administrative role that dominates all forms of political leadership. By monopolizing both the criteria for leadership and the organizational structure of succession, political leaders transform the privateness of social network into the publicness of administrative bureaucratic organization. This form of administrative rationalization is the means by which political leaders, lacking and seeking to avoid any formal organization such as political parties, proceed to perpetuate themselves organizationally. This particular relationship between succession and organization of leaders produces an administrative structure that must create a claim to a monopoly over political leadership.

This is so since the organizational structure of leadership is now centered on the publicness of the organization and its consequent knowledge of the public interest.

The relationship and structure of the administrative bureaucracy shifts somewhat when the organizational structure of leadership changes. Where there is a well-defined structure of leadership organization, such as a party, under conditions of high uncertainty, the strategy of rationalization is similar to the one described above. The main difference lies in the party leaders' desire to retain the party as the means for determining administrative eligibility and insuring accountability of implementation. The primary aim of the party under the conditions of total or critical succession is to remove challenges to power. Party leaders seek organizational rather than social network dominance and definition of information by a single party, their own. In doing so, party leaders distinguish between publicness or commitment to the public interest based on the representativeness of party and the publicness based on the collectively structured information characteristic of a rationalized administrative bureaucracy. In this strategy the aim of party leaders is to perpetuate party leadership by using it as the means for determining higher administrative positions (see the admirable description of this process in Gill 1990). In this sense, the party is the functional analogue of the bureaucracy in the preceding case—it is the means by which political leaders organize themselves and determine the rules for political succession. By utilizing the single-party dominance over administration, party leaders create a closed system of accountability and administrative career in which party and administrative leadership are synonymous.

Where uncertainty over political succession is low, where there are well-regulated rules for determining succession and leadership is organized on the basis of social networks, then the strategies of political leaders are aimed at reducing the uncertainties raised by the volatility of voters by displacing major contests over public policy. This is achieved by rationalization of the administrative structure based on a preprofessional training which holds high social status. Leadership organization here is based on social status as indicated by preprofessional training. Elected political leadership and administrative leadership are viewed as professional careers differentiated by a selection process—one elective, the other appointive. Both require the same standard of eligibility: a high-status educational experience. The strategy of elected political leaders here is aimed at producing a bureaucratic structure which is not autonomous but which is not easily permeated. At the same time, elected political leaders do not seek to use political party organization as the primary means for organizing political leadership. The main aim of party organization is to organize legislative voting. The shared exclusive educational experience and high status of party leaders and higher administrative officials provides the basis of an accountability achieved through consensus rather than through oversight and regulation. The result is the emergence of an administrative structure that is viewed as synonymous with the creation of a professional career. Service throughout the organization is what produces the professional, not prior training.

4) Finally, there is the low-uncertainty situation, characteristic of open elective systems, combined with the presence of formal structures of leadership organization, such as competitive political parties. The strategy of elective political leaders when faced with the problems raised by the conflicts of party contestation is directed, as in the preceding case, to the rationalization of administration in order to displace conflicts over public interest. The prior existence of party organization of leadership, however, produces a strategy aimed at maintaining the subordination of administrative office to party leadership. However, the inability to continue using party leadership as the means of determining administrative eligibility leads political leaders to utilize the existing structure of professional status as the criteria for appointment. The result is an administrative structure centered on job specification rather than organizational career.

What I have argued here is that there are two major modes of rational bureaucratic organization, determined in the first instance by the variable of uncertainty—high and low. Analysis of the two possible strategies and their outcomes leads to the conclusion that each strategy also had, in the second instance, two possible outcomes, depending on the nature of political leadership organization prior to rationalization of the bureaucratic role. This second variable emerges as a consequence of analyzing the difficulties of strategies in overcoming the problem of securing accountability of rationalized administrative roles to political leaders. There appear to be two basic strategies for securing a resolution to this problem, depending on the structure of leadership organization. This variable has two distinct modes. One is a structure of leadership based on informal social networks. These have systematic eligibility characteristics, usually derived from shared aspects of social status. In these structures, little attention is paid to formal organization of the networks. Indeed, the attempt is often made to avoid calling attention to what appears to be private criteria for exclusion. Accountability is secured through shared social status and experience of political and administrative leaders. The second mode is based on the formal organization of leadership, principally through political parties. The criteria for eligibility are public and well defined. Parties come to have explicit rules about entrance and selection for posts within the organization. Anyone who meets the criteria set by the rules may enter the party and seek access to its leadership structure. Election, seniority, and merit are some of the criteria used in determining party leadership. Accountability is assured through the intermingling of party leadership with administrative leadership. That is, party leadership assumes positions of administrative leadership according to well-understood rules.

The two outcomes, the organizationally oriented and professionally oriented roles, are thus each further determined by a second element—the presence or absence of formal leadership organizations. This second instance produces two types within each mode. This can produce the usual four-cell typology as shown in table 3.1.

Thus, high uncertainty, when joined with a political leadership based on informal social networks, results in the organizationally oriented bureaucratic role. Accountability is achieved through political leadership acceptance of high levels of bureaucratic autonomy based on Weberian-like internal rules of organization. Political leaders accept the arrangement since they have common social networks that allow bureaucratic leaders to move into positions of political leadership. Examples of this type are Japan in the pre–World War II period and Germany in the pre-Nazi period and, to some extent, in the postwar era as well. High uncertainty combined with party-organized political leadership produces single-party dominated, organizationally oriented bureaucracies. Accountability is assured by party organization of rules governing the selection of political leaders as senior administrators. Examples of this type are the former Soviet Union and other similar states dominated by the Communist Party where some form of *nomenklatura* provides for the systematic selection of party leaders for administrative posts. Nazi Germany might also be viewed as falling into this category, although a *nomenklatura* did not exist to translate party status into administrative status in a systematic way. Postrevolutionary France may also be in-

Table 3.1 Bureaucratic Structures

	LEADERSHIP STRUCTURE	
	Social Network	*Party Structure*
POLITICAL SUCCESSION	Japan (Germany)	France USSR
High Uncertainty	Social Leadership Organizational Orientation Bureaucratic Domination	Party Leadership Organizational Orientation Single Party Domination of Administrative Posts
Low Uncertainty	Social Leadership Professional Orientation Bureaucratic Consensus	Multi-Party Leadership Professional Orientation Party Domination of Administrative Posts
	UK	US

cluded in this category. The various assemblies that were the inheritors of the Third Estate acted, in effect, like a pre-existing party, which served to organize leadership.

When low uncertainty is combined with social-network organized leadership, the outcome is the professionally oriented role where the bureaucracy is dominated by a party system. Accountability of the bureaucratic role is assured by the homogeneity of the political and administrative leaders' educational experience and its accompanying socialization and status. Political and administrative leaders share the same understandings of the nature of professional responsibility and adhere to the same rules governing the use of information. Early twentieth-century Great Britain and Canada are examples of this outcome. Combining low uncertainty with a pre-existing structure of leadership organized on the basis of political party produces a professionally oriented outcome in which a party system dominates. Accountability is maintained by party appointment of professionally trained party supporters to the senior administrative posts. The United States and late nineteenth- and early twentieth-century Switzerland are examples of this kind of accountability.

Finally, this chapter has relied on the idea of strategic choices by political leaders as the agency of rationalization. Strategic choice is not conceived, here, as a series of independent choices. Put another way, I do not view strategies as independent. Rather, in the descriptions set forth in this chapter, strategic choices are constrained by the chain of choices to which each belongs. A problem is seen by political leaders as producing a particular resolution, which, in turn, creates new problems calling for new solutions. This process continues until there is a relatively stable collection of solutions or a structural equilibrium. The outcome is highly constrained but not completely determined by the original set of choices. The uncertainty to which political leaders respond becomes internalized or endogenous to the structure that emerges from the original problems and their solutions. That is, external uncertainties—political uncertainties—may change from one generation of political leaders to another, but these are viewed as belonging to a general category of uncertainty to which the strategic choices made by predecessors were basically appropriate. Successive generations of political leaders view the cost of producing past solutions as being too high to replace them with a new set. Instead, they build on the structure of solutions already in existence. The uncertainty political leaders become most concerned with is that generated by problems arising from existing structure, which were the result of earlier strategic choices. The process ends when closure occurs within the structure. This is a condition each generation of political leaders seeks. It is achieved, however, only when the accountability of the senior administrators is reasonably assured. Once this has occurred, exogenous political uncertainty—perturbations in the political environment—tends to be subsumed under the existing structure with relatively little effect on the structure of the bureaucratic role. The equilibrium arrived at—the "rational" bureaucratic role—has become institutionalized at this point. It is more than an organizational artifact, it has become a social value.

PART TWO

Strategies of High Uncertainty

FRANCE

4

Revolutionary Change and Structural Ambiguity: The Revolutionary and Napoleonic Transformations

Observing the Revolution of 1789 within the frame of reference outlined in the preceding chapters suggests the conclusion that France ought to be a case of bureaucratic development that is organizationally oriented. If organizationally oriented bureaucracies are the result of high uncertainty for political leaders, brought about by total or critical levels of leadership succession, then France during the revolutionary period certainly ought to fit. Those who sought to hold and exert power through the creation of new constitutional orders during the following decade were men who had not previously held power. Nor had they been selected by the means or criteria of leadership structure that had characterized the *ancien régime* (Giesselmann 1977; Sutherland 1986:40; LeMay 1977; Patrick 1972). The rapidity with which the Estates General was transformed into the National Assembly (17 June 1789), then to the Constituent Assembly (9 July 1789), and then into the Legislative Assembly (30 September 1791), finally culminating in the creation of the Republic (21 September 1792), surely reflects the dissolution of the old rules for determining political leadership.

The adoption of the elective principle for determining political leadership by revolutionary leaders seems to be at odds with any reasonable strategy designed to ensure incumbency and, indeed, it produced a powerful paradox. On the one hand, the Revolution seemed to be irrevocably tied to a system of leadership selection that was elective (Hunt 1984:125–26). Having been created by an elective assembly, neither the leadership of the constitutional monarchy nor of the First Republic could seem to lay claim to the right to govern without resorting to the notion of elective representation. Nevertheless, the very *act* of revolution, whether one places it in the Tennis Court Oath or in the act of the National Assembly reconstituting itself as the Constituent Assembly, was one which clearly could not be seen as a delegation of electors' or "the people's" wishes. In this sense, the members of the assemblies that brought an end to the monarchy as it had traditionally existed had acted as self-selected revolutionaries. At the same time, functionally, their transformation from an elected assembly into an organized body of self-selected revolutionary leaders resulted in the creation of a partylike structure of leadership. More important, no specific constraint (no notion of constituency or of contract) which could inhibit members of these assemblies from constantly redefining the goals of collective action emerged from this transformation. The great ambivalence surrounding the structure of political leadership in the nineteenth century was a consequence of this fact: *there was no revealed or seemingly necessary connection between elective structures of leadership and the acts of transforming the rules by which leadership and decision making were systematically organized* (Halevi 1988:74–75; Hunt 1987:404). Elections and decision making (or legislation) were two completely separate functions—the latter did not appear to be in any way accountable or subordinated to the former. The historical actions of the revolutionaries were institutionalized in the continuing separation of these two structural features.

The degree to which the inability to find a means to bridge the gap between election and self-selection of goals came to dominate much of the structure of nineteenth-century French politics is revealed in the roll call of assemblies and governments stretching from the Revolutionary Government of the Year II to the beginning of the Third Republic. In all of them, regardless of form, the elective principle of leadership was consistently negated. At the same time, while directories, empires, and monarchies came and went throughout the century, they were accompanied, ironically enough, by a constant expansion of franchise. By 1848, with the creation of the Second Republic, universal suffrage was established (Rémond 1969:II, 33–36), but the object of this was not clear. Coming at a time when the rules for selecting political leaders was, at best, fragile and without a firm anchor in widely accepted processes, universal suffrage could add little but greater uncertainty for political leaders. Indeed, the fragility of the leadership selection process was to be revealed in the ironic use of the universal suffrage to create an imperial system following the plebiscite of 21 and 22 November 1852. In short, the Revolution of 1789 clearly dissolved the old rules for determining leadership and decision making and thus created for political leaders a condition of high uncertainty that did not disappear for much of the century.

Equally important, the Revolution had not been preceded by any new organizational structure of leaders. Those who came to seek power after 1789 had no party organization. The Estates General itself had been organized largely around the principle of local notables (LeMay 1977). Despite the semi-party nature of the Jacobins, politics in France until at least midcentury continued to be predominantly a politics of notables (Rémond 1969:II, 12). Political leadership was not organized through parties but through status and wealth in a variety of social organizations such as family, community, and church. The emphasis on these socially based organizations of leadership and leadership succession created powerful obstacles to the creation of a national, integrated structure of leadership and leadership succession. Where leadership succession was constrained by family and family ties, then status and influence continued to be predominantly local in character. In the period after 1789, putative political leaders thus faced not only the problem of restructuring rules governing leadership and leadership succession, they also faced the problem of overcoming the localism of leadership—the problem of centralizing and integrating leadership.

Despite the high level of uncertainty and the absence of formal organizations or structures providing leadership integration, bureaucratic rationalization was slow in coming. If organizationally oriented bureaucracy is the outcome of high uncertainty for organizationally impoverished political leaders then the glacial-like character of French bureaucratic rationalization seems a denial of this claim. Yet, by the end of the century, between 1870 and 1895, the basic features of the French civil service structure had become institutionalized. The major changes that have occurred since came largely after 1945. These were primarily concerned with the rationalization of eligibility and training (the establishment of the École National d'Administration [ENA] per the Ordinance of 9 October 1945) and the creation of a general statute governing the bureaucratic role and career (Ordinance of 9 October 1945 and the Ordinance of 19 October 1946) (Kessler 1978:35–67; Thuillier and Tulard 1984:97–107).

Replacing the private École Libre des Science Politique with the ENA centralized eligibility and training under state auspices. With this reform, the ENA became the *grande école* for civil administrators. This did not, however, change the fundamental structure of the upper-level civil service career. Rather, this change only internalized and brought under direct state control the one aspect of the career structure that had remained outside of state direction: a *grande école* for nontechnical state administrators (Kessler 1978:38–39). The creation of a general statute governing the careers of all civil servants brought considerable uniformity to the role structure and, in so doing, reduced concerns among civil servants about the possible arbitrariness of ministerially determined career structures. Nevertheless, the main features of the pre–World War II structures remained intact: seniority, ministerial specialization, hierarchical definition of office rather than functional specialization (that is, the concepts of grade, cadre, and group as opposed to job specification) continued to be the basic elements defining civil service career and role, although they were now systematized and institutionalized (Grégoire 1954:122–44; Debbasch 1966:30ff.).

The basic features of the career and role structure of the modern French upper-level civil service that came into existence in the last quarter of the nineteenth century might be described as follows:

1. The civil service came to require higher education in law or the "public" sciences (that is, political science, economics, public finance, and public law), or the "civil" sciences (engineering, communications, education, and agriculture), or the military sciences.

2. In the case of central governmental nontechnical and nonmilitary administrative positions, successful candidates were required to pass a test of acquired knowledge generically known as the *concours*. By the end of the century, the *concours* included both a written and oral examination that covered a broad range of theoretical and cultural knowledge. Sufficient knowledge to pass these examinations or to be considered eligible to take them required the possession of the *baccalauréat* and in many cases a *licencié*.

3. Entrance into a distinct upper-level civil service career structure began usually with appointment as a *rédacteur* in the case of nonmilitary and nontechnical services. The latter services had equivalent upper-level grade distinctions.

4. Advancement to the penultimate highest levels (department heads or prefects and above) was largely based on seniority, and after this point a combination of free ministerial choice, passage of the *concours,* combined with seniority to produce a ranking that was applied to a table of advancement for the coming year.

5. The civil servant's career centered primarily within a single *corps* or a single ministry. That is to say, a career dominated not by technical or functional specialization but by departmental/group specialization.

6. There came to exist a uniform minimal career period entitling retirement with pension (thirty years service in central administration, twenty-eight in field service administration).

7. It was a career in which arbitrary dismissal was almost completely eliminated; moreover, the grounds for dismissal were carefully defined and delimited by a process largely in the hands of senior civil service members.

(Kessler 1978:15–25; Garas 1936; Vivien 1859:I, 182–305; Demartial 1909:1–81; Sibert 1912; Georgin 1911; Thuillier 1980:291–422; Sharp 1931:75–194; Lefas 1913; Anty 1936:22–23; Ferrat 1945:171–72; Osborne 1976; Osborne 1983:77–82).

This structure had nearly all of the features of what economists call an integrated internal labor market—a structure in which the price and allocation of labor was not determined by the market and in which skills were highly firm or organization-specific (Osterman 1984:2; Doeringer and Piore 1971). This was especially the case for the upper-level civil service. Entry here was governed by well-defined formal and informal rules. Furthermore, a major precondition of entry was the acquisition of the *baccalauréat,* which meant passing an exam covering a *lycée* education. This alone however, was not sufficient. By the last quarter of the century, a diploma from one of the *grandes écoles* (including the private École Libre des Sciences Politique) and/or education in one of the schools of application (École des Mines, or the École Ponts et Chaussées) and a diploma from one of the Paris law faculties was needed to gain access to the *concours* or a position in the higher levels of the civil service. The necessity of acquiring these specific forms of education meant the commitment of the individual to a public service career long before his entry into the civil service (Osborne 1974, 1976:157–59). Ezra Suleiman's description of contemporary elite careers fits just as neatly to the conditions of almost a century earlier:

School life itself becomes the beginning of one's career for there is no sharp break between school life and working life in terms of colleagues. . . . Thus upon completing their training in the specialized schools, the best graduates normally enter one of the *grand corps.* (1978:97)

Allocation of offices occurred through relatively well-defined internal rules. However, the rules differed considerably from ministry to ministry, and corps to corps (Thuillier 1980:363ff.; Lefas 1913:118; Demartial 1909:72–74; Georgin 1911:82–129). The result was that once a career began within a ministry or corps, there was little possibility of movement to another (Lefas 1913:118–19). Skills, thus, were not simply organization-specific but specific to ministries and corps. Specialization at the individual level did not grow out of pre-entry acquired skills. The absence of uniform rules governing the allocation of offices before 1945 tended to create considerable discontent among upper-level civil servants since their careers appeared to be dependant on an arbitrary set of rules emanating from the minister. The resistance on the part of ministers to supporting a general statute defining the civil service career led to "crises" of administration in the latter part of the nineteenth century and in the early years of the twentieth century (Thuillier and Tulard 1984:63–84; Cahen-Salvador 1911; Leroy 1906). These crises led to the formation of a wide variety of associations of civil servants in the early years of the twentieth century. Continued refusal to delimit ministerial power and establish a general statute finally resulted in the amalgamation of a number of these associations to form the Fédération générale des Fonctionnaires in 1909 (Thuillier and Tulard 1984:77–81; Cahen-Salvador 1911:55–183).

Despite the absence of a general statute, there appears to have been little in the way of major administrative purges or dismissals after 1852 (V.

Wright 1977). There were, however, a sufficient number to impress administrators with the understanding that, as individuals, their careers might well be dead-ended if they did not pay close attention to ministerial interests (V. Wright 1977). Despite the absence of uniform formal rules governing advancement at the senior levels of the upper-level civil service, careers tended to have at least minimal assurances of structure and form. These elements of predictability stemmed from the powerful organizational role of seniority and the growing and articulate discontent of civil servants at all levels during the last quarter of the nineteenth century and the early years of the twentieth century. Added to this was the general, if not unanimous, agreement within the ministries of the central government that individuals should serve in a hierarchy of offices and that there should be a minimal period of time served in each office (Georgin 1911:81–91, 687–725; Thuillier 1980).

It seems clear that by the end of the nineteenth century, despite the lack of uniform regulations and the seemingly arbitrary powers of the minister with regard to advancement, there was a relatively well-defined career structure (Wright and Le Clère 1973; Bottomore 1954; Rain 1963; Jacquemart, 1892; Massé 1908; École Polytechnique 1967; Shinn 1980; Osborne 1976). This career began with the *lycée* and moved through higher education in law and or the *grandes écoles* to the *concours,* appointment as a *rédacteur* or, perhaps if one had well-placed friends, a member of a ministerial cabinet; then on to promotions to *sous-chef* of a department or a *sous-préfet,* or an *auditeur* in the Conseil d'État; then to *chef* of a department or appointment as a prefect or one of the other equivalent positions in the other *grands corps.* The great mass of those who entered the upper-level civil service in the latter half of the nineteenth century could look forward with reasonable assurance to a lifetime career. They may not have been able to predict the course of their career with great precision, but the degree to which the civil service was able to attract graduates of the École Libre and the *grandes écoles* clearly indicates that there were strong incentives for individuals to pursue careers.

The creation of this internal or bureaucratized labor market was not achieved easily. The rationalization of administrative office-holding proceeded for almost a century before it arrived at a relatively stable institutionalized condition. The kaleidoscope of governments, which bemused and often mystified the French from 1789 until approximately 1880, reflected the continued failure of political leadership to solve the central problems created by the difficulty in constructing a new set of rules governing leadership selection and decision making. In turn, this difficulty emanated from the inability to overcome the problems posed by the creation of the revolutionary conceptions of equality, community, legitimacy, and history.

The Problem of Equality and Community

Civil Equality and the Problem of Administration

Those political leaders who came to and sought power after 1789 in the National Assembly, the Constituent Assembly, the Legislative Assembly, the Convention, and the Directory sought to establish a notion of equality not just because it was something they believed in and wanted. The very manner in which they had come to power or had become eligible for positions of power denied the possibility of continuing to utilize systematic, ascriptively determined, private social relationships as the means of determining public relationships between individuals. Once the National Assembly had taken the Tennis Court Oath and declared itself as representing the public and not distinct estates, then birth or social condition as a determinant of the weight to be given individual choice and preferences was abolished.

The problem arose immediately as to how equality should take form. The immediate answer was to abolish feudal rights on 4 August 1789 in return for just compensation, thus recognizing that (1) private social class rights were at an end; (2) the concept of property rights was inviolable; and (3) that it was the right of the state to determine the contents of the public domain. The abolition of feudalism was followed by the Decrees of 5–11 August and 15 March 1790 and the Declaration of the Rights of Man of 26 August 1789. Generally, these decrees created civil equality and removed all obstacles of birth and social status for entrance to all civil and military offices. These decrees also put an end to the sale of offices and any notion that offices were private property (Godechot 1968:35–40; Soboul 1977:62–65; Thuillier and Tulard 1984:11; Debbasch 1966:159). Civil and partial political equality were reaffirmed by the Constitution of 1791, but subsequent events were to place severe limitations on the freedom of the press, association, and petition (Godechot 1968:58–73). [1]

The elimination of venal office-holding had several important consequences for the development of administrative structure. First and most significant was an explicit commitment to the idea of office-holding as public rather than private in nature. From this point forward, office-holding at the central level became, at least in theory, contingent on evaluation of performance by those who had the legitimate power to appoint and dismiss. The elimination of patronage as proprietary right, however, made office-holding a much more arbitrary and contingent matter. The absence of an objective standard of evaluation in the patronage system raised the problem of deter-

---

1. For the most part, the poor and women were not given full political equality even though Robespierre proposed that the Constituent Assembly do so (Godechot 1968:50).

mining the standards by which appointment and performance was to be evaluated now that merit, in theory, was to be the standard for appointment (Church 1981:47–48).

The very uncertainty facing the political leaders of the various assemblies led them to make appointments largely on the basis of loyalties—both personal and revolutionary (Church 1981:70–71; Church 1983). This was all the more the case as France came to be faced with great perils from its European neighbors. The government of the Committee on Public Safety set aside, in its not totally paranoid fear of counterrevolutionaries, reliance on traditional administrative forms. Faced with the demands created by the wars of the revolution, the Jacobin government was forced to expand the number of officeholders as well as to experiment with the creation of new forms of administration (Church 1981:85–95). The expansion and reformulation of the administrative structure led directly to an enormous increase in the number of rules aimed at defining the duties of new officeholders and new offices (Church 1981:85–95). At the same time, expansion led to continuing reliance on patronage as the primary means of recruitment and appointment and on loyalty as the basic criterion.

The succession of governments from 1793 until the 18th of Brumaire perpetuated the emphasis on patronage and loyalty as the basic means and criterion for administrative appointment. Each new political crisis led political leaders to engage in purges and to engage in the process of "strategic replacement" (Church 1981: passim; Goyard 1977:5–7). On the one hand, this tended to undermine the notion of career but, on the other hand, it tended to stress the role of seniority as one standard for advancement and continued employment (Church 1981:75). The first consequence is easy to understand. The uncertainty of political leadership tenure led to a continual purging of officials in the first decade of the Revolution as different regimes of leaders sought to sustain their positions by appointing loyal supporters (Goyard 1977:5–6). Why seniority should emerge as an important feature of administrative structure is less simple. It appears to have arisen out of the fact that expansion of the central bureaucracy produced a real shortage of experienced lower-level and middle-level administrators. Officeholders from the old regime and from previous revolutionary regimes became increasingly important for administrative continuity as time went on (Church 1983:129–30). Surviving purges, in effect, became the criterion for advancement.

The inability to find any systematic structure for dispensing patronage appears to have led political leaders, especially during the period of the Directory, to fall back, increasingly, on prior experience as the means for selecting individuals to retain their positions. But seniority or prior experience did not become a criterion for advancement, at least not in any systematic way

(Church 1983:134). By the advent of the Consulate it is clear that (1) appointment to senior posts (*expéditionaire* and above) continued to be primarily based on patronage; (2) appointments were not based on any systematic structure of criteria for recruitment and advancement other than personal and political leadership regime loyalty; (3) there existed no systematic structure for organizing patronage—in effect, it was a system in which each minister had a more or less free hand and, therefore, a system which ministers were to jealously guard over the next century and a quarter; (4) lower-level officials found some level of security precisely because they were out of the running for senior positions, thus creating an informal distinction in the revolutionary administrative structure between an upper and lower administrative service; (5) finally, it seems clear that the reformulation of revolutionary governments led to increasing reliance on formal definitions of office and of role structure as each regime sought to spell out a uniform system of decision making and implementation.

One might conclude, then, that the very arbitrariness and unpredictability of office-holding at the upper level led to the utilization of two strategies by political leaders. The uncertainty facing political leaders led them to rely on seniority as an orderly means of filling positions in the hierarchy of lower offices where relatively little was at stake in terms of patronage. Further, the very high level of turnover of leadership regimes tended to produce an increasing reliance on rules as the only means of imposing order on administrative behavior (Church 1981:140–41). The continued importance of patronage was reflected in that seniority remained an entirely informal criterion while the increase in rule-making was anything but systematic. Thus, patronage remained the dominant mode of selection at the higher levels of office-holding. But the numerous reconstruction of leadership regimes further enhanced the power of ministers because of their continued reliance on patronage to help stabilize their control of office. The resistance of ministers to any formulation that might decrease their autonomy resulted in the persistence of patronage as the primary mechanism for recruitment and advancement. The reliance on patronage, based as it was on private privilege, resulted in the absence of a coherent theory of administrative law until the middle of the nineteenth century. The consequence of this was an increasingly wide divergence of practice in the various ministries and field services of the state administration (Demartial 1909:1–3; Georgin 1911:105–8). Indeed, diversity became institutionalized to such a degree that it became the major obstacle to the creation of uniform statutes defining the administrative role (Georgin 1911:105–29). When administrative law did emerge as a distinct area of legal theory, it stressed the authority and power of state officials rather than notions of uniformity inherent in the law (Lenöel

1865:110–20). Thus, while the resort to rules to define administrative roles and structure became increasingly characteristic of the Revolutionary period, the strategic necessity of political leaders to utilize loyalty as a basic criteria for appointment to office led them to support patronage and the supremacy of ministerial authority. With ministerial authority came ministerial diversity, which was to be the trademark of French administration throughout the nineteenth century.

Political Equality and the Problem of Administration

Although civil equality had been eagerly sought, political equality turned out to be an object of ambivalence on the part of succeeding parliamentary assemblies. The majority of the deputies to the early assemblies felt mass suffrage would produce very high levels of uncertainty with regard to their own fates if not everyone else's. The Constitution of 1791 thus had made a distinction between "active" and "passive" citizens, with the former being defined as those who paid the equivalent of at least three days labor in taxes (Godechot 1968:49). Deputies to future assemblies could only be chosen by active citizens, while to sit as a deputy required that the individual pay the equivalent of fifty days labor (D. M. G. Sutherland 1986:131). Indeed, as time went on and the revolutionary government came to face external threats while it had not yet fully resolved the problem of determining political succession, the qualifications for voters came to be markedly narrower. For example, the election law was changed by the Assembly under pressure and persuasion by the Feuillants in August 1791 in the attempt to limit the possibilities of radicalizing the Assembly. The new law limited the selection of deputies to those on the active list by citizens paying the equivalent of between 150 and 300 days work (D. M. G. Sutherland 1986:131). The August uprising in Paris in 1792 brought a swing of the pendulum. The new National Convention instituted universal manhood suffrage. Nevertheless, here too ambivalence was not absent as this suffrage was mediated by a system of electors who actually chose deputies (D. M. G. Sutherland 1986:156).

The pendulum was to swing in the other direction and more or less stay there until the advent of the Second Republic. The Constitution of the Year III produced a large basic electorate but a very small real electorate. The vote was possessed by anyone who paid a direct tax or who fought in the army. The actual power to choose deputies was restricted to individuals selected by the large base of voters, but these electors had to pay taxes equivalent to approximately 150 to 200 days of labor, which meant a direct electorate of about thirty thousand (Godechot 1968:461–62; D. M. G. Sutherland 1986:272–74). Moreover, the deputies of the Convention clearly feared that even with a limited electorate they might be evicted from office and thus resorted to the stratagem of requiring that the pool of nominees include at least two-thirds of the incumbent deputies (Godechot 1968:461–62). Even this stratagem failed to prevent an Assembly hostile to the Directory and its executive. In 1797, and again in 1798, the Directory executed coup d'états against the Assembly when elections produced hostile majorities. The unwillingness of the Directory to either adhere to its own rules or dispense with elections altogether provided the Assembly with the legitimacy to overthrow the Directory, only to be overthrown in turn by the Napoleonic coup of 18/19 Brumaire.

Despite the jaundiced view that struggling and conflicting political leaders came to have of elections as the means for determining political succession, the principle, if not the reality, was never abandoned, not even by Napoleon. Nevertheless, it is easy to see that the notion and practice of any form of political equality as the means of resolving the problem of how to choose leaders was suspect so long as it continued to be used to ensure their continued incumbency. Yet, political leaders over the next several decades could find no easy means to abandon ideas of political equality so long as civil equality reigned as a cornerstone of the irreversible Revolution. As long as civil equality remained unshakable, the absence of political equality always seemed an arbitrary condition imposed by those seeking their own interests. Whenever restrictions were placed on political equality, they always found a challenge and a challenger. Nor could elections as a form of public accounting or public legitimization of leadership selection be totally abandoned since to do so would immediately raise the challenge of "why should you govern and not us?"

If political equality provided little assurance to political leaders of their incumbency, why was it so difficult to find either a resolution to this problem or adequate alternatives? It is true that the Third Estate's grasping of the revolutionary bit in their collective mouth, combined with the execution of the king, meant that any notion of a monarchical/aristocratic solution was out of the question. Two other possible alternatives existed. First, leaders of the Assembly from 1789 could have utilized political equality in the form of the franchise to organize leadership and its selection in a systematic way through the development of a party or parties. Or, Assembly leaders could have utilized political equality to suppress organizations of leadership selection by reducing the number of elective positions and resorting to a plebiscitary concept of political equality. This latter form, in effect, could utilize the plebiscite to legitimize the civil and/or military bureaucratic seizure of power. In any case, one can't help but conclude that political leaders simply could not eliminate the franchise as the primary form of representation of the public interest.

The problem was exacerbated, and the ambivalence of political leaders about political equality was increased, by the franchise becoming inextricably intertwined with the problem of centralization and the creation of a unified national community as opposed to one based on the partial autonomy of local and regional communities. As it moved, in 1789, to try to reconstruct the administration and organization of the state, the Constituent Assembly dissolved the old local and municipal forms of royal governance and the Office of Intendant was eliminated. This left local government in the hands of more or less spontaneously elected local assemblies. The representatives of the provinces in the Constituent Assembly sought to institutionalize not only their form of self-government but also the privileges their localities held from the old regime (Godechot 1968:94–95; Chapman 1955:13–14; Mage 1924). It was clear to the majority of deputies, however, that to accede to these demands would have meant an end to the powers of the Constituent Assembly and to themselves as political leaders. This led them, in the first weeks of August 1789, to deny federalism in any form. In the same week the Assembly voted the Declaration of the Rights of Man it also decreed that:

A national constitution and public liberty are more advantageous to the provinces than the privileges which some of them now enjoy, and whose sacrifice is now necessary for the intimate union of all parts of the empire. It is therefore decreed that all particular privileges of the provinces, principalities, cities, corps, and communities, be they financial advantages or of any other kind, are henceforth abolished, and are merged in the common law of all the French. (as quoted in Chapman 1955:14; also Godechot 1968:95)

On 22 December, the Assembly chose to accept the recommendations of a commission and to redivide France into a more or less geometric structure of eighty-three departments, which were further divided into districts and communes. Each department was to have an assembly of thirty-six councilors elected for two years by the electoral assembly of the department, which was made up of those who paid taxes equivalent to ten days labor. These councilors, in turn, elected a Department Directory or executive committee to run the affairs of the department on a day-to-day basis. Districts had a similar organization. Direct administrative integration into the national structure was meant to occur through the election of a *procureur général syndic* at the department and the district levels. The department syndic was to represent the king (as the executive) in the departmental and district executive committees, with the latter being primarily accountable to the department syndic. The duties of the syndic were primarily to oversee the proper execution of the laws passed by the Assembly in Paris and to constrain the local assemblies from acting on their own initiative (Godechot 1968:101–12).

All of this is meant to point up the certainty with which it must be concluded that the political leaders of the new government viewed the franchise with a high degree of ambivalence. At the same time, the centrifugal tendencies of localism and regionalism would not, it was hoped, be simply encouraged by the resort to elections as the means for selecting local administrators and the central government's representatives. Indeed the franchise, utilized within a common and uniform structure of administration, appeared to the political leaders in Paris to be the only means by which centrifugal political forces could be suppressed. In the absence of any other means, the franchise became the primary mechanism for organizing the selection of political leaders at both the local and national levels. The political leaders of the Assembly had no choice but to rely on the franchise to organize their own legitimacy and incumbency. They tried to make sure that the same electors, the local notables, were responsible for selecting administrators and legislators at both the local and national levels of government.

Three aspects of this strategy are worth noting. The first is that the public good or interest was seen as residing in some form of franchise, restricted though it might be, and not in some form of superior knowledge. Administration was thus seen as best directed and supervised on a day-to-day basis by elected officials. Second, the integration of local offices of government and administration into the central state took place through an open "market" mechanism—elections—rather then through the process of internalization. That is, while a uniform hierarchy of offices was created, they were not defined or allocated on the basis of a systematic body of rules that produced relatively high degrees of predictability with regard to holding office or having decisions implemented. They were to be allocated instead by the electoral process. The third aspect to be noted is that the strategy was organized around the *social* organization of local leadership—the structure of local notables whose political role now came to be defined by their dominance in the structure of elections.

The weaknesses of this means of organization for those who held power in Paris became evident within a short time. The hope that a restricted and uniform body of electors might be sufficient to ensure legitimacy by providing predictability about the implementation of decisions proved to be a false one. Over the next several years, local and departmental assemblies became increasingly independent as they and the syndics sought to advance local interests, became instruments of individual interest, or came to be dominated by political factions and clubs (Bouloiseau 1983:15).

The majority in the Assembly, at the same time, could lay no essential claim to a monopoly on ascertaining or representing the public interest. Devoid of systematic organization which could ensure their dominance, they were open to challenges by those who claimed to truly represent the majority. The Girond was attacked on the ground that they restricted political equality through purely arbitrary restrictions. The Jacobins were ultimately successful in establishing themselves as a "majority." Seeking a new means to overcome the centrifugal forces inherent in the election of local administration, the Jacobins increasingly resorted to attempting to organize political leadership on the basis of a crude but relatively effective party organization. That is, they utilized local Jacobin clubs as a means to gain dominance over local elective offices and the election of deputies (Bouloiseau 1983:17ff.; Sydenham 1961; D. M. G. Sutherland 1986:161–247). Unfortunately, for the Jacobins, this loosely organized structure of clubs did not develop a systematic means for selecting and controlling leadership.

The Revolutionary government that followed from these events proclaimed itself as based on political equality but refused to put this notion to a test. Rather, they sought to solve the problem of administrative integration by removing administration from the hands of the legislative body and placing it directly in the grasp of the Committee on Public Safety. The committee then proceeded to send commissioners by the hundreds into local areas to oversee the implementation of the central government's decrees (Bouloiseau 1983:89–90). In this, the Jacobin-dominated government came as close as anyone would come in that decade to creating a party organization which would serve to subordinate both the administration and the franchise upon which it depended.

With the collapse of the Revolutionary government, the Directory which succeeded it once again had to fall back on the notable-mediated franchise and notable appointments to local assemblies as a means of organizing leadership and community (Lefebvre 1964a:164, 172–73; Lefebvre 1964b:251–53). Its fear of political equality led the Directory to refuse to recognize two elections held under its authority. This refusal to accept the results of elections carried out under its own rules undermined both the Directory and the franchise as a means of organizing leadership. As a result, the Directory's capacity to internalize the functions of local government within the central structure diminished rapidly (Lefebvre 1964b:427–45; Chapman 1955:16).

In short, political leaders and putative political leaders in the years after the fall of the Jacobins found themselves unwilling and unable, if they listened to the voice of strategic rationality, to utilize the notion of political equality as the means for organizing the structure of political leadership and the process of decision making. To seek to avoid this situation by relying on some form of restricted franchise that was defined by the social and economic structure of local notables was to openly accept political inequality. Accepting political inequality was always to invite challenge, opposition, and subversion (Lefebvre 1964b:456–57).

The Directory could not seek the bureaucratic solution for two reasons.

First, to do so would undermine the very basis on which they themselves had been chosen. That is, it would have required substitution of expertise and the publicness of that expertise for the criterion of representation of narrow individual, political, and class interests. Second, and perhaps more to the point, they had no administrative structure immediately at hand that represented publicness or the public in its organizational character. The existing bureaucracy was recruited largely on the basis of individual patronage. There existed no explicit standard of merit that could be measured objectively in any form except seniority (Church 1983:50–117). Nor did any of the political leaders between 1793 and 1799 seem to have any faith in the idea that their own incumbencies could be assured by abandoning local notables in favor of directly appointed state representatives as the means for internalizing the entire structure of local administration. To do this was to surely destroy the only political base that sustained the Directory. By Brumaire of 1799, the only solution seemed to be to seize power and have it legitimized not by a broad and deep exercise of the franchise but only by a broad one—a plebiscitary solution. In effect, the only solution political leaders had, if they wanted to stay somewhere in the vicinity of power, was to create a monarch who might then proceed, because of his great powers, to resolve the problems of equality and community. If there had been no Napoleon, the political leaders under the Directory would have had to create one.

Under Bonaparte's eye, the bourgeoisie continued its work: it was the bourgeoisie that established the institutions of the Consulate and the Empire, and drew up the laws, thus fixing the limits of the society it dominated. The eighteenth of Brumaire consecrated the Revolution in the form which the bourgeoisie had conceived it in 1789. (Lefebvre 1964b:456–57)

The Napoleonic Solution

No less than the Directory, Napoleon faced the problems of equality and community. The Napoleonic regime had to find some solution to the problem of the relationship between the revolutionary commitment to equality of individual preferences in economic and social life and the failure to provide such equality in political life. Equally, it had to find a means of reconstructing or constructing the national community. In the years between 1789 and 1799, the relationship between the two forms of equality remained evanescent. Political leaders were unwilling to test large numbers of voters with their incumbency. Nor was the Directory's experience with restricted voting any encouragement to depend on limited franchise. The Jacobin experience made the moderates and conservatives suspicious of parties and this forestalled further experimentation with party organization or the attempt to create an informal network of clubs. So long as political leaders suspected that the Jacobin presence would make itself felt again once restraints on voluntary organizations were removed, party organization was not likely to be viewed as a rewarding strategy.

The inability to create a party that might co-opt and impose discipline on local notables allowed centrifugal forces to dominate. The creation of a national community, even if only in formal administrative terms, could not be achieved through the mechanisms of franchise so long as there were no means of imposing discipline on local notables. The central problem was not, for the time being, why any one group of leaders should govern as against any other group. Rather, the problem was how to integrate the highly fractionated structure of local elites/notables into a community with national interests as well as local ones. Or, to put it another way, the problem was how to keep local notables from making the usual choice of the Prisoner's Dilemma—choosing one's own best interest regardless of anyone else's choice, even though this might lead to the worst outcomes. Caught between the pressures of local self-interest or the dangers inherent in the use of franchise as a means of overcoming self-interest, putative political leaders would have to subordinate local interest and its inevitable companion—notable franchise—to some principle of integration other than the franchise.

The Napoleonic strategy for resolving these problems was alarmingly simple. On the one hand, the problem of equality, that is, why anyone has the right to govern in the absence of any equally weighted aggregation of preferences, was to be resolved by shifting the right to determine preferences to an organizational structure that was not organized around any principle of private (notable) or local (notable) preferences. Instead of the varying and biased forms of preference aggregation, as encompassed in a seemingly infinite variety of ways in which the franchise could be organized, the answer was to make political equality a function of the administrative structure. This meant that the aggregation of equally weighted preferences was what defined Napoleonic administration. Such a notion required an ideal administrator—one who was capable of understanding the preferences of individuals and organizing them in a systematic manner along a spectrum of priorities. The idea also required a body of public, systematic rules that would govern the way in which preferences were distinguished, organized, transformed into policy, and implemented. Finally, this concept required those who would carry out the latter functions to be selected on the basis of criteria that reflected the publicness rather than the privateness of their interests.

Napoleon sought to create a state defined by the organization of administration. Rejecting the high risk to themselves of franchise and party as the mediation between individual and collective choices, the Brumaireans sought to substitute state organization as the mediation. Indeed, I would argue that the Napoleonic state was one which sought, with considerable success, to substitute administration for politics. Reacting to opposition to a bill he favored, Napoleon said that government aimed "to destroy the spirit of faction"—to govern through parties was to become dependent on them—"I am national" (D. M. G. Sutherland 1986:357). Napoleon came to be defined (and defined himself) as the ideal administrator.

It is not as a General that I am governing France; it is because the nation believes that I possess the civil qualities [earlier defined as 'foresight, power of calculation, administrative ability, ready wit, eloquence . . . and above all knowledge of men'] which go to make a ruler. (Sutherland 1986:361)

The Constitution of the Year VIII (15 December 1799), which created the Consulate, clearly showed Napoleon's and the Brumaireans' strategy of reducing two central risks to their leadership and dominance. As the historian Daniel Halevy wrote, "Every French regime since the Consulate has had 'two constitutions,'—its own and the Constitution of the Year VIII which hands the direction of the country over to the administrative corps" (Osborne 1983:20). The first strategy was aimed at eliminating the franchise as the means for selecting central administrators and legislators. This constitution, created by the venerable survivor Sieyes, provided for three levels of selection for eligibility for the legislative bodies. The first was at the communal level, followed by the departmental and the national levels. At the communal or *arrondissement* level, all citizens twenty-one years of age and over who had resided for at least a year in their place of registration voted for a list limited to ten percent of themselves. This ten percent reduced themselves to another ten percent at the departmental election. In theory, the Senate was to choose from this remaining group of notables to populate the Tribunal and the Legislature (Godechot 1968:564–65). In fact, such a selection took place only once, in 1801. After this one use of the lists, Napoleon eliminated the process and chose the membership himself. The Constitution of the Year X (4 August 1802) removed all real vestiges of the use of franchise as an organizing principle of leadership selection or succession (Godechot 1968:570–85). From this point on, Napoleon and his senior administrators, especially the prefects, would be responsible for determining the structure and content of leadership. This was to create, as we shall see, several major problems centering on the issues of selection and incentives.

The second strategy revolved around the problem of regionalism or federalism—the tendency of local governmental structures to end up pursuing local interests at the expense of central state interests. A major part of this

problem arose from the condition of either electing or appointing local notables to the positions of power in the departments and the communes. The
Constituent Assembly and its successors had sought to answer the problem
of integration of local government by appointing or allowing the election of
local notables as representatives of the central government. Elections were
seen as a necessary virtue or evil. They appeared to be the only means available of creating a national structure of leadership, one united by ties of loyalty, obligation, and pragmatic calculation to the central government. The
problem was, as we have seen and as central governmental political leaders
found to their continued despair, this often meant a disastrous weakening of
the central government's executive power.

The Napoleonic solution to this problem followed from the understanding arrived at by the creation of the Consulate. The creation of a singular powerful executive, by eschewing the franchise as the means for selecting leaders, immediately raised the problem of administrative loyalty. The
thin bond of unity and loyalty created by a system of notable elections was
now decapitated at the center. In its place, the Constitution of the Year VIII
created the basis for the structural autonomy of state administration. This
constitution provided for an executive that was responsible for the nomination, appointment, and revocation of individuals to public office (Godechot
1968:560). Equally important in the long run, perhaps, was the executive's
power to regulate the administration, to issue regulations at will with regard
to the definition of office without prior legislative action (Godechot
1968:563–64; Debbasch 1966:23–24). These prerogatives remained at the
heart of executive action and power over the next century. The capacity of
the executive to make administrative regulations was reaffirmed in the Constitutions of 1814, 1830, 1848, 1852, and 1875 (Debbasch 1966:24). In effect, administrative officials were directly responsible to the political will of
the executive, not to the representatives of the people. The underlying principle was clear: the execution of the public interest was too important to be
left in the hands of any group of representatives and their private interests.

In specific tactical terms, by eliminating the franchise, Napoleon was not
only faced with the problem of integrating local government into the structure of central decision making, he also faced the problem of a leadership
whose loyalties were predominantly local. Napoleon's answer to the problems of internalization of local government and loyalty was the creation of a
centralized system of local leadership selection—the prefect, sub-prefect,
and mayor. The law of 17 February 1800 (28 Pluviose, Year VIII) created
these officials to govern, respectively, the department, the newly created *ar-
rondissements,* and the communes. The prefect and sub-prefect were appointed by the central government, and in the first instance by Napoleon

himself, while mayors of communes with less than five thousand inhabitants were appointed by the prefect, and those with the larger populations were appointed by the central government (Godechot 1968:586–87, 592–94, 595–96; Legendre 1968:138–42; Chapman 1955:17–20). The law gave prefects extremely broad powers. The prefect was, in effect, the central government's representative on all matters. The sub-prefect and mayor were responsible and accountable directly to the prefect and he, in turn, was directly responsible to the Minister of the Interior and the Minister of Police. There was created, thus, a hierarchy of power and loyalty emanating from Paris (Vivien 1859:I, 72–75; Godechot 1968:586–96).

Napoleon sought, with a considerable measure of success, to remove the department from the realm of politics by the creation of administrative hierarchy. At the same time, he sought to reduce the risk to Brumairean government and political leaders by a process of strategic replacement. While the prefects he selected were drawn from a broad array of backgrounds (Godechot 1968:588), they had at least one thing in common: they had served in national capacities—although in very different ways—and, most of all, they were men who had risen above their local notable or particularistic backgrounds (Bergeron 1981:57–59). The Napoleonic compromise with local loyalties was revealed in the tendency to select the sub-prefects from local notables. Their complete administrative submission to the prefect, however, made it extremely difficult for the sub-prefects to pursue local interests at the expense of central ones.

In one decisive stroke, perhaps far more decisive than most historians of the French state have been willing to accede, Napoleon sought to resolve the problem of equality and community. His predecessors had sought to use the rule of civil equality and of political inequality. But, unable to escape franchise as the means for structuring leadership and leadership succession, Napoleon's revolutionary predecessors succumbed time and again to the contradictions the Revolution had bequeathed to them. Napoleon, creating a second revolution, swept aside the notion of community as dependent on the process of electing and, thereby, legitimizing the power of local notables. In providing a substitute for this conception of community, Napoleon responded to the very conditions of his self-selection as the prime political leader. As a result, he laid the foundations for the idea of community as arising from the administrative integrity, unity, and coherence of the state.

In this sense, the progression of Napoleon's status from First Consul, to Consul for Life, to Emperor was not a progression of hubris or charisma. While these were certainly present, the progression was primarily an administrative progression. In the absence of any basic structure of accountability, Napoleon had no choice but to find the source of his capacity to determine the public interest in his proximity to the integrated coherent national state. Seeking to avoid the clearly revealed uncertainties and disasters that awaited political leaders who wished to elude the logic of civil equality by relying on the arbitrariness of political inequality, he chose the strategy of depoliticizing administration. Political equality was now seen as being fulfilled in the ritual of the plebiscite.

Community was to be fulfilled in the orderly hierarchy of power and authority. But if Napoleon was to play the role of the administrative official capable of aggregating and ordering a system of desires out of all individual desires, then the following questions arise: How is this impartial administrator selected? Is he indispensable? If he is self-selected, what is there that makes others incapable of selecting themselves? Napoleon's primary strategy was to move progressively to the claim of indispensability. Any idea that the impartial arbiter of public interest was replaceable would have undermined Napoleon's position as the source and representation of the public interest. Life Consulship legitimized and crowned the administrative structure. Emperorship became the resolution of the problem of succession. No other resolution was possible for Napoleon. To be First Consul for Life with no provision for succession was to invite the struggle for succession to occur at once. Emperorship would put an end to conflicts over the question of succession. Depoliticization of administration would put an end to conflicts between center and periphery.

The Problem of Administrative Leadership

The creation of the prefect and its institutionalization by Napoleon and his successors may have resolved the problem of internalizing local government and brought into the realms of everyday action completely different conceptions of equality and community, but it also created a number of new problems. One of the most significant of these was the problem of internalizing and structuring a system of administrative leadership and leadership succession. Having created the administrative prefect and its subordinate hierarchy, the problem that then had to be confronted was the creation of a process by which such senior administrators might be systematically selected. The first group of prefects had been chosen on the basis of personal knowledge by Napoleon and his closest Brumairean associates. In effect, the system of patronage continued. Loyalty or the perceived capacity for loyalty and obligation clearly was one criterion. About twenty of the prefects were old acquaintances of Napoleon, another twenty or so were known and appointed by the other two consuls, Cambaceres and Lebrun (Bergeron 1981:56–57; Giesselmann 1977:420–23). But loyalty was not the dominant criterion.

This is clearly reflected in the diverse political backgrounds of the first appointees: sixty-two had belonged to revolutionary assemblies and had sported various political inclinations from the Mountain to liberal monarchism; sixty had served as members or presidents of departmental administrations under the Directory or held other important posts in the department; about twenty had served as administrators in the occupied territories, while a number had served as members of department councils (Aulard 1913:127–30; Bergeron 1981:58–59; Giesselmann 1977:420–23). In short, while the first group were seen as strategic replacements for the locally elected or based administrative officials, Napoleon sought to make it clear that he would not resort simply to the creation of patron-client relations. The strategy was clearly designed to avoid the accusation that these appointments were simply a means of maintaining personal power.

The problem with this arrangement was that it could not be systematized. That is, while the selection criteria sought to express a notion of public interest, the absence of clearly defined rules revealed that selection was, nevertheless, a function of personal and, therefore, possibly and probably private choices. For the process to continue in this mode would mean that the prefects could become the object of factional strife and patron-client structures by those seeking to ensure their positions in the government. At the same time, to continue to select prefects on the basis of ill-defined criteria would have left Napoleon open to charges of undermining the Revolution. It is not surprising then that within a relatively short period Napoleon sought to create a systematic structure of recruitment and training. His aim was to produce a career structure for the prefect and other senior positions—one which, by its formal structure and increasingly well-defined criteria based on experience and knowledge, reflected its public character.

The first step in this process was the creation of the position of *auditeur* in the Council of State (Conseil d'État) on 9 April 1803 (19 Germinal Year XI). The number of *auditeurs* was first set at sixteen, and their duties were to aid the Councilors of State in the development and formation of laws. From the very beginning, Napoleon meant the position to be one that trained young men for administrative and diplomatic careers. Napoleon felt the experiment worked well and in 1806 increased the number of *auditeurs*. In the same year, a decree regularized the practice of using the *auditeur* appointments as a step in an administrative or diplomatic career by requiring the position of ambassadorial and legation secretary to be filled by *auditeurs* with at least one year's service. The utilization of the *auditeur* appointment as the training ground for upper-level civil servants was greatly expanded after 1809. In that year, the number of prefects who had begun their careers as *auditeurs* was about eight percent; by 1813 the number had risen dramatically to twenty-five percent. The formalization of the auditorship as the beginning point of a prefectural corps career came in 1809 when a decree (26 December) set aside at least twenty-five percent of all sub-prefect openings for *auditeurs* (Durand 1958:10–24).

The concern about recruitment to the *auditeur* became evident as their number expanded and it became apparent that the position was seen as the entrance to the most senior careers. Napoleon began by using social status as one of the primary criteria for the appointment of young men to the office, in the hope and desire of thus co-opting the aristocracy to the new imperial regime, but he could not continue this kind of patronage. Not only would the problems of patronage be overwhelming as the number of appointments rose to over several hundred, but there would also be the problem once again of equality (Durand 1958:26–28, 33–34). This appears to be the major reason for the creation of a new criterion for appointment as *auditeur*. The same decree of 26 December 1809 that set aside twenty-five percent of subprefect offices for auditors also prescribed that from 1 January 1813 all candidates for the post of *auditeur* would be required to have a *licencié* in law or science. The decree also created the requirement for an examination, which was put in place in 1810, but which was defined quite loosely (Durand 1958:34–35). In the same decree, there was further definition of the *auditeur*'s role as the first step in a senior administrative career. The decree clearly prescribed the number of auditors to be assigned to different ministries and services, while at the same time it created two levels of *auditeur* rank (Durand 1958:34–35). In 1811, the number of classes was expanded to three, and the number of *auditeurs* in all three categories rose to 350 (Durand 1958:38–39). With this decree, the *auditeur* of the Conseil d'État became the basis of a relatively predictable career structure.

By 1812, the Napoleonic strategy of centralizing and integrating local administration by making local officials direct appointees of the central government had the effect of increasing the problems of recruitment, of incentives for attracting individuals, and of the organizational expression of equality in the absence of franchise. The appointment of prefects and subprefects on the basis of patronage and postrevolutionary administrative experience that transcended purely local service resolved the first of these difficulties. But this clearly could not be the basis of a systematic structure of selection for this most critical of administrative links to the center. Over time, the original basis of selection—participation in the attempt to create a new economic and political settlement at the national level in the revolutionary decade—would simply disappear by natural attrition.

To rely solely on the concept of patronage presented further difficulties.

On what basis would patronage be accorded? It could not be based on loyalty to party since this is what Napoleon and the Brumaireans sought to avoid. Patronage might have been distributed on the basis of individual loyalty. But how would anyone construct some appropriate test of personal loyalty which could get beyond the criterion of participation in the Eighteenth Brumaire? Even here, however, loyalty could not be loyalty to Napoleon as a person but only as a representative of the public and its interest. Any other form of personal loyalty would destroy the notion of the state as the representative and guardian of community in favor of some personalistic and private conception of community—just what the Revolution had sought to destroy and had done so with some success.

At the same time, any resort to personalistic patronage would undercut the resolution of the problems of political equality, if not of civil equality as well. Patronage as a function of political equality produces a *raison d'être* only where party is the mediating institution between individual choice and majority rule. Patronage can then be distributed under the argument that the majority should be represented in administrative offices in order to insure that the will of the majority is implemented. This can only be done where there is agreement that party is the central institution of political life and where party and party leadership succession is determined by an agreed-upon process of majority rule—exactly what the various pre-Napoleonic revolutionary governments had been unwilling and unable to achieve. Napoleon's unwillingness to resolve the problem of political equality by institutionalizing the franchise in the form of political parties left him with no rationale for the "publicness" of patronage. Thus, the elevation of the plebiscite served as one mechanism to resolve the problem of political equality. However, recruitment to the administrative structure, which was to substitute for politics, raised the problem in a different way—it reopened the question of why some individuals should govern and not others.

The very diversity of appointments arising from the resort to patronage also raised problems. In the absence of any uniform system of education and training, patronage could only produce a system of administrative conflict as officials placed different interpretations on the decrees and regulations emanating from Paris. As Church points out:

The concern for the execution of decisions was crucial and probably outweighed the distinctions he [Napoleon] drew between the various functions of government and between administrative and other acts. The preamble to the *loi 28 Pluvose VIII,* after distinguishing between communication, direct action, and procuring action, spends most time on the ways in which action can be procured. (1981:261)

The short-term solution was the specification of action by rules. The long-term solution was the creation of a uniformly trained body of officials.

The strategy with which Napoleon responded was to fall back on the idea of equality as represented in merit. It was, as Napoleon recognized, dangerous to conflate "merit-as-equality" with high birth as a necessary condition of the commitment to public service—the British idea of the gentleman as the only one committed by his social condition to public service. While he was partial to the notion, as we can see by his tendency to nominate young men from aristocratic families to *auditeur* posts, he was equally careful to attempt to construct a definition of merit which answered to the demands of equality and publicness. The strategy was aimed at accomplishing this without completely sacrificing the benefits of patronage. In basing a good number of his appointments on social status, Napoleon sought to gain the support of alienated social groups, notably the former aristocracy and the notables who had been locked out of local administration by the abolition of elected local administrators.

This kind of patronage was legitimated by the idea that social status, especially location in the former aristocracy and contemporary notables, resulted in the development of individuals who were or ought to have been committed to some idea of public service and public interest as part of their social condition (Dubois 1859, in Durand 1958:26; cf., 51–54, 65). This was not the idea of birth as a source of merit but rather the notion that class location brought with it the obligation to acquire knowledge and the obligation to participate in public, not purely private, affairs. The criterion was one of merit in the sense that anyone who was willing to engage in public service for reasons of public interest would not be excluded from access to senior positions. But this criterion alone would provide an overwhelming number of candidates and nominators since no one surely would be willing to admit to private reasons for public service. The answer to this dilemma was again a notion of merit closely associated with the idea of learned and acquired commitments to public service. The idea of a formal education which could be viewed as related to preparation for public service was one which stressed the equality of achievement and emulation. The former idea was reflected in the increasing stress Napoleon placed on education. The latter was reflected on the emergence, in the imperial period, of a stress on examinations *(concours)* as a measure of excellence.

This strategy was not simply or marginally reflected in the increasingly well defined structure of *auditeur* recruitment. The strategy was reflected with considerable force in Napoleonic educational policy. This policy had in mind, first of all, the creation of a system that would define merit in terms of the acquisition of knowledge, especially utilitarian knowledge founded on scientific or scientistic constructions of information, and an objective test of that achievement. It was also a system that sought to define equality as the absence of obstacles to acquiring such an education.

This aim can be seen quite clearly in the manner in which Napoleon reconstructed the educational system, which had been dismantled and only partially rebuilt in the first decade of revolutionary governments. The law of Floreal 10, Year X (1 May 1802) replaced the decentralized secondary school system with the *lycée*. Forty-five, less than two for each department, were authorized, but only thirty-six came into existence, making access to them even more contested and scarce (Palmer 1985:300–301). Access was by examination, but a large number of openings and scholarships were set aside for sons of civil servants and officers (Ponteil 1966:103–5). The *lycée* became the basic institutional structure for passage to higher education when the *baccalauréat* was revived in 1808. The decree of 17 March, which detailed the regulations of the Université Imperial de France, empowered the Faculties of Letters and Sciences (Articles 16 and 17) to grant the degrees after public examinations. Article 19 provided that candidates would be examined on what they had been taught in the senior levels of the *lycée* (Weiss 1984:18). "From the start, the baccalaureate was not a mere pedagogical examination, but a social institution, the condition for admission to civil offices" (Delfau 1902:62, as quoted in Vaughan and Archer 1971:186).

The second major aim of Napoleonic educational policy was state monopoly and control over education. This goal is reflected in the institutionalization of the *lycée* and the *baccalauréat* as the basis for the state monopoly on higher education. The persistence of these institutions over the next century and a half—indeed, up until today—established the basic means by which equality defined as merit became a dominant aspect of French notions of equality. But more than this, the *baccalauréat* became the basic test of achievement and merit and thus the key to not only civil office but social mobility in general (Vaughan and Archer 1971:186; Weiss 1984:21). The state's control over access to these tests of merit was ensured by the nature of the Napoleonic policy of monopolization of secondary and, especially, higher education. State domination clearly proceeded from Napoleon's concern about the basis of political and social stability. One could sum up the Napoleonic aim in the following manner:

Teaching is a function of the State, because schools should be State establishments and not establishments in the State. They depend on the State and have no resort but it; they exist by it and for it. They hold their right to exist and their very substance from it; they ought to receive from it their task and their rule. Then again, as the State is one, its schools ought to be the same everywhere. (Liard 1888–94:II, 35)

and again:

The men of the Revolution saw national education more than anything as a duty of the state toward its citizens. Napoleon saw in it primarily the interest of the State and its sovereign. To him, left to itself and free to dispense its own doctrines, public education could become a public danger very rapidly. Its real function and its real reason for existence was to serve as a moral support for the power inherent in and personified by the State. (Liard 1888–94:II, 69)

Napoleon thus saw the monopoly of higher education as central to any effort to create a new structure of uniform, or at least homogenous, leadership and as one of the primary means for resolving the problem of community.

The form which the monopoly over education took derived its character from the creation of three institutions: the *baccalauréat,* the Université, and the body of specialized schools usually called the *grandes écoles.* The first became, quite rapidly, in the first decades after its re-creation, the prerequisite for entrance into higher civil office and the liberal professions. The Université as a corporate structure embracing all of higher education eliminated, for all intents and purposes, the development of a competing private sector. Through its control of what was taught, who taught, and the whole structure of degrees and certification, this structure was successful in eliminating any private version of higher education and almost all other versions of secondary education (Ponteil 1966:123–43). In almost two centuries, only one nonpublic institution of higher learning of any significance was to emerge— the École Libre des Sciences Politiques. And this was an institution so closely in tune with the conception of education as a support of the state that it could not be, and was not, seriously viewed as an adventure in private education for private purposes (Osborne 1983:63–67). The public claims of the Université provided both the place and the opportunity for the creation of the *grandes écoles* as the dominating institutions of all the liberal and technical professions.

The *grandes écoles* emerged out of two closely related developments: the creation of specialized career and application schools of higher learning and the development of relatively specialized technical and administrative corps. The closeness of the relationship stemmed from the fact that the specialized career schools became, on almost all accounts, the certification units for entrance into the so-called *grands corps.* While Napoleon by no means created all of the *grandes écoles,* he was primarily responsible for institutionalizing them and expanding the notion of such certifying schools of specialized training to the liberal professions in general. Thus, under the *ancien régime,* the École des Ponts et Chaussées was created in 1747, the École Militaire de Paris was founded in 1751, and the École des Mines was founded in 1783 (Tranchant 1878:9). [2] Under the Jacobin Committee on Public Safety, the predecessor of the École Polytechnique (the École Centrale des Travaux Publiques) was founded in 1794. The Polytechnique was transformed by Napoleon, who sought to make it a general school of higher education aimed at providing recruits for the schools of application such as the École des Mines and eventually for the technical corps of the army (Shinn 1980: 24–30).

Napoleon not only continued these schools but established them on firm ground by ensuring their graduates military and civil careers. Further, he definitively reestablished the École Normale Supérieur, which had been created in 1794 but had lasted only until 1795 (R. J. Smith 1982:7–8; Ponteil 1966:142). Napoleon resurrected the school in 1808, intending it to serve as the training school which would create a uniformly prepared body of teachers, particularly for the *lycée.* Napoleon also created the military school of St. Cyr in 1802, as well as the naval school at Brest in 1810 (Tranchant 1878:11). Finally, but by no means insignificantly, in 1804 the Napoleonic regime created a faculty of law within the Université. The law curriculum was to follow the order established in the structure of the civil code: natural law, the law of nations, Roman law in relation to French law, criminal legislation, criminal and civil procedure, French public law and civil law in relation to public administration (Ponteil 1966:114). The aim of the curriculum was to prepare individuals for both judicial and administrative careers (Tranchant 1878:16–17). Entrance into these schools was almost universally by examination and, after the revival of the *baccalauréat,* possession of this sign of *lycée* education (Sibert 1912: 27–29). Furthermore, *concours* came to be required for candidates for teaching in the faculties of law and in the *lycée* (Sibert 1912:26–27).

As the various *grandes écoles* and the Paris law faculty came to be viewed as the apex of a hierarchical system of training, it was also evident that they would persist in this condition only insofar as they were linked to promising careers. The commitment to the *lycée,* the preparation for the *baccalauréat,* the preparation for the *concours* to enter the higher schools, the passage through the rigorous discipline of these schools and perhaps the schools of application to which some might aspire; all of this represented an enormous investment of time, effort, and, not least of all, money since tuitions at the

2. There are differences with regard to founding dates of the various old regime schools. Terry Shinn gives the date of 1715 for the founding of École des Ponts et Chaussées (Shinn 1980:9). Palmer gives the date as 1775 (Palmer 1985:44).

lycée and the higher schools were not low. The payoff for individuals engaging in this educational structure had to be the promise of a relatively rewarding career.

The emergence of the various *grands corps* under the Empire was the direct consequence of the necessity of producing rewards for entering the new structure of higher education that Napoleon had created. Thus the prefect became the basis of a corps, entrance into which began with the *auditeurs* appointments in the Conseil d'État, which in turn came to require a *baccalauréat* and certification from a law faculty. The same route was followed into the diplomatic corps. Over time, entrance into the Finance Inspectorate, the Cours des Comptes, as well as the Conseil d'État would come to require this path (Osborne 1976:157–58; Sharp 1931:144–54). Much the same occurred with regard to the École Polytechnique, which became the gateway to high careers in the army and in industry, as well as to the technical corps of civil administration. Napoleon, in creating the prefectural corps by establishing an educational and appointment route, had not created a highly specific or well-structured career. However, he had created and specified the place where individuals could arrive if they had the right education and the economic and social status necessary to acquire that education. The very ambiguity of the specific steps in the career of high officials made the development of the corps structure all the more necessary as part of the incentive structure. So long as the career was not defined by specific patterns of office-holding, the career predictability had to take some form that promised high status outcome.

In effect, the *grands corps* became a distinct level of administrative service appointment which, even at its lowest level (the sub-prefect, for example), was an appointment of very senior standing. It was here that the particular French administrative tradition of distinguishing between grade and class began: grade equaled place in the hierarchy of office, and class equaled place in the pay scale (Georgin 1911:398–99ff.); between *emploi* (position) and *cadre* (group): the position is not the specific job of work but the official's grade, while the cadre is the group of positions to which the individual may look forward to achieving (Grégoire 1964:123–30). Appointment to one of the *corps* thus promised a career of a superior nature regardless of the particular office the individual was called upon to fulfill.

This arrangement provided the basis for the emergence later in the century (certainly as early as 1870) of the practice of *pantouflage*—the ability to be detached for service in a private capacity to industry, commerce, or finance without losing one's membership in the corps (Lalumière 1959:69–70). Position in a *cadre* or *corps* being distinguished from any given position or rank made mobility without loss of original hierarchical position possible.

The emergence of *pantouflage* came as a result of the necessity to maintain the structure of incentives. The incentives of career and high-status positions were necessary if recruitment to the educational precareer, beginning with the entrance to the *lycée,* was to be maintained. As greater numbers of individuals entered such careers and the rate of administrative succession tended to decline, or at least the rate of advancement seemed to be less predictable, there was a positive incentive for younger officials to want second careers and for senior officials to allow such arrangements. Movement to the private sector provided a means for maintaining incentives where there was a surplus of officials. By allowing *pantouflage,* the existence of rewards was made clear-cut, and a means was found to maintain the cohesiveness of the corps, not to mention the influence of its senior officials.

In sum, Napoleon's educational policy went beyond producing a broad state monopoly over education. It sought to create a structured hierarchical relationship between various levels of education through a system of certification in which the *baccalauréat* would come to play the key and basic element (Vaughan and Archer 1971:186). The *baccalauréat* signified the passage of an "objective" test of merit. Equally objective tests of merit were utilized to determine entrance to the École Normal, the École Polytechnique, and the technical schools of application like the Écoles des Ponts et Chaussées and des Mines and others, and increasingly as time went on they also required the *baccalauréat* (Weiss 1984:24–28). The notion of a special examination—the *concours*—as the means of testifying to the possession of knowledge was consistently utilized as the Napoleonic strategy (Vaughan 1969:93). It was used not only as the means to test achievement, but also to link together various elements of education and career or, to put it another way, to link education directly to specific careers. In this fashion those who wished to pursue a senior technical career in the military or civil services now would have to commit themselves to the acquisition of a *lycée* education. Only such an education would provide sufficient training to pass the examination to enter the Polytechnique. Entrance to the Polytechnique would be the means for entering a military or civil career, going on to more specialized schools, and more specialized careers (Shinn 1980:29). In the same way, the examination, in conjunction with legal training, came to be used to determine entrance to the *auditeur* position. The examination thus became the chief sign of merit and the symbol of an idea of equality, not as the equality of chance but of civil equality—the idea of equality before the law.

At the level of higher education, the Napoleonic strategy was directed quite clearly at the creation of a system organized around utilitarian scientific or, at least, scientistic knowledge. With the exception of the École Normale, which emphasized the production of teachers capable of teaching clas-

sical ancient and French literature and philosophy in the *lycée,* training in
the higher schools of learning emphasized scientifically based knowledge.
This was a knowledge which had a public character in that it was not revealed to singular individuals, nor determined by faith, nor governed by
mysteries that could be known only to a few. This was knowledge that was
derived from, and utilized for, an empirical world where it met tests of its
validity in everyday affairs. In this sense, it was truly utilitarian. Napoleon
did not and would not accept the notion that the public interest was a function of individual subjective choices. The chaos and disorganization of a decade of revolutionary governments, in which uncertainty and instability were
constant companions of political leaders, led Napoleon to the conclusion
that where individual or factional choices were allowed to dominate, the outcomes were likely to be disastrous. Policy, in his mind, had to be judged by
its utilitarian consequences for the society.

Napoleon concluded that the public interest was a property that did not
emerge out of majorities but only out of mediations between individual
choices and public or state choices. Such choices, he concluded, could be arrived at only by interposing the perfectly empathetic administrator who
knows what goals are best for the greatest number and knows how they are
to be achieved. The achievement of these goals as well as the legitimacy of
their agent rested, Napoleon strongly believed, on the test of utility—the
greatest good for the greatest number. Thus, he was, more than any French
or continental leader, led to the conclusion that political stability rested in
good part on the ability of the political leader to utilize information that
seemed essentially public in character; that is, a body of information which
was readily accessible and completely independent of private will or desire.
It was no coincidence that Napoleon so assiduously sought to institutionalize "pragmatic" higher education (Vaughan and Archer 1971:184–85).

In terms of strategic action, this view followed from the desire to create
long-term solutions to the problems of cleavages—ideological, factional, and
religious, especially in the area of education. If the community were to be recreated it could not be done by party, or faction, or the Church—only by the
State. But, perhaps more importantly, this view stemmed equally from the
short-term desire to resolve the problem of how to construct an administrative
leadership that would appear to everyone to be constrained by a structure of
rules that insured the publicness, utility, and predictability of their acts. Publicness could only be assured by establishing explicit rules governing not only
the structure of decision making, but also the kind of knowledge used in the
decision-making process. The latter had to be of an order that achieved specified results in the least costly manner, thus producing the greatest net satisfaction spread over the greatest number. In short, as Napoleon sought to recon-

struct the rules of community with himself at the center of political leadership, he was led to a series of strategic choices designed consistently to answer the explicit and implicit challenges of the various would-be claimants to the mantle of the Revolution. In so doing, he created the basic elements of structural rationality that would dominate and come to characterize the French administrative system in the nineteenth and twentieth centuries.

5

The Post-Napoleonic Period

Administration as Politics: 1814–75

The period following the collapse of the Napoleonic regime was not to see a revision of the rules governing community and civil equality. The Napoleonic Code, especially the civil code, was to remain, as it still does, the basis for governing relationships between individuals and for defining the role of the state through the provision of sanctions and rights. All else might be shaken in the conflicts and tensions of the Revolutions of 1830, 1848, and the coup d'état of December 1851, but the inviolability of property and contract as encapsulated in the Napoleonic settlement would not be shaken. Napoleon's strategy for integrating control over local power also remained unscathed. The creation of the departmental structure, which served as the channel for central governmental influence and control, remained the key structure by which successive regimes could impose at least minimal levels of control over local interests. The so-called decentralization strategies of the Third Republic and its successors have not, strangely enough, sought to reverse the basic elements of the Napoleonic solution. This suggests that "decentralization" in the form of elected local officials and councils represents the strategy of political party organization rather than any ideological commitment to the weakening of state power in favor of the market (Schmidt 1990:41–69).

If the rules governing the relationships between individuals were unaltered, so were the rules governing the definition of roles. Napoleon's creation of the state monopoly over secondary and higher education and, perhaps more importantly, certification of educational level was to remain unchanged. The state's control over certification also gave the state a monopoly over almost everything approaching professional status. Under the first revolutionary governments, the professions and workers lost the capacity to govern the conditions of their occupations; as a consequence, the role structures organized around them were undermined. The professional and guild corporations were dissolved in March 1791 and the law of Le Chapelier of June 1791 not only banned interest group associations, especially workers' organizations, but also professional associations (Godechot 1968:213–20; Ramsey 1984:235–41). Physicians, for example, were not allowed to form legal associations until 1892 (Ramsey 1984:236). In their place, Napoleon had established a pattern of state control and regulation. The state came to set the standards, curriculum, and certification for engineering, medicine, law, and teaching. Napoleon's bequest, then, was the basis for social stability—relatively clear rules for social and economic succession. As a consequence, the state emerged as the major determinant of social status and prestige. What Napoleon failed to provide was a lasting set of rules governing the structure of political leadership and its succession.

The Parliamentary Monarchies

The 1814 restoration of the monarchy was clearly an attempt to solve the problem of uncertainty over political leadership succession. The return to what seemed to be the only historical principle of legitimacy was directed at resolving the problem of political leadership succession. The Bourbon Restoration and its Orleanist successor were, however, clearly incapable, whatever their wishes and fantasies, of reestablishing the king as the principle and principal of state administration. Louis XVIII understood that he could not restore a monarchy that subsumed both administration and politics (Bastid 1954:175–76). The establishment of parliaments, with an upper house of appointed peers and an elected Chamber of Deputies, reflected the commitment of post-Imperial political leaders as well as the victorious Allies not to permit the substitution of politics by administration. That most outstanding of Bonapartist principles had led, from the point of view of the notables, to a government in which the public interest was arrived at without much consideration for their understanding of what was necessary or beneficial. On the other hand, there was little desire either on the part of the Allies or the notables to create a republic resting on a wide and, therefore, volatile electorate. What emerged as the principle of the post-Imperial state might be said to be the idea of administration as politics.

The constitutions of 1814 and 1830 provided for governments in which the monarchs, like Napoleon, dominated the administrative structure. Not only were they responsible for the execution of laws, they were responsible for the organization and regulation of the administration (Bastid 1954:182–83). In this respect, as in many others, the monarchs owed much to Napoleon, who sought, successfully, to make administration responsible to the will of the executive. The constraint on the monarch resided in the creation of a parliament with limited powers. The lower house was elected but, in the cases of both the Bourbon and the July Monarchies, by a very restricted electorate. The Charter of 1814 set the eligibility to vote at the payment of 300 francs a year in direct (land) taxes and 1,000 francs a year for eligibility for election (Bastid 1954:221–22). This produced an electorate of less than 100 thousand and a candidature of about 20 thousand in a nation of about 26 million. There were further restrictions in 1820. Under the July Monarchy, the criterion were lowered a little, to 200 francs for voting and 500 for candidature (Bastid 1954:227–28). The upper house or Senate was selected by the monarchs from amongst peers and served for life. The two chambers, along with the monarch, had legislative powers as well as the power of ministerial interrogation. There were almost no restrictions on the ability of active civil, judicial, or military servants from serving in either chamber (Bastid 1954:264–65).

The monarchy and its political leaders thus sought to restrict the constitution of public opinion or public representation to the wealthiest segments of French society. In this arrangement, the monarchy sought to reassure the notables that their interests would be heard. At the same time, the monarchs sought to make it clear that they represented the integrity of the state. Indeed, they may not have represented the public, but they were the inheritors of the only historically sanctioned means of leadership succession by which they sought to establish their legitimacy through the representation of the public interest. This, however, created somewhat of a paradox. The parliament, especially the Chamber of Deputies, also laid claim to representing the only appropriate and responsible public interest—the oligarchy of landed wealth who had the most to lose under volatile and arbitrary systems of succession and power. In effect, the monarchies had two institutional claimants for the right to determine the public interest and two quite different methods of determining leadership succession.

There was little guidance as to how the two structures should be or could be related. Thus, for example, the monarchs selected their ministers, but it was not at all clear to whom they were responsible, although they could be impeached by the deputies. Nor was it clear what role the kings might play in regard to the formulation of policy. This confusion was especially critical since the monarchs had control over the administration and ministerial appointments as well as legislative and budgetary initiative. This ambiguity, of course, was equally true of the parliament. The Chamber of Deputies had legislative powers, the right to interrogate ministers and to impeach them, to veto legislation through a variety of tactics, but there was no requirement that the king or cabinet had to consult the legislature prior to the presentation of proposed legislation (Bastid 1954:270–88). It became clear within a very short time that the monarchs had to have some means of regulating the elected chamber or the latter had to have some means of regulating the monarchy and its powers. Unless a modus vivendi could be arrived at, there would be constant conflict.

The chamber had little effective means of leverage except by voting against all executive initiatives. The kings, however, had somewhat more effective possibilities. They could use administrative persuasion on voters at the local level and they could use parliamentary patronage. Since the former was not terribly predictable (Bastid 1954:96–98, 232–34), there was also a persistent attempt to control the elected chamber through a monarchical patronage system based on dual office-holding. The monarchs encouraged officials to run for office or, conversely, when it seemed required they provided offices for elected officials (Julien-Laferrière 1970:10–11). The only constraints were that prefects and general officers could not be elected from the departments where they served (article 17 of Election Law of 1817) and, after 1830, the requirement that elected deputies acquiring public office stand for reelection and officials being elected to office be confirmed in office (article 69 of the Constitution of 1830 and the law of 12 September 1830)(Julien-Laferrière 1970:13, 28–42). The result was a very large and increasing intrusion of government officials in the chambers of the two monarchies. Thus the last Chamber of Deputies under Charles X was composed of 38.5 percent higher officials, 41.5 percent large landowners, 14.8 percent in trade, finance, or industry, and 5.2 percent professionals (Cobban 1961:77). Under the Orleanist monarchy, the last chamber contained 287 or 62.5 percent members who were government officials (Julien-Laferrière 1970:180).

The attempt to dominate the Chambers of Deputies by the monarchs of both regimes was in the end an exercise in futility. The attempt to make administrative power into a political instrument that could be said to represent both public opinion and the public interest faltered and eventually failed over the problem of organization. While the monarchs and their ministers might well wield the power of patronage without much interference, it could only come to nothing unless it was systematically organized to provide a basis for predictable succession of political office and leadership. In short, patronage was not a substitute for some form of party organization. Patronage, as it turned out in this case, would have been more properly an incentive for party commitment since the numbers of people involved were simply too great to be the basis of a personal patron-client structure. With numbers so large, systems of surveillance and incentives were necessary to maintain discipline over individuals (the problem of free riders and shirkers in general). At the same time, without a rule system to provide predictability with regard to reelection and movement upward within the ranks of the patron-client structure, the tendency was for individual political leaders and actors to pursue their own interests in the most opportune fashion (Rémond 1965:I, 318).

The absence of real electoral disagreements [during the mid-1830s] produced a Namierite obsession with the spoils of office, as deputies abandoned ministers who failed to deliver expected sinecures and favours. (Magraw 1986:69)

The failure to develop a party left the monarchs with no real organizational base. There was thus little to assure anyone that the monarchical succession was in anyway related to the creation of stable political leadership or its selection and succession. In much the same way, the failure of the notables to create an integrated structure of political career left the question of political leadership and its selection in some dim never-never land. Under both monarchical regimes, political leadership seemed a function of arbitrary royal choices. These produced considerable ministerial shuffling and great puzzlement as to the degree to which any of the first ministers were, in fact, political leaders or royal clerks. In sum, the parliamentary monarchies produced no resolution to the problem of high uncertainty with regard to political leadership and succession.

The "Seconds": Republic and Empire

The Second Republic revealed the degree to which the problem of political leadership, succession, and decision making had become the critical question for the social order. Those who now sought political power and the means for restructuring political leadership and its succession turned to universal manhood suffrage. Universal suffrage was seen as the means by which the public interest could be legitimately determined (Rémond 1969:II, 28–29; Girard 1968:80–81). The Republic which emerged was the result of the efforts of putative political leaders who sought to avoid the constant temptation of the pleasures of short-term order and predictability inherent in rule by the executive, whether emperor, monarch, or committee. At the same time, they sought to place constraints on universal suffrage. The debates and compromises that produced the constitution of the Second Republic revealed the truth that political equality by itself, in the form of the franchise, could not produce a systematic structure of leadership selection.

In searching for the means to constrain their political opposites, the members of the Constituent Assembly created a political system which, strangely enough, appeared to presuppose a party system. That is, in their desire to limit the executive to administration, they created a presidency that was elected directly by universal manhood suffrage. He appointed ministers, but it was not clear to whom they were responsible (Girard 1968:156–57; Rémond 1969:II, 69–71). He could initiate legislation, although the Legislative Assembly had the power of initiative and veto. In short, the Constitution had provided no means at all of integrating the executive and the legislative branches. Furthermore, the mobilization of voters remained very much a local matter conducted by local notables, despite early republican attempts to utilize civil servants to organize voters against the right (Rémond 1969:82–85). The victory of Louis Napoleon in the presidential elections reflected the absence of any organization capable of mobilizing the voters, especially the peasantry. Against the opposition of all the parliamentary parties, Napoleon won with an overwhelming majority—his name and genealogy were sufficient to mobilize if not organize the voters. In effect, political leadership under the Republic continued to be an ad hoc matter. That is to say, political leadership did not emerge out of any structure that could provide predictability about the process of leadership selection or succession. Political leadership continued to materialize almost spontaneously out of highly contingent situations or alliances of individuals elected to the national assemblies.

The paradox could not be more plain. On the one hand, there was a president elected by an overwhelming majority (5.53 million votes as against 1.44 million for his nearest rival—Cavaignac [Rémond 1969:76]) without the help of any party. On the other hand, there was a legislative assembly dominated by intensely competing parliamentary rather than national parties whose leadership, therefore, was ambiguous when it came to the question of whom and what they represented. The so-called "Party of Order," on the Right, included the Orleanists and the legitimists. The Left was "irremediably divided between the Mountain [the Radical Republicans] and the moderates" (Rémond 1969:84); and the Assembly elections following the presidential one produced a Bonapartist faction. The partisan conflicts and the pursuit of seemingly private interests which absorbed the Assembly contrasted sharply with Napoleon's presentation of self. Here, as behooved the descendant of the greatest of French leaders, was a man who stood above all such partisan interests. As the first Bonaparte had said to Cambaceres, "Gouverner par un parti, c'est se mettre tot ou tard dans sa dépendance. On ne m'y prendre pas. Je suis national"; so his nephew, with clever apishness, echoed him with "La France m'a elu parce que je ne suis d'aucun parti" (Dansette 1972:107). His representation of the public interest was exhibited not only subjectively by his rejection of party but also objectively by the overwhelming nature of the vote.

Precisely because universal suffrage had shown itself to be capable of being mobilized by the Napoleonic symbol of standing apart from party, it could never truly be abandoned by the third Napoleon in favor of a party: "Le suffrage populaire est alors l'exacte expérience de la volonté populaire . . . voilà pourquoi le plébiscite et la plébiscite seul est une vérité" (Dansette 1972:52). If he had a party, he would be forced to destroy it to substantiate any claim to being the true representative of the public will and interest. Indeed, that is exactly what Louis Napoleon did after he became emperor—he simply refused to utilize the Bonapartist party committees as the means for selecting candidates for the legislative body and the party as such withered away (Zeldin 1958:23–26). The unfortunate congruence of illogical institutional arrangements, the political ambitions of a man with an extraordinarily well known inheritance enshrouding him, and a system of political competition which continued to be severely limited by its localized character produced what had become by now a typical resolution. Louis Napoleon saw every reason to attempt to reconstruct a rational system of political leadership—one founded not on the ad hoc structures of party represented by parliamentarianism in France but rather on the solid and predictable foundation of inherited principles and the hereditary commitment to "reconnaît, confirme et garantit les grands principes proclamés en 1789 et qui sont la base du droit public des Français" (article 1 of the Constitution of 1852; Dansette 1972:97).

The failure of the Republic to solve the problems of political leadership and therefore of the problem of national community led Louis Napoleon inevitably to seek to fulfil his ambition. The coup of 2 December 1851, in which Louis Napoleon proclaimed that the Legislative Assembly was the effective agent of anarchy and that the constitution needed to be revised, was the fulfillment of that ambition. What followed was the creation of a new constitution (14 January 1852), which set the groundwork for the proclamation of the Empire on 2 December 1852.

The Constitution (amended on 25 December 1852 by the Senate to transform the president into an emperor and expand the nature of his powers) sought to reinstate the essential characteristics of the First Empire's system. The basis of that system was to substitute administration for politics. Bonaparte had sought to do so through a strategy that was both complex and followed rationally from his assumptions about the utilization of organization as the response to the failure of the structure of political leadership. His nephew confounded both the assumption and the strategy by seeking to meet the demands of political equality by going beyond the plebiscite. Bonaparte had viewed the universal manhood suffrage plebiscite as the symbol, act, and institution of political equality and the delegation of popular will. The third Napoleon, going one better than his uncle, sought to institutionalize it in the form of a legislative body that continued to be elected by universal manhood suffrage. This presented a paradox—if the plebiscite was the source of the popular will and Louis Napoleon's right to govern, then what did universal suffrage mean when it came to the selection of a legislative body that had no real powers? How was it that universal suffrage was the transmission of sovereignty in one case but not the other? (see Girard 1964:63–64). It was a paradox that the structure of imperial leadership could not bear in the long run.

In seeking to reinstate the hereditary principle as the sole means of stabilizing and "guaranteeing" the revolution of 1789, Louis Napoleon's constitution provided him with wide-ranging powers: control of the legislative process, control of the entire administrative process, as well as complete control of the armed forces and conduct of foreign affairs (Girard 1964:62; Plessis 1985:16–17). His ministers were selected by him and were totally and individually responsible to him. The ministers were not even allowed to sit in the legislative body nor required to defend any legislation they proposed. In short, there was a total separation of the instruments of the executive from the legislative body (Plessis 1985:18). The Senate was composed mostly of members appointed for life by the emperor, who also appointed its president and vice-president. The Senate powers were few. Like the Conseil d'État, it was basically an imperial instrument and was not responsible to the public will in any form except through the emperor. The legislative body also had little power. Its consent was necessary for laws and taxes to be enforced, but that was the extent of the chamber's power (Girard 1964:70–71). As it turned out, the Assembly or legislative body came to acquire power by virtue of its character as one of the institutionalized forms of the plebiscite.

Napoleon sought to avoid the consequences of the paradox inherent in his insistence on having an Assembly based on universal manhood suffrage by deploying two strategies. The first was to make it illegal to run candidates as members of a party list (Plessis 1985:21–22). The second strategy was to create his own list without creating a party list. This was done by barbarizing the technique used under the parliamentary monarchies—using the administration as a political party. In this case, instead of the relatively sophisticated method of running active civil servants or giving deputies public office, Napoleon's prefects were given to understand quite clearly that they were to supply "official candidates." These candidates received the full support of the prefects and prefectural administration in getting elected. This support ran the gamut from influencing the local press, manipulating the ballots, to providing patronage for the candidates, and thus it is no surprise that official candidates tended to win in large numbers (Zeldin 1958:10–27).

Ironically, in endeavoring to avoid the emergence of centers of opposition, Napoleon III undermined any real Bonapartist party. In the selection of official candidates, as one might expect, prefects sought local notables who were sufficiently well known to attract votes. This most often meant that official candidates were not Bonapartists (Zeldin 1958:28–39). Thus, despite the desire to emulate the first of his name, Napoleon III ended not by substituting administration for politics but by continuing the monarchical practice of utilizing the administration as if it were a political party.

This strategy had profound defects. It failed to provide for an institutionalized structure of support for himself or his future progeny. There was great concern throughout the reign that he might die and leave the problem of succession in a complete muddle. Some anxiety was allayed with a birth of a son in 1856. The problem of creating a regency in the case of Napoleon's early demise, however, haunted the emperor and his ministers. Who would select the regent(s)? How would they govern? A political party that offered predictability in terms of leadership selection might well have resolved the problem. Indeed, as Zeldin paraphrases several members of the legislative body:

Napoleon and the creators of the empire were getting old. They must make provision for the future. The empire based on personal government would fall to pieces if Napoleon died without leaving an adequate heir. The empire must be made permanent and permanence could rest only on institutions and not on men. The youth of the country had not known the terrors of the republic of 1848 and therefore found no justification in the old despotic regime. (Zeldin 1958:134)

Viewing all this with alarm, parliamentary leaders in the late 1860s pressed hard for reform.

The strategy of utilizing the administrative structure as a political party had a second defect in that it made it impossible to establish the autonomy of the administration. Using the prefectural administration as a functional substitute for a political party resulted in the use of patronage in a broad but relatively unsystematic fashion (Zeldin 1958:52–56, 78–99; Plessis 1985:50–51; Wright and Le Clère 1973:36–40, 142–58). The imperial monopoly on ministerial and prefectural appointments and the minister's monopoly on appointments in his own ministry merely carried the pattern of administrative patronage up to the highest levels of the hierarchy (Wright and Le Clère 1973:19–34; Wright 1976:39–40). The political usages of administration necessitated by the requirement that universal suffrage be manipulated led to the persistence of the custom of patronage. Indeed, it produced a structure of personal patronage that was broader than the first Bonaparte's. He had rejected all forms of franchise because he was unwilling to compromise the notion of administrative autonomy and the state sovereignty he thought emanated from that autonomy. The patronage structure of Louis Napoleon, however, ensured that administration would not have autonomy or even relative autonomy from local notables or anyone else who had votes at their disposal. Thus, administration emerged as an institution that seemed to meld into the existing social and economic cleavages and structures.

The interpenetration of these spheres seriously undermined the very basis of the Napoleonic claim to represent the public interest. Politicizing the administration by making it function as a political party without making it accountable subverted the claim to administer in the public interest. Other choices were possible. Surely not all politicization of administration would have undermined the claim to representing the public interest. For example, if the prefects or members of the central administration were members of a dominant political party, they could claim to serve the public interest by representing the wishes of the majority. Thus, politicization of the administration might seem to be the means by which the appropriate distribution of public goods was insured in a system where there was agreement that the majority should get the majority of benefits.

Napoleon III, however, ended up with the worst of all the possible outcomes to imperial leadership succession and decision-making rules. What Napoleon III got was an administrative structure that was widely known to be an instrument not only of imperial and state interests but also one that appeared, because of widespread patronage, to be an instrument of private interests as well. The reforms of 1869 reflected the dilemma into which the regime had fallen. By the end of that year, the tensions created by the continued uncertainty over political leadership led the emperor to make deep inroads in the authoritarian structure of the Constitution of 1852 and its administrative regulations. While these tensions did not bring an end to the regime, they brought about a quite different imperial regime than that of 1852 (Rémond 1969:187–94).

Bureaucratic Change under Monarchical and Imperial Systems of Patronage

The travails and experiences of the two monarchies, the Second Republic and the Second Empire, reveal explicitly that not much progress had been made since the Revolution on the problem of reducing high uncertainty about political leadership. Held in abeyance for periods of time by the systematic use of patronage, uncertainty reasserted itself. No organization emerged which could use patronage to sustain and further political equality or leadership succession. At the same time, patronage undermined any notion that administration was a replacement for politics. That there was a clear, if piecemeal, understanding of this situation is reflected in the development of an increasingly rationalized administrative structure over the period of 1815 to 1870.

Interestingly enough, rationalization of the state bureaucracy in this period utilized strategies usually thought of as occurring in contexts where political parties played a major role. That is to say, the strategies of political leaders in this period revolved around the problems of patronage as the means of creating loyalty and reducing uncertainty. The first Napoleonic regime centered its strategies on administration and organization as the means of creating loyalty and reducing uncertainty. Thus, paradoxically, the first

Napoleonic regime emerges as both archetypical and atypical. Of all of the regimes of the nineteenth century, only Bonaparte's was truly centered on an organizational strategy for reducing uncertainty about political leadership and succession. Yet, that strategy is often seen as archetypically French in its emphasis on centralization and autonomy of bureaucratic action.

There are, then, three paradoxes to explain in the rationalization of the state bureaucracy in this period. First, why was the strategy of political leaders in this period predominantly influenced by the problems raised by patronage, despite the fact that political parties played a relatively minor role in determining political leadership, political succession, or decision making? Second, how did patronage produce the rationalizing administrative strategies and outcomes characteristic of this period? Finally, how is it that patronage produced, in this instance, not a professionally oriented bureaucracy but one that was organizationally oriented?

The resolution of the first paradox or anomaly focuses on the interplay between the uncertainties engendered by the cycle of revolutionary moments and the uncertainties concerning political role raised by the demands of equality. The first revolutionary "moment"—that of 1789—reflected the process by which putative political leaders came to be in a position to "select" revolution. They were not the products of spontaneous combustion— they were not a leadership thrown up by turmoil and violence. Nor were they primarily the products of any conscious and structured process of self-selection—they were not members of revolutionary groups or well-organized parties. They emerged, uniquely perhaps, as an elected group of revolutionaries. Elected for one purpose, they achieved another altogether.

This process constrained all further choices about the definition of political equality and participation. Whatever the definition of these terms in the succeeding revolutionary moments, they could never exclude the concept of some direct participation that reflected the equal weight of the participants' desires. Who was included might be the source of struggle between various political leaders or groups, but none of them could completely dismiss either the notion or the institution of franchise. Napoleon resorted it to it only once, and in its most diluted form—the plebiscite—but he could not completely eradicate it. We must conclude that the legitimacy of selecting revolution in France rested not simply on the rhetoric of public interest but on its institutional representation—the process of voting in which the participants have equal weight. Having been selected, even though for another purpose, the original leaders or "choosers" of revolution could and did claim legitimacy by virtue of the process. Political leadership, from that point forward, could and often did claim two sources of legitimacy: inherited commitment—in the form of either the constitutional monarchy or the constitutional empire—to the revolutionary settlements regarding property and civil equality; and franchise and political equality.

At the heart of these two forms of legitimacy or attempts to reduce uncertainty over political leadership lay the fear that the revolutionary settlements regarding the sacredness of property and contract might be overturned, now by the Right, now by the Left. The problem was that neither legitimating principle by itself, without mediating institutions, could reduce uncertainty about leadership or revolutionary settlements. Nor, despite the ingeniousness of the efforts of almost three-quarters of a century of French monarchs, emperors, and politicians, could the principle of inheritance become a mediating institution for franchise or vice-versa. For the two to work in tandem required other mediating institutions to which political leadership could be held accountable. Regardless of which way it was tried in nineteenth-century France, the strategy to which the participants consistently resorted was patronage. Why this should be the case is not so immediately evident. How is it that two seemingly absolutely opposing principles of leadership selection and decision making, inheritance and election, should end up with the same strategies?

One might very well understand the intentions of any set of elected officials in seeking patronage. After all, patronage ensured or at least helped to ensure an administration that would be supportive to individual elected officials in seeking reelection. But, it turns out that it is equally easy to understand why monarchs and emperors once committed to electing some form of national and/or local representation of the public interest, however that was defined, should also choose this strategy. If such elections were required to provide an institutional structure representing the public interest, then monarchs and emperors had no choice but to seek to rig the system so that public interest coincided with their own. If their interests did not coincide, then what function did monarchs and emperors fill, after all?

Two possible strategies were available. One was to turn to the administrative structure and attempt to make it represent the public interest by endowing it with the qualities of scientism and expertise. These qualities would represent the public interest by virtue of their inherent utilitarian nature or "neutrality" in terms of how and what goals were possible. The second possible strategy was to co-opt elected officials. Their election alone represented some form of the public interest. If they voluntarily chose to support the monarch's or emperor's views, then it would be clear where and what the public interest was. In this situation, possible disagreements between elected officials and monarchical desires are exacerbated by the problem of moral hazard. Elected officials have every incentive to conceal their true desires. By doing so, they can use their supposed qualms or differences to extract something from the monarch that would benefit them and their constituents. If co-option is the chosen strategy, then it requires the form of patronage demanded and patronage supplied.

But why did the restored monarchs and the reinvented Napoleon choose the co-option strategy despite the example of the first Bonaparte, and despite the clearly extractive and subversive character of the co-option strategy? Why not choose the administrative strategy, which would seem to require considerably less in the form of giveaways? Given a little thought, however, selecting the administrative strategy purely and simply appears to produce greater long-term, if not short-term, giveaways. The use of the administrative strategy must make the individual decision-making monarch or emperor (or president) a captive of his administrative structure. This follows from any move to create a structure of systematic rules for the selection of administrators and their decision making. The rules inhibit the capacity of the monarch to choose administrators and policy. Any attempt to control administrators directly by budget control and manipulation must immediately bring about a situation in which it appears that personal interest overrides the rules of the system. Arbitrary dismissals achieve the same result. Bonaparte's successors did not fail to learn the lesson taught by the refusal of the great majority of his prefects to support him during the One Hundred Days. Having been selected on the basis of organizational rules, they gave their loyalty to the organization when faced with the dilemma of choosing between it and Bonaparte (Richardson 1966:57).

The two alternatives placed the successors to Bonaparte in a situation where they had little choice but to try elements of both strategies. Unfortunately, it seems as if they chose the worst aspects of both as far as reducing uncertainty about political leadership and decision making. They chose to utilize patronage as the means for dominating elected representative institutions; in doing so, however, they refused to create any relatively independent long-term institutional arrangement for allocating patronage. Indeed, Napoleon III went so far as to ignore the beginnings of a Bonapartist party in favor of using his prefects, thereby insuring its dissolution (Zeldin 1958:23–27).

In the absence of any institutional arrangement to provide a systematic structure of elective leadership and support for a monarchical or imperial executive other than the state administration, the heads of the French state were unable to resolve the problem of uncertainty regarding political leadership. The postrevolutionary kings and Napoleon were thus led consistently to the principle of loyalty as a major criterion for selecting senior administrative officials. All the more so, as with Napoleon III, senior administrative officials were given the task of allocating patronage and administrative officials became agents of patronage loyalty. Thus, after 1815, we see the principle of open appointment by the executive of senior administrative officials. Throughout this period, senior officials (prefects and subdirectors of ministerial departments and above) were not required to meet any formal standards for appointment (Vivien 1859:I, 203–5; Church 1981:300–301; Sibert 1912:25–55; Vidalenc 1976:15–16; Tudesq and Jardin 1973:27–37; Wright 1976:42–43).

The principle of open appointment reached down from executive to minister/prefect. These senior officials had free appointment prerogatives within their jurisdictions (Wright 1976:42; Vidalenc 1976:15; V. Wright 1972: 36–51; Richardson 1966:23–30). Ministers and prefects theoretically had no constraints on their capacity to choose individuals for appointment or advancement. [1] It would appear that throughout this period the chief executives had been very careful to maintain for themselves full powers to indulge in a strategy aimed at creating an administration that would provide the basis for their continuing political dominance.

Despite this strategy, or perhaps because of it, several trends toward rationalization of the bureaucratic structure emerged. First, entry into the civil service narrowed considerably during this period. Through the imposition of informal rules regarding education, the number of individuals who could have possibly been eligible relative to the whole population was very small. The evidence, while not systematic, is very clear that entrance into the ranks of the upper-level civil service from the 1820s on came to require a *baccalauréat,* which was required to gain access to schools of higher education (Weiss 1984:22–23; R. J. Smith 1982:19–23; Goblot 1925; Meuriot 1919). Thus, for example, the great majority of directors of ministries, prefects, and councilors of state during the Second Empire had been educated at the École de Droit Paris (Wright 1976:52). While of the one hundred ministry directors during the period from 1852 to 1870 no less than thirty-five had been through the École Polytechnique, six had graduated from the École Navale, nine from the École Normale Supérieure and ten from St. Cyr (Wright 1976:52). Of the 222 prefects of the Second Empire, 206 had attended institutions of higher learning requiring a *baccalauréat* or its equivalent in sitting or passing an entrance examination. The breakdown is as follows:

1. The sub-prefect was the exception to this general rule. He was appointed by the government—the Minister of the Interior usually, however, with a recommendation from the prefect involved. This exception seems to be a result of the corps character of the prefectural service. As a corps, the head of the corps was the king or chief executive who had constitutional powers (even up to the present) to appoint all administrative officers. Thus while the prefect was nominally attached to the Ministry of the Interior for administrative purposes, he had considerable autonomy by virtue of the corps character of the service (see Henry 1950).

École Polytechnique	9
Faculté de Droit de Paris	130
Faculté de Droit de Poitiers	8
Faculté de Droit d'Aix	7
Faculté de Droit de Toulouse	6
Faculté de Droit de Strasbourg	5
Faculté de Droit de Caen	4
Faculté de Droit de Rennes	3
Faculté de Droit de Dijon	2
Faculté de Droit de Grenoble	1
Faculté des Lettres de Paris	1
Faculté de Médecine de Paris	5
Faculté des Sciences de Paris	1
École d'Administration	3
École des Chartes	1
Saint-Cyr	13
Other military schools	3
École Navale	3
École Royale Forestiere	1

(Wright and Le Clère 1973:189)

By the beginning of the Third Republic:

[T]he formally established path to high administrative office obliged the young aspirant to pass through a series of stages. Following his *baccalauréat,* the young man was required to obtain a law degree (often a mere formality) and to take the competitive examinations or *concours* given by one of the great corps of state. (Osborne 1976:157)

There seems to be little question that the seventy or so laws, decrees, and ordinances which defined the *baccalauréat* between 1820 and 1850 produced the primary entryway or obstacle to gaining access to the faculties of theology, law, medicine, and higher education generally (Ponteil 1966:180–81; Fox 1984:124; Weiss 1984:19). While the so-called *grandes écoles* did not require the *baccalauréat,* favoring their own exams, by 1860 and probably earlier, large proportions, more than fifty percent, of those admitted to the Polytechnique were *bacheliers* (Shinn 1980:51).

Not only did the *baccalauréat* become the gateway to higher education, it became a very narrow one. Preparation for the examination meant attendance at a *lycée* and this was never cheap. The number of those who received the degree was extremely small, as can be seen in table 5.1.

Access to the group going on to higher education was extremely limited. In 1820 there were approximately 3,100 *baccalauréats* granted in a population of over 30 million. The succeeding figures on the number of degrees per thousand at age seventeen means that the percentage of 17-year-olds who received the degree was .5 or less. By the end of the century, this proportion had more than doubled but still remained at only 1.2 percent of the age group. The narrowness of entry was not mitigated by access to the *grandes écoles*. Entrance to the École Normale required the *baccalauréat* and passage of a difficult entrance examination (R. J. Smith 1982:22–23). In the years between 1810 and 1869, only about thirty students a year were admitted in both categories of Letters and Science (R. J. Smith 1982:18). The Polytechnique admitted about two hundred students a year through its own rigorous examination system (R. J. Smith 1982:18). Total enrollment per year in the years between 1801 and 1870 ranged from 300 to 450 at the Polytechnique (Ringer 1979: 338–39). Ponts et Chaussées, which drew its students from the Polytechnique, also through examination, seldom had more than a total enrollment of seventy students a year until the 1870s (Weiss 1984:29). Total enrollment at Saint-Cyr between 1839 and 1865 was about 330 to 340 and went to about 750 to 800 at the end of the century (Ringer 1979:339).

Nor were the public faculties of law, theology, or medicine any more accessible. These too required the *baccalauréat* in order to matriculate. The number of degrees granted, thus, were not large through most of the nineteenth century (see table 5.2).

The educational structure the first Napoleon had created produced the effect of providing an extremely narrow entry for positions within the state administration. What is striking, of course, is the degree and speed with which these educational certifications became the informal standard for acquisition of senior civil service positions. The Faculties of Law and the *grandes écoles* especially came to play a major role as gatekeepers. In the absence

Table 5.1 Baccalaureates (Bacs) Granted by Age and Population

Year	General Population(m)	8–17-yr.-old Population(m)	Bacs (1,000s)	Bacs/1,000 (17-yr.-olds)
1820	30.3	—	3.1	—
1831	32.6	—	3.2	—
1842	34.5	6.1	2.8	5
1854	35.9	6.4	4.3	7
1865	37.9	6.5	5.9	9
1876	36.9	6.4	5.4	8
1887	38.2	6.6	6.6	10
1898	38.7	4.6	7.8	12

Source: Adapted from Ringer 1979, 316.

of a *grande école* for administrators, those who had aspirations for entering the prefectural corps or the central administrative offices came to utilize either their *grandes écoles* and/or legal education as their certificate of appropriate education (Vivien 1859:I, 191). In effect, the educational system came to be utilized in this period as the means for determining eligibility for holding higher administrative offices.

In so doing, the postrevolutionary monarchs and emperors created and confirmed the basic structure of career as characteristic of the administrative system. That is, the state's political leaders had come to rely on the state's social role in creating a meritocratic notion of educational equality. This educational system, with its emphasis on the development of professions, provided French society with a group of men possessing expertise. But the state control of education, especially professional education and certification, made it difficult, almost impossible, for these professionals to organize their own structure of training and to set the conditions and rules under which their expertise could be used (Léonard 1978:624–85; Suleiman 1987:40–45). They thus had strong incentives to seek some other organizational solution to the problem of repayment for high investment costs in education. This was partly resolved by seeking a monopoly over state employment and state subsidy of education and professional occupations. Furthermore, the expansion of state administration in the nineteenth century encouraged people to invest in education as the means for gaining eligibility, or increasing their chances for eligibility, for positions in the higher levels of the civil service.

In this regard, the strategy was, as was usually the case in nineteenth-century France, paradoxical. All of Bonaparte's successors were unwilling to create an autonomous civil service for fear of coming under its control. Nevertheless, the administration was consistently conceived of as the means by which executive power would both represent and dominate the state and the

Table 5.2 Public Faculty Degrees Granted

Year	Law(k)	Medicine(k)	Letters/ Theology(k)	Total Population(m)
1851	1.0	0.4	0.1	35.8
1856	0.8	0.4	0.1	36.0
1861	0.8	0.4	0.1	37.4
1866	1.1	0.5	0.1	38.1
1876	1.0	0.6	0.1	36.9
1886	1.4	0.5	0.3	38.2
1896	1.2	1.1	0.4	38.5

Source: Adapted from Ringer 1979, 335.

public interest. Yet, political leaders were equally reluctant, as time went by, to sustain their claims to representing the public interest by relying on loyalty—whether that loyalty was based on caste, party, or personality. Their solution was to utilize the state's role in the domination of education, especially higher and professional education, to produce a pool of eligibles who could meet the standard of expertise associated with their view of how the public interest should be arrived at. A group of eligibles was thus determined by the examinations and *concours* of the various stages of the educational system and professional certification. The executive was left free in this strategy to make selections without the hindrance of administrative sovereignty. They were often accused of corruption, but that accusation never became central to the problem of politics; that is, it never served as the focus of political contestation or engendered a structured reform or series of reforms.

The paradox emerges because such a system seems to rely on individuals as the source of theory, information, and decision-making rules, namely, the professional. But, as we shall see shortly, theory, information, and decision-making rules, while not in any sense uniform, were homogenous with respect to the degree with which they became organization-specific and generally nontransferable to the private sector or even other ministries. This was reflected in several other aspects of organizational development in this period. The first of these is the degree to which entrance into major areas of administration did, in fact, become limited to the increasingly autonomous control of civil servants themselves. But, this did not occur in any uniform fashion. Rather, entrance into these areas became highly specialized. These major areas were the corps—Public Works (Ponts et Chaussées), Mines (Mines), Council of State (Conseil d'État), Court of Accounts (Cour des Comptes), and the Inspectorate of Finance (Inspection des Finances). Three other corps—the prefectural corps, the central administrative corps, and the diplomatic corps—remained more directly under the aegis of executive intervention and control.

Entrance into Public Works was determined by the corps, which had its own director-general and for which recruitment to senior positions was entirely from the École des Ponts et Chaussées (Weiss 1984:29). Under the Second Republic, entrance into the Council of State as a lower-level *auditeur* required passage of an examination in 1845 and a *concours* in 1849, although it was eliminated in 1852 (Vivien 1859:I, 189–90). The *concours* was reinstated in 1854 and rewritten under the Third Republic, when the Law of 24 May 1872 established the Council of State as an autonomous body with powers to select its own personnel (Thuillier 1980:345; Freedeman 1961:27–28). Entrance into the corps from the time of Napoleon had required extensive legal training or at least a *licencié* from the Faculty of Law.

This pattern was reinforced by the examinations required from 1872 on (Freedeman 1961:29–30).

From 1830 until the establishment of the École National d'Administration after World War II, entrance into the Inspectorate of Finance was governed by examination and *concours* (Lalumière 1959:13). From 1842 on, admission to the *concours* required either a *licencié* in law or graduation from the Polytechnique and at least two instead of five years prior service (Lalumière 1959:14). From the time when Napoleon recreated the Cour des Comptes in 1807 (16 September), the corps of magistrates responsible for the nation's accounts had been autonomous in terms of its capacity to recruit (Vulliez 1970: 90). Admission to the corps required a *licencié* in law (Vivien 1859:I, 191). From 1816 on, those who sought to enter the corps had to pass a practical test by working on two different types of accounts under the observation of an official of the corps (Todisco 1969:39). Those seeking to enter the consular corps at the junior level from 1833 on were also required to take an examination. Those passing the exam were ranked according to their scores and were admitted to the service on the basis of these rankings (Vivien 1859:I, 190).

It is quite clear, then, that the relative autonomy of the various corps came to provide an increasingly homogenous commitment to high educational levels as a means of exclusion and eligibility. By midcentury almost everyone who sought any kind of career had to have passed the *baccalauréat*. At the same time, it was equally the case that each corps had different requirements for further education. And they had very different applications of this education than one might find in the private sector, where comparable organizations, for the most part, did not even exist since the *corps* operated in areas where the state maintained a monopoly or near monopoly. In short, by about 1850 entrance into one of the *grands corps* meant an early commitment to an educational career which, in turn, led to a life career of a very organizationally specific kind.

In the central administrative corps where patronage and executive control dominated, there was, surprisingly, steady movement within ministerial administration toward certification of new entrants via the *concours*. This brought with it not only some delimitation of ministerial power over appointment but also, as in the case of the *grands corps*, the utilization and acquisition of information in a highly organizationally specific way. Thus, in 1833, examinations were established for the positions of inspector in the newly established telegraphic service, for probationers, and for various officials in the tax services in the Finance Ministry (Vivien 1859:I, 190; Thuillier 1980:335). In 1844, the Ministry of War established an examination system for determining recruitment into the senior-level administrative service (Thuillier 1980:299). The installation of a *concours* for these levels of office was carried out soon after by the Ministries of Justice, Agriculture, and Commerce (Lanza 1976:307–10; Thuillier 1980:338). In each of these cases, however, the examinations were unique to the particular ministry and were, therefore, prologues to the development of skills that were very specific to each ministry and not capable of being transferred elsewhere.

The Constitution of the Second Republic continued this pattern. The political leaders of the Republic had committed it to recruitment of officials based on the concept that "[A]ll citizens are equally admissible to public employment without requirements for preference other than merit" (Thuillier 1980:339). Indeed, in its suspicion of the patronage structure of the restored monarchies, the political leaders of the Republic sought to remove this power from the executive by using the models of the *grands corps/grandes écoles*. By creating an École d'Administration in 1848, political leaders of the Second Republic hoped to put appointments in the central administrative corps out of the reach of executive-dominated patronage (Kessler 1978:10–12; Saurin 1964–1965:105–95; Legendre 1968:11–13). The experiment was short-lived. The École d'Administration lasted only until 1849. Nevertheless, the strategy was clear: political leaders sought to establish their autonomy by undermining the capacity of the executive to determine policy and select administrative leadership and by undermining the minister's capacity to maintain the autonomy of his ministry.

The onset of the Second Empire, with its curb on legislative political leaders, brought an end to overt attempts to impose a uniform constraint on the executive and his ministerial agents. Nevertheless, the Ministers of War, Agriculture, and Commerce continued to use the *concours* adopted in the 1840s. By the late 1860s, a *concours* was also in place in the Ministry of the Interior (Thuillier 1980:344). The Second Empire, then, which was clearly based on the principle of executive control over administration, was a period that saw increasing reliance on a system of written and oral examinations for recruitment for the junior levels of the higher civil service. The major reason for this seemingly anomalous behavior appears to be the attempt to overcome the problems of lack of continuity and the career arbitrariness of the patronage system. The absence of clear rules about appointment and promotion left ministers open to demands and pressure from those seeking patronage (Thuillier 1980:344). Furthermore, it aroused continued complaints from ministerial staffs concerned about their futures (Thuillier 1980:193–221, 567–76).

The desire to avoid the appearance of serving private interest by making room for patronage appointments and thus upsetting routines and lowering morale was reinforced by the desire to avoid the constant pressure of patronage demands. These pressures led ministers increasingly, throughout the period of the Second Empire, to adopt the *concours*. This resulted in the continuance of the pattern of the *grands corps* in a kind of isomorphic way. That is, the central administrative ministries, once they had instituted the *concours,* had reduced the arbitrariness of career by narrowing entry to an observable criterion. Furthermore, like the *grands corps,* they produced an increasingly organizationally and ministerially specific career structure (Wright 1976:53–54; Wright and Le Clère 1973:206–13). Precisely because each ministry was allowed, in the *grands corps* fashion, to regulate administration, recruitment, advancement, and dismissal in its own way meant that once an individual entered a ministry it would become almost impossible to transfer elsewhere without beginning from the very bottom of the seniority tier, unless, of course, he had friends. The ministerial boundaries to career was the result of the different pay levels, different patterns of promotion, different ways of doing things that were characteristic of each ministry. As time went on, individuals came to have knowledge and expertise that was not very transferable. Moreover, ministers were increasingly dependant on officials with seniority, since to replace them would mean administrative chaos. This element in itself provided a strong measure of predictability to careers. As long as ministers did not engage in wholesale dismissals, which they rarely did (Goyard 1977:1–48; Tulard 1977:49–61; Wright 1977:80), loss of position became increasingly unlikely as an individual's seniority grew. All of this strongly suggests the conclusion that by the end of the Second Empire two major aspects of the career structure were in place: early commitment to a civil service career prior to actually holding an office and organizational specificity of expertise.

This raises the central question of what were the incentives for this early commitment that clearly would preempt other careers? One incentive was the state's role as a primary employer in some professions such as engineering and law. If one wanted to pursue a career outside of the state, the risks were much greater, despite, or because of, the absence of well-defined career structures (Geison 1984:1–12). This situation, however, produces the problem of "moral hazard" and "inverse selection." Simply put, whenever there were jobs available in the bureaucracy, it would have been to the advantage of the least capable to fib as much as possible about their capacities in order to get the job. The most able would either be discouraged and be willing to take their chances in the private sector or would already have jobs elsewhere. In the 1830s and 1840s, this problem is what helped to produce the movement toward the use of examinations. This was especially the case as ministers were faced with the inverse selection process of patronage where the worst people (the better ones were more likely to use patronage to get better jobs in the private sector) were likely to be the ones everyone was trying to palm off on civil service positions (Lanza 1976:273–74; Thuillier 1980:567–73).

The executive in the restored monarchies and the empire pursued two strategies in this regard—both constrained by the desire to avoid giving into bureaucratic autonomy on the one hand and to the overwhelming and disorderly demands of patronage on the other. The first of these strategies was to encourage the autonomy of the emergent *grands corps,* all of which were concerned with regulatory or technical services rather than administration. [2] The tactic used to achieve this goal was the imposition of the rigid *concours,* which required that one take both written and oral examinations and be subjected to a close scrutiny of social background and convictions. This had the double consequence of providing for: (1) the technical expertise in the areas where such was needed without surrendering control over the implementing and distributing structures of the administration—the central administrative ministries and the prefectural system; (2) homogeneity of background and training, which produced highly predictable outcomes in the provision of technical and regulatory services. The outcome of this strategy was to solidify the basis for the development of the *grands corps* and to provide a career structure quite distinct from that of the more purely administrative structure where the ministers wished to retain discretion over the distribution of office and other public goods. Similarity of background and education, difficulty of entry, and small numbers combined to produce a sense of organizational community that put serious constraints on turnover or dismissals (V. Wright 1972:63–66, 188–207). The result was a career with considerable predictability and status.

This was reinforced by the development, possibly as a result of borrowing from the bureaucratic custom of the *ancien régime,* of the *stage* (Kessler 1977:16). The custom was in use at least as early as the first Napoleon (Church 1981:274; Armstrong 1973:196). Essentially the *stage* was a form of apprenticeship and probation in which an aspiring bureaucrat served with little or no pay for as long as six years, although it was usually no more than a year or two (Vivien 1859:I, 192–93). The position had different titles depending on which ministry or corps one served; student (consulates, medical corps), *auditeur* (Council of State), supernumerary (central ministries), auxiliary (Ponts et Chaussées, military health), attaché (Ministry of Interior and diplomatic corps) (Vivien 1859:I, 192; Kessler 1977:16–17). Sometimes the position was used as a substitute for an examination or *concours* and sometimes it followed upon the passing of the examination or *concours* as in the case of the Council of State (Vivien 1859:I, 193–94). Its importance, structurally, was that it came to serve quite uniformly throughout the upper-level civil service

---

2. The prefectural corps is not included here because it still did not have the autonomy of selection which characterized the *grands corps.* It was still considered to be a direct extension of the executive power (Wright and Le Clère 1973:46–80).

as a further exclusionary device that required high commitment from would-be officials. Since the young official had to find the means to support himself during this period, it meant that he had to be relatively well-to-do and to be willing to forego the benefits of some other occupation or career. The spread of this probationary-apprenticeship period throughout the civil service during this era reinforced the growing pattern of career structure and its emphasis on early recruitment, lack of permeability, and hierarchy.

The second aspect of ministerial strategy was aimed at the implementing and distributive elements of the administration—the nontechnical ministries. Here the aim was to reduce the arbitrariness, real or perceived, of life in the ministerial administrations but to do so without surrendering ministerial and executive discretion. Thus, in one direction, the executive and the ministers resisted the development of a unified administrative statute (Lanza 1976:283–85, 310–12). In the other direction, ministers were forced to resort more and more to examinations, if only to rationalize patronage. They used examinations as a means of reducing the number of eligibles seeking offices. Furthermore, the necessity of providing a minimal set of career expectations in order to maintain continuity and morale led the ministers to reluctantly utilize seniority and to delineate what one might expect of seniority. Thus, Vivien, the great analyst of French administration in the early nineteenth century, reports that, by the 1840s seniority played an important role in determining advancement (Vivien 1859:I, 207–11). Occurring at the same time in a number of ministries was the adoption of an informal rule that a certain number, often half, of all vacancies would be filled from within the bureau or ministry, thus tying seniority to a specific number of offices (Vivien 1859:I, 210–11; Thuillier 1980:368–75). Also during the same period, there was a growing adoption of the hierarchical rule—promotions from within had to be from positions immediately inferior to the vacancy (Vivien 1859:I, 210).

The hierarchical linkage of positions within a partial seniority structure was reinforced by the increasingly general rule that promotions could not take place until individuals had been in their present positions for a year or, often, two years (Vivien 1859:I, 211). By the 1870s the principle of seniority was well established. While there was no assurance that seniority would get one to the top, it became clear that it was a major means of getting there. The increasing utilization of examinations to determine entry, and of seniority to determine advancement, came to provide minimal assurances about tenure.

The ambiguity and ambivalence of the consequences of this strategy are reflected in the attempt to produce a distinctive set of career tracks within the central administration. Thus, for example, in response to a decade of bitter complaints about the lack of advancement and salary increases and the arbitrariness of career prospects, the administrative directors in the Ministry of War in September 1843 sought to introduce a formal structure of recruitment and advancement. They introduced a career distinction between three levels of administrative work: routine clerical *(expéditionnaire)*, senior clerical *(commis)*, and decision making *(rédacteur)*, each of which would be recruited for by candidates taking different *concours* (Thuillier 1980:293–300). The *concours* did not last long (1846). The bureau chiefs complained bitterly that they resulted only in attracting men who had failed in other careers or who had inappropriate training (Thuillier 1980:300). Nevertheless, the distinction between the levels spread in an informal manner throughout some areas of the central administrative corps. Thus, Vivien noted in his *Études administratives* of 1859, *rédacteurs,* along with *sous-chefs* and *chefs de bureau* at the Ministries of Justice and of Religious Affairs *(cultes),* were required to have *licencié des droits,* while *expéditionnaires* in various departments and ministries only required a *bachelier ès-lettres* (Vivien 1859:I, 191), thus clearly distinguishing the two levels of career.

Finally, however, this distinction in midlevel career tracks leading to senior ministerial positions did not spread, even after the demands for breaking up the "unity of career," which were voiced by the 1871–74 Commission for the Revision of the Administrative Services (Thuillier 1980:316–33). This development was largely undermined by the continued desire on the part of ministers to maintain as much control over the career structure as possible and the unwillingness of the executive to lose control of the central administrative organizations. The creation of separate tracks within ministries with distinct examinations would have meant a loss of ministerial control over placement. During the Second Empire and, to some degree, during the Third Republic, these attempts at systematizing or rationalizing careers were seen as particularly subversive to the very principles of executive versus legislative domination of administration. The end result of this strategy was to produce a career that was clearly second in status to those of the *grands corps.* Officials of the central administration lacked the assurances of a long-term career that had come to be more or less characteristic of the *grands corps.*

The attempt of the executive under the Second Empire to walk the line between a sufficiently predictable career structure and ministerial autonomy is again reflected in the creation of the first statute applicable uniformly to the whole civil bureaucracy, the pension and retirement law. Decreed on 9 June 1853, in the first years of the Second Empire, it was directly aimed at providing some general incentives for maintaining a steady flow of minimally adequate people. Interestingly enough, the law provided little incentive for early retirement—in fact, it provided just the opposite. The basic law provided that civil officials would have the right to a pension after thirty years of service at age sixty for "passive" service and after twenty-five years of service at age fifty-five for "active" service. The basic pension was calculated on the mean average of the last six years of service multiplied by one-sixtieth for every year of service (one-fiftieth in the case of active service) (Michel 1925:11; Rabany 1916). Since there was a flat rate of increase over the whole span of career, it was to the individual's best interest to stay in as long as possible, thus creating greater pressure for the recognition of seniority as the proper criterion for advancement. By the end of the imperial period, seniority had thus come to be the most important criterion of advancement to the senior levels of ministerial administration (Thuillier 1980:375).

In sum, the period between 1815 and 1870 saw the continued development of several major aspects of a rationalized bureaucratic administration:

First, two distinct career structures emerged. One was characterized by graduation from a *lycée,* passage of the *baccalauréat,* acquisition of a *licencié* in law (or passing the examination to enter the Polytechnique and then going on to Ponts et Chaussées or Mines), passing the *concours* for one of the emergent *grands corps,* appointment as a *surnuméraire,* and advancement within the corps in a more or less predictable fashion. The other career structure was characterized by the same beginnings but diverged with the failure to enter one of the corps, from which followed a much less secure or predictable future. Instead, one entered the prefectural corps or one of the central ministerial bureaucracies where there was greater competition from patronage appointments.

Second, the career structure was centered on ministerial or corps specialization. The wide variations between corps and ministries caused the emphasis on a departmental or bureau career, thus constraining individuals to become specialists within the area of their appointments. The acquisition of highly organization-specific information and expertise meant that specialization came also to be a means of underscoring security of tenure if not advancement.

Third, seniority became a major determinant of advancement both in the corps and the ministries.

Fourth, the creation of a pension and retirement system provided the basis for predictability as to how the career would end. That is, systematic retirement and pension arrangements provided for the definition of the career role from entrance to leaving. Dismissal was, thus, not the only systematic end of a career.

Fifth, These particular career structures required early commitment to an educational career beginning with the *lycée.* By the end of the Second Empire, if one desired entrance into any of the emergent corps, one had to pass out of one of the select Paris *lycées* (see V. Wright 1972:196, 64; Wright and

Le Clère 1973:188). Thus, access to the senior civil service positions, especially in the *grands corps*, meant early choices. This did not however, mean opportunity costs since the *baccalauréat* was required to enter into any higher profession. The final choice had to come, however, with the acquisition of the *baccalauréat*. At this point, the decision to go on to any profession had to be made since the paths now branched. With the entrance into the Faculty of Law or the Polytechnique, the commitment to a bureaucratic career was made, thus forgoing nearly all other opportunities.

The strategy of the various restored monarchs and the second Napoleon had been aimed at trying to ensure the predictability of political succession by co-opting the administration to the imperial executive. In so doing, Napoleon III and his monarchical predecessors had sought to make entry into the upper-level civil service appear to be a function of public interest by continuing to emphasize exclusionary access in the form of educational merit. However, this strategy could not make exclusion entirely dependent on the structure of an internal labor market organized and directed by civil servants themselves. To do so would have undermined the co-optive strategy of the monarchical or imperial executive. Unless the executive had patronage to offer, the bureaucracy might not support any particular leadership succession. But too much patronage would have destroyed the notion of the publicness of the executive, while at the same time it would suffer under a welter of patronage demands. Thus, the structure of the bureaucratic organization emerged by the 1870s as increasingly rationalized, but in a fragmented manner in which the chief principle was to allow the executive a range of discretionary choice among a group of eligibles who were determined by their success in gaining access to the highest educational levels. The result was, interestingly enough, the creation of an upper-level civil service structure with an astonishing degree of homogeneity in training and background prior to entry into the civil service. The autonomy of the *grands corps* and of the ministers tended to blunt that uniformity, but it did not eliminate it, as the creation of the École Libre des Sciences Politique in 1872 outside of the state monopoly was to reveal.

The Third Republic: 1871–1900

The Third Republic was dominated by the emergence of relatively well organized political parties. The thrust toward rationalization was confirmed by the ardent desire of political leaders to render the administration accountable to parliamentary rather than executive authority. The period from 1870 to 1879 (the Monarchist Republic) and the period from 1879 to 1899 (the Opportunist or Republican Republic) can, in one sense, be seen as a single period which saw the resolution of the problem of political leadership succession. The resolution of this problem made the Third Republic the longest lasting regime of modern France. Institutionally, this resolution was made possible by 1879 through the emergence of the Republicans as a national party—a party claiming the right to represent the public interest because it transcended class.

The collapse of the Second Empire left France once again to face the problem of political leadership. The failure, once again, of the imperial executive with birth as a solution to political leadership succession recreated the crisis of political leadership. As the liberalization of the empire in its last years had shown, the collapse of the imperial solution was not simply the fault of irrational decision making. Rather it was, in good part, the result of the failure to rationalize the relationship of the state bureaucracy to the imperial institution, or, one might say, the failure to create an imperial institution that was an integral part of the state administration. As each imperial or monarchical executive had found, the imperial or monarchical solutions to political leadership could be institutionalized only if the executive retreated to playing the role of symbol or of constitutional cog. Anything short of this required the executive to participate meaningfully in decision making.

The executive's will, as long as it was seen as somehow synonymous with that of the state's, had to be expressed in the administration and implementation of that will. Unless the executive was active in the direction of administration, there could be no assurance that his policies would be enforced. Thus, the imperial executive was forced to find means to make sure that officials reflected his views. This could be assured in only two possible ways: one, by unifying the imperial executive with administration through the process of institutionalizing loyalties, that is, the creation of a party with a monopoly over the process of patronage; or two, the creation of an autonomous administrative service whose training and career were centered on incentives and symbols which coincided with those of the imperial/monarchical executive. The latter, of course, meant the reduction of the imperial executive to symbol while the former meant its politicization.

The problem for nineteenth-century France and its would-be postrevolutionary monarchs and emperors was that they resisted the former and absolutely rejected the latter. The result was that these monarchical/imperial executives could never rise above their personal capacities or incapacities to become institutions within the context of the revolutionary social and economic settlement. This meant that the monarchical/imperial executive was never more than a stopgap measure in the search for a stable and predictable structure of political leadership and decision making. France stumbled haltingly through a good part of the century; periods of leadership stability built on monarchical/imperial executives, which were inherently unstable, persistently dissolved into a wilderness of uncertainty.

The attempts at republics fared little better, and for much the same reasons. These had failed because putative political leaders had not solved the problem of how to integrate the basis of their own power—an elected assembly—with the administrative structure. The solution the First Republic arrived at was the arrogation by an elected executive body of all administrative and legislative powers, and it sent shivers up the spine of middle-class France for the next century. Lacking any institutional accountability, the Committee on Public Safety could follow its powers to their logical and overwhelming conclusion. The Second Republic fell prey to the fears of the First Republic by seeking to make sure that powers were divided so securely that the executive would be only an administrative cog. Indeed, they went so far as to produce separate elective structures for the executive and the legislature. The problem here was that, like the First Republic, there existed no organizational structure through which political leaders could be integrated with the executive to insure the stability of their own political leadership. The latter problem, especially, was achingly reflected in the conflicts of the various groupings in the National Assembly. In short, the inability of would-be political leaders to organize a systematic structure of leadership selection left them at the mercy of the proclivities of contingently organized groups of claimants to political power.

Faced once again with the historic dilemma of leadership instability, the politicians of the National Assembly, after four years of dramatic struggle in the years between 1871 and 1875, finally arrived at what appeared to be a replay of the past constitutional, if not political, settlement of the problem. The laws of 1875, which created the machinery of government of the Third Republic, sought to constrain the executive—but not too much, out of the Right's fear of an excessive republicanism. The president was tied to the legislature by the slimmest of cords. He was elected by a joint meeting of the Senate and the Chamber of Deputies to serve a term of seven years and was not accountable to either chamber (Mayeur and Rebérioux 1984:24). He selected the ministers of state, who were not directly accountable to either chamber. The limits on his power came in the form of the requirement of a countersignature of a cabinet minister on all presidential decrees. The Chamber of Deputies was elected by universal manhood suffrage, while the Senate was to act as a counterweight, being chosen by indirect election with seventy-five of the three hundred chosen for life by the Senate itself (Mayeur and Rebérioux 1984:25). This original arrangement left the president with much the same powers and problems as the constitutional Bourbon and Orleanist monarchs. What it did reveal, however, was the final general commitment to a republican form of government.

The period between 1875 and 1879 was characterized by the conflict between the monarchist leaning executive and increasingly Republican legislature, which ended in a constitutional crisis. By 1879, the president of the Republic was faced with the dilemma of either resigning or refusing to govern with a cabinet made up of the majority Republicans. President MacMahon chose resignation rather than, as others before him had done, attempt a coup d'état (Anderson 1977:10–11). From this point forward, the office of President of the Republic became secondary to party majorities in the two chambers.

The victory of the legislature in this regard was the result of the electoral and organizational victories of the Republicans. Throughout the decade of 1869 to 1879, Republican leadership had consistently worked to create local organizations that could nominate appealing candidates and mobilize voters (Elwitt 1975:53–102). The party, although very loosely organized and without centralized machinery, provided the basic means for the selection of political leadership. By the turn of the century, party organization would become the central feature of politics (Mayeur and Rebérioux 1984:165–69, 214–24).

The emergence of Republican domination by 1879 was the result of three strategic thrusts: (1) the organization of local committees held together by the activities of a well-known national political leadership (Bury 1973:114–36; Elwitt 1975:54–59, 75–80); (2) the development of an ideology of property and progress, which quite successfully sought to transcend class at least with regard to farmers and petty producers (Elwitt 1975:54–55, 74–75; Anderson 1977:65); and (3) utilization of the constitutional and administrative structure to reduce the power of the Right by pressing the constitutional crises of 1876 to its conclusion (Mayeur and Rebérioux 1984:26–31). These three strategies led to the electoral victories that established the Republican majority after 1876, to the emergence of a party structure that served as the basis for the systematic selection of political leaders, and to the development of a conscious long-term strategy of restricting the constitutional powers of the executive (the primary institutional representation of the political Right, which lacked almost all party organization or orientation).

Restricting the powers of the executive was, of course, especially important in attempting to reduce the uncertainties about the future of Republican leaders and their movement. The strategy had its origins in the early years of the provisional republic, although its tradition reached all the way back to the Second Republic. In 1872 the National Assembly under Thiers had seen the constitutionalism of the Orleanists combine with the Republicans to reduce executive powers over administrative regulation. This was achieved on 24 May 1872 with the passage of a new law governing the organization and duties of the Conseil d'État. The law, in effect, made the

Conseil an autonomous juridical body rather than an aspect of executive power:

The Conseil d'État sits definitively on all cases in matters of administrative adjudication, and on all requests of annulment for *ultra vires* directed against the acts of the diverse administrative authorities. (quoted in Freedeman 1961:33)

This provision gave the Conseil the final power of decision over all cases of administrative controversy coming before it. Prior to this, decisions of the Conseil required the signature of the executive before they had the force of law, thereby leaving final say in administrative regulation to the executive (Freedeman 1961:33). Administrative regulation now became the subject of juridical autonomy, thus depriving the executive and the various ministers of considerable regulatory discretion. While this did not deprive ministers of the right to issue regulations under executive authority, it did deprive them of the right to make arbitrary or systematic exceptions without the issuance of appropriate regulations approved by the Conseil (Freedeman 1961:32–33).

The importance of this administrative autonomy of the Conseil lay in its role in delimiting the excessive use of power by the executive. The Conseil thus came to play an increasingly important role in determining the correct legal structure of regulations governing the process of the *concours,* the validity of general statutes governing officials, of the process of discipline and dismissal, and the legal coherence of the regulations governing advancement (Sibert 1912:56–158; Osborne 1983:108–11). One of the major results of this transformation of the Conseil's role was the increasing stability of career as the Conseil defined the legal forms of recruitment, advancement, dismissal, and retirement over the next three decades. Thus, while the requirement of an examination for appointment remained within the jurisdiction of the appropriate minister, how and under what conditions the *concours* were given were not. The violation of prescribed form became a major instrument in limiting the powers of the executive since it precluded exceptions made by ministers for protégés. At the same time, however, the Conseil became a powerful force in maintaining the fragmented character of the administrative structure. By refusing to allow any general statute to be implemented that did not recognize ministerial differences in requirements, the Conseil became the chief obstacle to the creation of a general statute of officials (Lanza 1976:338–39). The creation of specific and final jurisdictions for the Conseil d'État, along with the constitutional crises of 1876–79, laid the groundwork for the attempt of Republic leaders to sustain electoral control over the government.

The decade of the 1880s saw the final elements of the state bureaucratic structure put in place in a systematic way. Aside from the increasing predictability of the general civil service career made possible by the incremental decisions of the Conseil d'État, there were two other major developments. The first was the final institutionalization of the *concours*. The second was the founding and emergence of the École Libre des Sciences Politique as the essential gateway to the *grands corps* and the ministerial cabinets. The extension of the *concours* seems to have taken the appointment process out of the hands of party patronage, where it could have been used to acquire votes. The reliance on the École Libre, a private school, to provide training for passing the exams leading to the most important appointments in the higher civil service seems to have put the selection process outside the control of political leaders. Thus, both of these developments seem to be contradictions to the expected strategies of the Republican political leadership, if strengthening the party and retaining power were their goals.

The first contradiction can be dispelled, in part, by pointing out that useful patronage—that needed by deputies to help maintain local political machines—was of a lower level and primarily local in character (Ligou 1966:217–18; Combes 1956:217). Deputies wanted things for their constituents and these did not amount to senior civil service positions. Moreover, the *concours* were extended to the junior posts on the career ladder in the central ministries (Public Instruction, 1881; Public Works, 1885; Navy and Colonies, 1886; Interior, 1886; Agriculture, 1887; Finance, 1885, 1886, 1890; Cour des Comptes, 1886). This closed off the upper-level civil service as a base for party leadership patronage, but also closed off the worrisome problem of how to allocate senior positions. Moreover, the extension of the *concours* closed off senior positions from the worst excesses of the old, right-wing, social-status based, old-boy networks. The exams also established, with relative uniformity, the basic hurdle separating senior civil service careers from lower-level ones. All of this was entirely consonant with Republican rhetoric about careers open only to merit (Osborne 1983:89). Here, the Republicans met the problem of equality as had Napoleon: by reference to the equality of standards as against the equality of opportunity.

In 1871, Émile Boutmy, one of the founders of the École Libre des Sciences Politiques, wrote the following just after the Paris Commune had been put down with great bloodshed:

Privilege has gone, democracy cannot be halted. The higher classes, as they call themselves, are obliged to acknowledge the right of the majority, and they can only maintain their political dominance by invoking the right of the most capable. Behind the crumbling ramparts of their prerogatives and of tradition the tide of democracy must encounter a second line of defense, constructed by manifest and useful abilities, of superior qualities whose prestige cannot be gainsaid. (as quoted in Bottomore 1964:82)

Curiously enough, these attitudes about the legitimacy of status based on the acquisition of skills and expertise rather than on birth were echoed in the ideas and attitudes of the Republicans. The Republicans had come to power as a party and a movement, not simply as a collection of notables. It had done so by convincing peasants, landholders, and small producers, as well as urban bourgeoisie, that the party the Republicans had created was a public and not a private institution in pursuit of public and not private interests. It had done so by laying claims to transcending class, to commitment to the idea of equality as reflected in merit, and to the idea of community defined by Republican constitutionalism (namely, the notion of democracy constrained by reason) (Elwitt 1975:24–27, 305–7). Thus, the great spokesman of the early Republicans, Gambetta, announced on 26 September 1872 the arrival of a "new social stratum" *(couche sociale nouvelle)*—not classes, as he pointed out later, but stratum, by which he meant a coalition led by the Republican bourgeoisie (Elwitt 1975:54–55). Republicans, he said later, must exclude from their ranks "utopians and dreamers, showering the masses with unrealizable promises, incoherent and illogical programs, aiming at the division of classes, fomenting discord between one and another" (as quoted in Elwitt 1975:55). He went on to claim for the Republicans the role of the "party capable of directing the orderly business of government" (as quoted in Elwitt 1975:56). The Republican belief in the superior qualities of the bourgeoisie in organizing the society as democratic and egalitarian, is reflected again in Gambetta's words:

Only the Republic can effect the harmonious reconciliation between the legitimate demands of workers and the great respect for the sacred rights of property. . . . To attain this goal, two things are necessary: to dissolve the fears of one and calm the passions of the other; to teach the bourgeoisie to cherish democratic government and to teach the people to have confidence in their elder brothers. (quoted in Elwitt 1975:58)

In sum, I would argue, the Republican movement, as it unfolded ideologically, sought to transform the notion of the obligation of and fitness for public service inherent in birth into the concept of merit and expertise as the basis for the obligation to, and fitness for, public service. The concept of birth as the source of leadership had, as Boutmy had pointed out, crumbled. Publicness and public interest could no longer be reflected in the institutions of notability but now must be registered in the institutions of learning and of practical affairs.

Given this view, it is not surprising that the Science Po (École Libre de Science Politique), based on a curriculum dealing with real-world matters and policy, became, within a few years of its founding, an attractive means for exhibiting the standards of merit now seemingly required by the claims of public interest made by the supporters of the Republican movement and party. Founded and supported by Orleanist Republicans (Taine, Sorel, Guizot, de Lanjuinais, and others), whose views were reflected in Boutmy's ideas of a class sustained by its merit, the school soon found itself becoming a center of training for the senior civil service (Osborne 1983:57–58). In 1876, eleven of the seventeen places awarded by *concours* in the Council of State, the Finance Inspectorate, and the diplomatic corps were won by alumni of Science Po (Osborne 1983:64). Between 1876 and 1880, nineteen of twenty-four successful candidates for the Conseil d'État's openings and seventeen of the twenty-one entering the Inspectorate of Finances had attended the school (Osborne 1983:57–58). The degree to which Science Po became the point of entry into the nontechnical *grands corps* is striking. From 1899 to 1936, 97 percent of those admitted by exam into the Conseil d'État and the Inspectorate of Finance and 88 percent of those passing into the Cour des Comptes and into the diplomatic corps had attended the Science Po (Bottomore 1954:II, 145; Kessler 1977:32).

The success of Science Po in becoming, in essence, one of the *grandes écoles* is a result specifically of the growing uniformity among the *grands corps* of the *concours* and the necessity of finding some system of training which could produce a reliable and narrow flow of eligibles to take the examinations. This is reflected in the degree to which instruction at Science Po was staffed by members of the various corps. In 1872 there were two members of the corps also acting as instructors, Albert Sorel (diplomatic corp) and Anatole Dunoyer (Conseil d'État). They were joined in 1873 by Emile Flourens and LeVavasseur de Précourt (Conseil d'État) and Rodolphe Dareste (Cour de Cassation) (Osborne 1983:62–63). In following years, the school drew heavily from the Conseil d'État, the Cour des Comptes, and the Inspectorate of Finance (Osborne 1983:62–63). The board of directors of the school also drew heavily on members of the corps (Osborne 1983:62–63). The *grands corps* clearly sought to encourage the emergence of a barrier beyond that of the perfunctory attendance at the faculties of law, which were producing a large and increasing pool of eligibles (an average of almost twelve hundred degree graduates a year over the period of 1876 to 1906 and an average of over eight thousand matriculating students per year over the same period [Ringer 1979:335]), which had to be narrowed down somehow. More generally, the rather benign attitude taken by the Republicans toward the creation and growth of Science Po can be attributed to its meeting the party's requirement of a meritocratic higher officialdom. If the party's political leaders were to stay in power, they had to fulfill not only their pork-barrel promises but also the promise of an administration that by its organization and recruitment seemed committed to the public interest.

All three developments in the period from 1870 to 1899—the institutionalization of the *concours,* the autonomy of the Conseil d'État, and the emergence of the Science Po—all served to provide an almost untouchable career structure. Passage through Science Po established one's credentials, the *concours* established one's appropriateness, and the constraining legalisms of the Conseil d'État established organizational rather than ministerial rules governing promotion. All of this required an even greater commitment to the educational process than had been the case under the Second Empire. Now it became clear that if one wished to enter the central administrative upper-level civil service, it required commitment to an education that would ensure acceptance into Science Po, and this in turn required an educational track beginning with one of the select *lycées.* Entering Science Po meant giving up entering one of the professions or at least deferring it for several years. Clearly, this was a career track for well-to-do people—the lower classes need not apply. Nevertheless, the incentives for commitment to such extensive and costly educational careers must have been high.

What were these incentives? One of these was the strong possibility of eventually coming to hold high office and with it the honors of the state and perhaps the Légion d'Honneur. Given the middle-level status of the professions in France in the nineteenth and twentieth centuries in comparison with that of high official positions, this was a strong incentive. This was especially the case as upper-level civil service careers came to have high levels of predictability and security. Finally, the major problem which had caused considerable concern over the previous decades—blockage of careers created by slow turnover at senior levels—was resolved by the institutionalization of the system of *pantouflage* and detachment. *Pantouflage* allowed members of the *grands corps* to resign after a relatively short career so that they could enter private business (Lalumière 1959:69–74). This had the effect of allowing greater turnover within the corps, thus providing for incentives to enter the long educational and career process. *Pantouflage* offered a second and usually high-paying career. Thus the system tended to provide assurance that some kind of career advancement awaited everyone. Detachment emerged originally in the Inspectorate of the technical corps (Ponts et Chaussées and Mines), where it allowed individuals (usually with special technical or legal expertise) to take leaves of absence for prolonged periods to serve in other services and eventually in private capacities as well (Lalumière 1959:59). This had the additional effect of unblocking career paths in the *grands corps* without upsetting career structures in the central ministries since the positions were usually technical.

By 1890 the state administrative structure had acquired all of the major elements that have characterized it up to the present day, with some modifications to be sure, but not as many as one might think. Most of those characteristics were already in place by the end of the Second Empire. Despite the change in government, the rationalization of the structure proceeded with some speed, although, perhaps, with somewhat different intents by the political leaders of the two regimes. The trail had been a long one, beginning with the Revolutionary declarations eliminating public office as private property and ending a century later with the Republican idea of public office as the property of merit.

Conclusion

At the center of the bureaucratic structure which emerged was the principle that the role structure was the basic source for information and for the rules by which information was organized and utilized. The standard of professional certification came to have less and less validity for those who would and did become senior civil officials. The ideas that underlay the professional role were not recognized in any cardinal way as the basis for organizational or career structure. This seems to have been the result of the state monopoly on the organization and dispensation of professional knowledge and certification. Deprived of the capacity to control the very basis of their occupation, professionals in nineteenth-century France did not get very far in creating any sense of community. Loyalty to profession was not and still does not seem to be widespread in France. [3] The organizationally specific nature of information and the rules for its appropriate utilization emerged not just simply as the consequence of the absence of professional community. Constrained by the state monopoly or near monopoly on higher education and professional certification, individuals seeking higher civil service careers had little to say theoretically about the superiority of professionally autonomous systems of knowledge.

Organizational or "firm" specificity of knowledge was encouraged throughout the nineteenth century by the desire of political leaders as individuals to maintain control of their particular executive domains. This concern led ministers to resist any notion of uniformity. Ministers benefited by this arrangement. While it led to the growth of widely divergent patterns of administration as one moved from ministry to ministry and from regulatory corps to regulatory corps, it also provided the minister with the means to

3. This is reflected in the relative scarcity of professional as opposed to union forms of organizations among, for example, administrators and engineers (see Cahen-Salvador 1911; Wishnia 1978; Boltanski 1982). It is also reflected in the general tendency among administrators to view the problem of ethics as one to be derived from the general Christian rather than from specifically professional ethics (see, for example, de Calan 1953; *Cahiers* 1953–54).

maintain a considerable amount of autonomy and leverage against competi-tion. To enter one of these ministries was to learn a way of doing things and using information that was different from any other administrative unit. This had the twin effect of providing informal security to officials while pro-viding ministers with incentives to maintain a flow of officials without the danger of being held hostage by the threat from subordinates seeking better pastures. The outcome of this was an organizationally determined structure of information and its usage.

Here, it appears to be the case that the organizationally specific nature of information and its usage gave rise to the emergence of seniority, hierarchy, and the notion of expertise. Once in a ministry for a period of time, officials had considerable leverage over ministers who came and went. Dismissals could not be handed out with ease since it meant loss of critical expertise (the more so the longer the official stayed on) and disastrous drops in morale, as evidenced by the vocal complaints of officials in the late 1840s and again throughout the last decades of the nineteenth century and early decades of the twentieth century. Seniority became increasingly the primary means of moving people up without bringing forth charges of favoritism. With this came also the pressure to rationalize hierarchy so as to provide orderly move-ment both in salary and status. The variation in hierarchy between the regu-latory *grands corps* and the central administrative and prefectural corps is per-haps explained by the collegial nonadministrative character of the regulatory corps. Since many of the duties in these were categorical and thus performed by equals within each category (*auditeurs, maitre des requêtes,* for example), the hierarchies were arbitrarily organized around categories based on experi-ence and age and thus tended to be fewer in number. Once in place, how-ever, seniority and hierarchy became part of the incentive structure that con-vinced young men to commit themselves early on in their lives to a career in the higher civil service.

It is this condition of organizationally specific and dominated knowledge which, I believe, also goes a long way toward explaining why French officials throughout the nineteenth and twentieth centuries have shown enormous loyalty to the state administration while at the same time expressing bitter-ness about the conditions of their profession. Loyalty was, in effect, the only real alternative open to an official who had spent any time in the system. His expertise was useful, by and large, in one place and one place only. In a sense, there was no option but loyalty since there were few places to exit if one were in the central ministerial corps. Where this was not the case, as in some of the *grands corps,* loyalty was reinforced by the growth of the tradition of *pan-touflage.* This wonderful system of providing postcareer careers while in mid-career served not only to provide incentives for entering the career structure of the corps, it also produced a loyalty which was astonishingly similar to, and perhaps stronger than, loyalty to professions in societies like the United States or Great Britain (Suleiman 1978:96–97).

In conclusion, I think it is fair to say that the institutionalization of the French state bureaucracy had been largely achieved by 1890. Before the end of the nineteenth century, the French upper-level civil service had acquired all of the basic characteristics of the rational-legal organization described by Weber. It had arrived there not by any immutable development of industrial society. The major underpinnings of the system had been created by the first Napoleon when France had only the glimmerings of an industrial revolution. The structure which emerged out of the agonizing pendulum swings of the nineteenth century was created by political choices of political leaders who sought, without success for the most of the century, to reduce the uncertainty about political leadership and its capacity to stay in power.

JAPAN

6

The Meiji Restoration as the
Revolutionary Moment

The Failure of Traditional Leadership Roles

Within the thirty-two-year period between 1868 and 1900 there emerged in Japan, to the general astonishment of Western observers, a bureaucratic structure which bore a striking resemblance to Weber's rational-legal type. The creation of a modern administrative structure seemed all the more startling since Japan, in 1868, possessed a political and administrative system that had more in common with feudalism than with late nineteenth-century Western states. The Imperial Restoration of 1868 not only brought an end to this anachronistic structure, it also resulted in the dissolution of the rules governing the structure of political leadership selection. In their place, for the time being, the rules of the ancient hereditary court appointment structure were restored. The imperial court administration was thus headed by court aristocrats of ancient lineage. The offices, however, were staffed primarily by lower samurai who had been the leading activists against the Tokugawa regime (Silberman 1964:49–50; Hasegawa 1966:57–92).

For the preceding two hundred and fifty years, the Chinese-style imperial administration had languished in the ancient palaces of Kyoto, banished by the Tokugawa regime from participation in the political or administrative realities of the day. Thus, the court aristocrats (kuge) who now headed the new imperial administration had not held positions of real power under the preceding regime, nor had the samurai who now came to hold the lower-level positions under the hereditary court aristocrats. Under the old system, samurai status was such that they could never have come to hold these high-level offices. Within several years, no later than 1873, things would be very different. The kuge would be completely gone from administration—victims, not so much of incompetence, as of lack of any formal or informal relationships or networks outside of the sequestered court (Silberman 1964:50–72; Beasley 1972:375–78). The posts of the reorganized central imperial government would now be led and held predominantly by lower samurai (Silberman 1964:50–72).

Conclusively, the men who led and administered the new government could not have held such posts under the old regime. It is equally the case that the majority and, from 1873, all leaders were selected in a manner and by criteria completely different from that of the preceding regime (Silberman 1964:73–107). These men had not been selected by any formal criteria. They had passed no examinations. They had not been elected. They had emerged as claimants to positions of power on the basis of self-selection. They had been leading participants in the attacks on the old regime. Their claims to leadership in the new government were based on their self-pro-claimed leadership in bringing about the dissolution of the old regime. Their claims to leadership thus had no institutional foundation. This became pain-fully clear, especially in 1873 and in the years that followed. Challenges to their claims of leadership and power emerged from many quarters. These challenges took the form of both peaceful and violent demands for new in-stitutions and structures of leadership. The first decade of claimant power by the new leadership was decidedly one of high uncertainty and unpre-dictability about the future.

The Social Basis of Emergent Leadership

The putative leadership faced high uncertainty about their futures between 1868 and 1880 primarily because of the absence of any organizational basis for their interests and goals. These hopeful leaders had emerged out of the col-lapse of the Tokugawa regime with only the most tenuous and ambiguous in-formal ties to other groups. The existence of a formal organizational structure centered on interests might have reduced uncertainty. The absence of such a structure was a function of the social and political order of the Tokugawa re-gime, which has sometimes been characterized as "centralized feudalism."

Despite the oxymoronic character of this description, it does provide us with an intimation of the basic nature of the system. On the one hand, it did have a type of federalist governance structure. Their were 250 to 300 do-mains *(han),* each governing their local area with no direct intervention from the dominant Tokugawa domain. The Tokugawa domain was the largest and most powerful—a type of *prima inter pares.* With the aid of its vassals and allies, Tokugawa political supremacy had been acknowledged after a long competition with an opposing coalition of domains in the late sixteenth and early seventeenth centuries.

In victory, the Tokugawa House took for itself the obligations and rights of maintaining national defense, internal peace and security, and economic regulation. It was successful in institutionalizing the subordination of the domains through a variety of administrative and economic practices derived from this structure of translocal rights. The administration of these affairs was placed in a structure which bore the time-honored title of *Bakufu* or "camp-government" to show its difference from the government of the em-peror. Because the rights acquired by the Bakufu were interdomainal in

character, local direct administration outside of the Tokugawa domains remained in the hands of the domainal lords. [1] Each of the domains, including
the Tokugawa, governed in its own jurisdiction through an elaborate centralized, hierarchically organized administration largely patterned after the
Tokugawa domain system. There was, as a consequence, a high degree of informal administrative uniformity in this system that helped to overcome the
centrifugal tendencies of the federalist arrangement.

In contrast to the federalist character of the interdomainal system as reflected in the two levels of political and economic jurisdiction, the intradomainal system was highly centralized. While there was a significant degree of functional and decision-making differentiation in this local administration, its
outstanding characteristic was the high level of internal domain centralization.
Functional differentiation was organized on a hierarchical basis in which field
and central office roles provided the basic dividing point for hierarchical distinctions between offices but not for rank. Thus, those who occupied offices in
the domain administrative center tended to hold the highest offices, while
those who were relegated to the administration of local affairs generally held
the lowest ones. Rank in the administrative structure was not, however, determined by level of office or any internally organized system of movement
through offices. Rank was allocated on a completely different basis and one
completely unrelated to the hierarchy of offices or their functions.

In a seemingly contradictory or, at least, anomalous manner, the rationality of office differentiation was accompanied by a definition of administrative role in which status by virtue of birth was the central feature. Ascriptive
social status served not only as the test of eligibility for holding administrative office, it also served as the means for determining appointment to various ranks. One's status, in other words, was the test of holding a specific office. General status as a member of the samurai class or *shizoku*, as it later
came to be known, meant that one was eligible to be among the governing
class but was insufficient by itself to earn a place in the administrative structure. Administrative offices had specific samurai class status linked to them.
One could hold only those offices associated with one's rank. Specific status
in turn was a product of birth. At its core, office-holding within any structure of administration in the Tokugawa period (1615–1868) was dependent
on a specific inherited status within a privileged class.

This class was organized on a complex system of stratification originally determined by the intensity of loyalty shown by the original supporters of those

1. The term "Bakufu" is used hereafter as a synonym for the Tokugawa house or domain rule.
The system embracing the Bakufu and the domains or *han* has come to be known as the bakuhan
system *(bakuhan taisei).*

who came to be domain lords. The intensity of loyalty was determined in a fairly simple way—those who came first to support and sustain the winners in the conflicts of the sixteenth century were given the highest places. Those who came later and served in lower places because the upper ones were filled were assigned lower status. Exhibition of loyalty to the domain lord or *han* lay at the foundation of the structure that determined eligibility for office and the exclusion of all others from service and its rights. As peace prevailed, the continued exhibition of loyalty took the form of willingly preparing and presenting oneself to one's lord for service in any civil or military capacity.

The status structure became fixed with the coming of the *pax Tokugawa* at the beginning of the seventeenth century. The establishment of peace after almost three centuries of intermittent internal war fought by claimant lords was based on the differentiation of the political from the social and economic orders. This differentiation was achieved by separating the administrative role from the ownership of the means of administration. Or, to put it more simply, administrators were paid by a stipend, calculated in rice, directly from the domain treasury; the income of domain administrators did not come from possession of the income of the office, nor did they hold land as the form of payment for their services.

One must not be beguiled by this into thinking that this meets Weber's standard of rationalized bureaucratic role. Those who were appointed to office were not paid for performing the duties of their offices. On the contrary, they were paid because they held a social status. Stipends were a function of rank and thus inherited. The size of the stipend was a reflection and a symbol of the relationship existing between domain lord and retainer. Also, those who held a rank within the samurai class were generally forbidden to hold any land and its income or to engage in any kind of mercantile, artisanal, or industrial enterprise. Samurai, for the most part, were stripped of any direct ownership of the means of production as well as the means of administration. In economic terms, as a class they were determined by the possession of stipends paid by the domain lord out of systematic tax collections. This institutionalization of inherited rank as the determinant of political, economic, and social status brought an end to the ability of vassals to use their ownership of the means of administration to successfully challenge their superiors. Once the domain was considered as the generalized possession of the political order in the form of the domain lord's *(daimyō)* administration and not literally of any individual, the capacity for mobilizing resources by military entrepreneurs came to an end. [2]

2. Excellent descriptions of this system, usually referred to as the Baku-han system, can be found in the following: Tasaburo Itō 1980; Fujino Tamotsu 1983; W. G. Beasley 1972: chap. 1.

Although it appears that the domain administrative system has some of the characteristics of Weber's legal-rational type, namely the separation of the administrator from the ownership of the office, it is rather distant from the notion of bureaucratic role. The administrative role under the *bakuhan* system was largely without a career structure. There was no likelihood of advancing in any systematic way. Rather, the tendency was to remain in the same group of offices for which an individual's rank made him eligible. This is not to say that people did not get appointed to higher positions from lower ones. Toward the end of the period, when the demands for certain kinds of experience and skills were greater than the supply, people got moved up to posts that their rank would normally have made it impossible for them to hold. In order to do this, however, people had to be given temporary ranks. Temporary they were, since a family would generally have to have an appointment at that temporary level for several generations before its rank was changed permanently. It was equally difficult to lose rank. Several generations of failing to hold office was usually required before a family would suffer loss of rank and a lower stipend. Mobility, in short, did not occur systematically within a structure of offices. What mobility occurred did so within the relatively rigid structure of inherited family rank.

It is easy to see why politics and administration in the Tokugawa period have usually been viewed as synonymous. Access to any position of legitimate power was determined in a single, seemingly monolithic way. Birth determined access—the level of access was determined by the inherited relationship of retainer to lord. This was seen to be true not only at the intradomainal level but at the interdomainal level as well. The domains were divided into "inner" *(fudai)* and "outer" *(tozama)* lords *(daimyō)* or domains. The former were hereditary vassals of the Tokugawa before the great and critical battle of Sekigahara in 1600 that tipped the balance of power to the Tokugawa coalition. The *tozama* were those who had not been vassals at the time of the battle and thus included allies, members of the opposition, and those who were neutral. Only *fudai* lords and direct vassals could hold positions in the Bakufu administration. These offices were also, like those in the domains, allocated on the basis of the hereditary ranking and size of domains. Loyalty in its institutionalized and fossilized form was thus the basis of access to positions of power. No centers of power existed outside of the administrative structure. In a sense, it is possible to say that one of the major aims of the founders of the Tokugawa system was to reduce all politics to hereditary hierarchical administration. Having achieved this, they thought they had eliminated the dangers of continued political competition (Totman 1967:234–55).

Politics, or the propensity toward politics, survived. This was reflected in the shift of power within the Bakufu, as time went on, from *shōgun* and *shōgunal* officials to the direct medium and minor vassal *daimyō* (Totman 1967:249–51). It is also reflected in the domains in the emergence, by the beginning of the nineteenth century, of the search for men of "practical affairs" to fill administrative positions. "Practical affairs" largely meant men who had experience in the field administering domain laws and policies (Harootunian 1966). These shifts in the center of gravity of administrative power were derived from cleavages that, ironically enough, were incipient in the solution which the *bakuhan taisei* (bakufu-domain structure) represented.

The functional differentiation between national and local administration, and between central and field administration within the domain, produced the basis for cleavages that were to separate administrative from political roles. The catalyst for the emergence of political cleavage was the social organizational basis of leadership. The administrative role was organized around a set of exclusive properties (birth, loyalty, etc.) which determined social rank. These properties, however, were insufficient to answer all of the contingencies associated with administration. The financial problems brought on by economic development in the eighteenth and nineteenth centuries, population growth, urban expansion, the appearance of the West in the early part of the nineteenth century, all produced administrative problems and decision-making situations for which the system of hereditary rankings was incommensurate. The system simply could not provide enough people with sufficient skills or information at the appropriate levels of administration to allow social ranking to remain unchallenged as the source of the administrative role.

This situation provided the material for conflict between various groups within the governing elite over questions of policy and the nature of decision making. Local versus national interests emerged in the form of increasing pressure from vassal *daimyō* to dominate decision making within the Bakufu. This demand spread to the *tozama daimyō* by the 1850s with the opening of the country and the Bakufu's vacillating response. Within the larger domains, these same conditions of internal and external stress gave rise to conflicts over financial policy and administrative reforms. In these conflicts, the interests of field administrators came increasingly to be arrayed against those who held policy offices at the domain headquarters. Such divisions of interest became the object of manipulation by both senior and junior officials. These resulted in the emergence of clique politics at all levels of domain and Bakufu administration by the early nineteenth century.

The source of these cleavages was social rank. Access to decision making was determined by social rank at both the domainal and national levels of decision making. The politics of the late Tokugawa thus became a politics of exclusion and usurpation. *Fudai* lords sought to maintain the exclusion of *tozama*, while the latter sought to usurp the privileges of the direct Tokugawa vassals. The latter was a goal which, if accomplished, would have created a whole new set of rules governing participation in decision making at the national level. It is not surprising that the Bakufu and *fudai daimyō* fought such demands furiously.

At the domainal level, the same pattern of cleavage existed. Lower-level administrators in the domains were hereditarily locked out of systematic participation in domainal decision making. These administrators shared a common social status, which became the basis of the politics of exclusion and usurpation in a large number of domains in the nineteenth century. Conflicts emerged between lower- and upper-ranking samurai over questions of domainal policy and reform. In the course of these conflicts, politics as distinct from administration emerged, as nonoffice-holding, lower samurai attempted to forge new theories of policy and action and then proceeded to use these theories in attacks on the Bakufu and domain establishments.

In this type of politics, cleavage, organization, and leadership were all functions of social rank and status. At the interdomainal level, opposition organization centered on the largest domains excluded from Bakufu administration and decision making, mostly *tozama*. At the domainal level, active and often violent opposition emerged among groups of lower samurai who came to be known as *shi-shi* (men of spirit). While these groups sometimes recruited non-samurai to support their attacks on domainal and Bakufu authorities, they did not allow commoners access to leadership positions. Inter- and intradomainal levels of politics came to be integrated primarily as a result of pressures created by the lower samurai in the largest of those domains which participated in the demands for greater inclusion in national decision making—first, Mito, and then Satsuma and Chōshū, which were later joined by several others.

It is not surprising then that it was the lower samurai from these domains who came to play a major role in the Restoration and post-1868 politics. [3] Nor is it surprising that the basic aspect that served to integrate these groups of "men of spirit" was their social rank bounded by the network of domainal loyalties and relationships. The post-1868 claimants to leadership thus tended to identify themselves by their rank and domainal origins and these

3. The literature on the formation of politics at the end of the Tokugawa system is very large. The following are helpful: Tōyama 1951; Tōyama 1968; Sakata 1960; Sakata and Hall 1956:31–50; Harootunian 1970; W. G. Beasley 1972; Naramoto 1967.

became the basis for group identification in the new government. The immediate post-1868 period was a testing time not only for the new government and its putative leaders as a group, but it was equally a testing time for the viability of the small-group social network basis of leadership and its centrifugal tendencies.

Nevertheless, despite or perhaps because of the problems of leadership, role definition, and the atomistic character of the putative leaders' organizational base, there emerged within the span of their own generation an administrative structure that has continued to be the basis for civil service up until the present. Moreover, in spite of the great political and economic transformation that has occurred since the end of the last century, the civil service role and career structure created and institutionalized between 1868 and 1900 has remained essentially unchanged. The basic features of this upper civil service role might be described as follows:

1. Higher education in law or the so-called policy sciences; political science, economics, public finance as the basis for eligibility to the senior general administrative service. This is distinct from eligibility for the technical administrative roles in such areas as agriculture, communications, science, and public works where higher education in the civil sciences is the basis for eligibility.

2. Passage of tests, both written and oral, designed specifically for entry into the upper civil service. Passing these exams is essential for recruitment into the upper civil service. There is no linkage between the upper and lower civil service which allows mobility from the lower service to the higher one. These examinations originally centered on law but later came to include the policy sciences for those entering the senior administrative service. Furthermore, sufficient knowledge to pass these exams has required, in effect, the possession of a university degree from one of a limited number of universities. Possession of a degree from Tokyo University has had the greatest predictability aspect. Far more than a simple majority of administrative senior civil servants have been consistently recruited from the premier Japanese university. Smaller percentages are recruited from other state universities and several private universities.

3. Entrance into a distinct upper-level civil service career beginning at the lowest level of the upper civil service and moving through a series of hierarchically linked offices at a highly predictable rate.

4. Advancement largely on the basis of seniority until the middle levels (section chiefs or their equivalents) and, after this, as offices become fewer, selection by officials at the vice-ministerial level on the basis of performance and seniority.

5. A career primarily within a single ministry with specialization arising

systematically as a function of the degree to which individuals ceased to advance and remained in one office or section.

6. A servicewide uniform career period (twenty years service or sixty years of age), completion of which has provided the person with a vested interest in a retirement income or pension.

7. A career structure in which officeholders have been protected from arbitrary dismissal. The grounds for dismissal have been well defined in laws and regulations, and the administration of disciplinary measures has been in the hands of senior civil servants. [4]

The characteristics of this structure are very much like those of the French upper civil service. Like the French system, the Japanese structure was and is characterized by a highly insulated internal labor market. After entrance, allocation of offices is almost completely independent of external forces until a person reaches the highest levels of office as vice-minister. As a result, skills have been highly organization-specific. Moreover, the constraints of the career structure, which have kept most people within the same ministry throughout their careers, very often render their skills to be not only organization-specific, but specific to various subunits of the organization.

Entry into the civil service was, by 1900, governed by a set of clearly defined rules. An informal but major precondition of entry was training in law. This continues to be the case despite the growing inclusion of policy sciences. Legal or policy science training in itself has by no means been sufficient to secure entrance since passage of oral and written exams is essential. The ability to pass these exams, however, has not been widely distributed among graduates of a great many universities. Indeed, from the very beginning, graduates of the then Tokyo Imperial University (now less regally known as Tokyo University) have dominated the lists of successful examinees (Spaulding 1967:131–32; 267–70; Kubota 1969:67–76; Muramatsu 1981:56–82). Kyoto and several other state universities have made inroads over time, but they remain minority contributors to the lists of successful examinees.

Since the number of schools providing successful candidates has consistently been small and the desire for career so high, the demand for positions in the entering classes of Tokyo and Kyoto Universities have been proportionally high since the 1880s. Successful entry to these universities was, and still is, dependent on passage of an examination. Very early on, it became evident that significant numbers of successful entrants came from a relatively

---

4. Muramatsu 1981; Hata 1983; Tsuji 1968; Kubota 1969; Kawanaka 1972; Spaulding 1967; D. Itō 1980; Yamanaka 1974; Tsuji 1984; Silberman 1970; Koh 1985, 1979; Cicco and Ori 1974; Kubota 1980; Tsuji 1982; Hirano 1983; Koh and Kim 1982; Murobushi 1980; Kitani 1983; Koh 1989.

small number of higher schools—the "numbered" state higher schools which were the first to be established between 1877 and 1908 (Kubota 1969:60–63). Thus, if one had ambitions to become a senior civil servant, commitment to the career had to come at the point of entrance to one of the higher schools in the individual's midteens. Entrance to these schools became prized as well. Astute parents soon sought out middle schools that had reputations for preparing students successfully for entrance into the "numbered" higher schools. In effect, commitment to career was often not the choice of the person but rather of his or (only very, very rarely) her parents. However it occurred, the commitment to an upper-level civil service career had to be made long before a person came to sit for the civil service examinations.

Having successfully passed the upper civil service exams, the individual set out on a well-defined career course. One moved through a series of hierarchically organized offices at very regular intervals. This movement has been governed by adherence to the formal and informal rules of seniority. The career structure has assured everyone of a minimal level of promotion, usually to section chief or its equivalent (Kubota 1969:127–28). Specialization and differentiation have largely been a matter of internal training through career service and not a product of pre-entry training. The insulation of the career from external constraints was established in 1899 by the creation of autonomous disciplinary committees within the civil service (*Hōrei Zensho* [hereafter referred to in text and footnotes as H.Z.] 1899: Imperial Ordinance, 68, 69). These committees or their successors have, by and large, continued to be autonomous, being made up mostly of senior civil servants who have rarely dismissed anyone from the service except on grounds of illness and disability.

The creation of uniform retirement and pension rules, beginning in 1884 and revised in 1890, formed the basic continuing structure of career completion. This assured the senior official of a predictable career cycle very early on (*H.Z.* 1884: Dajōkan Ordinance 1; *H.Z.* 1890: Law 43; *H.Z.* 1923: Law 48). For those who were forced to retire early by rising to the highest posts, such as vice-minister, or by failing to achieve those posts when colleagues of equal seniority reached them, the completion of the career cycle has consistently been extended into the postcareer period through second careers (Johnson 1982:63–73; Johnson 1978:101–18; Silberman and Harootunian 1974:183–216; Seifu Kankei 1981; Ino and Hokuto 1972). In short, there have been very clearly understood rewards for early commitment and successful entry into the upper civil service since the completion of its institutionalization in 1899 through the *Chokunin* Appointment, Civil Service Status, and Civil Service Disciplinary Ordinances of that year (Silberman 1970:349).

The Problems of Equality, Authority, Community, and Legitimacy

Leadership Succession and Its Ambiguities: 1868–73

In February 1868, the Imperial Court, led by the young Emperor Meiji, stripped the head of the Tokugawa House, the Shōgun Keiki, of his court rank, and thus brought an end to *bakuhan* system. In its place, the emperor and the court administration were "restored" to govern a unified administration directly. The restoration of the traditional Chinese administrative structure to actual administration from its mothball existence in the formerly isolated palaces of Kyoto raised serious problems. The first of these was the absence of structures that bridged the gap between imperial administrative offices and the domains. The elimination of Bakufu administration left the archaic imperial administration dangling, so to speak, over an unintegrated structure of domains whose lords continued to hold direct power over subjects and taxation.

The second problem was that the Imperial Court ministers who were now formally vested with authority and power had, with a very few exceptions, little knowledge or experience in the realities of nineteenth-century Japanese political, social, or economic life. They were court nobles with no practical training or experience in administration or knowledge of the West. The latter had become especially important since 1853–54, when the Americans had forced Japan to open the country to trade. This event had precipitated the rapid development of the incipient cleavages in the governing classes. The question of policy in dealing with the West became one of the major sources of conflict (Harootunian 1970; Beasley 1972:82–116).

The first problem—administrative integration—raised the question of the nature of imperial administration. What did it mean to rule without the mediation of the Bakufu structure? Did the restoration of direct imperial rule mean a system of imperial administrators fanning out from the capital to govern administrative units and collect taxes without any limits on its right to penetrate local power and organization (Asai 1939 [1968])? The second problem—administrative leadership and structure—produced the equally compelling problem of what constituted the criteria for leadership in the government. Was hereditary status at court to prevail now that the Bakufu had collapsed? If so, where would the necessary information, skills, and experience come from just to deal on a day-to-day, much less on a long-term, basis with political realities?

The latter was resolved in a manner that raised severe internal contradictions to the whole notion of "imperial restoration." The gap between inheritance and experience was immediately filled by a group that included domainal lords and upper samurai but in which lower samurai dominated

(Silberman 1964:49–55). Approximately two-thirds of them had participated actively in the attacks on the old regime in the name of their loyalty to
the emperor (Silberman 1964:62–72). Altogether, almost 75 percent of this
group either had been politically active against the regime and/or had acquired some Western knowledge (Silberman 1964:62–72). Almost two-
thirds (62 percent) of this group, predominantly lower samurai (52 percent),
could not have held such posts under the preceding regime (Silberman
1964:57–72). In short, the appointment of lower samurai and some upper
samurai to imperial court positions revealed a revolutionary change: experience and achievement in the loyal service of the emperor was of more importance than rank accorded by birth.

The reasons for their appointment were clear enough. With no military
forces of its own, the court had to rely on the forces of those domains, primarily Satsuma and Chōshū, which had brought about the Tokugawa surrender. These domains had been politically manipulated to the support of
the emperor by the activities of groups of their lower samurai (Beasley
1972:214–99). The lower samurai thus represented a major liaison group
between the court and the domains. Furthermore, their activities and those
of their peers from a group of other domains revealed an asset relatively few
others outside of the court had—proven and tested loyalty. By their participation in terrorist attacks on the Bakufu, in attempted rebellions, in pushing
their domains to support "restoration" or at least to remain neutral, these
samurai had shown they were willing to pay a high price, as many did, for
imperial restoration. Having risked their lives by committing themselves to
the cause of the court, they could be trusted by the court to strenuously resist
counterrevolutionary efforts. Finally, those who were appointed had excellent knowledge of other loyalists who could be trusted to work on behalf of
the imperial government and would bring with them influence in their domains. If the imperial institution were to govern without the mediation of a
"camp government," it had to rely on court administrators who were both
loyal and experienced and who had access to others who were likewise.

The degree to which they were collectively essential in providing the mediating structure between court and domains is reflected in two developments in the period between 1868 and 1873. The first of these was the ability of the new appointees to marshal sufficient support from their domains
to convince all of the domainal lords to surrender their registers to the imperial administration in 1869, thus providing, at least in theory, a universal
commitment to the imperial restoration (Hasegawa 1966:93–110; Beasley
1972:325–35; Iwata 1964:143–47).

The second development was the gradual elimination of court aristocrats
and the domainal lords who had originally held senior positions in the new

government. This was accomplished by a series of governmental reorganizations of the court system beginning with the *san shoku* (three offices) structure of January 1868, followed by the *shichi ka* (seven offices) structure of June 1868, the revisions of 1869, and, finally, the reorganization of 1871. The latter saw the establishment of the Dajōkan cabinet structure as the system which was to last until the creation of the modern cabinet system in 1885 (Wilson 1957; Akita 1967: chaps. 1–2; Iwata 1964:116–48; Hasegawa 1966:56–183). As early as 1870–71, policy-making was in the hands of the ex-lower samurai. By no later than 1875, the leadership of the government was almost totally monopolized by former lower samurai primarily from the domains of Satsuma, Chōshū, Hizen, and Tosa, with the first two having the preponderant strength (Silberman 1964:73–97; Hasegawa 1966:56–183).

These two developments, while they helped define a new and coherent group of leaders within the new government, did not resolve the problem of equality. Rather, this problem was both revealed and exacerbated by the self-conscious and generally successful attempts of these lower samurai to hold leading positions in the new civil and military bureaucracies. Under the old dispensation they could not have come to hold these positions, and their rise to eminence clearly revealed the degree to which hereditary rank had been rendered meaningless by the Restoration. They were thus faced with the problem of defining or redefining the social basis of access to leadership roles. They could not return to some form of hereditary criterion since they had clearly set aside birth as a source of exclusiveness by their acts of self-selection. The rejection of the established social and organizational criteria for leadership in favor of self-determined and informal criteria that admitted commoners as well as the high born made it difficult, if not impossible, to reinstate the notion of birth. There were simply too many low- and relatively low-born participants in the Restoration to risk excluding them from leadership access by reinstating hereditary exclusiveness under which the putative new leaders themselves would be very notable exceptions. Furthermore, failure to provide redefinition of leadership could easily provoke reactions from a variety of sources challenging the legitimacy of the lower samurai occupants of the offices of the central government.

The only solution to the dilemma raised by their rather lowly origins was for the new leaders to eliminate the formal basis for social inequality; that is, it became necessary to remove the basis for occupational or role exclusiveness. They could not sustain the legitimacy of self-selection if they sought to resolve their problem by establishing both social and political equality. Establishment of the latter with no criteria for exclusiveness would have provided the opportunity for overwhelming challenges to the new leadership. The result was early recognition of social equality but no reference at all to

political equality. The emergence of social equality began with the formal
dissolution of the orders and hierarchy of nobility. The court aristocracy
(kuge) and the local aristocracy *(shoko)* were merged into one social class
known as the *kazoku* (flowery families) (*H.Z.*, Imperial Rescript 221, 26 July
1869). The abolition of the orders of nobility and their substitution by a ge-
neric category removed, with one stroke, the basic criterion for appointment
to the central government. The greatest challenge, however, came from the
problem of dissolving the numerically much larger and potentially more
dangerous lower levels of the elite hierarchy which dominated local government. The way was prepared by the "return" of the land registers to the emperor in 1869. Although theoretically the domains were now imperial and
the *daimyō* and samurai administrators were now officials of the central government, appointments continued to be made on the basis of hereditary
rank. The elimination of the hierarchy of ranks at the local level came shortly
after the return of the registers on 2 August 1869. All the various ranks were
replaced by two ranks that distinguished lower from upper samurai—*shizoku* for middle samurai and above, and *sotsu* for lower samurai (Beasley
1972:385). By the same legislation, former domainal lords, who now served
as governors, were placed on a hereditary stipend from the new government
equalling ten percent of the formally assessed revenue of the domain (Ishii
1958:90). Samurai continued to receive their stipends, although theoretically, but not in fact, these now came from the central government. In coun-
terpoint to this, commoners were given the right to have family names in
October 1870, and in the following year to marry into samurai and noble
families. *Shizoku,* including lower samurai, were allowed at the same time to
stop wearing their swords and enter all occupations without loss of status.
    The elimination of the ranks paved the way for the elimination of tradi-
tional hereditary criteria in the appointment of local officials. This action
also paved the way for the integration of local officials into the central governmental structure. This came with the abolition of the domains and their
replacement by the prefectures in 1871. The importance of the abolition of
the domains to the structure of social equality rested on the central government's assumption of all domainal debts from this time forward. By assuming the debts, the leadership of the new government made it possible to begin the process of eliminating the traditional economic bases of social
inequality, such as the entitlement to permanent stipends.
    Eliminating the bases of social inequality was finally accomplished in a two-
step process, beginning in 1873 with voluntary commutation of stipends in
which permanent stipends could be capitalized and ending in 1876 with the
compulsory commutation of stipends (Beasley 1972:388). With the end of the
stipendiary system, the formal legal economic basis of social distinction within

the former ranks of the governing elite came to an end. Consequently, the problem of formal, legal social inequality was largely resolved by 1876.

Although some formal social distinctions between the feudal class groupings continued to exist, these were insignificant. Informally, of course, the term *shizoku* or *kazoku* continued to evoke subservient behavior on the part of most commoners, even wealthy ones. The significance, however, of the new leadership's drive to eliminate formal social inequality was twofold. On the one hand, it made possible the elimination of a powerful burden on the new government's financial resources—the elimination of the stipends came as a great relief.

Equally important, on the other hand, was the redefinition of what constituted appropriate social status for entrance into leadership roles. The nature of the legislation that the new leaders promulgated suggests forcefully that its concern was not with the integration of *all* social classes into one category of social equality. The major concern of the social legislation of the first decade of the Restoration was the creation of minimal levels of social equality within the ranks of the former elite. The outcome of these efforts was the dissolution of the social basis of traditional elite network coherence. Hereditary rank and stipend no longer provided ready-made networks of interest and opposition. Nevertheless, at the same time, the dissolution of social inequality provided the general basis for claims of legitimacy by lower samurai leadership.

This stratagem may have provided the putative leaders with legitimate access to leadership roles but it did not, however, solve the problem of why this specific group of men should hold the positions of leadership and power. Indeed, the elimination of, at least formally, social inequality now made the solution of this problem imperative.

The Uncertainty of Office-holding: 1873–81

The total succession of leadership represented by the developments of 1868 through 1872 placed the putative leaders of the new government in a position where they were forced to make a series of strategic and tactical decisions about the nature of political leadership as well as the form and structure of the government. Having acquired the leading posts in the new government on the basis of self-selected criteria the exclusivity of which had little basis in a general test of loyalty, these lower samurai were immediately faced with challenges that rendered their positions precarious. The construction of social and civil equality between 1868 and 1876 may have made the lower samurai occupation of high offices seem legitimate, but it did little to specifically legitimate the new leaders' possession of those offices. Their rise to positions of eminence in the new government immediately raised the question among a large number of ex-samurai of, "Why them and not me (us)?" The manner in which the new government leaders had come to power raised voices of criticism, discontent, and envy. Equality, authority, and legitimacy continued to be central problems.

The lower samurai who held high government office were not the only men who had participated in the Restoration. At least hundreds, if not several thousand, could make the claim that they had committed themselves to the restoration of the emperor before the domains had provided an institutional and legitimate base for such behavior. As for their positions as former lower samurai with practical administrative experience, this criterion could easily apply to tens of thousands. That those who became the chief claimants of power came from a relatively small number of domains was a fact that was immediately and widely noted and that could not be easily translated into a criterion of loyalty to the imperial institution. Many samurai from other domains had also participated in the Restoration. Nor could these new officeholders claim a monopoly of Western knowledge. Many others had acquired various levels of Western knowledge.

The large numbers of new senior officials who came from a very small number of domains reveal the consequences of the unsystematic structure of exclusiveness. With the exception of domainal origin, the backgrounds of the men who claimed power in 1875 were not unique to them and, therefore, could not easily serve them as the basis for claiming the legitimate right to govern. That so many former samurai possessed these characteristics was the major reason for immediate challenges to the new leaders' right to hold the dominant positions of decision making. Beginning as early as 1870–71, these conflicts among the claimants to power led to an open breach in 1873 between several groups, both inside and outside the government.

An internal struggle over whether or not to engage in an invasion and subjugation of Korea led to the creation of two major challenges to those who remained in government. One group, which was led by Saigō Takamori and included Etō Shimpei and Maebara Issei, left the government to champion greater decentralization of power, better treatment of the samurai, and overseas expansion. Their resort to rebellion reached a climax in 1877 in the Satsuma Rebellion, which came close to dispossessing the reigning claimants to power. The other group, led by such men as Itagaki Taisuke, Goto Shōjirō, and, later, Okuma Shigenobu, sought greater localization and wider distribution of power through the creation of political parties and parliamentarization of the government. Their activities led to the creation of the political party tradition and the so-called "People's Rights Movement" (Jiyūminken undō) of the 1870s and early 1880s (Masumi 1965:118–369; Beasley 1972:400–404; Tōyama 1951:318–41; Ike 1950:47–59; Bowen 1980:107–15). The challenges to the would-be leaders, thus, were not purely rhetorical.

Under these circumstances, the new leaders were open to the charge, and were forcefully challenged on these grounds, that they had not achieved their positions by any singular selfless virtue but rather by political manipulation and maneuvering. Succession of leadership thus raised the question of authority: What were the rules governing the acquisition and possession of authority, and had the claimant leaders adhered to these rules? Without the establishment of such rules, no group of political leaders could expect consistent and predictable responses to specific acts of authority. The new leaders faced a quandary. They could not claim that the new government they had created represented a natural order of politics. The destruction of the old regime that had governed for 250 years on this basis precluded the use of this criterion of determining the rules for leadership and authority. There could not, after all, be two natural orders of politics. Moreover, the new leaders had based their right to attack the Shōgunate on an appeal to higher moral authority—the will of the emperor. In doing so, they implicitly argued that there was no natural order of politics, only a natural commitment to imperial will that superseded all political, social, and economic arrangements. In effect, all institutional arrangements were ephemeral. Any political arrangement could thus be utilized so long as it represented the imperial will to create a stable, harmonious, and independent social order.

The collapse of the Tokugawa order had opened the question of authority, leadership, and legitimacy in a manner that threatened to bring anarchy. By appealing to imperial will, the putative leaders denied the possibility of a governmental or political leadership based on a natural hierarchy of governing and governed. Their vision implied an emperor before whose awesome majesty there could be no "great" men, only subjects. Given their revolutionary impertinence, the new leaders had no choice but to proclaim an emperor before whom all men were essentially equal. As a consequence of their actions, they were led inevitably to claim that distinctions could no longer be based on birth. They were left with only the standard of ability and willingness to serve the emperor as the basis for differentiating between individuals. This view is summed up very well in the announcement of the Council of State (Dajōkan) on military conscription of 28 December 1872:

The samurai is no longer the samurai of former times and commoners no longer the commoners of the past. All are now equal in the Empire and without distinction in their duty to serve the nation.

The peasant and soldier should be unified to "bring about equality and make the rights of the people uniform" (Hackett 1971:65–66).

These circumstances made it impossible to restrain individuals from challenging both the policies and the authority of those claiming power by a similar appeal to moral authority. Although the new leadership clearly sought to distinguish between social and political equality, their opponents would have none of such fragile and self-serving distinctions: If we are all equal before the emperor, and we have served him loyally, they argued, in effect, then why is it that our voices are not heard? Leadership succession had raised not only the problem of authority and legitimacy but also the problem of equality, especially the problem of political equality.

A second problem created by the succession of leadership, and one intimately related to the question of authority and its predictability, was the lack of consensus as to what constituted the proper aims and goals of the administration and government. By eliminating birth as the criterion for recruitment to office, the homogeneity of leadership and leadership values was destroyed. Between 1868 and 1873, the leaders of the new government were, as we have seen, drawn from a variety of social and educational backgrounds. They included lower, middle, and upper samurai; daimyō; court aristocrats; members of the imperial family; and even a few commoners (Silberman 1964:49–50). Moreover, the samurai, who made up a majority of the new leadership before 1873, were drawn from at least thirty-five different domains, although the largest groups came from Satsuma, Chōshū, Hizen, and Tosa (Silberman 1964:74).

Equally important, there were major differences in education among the new leaders. A large number (29 percent between 1868 and 1873, 64.4 percent between 1874 and 1900) had, in addition to traditional education, acquired some Western knowledge. But neither of these patterns of education were homogenous or consistent. Traditional education had been acquired through a variety of domainal schools of very uneven quality, while Western education had been acquired in a more or less haphazard fashion from a wide variety of schools and circumstances (Silberman 1964:56–62; Silberman 1967). The classic statement of this problem is by Selznick:

Another development problem is that of creating an initial homogenous staff. The members of the core group reflect the basic policies of the organization in their own outlook. They can when matured in this role perform the essential task of indoctrinating newcomers along desired lines. They can provide assurance that decision making will conform, in spirit as well as letter, to policies that may have to be formulated abstractly or vaguely. The development of derivative policies and detailed applications of general rules will thus be guided by a shared experience. (Selznick 1957:105)

It was precisely this problem of leadership homogeneity and the absence of assurance about the uniform implementation of decisions that prevailed in the immediate post-Restoration period.

Nor was the lack of consensus limited to the central bureaucratic leadership. The same problem existed in the relationship between the central and local administrative leadership. In the years immediately following the Restoration, local government remained in the hands of the *daimyō* who were serving as imperial officials. Nevertheless, in the absence of any administrative constraints or redefined roles, they continued to govern as before. Yamagata Aritomo, one of the new leaders, summed it up well in 1871 when he wrote:

In order to realize the aim of the Restoration of the Emperor all orders must come from one source. If all orders are to emanate from one source we must eliminate the *han* (domains). . . . In abolishing the *han* it will be difficult to prevent the opposition of certain ex-*daimyō* and vassals. (Hackett 1971:58–59)

The ambiguity surrounding the goals of the new government, and the means for achieving them, created tensions and conflicts between the two levels of leadership almost immediately. These tensions were reflected in the dissolution of the domains. They were also reflected in the emergence of the *jiyūminken* (People's Rights) movement, whose leadership and support came predominantly from local leaders and notables opposed to the centralizing and monopolizing tendencies of the new central government leaders (Horie and Tōyama 1959: vols. 1 and 4; Bowen 1980; Masumi 1965:I, 118–369). In both of these leadership contexts, the potential for conflict was further exacerbated and, indeed, fulfilled by the capacity of individual officials to claim legitimacy for their acts by solipsistic appeals to the imperial will.

Finally, the new leaders were faced by a society rent by multiple cleavages: local as against central leadership; local economy versus central markets; lower samurai against upper samurai and *daimyō*; peasant against landlord. To overcome these conflicts, the new leadership turned to a conception of the emperor created by anti-Tokugawa ideologists and seized upon by the "men of spirit." This conception had transformed the emperor from the "principle" of politics to the "principal" of politics (Harootunian 1970:15). In the process, the emperor emerged as the prime actor, the source of action in the social order, and as community itself.

However appealing this notion of the emperor as the ongoing and immanent source of community was, it lacked any specificity. For the new leadership, the exalted role of the emperor thus became a two-edged sword. Apotheosized, he became capable of all things and no limits could be placed on his actions—the future was a clean slate on which could be written any form of politics. This was clearly perceived by the new leaders as an advantage. They were not compelled or constrained to conform to any past constitution of state or community. Immediately, however, it became clear that the blank check had all of the defects of its advantages. Having clearly defective claims

to being the sole interpreters of the imperial will meant that a host of competing visions of leadership and community were possible, and they were
quick in coming. The new leaders, if they were to retain their shaky hold on
the government, would have to transform themselves from politicians to imperial administrators whose special capacities in determining the public interest gave them a monopoly of interpreting the imperial will and thus make
them the molders of community.

The Rationalization of Power

Centralization, Strategic Replacement, and the
Emergence of "Emperorism": 1871–89

Very early in the life of the Restoration government, surely no later than the
early months of 1871, it had become apparent to the leaders of the central
government that their positions would remain insecure so long as the local
levels of administration were dominated by the traditional systems of leadership. They had little choice but to seek to integrate the structure of local government into a unified system. Furthermore, they had little choice, as Yamagata noted, but to structure that integration in a highly centralized form
(Hackett 1971:58–59). If they were to eliminate challenges to their authority
and sustain their claim to interpret imperial will, the new leaders had to engage in a systematic replacement of locally based administrative leadership.
This meant not only that local government had to be integrated with the central administration, it meant also that the means for doing so rested on the capacity of the central government to appoint local administrators.

The first major step in this direction came in 1871, when, with some
trepidation, the new leaders agreed to force the dissolution of the domains
and replace them with prefectures (*ken-fu*). On 14 July 1871, an Imperial
Ordinance proclaimed, in a few lines, the dissolution of the system of
autonomous local administration that had existed for over 250 years and replaced it with an imperial system (Yamazaki 1942:30ff.; Oshima 1981:50–
56; *H.Z.* 353, 14 July 1871). The process of dismantling the domains was
carried out quickly. By the end of 1871 the almost three hundred domains
had been reorganized and amalgamated to form seventy-five prefectures. [5]
These were reduced over the next two decades to forty-three prefectures
(*ken*) and three urban or metropolitan prefectures (*fu*).

The changed political situation was reflected in the redefinition of the

---

5. For the process by which this was accomplished, see *Hōrei Zensho* [hereafter referred to in
footnotes as *H.Z.*], Dajōkan Ordinances 566, 13 December 1871; 594, 595, 25 December 1871;
600, 601, 602, 26 December 1871; 608, 609, 31 December 1871; and 614, 2 January 1872.

prefectural structure in 1871 following the abolition of the domains. Under the new regulations, governors were to be appointed directly by the central government, a number of new positions were added, and all positions were assigned generally defined functions. However, prefectural functions and powers continued to be extraordinarily broad, thus providing newly appointed governors wide discretion in performing their duties. For example, the new regulations gave the governor full powers over the setting and collection of taxes, administration of laws and justice, the provision of rewards and punishments, control of trade in the open ports, and the selection, supervision, and promotion of local officials under his jurisdiction. The desire to move slowly in the process of integrating the structure of local government is reflected in the hesitation in defining the source of the governor's authority and his responsibility to the central government. Balanced against this continued ambiguity, however, was the imposition of the central government's authority on the local areas through the transformation of all of the village and district officials into government officials under the direct supervision and appointment of the prefectural government. [6]

Between 1871 and 1878, the process of defining prefectural administration and integrating it fully into the central government moved forward. But it was not until the major challenge to the new leadership and its attempt to monopolize administrative control—the Satsuma Rebellion of 1877—was successfully repressed that the process was basically completed. The Local Administration Ordinance of 1878 completed the metamorphosis of the domain into the prefecture. [7] The governor's functions and his responsibility to the central government were made explicit. The hierarchy of responsibility within the prefectural structure was also defined. The governor's powers were clearly defined and narrowed. The governor's term was specified and the power of removal at the pleasure of the central government was clearly spelled out. The implementation of the ordinance creating the district-city-town-village *(gun-ku-chō-son)* system was also provided by this reorganization. [8] Officials of these administrative units, while they continued to be appointed and supervised by the governor, were now defined as officials of the central, and not the local, government.

The result of the prefectural reorganization of 1878 was to complete, formally, the transformation of the local system of government from a diffuse, semi-autonomous structure to a relatively specialized administrative mecha-

6. *H.Z.*, Dajōkan Ordinance 622, 7 January 1872.

7. *H.Z.*, Dajōkan Ordinance 203, 30 November 1875; Imperial Ordinance 17, 22 July 1878; Imperial Ordinance 32, 25 July 1878.

8. *H.Z.*, Dajōkan Ordinance 17, 22 July 1878.

nism of the central government. The transformation had been carried out by increasingly specifying and defining the roles of local officials and their relationships to each other. By 1878, there was a seamless thread of hierarchy that stretched from the offices of the new leaders down to the smallest village by way of the prefectural governors.

This integration of local administration into the structure of the central government was the basis for the "strategic replacement" that accompanied the transformation. Following the dissolution of the domains, the new gubernatorial appointees were almost entirely (86.2 percent) drawn from the ranks of samurai (Silberman 1970:353). Only about one percent were drawn from the ranks of former *daimyō*. Almost three-quarters (73 percent) of the samurai had participated in the Restoration. Furthermore, about 40 percent of the samurai appointees were drawn from the four domains which had contributed the vast majority of the new leadership in the central government. [9] This evidence leads us to conclude that by 1868 the process of strategic replacement and integration of local administration had been completed. The suppression of the Satsuma Rebellion in 1877 had made it evident that the new government leaders had sufficient force and resources at their disposal to prevent the success of any locally based counterrevolution. The reliance on rules to specify and define the functions of all official roles in local administration made it possible for the new leaders to gain a monopoly over the administration of local power. In this process, the concept and direct challenge of semi-autonomous locally based power was largely put to rest.

Leadership Uncertainty and the Emergence of the Genrō: 1873–81

Faced with the exigencies of maintaining their own and the new government's status, the new leadership had been forced to replace the concept of leadership and authority based on "natural" hereditary relationships with one based on formal rules. The process of rationalization of roles was accompanied by the strategic replacement of personnel at all lower and local levels of administration in order to eliminate challenges to the new leadership. Although this process eliminated a serious immediate challenge, it by no means eradicated all challenges. Two severe tests remained. Both centered on the inability of the new leadership to provide a good reason as to why *they* should govern and not others possessing the same qualifications.

The first of these challenges came from sources external to the new leadership. The inability to provide a public and seemingly nonpolitical source for

9. For a description of the sample and the biographical materials used as the basis for acquiring this data, see Silberman 1970:352–53, fn. 11.

claims to leadership only fueled the growth of politics outside of the government. The rise of the People's Rights Movement and the political parties that emerged from it revealed two things. First, it revealed that the leadership in the central government did not represent an integrated leadership structure. Second, it showed that localism and local networks of leadership as the basis for claiming rights continued to exist and show great strength. Localism was now transmuted into the demand for representation in some form of representative government (Irokawa, Ei, and Arai 1970:159–62; Shōji 1956:188–236; Ike 1950). From the mid-1870s on, the mobilization of local farmers, former samurai, and local merchants, increased in tempo, finally forcing the government to accede, in 1881, to the creation of a constitution.

The second challenge was internal and stemmed equally from the lack of any systematic rules for the selection of leaders and for decision making. This was reflected in the internal leadership conflicts over the Korean Question, which led to the exodus of a number of leaders, followed by the conflict over representation, which led to the exclusion of Ōkuma Shigenobu from the leadership. The conflicts were reflected institutionally in the emergence of the domainal cliques *(hanbatsu)*. These internal conflicts and tensions over the nature of decision making were primarily the result of the dissolution of the traditional norms governing the selection of leaders and of those holding offices. The new leaders were individually and collectively very insecure in their offices. The ambiguities of the leadership structure were also aggravated by the lack of differentiation between bureaucratic administration and government. The inability to distinguish between bureaucratic and governmental decision-makers raised the problem of how to structure accountability and responsibility. It was this problem that left the new leadership open to charges of seeking power for private rather than public purposes.

The response to these challenges was, on an individual level, a series of strategic choices and actions aimed at providing as much security in office-holding as possible. At a collective level, it produced a series of choices, utilizing the individual solutions to the problem of reducing uncertainty over office-holding, to create an informal structure of rules governing leadership and decision making. The primary means by which both individual and collective uncertainty within the new administrative structure was reduced was through the mechanism of the *hanbatsu,* the so-called *han* cliques.

The most significant fact to which these cliques are traceable is that the largest single group of those who had been active in the Restoration were lower and middle samurai from the domains of Satsuma and Chōshū. Consequently, they received the largest number (although by no means a majority) of second- and third-level offices (the equivalent of department and section heads in the later administrative structure) in the new government in the period from 1868 to 1870. In this early period, their relatively low traditional rank appeared to be an inhibiting factor in their holding the highest offices. This was reflected, as we have seen, in the fact that the incumbents of these offices were drawn almost entirely from the court aristocracy, the *daimyō,* and the imperial family. The lower-ranking central and high-ranking local officials from the most active domains were recommended and sustained in office by their compatriots, who held the comparatively high-ranking central offices—the department heads who ran day-to-day affairs and soon came to dominate the policy-making process. The men who held these positions, men like Okubo Toshimichi, Kido Kōin, Saigō Takamori, and Itō Hirobumi, were not secure in their positions. They willingly became the focus of efforts by their lower-ranking domainal compatriots to sustain their positions by seeking ties with superiors (Hasegawa 1966:63–183; Silberman 1967, 1970).

This surely accounts for the fact that by 1873 samurai from Satsuma and Chōshū came to account for 40 percent of all the positions, from department head to vice-minister or their equivalents—with the greatest accretion coming as the consequence of the creation of the prefectural governors in 1871–72. This process of strategic replacement strengthened the positions of both superiors and subordinate officeholders from Satsuma and Chōshū, to the disadvantage of those from the other domains. The increase in Satsuma and Chōshū officeholders, especially at the key prefectural level, provided a broadened base of officials obligated to the Satsuma and Chōshū officials holding high positions in the central government. Through the development of this informal structure of solidarity, the leaders of these groups or factions were able to ensure—far more so than were their nominal aristocratic superiors—implementation of decisions in a more or less homogeneous fashion, thereby revealing themselves as indispensable. This process was, as a result, accompanied by the rapid exit from office of *daimyō,* court aristocrats, and the members of the imperial family. By 1873, this group ceased to be represented in the administrative governmental leadership. In this context, domainal identity came to serve a new function. Given the conditions under which the new leaders operated, they had no other sufficiently cohesive factor to fall back on in order to reduce the uncertainty surrounding their claims to office.

The exclusiveness of the domainal cliques provided assurance that selections for office would be loyal to the new regime and that leadership would have a minimal level of homogeneity of background and outlook. However, it did not provide stability or agreement on how the highest leadership would be selected. Nor did it provide a systematic structure for office-holding for second- and third-level officeholders, such as prefectural governors or ministerial department heads. Although attachment to one or another of the *han* cliques might serve as a basis for office-holding, it provided little in the way of providing any security of office-holding. Individuals might be dismissed at any time and have no redress.

The unsystematic character of office-holding and career structure in this early period is reflected in the wide variation in the lengths of time individuals held office. Thus, for those who held the office of prefectural governor (approximately the rank of a vice-minister) before 1900, the number of offices held prior to appointment as governor looks as shown in table 6.1. The wide variation in the number of offices held before appointment as governor reveals the unsystematic and therefore unpredictable character of office-holding. The same pattern is reflected in the pattern of appointments of those who came to hold the highest civil service positions (department head up to, and including, vice-ministers) between 1875 and 1900 (see table 6.2). The same unsystematic character of career structure is also reflected in the wide variation in the number of ministries served by appointees to the highest offices (see tables 6.3 and 6.4).

The data from tables 6.3 and 6.4, when taken with those on the length of service of gubernatorial appointments, clearly allow us to draw the conclusion that upper civil servants in the pre-1900 era, especially those who entered before the mid-1880s, did not have the comfort of a clearly visible career structure to support them as they considered their future (see table 6.5).

The level of office-holding uncertainty was increased by the inability to use either loyalty or *hanbatsu* membership as the basis for differentiating a

Table 6.1 Number of Offices Held Prior to Appointment of pre-1900 Appointees[10]

No. of Offices	N	%
0	31	38.7
1	10	12.5
2	7	8.7
3	11	13.8
4	9	11.2
5	5	6.3
6	4	5.0
7	1	1.2
8 and over	2	2.4
Totals	80	100.0

10. This data in this table is derived from an analysis of the backgrounds of a simple random sample of eighty (25 percent) prefectural govenors appointed to office between 1868 and 1900. The methods used to select the sample and the sources of information are detailed in Silberman 1970:352–53.

hierarchical structure of leadership. There was no simple or easy way to test levels of loyalty or group commitment. Nor could education or expertise be used to rank-order leaders. In the years immediately following the Restoration, there was not, by any means, complete practical agreement as to what constituted expertise or proper education, as can be seen in table 6.6, which

Table 6.2 Number of Offices Held Prior to Appointment to High Civil Service Offices of 1875–1900 Appointees[11]

No. of Offices	N	%
0–1	8	10.5
1	20	26.3
2	12	15.8
3	12	15.8
4	8	10.5
5	5	6.5
6	7	9.2
7–10	4	5.3
NA		
Totals	76	99.9

Table 6.3 Number of Ministries of Service for Those Holding the Highest Civil Service Positions, 1875–1900

No. of Ministries	N	%
1	1	1.3
2	2	2.6
3	7	9.2
4	10	13.1
5	13	17.1
6	13	17.1
7	12	15.8
8	5	6.6
9	3	4.0
10	1	1.3
11	2	2.6
NA	7	9.2
Totals	76	99.9

11. The data here is based on the analysis of those who entered the civil service prior to 1873 and achieved offices in the highest levels of the civil service. This group amounted to 50 percent of (seventy-six) the total population of those held such offices prior to 1900. The original group was selected on the basis of a simple random sample and would thus seem to be a relatively fair representation of the total population of the highest civil servants in this period (Silberman 1967:87).

Table 6.4 Level of First Appointment to Office of pre-1900 Gubernatorial Appointees

Level of Office by Civil Service Rank	N	%
Lower civil service *hannin* rank	11	14.0
Upper civil service *sōnin* rank, grades 8–6	16	20.0
Upper civil service *sōnin* rank, grades 5–3	17	21.0
Upper civil service *chokunin* rank, grades 2–1	20	25.0
Military service	7	9.0
NA	9	11.0
Totals	80	100.0

Table 6.5 Length of Service as Governor of pre-1900 Appointees

Years of service	N	%	Years of service	N	%
1 or less	13	16.2	11	0	0.0
2	15	18.7	12	2	2.5
3	6	7.5	13	0	0.0
4	5	6.2	14	2	2.5
5	13	16.2	15	2	2.5
6	3	3.8	16	0	0.0
7	2	2.5	17	1	1.2
8	3	3.8	18	1	1.2
9	2	2.5	19	2	2.5
10	1	1.2	20+	7	8.7
Totals				80	100.0

Table 6.6 Type of Education of Upper Civil Servants, 1868–99

	EDUCATION					
	Traditional		Western		NA	
	N	%	N	%	N	%
Sample I (central administration)	23	30.3	46	60.5	7	9.2
Sample II (prefectural governors)	58	72.5	18	22.5	4	5.0
Combined Totals	81	52.0	64	41.0	11	7.0

shows the data on the type of education of upper civil servants between 1868 and 1899.

The existence of at least two strong cliques of officials organized around origin in the domains of Satsuma and Chōshū eliminated the possibility of leadership exercised by a single group in which an informal hierarchy might have eventually been established. In sum, there were no criteria available by which a clearly defined hierarchy of governmental decision-makers could be selected in a systematic, routine manner from within the bureaucracy—that is, there was no systematic criteria for defining or allocating office. Government leaders were equally unwilling to turn to the political parties or to some form of suffrage as the means for selecting government leaders. This produced a situation in which all those who held positions of leadership in the administrative domainal cliques could and did claim possession of the proper credentials for participating in the decision-making process on the basis of equality.

The potential for conflict was limited by the progressive elimination, between 1868 and 1881, of minority views within the leadership. Furthermore, the combination of exclusion and "strategic replacement" at the local and prefectural levels of government resulted in the centralization of decision making in the hands of a relatively few men. Nevertheless, the cliques, and factions within them, continued to be an obstacle to systematic selection of the highest leadership and therefore presented the continuous problem of possible conflict. This was resolved by the more or less happy conjuncture of the centralization of decision making, the formation of domainal cliques in the attempt by the new leaders to reduce the uncertainty surrounding their positions, and the kind of decision-making situation that the new leaders faced in the years following the Restoration.

The type of decision-making situation that persisted after 1868 might be termed "judgmental." That is, there was consensus on goals but not on the means for achieving those goals. Nor was there adequate knowledge of means to achieve the selected goals. Decisions, in this situation, were primarily judgments about what means to utilize or where to go to get sufficient expertise, or both. By 1881, there had emerged, among the leadership of the administration and therefore of the government as well, consensus on the goals that the government ought to pursue. These goals can be briefly described as the pursuit of long-range industrial development as opposed to short-term commercial and agricultural development; long-range development of military strength through technological and organizational development as opposed to military adventurism; elimination of the unequal treaties; and the continued centralization and integration of political power as opposed to expanded participation in decision and policy-making (Masumi

1966:II, 5–55; Hackett 1971:50–89; Iwata 1964:143–206, 225–51; Tōyama 1968:191–231; 1966:425–35).

The rapidity with which consensus on goals was arrived at was made possible in large part by two factors. The first was the integration of local administrative offices into the central administrative structure, which made possible centralized decision- and policy-making. In the process, the number of people involved in making policy and major decisions was greatly reduced. The fewer the decision-makers, the greater the possibility of agreement. The second was that the men now holding positions of power in the new government, especially after 1873, had common social origins, values, and norms, thus radically increasing the possibility of agreement. Centralization and the resort to social networks, while originally the result of strategies to reduce uncertainty of office-holding by the new leaders, produced some of the necessary conditions—small numbers and similarity of background—for the solution of the problem of systematic leadership selection.

It is of great importance that the goals agreed upon required the use of Western models and therefore the use of Western systems of knowledge. The highest ranks of the new civil service were composed of men with varying educational backgrounds. Of those who came to hold higher offices in the new regime by 1873, two-thirds (66.4 percent) had some Western education in addition to traditional Confucian-oriented education, while the remaining one-third had only traditional education. When, after 1871, the prefectural governors are included, the proportions shift to 41 percent with Western knowledge and 52 percent with traditional education only (Silberman 1964:60–61; 1967:87). The lack of uniformity in educational background was exacerbated by the condition that the teaching of traditional or Western knowledge was not uniform or systematic in character. Training in Western knowledge, especially, was acquired in an ad hoc manner and thus was not very profound (Dore 1965; Kokuritsu Kyōiku Kenkyujo 1974: vol. I; Rubinger 1982; Huber 1981). The result of this confusion of education among the new leaders was a lack of consensus on, and absence of, knowledge necessary to achieve the goals on which they did agree.

Under these circumstances, decision making became primarily a question of what means were to be used to achieve specific goals, or where to go to acquire sufficient information to implement decisions, or both. Viewed in this light, decision making, in the absence of expertise, was continually a problem of choosing or judging between various systems and sources of knowledge. Such "judgments" could only be made by "wise and knowing" men. This immediately created the problem of determining the structure of the group and the criteria for inclusion. The emperor was automatically excluded from purposive decision making since birth was not so sufficiently refined a means of selection as to ensure that the throne would always be occupied by intelligence—as indeed history was to provide powerful support for this axiom. Nor, even if by some suspension of nature intelligence in emperors were to be always assured, would it be possible to turn decision making over to him. To allow the emperor to make mistakes would result in the vitiation of the very symbol of legitimation of the new regime and, as we shall see, of the new leaders as well.

Decision making could not be turned over to any other single individual since this would provoke charges of *lèse majesté*. Decision making thus had to be a group arrangement. Eligibility for entry into this group was limited by several factors related to administrative organizational development in the years up to 1880–81. By this time, as we have seen, decision making was already in the hands of the highest ranks of the civil service. Nonbureaucrats had to be excluded since there was no assurance that they would be committed to the goals agreed upon by the new leaders, much less committed to the retention of the government leaders. Eligibility, from the point of view of the new leaders, had to remain limited to those in the highest ranks of the bureaucracy. Furthermore, the group had to be small because of the following: (1) the necessity of arriving at decisions quickly in this critical period; (2) the members of the group had to have sufficient prestige to make their decisions binding on the lower ranks of the civil and military bureaucracy, a factor which automatically limited the number of eligibles; and (3) each putative member saw all the others as threats so long as no well-defined rules governing decision making or office-holding had emerged, and thus they sought to exclude as many claimants as possible. The type of group which emerged was, consequently, a collegial one that became known as the *genro* or "elder statesmen."

The group, as it emerged in the early 1880s, included seven men: Kuroda Kiyotaka (1840–1900), Matsukata Matsuyoshi (1835–1924), Saigō Tsukumichi (1843–1902), Ōyama Iwao (1842–1916), Itō Hirobumi (1841–1909), Inoue Kaoru (1836–1915), and Yamagata Aritomo (1838–1922). Two others, Saionji Kimmochi (1849–1940) and Katsura Tarō (1848–1913), were the only later additions to the group. All of the original seven members of the group held between them, at one time or another, all the major posts in the civil and military bureaucracy and the government (Hackett 1968; Bailey 1965; Oka 1963:I, 254–55). The origins of the group in the bureaucracy made the dividing line between government and administration indistinguishable over the next several decades. The group never had a formal status although each individual was named as an imperial advisor. Despite the informal nature of the structure, its prolonged dominance over the new state reflected the emergence of a set of rules governing the highest levels of decision making and political leadership. These rules might be summed as follows: equality of participation and voting, equal access and sharing of information, and acceptance of a majority decision as binding on all members. From the early 1880s until 1900, the *genrō* acted as the primary day-to-day and long-range decision-making body. In 1900 the original seven members retired from active participation in administration but continued to play the leading role in determining long-range policy and in solving leadership crises in the government and bureaucracy.

An analysis of the backgrounds of the original seven reveal the basis of their prestige and "wisdom." All were among the most active of those from the two most influential domains—Satsuma and Chōshū—involved in the Restoration movement and all had held positions in the new government from the very beginning. Being on the "right" or winning side in the Restoration struggle and committing themselves to the new government very early endowed them with an aura of wisdom and foresight. Their ability to hold off a succession of internal and external challenges and build powerful informal bureaucratic organizations further enhanced their prestige. All seven, furthermore, had acquired, by 1875, a comparatively extensive knowledge of the West or of various categories of Western knowledge, thus enabling them to meet the pressures emanating from overseas. The result was the emergence of a group of decision-makers and leaders who, by 1881 or thereabouts, had created a stable structure of decision making and established the basic criteria for political and bureaucratic leadership. In so doing, they had largely removed the distinctions between bureaucratic and governmental leadership.

While the emergence of the *genrō* resolved the immediate problems of uncertainty for the new leaders, it did little to resolve the long-term problems of uncertainty regarding the questions of authority and legitimacy. There was no way in which the *genrō* could be formalized or given constitutional existence if and when such a document were to appear. To do so would raise once more the question of equality of access to decision making. What criteria could be used to supplant one that would disappear with time (participation in the Restoration) and another that would be so generalized (Western education) as to no longer provide much of a level of exclusiveness. A new Restoration could not be created every twenty-five years as a kind of Darwinist test to determine who were the most successful and competent leaders. Who then would be responsible for choosing successors? Selection by co-optation would have left the members of the *genrō* constantly open to the criticism of dynasticism, of being self-serving, and even of *lèse majesté*. Any other method of selection would have opened the possibility that non-bureaucrats might be appointed—precisely what was to be avoided if uncertainty over office-holding were to be reduced.

In effect, the emergence of the *genrō* underscored the problems of leadership selection, power, and legitimacy. Was the *genrō* an indication that there was no distinction between bureaucratic administrative leadership and government leadership? If no distinction existed, then what was the relationship of the bureaucratic leaders to the emperor? Indeed, given the powers that the new leaders had arrogated to themselves, who and what was the emperor? Did not the self-selection of the new leaders suggest that they were not much different from the other historical mediations between emperor and society—one that isolated the emperor and reduced him to a "principle" rather than "principal" of politics? Moreover, the emergence of the *genrō* only heightened the problems of defining the nature of leadership roles. If the Restoration had been fought in order to bring an end to the private character of leadership and, therefore, the privacy of leadership interests, then what distinguished the new leadership from the old? The ascriptive and exclusive character of the old regime's definition of political leadership made it appear to be a system operating in the private interests of a group. The exclusiveness of the new criteria left the new leaders open to similar charges. This seemed all the more the case since recruitment to positions in the upper civil service (*sōnin* rank and above) continued to be completely in the hands of senior officials (Spaulding 1967:51). The stability of office-holding was dependent on the existence of cliques and their networks of loyalty, which seemed to reflect private interests.

In the same way, the *genrō* were accused of engaging in an equally exclusive definition of leadership. How then could the new leaders' determination to maintain control over decision making be defined as public in character? In short, the existence of the *genrō* raised the questions of what was the relationship between this leadership and society, and how could they be integrated. The new leadership had to provide some answer to the demand that leadership be a function of, and responsible to, the public interest.

7

The Resolution of Revolutionary Uncertainty and the Imperial State

The Construction of Authority and Legitimacy: The Emergence of the Emperor as the State, 1881–89

All of the achievements that the construction of the *genrō* represented would have been in vain if the new leaders had not proceeded to solve the problem of defining the relationships of leadership to community and society. The whole question of leadership authority, power, and legitimacy rested on their capacity to provide such. Unless the *genrō* were to resolve the problem of their accountability and the source of their authority, they remained open to the charge that they were engaged in, if not private politics, factional/domain politics, which amounted to very much the same thing. The *genrō's* solution to this problem was to place the government and themselves into the public realm. That is, they had to create a set of constraints or rules governing leadership recruitment and individual decision making that would seem to ensure that leadership behavior was in the public and not the private interest.

In pursuing this goal, the Meiji leaders had two possible choices. They could establish their public character by acceding to the notion of public sovereignty and its expression in public opinion and public will. Or, they could attempt to establish the publicness of their positions and roles by appeal to a higher transcendent moral order and embody this publicness in an institutional arrangement that would deny any notion of private interest.

The Meiji leaders' opposition to the first choice was vehement. They opposed any idea of submitting themselves to any form of electoral contest since they opposed any form of parliamentary domination of decision making and any form of leadership that derived its legitimacy from public opinion (Akita 1967:58–59; Inada 1960:I, 329–530). As Yamagata, fearing the spread of political parties and their demands for constitutional government, wrote in 1879: "Therefore every day we wait, the evil poison will spread more and more over the provinces, penetrate into the minds of the young, and inevitably produce unfathomable evils" (Ike 1950:93). They were, however, forced by the strength of public demands for some form of constitutional parliamentary government to accede to the idea of a constitution. In 1881, the leaders had an imperial proclamation issued, announcing the intent to establish a constitution in 1890 (Ike 1950:87–110, 148–68; Masumi

191

1966:II, 5–55). The drafting of the constitution was placed in the hands of one of the emergent *genrō*, Itō Hirobumi. While the new political parties saw this action as at least a partial victory over the new leadership, they, in turn, saw it as a means of defining the authority and legitimacy of bureaucratic leadership as nonpolitical in character. Thus, Inoue Kaoru, another member of the *genrō*, wrote to Itō pressing him to adopt a Prussian-style constitution:

To put into effect a Prussian-style constitution is an extremely difficult task under existing conditions, but at the present time it is possible to carry it out and win over the majority and thus succeed. This is because the English-style constitution has not become firmly fixed in the minds of the people. Among the samurai in the countryside more than one-half, no doubt, have a lingering desire to uphold the Imperial House. But if we lose this opportunity and vacillate, within two or three years, the people will become confident that they can succeed, and no matter how much oratory we may use, it will be difficult to win them back. Most of the political parties will be on the other side rather than ours. Public opinion will cast aside the draft of a constitution presented by the government, and the private drafts of the constitution will win out in the end. (quoted in Ike 1950:171–72)

The constitution was seen as the means by which the emperor could be defined in his relationship to government and society. At the same time, it would provide the means for securing and defining the relationship between the civil and military bureaucracy and the emperor (Akita 1967:58–66). Finally, there was little question in the minds of the leaders that the constitution was the means to delimit the role of public opinion in such a way so as to subvert any conception that it was synonymous with the public interest.

The Meiji leaders were equally well aware that they could not formalize the *genrō* structure in the constitution. Failure to do so, however, opened the door of uncertainty once again. The charge of pursuing private as against public interests would emerge with new vigor so long as the institution persisted in its informal character. The central problem for the leadership was to define bureaucratic leadership as the means for determining and carrying out the public interest. It was all very well for them to deny charges of private interest, in the words of the *genrō* appointee Kabayama Sukenori:

Who would accuse us of defiling the national honor? . . . The present government is the government which has succeeded in overcoming all external and internal difficulties the nation has confronted. Call it the Sat-Chō government [Satsuma-Chōshū clique government], or designate it by whatever name you wish; but who would deny its achievement in maintaining the security and well-being of 40,000,000 souls. (as quoted in Akita 1967:59)

Such denials were not enough. Nor could they wrap themselves in the emperor's cloak, since it was not altogether clear that this was sufficient to establish the publicness of their intentions.

In the early 1880s, the transcendent position of the emperor was by no means assured (Osatake 1939:II, 595–603). The public character of the emperor had not been well established in the decade since the Restoration. The task for the new leadership then was to link the emperor, the bureaucratic leadership, and the public interest in a seamless web that would exclude the political parties as the representatives of the public interest and brand political equality as the tool of selfish private interest. As Itō was to say in a famous speech in 1888, the emperor was the "axis of the nation" without which "the state will eventually collapse when politics are entrusted to the reckless discussions of the people" (Pittau 1967:177–78).

In 1881 this task of linking emperor, bureaucracy, and public interest was conceived as having several distinct parts. The first order of business was to establish the publicness of the emperor. This was to be followed by establishing the publicness of the imperial administration. Finally, these elements of publicness had to be made synonymous with the public interest so that the imperial institution could be integrated into social life. More specifically, this meant the construction of a formal legal structure of the state. Such a structure would, from the *genro's* point of view, necessarily include a legal definition of the relationships of emperor to state and society, administration to the bureaucracy, and the individual to the state. This kind of definition would establish, as incontrovertible, that the integrated nature of state and society rested on the public character of the emperor—"the axis of the nation." Beyond this, it was necessary that the leadership establish that the public character of the bureaucracy was not derived solely from the appeal to higher authority—the emperor. Rather, it had to show that the bureaucracy and, therefore, its leadership partially derived its public character from its autonomous capacity to determine and represent the public interest. Finally, the leadership had to show that the bureaucracy was public and representative in the sense that the rules of exclusiveness were not derived from class or status membership but from individual qualities.

With the Imperial Rescript of 1881 promising the promulgation of a constitution and the creation of a national assembly by 1890, the strategy of creating an integrated set of public institutions based on the emperor got under way. Itō Hirobumi, who had been entrusted with the task of creating the constitution, went off to Europe to go constitution hunting. His glance at the English and American systems was cursory as befitted a man who had been furious with Ōkuma Shigenobu for even suggesting that ministers be responsible to the parliament (Akita 1967:36). The speed with which Itō arrived in Germany, followed by a year-long stay listening to lectures from

Rudolf von Gneist and Laurenz von Stein on constitutional and state theory, reveals the degree to which the Meiji leaders were committed to something less than full parliamentary government (Pittau 1967:131–57; Inada 1960:I, 565–97). As Itō reported on his lessons from Berlin in August 1882:

The present situation of our country seems to be such that the writings of the radical liberalists of England, America, and France are mistaken as the golden rule to such an extent as to bring our country to ruin, but I have gained the principles and the means with which to save the situation, and I am inwardly quite prepared to die for my convictions. . . .

From what I see of the present situation of European countries, monarchical powers are gradually restricted and their governments have come to assume something like the posture of a servant towards the national assembly, so they have almost lost the actual power of rule. If this be true, they will never be in a position to develop national prestige and guarantee the people's happiness. Therefore, we propose to establish a constitutional monarchy with complete monarchic authority, and stabilize the legislative and administrative organizations so that the two work in parallel and smoothly. . . . Political scholars in Europe have argued that sovereign status is placed above the constitution; there can be no question, in the case of our Imperial Household. (Centre 1972:118–21)

While Itō was learning the rhetoric of positivist imperial law and power, his colleagues at home had taken up the task of elevating the emperor. Between 1871, and the rescript on establishing the constitution of 1881, the new leadership had industriously trotted out the emperor to be seen by the populace—something entirely novel (Titus 1974:48–49). The aim was to popularize a figure of whom Japanese were only vaguely aware of and to whom they had relatively little commitment in order to demonstrate in the flesh the replacement of the old regime by direct imperial rule. In supporting the imperial travels of 1878, Inoue Kaoru argued that:

the emperor's visiting all parts of Japan not only informs the people of the emperor's great virtue but also offers the opportunity of displaying direct imperial rule in the flesh, thus dispelling misgivings regarding monarchical government. (quoted in Gluck 1985:75)

After 1881 the emperor's outings were drastically curtailed. Between 1871 and 1881, there was an average of over ninety imperial tours a year; but from 1882 to 1888, the average dropped to about sixty-seven per year; and from 1890 to 1900, the average dropped to about seventeen per year (Titus 1974:48–49). The reduction in exposure coincided with the attempts of the leadership to construct a legal conception of sovereignty that would once again elevate the emperor "above the clouds."

As they restricted his appearances, the leadership began the process of constructing the emperor as a sovereign who was both ideologically and legally the ultimate source of authority and, at the same time, the embodiment of the national interest. Itō was off learning the language of imperial sovereignty, which would be embodied in the constitution. His colleagues at home, especially Yamagata, now began the production of the imperial sovereign whose will had no natural obstacles, who ruled directly. This was reflected in a line of Imperial Rescripts that were not merely moral invocations but legal prescripts, shaping the social world of the Japanese subject. They were clearly directed at establishing the validity of social, but not political, equality. The first of these was the Soldier's and Sailor's Rescript promulgated on 4 January 1882. The rescript begins with a description of the manner in which the original emperors ruled the military forces directly and how this imperial authority was corrupted in the Middle Ages by the adoption of Chinese forms of administration. The collapse of the Tokugawa usurpers led to the restoration of direct imperial rule.

Now the supreme command of Our forces is in Our hands, and although We may intrust subordinate commands to our subjects, yet the ultimate authority We Ourself shall hold and never delegate to any subject. It is Our will that this principle be carefully handed down to posterity and that the Emperor always retain the supreme civil and military power, so that the disgrace of the Middle and succeeding Ages may never be repeated. Soldiers and Sailors, We are your supreme commander-in-chief. (Centre 1972:237)

The remainder of the rescript described the moral precepts by which soldiers and sailors were to be guided: loyalty, discipline, valor, faithfulness and righteousness, and simplicity (Centre 1972:237–41).

The rescript thus joined the definition of the emperor as the source of authority with what appeared to be the natural essence and right of the sovereign to prescribe the correct moral behavior. These precepts held true for all ranks regardless of social origin. The emperor's power and will held true without regard to social origin. The rescript thus removed all feudal restraints on the imperial will. No act could more plainly set forth the limits placed on any attempts by political parties to carry forward the idea of parliamentary authority over the civil and military administrations. These administrations were, here, legally designated to be within the realm of imperial authority and not subject to any structure of representation.

Equally important, the rescript sought to establish the emperor as the appropriate source of moral social behavior. In this aspect, the emperor was seen as the incarnation of the public interest. Not yet divine, as he was to be shortly, he was nevertheless made the true arbiter of the public interest by virtue of his "unbroken" descent from the first emperor. The rescript was thus a major step in reducing the potential power of the political parties and in isolating them by undermining their claim to represent the public interest. Stripped of any moral claims that might be made on the basis of representing public opinion, political parties were being reduced to crass representations of private interest.

The process of weaving a seamless web of imperial authority and public interest which would isolate the parties while legitimizing the new leadership continued unabated throughout the 1880s. Itō returned from Europe in 1883 carrying with him as part of his baggage the rhetoric of constitutional imperial sovereignty learned at the feet of his Prussian tutors. He immediately set to work creating the structural underpinnings of a regime that centered on an emperor elevated above the political issues and insulated from public partisan politics. As head of the Bureau for the Investigation of Administrative Reforms, which he had created in 1884 while he was also head of the Imperial Household Ministry, Itō was responsible for the constitution of a new peerage. In July 1884, a new peerage was created which would stand against the parties as a competing form of representation of public interest (Inada 1960:I, 691–92). The peerage was seen, so to speak, both as a monarchical constituency and as the reflection of the emergence of the emperor as the fount of public honor and status.

The completion of the strategy to make the emperor synonymous with an immanent and transcendent public interest came with two events: the promulgation of the constitution in 1889, which Itō was largely responsible for formulating, and the Imperial Rescript on Education of 1890, which Yamagata was largely responsible for bringing into being. The first of these, the Meiji Constitution, was conceived of as a gift of an emperor who was successfully apotheosized by the document. The constitution implicitly recognized the divinity of the emperor by proclaiming that his sovereignty emanated from the "lineal succession unbroken for ages eternal" (Fujii 1965:297). It explicitly defined him as divine by virtue of Article III: "The Emperor is sacred and inviolable." His divinity was thus both historical and immanent. Such a definition allowed Itō to formulate a description of the monarch that had no precedent in the lectures he received from Gneist and Stein: "The Emperor stands at the head of the Empire, combining in Himself the rights of sovereignty and their exercise according to the provisions of the present Constitution" (Article IV). In this definition the emperor was, in fact, the state. The powers formally accorded to him gave substance to this prescription: his was the sole power of initiating amendments (Article LXXIII), he had complete powers of administration (Article X), he was the supreme commander of the Army and Navy and determined their organization and disposition (Articles XI, XII), the emperor made war, peace, and concluded treaties (XIII), he had expansive legislative powers (Articles V, VI, VIII, and IX), which left the newly created Imperial Diet with few powers of legislation or legislative initiative (XXXVII, XXXVIII, XXXIX, XL), he was the fount of honor (Article XV) and the bestower of mercy (Article XVI). So vast were his powers that divinity was a necessary corollary to their possession and dispensation.

In bestowing these powers on the emperor, the Meiji leaders ensured for themselves and their civil bureaucratic colleagues the isolation of the political parties from effective control over policy-making and administration. These were in the hands of the emperor and his administrators, who were legally his servants. The constitution was the culmination of the rationalization of imperial sovereignty and power. On the one hand, it rendered the emperor divine, while on the other, it carefully delineated the powers which made him synonymous with the public interest and, indeed, defined him as encompassing the public. His will was expressed through his servants—the civil and military bureaucrats whose selection and careers had come to be organized in such a manner as to reflect an equality and publicness which provided high and persisting walls against outside interference.

The Rescript on Education followed swiftly on the promulgation of the constitution. It had less to do with education as such as it had to do with establishing the emperor as the source of moral authority and the educational system as the means of its extension. In general, the constitution was constructed to reveal the will of the emperor as providing for a structure by which the public interest would be achieved by servants trained to mediate between the imperial will and specific policies. The Rescript on Education was specifically constructed to reveal the will of the emperor as providing for a structure by which the ordinary citizen could learn to rise above his or her personal interest and sustain the public interest.

Concerned over the elections to the first Diet of 1890, the prefectural governors at their conference in Tokyo, in February 1890, made education their primary concern. They submitted their Memorial on the Cultivation of Moral Education to Yamagata, then to both the Prime Minister and the Home Minister. Worried that the new parliamentary elections would reinforce the commitment to political parties, the memorial complained that as a result of an overemphasis on knowledge and skills and "a complete lack of attention to moral education":

. . . pupils are proud of whatever small skills they gain in theory and mathematics. . . . Those who graduate from upper elementary school forsake their ancestral occupations and wish to become officials or politicians. If they continue further to middle school, even before they have graduated they begin to discuss political affairs . . . At the worst, they leave school and take up political activities. Although teacher training is in part to blame, so, too, is the educational system. As this situation continues, youth will not value enterprise and will resort instead to lofty opinion. With immature learning and knowledge, they pursue fortune and scorn their elders, thus bringing the social order into confusion and endangering the nation. (as quoted in Gluck 1985:117)

Yamagata and the Meiji leaders were of like mind about the need to establish the emperor as the source of moral authority and to establish social morality as a consequence of the direct relationship between emperor and subject. Out of this emerged the rescript of 30 October 1890, which enjoined:

. . . Ye our subjects, be filial to your parents, affectionate to your brothers and sisters; as husbands and wives be harmonious, as friends true; bear yourselves in modesty and moderation; extend your benevolence to all: pursue learning and cultivate arts, and thereby develop intellectual faculties and perfect moral powers; furthermore advance public good and promote common interests; always respect the Constitution and observe the laws; should emergency arise, offer yourselves courageously to the state and thus guard and maintain the prosperity of Our Imperial Throne coeval with heaven and earth . . .

The Way here set forth is indeed the teaching bequeathed by Our Imperial Ancestors, to be observed alike by Their Descendants and subjects, infallible for all ages and true in all places. (as quoted in Gluck 1985:121)

The rescript established the emperor as the source of moral authority, but, equally important, reinforced the understanding, already inherent in the early rescripts and in the constitution, that the emperor was the only *natural* institution and that all other institutions existed as a function of his will, mediated by his civil and military servants.

The promulgation of the constitution and the Rescript on Education produced an emperor who was unassailable. By 1890, the Meiji leaders had defined the institutional structure of imperial will in such a way as to reduce phenomenally the insecurity that had beset their places only a decade earlier. Now, all that remained was to create an institutional role that reflected the publicness which emanated from the imperial will.

The Rationalization of the State Bureaucracy, 1881–1900

The challenges to the new leadership's claim to govern by the People's Rights Movement of the 1870s, and the parties emerging from such, had, in 1881, produced a promise of a constitution. However, it also tended to concentrate the attentions of the leadership wonderfully on the attempt to construct a system of authority and power that would isolate the parties. More to the point, the system the Meiji leaders sought to construct was one which would also legitimize their control of state authority and power. By 1881, the leadership had traveled a considerable distance in this direction. They had managed to stabilize their control of the central government, to integrate local administration and power into the central governmental structure, to integrate the old elites, to establish social equality, and to establish the emperor as a presence and source of direct rule.

However, the Meiji leaders were not out of the woods yet. Their elimination of Ōkuma Shigenobu from the oligarchy in 1881 revealed just how far they still had to go before they were secure. Ōkuma's expulsion only confirmed to many that the oligarchs were pursuing their own parochial interests (Masumi 1966:II, 5–20). Ōkuma and the political party, the Kaishintō, which he had created upon his expulsion from the oligarchy, joined the opposition and reinforced their position against the seemingly personal rule of the oligarchs. The continued domination of high- and middle-level administrative appointments on the basis of personal networks, which emphasized traditional samurai rank and domain origin, provided the opposition with more and quite usable ammunition (Suzuki 1948:374–404). Several major incidents of rebellion and violence in the years between 1882 and 1885 centering on political opposition to the oligarchs by local organizations of political parties show clearly that the oligarchs had not yet resolved the problems of legitimacy and authority that surrounded their claims to leadership (Bowen 1980:8–69).

Concurrently, Ōkuma's expulsion had clarified and defined more clearly the nature of the oligarchic leadership. From this point forward, membership in the leadership was to remain quite stable until the end of the century, and the rules for decision making within the group now emerged to provide for consistent patterns of decision making. This stabilization had, however, serious defects. The rationalization of the informal structure of political leadership did not provide any basis for its legitimacy—that is, the leadership had to continue to rely on the informal structures of cliques or factions to provide any semblance of predictability about the enforcement of rules and decisions. While this strengthened each member's claim to participate in the leadership group, it also proclaimed just what the opposition continued to hammer away at; government by the Meiji leaders was government by parochial and private interest.

The nature of the dilemma and its unsolvable character is plainly revealed in the manner in which the emperor was made to be the chief decision-maker in the Constitution of 1889. As wonderful an instrument of imperial sovereignty as the constitution turned out to be, it did not solve one major problem—the ultimate *exercise* of decision making, especially in relation to the appointment of the decision-makers. The constitution merely provided that the emperor "determines the organization of the different branches of the admini-stration . . . and appoints and dismisses the same" (Article X). This seemed to force the issue of cabinet appointment on the emperor directly and with no mediating element (Minobe 1928:170–71). In fact, however, the constitution made it impossible for the emperor to engage directly in political acts. What the constitution gave, it also took away. It required that the ministers advise the emperor and accept the responsibility for the consequences of their advice (Ar-ticle LV, para. 1) and that "[A]ll laws, Imperial Ordinances and Imperial Re-scripts of whatever kind, that relate to the affairs of the State, require the coun-tersignature of a Minister of State" (Article LV, para. 2). By these restrictions, the emperor was not free to choose anyone he wished to assume ministerial or administrative office. The constitution thus left a significant gap in the formal structure of leadership succession and decision making.

This was not an accidental lapse of attention or rationality. The Meiji po-litical leaders had been faced with a dilemma. To specify a mediating deci-sion-making structure which could select a cabinet on some systematic for-mal principle would have threatened the continued existence of the emergent *genrō* structure of leadership and decision making. Any external source for such selection, such as parliamentary or direct elections, would give parties far more power than the Meiji leaders were willing to risk. Only imperial selection, which could then be delegated to the *genrō* or the "senior advisors," could assure the leaders of their role in decision making and de-termining leadership. In the short run, this unwillingness to subject their leadership to any externally determined test left the emergent *genrō* structure with only one solution; total imperial sovereignty, which would then be delegated to the imperial advisors. This gave the leadership such vast powers that they had no choice but to invent an emperor who *was* the state and en-compassed the public realm, not just a monarch or an instrument who wielded the sovereignty on behalf of the state and merely *represented* the pub-lic realm. The former conception would allow the leadership to persist, ac-countable only to an emperor whose instrumental powers were limited.

The Creation of the Cabinet Structure: 1881–85

This position required the Meiji leaders to work out the solution to two im-mediate problems in the period before the promulgation of the constitution if they wished to reduce the uncertainty surrounding their positions and their claims to leadership. The first was that the decision-making structure which made the political leaders accountable only to the emperor had to be regularized and rationalized. The second was that the problem of leadership selection and succession had to be transformed from what appeared to be a private, factional, and parochial structure into what would appear to be a public, integrated, and universal one. The first problem centered on the rationalization of administrative structure, while the second centered on the rationalization of the bureaucratic role.

The structural problem involved two tactics. First, the emperor had to be elevated to the ultimate source of decision-making authority. This had the virtue of helping to advance the strategy of making the emperor synonymous with the public and thus the source of the public interest. The first step in this direction was, as we have seen, the Soldier's and Sailor's Rescript of 1882. The rescript had not only implied the emperor's divinity, it also established or "confirmed" the emperor's role as the direct authority over the civil and military orders. This was followed by the reorganization of the central administrative structure with the elimination of the Dajokan system and its replacement by a Western-style cabinet system on 22 December 1885 (*H.Z.,* Imperial Ordinance 69, 22 December 1885).

The creation of the cabinet system had significant advantages for the leadership in stabilizing its relationship to decision-making authority and its capacity to secure domination over the decision making. The Dajōkan (Council of State) system had been a somewhat cumbersome apparatus. In theory, it provided that advice and access to the emperor be limited to three people—the Chief Councilor *(dajōdaijin)*, the Minister of the Left *(sadaijin),* and the Minister of the Right *(udaijin).* The other members of the council assisted them and participated in deliberations only when requested. The ministers of the various executive departments were not members of the Council and could not formally participate in its deliberations. Furthermore, they were under the direct jurisdiction of the Council and they were at the disposal of the instructions of the Council. All reports to the Throne had to be channelled through the Council and then through the three primary councilors responsible for presenting advice to the emperor (Suzuki 1944:57–80). The arrangement had caused no end of problems, since it meant that the advice of executive ministers might be ignored or that outsiders or members of the imperial household might have access to the emperor through the Council of State.

The Meiji leaders wanted to rationalize the structure so that the ministers of the executive departments would be synonymous with a council of state (cabinet). Under such an arrangement, they could eliminate all other access to imperial authority. As the memorial to the throne explained:

This system, although suited as a temporary expedient to the exigencies of the time, is opposed to the principle of personal government by Your Majesty; it has tended moreover to lessen unduly the responsibilities of the ministers of the departments, and has caused obstruction in the public business . . . With this end in view it appears desirable to Your servant that the system under which the Council of State exercises direct control over the various public departments should be revised; that the various functions of the Council of State be abolished; that the cabinet should be made a supreme council of ministers with authority to communicate directly with Your Majesty. . . . It appears desirable, moreover, that one of these ministers should be specially selected to receive and promulgate Your Majesty's commands. (McLaren 1914:91–92)

The cabinet system brought the *genrō* to complete control of decision making through their domination of the ministerial offices and their ability to appoint all senior officials. The selection of the prime minister was a function of *genrō* advice. The collegial nature of the informal structure of decision making was reflected in the absence of cabinet responsibility. Each minister was, in theory, responsible to the emperor and not to the cabinet or its first minister. Cabinet reorganization made the *genrō* into a self-selecting and self-regulating structure of decision making without any formal recognition of the exclusivity that marked the group. The constitution was to do nothing more than to confirm this arrangement by reiterating the relationship of the emperor to his cabinet and administration.

The Civil Service Examination System: 1881–94

The resolution to the problem of legitimacy and equality—the problem of bureaucratic role appearing to be a function of private interest and privilege—was achieved by rationalizing the process of recruitment and appointment. The rationalization process centered on the development of two aspects: education and examination as tests of capacity and the delineation of lower and upper civil service roles. Prior to the early 1880s, appointment to the upper ranks of the civil service was still largely a function of patronage. Nor was there any distinction made between entry levels. People appointed as *hannin* (lowest rank of administrative office) officials faced no legal obstacle to being promoted to the next rank, *sōnin;* and in theory they could then reach the very senior level, *chokunin.* Basic literacy examinations, it is true, had been introduced at the lowest ranks *(hannin)* in some ministries quite early (Spaulding 1967:51); but the upper ranks were left free, primarily as a consequence of the new leadership's attempts to ensure their own positions by creating patronage constituencies.

There were three distinct sources of uncertainty for the leaders of the new government in the early 1880s: (1) the challenges of parochial interest presented by the People's Rights Movement and the political parties; (2) the uncertainty about the basis for further leadership recruitment; and (3) fears on the part of second- and third-level leaders and new entrants over the future engendered by the absence of any systematic career. The congruence of these three forces now led the Meiji leaders to directly confront the issue. In 1884, the Administrative Reform Investigation Office *(Seido Torishirabe Kyoku)*, under Itō's supervision, produced the first two steps in the direction of resolving these problems. One of these was development of plans for systematic examinations designed specifically for upper civil servants in the judiciary (Spaulding 1967:53–56). Such examinations would help resolve the problem of extraterritoriality by producing judges trained and examined in Western jurisprudence. At the same time, the examinations would provide a response to the parties on the question of patronage and the pursuit of clique and private interest. Regulations for the recruitment and appointment of judges were promulgated on 26 December 1884 (*H.Z.*, Dajōkan Notice *[tasshi]* 102). Judges (*sōnin* rank) could be recruited from past or present judicial officials with five years service and those who had passed the bar or passed the new judicial examinations. One year of in-service training was required. Perhaps most significant was the provision that graduates of Tokyo University (Imperial University, 1886–97; Tokyo Imperial University, 1897–1947; Tokyo University 1947–present) were exempt from the examinations.

The second step taken by Itō's committee was the creation of a pension plan. This was aimed at calming fears about the future, especially for new entrants. Incentives for the latter were important as the supply of former samurai who could be relied on by those in the upper reaches of the central government now steadily diminished with the passage of time. Early in 1884, the first systemwide pension arrangements came into existence. [1] The system was to remain the basic one until the end of World War II. It provided for full retirement at the age of sixty, with at least fifteen years service. Ministers of state or their equivalents were eligible after two years service at that rank. The basic pension benefits provided one-fourth of the annual salary at time of retirement and an increment of only 1/240 for each additional year after the first fifteen, up to thirty-five years. The highest total pension one might get was, thus, one-third of the annual salary. The system was revised only slightly in 1890 to allow full eligibility for pensions after fifteen years service, without requiring that any particular retirement age be reached. [2] The main purpose here was to allow full eligibility for those whose movement through the system was relatively rapid. This arrangement allowed for relatively high succession rates for senior civil

1. This was embodied in *H.Z.*, Imperial Ordinance 1, 4 January 1884. Some provision for retirement had been made as early as 1878. It was not, however, systemwide. It applied only to prefectural governors and did not provide for systematic benefits.

2. The revisions were embodied in *H.Z.*, Law 43, 20 June 1890. The law was revised again in 1923, primarily to increase benefits to one-third of annual salary plus 1/150 for each year after fifteen up to forty years. The highest pension thus became equal to one-half of the annual salary (*H.Z.*, Law 48, 13 April 1923).

servants, which, in turn, provided a steady flow of openings to provide incentives for individuals to commit themselves to the bureaucratic career. By 1884, then, the first steps toward the creation of a career structure had been taken.

These regulations were followed in 1887 by the establishment of a system of requirements and/or examinations clearly distinguishing entry into the upper civil service.[3] Itō's concern about the lack of uniformity within the administration and the challenges from the parties is reflected in his "Instructions Addressed to the Governors of Cities and Prefectures," 28 September 1887:

Administrative affairs ought to advance hand in hand with the march of social improvement. Since the Restoration the condition of society has been greatly changed with the downfall of the feudal system and the mode of living has assumed an entirely new character and is now in a career of striking progress. Now in this transition from the old to the new order of things, we inevitably find many forces in a stationary and unprogressive state, while other elements and antagonistic tendencies may be found perpetually in conflict with each other, thereby preventing a harmonization of social life. . . . Under these circumstances those engaged in the work of administration ought to make stability and permanence their object . . . were the scheme of administration planned during the last twenty years to be left to take care of itself, what would become of the future of the nation? (McLaren 1914:324–30)

The new regulations provided for entry directly into the upper civil service at *sōnin*-level positions based on a range of educational and service criteria. The most significant of these was the establishment of a higher examination composed of a written and an oral section. Success in this examination allowed appointment as *sōnin* officials to those who had passed the bar examinations and served three years as an attorney, former *sōnin* officials with five years service, male graduates of higher schools or foreign universities and some special higher schools (plus three years in-service training), and male graduates of approved private law schools (plus three years in-service training). Professors (plus three years experience in office) and graduates of Tokyo University and Tokyo and Sapporo Agricultural Schools (plus three years in-service training) and former judicial and Justice Ministry *sōnin* officials with four years service were exempt from the exam.

The exemption rules for Tokyo graduates soon produced a situation in which there were very high incentives for Tokyo graduates to enter the civil service. Not only did they not have to take the examination, but they could be

3. *H.Z.*, Imperial Ordinances 37, 38, 23 July 1887; *H.Z.*, Cabinet Ordinance 20, 23 July 1887; *H.Z.*, Imperial Ordinances 57, 58, 5 November 1887; *H.Z.*, Cabinet Ordinance 25, 21 December 1887; *H.Z.*, Imperial Ordinances 63, 64, 24 December 1887; *H.Z.*, Cabinet Ordinance 28, 28 December 1887.

readily assured of appointment to the upper civil service. The new regulations had provided the means for by-passing the examinations for those who came to hold Tokyo University degrees. This produced not only an increased demand for entry into Tokyo University and more graduates, but it also created protests from graduates of the private approved law schools whose candidates consistently failed the examinations. The pressure for finding offices for Tokyo graduates soon produced more applicants for offices than there were offices (Spaulding 1967:93–98). The alternatives were few: eliminate the exams and rely completely on Tokyo graduates; return to patronage; remove the exemption for Tokyo graduates. At the head of the government, Itō finally decided that the latter was the only course that would resolve the demands for equality of treatment while at the same provide the government with some gatekeeping mechanism over the numbers of Tokyo graduates for whom they had to find offices.

The result of these developments was the revision of the upper civil service examination system in 1893–94, which served as the basic structure of recruitment and appointment over the next fifty years. [4] The revised structure was not strikingly different from the 1887 system, with several important exceptions—one being that Tokyo graduates were no longer exempted from examinations except in the judicial exams. The new regulations, however, did create a set of preliminary examinations from which Tokyo graduates were exempt. Tokyo graduates thus retained a considerable degree of exclusiveness in the examination system. In-service training was, for the most part, eliminated from administrative appointment and there ceased to be any significant number of appointments without salary (probationer appointments). This significantly increased the incentives to seek appointment. Finally, the creation of a diplomatic examination provided a career-track entry into the diplomatic service.

The Examination System and Career Commitment: 1886–94

The 1894 reorganization firmly established the distinction between the lower and upper civil service as career entry points. The revision also created a diplomatic track in addition to the administrative and judicial ones. While the regulations did not formally require any level of education to enter the upper civil service, the nature of the exams made it more than self-evident that a university education in law was a prerequisite for entry into any of the three career tracks. Between 1894 and 1928, the administrative exam in-

4. The revisions are encompassed by the following regulations: *H.Z.,* Imperial Ordinances 126, 183, 187, 197, 31 October 1893; Imperial Ordinance 54, 24 May 1894; Cabinet Ordinance 2, 7 May 1894; Foreign Ministry Ordinance 7, 22 June 1894.

cluded the following subjects: constitutional, administrative, criminal, civil, and international law; economics; and one elective chosen from criminal or civil procedure, commercial law, and finance. In 1928, international law and criminal law were made electives, but the exams remained very heavily based on legal and constitutional education (Spaulding 1967:210–11). Much the same was true for the diplomatic exams, which expanded electives into a few areas of the social sciences after the turn of the century. Basically, however, an advanced legal education was needed for passing the higher civil service examinations.

The new preliminary examinations also did not require a formal level of education. Nevertheless, their contents were such that it would have been extraordinarily difficult to pass them without having passed through a higher school education *(kotogakko)*. The preliminary exam consisted of a home composition written within a specified period of time, a supervised composition written within a few hours, and an oral examination, which was replaced in 1906 with an examination in a foreign language (English, French, or German). After 1909, the home composition was eliminated, leaving the foreign-language examination (Spaulding 1967:197–98).

With the 1894 examination regulations, the path to a bureaucratic career became relatively well defined, well known and, within a very few years, highly predictable. Bureaucratic recruitment at the senior level now came to require not only a university education in law, but also, as a prerequisite to university entrance, a higher school education as well. This was true despite the fact that Tokyo Imperial University graduates were exempt from the preliminary examinations. Entrance into Tokyo and, later, other imperial universities was dependent on passing an examination that required higher school education. The exclusiveness of these criteria was intensified by the Meiji leaders. They sought to create an eligibility pool for administrative office that was very homogenous in character and that excluded as much as possible those trained in private universities where faculty selection was outside of government regulation. Thus, the exams were based on the level of difficulty of Tokyo Imperial legal training, and the answers had to fall within the interpretations and readings provided by Tokyo Imperial professors. This is clearly mirrored in several significant facts concerning the carrying out of the exams over the next four or five decades.

First was the degree to which the Higher Civil Service Examination Committee was dominated by either graduates or professors of Tokyo Imperial University Law Faculty. This was, in part, a function of the carefully designed law which limited appointments to the committee to upper civil servants (Spaulding 1967:237). This allowed examiners to be chosen from the imperial universities since faculty members were legally senior civil servants.

Since, as will shortly be evident, a vast majority of senior civil servants were recruited from Tokyo Imperial, the examining committees were heavily biased in favor of the training received at Tokyo Imperial. These patterns of examiner recruitment are reflected in tables 7.1 and 7.2.

The dominance of Tokyo Imperial University as a source for examiners is also mirrored in the dominance of its students among those passing the examinations (see table 7.3). The degree to which Tokyo graduates came to dominate the upper civil service after 1900 is suggested by their dominance among those who came to hold appointments as prefectural governors between 1900 and 1945 (see table 7.4). Again, in 1949 when nearly the entire upper civil service had been recruited during the 1930s, data collected by

Table 7.1 Recruitment of Administrative Examiners, 1894–1941

Status at time of Appointment	1894–1905	1906–1917	1918–1928	1929–1941
Professors				
Tokyo Imperial University	46.0	66.0	44.6	41.2
Kyoto Imperial University	3.7	19.1	22.8	24.9
Other Public Colleges	2.1	4.1	2.2	14.8
Other Universities	0.0	0.0	0.0	8.0
Serving Officials	48.2	10.8	30.4	11.1
Total	100.0	100.0	100.0	100.0
N	189	194	224	687

Source: Modified from Spaulding 1967, 249.

Table 7.2 University Training of Higher Examiners
(in percentage of total number of appointments to committees)

	Judicial		Administrative			
Education	1893–1907	1908–1922	1894–1905	1906–1917	1918–1928	1929–1941
Tokyo Imperial University	44.8	78.0	72.5	95.9	85.7	67.5
Justice Ministry Law School	41.4	6.4	19.0	3.1	0.0	0.0
Kyoto Imperial University	0.0	5.2	0.0	0.0	8.9	24.2
Other State Colleges	0.0	0.0	0.0	0.5	0.0	3.2
Private Universities	0.0	7.5	0.0	0.0	5.4	5.1
Foreign Universities	0.0	0.0	4.8	0.0	0.0	0.0
No Higher Education	13.8	2.9	3.7	0.5	0.0	0.0
Total	100	100	100	100	100	100
N	174	173	189	194	224	687

Source: Modified from Spaulding 1967, 251.

Kubota shows the persistent dominance of Tokyo graduates: two-thirds of the upper civil service had attended Tokyo Imperial University (Kubota 1969:74).

The path to bureaucratic recruitment did not simply become a monopoly of higher school-university graduates but increasingly a near monopoly of higher school-Tokyo Imperial University graduates. By 1900, the examination system the Meiji leaders had created produced strong incentives for in-

Table 7.3 Administrative Examination Results, 1894–1901
(by Tokyo Imperial University graduates versus others)

Year	University	Taking Prelim Examination	Taking Main Examination	Passed Main Examination
1895	Tokyo	0	42	25 (59.5)
	Other	84	39	12 (30.7)
1896	Tokyo	0	66	42 (63.6)
	Other	144	43	8 (18.6)
1897	Tokyo	0	51	26 (51.0)
	Other	259	95	28 (29.5)
1898	Tokyo	0	51	26 (51.0)
	Other	373	163	18 (11.0)
1899	Tokyo	0	71	22 (31.0)
	Other	344	103	9 (8.7)
1900	Tokyo	0	94	39 (41.5)
	Other	377	94	19 (20.2)
1901	Tokyo	0	70	16 (22.8)
	Other	396	101	26 (25.7)
Totals	1894–1901			
	Tokyo	0	450	193 (42.9)
	Other	2022	657	126 (19.2)

Source: Modified from Spaulding 1967, 131.

Table 7.4 University Education of Gubernatorial Appointees, 1900–1945

University	N	%
Tokyo Imperial	115	85.2
Kyoto Imperial	10	7.4
Hitotsubashi (state university)	2	1.5
Hosei (private university)	1	.7
Foreign	2	1.5
No Degree	5	3.7
Totals	135	100.0

dividuals seeking high-status positions in the bureaucracy to seek entry into Tokyo and later Kyoto Imperial Universities' Law Faculties (1899). The entrance examinations to the Imperial Universities proved to be another obstacle to be overcome in the pursuit of a bureaucratic career.

The demand for preparation to pass the examinations was met by the creation of the upper middle schools *(kōtōchugakkō)*, which later came to be known as upper or higher schools *(kōtōgakkō)*. Originally, they were designed in the early 1880s to resolve the problem of transition from primary compulsory education to higher education (Roden 1980:35; Motoyama 1965:34–35). With the establishment of the cabinet system in 1885, the new Ministry of Education came to be headed by Mori Arinori. He made it clear that the Meiji leaders sought to establish an educational system that served the national before the private interest. To this end, Mori viewed the educational structure as having differentiated functions. Primary school students were seen as providing the social base of the country but were not able to get more than a rudimentary education because of their economically dependent status. University students, however, were seen as performing the significant leadership functions of the society (Hall 1973:409–13).

Bridging the gap and providing the means for producing distinct streams for technical colleges *(semmongaku)*, professional schools and the Imperial Universities were the middle schools. The legislation created by Mori in 1886 produced two distinct middle school streams—the ordinary middle schools *(jinjōchūgakkō)* and the higher middle schools. The ordinary middle schools were for students from twelve to seventeen years of age, and the higher middle schools were for students seventeen to twenty years of age. The two structures had different financial bases and supervision. Ordinary middle schools were to be financed primarily from local sources, while the higher schools were to be national institutions supported completely by the central government (Roden 1980:39–40). The number of higher schools was kept intentionally small (five at the beginning, expanded to seven by 1888, to eight by 1901, and to fifteen by 1920). This is particularly noticeable when compared to the number of ordinary middle schools (see table 7.5). The intention was clear. The higher schools *(kōtōgakkō)*, as the higher middle schools were to be renamed in 1894, were to narrow the gate for entry into the higher levels of business management or universities, especially into the imperial universities. In a speech to a conference of school administrators in 1887, Mori characterized the ordinary middle schools along with the primary schools as dispensing ordinary practical education. The higher schools did something significantly different:

Those who study in the higher school may, upon graduation, move immediately into business or pursue a specialized course of study. In either case, they will enter society's upper crust. Namely the higher schools should cultivate, among those who are headed for the upper crust [of society], men worthy of directing the thoughts of the masses: be they bureaucrats, then those of the highest echelon, be they businessmen, then those for the top management, be they scholars, then true experts in the various arts and sciences. (as quoted in Roden 1980:40)

By 1900, when the technical courses were largely eliminated from the higher-school curriculum (Kokuritsu Kyōiku Kenkyūjo 1974: vol. 4, 454), the vast majority of students in the higher schools were entered in the university preparatory curriculum: in 1899, 62.2 percent were taking university preparation (Kokuritsu Kyōiku Kenkyūjo 1974: vol. 4, 463). In 1900, the Ministry of Education gave up on the technical education stream for the higher schools, and they became solely entryways to the universities and professional schools (Kokuritsu Kyōiku Kenkyūjo 1974: vol. 4, 460–61). These numbered higher schools (they were named one through eight: *dai ichi kōtogakkō, dai ni kōtogakkō,* etc.) thus became the only path of entry into the imperial universities and the major private ones as well. They became an integral part of the career recruitment path.

In 1900, the commitment to a bureaucratic career had to be made before the age of seventeen, when one sought to pass the examinations providing for entry into one of the numbered higher schools. Without entry, one's chances of gaining access to the imperial universities were small indeed, even when the number of national state universities increased to five by 1918. The degree to which the examination regulations of 1887, 1893–94, and the middle school regulations of 1886 narrowed access to the bureaucratic career can be seen when we combine the enrollment data for primary, ordinary secondary, higher schools, and imperial universities (see table 7.6).

Thus, at the beginning of the century, access to the higher schools and imperial universities was less than one-tenth of one percent of those who entered at the primary school level. Much has been said and written about the Imperial Rescript on Education of 1890 and the Meiji leaders' decision to make emperor-centered moral teaching a major aspect of the educational system (Kaigo 1965; Inada 1971). However, the major characteristic of the educational structure as it emerged from the fashioning of the Meiji leaders was its exclusivity, once one was past the compulsory primary years. By 1902, those entering the ordinary middle schools only accounted for less than two percent (1.8 percent) of primary school students, and those entering the higher schools were only five percent of those at the ordinary middle school level. It was this exclusivity, this straitness of the gate, that made early commitment an absolute necessity if one wished to enter a bureaucratic career.

Furthermore, it was an education aimed at producing a relatively homogenous group of men whose experiences for a period of eight or nine years would be much the same (Roden 1980:230–53). The higher schools aimed at producing a *shi* (samurai in the sense of gentleman) or *zenturomen* (gentleman)—one who was above the lure of personal gain and who embodied the ideal commitment to the public interest (Roden 1980:46–47). The imperial university took this student and provided him with the materials and expertise for fulfilling a public role. Education in law provided the public-spirited man with a body of theory which enabled him to express his commitment to the public over his private interests in a self-evident and systematic way. Decisions would not be made on personal subjective grounds, but on those provided by a systematic body of public knowledge.

Table 7.5 Comparison of Ordinary to Higher Middle Schools by Number and Enrollment, 1886–1902

Year	Ordinary		Higher	
	No.	Students	No.	Students
1886	56	10,300	2	1,585
1889	53	11,530	7	3,837
1892	62	16,189	7	4,443
1895	96	30,871	7	4,289
1898	169	61,632	6	4,664
1901	242	88,391	8	4,361
1902	258	95,027	8	4,781

Source: Kokuritsu Kyoiku Kenkyūjo 1974, vol. 4, 13–15.

Table 7.6 Enrollment at Various Levels of the Educational System, 1886–1902

Year	Primary	Ordinary Middle	Higher	Imperial Universities
1886	2,802,639	10,300	1,585	875
1889	3,031,928	11,530	3,837	774
1892	3,165,410	16,189	4,443	1,308
1895	3,670,345	30,871	4,289	1,620
1898	4,062,418	61,632	4,664	2,560
1901	4,980,604	88,391	4,361	3,612
1902	5,135,487	95,027	4,781	4,046

Source: Kokuritsu Kyoiku Kenkyūjo 1974, vol. 4, 15–16.

The Completion of the Bureaucratic Career Structure: 1894–1900

The examination system as it was organized between 1884 and 1894 created a well-defined preservice career structure and entry-level career paths for the lower and upper civil service. Two new sets of pressures now emerged and led to the development of an internal career structure that was equally well defined. One was created by the necessity for providing a systematic predictable pattern of possible careers, and the second was the continued challenge of political parties to the Meiji leadership. The almost total dependence on Tokyo Imperial University as the source for new recruitment to the upper civil service after 1887, combined with the emergence of the higher schools as a major source for university recruitment, produced the necessity for clearly specifying the rewards for such early preservice commitment. Assurance of entrance into the upper civil service could not be a sufficient incentive in light of the early commitment and subsequent high opportunity costs required.

The first consequence of the ensuing pressure was the specification of movement upward within *sōnin* appointment ranks. Beginning in 1892, a series of ordinances created a system in which seniority came to play a major role. [5] At least two years of service in each *sōnin* rank came to be required for promotion to the next higher rank. By 1895, free or patronage appointment at *sōnin* rank had largely come to an end, at least, formally. The requirement of remaining in rank for at least two years put the emphasis on seniority as a primary means for determining upward movement. The emphasis on seniority also tended to raise the costs of transfers from one ministry to another. Seniority produced a rank-order structure of expectations which transfers would upset considerably. Moreover, the longer one stayed in a ministry, the greater the cost of transfer for the ministry and the transferee. The ministry lost an individual with considerable ministry-specific training and information, while the transferee was behind his new colleagues in the possession of important information and training. The tendency, thus, was to create an increasingly specialized and differentiated role structure emerging out of ministry- and even department-specific service.

The final elements of the career structure were put in place in 1899, primarily as a response to political party attempts to gain control of the administrative structure through parliamentary majorities. After 1895, the highest levels of administrative appointments or *chokunin* (prefectural governors, vice-ministers, ambassadors, and a few department heads) continued to be

5. The following ordinances are important: *H.Z.,* Imperial Ordinance 96, 14 November 1892; Imperial Ordinances 123, 124, 21 September 1895. These were followed by: *H.Z.,* Imperial Ordinances 196, 197, 22 June 1897.

open to the patronage of the *genrō*. Indeed, the ability of the *genrō* to select, at will, the highest levels of the administration was central to their capacity to enforce their decisions. Their powers would, of course, be undermined if the cabinets came to be chosen on the basis of parliamentary majorities. Itō's carefully written constitution had seemed to make this eventuality unlikely. The cabinet and the bureaucracy were servants of the emperor and were to be selected by him. No such powers were given to the Diet. Nevertheless, the constitution had provided the Diet with some powers, although they seemed relatively trivial at the time. The most significant of these was the power to reject a budget. The Meiji leaders sought to trivialize this power by explicitly allowing the cabinet to bring the previous year's budget into existence (Article LXXI). Furthermore, the cabinet could take emergency financial measures, so long as these were approved by the next meeting of the Diet (Article LXX). By then, of course, the Diet would be facing a *fait accompli*. This did not stop the parties in the Diet from rejecting budgets for a variety of reasons, all of them having to do essentially with the demand of parties for greater access to decision making. The tactic had more than nuisance value, as it turned out. The increasing complexity of government budget-making, centering on the process of negotiations within the bureaucracy, made each year's budget the result of long, drawn-out deliberations and a delicate balance of forces. Rejection of the budget meant that everyone had to start from scratch and new demands would have to be based on emergency powers using imperial ordinances. The result was the capacity of the parties to force delays and raise public opinion against the Meiji leaders to such a degree that they had to come to terms with parties (Masumi 1966:II, 148–244).

In 1898, the contingent arrangements between the *genrō* and the parties broke down over demands by the parties for greater and more institutionalized access to senior civil service appointments. There were some demands for an end to the examination system but most sought free nonexamination appointment of lower house and prefectural assembly members to *sōnin* rank offices (Spaulding 1967:112). Itō, then acting as prime minister for the third time, found it impossible to maintain a working relationship with the Diet parties. Itō's solution was to attempt to create a government party. This was adamantly opposed by Yamagata, who refused to attempt to form a new cabinet (Masumi 1966:II, 292–98). With some trepidation, Itō played out his cards and asked the opposition leaders, Ōkuma Shigenobu and Itagaki Taisuke, whose parties had just merged to form the Kaishintō, to take over the cabinet. On 30 June 1898 the first party cabinet came to power.

Rent by internal tensions and facing the opposition of the bureaucracy, the first party cabinet did not last long, and on 8 November 1898, it was replaced by the second Yamagata cabinet (Masumi 1966:II, 298–300).

While the party cabinet had not engaged in any attempt to open the civil bureaucracy to party patronage, Yamagata was concerned that the future might bring parties into control of the cabinet which would not respect the autonomy of the civil bureaucracy. Seeking to protect and maintain *genrō* control over leadership and leadership succession, Yamagata instituted a series of regulations which completed the structure of an "internal labor market"; that is, a career structure which linked all offices from beginning *sōnin* rank up through the highest levels of *chokunin* rank. The Civil Service Appointment Ordinance of 28 March 1899 integrated *chokunin* to the *sōnin* ranks below them. [6]

There were three significant consequences of the limitations created by the ordinance of 1899 and its successors. The first was that the regulations generally restricted *chokunin* selection to former and incumbent *chokunin* or the highest-grade *sōnin* officials. The second consequence was that the new regulations partially integrated the two levels of the upper civil service by providing for the possibility, now stated formally, of advancement from *sōnin* to *chokunin* rank. Finally, by restricting new *chokunin* appointments primarily to *sōnin* officials of the highest grade or to former *chokunin* officials, the regulations established two basic criteria for advancement or appointment at *chokunin* rank: passing of the higher civil service examinations and/or extensive service as reflected in the seniority requirements. Since the number of *chokunin* appointments available without prior *sōnin* service was limited and the number of *chokunin* who had achieved this rank without prior *sōnin* service would decrease with time, *chokunin* officials would have to be increasingly appointed from the ranks of *sōnin* officials. When the new regulations were linked to the requirement, under the rules of 1894, that *sōnin* officials be recruited by examination, this had the effect of making advancement dependent on the dual criteria of examination and successful

---

6. *H.Z.,* Imperial Ordinance 61. Specifically, the ordinance provided that *chokunin* officials could be recruited only from the following: (1) former and incumbent *sōnin* officials of the third grade (highest *sōnin* grade); (2) former *chokunin* officials with at least one year's service in *chokunin* rank, excluding the years served as a technician or teacher and excluding those appointed under special regulations; (3) former *chokunin* officials who had passed the higher civil service examinations or had two years' service as a *sōnin*-rank official; (4) former or incumbent *chokunin* procurators; (5) former and incumbent *chokunin* judges who could be appointed in the Ministry of Justice only; (6) former and incumbent *chokunin* professors who could be appointed *chokunin* only in the Ministry of Education; (7) flag officers who could be appointed as *chokunin* only in the Army or Navy Ministries.

These regulations were changed slightly in 1913 to include those who passed the newly instituted diplomatic examinations and approval of the Upper Civil Service Commission for the reinstatement of ex-*chokunin* officials. See *H.Z.,* Imperial Ordinance 261, 31 July 1913.

sōnin performance. "Successful" came to mean, at least for the lower- and mid-*sōnin* ranks, seniority.

To protect the upper civil service from the putative depredations of party politicians, Yamagata also created what was, in effect, a tenure system through the promulgation of the Civil Service Discipline Ordinance and the Civil Service Status Ordinance. [7] The Status Ordinance limited dismissal to specific causes thought to make adequate performance impossible: criminal conviction, insubordination, physical or mental incapacity, and surplus personnel. In order to protect those dismissed for the latter cause, officials first had to be placed on the inactive or "suspended" list. Officials placed on this list could be reappointed at any time, but could not be retired permanently until they had been on the list for two years at full pay. Two years having passed without reappointment, the official was then required to retire but was eligible to receive the full retirement benefits of his rank and length of service.

Protection from the possible tactic of dismissing senior civil servants on charges of incompetency or incapacity was provided by the Disciplinary Ordinance. Under its provisions a Higher Civil Service Disciplinary Committee was created to provide the machinery for investigation, hearing and rendering judgments, and fixing appropriate punishments with regard to charges brought against senior civil servants. To provide further protection against possible attacks by political parties, the ordinance required that committee members be selected from the ranks of permanent upper civil servants, while the chairman had to be selected from the ultraconservative Privy Council, which had broad but ambiguous powers of legislative review. This requirement, when combined with the status ordinance, made the upper civil service almost completely autonomous. Under these regulations, outright dismissal of an upper civil servant was rendered impossible. Only the inactive list allowed for the appointment of new vice-ministers by an incoming minister. But, even here, the selection had to be made from among incumbent senior civil servants in the ministry.

Yamagata sought to plug any possible loopholes in the autonomy of the upper civil service. As insurance against any possible attempt to revoke the regulations by future party cabinets, Yamagata resorted to the stratagem of having the emperor issue an imperial message *(gosatashō)* outlining categories of legislation requiring Privy Council approval. Included in these categories were all ordinances and legislation relating to the appointment, examination, discipline, dismissal, and ranking of civil servants (Fukai 1953:472–75). While the imperial message did not have the force of law as

7. The Discipline Ordinance is embodied in *H.Z.,* Imperial Ordinance 62, 28 March 1899, and the Status Ordinance is in *H.Z.,* Imperial Ordinance 63, 28 March 1899.

would have a rescript, there was very little chance that a future cabinet would take upon itself the onus of ignoring an imperial wish—that would be getting much too close to *lèse majesté*. Since the Privy Council was made up largely of former high-ranking civil servants who had been rewarded for their faithful performance by appointment to the council, no more appropriate body could be found to protect the status and autonomy of the civil service career.

At the beginning of the new century, the upper civil service had been legally formulated in such a way as to create a highly hierarchic, autonomous role. Entry was extremely narrow. One could only enter at the lowest level of the upper civil service. One could only do so upon passage of an examination that primarily tested the individual's knowledge of Japanese and foreign jurisprudence. The passage upwards was legally structured on the basis of performance as reflected in seniority and one's superior's judgment. Protection from external intervention was almost but not quite complete. Party cabinets could distinguish between those who received promotions and those who didn't and, in this way, had some effect on bureaucratic attitudes toward political party ministers. All told, however, this had relatively little effect on the nature of the bureaucracy as an organization. Party politicians serving as ministers had to choose from among officials who had similar training and service backgrounds. There was no autonomy of choice as in a patronage system. The effects of this legal structure of autonomy became evident within a short time. It produced an extremely systematic and predictable career structure characterized by the dominance of seniority as the criteria for advancement, by service in a single ministry, which became the source of administrative specialization, and by relatively high rates of turnover as a consequence of the relatively rapid movement upward and the growth of the tendency of the very senior civil servants in a ministry to resign when one member of their cohort achieved vice-ministerial status.

These patterns are clearly reflected in the careers of prefectural governors appointed after 1899. We have already seen the degree to which the career required a university degree primarily from Tokyo Imperial University: 85 percent of those who rose to be governors after 1899 were graduates of Tokyo Imperial University, while only 1.5 percent came from private universities. Furthermore, 91 percent graduated from law faculties. Clearly, the legal criteria were translated into actuality by 1900, and the systematic character of the career is seen in table 7.7. Entrance, thus, was largely limited to the lowest grades of the upper civil service. The number of offices held before appointment as governor also reflects the systematic structure of career movement (see table 7.8). Seniority, or at least movement through a minimal number of offices, now had become standard, since only 7.2 percent were promoted to this office with less than six appointments. The importance of seniority can be further demonstrated in table 7.9. As can be seen from the data, appointment to high office only came after at least eleven years of service and, generally, five previous appointments, beginning with the lowest *sōnin* grade. Equally important, the length of time in each office for the vast majority (73 percent) was about two years, revealing a relatively high succession rate.

The degree to which the regulations governing dismissal produced a highly predictable career length is reflected in table 7.10. These data suggest that not only did the upper civil service career become safe from random and arbitrary dismissal, it also suggests that the retirement system was important in shaping the structure, since almost no one after 1900 retired before the fifteen-year minimum. Indeed, the reward structure seems to have been sufficiently high so as to keep 63 percent in service for over twenty years.

Finally, the age of upper civil servants at retirement, as represented here

Table 7.7 Level of First Office Held by Gubernatorial Appointee, 1900–1945

Level of Office	N	%
Lower civil service, *hannin* rank	0	0.0
Upper civil service, *sōnin*, grades 8–6	111	82.0
Upper civil service, *sōnin*, grades 5–3	13	10.0
Upper civil service, *chokunin*, grades 2–1	0	0.0
Military service	0	0.0
NA	11	8.0
Total	135	100.0

Table 7.8 Number of Offices Held prior to Appointment as Governor, 1900–1945

No. of Offices	N	%
1	0	0.0
2	0	0.0
3	2	1.5
4	1	0.75
5	7	5.0
6	21	15.5
7	31	23.0
8	21	15.5
9	14	10.0
10	12	9.0
11	9	6.5
12	5	4.0
NA	12	9.0
Total	135	99.775

by prefectural governors, provides further evidence of the systematic structure of careers created by the Meiji leaders (see table 7.11). It seems to have been the case that high rates of succession became the norm after 1900, thus forcing relatively early retirement of senior officials. This had the consequence of providing for a constant flow of openings at the lower level,

Table 7.9 Years of Service by Number of Offices Held prior to Appointment as Governor, 1900–1945

No. of Offices	Years of Service prior to Appointment							Total	
	0–5	6–10	11–15	16–20	21–25	26+	NA	n	%
1	0	0	0	0	0	0		0	0
2	0	0	0	0	0	0		0	0
3	0	1	1	0	0	0		2	1.5
4	0	0	0	1	0	0		1	0.75
5	0	0	5	2	0	0		7	5.0
6	0	0	10	10	1	0		21	15.5
7	0	0	14	13	4	0		31	23.0
8	0	0	9	10	2	0		21	15.5
9	0	0	2	10	1	1		14	10.0
10	0	0	2	9	1	0		12	9.0
11	0	0	0	6	3	0		9	6.5
12	0	0	0	3	1	1		5	3.75
NA								12	9.0
Total n	0	1	43	64	13	2			
%	0	0.75	30.5	47.5	10.0	1.5		9.0	99.75

Table 7.10 Length of Service of Governors, 1868–99; 1900–1945

Length of Service in Years	Period of Appointment			
	1868–1899		1900–1945	
	n	%	n	%
1–5	20	25.0	0	0
6–10	16	20.0	3	2.0
11–15	4	6.0	0	0.0
16–20	4	5.0	28	20.5
21–25	11	14.0	47	35.0
26–30	10	12.0	17	13.0
31–35	5	6.0	12	9.0
35+	3	4.0	2	1.5
NA	6	8.0	26	19.0
Total	80	100.0	135	100.0
Median	10.5		23.0	
Mean	18.0		25.4	

which, in turn, provided incentives for individuals to continue to commit themselves very early in their educational careers to seek to enter the civil bureaucracy.

The high succession rate also led to the development of post-civil service careers. Since most of those who retired did so at the age of fifty or slightly over, their pensions were not generous. At fifty, with approximately twenty-five years of service, an official would receive a pension equal to about two/fifths of the annual salary. This would come at a point of an individual's family development where his children would just be entering higher school

Table 7.11 Retirement Age of Gubernatorial Appointees, 1900–1945*

Age in 5-year interval	N		%	
20–24	0	(0)	0.0	(0.0)
25–29	0	(2)	0.0	(2.5)
30–34	3	(5)	2.0	(6.0)
35–39	0	(5)	0.0	(6.0)
40–44	16	(6)	12.0	(7.5)
45–49	48	(2)	35.5	(2.5)
50–54	42	(10)	31.0	(12.5)
55–59	15	(24)	11.0	(30.0)
60–64	5	(9)	3.5	(11.5)
65–69	0	(3)	0.0	(4.0)
70+	0	(1)	0.0	(1.5)
NA	6	(13)	4.5	(16.0)
Total	135	(80)	99.5	(100.0)
Mean	46.6	(55)		
Median	49.0	(56.8)		

*1868–89 figures are in parentheses.

Table 7.12 Post-service Occupations of Governors, 1900–1945

Occupation	N	%
Business-Industry	30	22.0
Politics—Local and National	38	28.0
Law Practice	6	5.0
Government Advisor	8	6.0
Volunteer Activities	11	8.0
No Occupation	11	8.0
NA	31	23.0
Total	135	100.0

Source: Silberman 1973, 202.

or university, both quite costly events. The result was the search for second careers before retirement. Out of this emerged a pattern of second careers that still persists. In the period from 1900 to 1945, the pattern of second careers is very evident, as is shown in table 7.12.

In sum, the phalanx of civil service regulations put into force between 1884 and 1899 produced a career structure that was characterized by its emphasis on an objective test of knowledge for entrance and on seniority, hierarchy, highly organization-specific specialization and differentiation, and career as integral elements of the role.

Conclusion

The men who sought to monopolize the structure of leadership in the years immediately following 1868 were not few in number nor were they well organized. The old regime had given way before a combination of attacks from small groups of men (mostly lower and middle samurai) and a few women who were organized along social networks usually informed by domainal origin and social status. Other forces entered the picture as well, *daimyō* and some court aristocrats, attacks from peasants usually organized by lower samurai, but the shell was pierced by the attacks of the "men of spirit" or the *shi-shi*. Once the old regime had collapsed, these individuals had no formal organization of their own that could be used as the basis for a structure of leadership or for allocating leadership in a more or less systematic way. Nor did they, in any of their various factional incarnations, have any overwhelming claim to a monopoly of leadership. The most ambitious of them sought positions in the new Restoration government. Serving as underlings to a court bureaucracy that had little in the way of either ability or capacity to deal with the day-to-day problems of administration, they soon became indispensable. Their indispensability arose from their ability to serve as mediators between their not-so-capable superiors and the necessity of recruiting officials loyal to the new regime. They not only became the arbiters of loyalty, selecting subordinates on the basis of social networks, but they also, by the same token, became the heads of cliques which became the major means for implementing decisions. By 1873, their aristocratic superiors had, by and large, disappeared from administrative office and the putative leaders had taken their place.

Despite the fact that this group of men had come into positions of great power and were the inheritors of the Restoration, the very absence of any formal or systematic structure of leadership selection produced internal tensions that led to a long series of challenges to their power. Some of these challenges, indeed, perhaps most of them, were mounted by former peers and colleagues who now found themselves without constituents inside the bureaucracy. Some now sought to create, with considerable success, an alternative claim to leadership—political parties and an elective principle of leadership selection. Others sought, with less success, to create an alternative based on localism. In raising challenges to their colleagues in the new government's administration, it became clear that no one's claim to leadership was secure. This fact of political life was reflected in a large number of incidents and rebellions aimed at dislodging the putative leaders, who continued to hold office.

From the mid-1870s, those who continued to hold offices sought to utilize the administrative role as the basis for the creation of a systematic structure of leadership. The central problem for them was how to transform the role from one that was characterized by domainal and personal loyalty to one that appeared to be dominated by transcendent public interest. They pursued, with extraordinary single-mindedness, strategies which would make the bureaucracy the primary structure of political leadership. They created an emperor whose powers were limitless and who was defined by his embodiment of the public interest. At the same time, the putative leaders sought to show that they alone were capable of serving this divine embodiment of Japanese society before whom all men were equal. To do so, they transformed the role of the official from one with an essentially private basis to one which was public in character. Its publicness was derived from the requirement that officials be trained experts—experts possessing a knowledge that was by its nature public and not private or magical in character or form.

By imposing the qualifications of higher education, the Meiji leaders maintained exclusiveness and rejected the elective principle while, at the same time, they maintained the ideal of equality before the emperor. Anyone who was qualified could enter the ranks of the emperor's servants. But to become qualified required (considerably before the end of the century) an early commitment to an expensive educational career. To provide incentives to maintain a flow of eligibles, the leadership had to create a systematic structure of rewards. Out of this emerged a bureaucratic structure that possessed all of the characteristics of Weber's legal-rational organizational structure. Uncertainty over their positions had led the Meiji leaders increasingly to formulate and pursue strategies that would secure them uncontested control over decision making. In this they were wonderfully successful. However, in the process of assuring their, and their bureaucratic successors', control over decision making, they had to depend on a purely informal structure of bureaucratic leadership—the *genrō* structure. The structure simply could not

be perpetuated without once again returning to the principle of private selection and interest. Nevertheless, the civil bureaucracy had emerged by
1900 as the primary instrument of decision making and the primary structure of political leadership selection. The challenge of parties continued, but
they remained isolated from independent sources of power. Eventually, their
subordination to bureaucratic power became so powerful that they seemed,
by the 1930s, to have faded into pale ghosts of their Meiji progenitors. The
bureaucracy remained as the premier institution of public interest.

PART THREE
Strategies of Low Uncertainty

UNITED STATES

8

Political Parties, Patronage,
and Administration

The United States stands at one extreme of the continuum of uncertainty regarding leadership succession. The rules governing political leadership succession were settled fairly early in its history. Certainly by the 1830s all of the basic precepts and elements that have governed political leadership selection until the present day were in place. Universal white manhood suffrage, which would serve as the basis for an eventual universal suffrage, the multiplicity of elective offices, the rise of political parties as the means of regulating nomination and mobilizing voters, majority notions of determining winners, and the maintenance of the rights of losers were precepts that had wide support and were firmly anchored in the legal, social, and economic structures. As the emergence of party organizations in the 1830s and 1840s indicates, the prime concern of political leaders was in finding the means to reduce uncertainty about individual and party incumbency. One of the primary means for doing so was for the party to organize recruitment to the administrative service, thus ensuring that the will of the majority party would dominate in the administration and that faithful retainers would be rewarded. Out of this emerged a powerful link between party leadership and the organizational fate of state administration in the United States. Political party leadership succession and the nature of the federal state administration were inextricably tied together so that any changes in the level of uncertainty for the former would produce changes in the latter.

The Nature of the American State Bureaucracy

Between 1883, when the Pendleton Act created the so-called merit system, and 1923, when the passage of the Personnel Classification Act formalized the nature of the role structure, the basic elements of the modern American civil bureaucracy came into being. While it has changed considerably in its details and complexities since 1923, the essential character of the structure remains largely intact today. That structure has been characterized in a number of ways. Hugh Heclo has portrayed this civil bureaucracy as "an unmanaged affair, weak in the central executive apparatus and extensive in horizontal links to the larger political society" (Heclo 1984:30). Frederick Mosher argues, in seeming contradiction, that "the characteristic of the public service—and in-

227

deed of a great part of the rest of society—which seems to me most significant today is *professionalism"* (Mosher 1968:101; italics in the original). "For better or worse—or better *and* worse—," Mosher says further,

much of our government is now in the hands of professionals (including scientists). The choice of these professionals, the determination of their skills, and the content of their work are now principally determined, not by general governmental agencies, but by their own professional elites, professional organizations, and the institutions and faculties of higher education. (Mosher 1968:132; italics in the original)[1]

Upon closer examination, we can see that these two descriptions are not mutually exclusive. In fact, to the degree that Mosher is right, then the structure of the civil service ought to look ambiguous, permeable, and underdirected—just what you might expect from an organization dominated by professionals whose organizational, as against their professional, commitment is relatively low. As Heclo puts it:

In contrast to the results produced by a patronage operation, the in-and-outers are a technocratic group called upon to fill jobs that are far from routine. They are asked to play challenging roles as policy managers and administrative leaders. Their previous involvement in policy matters is often substantial, but their attachments to government or politics as organizational enterprises are always transient. . . . The in-and-outer system, with its mixed emphasis on technical competence and political responsiveness, seems well fitted to the American political context. However, Americans can expect serious problems in government if this system is allowed to continue just growing. (Heclo 1987:196–97, 215)

Finally, it seems fitting to quote Heclo again as he goes on to say in a somewhat bemused manner about the "in-and-out" professionals:

The profile of the senior bureaucracy is, therefore, etched by the interaction of powerful external agents on the hard surface of government expertise. The great strength of this system is its capacity to make government accessible to those who are actively interested in affecting its work. The great dangers are that the

---

1. Mosher points out that there are five major avenues to political power: (1) election or appointment to high office (dominated by lawyers); (2) effective control by a profession of senior managerial positions in a department (educators in the Office of Education; engineers in public works agencies; lawyers in the Justice Department); (3) professional presence in an agency but without professional domination (the presence in all agencies of legal counsel, personnel specialists, budget and planning specialists); (4) an ability to generate pressure on decision-makers from the professional community outside the government; and (5) collaborating with fellow professionals in other units of government to affect policy decisions. All of these have some component of the professional role as the basis for gaining access to political power (Mosher 1978:145–46).

government will be unable to act as a collective enterprise with institutional con-tinuity and with some sense of purpose that is more than a reflection of the pref-erences held by those who happen to be mobilized to affect its work. No nation seems likely to reverse the growing trend for technical expertise at all govern-ment levels. What America's "non-system" of public careerists may have to offer are some hints about tilting the inevitable technocracy in more broadly demo-cratic directions. (Heclo 1984:30)

In essence, Mosher and Heclo seem to make it clear that, in their view, the professionalism characteristic of the upper civil service is not synonymous with the idea of the civil service career as a professional career. Rather, what they mean is that the upper civil service is dominated by those trained in a variety of professions (law, science, engineering, social sciences, etc.). It seems equally plain that they believe that this form of professionalism and the ambiguous and ambivalent structure of the civil bureaucracy are linked in some way. How they are linked has not, however, been very well articulated. Earlier I suggested that they were not linked primarily through any secular process of rationalization or by functional system requirements. Instead, the argument was that they were linked through strategic decisions by party leaders to stress certain struc-tural characteristics which would place constraints on the emergence of bu-reaucratic autonomy. The outcome of stressing some organizational features as against others, with the degree of autonomy as the criterion for selection, pro-duced a set of characteristics which have continued in most ways to inform the upper civil service structure. These general characteristics might be summed up in the following manner:

1. A role structure centered on job description and the individual's ap-propriateness for the described position. Thus the major concern is "finding the right person for the right job."

2. Entrance into the role structure is based on the acquisition of specific skills or expertise rather than a set of general skills.

3. As a consequence of the second characteristic, entrance into the bu-reaucracy at all levels is relatively easy. Depending on skill level or skill cer-tification, putative entrants have access to a wide range of positions at all lev-els and grades.

4. There is a major distinction, if not a very clear one, between the upper and lower civil service structure. Ambiguity between the two structures is, in good part, a function of the first two characteristics, that is, the emphasis on specific jobs or occupations rather than on a clearly delineated linked series of positions such as the French *cadre* for which a certain level of education is required. Barriers between the two strata are, as a consequence, permeable, depending on the individual's acquisition of specific skills or expertise for a position.

(5.) Entrance into the senior civil service is achieved by both examination (classified) and appointment. The former is not a general examination for all entrants. Rather, the examination system is a test of specific skills (including technical, scientific, and professional) or capacities (namely, managerial capacities), which does not provide access to a well-defined career but to a job classification, a promotion tree, and a salary grade. Appointment as the means of entrance is based on party membership, party activism, and, nearly always, an exhibited level of professional or work experience.

(6.) Service tends to be within the same department (ministerial department) or agency but is not the only or, perhaps, even primary source of specialization since skill levels are required to be acquired and exhibited prior to holding a position. This is reflected in the system of grouping positions in classes horizontally across the entire structure.

(7.) Tenure of office in the senior civil bureaucracy is variable and dependant on whether the individual holds a position within the examined or appointive group of positions. The former tend to stay in the service for relatively long periods of time. Although there are no well-defined career lines, individuals can create careers for themselves by pursuing higher levels of skill, experience, or professional certification. Those in appointive positions tend to move in and out of office with no prolonged periods of service. They tend to pursue careers centered on their professional status rather than in any specific organization.

(8.) The completion of service is indicated by specific retirement and pension benefits which provide incentives primarily for lower- and middle-level civil servants. For upper-level civil servants, the incentive of a specified end-of-career retirement benefit is offset by the possible rewards of pursuing one's professional activities outside of the bureaucracy after a relatively short period of service.[2]

In sum, the system is conceived of as having relatively wide entrance gates, allowing access based on skill levels at almost any point in the hierarchy of job classifications. Specialization and differentiation are not basically determined by career service but fundamentally by previously or extra-service acquired expertise or skills. Well-defined career paths are not numerous. Careers are the products of individual choices and job classification requirements and are, consequently, highly variable. Promotion is theoretically a function of the acquisition of greater skills or expertise and not merely as a matter of seniority.

2. Heclo 1977, 1984, 1987; Mosher 1982, 1978; Fisher 1987; Brauer 1987; Mayers 1922; Betters 1931; Cayer 1987; Warner, Van Riper, Martin, and Collins 1963; Corson and Paul 1966; Van Riper 1958a, 1958b; Stanley 1964; Bendix 1949; Stanley, Mann, and Doig 1967; Murphy, Neuchterlein, and Stupak 1978; U.S. Civil Service Commission 1972; Federal Council for Science and Technology 1962; Grandjean 1981; DiPrete and Soule 1986; Granick 1972:50–64.

Because of the emphasis on previously acquired skills, professional qualifications receive the highest rewards. At the same time, however, those possessing professional qualifications have high incentives to leave government service after acquiring some experience to gain the greater rewards of private service. Permeability thus seems part and parcel of the organizational structure. Finally, it is plain that in the absence of well-articulated career lines, hierarchy is deemphasized in favor of skill or professional standing.

The Problem of Political Leadership and Administration

The general agreement as to the absence of organizational integration, to well-specified leadership and responsibility, and to the existence of permeability reveals the consistently normative stance taken by analysts of American administration. The view, best expressed by Skowronek, perhaps, is that any description of American administration cannot help but be placed within the context of the failure of administrative rationalization:

The outstanding characteristic of Progressive state building was neither efficiency nor rationality. Although the capacities of the new order to meet the growing demands on the national government clearly surpassed those of the old, the American state was also newly constricted in action by the repoliticization of its national bureaucracy around a constitutional stalemate. . . . A struggle for political power and institutional position within the state apparatus mediated the modernization process and defied both the ideology of efficiency and the developmental imperatives for rationality. (Skowronek 1982:210)

At the heart of these normative concerns is the understandable desire to provide some basis not only for a critical appraisal but also for a solution to what appears to be a dangerous condition. The dangerousness of the condition, it is argued (Skowronek 1982:211; Heclo 1984:30–32), stems from the failure to find an integrating mechanism for policy-making. Roughly stated, the argument is that although political parties have declined since the end of the last century, they have continued to be strong enough to make sure that the civil bureaucracy would not be sufficiently rationalized to replace them as the primary structure of leadership integration and policy-making. Underlying this argument is the seemingly respectable assumption that the bureaucratic structure which evolved is disorderly—it lacks a structural discipline which would make it operate more efficiently or, at least, more decisively. The political parties are cast as the villains or, less pejoratively, as the principal actors in keeping the administrative structure from fulfilling "the developmental imperatives for rationality." While it is not at all clear that such imperatives exist in some secular way in the development of capitalism or in the modern state system, it does seem to be an undeniable fact that the major actors in determining the structure of the civil bureaucracy were political party leaders.

This raises the question of why political leaders would evolve a strategy or engage in a series of tactics which would produce the kind of structure described above. Reasons often cited are: the growth in demands for greater and more consistent services, the growing concern over disorder, and the search for more rational organization of political party resources (Skowronek 1982; Wiebe 1967; Shefter 1978a). These supply some, if not too many, reasons why politicians who had hitherto depended on patronage as the main personnel system for state administration should turn to another system. They do not, however, suggest why politicians ended up selecting this particular set of arrangements. That political party leaders wanted to make sure that the administrative structure did not acquire a great deal of autonomy is entirely comprehensible. However, why they ended up limiting autonomy in this seemingly unique fashion is not revealed by their intentions about autonomy.

The road to understanding this mystery is located, I believe, in the continuing problem facing political leaders since the early decades of the nineteenth century. With the extension of suffrage and the enormous growth of elective offices in the period between 1800 and 1830, political leadership ceased to be a function of social organization and status. Or, to put it in plainer language, political leadership ceased to be dominated by notables. The notables came to be replaced by a leadership selected by political parties. The problem facing political leaders selected in this manner was not, as in the case of France, for example, how to create a systematic and predictable structure of choosing political leaders. Rather, the problem was how political leaders—in search of a means by which they could organize voters and reduce their volatility, and who were selected through a highly decentralized party system—could come to control administration in a long-term systematic way.

This problem has had several aspects. The first centers on the absence of political parties from the formal constitutional order. That is to say, while parties resolved the problem of leadership succession in a more or less orderly and disciplined manner, they had few resources at their disposal to maintain or institutionalize themselves. Pursuing systematic control over administration of public assets could solve the problem of resources, and this, in turn, would provide the stability as well as the assets needed to help organize the voters. The absence of any specific constitutional arrangement for controlling or organizing the administration of the state except through the general appointment and executive powers of the president placed him in somewhat of an institutional quandary as to how he should go about organizing recruitment and administration. The party was a nice neat solution from the standpoint of party leaders. Parties were, however, private associations. This produced a continuing structure of tension not only between political parties and the American state organization, but also among party political leaders themselves, who were often at a loss to know when or whether they were acting in the public or the party interest.

These tensions were exacerbated by the fact that the parties which emerged were national only in an ephemeral sense. Once the national convention system had come into being after 1831–32, there could be said, with some degree of accuracy, to be a national party, but only once every four years. It would be far more difficult to sustain the assertion for the times in between the presidential elections—a condition which still holds true to a very considerable extent. This meant there were no national party organizations that might organize control over the staffing of the civil bureaucracy and the direction of its implementational policies as was the case in nineteenth-century Britain, where a patronage secretary performed these functions.

The parties at the state level were the organizations that had continuing existence and were more or less institutionalized. Their access to the resources of the national administration was, however, limited to the Congress. The party leaders or their representatives in Congress had to rely on congressional organization to channel national government resources to the state parties. Whatever virtues Congress had or has as an organization of legislators, they do not contribute much as an organization capable of efficient administration. Congress simply was and is not suited for the well-oiled administration of anything, including patronage. The result has been that party control over the bureaucracy through Congress (or even congressional control *per se*) has never been deeply institutionalized and has always had something of the purely contingent about it.

The absence of formal public and national constitutional status has rendered the political parties both vulnerable and sensitive to the uncertainties of voter volatility. Major shifts in party preferences by the voters both threatens and predicts reform of existing arrangements for party management of administrative activity. The history of the development of the bureaucratic structure may then be seen as the history of party attempts to institutionalize their control over administration under the effects of major changes in voter preferences. This has produced, among political leaders, an ex post facto pattern of strategic choices. The very unpredictability of voter volatility has led to attempts either to repair the damage or institutionalize the gains—depending on whether your party won or lost. Unlike the preemptive strategies of postrevolutionary political leaders in France and Japan, successful political leaders in the United States seem to have been constantly running to catch up with the direction of the voters and then seeking to freeze voters in their choices.

The bureaucratic structure which emerged may thus, in some sense, be seen as a consequence of the complex interplay between voter shifts in party preferences and party attempts to reduce the uncertainties over the incumbency of political leadership raised by such shifts. Analysis of the way in which the tensions existing between these various elements of the political structure should bring us to an understanding of how they produced the particular nature of the American civil bureaucracy.

Jacksonian Democracy and the Restructuring of the Civil Bureaucracy: 1828–32

Two systems of rules governing the relations between individuals were well established in the United States by the end of the second decade of the nineteenth century. One of these was the system of legal rules, the basis of which had been inherited from English law. By the end of the 1820s, this law had become sufficiently uniform within the American context so as to allow state jurisdictions to function without creating serious conflicts over the meaning, content, and operation of the legal system. By the same time, the laws governing property were pretty much Americanized and were more or less uniform across state lines (Friedman 1973:206–9). The laws of contract inherited from England also prevailed in a relatively uniform manner, recognizing and regulating the equality of individuals before the law (Nelson 1975:126, 154–56; W. Nelson 1982:30–34). During the same period, the courts had become, in the absence of large state or federal civil services, the means by which law was enforced:

Basically, the law left it to private persons to enforce what regulation there was. If no one brought a lawsuit, or complained to the district attorney about some violation, nothing was done. The state did not seriously try to administer, or carry through independently, what the statutes decreed. (Friedman 1973:165)

Law as administered by the courts became the chief means of individual redress. The system of local, state, and federal courts, while neither perfectly uniform nor perfectly hierarchical, formed a network of redress and enforcement that had become national in character. While variations existed, the basic rules governing property, contract, and procedure were well set and, by and large, just as recognizable to a citizen of Massachusetts as they were to a citizen of Pennsylvania or Georgia. By the time of Jackson's election to the presidency in 1828, the rules governing relationships between individuals in their economic life and, to a considerable degree, their social life were well defined and moderately well regulated without resort to large state bureaucracies. This structure of law provided a common basis for the association of states and, indeed, might be said to have made possible the relative stability of the decentralized federal system.

This structure also provided the basis for arriving at and maintaining agreement on the political process. It was the relatively well regulated nature of civil life which made possible the rapid and mostly smooth transition from restricted notable democracy to a much more open mass democracy which Jackson's election is often said to symbolize. In this respect, the Constitution and the Bill of Rights outlined a structure of due process and provided a basic mechanism for the conduct of political life. Nevertheless, despite the ingenuity of its drafters, the mechanism had its weaknesses, one of which was the failure to foresee or provide for some means by which to systematically reduce the number of candidates for the presidency (Chase 1973:xvii; Lowi 1975:247). Until the election of 1820, the congressional caucus, organized primarily on the basis of social notability, served this purpose. But the extension of suffrage brought with it an end to the consensus built on social status which organized parties in the Congressional caucus (Shefter 1978a:215–16; McCormick 1966:30, 348). The infighting and factionalization of the caucus system which accompanied this change in the social basis of politics finally led to its dissolution (Chase 1973:24–28).

The problem of candidate competition became endemic at every level of elective office-holding as white manhood suffrage became almost universal before the end of the 1830s. The problem was exacerbated in part by the rapidly expanding number of state and local elective offices in the first decades of the century (McCormick 1966:29–30; Ostrogorski 1902:II, 55; Kaufman 1956:1,059). At the local level, this was resolved relatively early by the development of local and district delegate conventions, followed by state conventions (Chase 1973:28–29; McCormick 1966:24–25). The state delegate conventions were organized primarily to meet the problem of the collapse of the congressional caucus. The caucus failure left presidential hopefuls with the only alternative of organizing voters and electors on their own. The first of these hopefuls to turn away from dependence on notables as a basis for party was Jackson and his party organizer Martin Van Buren in the election of 1828. The development of party organization by Van Buren, especially after the election of 1828, created a totally new procedure and structure for the selection of political leadership.

The parties which emerged from the Jacksonian period were built on state organizations in which leadership operated through, and eventually came to be selected by, a system of party conventions (McCormick 1966:346–47; Marshall 1967:453–54). They became the major procedural means for rationalizing the selection of candidates for the otherwise bewildering array of offices and possible candidates. This system produced a new type of political leader—one who centered his activities on his role as a member of an organizational structure rather than on his social role as a notable (Marshall 1967:452; Meyers 1957:7). By the end of the 1830s, "parties everywhere confronted broadly similar tasks" (McCormick 1966:344). The two parties—Whigs and Democrats—were now established in every state and played the dominant role in determining candidacy and voter organization. "There was, indeed, a nationalization of institutional forms and political styles. There was also a nationalization of political identities" (McCormick 1966:342; Silbey 1985:35–36).

The first third of the nineteenth century saw the emergence of well-defined and understood systems of rules governing both economic and political relationships (and social ones as well if we are to believe Tocqueville). There had never been serious questions about the nature of property during the Revolution and there was, thus, no property settlement for the upper and middle classes to be seriously concerned about in connection with democratic politics. By Jackson's second term, the course of political development was clearly set.

Government by the people was largely a matter of consensus and of wont. Basic principles and institutions were firmly settled; only their legal elaboration—for example, in suffrage extension and the increase of elective offices—was recent and still in progress. There was some party conflict over details, none over the general democratic direction. . . . The new party democracy, like democracy in the abstract, was a common element of politics and raised no substantial public issues between Jacksonians and their rivals. (Meyers 1957:7–8)

The essential features of the American political process as it was to operate over the next century had begun to emerge by 1828 and was largely completed by 1840. A national two-party system based on party organization at local and state levels was the focus of the politician's role. Notable status was no longer a sufficient criterion for entrance into political life—political activity on behalf of a party became the basis of access to political leadership. Political parties thus became the central institution in the political process and procedure so sketchily outlined in the formal constitutional order. There was general agreement on this process and procedure and its effect was, as Ostrogorski noted so astutely and acerbically, was critical and long-lasting:

The separation of society from politics became the leading fact of the situation; the nation had, as it were, split into two distinct parts: a large majority, which was toiling, developing, and growing rich, and a small, active minority, full of passions and still more appetites, which was monopolizing political action. (Ostrogorski 1902:II, 70)

The advent of the Jacksonian democracy based on party organization and mobilization of the electorate resulted in the emergence of what McCormick has called the "second party system." Jackson's victories and that of his successor Van Buren resulted in the creation of a national politics, the nature and process of which solicited a consensus. For at least the next half-century or so, the rules of the game concerning the selection of political leadership were agreed upon with a startling absence of dissent. The rules of the game now constrained the political contest to a specific political arena in which the contest was played out between political parties.

The emergence of national parties ended a period in which political leadership was a function of social organization and networks—a spill-over of social status; it ended a period in which contestation was a function of conflict among notables with differing views as to the nature of political, but not social, organization. In its place emerged a new conception and structure of political leadership—one based on the view that politics was a full-time occupation, if not a profession, and that political leadership meant a full-time commitment to a party. By midcentury, the road to political leadership was relatively well defined. It meant laboring in the vineyards of local politics through the medium of party organization in order to get nominated for local office; it meant getting elected and utilizing the appointment and implementing powers of the office to reward both past and future party supporters; finally, it meant repeating this process at the county and state levels. The winnowing process was severe. Those who survived it were wily and extremely self-conscious about strategies of choice (R. P. McCormick 1966:347–49; R. P. McCormick 1975:110–11; Remini 1981:382–84; White 1954:13–16).

Central to this new game of politics was the creation of a new set of rules governing the relationship between the political parties, the administrative structure, and public policy. These rules might be summed up in the following way:

1. Selection of the presidential candidates was the function of state party organization and party leaders organized nationally every four years, rather than that of a congressional caucus.

2. Selection of candidates for congressional, state, and local offices were functions of the state party hierarchies of political leaders, which had more or less continuing corporatelike existence.

3. Contestation between the existing two parties in the 1830s led to the institutionalization of the effort to limit competition to two parties.

4. Party and majoritarian politics became generally, although by no means universally, synonymous.

5. Majority-party domination at all levels sought to perpetuate itself by

the means available to it: distribution of public goods through the party-dominated legislatures (the pork barrel) and distribution of nonelective public offices through party-dominated executives (the patronage system)(Lowi 1975; Chambers 1975; R. P. McCormick 1975; Shefter 1978a).

Jackson's accession to office in 1828 produced three important areas of activity on the part of the new administration which reflected the emergence of these rules. The first was the informal national committee of the new party—Jackson's famous, or infamous, Kitchen Cabinet sought further development of the party organization and structure. The second was that Jackson and his advisors immediately set to altering and restructuring administrative organization, recruitment, and appointment. Finally, Jackson singled out as his most important general policy—elimination of monopoly charters, both public and private, such as the Bank of the United States (Marshall 1967:446–55; Crenson 1975:51–71; W. Nelson 1982:22–30; Shefter 1978a:218–22). The first was clearly directed toward confirming and expanding the means by which the Jacksonian Democrats had achieved victory. This entailed the development and expansion of state and local party organizations and support and encouragement of reforms in the electoral process, such as: expanded suffrage; direct election of presidential electors, governors, executive heads of state departments, and of an enormous range of formerly appointive local offices (Ostrogorski 1902:II, 52–60, 63–69; Marshall 1967:454; McCormick 1975:105–6).

The second area of activity was directed toward reform of nonelective administrative office-holding. Jackson's views on office-holding through appointment were expressed in his famous message to Congress in 1829:

There are, perhaps, few men who can for any length of time enjoy office and power without being more or less under the influence of feelings unfavorable to the faithful discharge of their public duties. Their integrity may be proof against improper considerations immediately addressed to themselves, but they are apt to acquire a habit of looking with indifference upon the public interests and of tolerating conduct from which an unpracticed man would revolt. Office is considered as a species of property, and government rather as a means of promoting individual interests than as an instrument created solely for the service of the people. Corruption in some and in others a perversion of correct feelings and principles divert government from its legitimate ends, and make it an engine for the support of the few at the expense of the many. The duties of all public offices are, or at least admit of being made, so plain and simple that men of intelligence may readily qualify themselves for their performance; and I cannot but believe that more is lost by the long continuance of men in office than is generally gained by their experience. I submit, therefore, to your consideration whether the efficiency of the government would not be promoted, and official industry and integrity better secured, by a general extension of the law which limits appointments to four years.

In a country where offices are created solely for the benefit of the people no one man has any more intrinsic right to official station than another. Offices were not established to give support to particular men at the public expense. No individual wrong is, therefore, done by removal, since neither appointment to or continuance in office is a matter of right. The incumbent became an officer with a view to public benefits, and when these require his removal they are not to be sacrificed to public interest. It is the people, and they alone, who have a right to complain when a bad officer is substituted for a good one. He who is removed has the same means of obtaining a living that are enjoyed by millions who never held office. The proposed limitation would destroy the idea of property now so generally connected with official station, and although individual distress may be sometimes produced, it would, by promoting that rotation which constitutes a leading principle in the republican creed, give healthful action to the system. (as quoted in Fish 1904 (1963):111–12)

In many ways this is a classic formulation of the reasons for establishing systematic regulation of administrative appointment and dismissal. Jackson clearly provides the basic legitimacy for regulation. The conception of office as property, although under attack in the 1820s, was by no means completely dead. The "decision of 1789" had given the president the power of removal of department heads, thus adding to his constitutional powers of removal over those not appointed with the advice and consent of the Senate. Nevertheless, the tendency had remained for appointees to stay in office as long as they were not wildly corrupt or openly opposed to the politics of the incumbent president (Rosenbloom 1971:26–28; Prince 1977:268–79). It was equally clear that preceding presidents had made appointments on the basis of their politics, thus locking officials into office regardless of the politics and policies of those who later came to hold power. The property right seemed especially imminent and conspicuous in light of the fact that no retirement system existed, nor was there any statutory age of retirement.

At the same time, Jackson addressed the problem of dismissal, which was seen as a purely presidential prerogative. Previous presidents had engaged in arbitrary dismissals with a variety of ends in mind. John Adams had dismissed several high-ranking appointees for failing to support Federalist policy and had also dismissed several appointees for simply belonging to the wrong party (Rosenbloom 1971:37–38). Jefferson engaged in the same practice but on a somewhat wider scale (White 1965:347). There was no standard rule governing dismissals other than self-imposed constraints of the president. This provided an opportunity for the opposition to charge incumbents with pursuing purely party interests as against the public interest (Fish 1904:46).

In 1820, an attempt was made by William H. Crawford, then Secretary of the Treasury, to curb the president's power over dismissal. He successfully urged his supporters in Congress to pass the "Four Year's Bill," or Tenure of Office Act. This provided a fixed term of office for appointees having responsibility for collection and disbursal of funds. The idea, supposedly, was to make sure that accounts were rendered at least every four years. Whatever Crawford's intentions, the legislation would also have reduced the president's capacity to lock in officials of his choice and party (Fish 1904:66–68; Rosenbloom 1971:42; White 1965:390). If used consistently and broadened to include all appointments, it would reduce the capacity of a president to determine the long-term character of the civil service since it meant that no one was safely in possession of an office. Furthermore, since the senior posts required the consent and advice of the Senate, it meant an expansion of Senate power at the expense of the president, hence as Jefferson complained over a dismissal:

This is a sample of the effects we may expect from the late mischievous law vacating every four years nearly all the executive offices of the government. It saps the constitutional and salutary functions of the president, and introduces a principal of intrigue and corruption, which will soon leaven the mass, not only of Senators, but of citizens. . . . it puts all appointments under their [Senate] control every four years, and will keep in constant excitement all the hungry cormorants for office. (quoted in Fish 1904:67)

Why did Jackson want this kind of regulation if it weakened, as Jefferson claimed, presidential power? The answer, I believe, is that it enhanced two Jacksonian goals at the same time: the desire for an impersonal system of tenure and appointment which appeared to use a more "republican" criterion for appointment than social class or its corollary—college education; and his belief that party activism was the appropriate indication of public spirit, so long as it did not subvert the rights of majoritarian election victories. The only way of fulfilling majoritarian expectations was by insuring that implementation of policy would be carried out by those with a vested interest in the government's policies. This was, after all, an old notion going back to George Washington, who had written in 1795:

I shall not, whilst I have the honor to administer the government, bring a man into any office of consequence knowingly, whose political tenets are adverse to the measures which the general government are pursuing; for this, in my opinion, would be a sort of political suicide. (as quoted in Rosenbloom 1971:36)

In this sense, Jackson was arguing that party, rather than social class as evidenced in the idea of "fitness of character," (Rosenbloom 1971:35; Aronson 1964:3–5) provided the best means of ensuring the commitment of the official to the public interest. The public interest coincided, after all, with majority party interest. Or, in Van Buren's words: [Patronage power should be] "put in the hands of the executive, not for himself, but to secure to the majority of the people that control and influence in every section of the state to which they are justly entitled" (quoted in Meyers 1957:252).

Indeed, subjecting the appointment to four-year terms or rotation meant that specific jobs rather than lifelong careers became the primary object of definition as well as of aspiration. This seems to help account for Jackson's statements regarding the evils of prolonged careers and the superiority of office-holding by terms. Once jobs were well defined, they might not only be filled by any intelligent person, but the officeholders were also more easily held accountable for their performance (Crenson 1975:56–57). Thus any efficiency gained by lifelong tenure in office was offset, in Jackson's view, by the absence of any coherent means of making individuals account for their actions and the interests which underlay them.

Equally, however, it was clear that the legislation could provide incoming presidents or departmental heads with the capacity to determine the short-term character of the civil service—or at least a good part of it. The rule had the added advantage of confirming the notion that office-holding was not a property right. In short, specific terms on office-holding provided contemporary political leaders with a rule governing tenure and exit from office that was systematic and relatively predictable, if not conducive to the idea of career. Jackson's commitment to the idea of systematic rotation or definite terms of office was not without precedent. Rather, his innovation was the attempt to elevate the conception to a general principle of appointment.

Jackson sought, and accomplished to a considerable degree, the rationalization and legitimation of patronage in the form of term appointments as the means for ensuring the "publicness" of the administrative system. This was accomplished by using the political party as the mechanism and the mediation for this rationalization. Party provided the means for restraining the individual from pursuing his own interests without limit. Party provided the means, public in character, for rising above the personalistic and idiosyncratic means of filling out the administrative structure utilized by his predecessors. Party regulated not only in the sense of individual behavior but in the institutional sense as well. As long as appointment coincided with the rotation of terms and majority parties, civil administration could not come to have an interest of its own. Where this condition prevailed, officials were, as Jackson had put it in his inaugural speech, "apt to acquire a habit of looking with indifference upon the public interests and of tolerating conduct from which an *unpracticed* man would revolt" (italics inserted).

In sum, the expansion of the franchise, the great growth in the number of elective offices, the development of the convention system, and the powerful contestation over the nomination and election of presidents were major factors bringing about both the decline of the notable basis of the first party system and the emergence of the second party system. The second party system had at its base the development of relatively well organized state parties working in coordination to nominate and elect presidents at the national level. The victory of the Jacksonian Democrats reflected the efficacy of the new view of party as a full-time, continuous organization in local and state politics. It was the victory of the new politician: the professional who saw himself as a political activist on behalf of a party which reflected the public interest and not a statesman who reflected the public interest by virtue of his social standing and its corollaries. The publicness of administration could only be maintained, from the point of view of party leaders, by placing severe limits on the self-perpetuation of civil administrators through the existence of lifetime employment—a view which came to be shared by Jackson's and Van Buren's competition, the Whigs.

Concurrently, the party came to serve as the sole means of mediating between individuals and public policy by providing a structure for producing meaningful majorities. The means by which it did so was through an organizational structure that did two things very well: it mobilized voters and reduced the number of candidates so as to reduce the number of choices open to the voters. This kind of organization was able to reduce voter volatility considerably, to the relief of party leaders, and limit it by and large to changes in majorities between two parties. Party organizations, however, did require large amounts of resources to maintain activists. What more efficient and benign means of sustaining the institutionalization of the party while legitimizing its public role than resorting to patronage in a systematic rotational pattern? The Whigs attacked term rotation and patronage violently after the 1828 election (but were to engage in it when their turn in power came in 1840)(Fish 1904:140). The Jacksonian Democrats were able to legitimize their behavior precisely because term dismissals and patronage appointments were no longer based on what appeared to be the willfulness of individual presidents seemingly consulting no one but themselves and their interests. The presence of party organization, which sustained a public administrative organization through patronage and term appointments, was itself sustained by the resources patronage represented. Out of this situation, then, term appointments emerged as the solution to the "publicness" of the civil service, while its corollary, party appointments or patronage, became the solution to the problem of resources for party leaders.

Party and Patronage: 1840–83

Party patronage and the term or job appointment as solutions to the problem of integrating parties and party leadership to the structure of government was not without its problems. Not the least of these was the absence of any central organization for the selection of patronage appointments, nor any criteria for that selection which might produce a pool of eligibles of manageable size. Although Jackson and Van Buren did not engage in wholesale rotation of offices, their successors increasingly did so. Polk, Taylor, Pierce, Filmore, and, finally, Buchanan all engaged in increasingly expanding purges of their predecessors (Fish 1904:158–72; White 1954:325–46; Rosenbloom 1971:55–69).

Buchanan is sometimes thought of as having reached the heights of rotation and patronage logic by turning out almost the entire range of his predecessor's presidential appointments, even though he was of the same party (Fish 1904:166–69; White 1954:313). Buchanan's action thus revealed that patronage and rotation had become the means not simply of party maintenance but the means by which party factions sought to strengthen their positions and dominate the party. Lincoln's sweep of Democratic officeholders in 1861 and after completed three decades of the growth and institutionalization of term appointments as the means of providing patronage for party leaders to secure their place as well as that of their party's (Fish 1904:171–72).

The 1840s, then, saw presidential-party selection emerge as the primary, indeed the only, systematic means of appointment to the civil service. No test of basic skills or capacities related to job performance was required until 1853. Even then, the requirement was only a minimal pass examination, not a competitive one. At any rate, this examination apparently proved to be no obstacle to any reasonable patronage appointment (Van Riper 1958a:52–53; Fish 1904:182–83). It seems clear that the examination was primarily aimed at eliminating the most grossly illiterate applicants (Hoogenboom 1961:9). The system of recruitment to the civil service thus had mostly to do with party activity and not with any standard of skills. Although terms of appointment did not require dismissal at the end of four years or the completion of a presidential term, it became increasingly the case that four years was the longest one might prudently count on to hold office, unless it was largely technical in character. But even technical offices were also subject to patronage considerations—party loyalty in some fashion determining choice among those who might possess certain skills (White 1954:357).

As a consequence of this periodic replacement system, the number of appointments to be made did not decline over time, since they were not a function of a career structure with a retirement or, for the most part, any natural attrition system. A newly elected president, thus, in theory, had at least as many or more appointments to make as his predecessor. In fact, throughout the nineteenth century, the number of patronage appointments grew with each president. Between 1792 and 1871, the civil service increased from approximately one thousand to over fifty thousand employees (U.S. Bureau of the Census 1960:710; Peters 1985:230–33). The vast majority of these positions were in the field services—primarily the post office (U.S. Bureau of the Census 1960:710). Polk, for example, appointed more than 13,500 postmasters during his four-year term—filling vacancies created by nearly 10,000 resignations, 1,600 removals, and the addition of new post offices (White 1954:312).

The very high level of rotation achieved in the system by 1860 meant that the conception of career—in the sense of a structure of offices linked hierarchically with a specific point of entrance and exit, movement through which was relatively predictable—simply could not be said to exist. Assuredly, there were a number of individuals, primarily chief clerks and a few clerks in the Washington departments, who held office for almost their entire adult lives (White 1954:352–57). This longevity was not achieved by any formal or informal rule governing seniority or promotion. Seniority played a role in the promotion of a few clerks to senior clerks, but they were by no means the great majority of cases (White 1954:352–57; Hoogenboom 1961:3–4). Scientific officers did have some prospect of tenure; however, these were relatively few in number (White 1954:357–58). It is just to say that the rather small numbers of individuals who managed to stay on in office for a long period of time did so as a function of the high rate of turnover all around them, especially above them. The high rates of turnover of senior presidential appointees in the departments (the secretaries) meant that authority and expertise tended to slip downward to the chief clerk who served as the chief administrative officer under the secretary (except in the Treasury Department). The high rate of turnover would require at least a few souls who had knowledge of office affairs, and these would generally be the individuals who had the longest service. The consequence was that those individuals who, by happy coincidence, happened to have the longest tenure in a department at times of high turnover were likely to keep their positions. Those with the shortest service were viewed as the ones most easily dispensed with, if only because they had been appointed by an immediately preceding secretary.

This condition was little changed by the legislation of 1853, which created the pass examinations and, at the same time, the first system of job classifications. The act of 3 March 1853 required that all heads of departments (with the exception of the State Department, which was included two years later) group their clerks into four classes. Each class was distinguished by differing ranges of salary but not carefully defined job distinctions (Van Riper 1958a:54). There was no provision for promotion linkage between classes—individuals could be appointed to any level without regard for seniority (White 1954:371). Despite the absence of any reference to linkage between offices by promotion, that there were four defined classes seemed to suggest a ladder of promotion. All in all, however, rotation clearly meant careers were not a dominant characteristic of the patronage recruited civil service. Rather, rotation patronage defined civil service as a job not a career role.

The sheer number of possible appointments meant that those who dispensed them were the object of continual pressure—not only from job seekers, but also from party leaders at the state and local levels who wished to maintain their positions through the dispensation of rewards and the resources that accompanied them. Presidents, especially, faced great demands. When the Whigs won the election of 1840 and Harrison became president, he was greeted on his arrival in Washington with such a great crowd of office seekers that he could not attend his first cabinet meeting because every room was filled. Nor would they leave until he had accepted all of their papers (White 1954:304). When the Democrats returned to office in 1845, Polk was greeted with demands that lasted for the entire four years of his term. On the first anniversary of his inauguration he wrote in his diary:

I am ready to exclaim, will the pressure for office never cease! It is one year today since I entered on the duties of my office, and still the pressure for office has not abated. I most sincerely wish I had no offices to bestow. (as quoted in White 1954:304)

In 1847 he predicted that no president would ever be reelected.

The reason is that the patronage of the Government will destroy the popularity of any President, however well he may administer the Government. The office seekers have become so numerous that they hold the balance of power between the two great parties of the country. (as quoted in White 1954:304)

President Taylor was reported to have said that office seekers had become so importunate that if he did not kick a man downstairs, he went away believing he had a promise of office (White 1954:304). Congressmen and senators were also pressured and they, in turn, pressured the president.

The party as an organization could offer little relief from this pressure. Lacking a permanent national organizational structure meant there was no patronage secretary, as in England. Even if one had existed, it is doubtful that a president would have yielded the leverage of patronage except to a machinery controlled by himself. To do otherwise would have meant the loss of any real power. Nevertheless, presidents simply could not handle the requests all by themselves. If positions were to be given out on the basis of deserving service for president and party, then something had to be known about applicants and local nominees, especially since there were often hundreds of applicants for every position.

Presidents had early taken to asking the advice of trusted people. After rotation patronage came into full swing, however, presidents were forced to delegate advisory functions in a more systematic fashion. Minor offices in congressional districts generally came to be given to congressmen of the presidential party, while senators were consulted for more important state positions or offices in major urban areas (Fish 1904:173–74). By the time of the Civil War, the state congressional delegations had come to act as the major channel for patronage appointments within their states (Fish 1904:173–74). Where there were no delegations, or there were factions within the state, the president had to hunt for other sources of information (Fish 1904:175). In larger urban areas where there grew significant autonomous organizations, such as Weed's organization in New York in the 1840s and 1850s, the organization boss had access to local patronage (Fish 1904:175).

The system had its advantages for a president seeking a second term. He could use patronage not only to reward the party stalwarts who had put him in office, but also those who might be instrumental in returning him. The patronage was also of great help in cementing relationships between party leaders and their factions. The importance of patronage did not stem merely from the capacity to "reward friends and punish enemies." In good part, the importance of patronage stemmed from the party leaders' ability to assess patronage appointees for party treasure chests. The assessments ran from one to six percent of the appointee's annual salary (Rosenbloom 1971:62–63; White 1954:334–37; Ostrogorski 1902:II, 143–48). Patronage appointees were not only expected to vote early and often, they were also expected to work hard to get out the vote at all the various and sundry elections which occurred where they lived (White 1954:337–40).

Nevertheless, as time went on it became more and more apparent that patronage was a source of friction as well as a source of integration. The absence of any clear explicit rules for handing out patronage, except the very general one of party loyalty and activism, meant that the allocation of patronage was highly contingent. A variety of contingent matters, such as presidential aggressiveness, whether the president was in his first or second term, party strength in Congress, and factionalism in state party organizations, all entered into the way in which positions were passed out. These same factors also produced conflict over patronage allocations. Since patronage represented party funding as well as the source for maintaining party workers, patronage allocations were the object of increasingly sharp and bitter conflict. Such positions as the Collector of Customs for New York were major political plums which were eagerly sought (Hoogenboom 1961:35; Fish 1904:139–40, 177). Postmasterships were also a potential source of conflict for every member of Congress (Fish 1904:176; Norris and Shaffer 1970:xxiii, 67–68). Factions within parties also came to fight over important patronage positions (Doenecke 1981:33–34, 41–45; Fish 1904:186–206).

The problems of regulating and controlling patronage were exacerbated by the absence of any homogeneity among patronage appointments. Since minimal, if any, literacy was required in the field services, the range of training and skills was extremely wide. This was somewhat less so in the departmental bureaucracies in Washington where seniority had produced a few career men. On the whole, however, public duties were performed by individuals who tended to have little in common except their party. This resulted in the development of the bureau system, where specific areas of functions came to be defined. Absence of any uniform training, combined with rotation, meant an increased reliance on formal and informal rules. Without any general departmental rules, the bureaus within the departments developed their own. They came to have highly parochial systems of organizing their work—so much so that they were consistently the object of complaints about their autonomy from departmental direction (White 1954:536–40; Crenson 1975:104–39). As a result, highly centralized direction of departmental activities and policies was absent and this state of affairs became increasingly institutionalized.

By the end of the Civil War, party and civil service had become inextricably bound together. Beginning with the Jacksonians, political leaders had become party leaders. The party had become the means by which the expanded suffrage was organized to end the dominance of the notables. To maintain themselves in power, party leaders sought to create a civil bureaucracy free of individual patronage with all of its overtones of privateness and private interest. Furthermore, they sought to provide for the party and for themselves a continuing fountain of resources that would allow the perpetuation of the party as an organization. Party leaders had few other choices than to link rotation and patronage. Each element alone would have provided little. Together, they provided party leaders with the means to ensure implementation of party policies and distribution of public goods in a manner designed to maintain the state structure of parties. No other solution was available if party leaders' major aim was to remain in power and reduce voter volatility (Shefter 1978b:413–15). Buchanan's and Lincoln's presidencies both showed, in different ways, how party leaders had become almost completely dependent on patronage and rotation as the means for providing resources and manpower to organize the voters and sustain the party. Indeed, they had become the primary means by which to travel the road to political leadership itself.

Although rotation and patronage meant party loyalty was the primary criterion for appointment, this did not mean there were no constraints on the performance of public duties. The party posed not inconsiderable constraints on individual interests. The party, as represented by its congressional delegation, its statewide representatives, and its local activists, had to produce. It became a general assumption that winning parties had to bring development funds to local areas through the "pork barrel." This meant that efforts had to be made to ensure the implementation of distribution policies. Substance may have been important when it came to public policy, but it was clearly secondary to the distributive/proportional apportionment aspects of policy (Lowi 1975:254–55; McCormick 1986:206–14). Thus, there appeared the notion of fair distribution of public goods such as patronage (White 1954:396–98).[3] To this end, patronage appointees had to be careful about implementing public works projects or face the possibility of voters switching loyalties. Furthermore, too much skimming of public funds, too much corruption in the form of kickbacks, too much scandal, too much inefficiency, all tended to put the party and, specifically, the appointers of such corrupt officials in a bad light (Norris and Shaffer 1970:xxi–xxii). There was, thus, some considerable concern to find capable people who would enhance the reputation of the appointer.

Out of this situation emerged a civil bureaucracy characterized by an absence of career structure, by a concern for job, by job description and appointment, and one in which entry and exit could occur at any level. High rates of turnover at the most senior and lucrative levels meant that ongoing authority and decision-making tended to move down to middle levels. This resulted in the maintenance of a small number of bureau officials who served for life but who were not the possessors of careers. High rates of turnover also produced reliance on bureau organization and rule-making. These came to be the means of maintaining order and system in everyday affairs among lower-ranking positions, where rotation was high, and among middle-level

3. In May 1853, Secretary of the Interior Robert McClelland instituted an apportionment rule for his department. Henceforth clerkships would be distributed among the states in proportion to the size of their congressional representation. Other departments soon followed so that by the end of the decade it had become an informal rule (White 1954:398).

positions, where rotation grew increasingly along with the century. The civil bureaucracy had little, if any, autonomy by the end of the Civil War. However, the necessity on the part of party leaders to maintain the legitimacy and publicness of party acted as a constraint, if not always very successfully, on the temptation to pursue individual interest. All of this, however, was to change under the intense pressures of the changes wrought by the Union's and Republican Party's victory in the Civil War.

9

Political Leadership, Party Contestation, and Reform: 1865–1925

Party Conflict and the Attack on Patronage: 1865–83

The politics of the post–Civil War period, until the critical elections and re-alignments of 1893–96, was dominated by the institutional arrangements of party that had originated in the second party system. These arrangements were characterized by party activist or leader control of nominations through the convention system, a large number of elective offices which served as a structure of leadership career, patronage control by party leaders of most appointive offices, and full mobilization of voters by party organizations that produced high levels of competition (Burnham 1970:72). The Civil War had confirmed the role of the party as the essential mediator. Lincoln's war machine had been a party machine not an administrative one (McKitrick 1967:117–51; Skowronek 1982:30). The resources mobilized by the North were enormous. "[B]ut . . . , the state's power was anchored in the new Republican organization and its capacity to channel the actions of governing elites" (Skowronek 1982:30).

The party system emerged strengthened rather than weakened from the Civil War. In the following decades it produced an almost evenly matched competition between the Democratic and Republican parties. This competition has been styled as "militaristic" (Jensen 1968:2–10). The term was prompted by the nature of the two highly organized parties, with their well-disciplined and motivated staffs, supported by financial and communications resources, ready and willing to engage in combat like armies.

On the face of it, the organization of the two parties around the resources provided by elections and, especially, patronage appears to have been sufficiently well regulated so that political leadership faced few challenges to the existing rules. But the passage of the Pendleton Act in 1883 and the move toward greater rationalization of the bureaucracy over the next thirty years suggests this was not completely true. The creation of the merit system seemed to be aimed at challenging party leaders' control over access to resources provided by the patronage system. This meant, in turn, an attack on the very nature of party organization or, at least, on the basis of political party leadership. How then, did patronage, which seemed so well anchored in the most widely accepted American institution—the political party—

come to be severely constrained by the very men—party leaders—who benefited the most by this arrangement?

The answer lies in three closely related developments of the post–Civil War
period. The first of these was the unsettled nature of Republican Party leadership. With the end of the Civil War, the unintegrated factions of an expanded
party revealed themselves. The most bitter and contentious of these was the so-
called mugwumps, who were to challenge the party professionals until their
partial victories at the end of the century. The second political development
was the emergence of the Democrats by the late 1870s as a party with sufficient
strength to win not only state but national elections. This equality of resources
and voters made it possible for small groups in either party to carry greater
weight than their numbers. In the tight contests of the late 1870s, 1880s, and
early 1890s, even small defections were viewed as disastrous. The third development was the growth of patronage and increasing difficulties in finding a
harmonious arrangement for its distribution. The reliance of party leaders on
patronage encouraged the growth of civil service jobs in the federal and state
governments. Along with this, industrial and commercial growth produced
demands for expanded services in such areas as the post office and the customs
service. The combination of these developments produced conditions which
led party leaders to follow a strategy which led, unintentionally, to the rationalization of the civil service bureaucracy.

At the center of this almost dialectical change was the contest within the Republican Party and, finally, within the party system as a whole, over the nature
of party and, therefore, political leadership. The conflict over party leadership
among the Republicans stemmed in large part from the group of antislavery,
free-trade reformers who had joined the Republican party and helped bring
the party to power under Lincoln. They were generally anti-labor, advocates of
hard money, and believers in "good," efficient businesslike government
(Sproat 1968:6). These predominantly Northeastern liberal free-labor, free-
trade proponents had originally entered the Republican party because they saw
it as the only possible vehicle for their antislavery views. In doing so, however,
they came with no organizational structure of their own, nor any willingness
to spend time and effort in creating a party organization similar to those of the
major urban areas from which they came (Sproat 1968:47–69; McFarland
1975:12, 20–21). The bossism they felt characterized the structure of party
politics was distasteful to them (Sproat 1968:48).

It is not easy to locate the precise source of their seemingly aristocratic
disdain for the low, hardworking side of politics nor for their early assumption of civil service reform as their major goal. The burgeoning industrialists
of the age were not so tender about with whom and how they had to deal to

get their way (Sproat 1968:46–47). The vast majority of Americans in the last third of the nineteenth century did not appear to view patronage politics as inherently immoral. This small group of men, however, once antislavery reformers, now, with the end of the Civil War, became antipatronage. Carl Schurz, the early leader of the liberal Republicans made this explicit when he wrote that slavery had been replaced by spoils politics as "the greatest danger threatening our republican institutions" (as quoted in McFarland 1975:12). This shift to the view that spoils politics was the great crisis to be met if the republic was to survive appears to have had no immediate cause or provocation. No major historical event of the late 1860s or the 1870s could be said to cry out that the republic was endangered by the patronage system.

That the liberal Republicans or mugwumps chose the spoils system as their object of attack, and then proceeded to attack the existing party leadership by attempting to organize their own presidential nomination in Cincinnati in 1872, suggests that their struggle was over the question of what constituted political leadership and how it should be selected (Sproat 1968:80–81). That is to say, an end to the spoils system was not the solution to any specific institution-grinding crisis. While labor unrest emerged in the 1870s along with an economic depression, there was no real belief that revolution was in the offing. Nor would an end to patronage resolve those particular problems. Rather, an end to patronage was seen as the solution to the problem of the "best men" and why they did not hold the positions of political leadership (Sproat 1968:48–50, 55–61; Keller 1977:272–75).

The liberal Republicans wanted government to be run by moral men. But it was not immediately clear what defined morality other than the rather self-serving notion that the "best men" possessed this virtue. In the decade between 1865 and 1875, the reformers came to define moral leadership in more precise, practical, if not theoretical, terms. The moral stature of the individual could be measured in a practical sense by the organizational structure which brought him to positions of social status. Political leadership thus became, in their eyes, a function of a moral *organizational* life.

What then was the proper road to political leadership if it was not through the increasingly complex and skillful manipulation of patronage? It was clear that the challengers opposed large-scale organizational structures as the source for moral leadership. They were not only opposed to the organizational structure of the parties with their demands for discipline and hierarchy, they were also opposed to monopolies and viewed big business generally with suspicion (Hoogenboom 1961:22). The mugwumps believed these organizational structures deprived men of their independence and forced them to act in the interests of organizational rather public interest. Individual independence was construed as synonymous with the capacity for a public life in a manner similar to the idea of "republican virtue" which informed some of the Founders (Sproat 1968:60–63). These views clearly mirrored the organizational life with which the reformers themselves were endowed. Coming largely from the professional middle class (lawyers, doctors, clergymen, editors, and professors, as well as mercantile and financial businessmen), their experiences had all been in individually oriented professions or small organizations (Hoogenboom 1961:21; McFarland 1975:24–25; Skowronek 1982:53).

The aspirations of professionals and would-be professionals, especially the desire to control the conditions of their occupation, led them to view ethical behavior as a function of individually internalized rules derived from the nature and essence of their training and not from organization. Where organizational ethics dominated, they believed, there could be no adequate commitment to the public interest (Bledstein 1976:87–92). Seen from this point of view, the proper organizational structure was not one that centered on hierarchy, discipline, and incremental levels of organizational experience (seniority). These characteristics subordinated knowledge or expertise to organizational and, therefore, private interests. Rather, the only appropriate form of organization was one which recognized the independence of the professional. Such an organization would be more like a community of equals rather than a structure of hierarchy. It would be an organization of voluntary association which expressed the independence and professionalism of the individual. Finally, it would be an organization which was epiphenomenal to their professional career not the source of the career. In short, the moral organization was one which stressed the independence and equality of those possessing the requisite knowledge to claim professional status.

It is, thus, no coincidence that the first nationally oriented organization with which the reformers found themselves closely associated was the American Social Science Association, founded in 1865 (Hoogenboom 1961:54–55, 64–65; Silva and Slaughter 1984:39–68; Sproat 1968:56–57; Haskell 1977). Its aims included a broad spectrum of public interest issues, not the least of which was civil service reform (Silva and Slaughter 1984:39–68). Nor is it coincidental that the other major form of organization they turned to were local clubs formed by professionals aimed at reforms of various kinds (Sproat 1968:55–60; McFarland 1975:14–15). All notion of coincidence must disappear when we note that the early 1870s until the end of the century was a period when professional associations flowered (Bledstein 1976:84–87; Choi 1985). Other public policy oriented organizations founded and inhabited by professionals emerged in the 1870s and 1880s. Such groups as the New York Civil Service Reform Association (1877), the forerunner of the National Civil Service Reform League (1881), the Massa-

chusetts Reform Club (1882), the American Free Trade League (1867), the
Boston Reform League (1869), and the Taxpayer's Union (1871) became
rallying points for professionals. In sum, the highly individually oriented
and essentially private nature of professional training produced an expanding group of middle-class professionals whose social and economic role led
them to adopt an organizational style that was in direct opposition to that of
the political parties and the industrial sector.

The liberal Republicans had entered the party with no organizational
base. The end of the war found them in no better position. Nor had they
served in the trenches of the urban or state parties sufficiently long to acquire
either patronage resources or party organizational position. By the beginning
of the 1870s, these men were faced with only three possible courses if they
wished to gain access to political leadership, which meant, in effect, party
leadership. They could join the regular state and/or local party organizations
and acquire the resources which would provide them with the leadership
base, or they could stay within the party and gain access to leadership by undermining the basis of the regular party leadership—that is, by attacking patronage and seeking other forms of organization which would sustain the
party. Lastly, they could attack the existent party structure as corrupt
through the medium of a new party.

For the liberal Republicans the first alternative was out of the question on
several grounds. To join the party on terms of the regulars meant abandoning the very role construct that distinguished them from the regular party
leaders. Their claims to leadership were based on their distinctiveness as
nonregular politicians. This claim to legitimacy was not simply based on opportunistic criteria since, as individuals in pursuit of political power, playing
the regular party game might have been the most efficient way of gaining
leadership. In good part, their claim to leadership also rested on their repug-
nance of organizational ethics. "People seem to think they are citizens of the
Republican Party and that is patriotism and sufficiently good patriotism."
And again, "I prefer to be a citizen of the United States," wrote Mark Twain
on becoming a mugwump in 1884 (quoted in Sproat 1968:61). "I am persuaded," Mark Twain said during the presidential campaign of 1884, "that
this idea of *consistency*—unchanging allegiance to *party*—has lowered the
manhood of the whole *nation*—pulled it down and dragged it in the mud"
(italics in the original, as quoted in Sproat 1968:128). As men who had
emerged out of the professional role, they had, aside from their strategic objections to regular party leadership, an abhorrence for party organization
that underlined their commitments to the norms of profession and its community egalitarianism.

The liberals tried the third alternative very early. In 1872, out of disgust with Grant's coziness with big industry and big finance, not to mention the scandals associated with Grant's first term, the liberals sought to pressure the regular Republicans by creating a new nominee, if not a new party. This "convention of idealists and professors and soreheads" as Roscoe Conkling, senator from New York, described it (as quoted in Josephson 1938:163) were joined by some old regulars who had it in for the Stalwart faction supporting Grant to nominate Horace Greely for president. The Democrats, smelling a chance at upsetting the Republicans, also nominated him, thus co-opting many liberals and eliminating a third party at the same time (Josephson 1938:153–64; Jordan 1971:178–81). Grant's large victory revealed the organizational weakness of the liberals not only within the Republican Party but as putative political leaders.

This position left them with only one strategy other than simply resigning any notion of acquiring political leadership. Lacking the means, capacity, will, and desire to engage in the struggle for patronage, the putative liberal leaders now returned to the party and attacked its leadership structure as corrupt, and patronage as the source of corruption. Martin Shefter's observation applies quite well, albeit in a slightly different context:

Because they are established by outsiders . . . [they] do not enjoy access to state patronage at the time of their founding and perforce are compelled to rely upon other means to acquire a following . . . they will find it necessary to rely upon other appeals to mobilize supporters . . . the leaders and cadres . . . themselves will comprise a constituency for universalism, and the party will not be beholden to any constituency for patronage. . . . The leaders and cadres . . . are likely to be committed to an ideology—a vision of society—and once they come to power, they are not going to be willing to fritter away in patronage the authority they now have to remold society. (Shefter 1978b:415, 417, 419)

In short, where exit and loyalty are self-destructive strategies, voice becomes the only viable strategy if putative leaders want to stay in the game. The liberal Republicans thus had little choice. As outsiders they had no access to the machinery of power. They were thus led inevitably by both the strategic situation and their belief in the superiority of their structure of leadership to challenge the "ins." Benjamin Butler, one of the great spoilsmen of the Gilded Age, got it more or less right when he said succinctly, "Civil service reform is always popular with the 'outs' and never with the 'ins', unless with those who have a strong expectation of soon going out" (as quoted in Hoogenboom 1961:ix). The liberal Republicans, dominated by professionals, thus became strong advocates of civil service reform. They wanted an end to large-scale patronage, especially patronage at the lower levels, since this is what provided the resource base of the regular party leaders. They didn't want an end to all patronage, merely that which enabled the professional regular party leader to continue to dominate (Shefter 1978a:227). As one of the leading reformers, George W. Curtis argued, reform was not aimed at eliminating political parties but at returning parties to their proper role.

What is the legitimate sphere of party action? Parties divide on questions of national policy. In a free country they appeal by public speech and in the public press to the judgement of the people. . . . But they succeed only by legislation. Consequently each party strives to elect to the various legislatures representatives who will put its policy into law, and to commit the chief executives offices . . . to friendly hands. This is the legitimate scope of party action. (as quoted in White 1958:300)

The charge that corrupt leadership was engendered by a corrupt system of allocating office would have meant little to Republican party leadership if it had not come at a time when the two parties were about evenly matched. Major issues between the parties gradually diminished in the 1870s, especially with the end of Reconstruction and the redemption of the Southern states, following the extraordinarily close election of 1876 (Dobson 1972:43–44). This meant that challenges to regular Republican party leadership from within or without had a relatively narrow range. Corruption was always an excellent choice since it was both an issue of moral principle and a challenge to the legitimacy of leaders. The evenly balanced political situation of the next two decades encouraged the emergence of groups who sought to use their small numbers to gain major influence.

The depression of 1873 had helped produce the first postwar Democratic majority in the House of Representatives in the following year. The close election of 1876, in which Tilden won the popular vote, was won by the Republicans only because they achieved a majority on the commission which certified the disputed electoral votes. The Republican victory in the presidential election of 1880 was also very close, with Garfield just barely winning. The Democrats won control of the House of Representatives in the elections of 1882, winning key elections in states where liberal strength was greatest (Hoogenboom 1961:233–34). It was, then, entirely possible that a Democrat could take the White House in 1884. The liberals were in an excellent bargaining position for challenging the regular leadership and making progress toward undermining their basis of power. Simultaneously, the threat of losing patronage control, of having all the patronage turned out of office with its assessments and activists, put the regular party leaders in the mood for compromise on the reform issue.

Not only did the electoral situation put them in mind of reform, but the whole problem of party factionalism centering on patronage allocation put them in the mood for considering some way of handling patronage on a less conflictual basis. The problem was not one simply of size, even though the large numbers of appointments available meant an enormous investment of time—it has been estimated that each congressman had several hundred appointments to dispense (Dobson 1972:56). More important, the distribution of the patronage plums brought on powerful conflicts between factions and between members of the same party in the executive and Congress (Kaufman 1956:1,068–69). The most notable and archetypical of these was the struggle between the Stalwarts, led by Roscoe Conkling, and Hayes and the Half-Breeds over the dispensation of the New York Customs House. The latter had been in the hands of Conkling, who had used it well in maintaining his dominance over New York Republican politics. Hayes had no use for Conkling, whom he viewed as an enemy. The upshot was that Hayes removed Conkling's appointments and sought to turn them over to his supporters. While the Senate voted to support senatorial courtesy, Hayes merely waited until the Congress was out of session to defeat Conkling. This drama was repeated when Garfield was elected in 1880. Despite Conkling's fierce opposition, Garfield gave another set of anti-Conklinites the Custom House plum. This conflict and its repetition within a five-year period revealed the degree to which the party remained unintegrated and the subversive role played by a patronage system over which there was no institutional control. It also produced a situation in which the liberals' power was enhanced despite their relatively small numbers and resources (Dobson 1972:64–67; Josephson 1938:238–53; Marcus 1971:29–58; Doenecke 1981:43–45).

Finally, the patronage system had genetic failings as a support for party politics. The growth of the federal field services, especially the postal service, the customs service, and the land office service, produced an increasing level of demands on the existing system of recruitment through the patronage system. By 1881, the total number of civilian federal employees had risen to 100,020, of which 86,896 were in field services. Of these, over fifty-six thousand were in the postal service and approximately twenty thousand were in the other two services (U.S. Bureau of the Census 1960:710). The number of appointments available for each member of Congress (several hundred) and the executive branch (several thousand for the president directly, and well over several hundred for each department head outside of the postal service) to make was large and time consuming. There was no systematic way for these individuals to ensure that appointments met minimal qualifications. A rather haphazard system grew up in the 1870s, in which congressmen and senators came to rely on principal agents to make recommendations, but here, too, the system was entirely *ad hoc* (Norris and Shaffer 1970:ix–xxix; Thompson 1985:248–49).

Not only did the jury-rigged nature of the appointment system create problems in finding minimally capable people, the necessity of relying heavily on loyalty as a criterion meant that the standard of quality was, at best, variable and, at worst, dismaying. As Garfield's diaries and letters have shown, there was very great concern over the quality of patronage appointments since they reflected on the ability of elected officials to serve their constituencies (Thompson 1985:220–21; Norris and Shaffer 1970:ix–xxiv). There is little doubt that, by the 1880s, the problem of maintaining a group of minimally capable federal appointees at the field service level had reached a point where it was a constant source of concern for members of Congress (Skowronek 1982:51–52; Thompson 1985:117–44). By the early 1880s, patronage had helped undermine the party structure by its failure to provide minimally standard tests of competence for patronage appointments.

The congressional elections of 1882 brought some of these concerns very directly into focus. The Republicans suffered serious losses. Republicans were defeated by large majorities in Pennsylvania, Indiana, Connecticut, New Jersey, and even in Massachusetts; moreover, they were not only defeated in New York—a Democrat, Cleveland, was elected governor. Nearly all of these were states in which the liberal Republicans had been strong (Hoogenboom 1961:234). The losses clearly were related to the apparent success of the liberal Republicans in organizing a sufficient number of voters to make civil service reform an issue that could make a major difference in the presidential elections of 1884.

On the part of the regular Republican party leadership, civil service reform appeared necessary for two reasons: first, because it appeared that the liberal Republican challenge was sufficiently strong so as to make their threat of defection to the Democrats in the 1884 presidential elections a powerful one; second, reforms of a certain kind, especially those pressed by the reformers, would help soften the blow if the Republicans did lose the White House in 1884—that is, by putting large numbers of patronage Republicans under protection from dismissal. For the Democrats, reform was an issue that might provide them sufficient votes to win the White House for the first time in the post–Civil War era. Charges of corruption and the inability to distinguish private from public interest were strong issues in an otherwise issueless period (Dobson 1972:66–71; Hoogenboom 1961:236–38). Moreover, the Democrats had something to gain by a reform that outlawed forced assessments from patronage officeholders. The Republicans had a considerable edge on federal patronage assessments, and the loss of such funds might help redress the balance (Hoogenboom 1961:236–38). All in all, the regular Republican party leadership, along with a number of Democratic leaders now found it to their real interest to pass specific kinds of civil service reform.

The result was the passage of a bill submitted by Senator George Pendleton of Ohio, and actually written by Dorman Eaton, a leading reform advocate (Dobson 1972:69). The final version, which passed the House and Senate in the early days of January 1883, was signed on the 16th by President Arthur, a very prominent spoilsman. The bill basically provided for the following arrangements (Hoogenboom 1961:236–52; Sageser 1935:52–62, 241–44; Van Riper 1958a:96–112; Skowronek 1982:64–68):

1. It generally recognized the president's dominance in the appointment process by providing for an executive service staff—the Civil Service Commission—to regulate and regularize appointments. The commission would recommend rules for the regulation of the executive service, create and supervise examinations, conduct investigations, and submit an annual report to the president. Enforcement of the provisions rested with the president and heads of departments. The original bill provided for a bipartisan commission of five members appointed by the president and serving at his pleasure. The final version reduced this to three members, with no more than two from one party appointed by the president with the advice and consent of the Senate. The commission was given no powers over dismissal. These powers were to remain in the hands of the chief executive and his department heads.

2. The bill established the basic principle of competitive examination as the means for entry into lower-level civil service positions. Examinations were to be based on practical demands of the positions rather than on ideas of education for leadership or some other general conception of appropriate education. Exemptions were to be allowed at the request of department heads. Noncompetitive examinations were to be allowed wherever sufficient competent persons did not compete.

3. While the original bill provided for the basis of a career structure by requiring entrance into the civil service at the lowest grade of any given service, the final version allowed entry at any point so long as the individual fulfilled the examination requirements. Promotion was to be based on merit and competition wherever practical. There were no requirements that appointments above the lowest grade had to be selected from immediately lower offices or grades.

4. Appointments were to be made by appropriate executive officers from among those holding the highest scores. Appointments to departments in Washington were to be further constrained by the requirement that they be apportioned among the states on the basis of population. The merit exams were to be applied to appointments of clerks in Washington departments and to all post offices and customs houses employing fifty or more individuals.

There were also several provisions which applied to all civil service em-

ployees and not just to those who would be classified under the provisions
of the bill. Compulsory assessments were made illegal, as was any attempt at
coercing individuals to perform any political action. It made acceptance of
such assessments and any punishment for failing to provide service or money
illegal as well. The law also made it illegal for elected federal officials to provide written recommendations, other than statements regarding character
and community standing. No more than two members of the same family
could hold positions in the federal service. Violation of any of these was pun-
ishable by fines and a possible prison sentence.

The act, along with the commission rules specifying the examinations
later accepted by the president, made it very clear that political leaders did
not want an autonomous, well-insulated career structure to be characteristic
of the civil service. They created a job structure in which there were no necessary links between offices in any service in the civil administration. Entrance into the various departments could occur at any level and would require an examination only in those positions which had been placed in the
classified category, namely, the merit category. This meant examinations
had to be, indeed, practical in character. Since entrants did not necessarily
start at the same level, no single uniform examination could test for various
levels of experience and ability. Nevertheless, since most of the 13,924 positions placed in the merit category were lower-level offices (clerks, postal and
customs workers), it is not surprising that the early examinations created by
the commission were basically tests of literacy in writing and arithmetic
(White 1958:348–49; Sageser 1935:62–63). The special examinations were
applied primarily to filling offices which required special qualifications, such
as languages and scientific, medical, or legal training, and these were often
noncompetitive (Sageser 1935:94).

Recruitment in this sense, then, was not recruitment to a career. Nor did
the examinations require, at any level, a degree of education that required
much in the way of possible opportunity costs. Lower-level exams required
a degree of literacy that surely did not need much more than a grammar
school education. Special examinations were for positions at levels which did
not impose opportunity costs on individuals. Since these were not positions
at the lowest grades, costs were minimal or nonexistent (Sageser 1935:62–
63). The amorphous character of federal service employment is further reflected in the absence of any rules on tenure. Reformers had always argued
that if they could close the front door, the back door would take care of itself
(Van Riper 1958a:102). The regulation and depoliticization of the former
would remove the incentive for the abuse of the latter. The length of tenure
was thus left to the pleasure of the executive. Placing offices under classification meant that the president sought to remove these offices from patronage

and political considerations. In this way, there was less incentive for rotational removal and greater chances for longevity in office. But the absence of any linkage in offices and the lack of privilege for seniority meant there were no powerful incentives for career commitment. Absence of pension arrangements further contributed to the institutionalization of an administrative structure primarily directed at specific jobs and not careers.

The Pendleton Act created no new structures of hierarchy. Examinations were aimed primarily at lower-level clerks and field workers. Over time, presidents did place new segments of federal workers in the classified service, but these too were primarily lower-level clerks and workers (Sageser 1935:107, 162, 246; Skowronek 1982:69–73). Since entrance could take place at any level, examinations did not serve to distinguish between hierarchical levels of career, as in the cases of France or England, for example. The emphasis of the reform on filling individual positions helped to institutionalize a structure in which there was a unity of a kind, insofar as there were no restrictions on moving upward once one was inside the system (Hays and Kearney 1982:27). At the same time, the utilization of literacy examinations for lower-level workers and of special examinations or certifications for professionals with specialized skills laid the groundwork for the professionalization of areas of specialized administration and the rationalization of appointment in areas of white-collar administration. In the long run, this would mean the creation of distinctions between white-collar, professional, and policy-making job structures.

Interestingly enough, unlike the experiences in a number of other states, in the United States it would be the policy-making positions that would remain open to patronage. Both white-collar and professional employees under the classified system would come to serve for long periods in a variety of offices, but it was not very likely that they would have careers of a systematic character that would lead to the highest positions. The emphasis in the law on open access to all positions, when combined with the loss of pure patronage for positions could provide the basis for long-term careers because it did remove most of the incentives for rotation of technical positions requiring professional or near professional skills. Such careers did emerge toward the end of the century. However, these careers were limited in terms of vertical mobility. They very rarely rose above the rank of bureau chief (MacMahon and Millett 1939:307–50). The ability to fill positions from the outside produced further competition for career structures. Here, too, by the end of the century a significant number of positions were filled from the outside on the basis of special examinations or noncompetitive evaluations (U.S. Civil Service Commission, Annual Report, 1893–1894, 1894–1895, 1895–1896: statistical section on examinations, tables on noncompetitive exams, pagination varies).

The assistant secretaries of the departments were mostly chosen on the basis of political patronage. Thus, in the Treasury Department, the assistant secretaries throughout the nineteenth century, and during the first third of the twentieth, were drawn primarily from non-civil servants, and at least three-quarters were appointed on the basis of political patronage. Most were lawyers, and only ten of the fifty-five who held these offices between 1849 and 1909 rose from the ranks of the clerks' service within the department (MacMahon and Millett 1939:183–96, 474–76). For assistant secretaries, the pattern is repeated in all of the various departments (MacMahon and Millett 1939:290–303). Surprising is the degree to which professionals, especially lawyers, dominated the position throughout the last half of the nineteenth century (MacMahon and Millett 1939:183–96, 474–76).

In short, the reforms resulted in basing the role structure on positions and not careers. In so doing, the reforms created no incentives for individuals to pay opportunity costs with regard to education and training. Education came to have either general literacy value, or its value was to train individuals to fulfill specific roles or occupations. In the absence of incentives, individuals did not invest heavily in education with service in the civil bureaucracy in mind. People acquired education with occupational levels and status in mind (Bledstein 1976:39, 111–12). Individuals moved from specific educational levels directly into various administrative positions. This is reflected in the civil service in the average age at which the various exams were taken. The average age of successful competitors in the general clerical examination of 1886–87 was 27.4; in that of bookkeeper, 33.2; and in that of customs examiners, 35.9, and these averages remained roughly the same over the next decade (U.S. Civil Service Commission, Annual Report, 1886–87:33; 1895–96:175, 176, 222, 223). The average age of individuals successful in the noncompetitive evaluations—the positions most often technical—was over 34 in 1893–94, and this represented the general average over the decade between 1890 and 1900 (U.S. Civil Service Commission, Annual Report, 1895:178–79).

Individuals at the lower and technical levels of the civil service did not prepare themselves specifically for civil service careers. Instead, they viewed the civil service as one place where they might find long-term positions or move on to other situations. This condition encouraged the employment of technical professionals. The federal service paid no opportunity or incentive costs by recruiting professionally or technically trained individuals. In effect the "market" picked up the costs of training for the civil service under this arrangement. At the same time, access to varying levels of office provided incentives to those with experience because, if they were successful in getting the position, they neither paid opportunity costs nor suffered significant losses on their acquired experience. Indeed, because of the inevitable problem of moral hazard—the tendency of individuals to overstate their abilities when applying for a position—individuals with technical or professional training probably profited from the system if they got the position. The result was, as Van Riper has put it:

The entry of such men continued apace and in 1900 they provided approximately 3.43 per cent of the total intake. The trend was clear, with a reciprocal affinity between the merit system and scientific and technical work well established by 1900. (1958a:161)

By the end of the century, the merit system as constructed by the Pendleton Act had produced or, at least, strongly encouraged the development of an organization oriented toward the utilization of individual skills, without much regard to whether they were acquired outside of or inside the organization. This meant there were either relatively low levels of firm-specific knowledge or that this kind of knowledge had less leverage and importance in determining salaries than professionally specific knowledge. One result was the creation of the basis for relatively easy movement between public service and the private sector—a basic institutional characteristic of the Civil Service until the present time.

Interestingly enough, in this respect the reforms of 1883 changed the basic structure of the civil bureaucracy perhaps relatively less than is usually thought. They tended to formalize the structure of the administrative role that had existed since the reforms of the Jacksonian period. Patronage and the rotation of office had broken down any notion of predictable systematic careers. They had placed the emphasis in administrative role on the single position and finding the appropriate person for it. By emphasizing the lack of special training required for most positions, majority party patronage was easily substituted. In terms of organizational structure, the Pendleton Act did little better than provide a more rationalized and coherent structure for recruitment and appointment than that provided by the patronage structure.

That political leaders of the Democratic and regular Republican Parties were brought to it unwillingly is reflected both in the numbers of workers brought under the system and the degree to which they rejected the notion of a relatively exclusive, integrated internal labor market. The act provided almost no insulation for civil servants except against the most predatory forms of coercion and dismissal. The progress in numbers brought into the merit system clearly indicates the desire of political leaders to avoid the worst aspects of patronage loss while gaining the greatest benefit from classification. The strategy emerged out of the peculiar circumstances the reforms had produced with regard to the president's role in reform. The act provided institutional arrangements for the president to carry out his constitutional duties to provide appointments for the executive branch. The extent to which the reforms would be carried out rested on the president's good will. In effect, the reformers found that the reforms were now at the mercy of presidential choice. The gray area of authority over recruitment and appointment that existed between president and Congress was clarified to some extent by the act. The president's power over the organization of appointments was recognized, while Congress's arm's length authority was recognized by the law's requirement that the Civil Service Commissioners be included among those whose appointment by the president required the advice and consent of the Senate (Van Riper 1958a:100–110).

This formalization tended to provide the president with a somewhat sharper edge in his dealings with party leaders. He could provide cover for a large number of party patronage appointments by simply classifying whole categories of positions as protected after a period of rotation. He could also do so as a reward for renomination or as a promise for nomination. Bringing too many under protection, however, would reduce the clout that patronage provided both for the president and his party. Thus, the only strategy presidents representing regular party leaders could pursue was incremental classification combined with an expanding civil service in the patronage categories. Arthur covered in an additional 1,649 (total: 15,573); Cleveland added 11,757 between 1 March 1888 and 5 December 1888 (total: 27,330) in the last year of his first term as he tried for renomination and, failing to win, locked in a number of Democratic patronage appointees; Harrison added 10,535 between 13 April 1891 and 5 January 1893 (total: 37,865) with 7,924 of these coming on the later date just before leaving the office for a Democrat—Cleveland. In his second term, Cleveland added 49,179 (total: 87,044), with 10,396 coming in his first three years (about 10,000 just after the Republican victories in the 1894 Congressional elections) and the bulk of the remainder in 1896 (about 27,000 came just before the Democratic convention and another 6,549 just after the election) (Sageser 1935:68, 107, 162, 246; Skowronek 1982:69–73). McKinley, a Republican riding to power on a major shift of voter preferences proceeded to uncover about 9,000 positions immediately, and then later added 10,361 Republican appointments (Skowronek 1982:71, 73–74). In the meantime, in the decade between 1891 and 1901, the number of federal service positions had increased by 80,212 and the number of patronage positions was 124,851, an increase of 7,880 (U.S. Bureau of the Census 1960:710).

Was there a different strategy party leaders might have used? In one sense, the bill which emerged was an alternative strategy to that pursued by the liberal/mugwump Republicans. The latter sought to attack party leadership by separating the civil service from patronage and patronage from party leaders by

creating the basis for a career structure system with narrow entry—by examination in the lowest grades of the various services. The regular party leaders saw
through this and amended Pendleton's original bill by allowing access at any
level with the appropriate examination scores or professional credentials. They
also got their way by outlawing only *forced* assessments to party coffers, thus,
leaving patronage as a source of party funding—at least in the short run.

There was no way in which party leaders could have rejected the demand
for reform. For either party leadership to do nothing, or oppose reform, left
too good an opportunity for one's opponent. Furthermore, if the regular Republican Party leaders failed to support some version of the bill, they would
be courting the loss of the liberal Republican vote in key states in what was
clearly going to be a very tight election in 1884. The Democratic leadership
had considerable to gain by supporting the revised version, since it might
give them enough votes from liberal Republicans to bring the White House
home to them if they had a candidate relatively unsullied by patronage ma-
nipulations, such as Grover Cleveland, the governor of New York.

In effect, patronage was rejected at this particular time precisely because
the immediate struggle was over the question of political leadership and the
process and criteria by which it was to be selected. Traditional political leaders sought to maintain as much control over public goods—appointments
and the pork barrel—as they could in order to ensure their continued dominance of political leadership. The mugwumps or liberal Republicans sought
to gain control over party leadership and establish a new basis for leadership
and leadership selection: reform. Reform became a kind of public good in
the sense that it would lead to redistribution of public goods for the "public
interest" and not just for individual and party interests (McCormick
1986:207–24; Sproat 1968: especially chaps. 1, 6–9).

Reform also became the means of recruiting and organizing new leadership—a leadership that was not rooted in party professionalism. This leadership instead was to be rooted in a range of voluntary public interest or professional associations aimed at constantly reforming the structure of
government on behalf of the public interest. Such groups as the United
States Sanitary Commission of the Civil War period, the American Social
Science Association (1865), the New York Civil Service Reform Association
(1877), the National Civil Service Reform League (1881), and the Association of the Bar of the City of New York (1870) were all organizations aimed
at reform in the name of the public interest. The leadership of these organizations would produce the "best men." It was not wholly coincidental that
the "best men" were drawn primarily from professionals such as lawyers,
doctors, editors, and ministers (Hoogenboom 1961:179–97; Skowronek
1982:52–53; McFarland 1975:24–25).

The claim to leadership did not arise simply out of claims of moral superiority, but also out of their definition of what constituted moral behavior in the public sphere. It was not merely that they did not live off of the public coffers in some manner which made them moral men. Rather, the moral position of antislavery that had prompted the early liberals to participate in the public and political arenas now came to be transmuted into a notion of public service. Public service became the link between individual moral behavior and the public interest. The measure of the publicness of public service was, as in the case of individual moral behavior, a principle which transcended private interest. In private affairs, that idea was reflected in the disinterested adherence to religious (Christian and, perhaps, predominantly Puritan) principles. In public affairs, this came to be transmuted into a collective morality reflected in the disinterested adherence to associative *professional* principles. In both the cases of private and public morality there was adherence to a body of seemingly transcendent principles—religious ones on the one hand, scientific (or scientistic) ones on the other. The latter allowed justice, honesty, and efficiency to follow naturally in the public arena, just as the former allowed honesty and fairness to follow naturally in the arena of private affairs (Karl 1963:18; Sproat 1968:6–7, 9; Bledstein 1976:87–92; Hays 1972:1–15; Szasz 1972:95–96; McFarland 1975:49–50; McCormick 1986:270–71; Griffen 1970:120–49; Crunden 1982).

The real problem for this new leadership was to establish a link between themselves and the voting public, thus bypassing the traditional party patronage structure that had hitherto been the main mechanism of voter mobilization and organization. This was not to occur, however, until the critical elections of 1893–96 created the conditions for a renewed thrust of liberal Republicans to gain control and reshape the structure of party politics. In the meantime, the only strategies available to the liberals were either to attempt to influence the selection of presidential candidates and candidates generally by threatening to shift their votes or to continue to use the public media to reveal and demand investigation of the corruption of patronage politics.

The first tactic was useful only so long as the two parties were evenly matched, as in the case of the 1884 election, which saw the defection of the liberals in several key states to give the Democrats their first postbellum victory. But the defection left the mugwumps and Independent Republicans in somewhat bad odor with the regular party leaders, who accused them of treason. A number of liberal Republican supporters who had voted for Cleveland in 1884 drifted over to the Democratic Party when Cleveland ran again in 1892 (McFarland 1975:55–80). They found the Cleveland positions on civil service reform, the tariff, and silver very sympathetic (McFarland 1975:55–80; Sproat

1968:267–69). But a large number of reformers and their supporters had remained in the party or on the sidelines, splitting the group and thereby reducing the efficacy of the reform threat to shift votes. Only with the critical elections of 1893, 1894, and 1896, especially with the Democratic nomination of Bryan, did the liberal Republicans and many of the old mugwumps find themselves once again reunited in the Grand Old Party.

The second tactic took place largely at the local level, especially in urban politics. Reformers and their associations emerged in all the major cities of the Northeast, in some cities along the South Atlantic tier, and in the Midwest (Schiesl 1977:25–45; Teaford 1984:187–98). Their activities provoked investigations which provided considerable food for voters to think about in city and state elections (Schiesl 1977:33–67; McFarland 1975:81–106). Throughout the 1880s and 1890s, reform movements and reform slates made the cities a venue for the training and activities of a new and expanding generation of leaders opposed to party professionals (Schiesl 1977:33–67; McGerr 1986:59–62). They sought, with varying degrees of success, to undermine the structure of party machines and the basis of party machinery. Publicity was a major element in their activities since reform not only made good headlines, it was usually supported by the publishers themselves (Schudson 1978:107–20; Hoogenboom 1961:191; McCormick 1986:272; McGerr 1986:45, 59, 113–37; Filler 1976). Neither of these tactics, however, provided sufficient resources as a base for the development of an organizational structure that might match and compete with the regular party organizations.

In sum, the Pendleton Act formalized the basic orientation of the civil service. In emphasizing the individual role, it provided strong incentives for professionals to enter the system. This provided a neat solution to the political leadership dilemma of how to avoid charges of pursuing private interest without giving up control of the implementing structure of government so essential to filling constituent needs. The answer, as it emerged from the Pendleton Act, was the job- or occupation-oriented organizational structure. In this sense, the outcome was not directly tied, as some have argued, to the growing demands of efficiency emanating from an industrializing society. These demands had effects not because of their inherent appeal, or because of the numbers of voters involved, but because incumbent politicians were sensitive to discontent of any kind if elections looked close. Such demands were not the only pressures producing a crisis for patronage. The system itself had become a major source of factionalism within the parties and a source of conflict between president and Congress. There was, thus, good reason for a new leadership arising out of the abolitionist reformers to seek civil service reform—it was a clear and attractive target. This was especially the case for professional base of this leadership. Professionalism provided the basis for a critical stance with regard to professional party politics and its approach to public policy and the public interest.

The Critical Elections of 1893–96 and the Rooseveltian Confirmation of the Pendleton Structure: 1893–1909

Between 1893 and 1896, a series of local, state, and national elections revealed a powerful shift in voter party preferences. What had been a more or less evenly matched contest between parties now became a mismatch as the Republican Party established its dominance nationally over the next decade and a half. Beginning with the election of a Republican Secretary of State in New York in 1893, and ending with smashing Republican victories in the congressional elections of 1894 and the presidential election of 1896, the Democrats as a majority party were limited largely to the states of the old South. These victories, or their extent, had not been foreseen by Republicans, although they certainly had hopes that the depression under Cleveland would help shift enough votes for victory.

The Republican victories at the national level were matched at the state level almost everywhere but in the South by Republicans. At the local level, they were matched by the victories of city reform candidates who were predominantly, although by no means completely, liberal "progressive" Republicans. The latter included the older liberal and mugwump Republicans and a whole new group of reformers the liberal associations had recruited and organized over the preceding decade. Thus, for the period which followed, perhaps up to the eve of the First World War, the interests of reformer leaders at the local level and Republican leadership at the state and national levels coincided to a considerable degree.

Their interests coincided at several levels. First, their interests ran together in the attempt to restructure the patterns of voting so as to ensure or, at least, stabilize the victories that had been won. In the face of voter volatility, both reform and regular Republican leaders sought ways to reduce the possibility of an equally major shift in the opposite direction. At the city level, reformers sought to remove city administration from patronage, indeed, from all politics, by introducing civil service reforms, nonpartisan elections, citywide voting for council members; by creating a strong executive; and by appointing and requiring professionals for city management, finance, and technical offices (Schiesl 1977:25–132; Teaford 1984:103–214; Hays 1964:162–69). These reforms, many of them successfully introduced in the two decades between 1890 and 1910, were clearly aimed at destroying the hold of the professional politician over the resources necessary to organize and mobilize voters.

The interests of reform leaders and regular Republican leaders coincided also at a second strategy—regulating voters, or at least seeking to gain some control over the shape of the actual electorate. The strategies evolved here were aimed partly at attempts to break party identification and solidarity through such tactics as the nonpartisan elections and through breaking up election times so that national, state, and local office elections did not coincide, thereby allowing and encouraging ticket splitting (McCormick 1981:54–55; McGerr 1986:64–65; Burnham 1970:75–76; Key 1956:67).

Another tactic in the same direction was ballot reform. Before 1889, ballots were published by the political parties and distributed to voters before election day. They were usually printed on distinctively colored paper so that a voter's preference at the voting booth was readily known. Furthermore, the ballot contained only one party's slate, thus encouraging straight ticket voting (McGerr 1986:63–64; Rusk 1970:1,220–38; Argersinger 1980:290–91). But beginning with Massachusetts in 1889 the secret, officially published Australian ballot system spread so that almost every state had adopted the system by the end of the 1890s. The Australian ballot served to help narrow the voting base. Since it required that the voter not receive the ballot until entry into the voting station, he normally could not receive help in understanding the ballot. This meant that immigrants and those of limited literacy had difficulty in casting votes. The Republicans at the state level benefited from this since they had come into control of most of the state governments.

The use of the Australian ballot had the effect of limiting the influence of Democratic control of some major New York and Northeastern cities where recent immigrants provided much of the voting power. It also allowed Republican state leaders to modify the ballots to discourage the Democrats from joining with third parties. This was done by not allowing a person's name to appear more than once on the ballot, with the result that no fusion party could appear on the ballot (Argersinger 1980:292).

The direct primary system adopted by many states in the period from the mid-1890s to 1913 was another tactic of reform and attack on regular party leadership. This system was aimed at turning general election competition in one-party states into intraparty competition. The impetus to its spread came with the emergence of sectoral one-party systems in the North and South after 1893–96. The direct primary tended to reinforce one party domination by "stripping the minority party of its sole remaining resource, monopoly of opposition" (Burnham 1970:75; Key 1956:85–132; Kousser 1974:72–75). The local city form of this was the citywide election for aldermen instead of ward representation. The aim here was to break down the dominance of representation by limited constituencies that provided support for the patronage system of party politics. Under the direct citywide councilman vote, reformers sought to replace the system of ward patronage with their own system of citywide policies, with the hope that this would constrain the influence of voters supporting the patronage structure (Hays 1964:163–65). Although this system did not promote one-partyism, it did tend to support Republican administrations in several key cities in the Northeast (Hays 1964:163–65).

The attempt to restrict voting through the creation of registration laws was also a tactic reform and regular Republican leaders saw as mutually beneficial. City reformers and state leaders sought to use registration, for city populations primarily, as a means of regulating immigrant and lower economic class voters (Burnham 1970:79–83; Klepner and Baker 1979). In the South, this took the form of poll taxes and literacy tests, both of which tended to eliminate nearly all blacks and poor whites (Kousser 1974:63–82). Registration and other forms of voter regulation then tended to sustain one-party domination where there were significant differences in the social bases of parties.

By 1900, the city reformers, utilizing a base of independent voluntary associations many of which were professional, had evolved a whole set of tactics aimed at undermining the structure of leadership of the old regular party organizations. The elections of the preceding five or six years had revealed that a number of these tactics not only served to undermine party patronage, but they also served to undermine, specifically, Democratic Party patronage. These same tactics also were directed at narrowing and regulating, thus stabilizing, voter behavior. Simultaneously, a number of these reforms were aimed at regulating and narrowing party behavior. Civil service reforms along the lines of the Pendleton Act allowed not only for the reduction of patronage but also encouraged the appointment of professionals in the system of city-provided services (Teaford 1984:132–73; Schiesl 1977:32–45; Wiebe 1967:168). The city manager movement also reflected the desire of reformers to move as much of politics as possible into the realm of administration (Schiesl 1977:173–88).

Pressures for reform also emerged at the state level. In the two decades between 1885 and 1905, almost every state found itself locked in struggles over railroad regulation. Many states established their own railway commissions with varying degrees of administrative powers (Hays 1957:54–57; McCormick 1986:278; Mowry 1958:82; Wiebe 1967:53). The struggles for regulation of rates lasted into the second decade of the new century, centering in the Interstate Commerce Commission rather than in Congress. Utility regulation also emerged as a major concern in many states. City reform leaders, especially, sought to gain control over the extremely profitable traction and, later, power suppliers whose deals with the patronage parties, they argued, had proved costly to consumers and businessmen alike (Mowry 1958:80; Teaford 1984:234–35; Schiesl 1977:84–87). Much the same occurred in the area of insurance (Keller 1963:256–59).

Out of this emerged the increasing suspicion that unregulated big business not only impinged on the autonomy of the community, it also rendered the individual helpless in the marketplace (Wiebe 1967:71–74; Hofstadter 1955:213–56; Unger and Unger 1977:102–8). The fear of the "trusts" produced first the antitrust law of 1890 and, with the growth of monopolies and near monopolies near the turn of the century, increasingly strong prosecution. In short, the last two decades of the century saw an increasing demand for reform that produced the new organizational means for depoliticizing the conflicts inherent in the restructuring of the market. The administrative commission emerged as the primary means of taking these conflicts out of the domain of political conflict and increasingly reduced them to questions of a technical character, which could be settled by agreements between the state and the regulated (McCormick 1986:345–46; Hurst 1956:88–107). As Wiebe has put it:

After 1900 the dynamics of American politics increasingly concentrated in administration, where businessmen sought freedom from antimonopoly rules, farmers the basis for modern marketing, urban reformers the techniques for economy or systematic law enforcement, professionals the right to police their fields, and countless conflicting interests the mechanisms for adjustment and compromise. To a striking degree, the major legislative battles now involved which administrative agencies would receive what mandates under whose supervision. (1967:185)

At the national level, the Republican recapture of the White House in 1896 was proven to be no fluke in 1900, when it was repeated. That the Republicans were able to do so was due in part to the sometimes hesitant and grudging support of independent-minded reform/liberal/mugwump/progressive Republicans. Under these circumstances, party leaders had little choice but to pursue some elements of reform in the attempt to stabilize their control of national politics. That the agent of these reforms was Theodore Roosevelt was in part accidental. His selection to run as vice-president under McKinley came as result of his ability to manage reforms in New York while serving as governor without making significant contributions to the decline of the regular party leadership (McCormick 1981:129–33; Mowry 1958:108–9). His appearance as president came only as the result of an assassin's bullet which felled McKinley in September 1901. Roosevelt's selection as vice-president, however, had been made partly to satisfy independent and reform voters. Thus Roosevelt's appearance on the national political scene was not accidental, although his rise to the presidency was certainly so. However, despite the contingent appearance of a somewhat reform-minded president, there were already strong structural pushes toward reforms, some of which might help institutionalize Republican control over the White House and the Congress. Roosevelt's behavior as a champion of Progressive reform, thus, was not conditioned solely by a tendency toward reform nor simply by the desire and ambition to make great waves. In a sense, he was committed to reform not only because he believed in it, but because it was essential to securing his place as leader of the party to which he had accidentally fallen heir.

Roosevelt's elevation to the presidency proved to be the event that precipitated the convergence of several pressures and their solutions. Coming to the presidency with no organization of his own left him vulnerable to powerful congressional, especially Senate, leaders (Mowry 1958:115–20). At the same time, the urban reform movements, with their emphasis on association and organization, had become sufficiently significant in a number of states. This made it possible for them to seriously undermine the regular Republican Party when they were displeased, as they did in New York and Wisconsin in 1897 (McCormick 1981:107–26; Thelen 1972:290–308). By the end of the century, reformers and their organizations were numerous enough to provide the basis for political mobilization.

The desire on the part of party leaders to stabilize what appeared to be an arbitrary shift of voters' preferences left them vulnerable to demands for reforms. It especially left them sensitive to the possible consequences of the continued politicization of economic conflicts. Regular party leaders came to appreciate the virtues of administrative solutions. Under these conditions, Roosevelt, if he wished to be nominated for a term of his own, had little choice but to carefully seek the support of reform-minded Republicans as an organizational base while exploring those reforms which could be seen as instrumental to maintaining Republican Party dominance. Sensitive to the widespread demand for reforms which would regulate parties, big business, and voters, regular party leaders also had little choice but to seek reforms that would remove these issues from the arena in which the volatility of voters might find expression.

In order to secure his place in the party structure of leadership, Roosevelt had to engage in several strategies at the same time. Central to them all was the condition that he had to establish the strength of his position vis-à-vis congressional party leaders. There were only a limited number of strategies available for achieving this goal. The boldest of these was to increase the strength of the executive at the expense of the congressional leaders. That is, he could seek greater control of the administrative structure, making it more independent of congressional control. Alternatively, he could seek the support of the liberal/Progressive Republicans. By pushing reform proposals, Roosevelt could attract the support of liberal/Progressive organizations, such as the Municipal Reform League and the National Civil Service Reform League, and use them as leverage against the regular party leaders. Finally, he could attempt to strengthen his position by pursuing reforms that helped stabilize Republican Party dominance and therefore regular party leadership. Since none of these strategies were mutually exclusive, it is not surprising that Roosevelt engaged in all of them.

In his first two years as president, Roosevelt worked with great success at strengthening his position as head of the party. By spring of 1903, Roosevelt had successfully undermined Mark Hanna's considerable power in the party by his skillful use of the patronage (Mowry 1958:172). Equally important, he worked carefully to increase the gulf separating administration from party patronage control and use. Thus, in 1901 he ordered the Comptroller of the Treasury to withhold salary payment to any merit employee whose appointment violated the civil service rules. Under McKinley, the comptroller had ruled that he would not go beyond the certification of the appointing officer to see whether an employee had been hired according to the rules. This made it difficult for the Civil Service Commission to police appointments in the classified service (Van Riper 1958a:189). The new ruling gave the commission powers to police appointments in a much more rigorous fashion. This power was enhanced by Roosevelt's order that all employees would now be required to testify before the commission when so ordered or face dismissal. As a result of these orders, patronage appointments could no longer be hidden behind officially certified appointing officers.

These moves were followed in 1902 by Roosevelt's insistence that the Attorney General rule that written solicitations for funds between two federal officeholders was illegal (Van Riper 1958a:187). In the same year, Roosevelt made further inroads on political use of officeholders by outlawing any political activities for those in the classified service (Van Riper 1958a:187). Finally, Roosevelt, also in 1902, ruled that an appointing officer could remove a merit employee for any cause, excepting political or religious affiliation, that would promote efficiency, and the individual would have no right to a hearing (Rosenbloom 1971:102; Skowronek 1982:179–80).

The attempt here was to cut off the classified service from as much patronage manipulation as possible and, at the same time, make it an instrument of executive authority. The absence of appeal rights on dismissals, when combined with the absence of patronage support, meant that the officeholder was much more directly under the aegis of the president or the department heads and their supervisory personnel. Concomitantly, strengthening the policing powers of the Civil Service Commission served to undermine congressional party influence within the administrative structure. The so-called neutrality of the bureaucracy to which these rules were directed meant neutrality with regard to party usage. The fact was, however, that in the short term, placing officeholders under the merit rules meant covering in patronage appointees and that the "rule of three" governed selection (appointing officers could choose among the top three scorers). When this was combined with the relatively low level of literacy required to pass the basic tests, it then became relatively easy to make what amounted to patronage appointments.

Thus, although the rules did not ensure the neutrality of officeholders vis-à-vis policy preferences, they did undermine congressional party leaders' ability to influence administrative implementation in specific interest matters. That this was Roosevelt's object, at least in good part, is reflected in his rather surprising imposition of a gag rule on public employees, forbidding them to solicit, directly or indirectly, Congress in support of pay raises or any other benefits (Skowronek 1982:180). Roosevelt was not especially anti-union so that the gag order did not stem from strong principles or outside pressures. The rule did, however, erect barriers between Congress and the civil service.

These reforms had relatively little effect on the internal structure of the civil service. While they did provide some protection from congressional intervention and influence, this did not change either the structure or nature of civil service roles. Rather, the reforms placed a greater share of the fate of those roles in the hands of the executive. In this process, Roosevelt materialized as a champion of the public interest as against the demands of private and factional interest. As a result of this strategy, Roosevelt had emerged, by the end of 1903, as the strongest of his party's leaders. So much so, that his nomination for the presidency, in doubt at the year's beginning, was no longer so by its end. Moreover, by his strengthening of the Civil Service Commission and the weakening of congressional influence, Roosevelt won much support among the liberal/progressive Republicans (Foulke 1925:52–53). Having established his leadership and carefully avoiding any major conflict with regular party leaders, Roosevelt won the nomination unanimously. Running against a rather colorless Democratic candidate, Alton Parker, Roosevelt won the presidency with little trouble, getting strong support in the areas where progressive reform had moved from local to state levels.

Roosevelt's attempts to retain both his and his party's dominance were reflected in the policies of his second term. On the one hand, he was responsible for covering in (placing in the merit system) over sixty thousand positions between 1905 and 1909 (U.S. Bureau of the Census 1960:710). By the end of his second term, approximately two-thirds of the civil service had become classified. Nevertheless, there remained at least 100 thousand patronage positions available in the executive civil service at the end of Roosevelt's term in 1909 (U.S. Bureau of the Census 1960:710). Over the seven and one-half years in office, he had covered in approximately 100 thousand good Republicans.

Roosevelt was also responsible for the creation of important technical bureaus: the Department of Commerce and Labor, a permanent Bureau of the Census, the Bureau of Food and Drugs, the Bureau of Corporations (Department of Commerce and Labor), the Reclamation Service, and the Isthmian Canal Commission, all of which provided for professional and technical offices in growing numbers (Mowry 1958:207–16; Van Riper 1958a:201–2). Both the Food and Drug and Reclamation Bureaus were created to remove public concern over impure foods and conservation from the political arena. Creation of the Bureau of Corporations in 1903 had much the same purpose. The legislation creating the Bureau of Corporations gave the president considerable powers to investigate and deal with big business. It was expected that its investigations would help the president in shaping public opinion, in recommending regulatory legislation and, consequently, strengthen the president's capacity to monitor and influence big business behavior (Sklar 1988:186).

More important in this regard, perhaps, was the successful recasting of the Interstate Commerce Commission. Roosevelt's bill, known as the Hepburn Bill, was approved by the House with only seven dissenting votes and, after a battle with conservative senators, a compromise version favoring the president became law in the summer of 1906. The bill gave the ICC, whose powers had been almost eliminated by the courts, the power to set aside rate schedules on complaint and issue new ones subject to court review. The act permitted the commission to examine railroad books and prescribe uniform bookkeeping and placed some aspects of railroad service directly under commission supervision (Mowry 1958:204–6). This not only created a new set of offices at the professional and technical level, it also created or recreated an agency that removed a major issue that threatened to sunder the Republican Party. Moreover, it established a precedent for dealing with especially fractious problems that was to be followed by a number of Roosevelt's successors, not the least of them being his younger cousin.

The basic result of Roosevelt's strategies was to attract the support of the rising tide of Progressive and liberal Republicans not only to himself but to the party as well. He successfully kept both wings of the Republican Party together (Hays 1957:147). In the long run, this was to prove destructive for the party. The support for reform and Progressive action grew sufficiently so that it tempted Roosevelt to try to create his own party for the election of 1912. This led to a three-party election, splitting the Republicans, which allowed the Democrats to win the White House. Nevertheless, for the time being, Roosevelt's strategies allowed the Republicans to take advantage of the Progressive reform movements in the various states to sustain their dominance.

Roosevelt's policies with regard to the bureaucracy had relatively little effect on the nature of the bureaucratic role, with one exception. His strong commitment to the development of technical bureaus as a means of attacking various political and economic problems and removing them from the political arena provided strong incentives for professionals to enter the civil service and, indeed, provided impetus for the further development of the professional role (Kaufman 1956:1,061).

At the center of this revolution lay the same flexible, adaptive approach that characterized the reforms in city and state government. Each new administrative power, from the expansion of Pinchot's conservation program to the birth of an effective Interstate Commerce Commission, was predicated upon the continuous, expert management of indeterminate processes. (Wiebe 1967:193)

His greatest effect may have been indirect. His policies certainly had a long-range effect on the relationship of the bureaucracy to the constituent elements of the federal state. The bureaucracy, somewhat more professionalized, emerged from the Rooseveltian experience a much more executive-oriented body. As long as presidents would not surrender to Congress on the issue of the "neutrality" of the civil service, and as long as they had scruples about maintaining some barriers to entrance, then the possibility of long-term service in the administration rose considerably. That this was at least partly so is reflected in the increasing degree to which bureau chiefs, by the 1920s and early 1930s, were being selected from among individuals who had been in the service in only one department for long periods of time (MacMahon and Millett 1939:319–50).

Perhaps equally important is the way in which certified professional and technical expertise had relatively easy access to various levels of office-holding. This made possible the creation of administrative agencies almost at will, if not at whim, since professionals, such as lawyers, could be used to staff them. T. R. showed the way in which such administrative agencies could be created by the executive. His successors, especially Wilson and Franklin D. Roosevelt, did not overlook this lesson. They used the technique with such success that it has become a landmark of American administrative development. That this technique helped to fragment the bureaucratic structure also become a landmark of American administrative development. By producing a range of agencies whose technical and professional staff led them to resent interference from their senior but more amateurish directors and executives, it became possible for such agencies to seek alliances in Congress. This body's eternal suspicion of the executive led them to receive such overtures with joy. One result is that there is no organizational structure which integrates these agencies and makes them toe the line (Kaufman 1956:1,062; Skowronek 1982:290–92).

Roosevelt helped to stabilize and institutionalize the Pendleton Civil Service. He made no effort, however, to transform the basic nature of the administrative role from position to career orientation. His effort to rationalize the civil service structure through the creation of the Commission on Department Methods (Keep Commission 1905) produced proposals for a more sophisticated and uniform system of job classification and for more efficient handling of departmental business rather than proposals for creating an integrated career-oriented system (Kraines 1970:5–54; Arnold 1986:24–26).

Roosevelt is important, then, because he confirmed the reformist tendencies which had brought the Pendleton Civil Service into being. In doing so, he confirmed the boundaries within which discussions of civil service development would take place. From this point on, party leaders would accept the notion of a minimally politicized service while reformers would accept the notion of a permeable service with low entry barriers, where career autonomy did not exist. Party leaders would continue to have patronage at the upper levels. Reformers would only object to large fields of patronage at the lower levels, where it might be used for party patronage purposes.

Organizational Capstone: The Personnel Classification Act of 1923

The period between 1909 and 1920 produced little in the way of tests of party leadership. Wilson and the Democrats had absorbed some of the tenets and attitudes of Progressivism. To a certain extent, Progressivism, especially in its tendency to seek reform via the professional technical administrative agency, became part of the lore and beliefs of both parties. America's entry into World War I encouraged the flow of professionals to Washington. This made the in-and-outer highly visible and emphasized the job- versus career-orientation of the bureaucracy (Van Riper 1958a:259, 261–62; Skowronek 1982:200). The end of the war saw the reemergence of two issues that had been of concern prior to the war: pensions and retirement, and personnel classification.

The problems of pensions and uniform retirement age became acute as the postwar revulsion to the profligate spending of the war years took hold of the resurgent Republican Party. Retirement as an issue emerged as the consequence of the convergence of three pressures. Partly as an inheritance from the Progressive urge toward efficiency and economy, partly as a move toward economy as an issue to secure Republican resurgence, and partly as a consequence of pressure from members of the civil service in the form of the United States Civil Service Retirement Association (1900), retirement became an issue to be dealt within the civil service.

The proponents of economy and efficiency were interested in a formal retirement structure because the absence of a retirement age tended to produce an older civil service. An older civil service was also, in their eyes, a costlier one, because it paid higher wages for less work (Graebner 1980:117). Earlier discussions of retirement schemes aimed at increasing efficiency had provoked the creation of the United States Civil Service Retirement Association by civil servants. Their aim was to avoid a forced retirement policy which did not provide for a salary (Graebner 1980:120). Schemes had been bruited about since McKinley's presidency, but resistance from those representing rural constituencies kept legislation from emerging (Graebner 1980:128). The World War hastened the acceptance of pensions and retirement because it aged the civil service and it had seen the growth of unions to the point where they were considered dangerous—a retirement pension scheme was seen as one means for reducing their aggressiveness (Graebner 1980:128–29).

The act of 22 May 1920 provided for the retirement of civil service employees at age seventy if they had at least fifteen years of service. Those engaged in more physical work, such as mechanics, letter carriers, and postal clerks, were eligible at sixty-five, and railway clerks at sixty-two. Annuities were based on years of service. The maximum for those with more than thirty years of service, was $720 per year, and the minimum was $360 per year for those with fifteen to eighteen years of service (Graebner 1980:130). The plan was designed to cost the federal government almost nothing until 1929–30. The system was to be financed by a two and one-half percent deduction from salaries until the fund began to pay out more than had been collected (Graebner 1980:128–29). The act allowed extensions, but after 1930 extensions were severely limited (Graebner 1980:128–29).

The pension system was clearly designed to provide a cut-off time for employment so as to allow greater turnover and the employment of younger and cheaper personnel. Since employment was allowed until at least age seventy-four in many cases, it is clear that the retirement structure offered relatively small incentive to leave the service early—those holding the better-paying jobs preferred to stay as long as possible (Mayers 1922:512). Indeed, the pensions were so small for those at the more senior and professional ranks that they further reduced the incentive to retire at an early age (U.S. Civil Service Commission 1922:xiv). Thus, based on the relatively homogenous classification of salaries of 1928, individuals in the clerical service could earn, at most, between forty and fifty percent of their annual salaries. However, for the senior professional grades (grades 4 through 9), retirement pensions ranged from seven to eight percent of annual salary for grade 9 to about twenty-five percent for grade 4 (Betters 1931:120–30). The retirement system played a relatively minor role in producing incentives to enter the services for senior or professional careers. In fact, the pension system probably provided incentives for people with professional skills to acquire experience in the service and move on to other private positions (Mayers 1922:513–14). This is also reflected generally in the relatively high rates of turnover for the departmental services, a fact which caused considerable concern (U.S. Civil Service Commission 1931:3).

In short, the retirement system was not designed to encourage a coherent and appealing career structure. Those who had professional and/or technical skills that had applicability in the private sphere had every incentive to pursue these opportunities relatively early in their own careers. The system, in some ways, appeared to have been designed to encourage exits at that point where experience in the service had added value to skills. Since private industry or other public services had equally accessible entry points throughout much of their job structures, especially for professionals, this offered no obstacle to movement (Meriam 1938:327).

The Classification Act of 1923 confirmed indelibly in law the position-orientation of the civil service. The classification system adopted in the legislation created a system of classes, grades, and services. Classes were the basic unit of job descriptions. All positions throughout the service requiring the same basic general training and skills (such as training in secretarial skills or training as an economist) were grouped by class. The class was a category that went horizontally through the service. Grades were hierarchical distinctions within classes. Classes were divided into positions that required differing levels of skills and experience building on the same basic training. Classes and grades were grouped together by their function, general skill, and education levels: professional and scientific; subprofessional; clerical, administrative, and fiscal; custodial; clerical-mechanical (U.S. Civil Service Commission 1923:127–35). The legislation also created the Personnel Classification Board, which created the rules for classifying and allocating each position to the appropriate classes, grades, and services (U.S. Civil Service Commission 1927:127–35). The classification board then created a total of 1,633 classes, each with a description of duties, required training, and several possible directions for promotion (Betters 1931:47–62). The Classification Board was also allowed to develop a system of efficiency ratings which would establish a record for each individual in each position and which followed the individual (Betters 1931:62–63).

The classification structure emerged as a result of the desire by Republican Party leaders to put into effect the recommendations of the Keep Commission and President Taft's Commission on Economy and Efficiency. The aim was to bring about order in the anarchy of positions and salaries attached to them. The prior absence of any uniform standard had produced wide variations in salaries for roughly identical work. The hope was that uniform classifications would bring an end to the constant bidding within the service for positions paying higher salaries for the same work. Indeed, the number of transfers did decline (U.S. Civil Service Commission 1929:33). The legislation, however, fully confirmed the emphasis on position and its qualifications. It undermined or underplayed the idea of career by indicating only immediate possible promotion chains—one subordinate and one superior office. While it was possible to construct a career by linking various groupings of positions in a service, this was left to individuals in pursuit of careers. Such linkings were not seen by the system as forming systematic and predictable careers.

Furthermore, the legislation made it clear that Congress sought to rely on external sources of training to provide individuals with appropriate qualifications (Meriam 1938:326). While doing the research for the Classification Act of 1923, the congressional committee made comparisons of salaries of professionals and technicians, not to equivalents in industry, but to university salaries. From this it seems equally clear that Congress understood that many professionals sought public service as a means of enhancing their professional and/or technical standing, that is, as a means of pursuing their professional careers, not specifically a government career (Meriam 1938:116–17). In this sense, the Classification Act made movement from university to government, and government to university, relatively easy, thus encouraging the notion of professional rather than governmental career. The wide disparities in salaries between equivalent positions in private industry also must be seen as encouraging movement from the civil service once increased experience had been acquired (Meriam 1938:114–15). Conversely, however, the increased value of experience to a professional career in the private sector encouraged young professionals to enter government service for at least a short period. In sum, the position orientation of the classification structure provided incentives for movement back and forth between public agencies and between public and private service.

We must also remember that the classification scheme applied to only about two-thirds of the civil service. Moreover, the vast majority of these, perhaps as much as ninety-nine percent, were in the lower-ranking services or the lower grades of services with administrative leadership possibilities. In the 1920s and 1930s, only about two thousand positions within the classified service could be viewed by their classifications as professional or senior administrative (Meriam 1938:318). The remainder of the senior administrative offices remained patronage positions. Here, of course, there was little question of holding positions as a stage in a civil service career. Nevertheless, the nature of the careers of assistant secretaries, while revealing movement back and forth between public and private careers, also reveals that, for the most part, they were professionals (MacMahon and Millett 1939:290–95). Lawyers predominated, revealing the continued close connection between legal education and political careers, which had been in evidence since the nineteenth century. More important, the predominance of professionals in the patronage appointments reveals the emergence of certification as a criterion for holding senior administrative office.

The bureaucratic structure which emerged from this position-oriented arrangement of the administrative-public service role was characterized by its emphasis on the acquisition of skills, but not necessarily or primarily within the organization. Permeability or multilevel access was also characteristic, and this tended to undermine the role of seniority. Hierarchy existed, but it was not very rigid and it was bridgeable. Individuals could move from classes which required no administrative skills or experience to those that did and, in doing so, could move up grades in the same or different services. The main and almost unbridgeable gap between levels of hierarchy existed between the classified and the senior patronage-dominated positions. As a consequence, it was very rare for someone to have spent a lifetime in the service and have it culminate in holding the highest offices in a department. Here, however, by the end of the nineteenth century, political loyalty, although necessary, was not a sufficient criterion for holding senior offices—professional standing had also become important.

By the end of the 1920s, the system of role definition that had emerged with the Pendleton Act had clearly encouraged the movement of professionals into the decision-making positions of the public service, both classified and unclassified. The Classification Act of 1923 confirmed the almost complete accessibility to all levels of office without beginning at the lowest grades within the service. The desire of political leaders, even those whose challenge to regular party leaders in the nineteenth century had led to the creation of the classified system, to limit as much as possible the autonomy of the civil service had led them to create an organization which encouraged movement in and out of the structure at many levels. This explicitly provided few incentives for preparing oneself for a government career. Rather, it took advantage of the growing tendency of the middle class in America to construct roles around the idea and structure of the profession. Individuals prepared themselves for careers as professionals and practiced *that* career wherever there were opportunities.

The civil service reflected this ubiquity of the professional role. At the most senior decision-making levels, patronage professionals dominated. Lawyers, bankers, some educators, and a few technical professionals had utilized their professional training as a means for entering politics. In turn, they often used politics to further their status as professionals—this was especially the case for lawyers (MacMahon and Millett 1939:290–95; Schlesinger 1966:177–79). At middle levels (bureau chiefs and professional/technical positions), merit professionals tended to be increasingly typical, although professional careers were not (MacMahon and Millett 1939:318–75). Party leaders had feared an autonomous bureaucracy. If patronage were to go, then, they insisted, regardless of party and faction, that the bureaucracy be permeable and that no incentive be given to create a system of careers that would lead to administrative independence. In this they largely succeeded.

Conclusion

The bureaucracy that Heclo and Mosher described as malintegrated, highly permeable and mobile, and very professionally oriented in its middle and higher reaches emerged out of the conjunction of several crises in the structure of party leadership. The increasingly fractionating power of patronage, the increasing unmanageability of patronage, the unreliability of political loyalty as a criterion for holding office, the rise of new sources of political leadership, especially in the Republican Party in the postbellum period, the equal balance of power between the parties in the Gilded Age: all of these conjoined to help to produce this crisis. The crisis pressed upon regular party leaders ever more intensely as the reform leaders of the abolition movement turned on patronage as the next step in the reform of public life. Reform leaders gathered strength from a new resurgence of professional life, which now became the model of a moral middle-class life. Building an associational base in the expanding cities of industrializing America, these reformers attacked the very foundations of regular party leadership: the patronage, party loyalty, local machines, state machines, and unregulated voting.

Their first successes came in the attack on federal patronage with the appearance of the Pendleton Act of 1883. It was an imperfect instrument for reformers and regular party leaders alike. The reformers gave up, without much struggle, the notion of a bureaucracy with linked careers and narrow entry. The regular party leaders gave up some patronage, without much struggle, but clung tenaciously to the ideas of free accessibility and patronage at the top. There was probably some relief on both sides that each failed to achieve their complete desires. The reformers soon realized that they had given the executive somewhat more power than they had reckoned with. It might indeed be wise to leave senior positions open to the ambiguities of party politics, not to mention the serendipitous encouragement the legislation gave to professionalism. The politicians had found a relatively simple and not very devastating way to handle the problem of patronage. They could now escape the worst problems of attempting to thread their way through the thickets of party loyalty and patronage. Now when people complained about not receiving the appointment they deserved, Congressman Jones, or whomever, could simply say that it was no longer in his hands and thus escape the otherwise inevitable calumny.

The Progressive inheritors of the mugwumps of the Gilded Age continued the attack on the organizational basis of party leadership. Utilizing a variety of means (the secret ballot, direct primaries, municipal reform, regulation of monopolies, voting registration, decreasing the number of elective offices), the new generation of reformers came to be a threat to the regular party leadership in the Republican party. Theodore Roosevelt was, in many ways, the high point of reformist leadership power. He came increasingly to pursue strategies that would not only give him control of the party after his elevation to the presidency in 1901, but also would attract the independent Progressive voters. In doing so, he strengthened the executive by building a wall between Congress and the civil service. He did so, however, without increasing the autonomy of the service; rather, he made it more of an executive creature than a creature of its own. He thus confirmed the structure that the Pendleton Act had created. He gave neither the reformers nor the regular party leaders great victories.

Party leaders adapted extraordinarily well to this situation. They came to understand that patronage and its resources would not be the major basis of party leadership in the future and turned to organized interests as the source of party organizational resources. The reformers were co-opted. The reformers saw in the turn to organized and associated interests the possibility of organizing leadership around policies and not simply over spoils. It is perhaps the true nature of American politics that neither the reformers nor the regular party leaders have gotten their way. Throughout it all reform remains the means of attracting new kinds of leadership.

GREAT BRITAIN

10

Parliament, the Crown, and the
Problem of Patronage

The Paradoxes of the English Civil Service

In many ways, the institutionalization of a "rational" state bureaucracy in Britain is the most difficult case to unravel. There are several glaring anomalies or paradoxes. The creation of the formal organizational structure of rationality was not the result of a revolutionary moment, nor was it a central issue of political contest, nor was it the product of a great public hue and cry about corruption or inefficiency. Rather, it was the product of demands by political leaders whose incentives seem to be somewhat of a mystery since their constituencies did not seem to demand such action.

A second puzzle is evident when we observe the apparently depoliticized and closed nature of the higher civil service structure that emerged in the latter part of the nineteenth century. It has nearly always been characterized, and praised, by its members as "professional." Yet the dominant ideology governing the norms of training has emphasized the ideal of the "generalist" or the "amateur." Thus, the English case seems, from some points of view, to be closer to the French and other Continental systems in that they were, first of all, not a product of public contention but of elite concerns and, secondly, because of the emphasis on the senior bureaucracy as a closed or impermeable internal labor market.

Yet, the evolution of the English civil service also bears strong family resemblances to that of the United States. The rationalization process was not associated with a major or even minor replacement of elites. It appears to have been the product of evolutionary rather than revolutionary energies. In this regard then the English case appears to belong to a unique category—a case of low uncertainty that produces an organizationally oriented bureaucratic structure. However, closer examination of the critical aspect of the "amateur/professionalism" anomaly reveals that the English case belongs to the category of professionally oriented bureaucratic structure.

The Paradox of "Amateur" and "Professional" in the
English Higher Civil Service

The hundred years between, approximately, 1790 and 1890 saw the emergence of those basic aspects which characterize the role structure of the modern British civil administrative organization (one could hardly speak, even in

287

1870, of an integrated "civil service" as such). Since about 1890 the role structure has usually been viewed as one dominated by the idea of professionalism. The British civil servant has come to be described in terms which are often counterposed against the civil servant in the United States. One commentator and analyst of the higher civil service in Britain put it this way some years ago:

> The British case is in striking contrast to that of the Federal administrators in the United States, who are still, it is said, not accepted as professionals. . . . In their case there has been a marked diversity of social origin and educational background. Instead of a career-service mainly recruited by a standard selection procedure on completing a university education, there have been informal methods of selection, widely varying ages of entry, and insecurity of tenure. Very many of those recruited have already been in other professions, and tend to identify themselves with these organized groups outside the Service. It is not surprising that there has so far failed to develop among them "the social cohesion and common outlook which has characterized, for example, the higher civil service in England or in pre-Hitler Germany [Bendix 1949:90]." (Kelsall 1955:178–79)

The crucial difference, as Kelsall, Bendix, and others have seen it, lies in the idea of the bureaucratic role as a lifetime career—a career encompassing the acquisition of a body of information derived almost completely from organizational experience. Indeed, Americans have tended to adopt similar attitudes about Anglo-American bureaucratic differences, noting that in the United States bureaucrats often acquire their expertise outside of organizational experience. This is reflected in the arcane methods of position classification recruitment utilized by the U.S. Civil Service (Heady 1966:46–48; Shafritz 1973:13–34; Heclo 1977:120–33).

Why then, despite these contrasts, does England belong to the same category as the United States as a *professionally oriented* rather than an organizationally oriented bureaucracy? There are several reasons. There is the persistent emphasis in British writing and analysis, going all the way back to the Northcote-Trevelyan Report of 1853–54 (Great Britain, Parliamentary Papers 1854–55 [1713]: vol. 27) and to the Macaulay Report of 1854 (Great Britain, Parliamentary Papers 1854–55:34/LV; Dewey 1973:262–85), on the notion of the policy-making civil servant as one whose essential training is that of a "generalist." That is to say, that training is based on the acquisition of a body of knowledge by the individual prior to his entry into office. The body of knowledge required is explicitly seen as providing relatively little in the way of specific information on the performance of administrative duties but which appears to be a general paradigm for the analysis of day-to-day administrative problems. Thus, the Report of the Fulton Committee, issued in 1968, felt compelled to say:

The Home Civil Service today is still fundamentally the product of the nineteenth-century philosophy of the Northcote-Trevelyan Report. . . .

Northcote and Trevelyan were much influenced by Macaulay whose Committee reported in the same year on the reform of the India Service. . . . There emerged [from these reports] the tradition of the "all-rounder" as he has been called by his champions, or "amateur" as he has been called by his critics. . . .

First, the Service is still essentially based on the philosophy of the amateur (or "generalist" or "all-rounder"). This is most evident in the Administrative Class which holds the dominant position in the Service. (Great Britain, Fulton Committee 1966–68: command paper 3638:9–11)

In the conception of the generalist, the key notion was that individuals would come to the civil service with an education that made it possible for them to reason through everyday decision-making situations. Underlying this concept of education were two elements. On the one side, there was the idea that problem solving was not a function of a body of easily available data categorized by well-defined theories of the social, economic, and political world. Rather, what predominated was the nineteenth-century view that the main task of education was to improve the inferior faculties in such a manner as to expand the capacities of the superior faculties—imagination, and especially understanding and reasoning (Rothblatt 1976:128–29). Faculty psychology, as this conception has come to be known, was given strong underpinning in Kant's delineation of the faculties of the brain as having two divisions—superior and inferior (Rothblatt 1976:128–29). The individual, as an educable object, required the development of the faculties of reason, which made it possible to generalize decision making.

A liberal education, then, was a matter of mind training. The value of a particular object or discipline lay in the number of faculties it could cultivate, so that classical languages could be said to stimulate the logical faculties, and especially the faculty of memory, classical poetry the imaginative ones, classical rhetoric the moral faculties, and so on. (Rothblatt 1976:131)

Or, as Leslie Steven wrote in 1863:

I believe there is no better intellectual training than that which is necessarily undergone by a man who takes good . . . mathematical honors. (as quoted in Garland 1980:117)

Of course, Steven had strong associations with mathematics-oriented Cambridge rather than Oxford, where the classical ideal was dominant.

Thus, the basic capacity to make sense of information and to organize it for decision making came, as in the United States, from the preorganizational training of the individual. It is this aspect which leads to a second reason for viewing the English civil service as falling in the category of professionally oriented bureaucracy. The individual acquisition of the means for organizing data for decision making became, in England, the prerequisite for professional status. John Stuart Mill summarized this view very neatly in his rectorial address to the University of St. Andrews in 1867:

The proper function of an University in national education is tolerably well understood. At least there is a tolerably general agreement about what an university is not. It is not a place of professional education. Universities are not intended to teach the knowledge required to fit men for some special mode of gaining their livelihood. Their object is not to make skillful lawyers, or physicians, or engineers, but capable and cultivated human beings. . . . Men are men before they are lawyers, or physicians, or merchants, or manufacturers; and if you make them capable and sensible men, they will make themselves capable and sensible lawyers and physicians. (as quoted in Engel 1983a:294)

The professionalism of the civil servant, like that of the lawyer (barrister rather than solicitor), was based on the acquisition of a generalist education. This education provided the individual with the capacity to make sense out of the nitty-gritty substantive aspects of the occupation that could easily be learned through apprenticeship and service in the organization. Thus physicians, in the nineteenth century, learned their craft by walking rounds at teaching hospitals, lawyers learned their profession by serving apprenticeships at the Inns of Court, clergymen took curacies before getting benefices of their own. In the same way, civil servants came to know administrative detail by serving in the lower ranks of the upper civil service (Engel 1983a:294–95; Rothblatt 1968:88–92).

In the nineteenth century, those who entered the highest divisions or, rather, acquired the highest status in the liberal professions were expected to have a liberal education such as that provided primarily by public schools and Oxford or Cambridge (Reader 1966:45; Parry and Parry 1976:131–32; Rothblatt 1968:88–89). Professionalism in the civil service continued, through the twentieth century, to mean preparation by the individual in some form of liberal education and, to a surprising degree, predominately at Oxford or Cambridge (Drewry and Butcher 1988:71–72; Kelsall 1955:136–45; Great Britain, Fulton Committee 1966–68: command paper 3638, 4:335–39).

The apparent continued belief that liberal education provided the individual with training in the higher faculties of logic, reasoning, and decision making meant that the individual remained at the center of the information process. The civil service organization was seen throughout the latter half of the nineteenth and much of the twentieth centuries as the basic structure for collecting but not for organizing information. Nor was the organization seen as possessing the capacity for providing an explicit pattern of rules that could govern decision making. Thus, the peculiar paradox of a "professional" bureaucracy dominated by "all rounders" or "amateurs." Professionalism was, and, indeed, seems to continue to be, viewed as stemming from the training of the individual's faculties through a liberal education. The individual's possession of the faculties of logic and reason is what allowed the person to become a professional—whether civil servant, barrister, or physician made and makes little difference.

Seen from this vantage point, the English conception of the bureaucratic and professional role is strongly similar to that which prevails in the United States, despite some very significant differences in structure. The emphasis in both societies on the role of the individual, as opposed to the organization, as the primary means of ordering and processing information for decision making is a distinctive, if not the most distinctive, aspect of their view of the bureaucratic and professional role. This provides a very powerful reason for viewing the English and United States bureaucratic structures as products of similar energies and constraints.

The Bureaucratic Role in the English Civil Service

While it is perhaps somewhat of an exaggeration to say, as the Fulton Report did in 1968, that the English civil service is still dominated by the principles of the Northcote-Trevelyan and Macaulay Reports, it is not too much of one. The present delineation of the upper civil service role, which had become institutionalized by 1890 at the latest, still possesses the general outlines of its historical period of institutionalization. The role can be characterized in the following way:

1. Possession of a generalist or liberal higher education, which includes the social sciences, humanities, and, to a degree, the arts. This type of education is the primary basis for eligibility in the top civil service grades, especially in the highest three grades of permanent secretary, under secretary, and deputy secretary, which used to constitute the peak of the administrative or policy-making class.

2. Passage of tests, both written and oral, designed specifically for determining entry into the senior civil service grades. There is no direct career linkage in the form of rules requiring the recruitment of individuals from lower grades. The structure does not exclude such recruitment but is clearly designed to discourage the notion that one can begin at the bottom and rise

to the top. Entrance into the top levels of the senior civil service must be through the examination route. Passing the examination clearly requires a university education. The examinations are not designed to test any specific expertise. Over the past century, despite efforts in the period after the Fulton Report (1968), the possession of a respectable (a first or second honors) degree from Oxford or Cambridge has the highest predictability for successful entry. A very much greater percentage of "Oxbridge" graduates compete successfully for entry than those from all other universities.

3. Entrance into a distinct upper-level civil service career begins at the lowest level of the upper civil service and moves through a series of hierarchically linked offices. These offices are not defined in terms of job descriptions or position classifications. Rather, they are defined in terms of grades, which are distinguished from the occupational classifications of lower-level offices.

4. The linkage of offices, that is, through the seven highest grades from principle to permanent secretary, in a formal fashion provides general predictability about career at the lower levels, primarily on the basis of seniority. At the three or four highest grades, seniority plays a role, but it tends to be secondary to the process of senior evaluation of merit in the form of collegial departmental promotion boards. Here promotions are reviewed by the board on an individual basis and not passed on automatically by a single senior officer. This seems to be at least sufficiently the case so as to produce some tensions about the predictability of the rate of upward mobility.

5. Career within the senior levels of the upper civil service (the old administrative class and the present top three or four grades) is not centered in one department. Rather, the individual's career is topped by the acquisition of experience in more than one ministry. Departmental specialization is, however, characteristic of the lower levels of the senior service.

6. A servicewide uniform career exit structure is maintained. The career is tenured and fully vested at sixty, with compulsory retirement at sixty-five years of age.

7. A career structure in which officeholders at the senior and other levels have been protected from arbitrary dismissal through the existence of elaborate structures of promotion boards, hearing and grievance councils. At the highest levels, the tenure of officials is protected by the formal hearing procedures required by law.

Finally, it should be noted that the upper civil service has increasingly, in the period after World War I, become divided informally into two career structures. At the lower level, the bottom three grades of the now-open structure of senior management, there is greater access for those promoted from the former executive grades (supervisory non-policymaking offices).

Relatively few of these, however, progress to the highest grades—these tend to be dominated by open competition, university trained nonspecialists, often from Oxbridge.[1]

The role structure has considerable similarities to those in France and Japan. The English organizational pattern is similar to those of the French and Japanese in that it has a highly insulated internal labor market. After entrance, the movement through offices is completely independent of external market forces. Nevertheless, the English pattern does share a number of characteristics with that of the United States. It is less concerned with hierarchy, except at macrolevels where the hierarchy is, or seems to be, closely linked to educational distinctions and qualifications. Hierarchy as a function of seniority has lesser force at the senior levels of the higher service. Like the senior-level civil servants in the United States, and to some degree in France as well, the very senior English civil servants have considerable horizontal mobility. Also like their American counterparts, English higher civil servants do not make early organizational career commitments. Such commitments are rendered unnecessary by the commitment to the normative pattern of professional career.

Throughout the last half of the nineteenth and the first half of the twentieth century this commitment meant preuniversity training at a public school, as opposed to state grammar and higher schools. Neither this commitment, nor one to Oxbridge training, produced opportunity costs except to what has traditionally been viewed as lower-status occupations and professions. Indeed, since the middle of the nineteenth century, commitment to public school and Oxbridge training has been seen as expanding the range of opportunities available to the individual. With such training and certification, the individual had, and continues to have, the opportunity of going on to enter a number of high-status professions.

As with the case of university students in the United States, the career choice did and does not have to be made early; it can wait virtually until the end of university training (Chapman 1970:50–52; Great Britain, Fulton Committee 1966–68: command paper 3638, 3:323). In effect, the individual who has gone on from the liberal education public school to nonspecialist university training is able to postpone career choice considerably longer than those who choose specialist careers or occupations. As a result of this postponement, the individual suffers little or no opportunity costs. The individual who follows this educational pattern and takes and passes the so-

1. Chapman 1970:48–49; Drewry and Butcher 1988:106–7; Greenwood and Wilson 1984:92–93; Great Britain, Fulton Committee 1966–68; Kellner and Crowther-Hunt 1980; Kelsall 1955; Heclo and Wildavsky 1974; Fry 1969; Page 1985b; Sheriff 1976.

called Method I examination is usually assured of selection by the FSB (Final Selection Board) to enter one of the lower grades of the upper civil service (Drewry and Butcher 1988:97–110). Once inside, it is a rare individual indeed who does not move up the ladder to at least grade 3 or 4 (Permanent Secretary, Deputy Secretary, Under Secretary, Assistant Secretary). Thus, the system is structured to provide strong incentives for Oxbridge, nonspecialist trained, university graduates to enter a career designed to follow the pattern of the traditionally higher-status professions.

Low Uncertainty, Social Organization, and the Problem of Political Leadership

The outstanding characteristic of the history of the rationalization of the civil service in the nineteenth century is the degree to which it was almost completely unaccompanied by public clamor and controversy (Chapman and Greenaway 1980:45, 201–2; Anderson 1974:266–67). Yes, it was certainly the case that the Crimean War helped to provoke the creation of the Administrative Reform Association by businessmen in 1855 (Anderson 1965:233–35). It is equally clear, as Olive Anderson has shown, that the association was not really interested in the civil service but rather in ministerial and parliamentary reform (Anderson 1965:231–42). The Northcote-Trevelyan Report was a product of departmental evaluation which predated the Crimean War and was produced by an administrative commission, not a parliamentary or royal commission (Hughes 1942:61–62; Hart 1972:63–81). It was thus not the product of parliamentary debate or party contestation focused on administrative corruption. The commission was created as part of a series of evaluations of various departments that began in 1848 and were centered on the question of efficiency (Hughes 1942:61–62; Cohen 1941:87–88). The same can be said of the introduction of examinations in 1870–71, which determined the differentiation of the higher from the lower civil service (Chapman and Greenaway 1980:48; Wright 1969:74–80; Winter 1976:263–64).

The reforms that emerged from the report in 1855 were given force by Orders in Council; that is, through administrative prerogatives of the government and not through legislative acts of Parliament. In fact, all the major civil service reforms throughout the century were issued as Orders in Council. Thus, like the Northcote-Trevelyan Report, they were not the subjects of major parliamentary debates or party contests. This is reflected as well in the Orders in Council of 1870 and 1871, which established a hierarchical examination and entry system for much of the civil service (Great Britain, Civil Service Commissioners 1872:1–10). Civil service reform was, therefore, not the consequence of public outcry with regard to questions of corruption or inefficiency. Nor does it appear to have been the consequence of party conflict with the issue of corruption being used as a focus for attack.

However, before 1939 the political parties seem in general to have displayed little interest in the civil service. In contrast to local government reform, the organisation of the central government did not feature in the 'Newcastle Programme' of 1891 nor in any of the other radical Liberal agitations or manifestos of the period. (Chapman and Greenaway 1980:202–3)

In the absence of compelling public demands and forces, what then was the engine that drove civil service rationalization and reform, and why did it take the form that it did? Interestingly enough, despite the centrality of the central bureaucracy in the development of modern Britain, there have been relatively few attempts to understand why the civil service became institutionalized when it did and in the form it did. Those works which have taken the subject seriously as an object of analysis have provided three basic types of explanations. One is the class transformation argument. The rise of the middle classes with their demands for greater equality with the traditional elites are said to have produced not only pressures for expansion of the franchise but also for greater access to the instruments of political and social power. The result, it is argued, was the emergence of new criteria for access to administrative office which rejected the personal networks of patronage and their exclusiveness (Kingsley 1944; Shefter 1978b:434–41; MacDonagh 1977:202–3). The reformed structure took its shape primarily from the rise of essentially middle-class ideals of professionalism and rationalization (Perkin 1969:252–70).

The second type of argument is largely a differentiation and specialization argument. This view sees the civil service emerging from the increasingly dysfunctional character of patronage as a system of selecting administrators and as the basis of political power and leadership generally. The settlement of 1688 and the ensuing institutional contradictions, which were exacerbated by the transformation of British society in the late eighteenth and nineteenth centuries, produced a specialization and differentiation of political institutions. Parliament came to control the executive; Parliament came to be controlled by parties which needed permanence in administration; permanence meant the emergence of stable institutional arrangements shaped by a variety of social, political, and economic pressures (Parris 1969:29–79; Chapman and Greenaway 1980:183–237).

Lastly, there is the argument that England's political and expansionist wars of the late seventeenth and much of the eighteenth centuries required the expansion of financial and administrative capacities. This expansion, it is argued, produced the institutionalization as well as the origins of rationalization of the administrative role (Brewer 1989:64–87).

The first of these arguments is difficult to sustain. Aside from the abortive Administrative Reform Society of 1855–57, there seems to have been no major agitation of a collective nature on the part of the middle classes for either the reform of the civil service or for the creation of a "professionally oriented" civil service. Nowhere do we see any inclination on the part of groups which were middle-class in character to demand access in any systematic way to administrative positions. That is to say, before 1870 there does not seem to be any evidence that the middle classes viewed structural changes in administration as the means for gaining access to administrative positions. Nor is it clear why the middle classes, whether entrepreneurial or professional, should have automatically viewed certifying examinations and hierarchical organization tied to highly exclusive educational qualifications as essentially attractive. It would seem more likely that, as in the United States, middle-class ambitions might be better served by systematic rotational patronage tied to political parties, where professional certification served as the means of rationalizing exclusiveness.

If the argument is that the civil service was the object of an emergent *professional* middle class that was becoming self-conscious, then the evidence is singularly scarce. Before 1870 the professional associations were primarily interested in attempting to establish monopolistic control over their professional occupations in contest with more pluralistic colleagues (Carr-Saunders and Wilson 1933:45–51, 70–102; Reader 1966:45–165; Parry and Parry 1976:104–61). There was no general collective effort to place some occupations within the sphere of professions. Nor was there any specific proto-profession which sought to monopolize senior civil service positions by means of a credentialing system, in the effort to establish themselves as a full-fledged liberal profession. Those who held positions in the civil service, at the middle levels especially, were strongly opposed to the whole tenor of the Northcote-Trevelyan Report and the proposed introduction of examinations (Cohen 1941:104–9). In sum, the argument of class pressure and consciousness appears to stem largely from the notion that some political leaders sought to reform the civil service, and many of these leaders were drawn from the middle classes and thus represented their interests. There is little evidence to support the idea of representation except in some vague and general structural argument. It might be equally argued that such men represented in some degree the interests of political leaders and actors as a group.

The problem with the differentiation argument is that it is very vague on the forces most important in producing reform and almost completely silent on why the civil service should take on its particular form. The settlement of

1688 did not completely resolve the contradictions inherent in the monarch as executive, but it provided Parliament with the means by which it would separate, over the next century and a half, the executive from the monarch. The settlement may have contained the logic of contradiction, but it did not possess necessity. This had to be supplied by the actions and interests of those who were in Parliament or, to be more exact, the leaders of Parliament. What drove them to this differentiation and then to greater differentiation in Parliament between legislation and policy-making and administration is not at all clear. Nor is there a logic of professionalism that explains why the bureaucracy was institutionalized in a particular way.

The argument that rationalization of administration was essentially institutionalized in the eighteenth century simply confuses size and administrative differentiation with bureaucratic rationalization. There can be no doubt, however, that England in the eighteenth century continued to be a proprietary state where officeholders outside of Parliament had legal property rights to the offices they held (Brewer 1989:70–72). So long as this was the case, there could be no systematic predictable structure of administrative role.

Finally, in addition to these explanations, it has sometimes been suggested that civil service reform was a product of the emergence of Benthamite rationalism. At the heart of this idea is the view that utilitarianism provided a social basis for judging efficiency which might be calculable. After all, the dictum about the greatest good for the greatest number easily could be seen as the basis for efficiency comparisons and judgments (Ryan 1972:39–51). While this may be so, it is extraordinarily difficult to define the degree to which these views had effect. Generally, the tendency has been to suggest that various political leaders (Mill, Cobden, Chadwick, Trevelyan, Macaulay, and Northcote, and other Liberal politicians) were strongly affected by Benthamite views (Perkin 1969:318–39). That they were so influenced does not explain what problem they thought they were addressing when bringing these views to bear. Efficiency is generally seen as the problem to be addressed (Ryan 1972:39–51; Perkin 1969:318–39). But did this simply mean good management in the sense of hiring people with appropriate skills to gather information and make decisions? Or did it also include the idea of efficiency and good management in the more complex sense of the structuring of responsibility and accountability so that administrators were constrained from making decisions in their own interests rather than in the public interest? To the extent that either or both of these were the problems being addressed then, there are still the questions of why these problems were seen as especially acute in the early 1850s and why some people thought they could be resolved by the proposed reforms.

The answers to these questions can be found by examining closely the one aspect all of these explanations have in common—the dominant role played by political leaders in bringing about reform of the civil service and institutionalizing it in the manner which persisted until the present. To the extent that this is the case, we might then ask what was the problem to which political leaders were addressing themselves in the creation of the civil bureaucracy in the nineteenth century? That the problem was closely related to the issue of the level of integration of political leaders, party, and administration is exhibited in the beginning section of the Northcote-Trevelyan Report, which stresses the problem of providing an administrative role that is accountable, efficient, public in character, and possesses appropriate expertise:

It cannot be necessary to enter into any lengthened argument for the purpose of showing the high importance of the Permanent Civil Service of the country in the present day. The great and increasing accumulation of public business, and the consequent pressure upon the government, need only be alluded to; and the inconveniences which are inseparable from the frequent changes which take place in the responsible administration are a matter of sufficient notoriety. It may be safely asserted that, as matters now stand, the Government of the country could not be carried on without the aid of an efficient body of permanent officers, occupying a position duly subordinate to that of the Ministers who are directly responsible to the Crown and to Parliament, yet possessing sufficient independence, character, ability, and experience to be able to advise, assist, and to some extent, influence, those who are from time to time set over them. (Great Britain, Report on the Organization of the Permanent Civil Service 1854–55 [1713]:3)

The close relationship of this problem to that of patronage is reflected in the commentary of Edwin Chadwick, the primary author of the influential *Report on the Sanitary Condition of the Labouring Population of Great Britain* (1842), who wrote the longest paper commenting on the Northcote-Trevelyan Report and ended by saying:

Mr. Burke, in his speech on economical reform [1782], says—"What I bent my whole force of mind to was, the reduction of the corrupt influence which is itself the perennial spring of all prodigality, and of all disorder, which loads us with two million of debt, which takes away vigour from our arms, wisdom from our councils, and every shadow of authority and credit from the most venerable parts of our Constitution."

The late Sir Robert Peel, speaking of the Encumbered Estates Act, said it was "so very good a measure that he really wondered how it passed." Nevertheless, great faith and hope may be had in the public and private integrity, to which the proposed measure for the relief of the Civil Service from its encumbrance appeals, against narrow views and feelings and sinister interests, in behalf of the extended relations and the most important interests of the empire. (Great Britain, Report on the Organization of the Permanent Civil Service 1854–55 [1713]:221–22)

The integration of executive and legislative powers in the hands of ministers was a major goal for political leaders in the 1850s. Or, to put it in structural terms, the problem of greatest moment for parliamentary leaders was how to integrate the parliamentary cabinet/executive with the administrative organization. Having won the victory of establishing the cabinet as the real executive in place of the monarch, parliamentary political leaders now had to solve the problem of building indissoluble and controlling ties to the administrative system.

The institution of patronage was central to the whole issue. But patronage had emerged out of the eighteenth century Janus-faced. The attack on the monarch's chief instrument for molding Parliament to his will meant that patronage was cast as the dark side of politics and the major obstacle to the achievement of parliamentary power. As is clear from Chadwick's quotation of Burke of more than a half century earlier, patronage had long been considered by some as an evil of constitutional and not individual corruption.

But why the early and concerted attack on patronage by political leaders in the nineteenth century? In other contexts, and in the English context of the early nineteenth century, patronage served as a sometimes means of integrating governing party and administration while simultaneously serving as a powerful tool for incumbents to retain office. As a consequence, politicians generally and English politicians specifically were loath to give up patronage. Why then the attack on the idea of patronage in the English case, and why was it so closely tied to the rationalization of the civil administration? I would like to suggest that the rationalization of the civil service emerged in the period between 1850 and 1870 as a consequence of the long process in which political leaders sought to reduce the uncertainty of their positions by expanding their control over the parliamentary cabinet/executive through the mechanism of party discipline. It was the unsystematic character of patronage which over time made it difficult for any individual putative or incumbent political leader, as well as party leaders, to predict with any degree of high probability the outcome of leadership competition and succession. The institutionalized uncertainty created by patronage thus came to be seen as a prime obstacle to greater predictability about the nature of political leadership succession and capacity.

The problem stemmed originally from the manner in which the settlement of 1688 left unresolved the problem of how to integrate the monarch, the Crown, Parliament, and the administrative structure. Or to put it some-what differently, how could the monarch as the executive (Crown) with in-stitutional interests to protect, and the monarch as the sovereign with policy views to push, achieve these aims without direct control over the means of administration? The monarchs' only means for achieving integration of ends and means was through parliamentary agreement to fund the executive. The only road to this agreement lay in influencing Parliament. The monarchs had two devices for this in the eighteenth century. One of these was through the selection of the Crown's executives—the selection of the first minister who could use his powers to try to organize a majority. The second means of influencing Parliament was through the use of patronage via the mon-arch's capacity to control appointments to the civil list. As long as there were no well-organized parties capable of garnering majorities and providing for systematic leadership and leadership succession, the monarchs' powers made political leadership in Parliament relatively unpredictable.

The monarchs could choose as first minister, if so minded, someone of their own persuasion and then, through the use of patronage, that minister could produce a majority. While this might produce an opposition, it was one without significant powers. In the absence of party organization, it had little hope of producing a leadership that could systematically bring down a government majority. In effect, the settlement of 1688 had the strange con-sequence of doing what earlier and less fortunate monarchs had hoped for—the ability to divide and conquer in Parliament.

This situation created several problems, primarily after the accession of George III, who tended to pursue his prerogatives rather aggressively. The first of these was that the structural conditions inevitably encouraged a strong-willed monarch to seek to create political leadership in his or her own image and thus raised the level of uncertainty about leadership. The second problem was that the monarch's direct expression of will with regard to po-litical leadership in Parliament raised the question of distinguishing between personal and public interest—the problem which had done much to pro-duce the conflicts of the seventeenth century.

The resolution of these problems took the form of attacks on the monar-chical structure of patronage. Between 1780 and the 1820s, political leaders in Parliament, especially the Rockingham Whigs with Burke as one of their major spokesmen, attacked the monarch's structure of patronage and de-stroyed it. The civil list became the property of Parliament. This solution did not resolve the central problem for political leaders, however. Indeed, it in-tensified the problem. The dissolution of the monarch's control over patron-age left patronage without any systematic rational structure. It dissolved the thin cords of attachment between civil list patronage and parliamentary membership purchase and influence. This created the problem of the systematic organization and use of patronage by political leaders in Parliament. Its use became decentralized, falling under the control of a variety of administrative officials on the one hand, and, on the other, to individual backbencher MPs who, by the early 1800s, had acquired the right to nominate local appointments. Parliamentary acquisition of patronage thus further destabilized the leadership structure.

By the end of the 1820s, the monarch had become a relatively insignificant factor in determining political leadership. Parliament was now left to its own devices to find a systematic and predictable structure of political organization and leadership. The issue was made more complex by the fact that Parliament was not a very sharp instrument of administration. The elimination of the only constitutional arrangement for controlling and organizing the administration of the state, the direct intervention of the monarch as an organizing principle, left political leaders in somewhat of quandary as to how to organize recruitment of officeholders and administration. Parties might have been a solution, but the independence of the backbench from political leaders was a powerful obstacle to the formation of well-disciplined party organizations. This independence was based on a number of aspects of the unreformed political and administrative system. Not the least of these was the existence of significant numbers of parliamentary seats, which were at the disposal of single individuals or available literally for purchase. Their existence only deepened the problem of uncertainty for political leaders since such seats represented individual arbitrary choices. These individuals were, theoretically, unconstrained by any organizational interest or power. This left such interests open to the charge of the pursuit of personal interest. But the constitutional order did not prohibit such behavior and it was, in some ways, self-validating—by virtue of its constitutionality it was legitimate.

Furthermore, patronage existed not only in the political world but pervaded all social relations in the eighteenth and early nineteenth centuries. As a consequence, it was the basic means by which political leadership itself was determined (Perkin 1969:37–62). Or, to be more accurate, political leadership prior to the 1830s was a consequence of a structure of personal relationships and networks which were held together and reinforced by various forms of patronage (Richards 1963:20–31; Kingsley 1944:30–45; Aspinall 1926:389–411; Foord 1947:484–507). Moving upward in terms of political leadership meant cultivating and maintaining a large body of social relationships, the glue for which was patronage in a wide array of forms. To the extent that political leadership was dependent on this tightly woven fabric of patronage, it was an obstacle to the formation of less particularistic forms of organization.

Parliamentary political leaders in the early 1820s thus faced a bundle of problems which made for uncertainty. At the core of this bundle was the problem of freeing parliamentary representation from the grips of single individuals and from small groups such as the close corporations which conceived and treated parliamentary seats as individual rather than organizational resources. So long as significant numbers of seats were subject to such conditions, they were not capable of being molded to any collective purpose. They could only be shaped to such purposes if representatives represented a constituency or an interest. Only when capable of being held accountable by a constituency would members of Parliament have sufficient incentives to actively pursue collective behavior and organization. Only then would putative political leaders have the opportunity to forge collective organization. Once given the opportunity, however, political leaders would find themselves faced with the problem of how to take advantage of the opportunity to forge a systematic structure of collective action.

Without the solution to the problem of representation there could be no solution to the problem of integrating administration into the parliamentary executive except in a fitful unsystematic way via patronage. The problem for political leaders was thus extraordinarily complex. To reduce uncertainty about political leadership, political leaders had to eliminate arbitrary aspects of parliamentary representation. Once this was achieved, political leaders might have greater control over their own fates, but they still faced the problem of making administration an instrument of parliamentary executive will. Without this, the delivery of promises to constituencies would be unpredictable and leadership uncertainty would continue only slightly unabated.

The arbitrariness of representation emerged almost untouched from the settlement of 1688–89. The enhanced and differentiated role of Parliament vis-à-vis the executive had earlier raised the problem of the independent source of its power and authority. The agreement that Parliament should have this role gave legitimacy to the pragmatic fact that Parliament's source of power did not lie in the royal prerogative but in its role of representation, which was expressed in its virtual control of state finances. The existing structure of representation, however, had only a customary constitutional basis, no well-rationalized criteria, and no inherent logical claim to executive powers. That is, the constitutional settlement of 1688–89 failed to bridge the gap between representation and governing except through limiting the monarch to selecting his ministers from Parliament.

To eliminate this arbitrariness, political leaders had to pursue a policy of rationalizing—in the sense of making more predictable through uniform rules—the system of representation. To do so meant making every representative somehow accountable to a body of interests or an interest. This implied the expansion of franchise, not out of democratic principles but out of principles of uniformity with regard to organizing collective action. Expansion of the franchise was in this sense epiphenomenal to the problem of political leadership and organization. But it was neither trivial nor insignificant as a problem. It raised uncertainty to a different level. Now political leaders had to deal with the problem of voter volatility. This made the problem of integrating the parliamentary executive with administration an even more difficult problem, which they sought to resolve through the linking of party with the mechanism of patronage. Patronage, however, had a number of drawbacks as a mechanism for satisfying constituents and imposing discipline on MPs. On the one hand, since patronage remained decentralized (only partially controlled by political leaders), it created new uncertainties over the imposition of discipline. On the other hand, political leaders had to be careful in attempting to make it the chosen weapon of discipline since this would leave them open to the charge of corruption. Once again, the question of private versus public interest emerges.

Ironically, without the discipline of party, political leaders could not move to periodic rotation of public offices, as in the case of the United States throughout much of the nineteenth century. Rotation could not be evoked until there had emerged some criterion for such systematic change. The one criterion that was unproblematic required a large franchise whose organization and shift in choices could be used to determine who was deserving and who was not. Large franchises, however, were even more unsettling for political leaders, since it was not clear how larger numbers of voters might transform the nature of political leadership and succession. Parliamentary leaders, in the first three-quarters of the nineteenth century, thus found themselves engaged in preemptive ad hoc tactics in the attempt to control and rationalize constituency volatility and at the same time rationalize and control representative volatility. The particular solution to the problem of administrative integration—the rationalization of the civil service—was in this sense a consequence primarily of the strategic necessity of political leaders to rationalize the parliamentary structure of power. Analysis of these dilemmas and their resolutions should bring us to a better understanding of how they resulted in the emergence of the rationalized, professionally oriented civil service characteristic of the British administration since the mid-nineteenth century.

The Settlement of 1688 and the Rationalization of Parliamentary Power: 1688–1830

If the emphasis on the individual as the means for transmitting and organizing information in the decision-making process is one source of similarity between the United States and Great Britain, then low uncertainty with regard to leadership succession is another central feature of similarity between the two countries. The relative stability of English politics after 1688 can be attributed to the emergence of two systems of rules which increasingly came to govern the relationships between individuals.

I think it may be argued that the social stability of the eighteenth century, which both sustained and was sustained by political stability, was, in good part, the product of the emergence of contract as an extraordinarily well-defined body of rules governing the relationships between individuals. Habermas has put it basically correctly, if in somewhat exaggerated language, when he says of England in the late seventeenth and eighteenth centuries:

The conception of the legal transaction as involving a contract based on a free declaration of will was modelled on the exchange transaction of freely competing owners of commodities. At the same time, a system of private law that in principle reduced the relationships of private people with one another to private contracts operated with the assumption that the exchange relationships that came about in accordance with the laws of the free market had model character. Of course, parties to a contract were not in every case also exchange partners, but the relationship of the latter, which was central to civil society, supplied the model for all contractual relationships. With the fundamental liberties of the system of private law, the category of a general legal standing—the guarantee of the legal status of the person—was articulated as well: the latter was no longer defined by estate and birth. The *status libertatis,* the *status civitatus,* and the *status familiae* gave way to the one *status naturalis,* now ascribed generally to all legal subjects—thus corresponding to the fundamental parity among owners of commodities in the market and among educated individuals in the public sphere. (Habermas 1989:75)

In essence, as Habermas points out, there emerged from the end of the seventeenth and beginning of the eighteenth century a body of civil law centered on the laws of contract which provided a relatively predictable pattern of behavior and relationships between individuals. In speaking of England, E. P. Thompson sums it up in the following way:

I have shown . . . a political oligarchy inventing callous and oppressive laws to serve its own interests . . . for many of England's governing elite the rules of law were a nuisance, to be manipulated and bent in what ways they could . . . But I do not conclude from this that the rule of law itself was humbug. On the contrary, the inhibitions upon power imposed by law seems to me a legacy as substantial as any handed down from the struggles of the seventeenth century to the eighteenth, and a true and important cultural achievement of the agrarian and mercantile bourgeoisie, and their supporting yeoman and artisans. (1975:265)

This body of rules was incrementally defined and sustained by the courts.

The courts had the ultimate sanction of force provided by the state, but, at the same time, they provided the means by which the state was constrained from randomly exercising its powers in relationships between individuals (Atiyah 1979:71–76; 95–97). The constitutional settlement following 1688 emphasized the restraints placed on the executive. The enhancement of Parliament's powers and its rejection of a powerful and numerous central administration had profound consequences. Not the least of these was that private arrangements, initiatives, and incentives played an ever more important role in the process of maintaining law and order. Public law became almost exclusively based on and legitimated by the common law (Shapiro 1986:51).

Equally important, perhaps, was the increased emphasis placed by elites on the power and majesty of law itself, not only through the ultimate sanction of the state but also through the elevation of law as a structure of values and norms (Atiyah 1979:98). "The whole judicial process, both civil and criminal, depended throughout on private initiative to set it in operation and keep it going" (Atiyah 1979:98–99). In effect, in the absence of anything but the smallest and crudest forms of civil and police administration, contract and its rules became the means by which this private behavior came to be increasingly orderly and disciplined in the latter part of the eighteenth century.

As I have pointed out in discussing the case of the United States, the dominance of contract in the organization of social and economic relationships also implied the equality of the individual, at least within the terms of the market. Participants in the contract must be of equal standing before the law, especially with regard to commodities and property. Without such equality, it is some form of public authority and power which drives and organizes the relationship rather than consent. This is reflected in the characteristics of the "model" of contract: each individual must deal with each other at arms's length, each individual relies on their own skill and judgment unhampered by obligations as if they are as strangers to each other; the parties are free to haggle and negotiate with no obligation incurred; the participant's equality is further recognized in the condition that individuals do not owe each other any information but are required to maintain the integrity of information, agreeing not to misrepresent or falsify; a deal is struck when the parties indicate agreement and the agreement is voluntary—consent is not enforced by social or political condition; the terms of the contract are the perquisites of the participants because it is assumed that they know their own minds and are the best judges of their needs and requirements, thereby recognizing the basic equality of the participants in entering and organizing the contract; finally, the agreement is binding and has pecuniary consequences for failure to perform regardless of the individual's social or political status

(Atiyah 1979:402–3). As contract replaced custom as the basis of law in the eighteenth century, individual equality replaced status as the basis of relationships in the marketplace. But it was not until the latter half of the nineteenth century that political equality would be erected on these foundations.

By the time of George III's accession to the throne in 1760, the rules governing relationships between individuals in economic life, and to a very considerable degree in social life as well, were relatively well defined and people's lives, insofar as they were affected by economic exchange, were moderately well regulated by these rules.

When seventeenth and eighteenth century Englishmen thought of the law, they thought not only of the criminal law and its preoccupation with theft, but of the common law in its broadest sense and of the body of regulation and equitable practice which oiled the social mechanism and mediated disputes of all kinds, including those that occurred within as well as between classes. (Brewer and Styles 1980:19)

Private arrangements utilizing contractarian law substituted for state administration to a considerable degree. As a consequence, the English administrative structure was very small, with most enforcement carried out by local magistrates and officers utilizing common law who, although serving at the monarch's pleasure, were not employed by the central state (Chester 1981:24–68, 166–67).[2]

The rise of a common law based on contract also provided the basic rules for bringing an end to sinecures and other forms of proprietary rights to office and for rationalizing the relationship of state officers to the Crown and Parliament. By the end of the eighteenth century, the rules of contract came to be utilized increasingly as the means for regulating private employment. While contracts for long-term employment often had fixed periods, it was already perfectly acceptable not to specify the time period. In the absence of a fixed term, the contract was normally capable of being brought to an end by giving reasonable notice. This rule is the modern one, and it only binds the future conduct of the parties to a minimum degree (Atiyah 1979:197). Until such rules had become well settled, public offices could only be thought of as property rights in which the official owned the means of administration. In this sense indeed, England was a proprietary state. How-

---

2. In 1797, the total number of public employees, excluding the armed services, was approximately 17,600, of which almost 15,000 were employed as collectors of various types of revenues. Only about 3,000 were employed in the central offices, and the vast majority of these were engaged in relatively menial work. Thus, even as late as 1829, the Home Department employed thirty and the Foreign and Colonial Departments forty-seven and thirty-three respectively (Chester 1981:166–68).

ever, once employment could be defined by contractarian rules, Parliament was provided a means by which employment might be regulated without succumbing to the sovereignty of property rights.

The rise of contract law as the basis of common law in the eighteenth century thus provided the basis for the elaboration of orderly rules governing political leadership succession or, to be more precise, governmental leadership succession. The two were close but not quite synonymous. The emergence of contract to regulate the succession of positions under employment established the basis for the structure of succession in public office. Beyond this, the relatively well regulated nature of civil life, which was based on a predictable set of rules, made possible the transition in the eighteenth century from the conflict-generating, paternalistic seventeenth-century monarchy to the ruleful, legally regulated Victorian state.

The rulefulness that came increasingly to govern the relations between individuals made the task of settling the ambiguities of the constitutional settlement of 1688–89 considerably easier. The conflicts which engaged the monarchs and Parliament in the latter half of the eighteenth century were kept within bounds of rhetorical conflict by the existence of a broadly ranging body of rules governing civil society. As Dicey argued, the rules of law which informed the constitution were the direct consequence of the existence of a body of individual rights defined and enforced by the courts. The principles of private law had been extended through the courts and through Parliament so as to define the position of the monarch, the Crown, and its servants (Dicey 1982 [1915]:115–16).

Certainly after 1688, and until as late as 1834, the selection of the leadership of the administration was both formally and actually, although not uncontestedly, the monarch's (sovereign's *and* the Crown's) prerogative (Le May 1979:22–41; Williams 1960:67–73). There was general agreement as to what constituted the constraining rules. In the absence of any parliamentary structures, such as organized parties that could provide leadership in a predictable and systematic fashion, much initiative in the selection of the Crown's ministers was left to the monarch in the eighteenth century. The Hanoverians, especially George III, tended to be highly aggressive in this regard (Clark 1980:306–9; O'Gorman 1982:passim; Wright 1970:4–5; Bulmer-Thomas 1965:17–30).

The selection of chief minister was by no means totally arbitrary or random, however. Most important, the monarch was not free to choose outside of members of Parliament—peers and elected members. Other than this, however, there was little, in a legal way, to direct selection. There was, of course, the necessity of selecting someone with sufficient recognition and status who possessed a core of supporters that could serve as a foundation on which to build a government majority. Once selected, however, the procedures for serving in office and leaving were relatively well defined. The chief minister and his cabinet could serve until he met with stubborn demands from the monarch or majority opposition in Parliament (Namier 1955:28–31). How long a first minister and his cabinet might serve was not predictable, but the means and procedures for transferring power were clearly understood. A monarch had to choose a first minister with the appropriate formal and informal qualifications, and he, in turn, had to put together a cabinet and a majority in Parliament by the process of appointment and preferment. First ministers and cabinet members forced to leave office did not lose their places in Parliament, nor were they in danger any longer of being declared treasonous and then dispatched.

The procedural stability that accompanied the post-1688 constitution and its Bill of Rights was made possible or, at least, was sustained primarily by the rise of contract. The combination of constitutional delineation in 1688–89 and the rise of contractarian law in the following century served to provide the basis for considerable certainty, discipline, and predictability in both public and private and in political, social, and economic life. These developments, nevertheless, also had a side to them which produced serious but not critical public uncertainties as the eighteenth century wore on. One of the central problems or, perhaps, *the* persisting problem of English politics emerging from the constitutional settlement of 1688 was the absence of a systematic structure that would provide predictability for the *selection* of government and political leaders. Such structures did not emerge until the last half of the nineteenth century in the form of political parties. The rise of political party organizations was accompanied by the emergence of increasingly well defined expectations concerning the career experiences and social status of leaders. The rationalization of parliamentary politics in the late eighteenth and early nineteenth centuries preceded and finally led to the rationalization of franchise, voter mobilization, and political leadership in the last part of the nineteenth century.

One of the outstanding characteristics of this rationalization process was the long time it took for it to occur. The constitutional settlement of the late seventeenth and early eighteenth centuries had produced a parliament in which there was always an opposition of some kind to the existing government. One might have expected that highly contingent, ad hoc arrangements for selecting political leaders would have caused great political instability and, as a consequence, great social instability. If this were the case, we would also expect some strong impulse toward the solution of the problem. It does not seem illogical to conclude that, in the absence of organizations that could reduce the level of competition for leadership and its rewards, factionalism would play a powerful and unsettling role. Although factionalism existed in the opposition all the way past the middle of the nineteenth century, it does not, however, seem to have been a threat to the structure of parliamentary governance (O'Gorman 1982:16–17, 24–25, 53–54, 106–7; Gash 1953:xix; Southgate 1962:317–18).

The consensus on the procedural or constituent elements of leadership succession surely played a major role in this regard. It did, nevertheless, both reflect and produce uncertainty about the selection of government leaders. Government political leadership was contingent—up through William IV, the last Hanoverian—on the monarch's choice. That is, the selection of the chief minister was still, to a considerable degree, an expression of the monarch's will and desire, not that of Parliament's. In the absence of a relatively rationalized party structure or a similar mechanism, the ambiguities surrounding the specifics of leadership succession continued to produce a level of uncertainty for actual and putative political leaders. Or, as Moore has put it:

The governmental system failed to provide adequate nexus between Ministers, Members of Parliament, and the leaders of the significant groups or communities throughout the kingdom. (Moore 1976:190)

The result was a system in which everyone understood and could predict the procedural structure of governmental leadership succession—there was no question of how to go about selecting a government leader or first minister. There was, however, considerable ambiguity at the end of the eighteenth and beginning of the nineteenth centuries about how political leaders emerged and succeeded each other, a condition which was reflected in the emergence of personal factions or groups such the Rockinghamites, Foxites, and others (Aspinall 1926:389–94; O'Gorman 1982:17–55).

Equality, Stability, and Uncertainty in the Political Leadership of the Eighteenth and Early Nineteenth Centuries

Standing at a distance, both temporally and culturally, one must be rather puzzled by the degree to which political stability was maintained between 1700 and 1850 in the face of the almost completely ad hoc arrangements for the specifics of political leadership. Equally bemusing, given the history of political and social conflict in the seventeenth century, is the degree to which society in the late nineteenth and early twentieth centuries seemed to often approach structural instability. One might very well think, given a glance at the nature of political history in other parts of the world during the nineteenth and twentieth centuries, that such ambiguity about the political leadership and its succession would produce highly centrifugal results. Yet, as

British and North American commentators are wont to say, the process of political development was evolutionary not revolutionary.

There were several reasons for avoidance of overwhelming political instability stemming from uncertainty over the institutions of political leadership and succession. Surely, the emergence of a body of rules and a set of institutional arrangements which defined and rendered predictable individual relationships helped reduce the consequences of this ambiguity. Surely, however, while this may have been a necessary cause, it hardly seems a sufficient one. The crises of the seventeenth century were brought about in good part by monarchs having quite different interpretations from those of Parliament as to what the common law meant with regard to restraint of Crown power.

The settlement of 1688–89 did expand the powers of Parliament at the expense of the monarch. However, the definition of the division of powers was very vague—sufficiently so as to provide the Hanoverians with considerable room for maneuver. The eventual definition and limitation of monarchical executive power came not as a result of the settlement of 1688 but of the continued existence of an opposition in Parliament; an opposition sufficiently strong on an increasing number of occasions to bring the government to heel, if not to new elections. Curiously enough, this suggests that the opposition came to possess a sufficiently well defined leadership so as to make it a powerful player despite the seeming absence of well-defined rules governing political leadership. In other words, while putative and actual political leaders faced considerable uncertainty with regard to power and position within the confines of formal structure, uncertainty appears to have been significantly reduced by some features of the leadership structure not present in formal organization.

What limited competition for leadership and reduced uncertainty? What informal structures existed for determining leadership which kept it from being a war of all against all? Central to understanding these questions is the structure of patronage, or patterns of social networks in which patronage played a major role. In the most general sense, the level of uncertainty for political leaders or putative ones remained low, in good part, because leadership was a function of social organization. Access to political leadership via parliamentary membership and experience was highly exclusive from the seventeenth to the twentieth centuries. While the specific criteria for access may have changed in the nineteenth century and perhaps again in the twentieth, it nevertheless was a function of a consistently narrow set of social experiences and relationships. Thus, one early twentieth-century commentator could write that:

The governing cliques can govern because they see one another daily: they are always calling on each other, or lunching, or dining, or attending receptions together; they have been at the same schools and colleges; they have shot together, hunted together; yachted together; they stay at the same country houses, when they leave the dozen or so of streets and squares in London in which they all live; and about half of them are more or less closely connected by the ties of blood or marriage. (as quoted in Le May 1979:11)

In some ways, it seems that so deep were the informal networks that tied politics to society that it was extraordinarily difficult for a systematic party organization to emerge. So long as patronage provided a more or less predictable means of organizing influence and recruiting individuals to public and private offices, there was not much incentive to find some other mechanism. The role of patronage in the rationalization of the civil service can be observed at several levels. First, social networks and patronage in the latter part of the eighteenth century served as the basic glue of social and political activities. Patronage stemmed primarily from property and the two were inseparable (Owen 1972:369–87; Perkin 1969:38). The aim of those seeking patronage was the advancement of their property and station. The aim of those bestowing patronage was to maintain and elevate their station and serve a social interest, that is, to maintain the appropriate social order in which everyone was "virtually" if not really represented (Moore 1976:192; Young 1794:106 in Perkin 1969:39; Habermas 1989:12–13). These aims were summed up and expressed in individual terms by Edward Gibbon writing to his father in 1760:

But I hear you say It is not necessary that every man should enter into Parliament with such exalted hopes. It is to acquire a title the most glorious of any in a free country, and to employ the weight and consideration it gives in the service of one's friends. (quoted in Namier 1957:18)

To use one's position "in the service of one's friends" was recognition of the role of patronage in society. One might rise in the world by virtue of patronage, whether it came from one's family or friend. "If successful the search for place yielded economic security and therefore self-esteem—the two were inseparably connected" (Rothblatt 1976:28). To help someone else up the ladder affirmed and enhanced one's position.

Patronage was the basic, if informal, structure of politics and power. This is expressed well, if in a somewhat excessive rhetoric, by the historian J. H. Plumb:

Patronage has been, and is an essential feature of the British structure of power, no matter how various the costumes it may wear. In the eighteenth century it scarcely bothered to wear a fig-leaf. It was naked and quite unashamed. . . . It was patronage that cemented the political system, and made it an almost impregnable citadel, impervious to defeat, indifferent to social change. . . . Place was power; and power is what men in politics are after. After 1715 power could not be achieved through party and so the rage of party gave way to the pursuit of place. (Plumb 1967:188–89)

Political patronage at the end of the eighteenth and the beginning of the nineteenth centuries took several forms: nomination or influence over parliamentary membership; nomination or appointment to civil list offices, to church positions, and, to varying degrees, nomination for service commissions (Richards 1963:20–25; Namier 1957:1–43; Phillips 1982:47–48; Parris 1969:50–79; Reitan 1966:318–37).

Administrative Patronage

In the latter half of the eighteenth century, all administrative positions were effectively filled by appointment of the Crown, which meant they were patronage appointments of government ministers and department heads (Chester 1981:13–14, 24–25; Reitan 1966:318–19). The government ministers used them not only to satisfy personal social networks but also political ones. Appointments were often used to help secure the support of members of Parliament by establishing ties of obligation that required reciprocity (Richards 1963:22–25). In 1797, Crown appointments amounted to over 17,500 offices (Chester 1981:166). While this seems like a large pool, in actuality it was rather small, since life tenure in most positions meant there were relatively few positions open at any given time.

At the beginning of the nineteenth century, little had changed. Recruitment to government offices was entirely a matter of patronage. As such, the notion of careers in offices simply did not exist. A large number of offices, especially many associated with the monarch's household, were not associated with any structure of associated offices through which individuals moved in a more or less predictable manner. Individuals were simply appointed to them without any basic criteria other than the individual's place in constructing an edifice of deference, status, loyalty, and parliamentary power. These were, many of them, sinecure offices to which the appointee held actual if not formal life tenure and thus were considered a form of property right (Chester 1981:18–19). Appointment rested on no specific criteria other than a monarch's or a department head's or a minister's need to meet the demands of constructing a parliamentary majority. No specific education standards were required, which might have created a standard entry age. In some of these offices, no real duties were required. In others, deputies or substitutes were employed by the officeholder to perform the duties. The main point of holding the office was not to pursue a career leading to an office which capped a lifetime of service and experience. The object of holding office for the individual was to have an assured source of income in a wildly contingent world. The object of office-holding socially was to provide the offspring or dependents of the upper classes with a living. This was generally thought to be legitimate since it was these classes which were the main support of the monarchy.

There was also a large and increasing number of appointments in the last half of the eighteenth and early nineteenth centuries to positions which were not offices in the legal sense of having a Crown or Treasury Letter of Patent establishing the office within the Civil List. Most of these were employees in Customs or Land Revenue. These were also appointed on the basis of patronage by department heads. Like sinecures, they came to be viewed as lifetime appointments carrying with them the implication of property right. Here, too, offices did not exist in any pattern of interdependent role relationships. Individuals did not move from one position to another as they acquired knowledge or experience which enabled them to perform another office. Each of these offices was viewed as being discrete, and thus no pattern of systematic promotion existed. Finally, there was the category of public employee that emerged in the Treasury and the Offices of the Secretaries of State to conduct the record keeping and communication of administrative orders and accounts—the clerks. These, like the customs and revenue officials were not legally officeholders but like the others came to view their offices as having lifetime tenure.

Once again, there were no standard criteria for appointment to these offices other than meeting the demands of the patronage network structure. In these offices, however, there emerged an interrelated hierarchy of positions—a general division of junior and senior clerks. It is not clear what generated this division originally, but seniority quickly dominated the promotion of individuals to senior clerkships (Sainty 1972:5–6; Sainty 1975:3–5; Sainty 1974:5; Sainty 1976:3–4). This suggests that the division stemmed from the arbitrariness of criteria combined with differentials in time of employment. Absence of preentry training and the periodic need to replace people or expand the number of clerks meant that some offices had to be designated as ones in which appropriate experience and skills could be acquired before advancement took place when openings occurred. In the absence of any recruitment criteria other than patronage, seniority became the default means of filling the senior-level clerkships, where experience was necessary. This, of course, limited the discretion and power of ministers and the heads of the various boards. Ministers, as political leaders, sought increasingly to avoid the consequences imposed by seniority. As early as 1782, the Treasury sought to establish the principle that promotions among the lower-level clerks should go to those "who have distinguished themselves most by their Diligence, Attention and Acquirement of the Knowledge of Business without regard to Seniority" (Roseveare 1969:122). In this effort, however, they were not very successful. Without any criterion as to what constituted merit, except in the grossest fashion, ministers found themselves faced with severe resistance from their clerks to the use of arbitrary "merit" selections for promotion (Roseveare 1969:123).

The central feature of the administrative role at the end of the eighteenth century was the concept of lifetime tenure. The main concern was appointment, not movement through a series of hierarchically arranged and rewarded offices. This absence of career structure is reflected in the wide variations of tenure in office of a variety of offices in the late eighteenth and early nineteenth centuries. Thus, the eighteen Colonial Office clerks between 1794 and 1822 held office for an average of 9.8 years, but their tenure ranged from one year (two people) to twenty-eight years (one person).[3] A similar pattern is reflected in the wide variations of age of appointments by the Treasury to clerkships in the Census Office as of 1851 (see table 10.1). The wide distribution of ages of first appointment clearly reveals the degree to which career structure was absent. Looking at the previous occupations of this group reaffirms the absence of career preparation and structure (see table 10.2). Holding an office was, thus, more important generally than the idea of advancement. This view of office was supported by the utilization of fees to supplant or subsidize salaries. In a great many cases, the holding of an office meant *de facto* and, very often, legal rights to the fees associated with the work of the office. Holding an office often meant ownership of part of its income. Movement from the office would mean forfeiting these rights. As a consequence, everyone saw the office one held as a sure thing not to be traded for prospects. The absence of any specified criteria for holding office also contributed to the lifetime tenure concept of the administrative role. Since there was no basis of appointment other than personal relationships, it was impossible to specify a criterion for ending tenure other than physical or mental inability to perform duties. The absence of contractual elements thus made it appear that the relationship of individual to office was a proprietary one. Office was property, not career.

To a considerable extent, this autonomy or independence of office was reflected in the autonomy of departments. Since each department's offices were like archeological layers of artifacts reflecting the time of their creation and frozen by the proprietary nature of the office, the departments were all very different in structure, organization, and operation. Or, to put it some-

---

3. Standard deviation = 8.162, based on Sainty 1976.

what differently, the creation of each office or groups of offices as distinct unique entities made every office more or less specific to one department. This made the notion of movement from one department to another, except at the ministerial and subministerial levels, simply mind-boggling. Over time, the distinctive differences of departments and their offices were institutionalized. This autonomy of development became the chief characteristic of Victorian administration:

Table 10.1 Age of Census Office Clerkship Appointments, 1851

Age at Appointment	N		%
14–18	19		18.0
19–23	22	60%	21.0
24–29	22		21.0
30–34	14		13.0
35–39	10		9.5
40–44	6		5.5
45–59	7		6.0
50–54	2		2.0
55–60	4		4.0
Totals	106		100

Source: Data from *Great Britain, Parliamentary Papers: Report from the Select Committee Report on Civil Service Appointments,* 1860 (440) IX: 344.

Table 10.2 Previous Occupation of Census Office Clerks, 1851

Occupation	No.	Occupation	No.
Barrister	1	Merchant Service	1
Bookkeeper	1	Newspaper Reporter	1
Bookseller	1	Plantation Overseer	1
Clerk (various types)	51	Scholastic	5
Merchant (various types)	6	Silk Merchant	1
Colliery Agent	1	Solicitor	3
Dissenting Minister	4	Ship Agent	1
Engineer	1	Surgeon	1
Farmer	2	Writer	1
Grocer	1	Tailor	1
Surgeon Assistant	1	W. I. Planter	1
Workhouse Master	1	Italian Teacher	1
Wood Engraver	1	No Occupation	16

Source: Based on *Great Britain, Parliamentary Papers: Report from the Select Committee Report on Civil Service Appointments,* 1860 (440) IX: 344.

Indeed perhaps the most striking feature of Victorian administration was the comparative autonomy of the various departments of state. These often had had very venerable and varied origins, and the development and history of each was "almost as complex as the history of the constitution itself." Apart from the marked difference in tone—some aristocratic, some businesslike, some slack—each department had evolved its own procedures and organisation to meet the widely differing tasks which it had to face. (Chapman and Greenaway 1980:17)

If patronage was the central feature of the administrative role at the end of the eighteenth century, it was also the central feature of the administrative structure. This was a consequence of the manner in which patronage was the main resource of political power. Since patronage was the only means of recruitment to office by the monarch or the Crown, its greatest advantage as a resource lay in the office's absence of accountability to Parliament. Accountability was insured only by law, that is, by prosecution for failure to perform one's duties (Chester 1981:27–28). In this situation, it was the legal structure of the office that determined the boundaries of performance. This made it difficult, if not impossible, to create systematic hierarchical structures of authority. Accountability and oversight were, at least formally, functions of the legal and justice systems, not of administrative hierarchy. The instruments of accountability were not to be internalized until the mid-nineteenth century.

It is not surprising, then, to note that one of the chief characteristics of pre-nineteenth-century administration was the use of corporate bodies as the basic structural building block of administration. Even through much of the nineteenth century, corporate bodies—boards and commissions—continued to be used as administrative devices rather than hierarchically organized units (Chester 1981:221–81). That they persisted is testimony to the way in which patronage and its control was a central concern of parliamentary leaders. So long as patronage continued to be the major means of recruitment and so long as the means of exerting control and accountability was through external rather than internal mechanisms, then Parliament's control over administration was best served by corporate management. Accountability and control could be imposed by having equals set to watch over each other. Such an arrangement was far better than the appointment of administrators who then might possess almost autonomous power over an administrative unit through hierarchical authority delegated by legislation. In the absence of any systematic uniform means of recruitment, the possibility of idiosyncratic and independent administrators was simply too great to allow hierarchical authority to be the central feature of administrative organization.

By themselves, these elements of control over officeholders were not powerful since they did not provide immediate sanctions or incentives to act on behalf of the state's rather than the individual's interest. The absence of ways to integrate roles into a coherent organizational structure to which individuals might be loyal and on whose behalf, rather than their own, they might act, led in the eighteenth century to the use of sinecures as a means for resolving this problem. Sinecures were often recognized as a form of pension which would provide incentives for appropriate performance (Chester 1981:129). The form of the sinecure—a specific rather than general appointment for service—made it especially useful in the eighteenth century for the monarch and the government in creating parliamentary majorities. The attack on monarchical influence after 1780, however, led increasingly to the creation of generalized rather than individual pension grants. The first major such scheme was created in the customs service, one of the largest areas of state employment, between 1791 and 1803 (Raphael 1964:68–84). The development of the pension structure in the customs service provided the first step toward the creation of an internal source for the integration of public service roles. In nearly all other cases, however, pensions were granted on individual terms (Raphael 1964:127–29).

In the final analysis, despite the emergence of pensions as a source of organizational integration, administration at the end of the eighteenth and beginning of the nineteenth centuries was a function of considerations external to the administrative structure. Patronage—the construction of social networks of allocating power and resources—was the most significant determinant of administrative role and organization. Control over individual opportunism was exerted, with the exception of the use of sinecures and pensions, only by the external constraints of law and the informal constraints of corporate watchfulness. Neither of these were powerful deterrents to collusion or opportunism on the part of life-tenured or long-term commissioners, board members, and senior officials generally. At the end of the eighteenth century, the reliance on patronage as the major means of recruitment and appointment to office at all levels provided a powerful obstacle to the emergence of an integrated, systematic, and predictable structure of administration.

Political Patronage

Patronage in the selection of parliamentary candidates was also widespread in the eighteenth century. Namier calculated that in 1760, 55 peers had the ability to select outright or heavily influence the selection and assure election of 111 parliamentary seats, while 56 commoners could affect 94 seats in the same way (Namier 1957:148–49). When the 30 or so seats dominated by any government ministry through influence in boroughs where government interests were heavy are added, the total number of seats subject to direct and indirect patronage came to about half of the English representation (489) (Namier 1957:148–49).

When the patronage of the Church of England hierarchy was added to many of the senior promotions in the services, it is easy to understand why the importance of the role of patronage has so often been stressed. Patronage was the dominant means for recruitment to political, administrative, and even religious and military offices. The system worked with relatively little friction up through most of the eighteenth century. There were several reasons for its success. The first was the decentralization of the means of acquiring political power. This decentralization was based, in the first instance, on the nomination powers of great aristocratic magnates and country gentry. This was reinforced by the expanded powers of Parliament after 1688. These two factors made it very difficult for power to be overwhelmingly centralized in the hands of one or a very few figures. Decentralization was further enhanced by the custom of viewing office as a property right. Proprietary rights were often reflected, as we have seen, in the ownership of any fees associated with the office and the right to hire others to actually fulfill the duties of the office (Chester 1981:14–18). Those who came to hold offices in the administration by virtue of patronage could not easily be ousted. Thus the resources available for distribution at any time were not anywhere near as great as the demand, thereby limiting the government's capacity to influence nomination (Chester 1981:18–20). Furthermore, in the eighteenth century political power had come to be distributed rather broadly in geographic terms but within narrow social bounds of peerage and property holders who numbered not much more than four thousand families by the beginning of the nineteenth century (Gash 1979:18). This decentralization meant that no single individual could dominate Parliament by virtue of wealth and property. Thus, the largest number of seats in Parliament held by the patronage of a single person was twelve—by the Duke of Newcastle at the end of the eighteenth century (Namier 1957:9).

The only close exception to this rule was the monarch. The monarch, by virtue of control of the civil list (the appointments and pay of the vast majority of administrative positions), had considerable potential resources available to be given to those who might be selected as first minister and heads of departments. When this was combined with those large numbers willing to support the Crown as a matter of principle, there was usually more than enough to produce a solid government majority. But even here the absence of a systematic structure of leadership selection and succession meant that political power would remain relatively diffuse. Thus, when the Rockingham Government seemed on the verge of dissolution in January 1766, its leaders described their position:

Those who have hitherto acted upon the sole principle of attachment to the Crown. This is probably the most numerous body and would on trial be found sufficient to carry on the publick business themselves if there was any person to accept of a Ministerial office at the head of them, and this is all they want. (as quoted in Namier 1965 [1955]:29)

As Namier concluded, "the Court could supply numbers and workers but not political leaders and a parliamentary facade—for this it had to turn to the Rockinghams, or the Grenvilles and Bedfords, or to Chatham" (Namier 1965 [1955]:29).

Despite the strong centrifugal forces which kept patronage from serving centralized political power and leadership, patronage did provide a base for aspiring political leadership. Patronage, along with family ties, bred a network of social relationships that made it possible to create influence beyond the direct control of any single individual. Each individual included in the network of patronage and obligation also had a network of ties. Within Parliament this meant that the patronage of an active pursuing political aspirant might be sufficient to set in motion a network which would vault an individual to leadership or at least to make him noticeable. The centrality of patronage and its social networks to political leadership is described with great nicety and irony by Sir Henry Taylor, a senior official in the Colonial Office for almost fifty years, in his book of practical advice, *The Statesman*, published in 1832:

It is of far greater importance to a statesman to make one friend who will hold out with him for twenty years, than to find twenty followers in each year, losing as many. For a statesman who stands upon a shifting ground of adherency, requires incessantly renewed calculation to inform him where he is as to means and powers; and perpetual management at the hooking and dropping of dependencies; and he must be always sacrificing his own unity of purpose, and the strength he might derive from it, in order to avail himself of the varying support. (1927:18) . . .

Whilst he [the political aspirant] has his way to make in the world he should not be afraid of incurring obligations towards men in power; still less should he be afraid of avowing those which he does incur. On the contrary, he should be more ready to imagine a benefit when there is none, than to disavow or to extenuate (as men will sometimes do through the mistakes of an unintelligent pride) any real service. He should indeed be prodigal of thanks to every body who can be implicated in a benefit conferred on him. (Taylor 1927:69)

The role of patronage for sustaining political leadership was reflected in the ability of those who had served as a monarch's first minister to come away with a relatively well settled core of followers whose commitment was preserved and nourished by patronage (Perkin 1969:47–48; O'Gorman 1975:46–66, 478–82; Foord 1964:338–45, 404–9; Beckett 1986:434–35).

While patronage and social networks provided a relatively well understood principle and structure for the development of political leadership, it by no means offered the solace of predictability. Nor did one's emergence as the leader of a group in Parliament provide any assurance that one might come to govern or provide any means by which to construct a majority. Indeed, one of the most important political lessons of the late eighteenth and early nineteenth centuries was that while the king might not be able to run politics as he wished, he could make it difficult or impossible to run it without him. Patronage as a political institution thus seemed consistently to provide an advantage to the monarch and the executive against Parliament and the legislative and taxing power.

In the absence of any day-to-day organizing principle other than patronage and its social ties, parliamentary political leaders were unable to make their futures wholly predictable. In effect, then, patronage and its social ties provided for a structure of political leadership that had strong elements of rulefulness but which, by virtue of its localized face-to-face character, made the process of political leadership and succession an uncertain one. Political leadership in Great Britain at the end of the eighteenth and beginning of the nineteenth century was thus a function of social organization tied inseparably to property and social status. So closely was political leadership tied to social organization that until the franchise became considerably larger, there was little incentive to form political party structures outside of Parliament. The absence of such organizations made it impossible to aspire to political leadership outside of the patronage structure.

11

Patronage, Representation, and Administrative Reform

The Problem of Representation

At the end of the eighteenth century, two rule systems—contractarian law in the marketplace and the rule of deference and patronage in the network of social relations—existed side by side in an increasing state of tension. The tension arose from the requirement of individual equality that was a condition of contract and the inequality that was a condition of patron-client relations. This contradiction took on a myriad of forms of conflict in the nineteenth century. Two of these—representation and publicness or public interest—were of the greatest importance for incumbent and putative political leaders in Parliament. The Crown's use of patronage to produce a government party in the eighteenth century, especially under George III, continually confronted political leaders with arbitrariness in the process of leadership succession.

The response of political leaders was to raise the question of whose interests were being represented. That is, the absence of a systematic and relatively predictable method for determining leadership and, therefore, leadership succession raised the questions of where the ultimate responsibility of policy formation lay and how it was formed. Was policy-making a function of the executive? If so, how was the executive made accountable for its policies so that they were not idiosyncratic or, worse, selfish? To reduce uncertainty about leadership and leadership succession, parliamentary political leaders sitting in the opposition had few choices. Indeed, short of redoing the settlement of 1688–89, nongovernment leaders really had only one choice, and that was summed up in Dunning's famous parliamentary resolution of 1780: "The influence of the Crown is increasing, has increased, and ought to be diminished" (Richards 1963:34). They could attack the Crown for pursuing its selfish interests through the use of corrupt practices—corrupt because patronage allowed the monarch to pursue his interests without regard to the constitutional requirement that parliamentary legislation should be the product of representation of social interests.

The quarrel over the nature of leadership succession and the control of decision making was not only between the Crown and Parliament but was also internal to Parliament. As the eighteenth century wore on, the electoral system became increasingly oligarchical. Oligarchical tendencies were encouraged by Parliament's conservative attitude toward franchise. Since Parliament had the sole right of determining the franchise in boroughs where the vote was disputed, it could and did tend to opt for narrow franchises (Cannon 1973:33–34). These franchise determinations were frozen by the so-called "Last Determination Acts" of 1696 and 1729 (Cannon 1973:33–34). These actions tended to force up the price of electioneering by making boroughs with small numbers of voters inviolate to change and thus able to enforce monopoly conditions on putative candidates. The property qualification introduced in 1711 further enhanced the exclusivity of parliamentary access by requiring that a knight of the shire possess land paying £600 and that burgesses pay £300 per year to be eligible for candidacy (Cannon 1973:36).

All of these factors tended to favor the wealthier landowners as against the country gentry in the process of nomination and candidacy. By the first decade of the nineteenth century it has been estimated that peerage patronage in Parliament had reached over 200 members (210 in 1786, 226 in 1802, and 236 in 1807) (Sack 1980:913–37). The expansion of peerage patronage was due in no small part to the great number of boroughs in which the franchise was sufficiently limited as to make the electors acutely aware of the benefits that might come as a consequence of their small numbers. Small numbers of electors provided a strong incentive for the wealthy to make parliamentary seats the object of purchase. The result was the emergence of wealth, especially, but not solely, landowning wealth, as a major means of nominating or selecting candidates for House of Commons contests. This ran directly into the older traditional manner of nomination by customary status or, if you will, nomination by means of the local structures of deference.

This growth of peerage patronage power not only created new and very individualistic modes of candidate nomination, it also raised the question of representation. Was Parliament merely an instrument of representation of the great aristocracy (Cannon 1973:40, 50–55)? In its broadest sense, the problem of patronage and representation provided political leaders with a potent weapon: the idea of the public interest and how it was to be formulated and pursued as opposed to the "corruption" of private desires and interest. By the 1760s, monarchical patronage was seen as the corrupt means by which the opposition, especially the Rockingham Whigs, were kept from achieving their rightful majority in the Commons (Christie 1962: chapter 2; Cannon 1973:73; O'Gorman 1975:393). At the same time, the patronage of the aristocracy as a central feature of the political makeup of the Commons began to provoke similar claims of corruption (Christie 1962: chapter 2). The transformation of patronage into corruption stemmed from the growing claim emanating from the parliamentary opposition that patronage was the means by which true representation was distorted and private interest prevailed over public interest. Thus the Wilkites, the supporters of John Wilkes, the editor of the *North Briton* whose writing in 1762–63 provoked the authorities to attempt to jail him and exclude him from his seat in Parliament, saw the attack on Wilkes as an indication of the overweening powers of the Crown. They came, in the following years, to attack royal and aristocratic power in the Commons, demanding that MPs be prohibited from holding Crown offices, that rotten boroughs be eliminated, and that perhaps a wider franchise be created (Christie 1962: chapter 2).

In this fashion, parliamentary political leaders in opposition to the Crown rapidly came to view patronage as the basis of a strategy by which they could raise the questions of representativeness and public interest to their benefit (that is, to remove the Crown as a source of arbitrary determination of political succession). Concomitantly, the increasing prominence of the contractarian requirement of equality in the marketplace, and in the law governing private transactions and relationships, provided political leaders with tactical instruments by which patronage might be rationalized and removed from the grasp of the Crown. Parliamentary opposition political leaders had little choice over the means for doing so. In the absence of strong, well organized parties capable of organizing voters, political leaders had no choice but to construct Parliament as a collective body as the aggrieved party. They were forced to construct a view of the monarch as a corrupting influence on the constitution itself. The solution was to sever the monarch from direct control over the appointment process and to interpose Parliament between monarch and administration. The tools for achieving this were close at hand. Parliamentary leaders turned to the now relatively well developed contractarian doctrine that employees of the government existed on a basis of equality with all other contracting parties in employer-employee relationships. In effect, they would argue that the Crown's appointment powers could be no exception to these rules and, therefore, state employees did not have proprietary rights to their offices. Under these circumstances, the contracting party had to be defined as the Crown in Parliament, not the Crown as the monarch. In this view, Parliament had the power to control the Civil List and the whole structure of appointments.

The development of this approach is reflected in the conflict over the Civil List debts. The Civil List revenues had been transferred to Parliament in 1760, in return for which Parliament had granted George III a fixed amount per year—£800,000 (Reitan 1966:323). The problem arose from the increasing costs of the Civil List in succeeding years. The discrepancy between budget and actual cost required the Crown's first minister to ask Parliament for relief. This provided the basis for the opposition's attack on Crown influence. Thus, in 1777, when Lord North prevailed upon Parliament to pay the debts incurred over and above the amount accorded to the Civil List, Burke's reply was that the debt must have been incurred "for purposes not fit to be avowed by ministry, and therefore very fit to be inquired by this house" (Reitan 1966:326). At stake here obviously was the independence of the Civil List from parliamentary control. The debates on the Civil List debt in 1777 resulted in laying the foundation for a purely contractual view of the Crown's appointments.

The principle was firmly established by Burke's Economical Reform Act of 1782. Between 1780 and 1782, aided by external attacks on the cost and depth of Crown influence in Parliament made by followers of the Reverend Christopher Wyvil of Yorkshire in late 1789, the opposition in the House of Commons sought to constrain the Crown's powers over appointment. Thus, in the debates on the issue of Civil List reform, Burke, who had become Paymaster General in the Rockingham Ministry, in his famous argument for eliminating sinecure offices, emphasized the corrupting influence of Crown patronage:

But what, I confess, was uppermost with me, what I bent the whole force of my mind to, was the reduction of that corrupt influence, which is itself the perennial spring of all prodigality, and of all disorder; which loads us more than millions of debt; which takes away vigour from our arms, wisdom from our councils, and every shadow of authority and credit from the most vulnerable parts of our constitution. (quoted in Reitan 1966:331)

The act passed in 1782 and eliminated, for the first time, on parliamentary command 134 sinecure offices (Richards 1963:26; Foord 1947:499).

This process of placing state employment within the bounds of contract law was pursued with considerable energy throughout the remainder of the decade by the Commissioners on Public Accounts. They attempted to find a means for overcoming the proprietary rights to office without subverting property rights. In their Eleventh Report of 1784, the commissioners presented their quandary:

We do not mean to violate in the slightest Degree, any Right vested in an officer by virtue of his Office. The Principles which secure the Rights of private property are sacred, and to be preserved inviolate; they are Land Marks to be considered as immovable. But the Public have their Rights also; . . . If a useless and expensive Office cannot be suppressed . . . be the Necessities of the State ever so urgent, without intrenching upon the right of the Possessor . . . the evil must be endured, until the Power of the Legislature can, without the Imputation of Injustice, be exerted for the Relief of the State. (as quoted in Chester 1981:125)

The answer to their problem was constructed out of contract law. The commissioners earnestly sought to remove offices from the realm of property and place them in that of contractual relations, as can be seen very clearly in their argument presented in the Fourteenth Report of 1785:

A Freehold held under the Grant of the Crown, is a solemn Right, to be treated with Respect, Delicacy and Caution; but if the Subject of that Grant be a Public Office, and a stipend be annexed to it, payable out of the Revenue of the Public; if rendering a service useful to the State, as the Consideration for the Stipend, be of the Essence of such an Office . . . where the Utility of the Service is either wanting at the Time of the Grant, or in the Process of Time ceases to exist, the Grant either had not at first, or has lost, the Quality essential to its Support; and no Power of the Grantor, . . . or Duration of the Interest, can supply the Defect. (as quoted in Chester 1981:126)

The commissioners went on to recommend to Parliament that sinecure offices should be totally eliminated. They put forward a fourfold principle by which to define the nature of the role of public officials:

First, No office should be holden by Legal Tenure; Secondly, Every Office should have a useful Duty annexed to it; Thirdly, Every Officer should execute, himself, the Duty of his Office; Fourthly, Offices where the duty was of the same Kind should be consolidated. (as quoted in Cohen 1941:39)

These principles became the basis for further attacks on sinecure offices. By the turn of the century, over twelve hundred offices, most of them sinecures, had been eliminated (Foord 1947:500). The first decade of the nineteenth century saw the death of the concept of property rights to public office. Sinecures as a means of influencing votes simply disappeared as an effective political weapon on the part of the Crown. Certainly by no later than 1830, Parliament could be said to have transformed public proprietary officeholders into employees whose relationship to the state was essentially a contractual one (Chester 1981:131–55).

The contractual nature of the relationship was further reinforced by the progressive elimination of both the proprietary right to the fees of office and to the use of fees as a form of direct salary payment. In both cases, fees represented the independence of the officeholder from parliamentary control of office. The first of these was most subversive to parliamentary control since it meant that individuals owned the means of administration so long as they lived. These were assailed early as part of the attack on sinecures. Each elimination of sinecures carried with it the abolition of fees, perquisites, gratuities, allowances, emoluments, as well as salaries (Chester 1981:138). The attack on fees as salaries was accomplished by administrative acts beginning, as with the attacks on sinecures, with the Rockingham Ministry. In 1782, a minute of the Treasury Board abolished the fee and gratuity structure in regard to salaries in the department. This was followed by the same in other departments between 1795 and 1800 (Chester 1981:139). While fees continued to be collected, they eventually were absorbed into general government revenues. The last formal vestige of the relationship of office to fees came to end in 1849–50, but any real relationship had ceased to exist considerably earlier (Chester 1981:140).

This separation of the control of office appointment from the monarch and its absorption by Parliament rationalized the relationship of officeholder to the state, thus appearing to resolve one of the major sources of ambiguity and uncertainty for political leaders. This may well have been the case, but the shift from proprietary to contractual bases for office-holding produced other difficulties while leaving some sources of uncertainty untouched. Within the administrative structure, the changeover to contractual relationships governing administrative roles helped to weaken seniority as the basic element in determining appointments to those offices which had customary proprietary claims to promotion. At the end of the eighteenth and the beginning of the nineteenth centuries, seniority as the basis of promotion was a function of proprietary rights to any office in which upward movement had become customary. The elimination of proprietary rights, which accompanied the transfer of patronage from monarch to Parliament, meant there was no longer a necessary link between subordinate and superordinate offices. Promotion thus came to be seen as an opportunity for patronage (Hughes 1942:56; Parris 1969:62–63).

As a consequence, by the 1830s and 1840s higher positions in the various departments were increasingly awarded to outsiders—men like Trevelyan, Kay Shuttleworth, James Stephen, Chadwick, and a host of others (MacDonagh 1977:200–201). While a number of these appointments produced important innovators, they also produced officials who took great care to establish *their* autonomy by perpetuating departmental patronage appointments through control over promotion (MacDonagh 1977:200–201). The desire for departmental control over its patronage by party leaders holding ministerial positions, as well as by senior officials, contributed greatly to the emergence of the idea that appointment and promotion should be based on merit. The use of the idea of merit—only very vaguely defined if defined at all—allowed department heads to utilize patronage to sustain their positions while at the same time reduce the possibility of charges that they were pursuing private interests. So long as merit was not determined by well-defined rules and systematic role behavior, ministerial heads were free to pick whomever they liked so long as the individual showed at least average intelligence and capacity. This, however, created several problems. It raised, on the one hand, the question as to what constituted the minimal conditions of merit. On the other side, the breakdown of seniority undermined the morale of those who had been passed over. The use of patronage to fill positions in the hierarchy of ministerial offices produced great unease and a sense that administrative appointment and promotion was largely arbitrary (Parris 1969:65–66; MacDonagh 1977:201).

The dissolution of the hierarchical links in the proprietary-based system of patronage also produced the informal beginnings of the distinction between a lower and upper civil service. Bringing in outsiders to hold the upper-level offices resulted in the emergence of distinct office-holding opportunities—one for junior clerks and one for senior positions. Thus, by the early 1850s it was rare for a permanent head of a department, namely, the senior official whose position was not automatically vacated with a change in government, to have started official life as a junior clerk who worked his way up. At the Treasury, of the first six assistant secretaries who held office from 1805 to 1870, only two had begun as junior clerks, and these had served for only six years of the entire period (Chester 1981:310). In 1850, the senior permanent heads at the Foreign, Colonial, and Home Offices had all been recruited from outside department ranks (Chester 1981:310). By the time of the Northcote-Trevelyan Report of 1853, there was already an informal division of labor between what the report would describe as "mechanical" and "intellectual" labor, but which was in essence a distinction between higher and lower patronage awards by departmental heads.[1]

Finally, the dissolution of seniority rights to promotion, while problematic with regard to morale, allowed department heads to extract an increased degree of accountability from officials. Under the proprietary conception of office-holding, there was, as we have seen, relatively little leverage to be exerted on officials except through the granting of pensions. By establishing

1. The Report itself called attention to this distinction as it tried to use the examination system as a means for transforming the distinction into a merit standard.

"It is of course essential to the public service that men of the highest abilities should be selected for the highest posts; and it cannot be denied that there are a few situations in which such varied talent and such an amount of experience are required, that it is probable that under any circumstances it will occasionally be found necessary to fill them with persons who have distinguished themselves elsewhere than in the Civil Service. But the system of appointing strangers to the higher offices has been carried far beyond this. In several departments the clerks are regarded as having no claim whatever to what are called staff appointments; and numerous instances might be given in which personal or political considerations have led to the appointment of men of slender ability, and perhaps of questionable character, to situations of considerable emolument, over the heads of public servants of long standing and undoubted merit." (Quote from Great Britain 1854–55 [1713]: vol. XXVII, 7.)

the principle of appointing outsiders, ministerial department heads were able to exert more party and individual influence over decision making (Hughes 1942:56–57). But here too there existed tension-creating contradictions. While using patronage to fill promotion positions enhanced the power and influence of department heads both within the department and in relation to other political leaders, it did not provide them with the ability to remove men appointed by others. In the absence of clear standards of merit, so long as officials were not completely and visibly incompetent, there were no easy means to create vacancies, especially since there was no standard term for the tenure of department heads. Thus, while unlinking promotion appointments might give a department head some immediate leverage over officials, this by no means amounted to a long-term continuing means of imposing accountability and homogeneity of outlook.

The problem was not a terribly significant one in the early decades of the century. At that time, the function of accountability of officials was met by reference to the personal character of the individual as assured by the structure of patronage. The "gentlemanly" and, indeed, aristocratic origins of the great majority of members of Parliament and members of the government on both sides of the aisle, but especially among the Whigs, meant that patronage appointments went to individuals of the same class, from whom a minimal level of predictable kinds of behavior could be expected (Beckett 1986:403–35, 456–63).

The issue of accountability became an increasing source of concern, however, with the expansion of franchise after 1832. The reform created, among many parliamentary leaders, the anxiety that further franchise reform might be forthcoming since it seemed to be a possible source of party energies and dynamics. The reform movement and the expansion of franchise forced politicians to pay more attention to constituencies, and this brought with it the apprehension that standards other than the station of "gentleman" might be used in appointments to office and in politics generally.

Peel's concern over the problem of accountability is reflected in his comments to Goulburn, his Chancellor of the Exchequer, in 1842 concerning an incipient scandal in Customs: "I think there is a strong presumptive evidence of gross neglect on the part of superior officers," and later in writing, "I have a strong impression that there has been systematic corruption on the part of the lower class officers, systematic fraud on the part of merchants and that the customs' revenue has most materially suffered" (Hughes 1942:58). A decade or so later, Chadwick was to complain that in the smaller parliamentary boroughs patronage was being passed out to people of low social status (Hughes 1942:58). Trevelyan, in defending his and Northcote's report against the criticisms of Captain O'Brien in January 1854, wrote with characteristic bluntness about the same problem:

At present a mixed multitude is sent up, a large proportion of whom, owing to the operation of political and personal patronage are of an inferior rank of society . . . *and they are, in general, the least eligible of their respective ranks.* (as quoted in Hughes 1949a:72)

In many ways, this concern was best expressed by Gladstone in a letter to Lord John Russell written in January 1854 when the Northcote-Trevelyan Report was being considered:

I do not hesitate to say that one of the greatest recommendations of the change in my eyes would be its tendency to strengthen and multiply the ties between the higher classes and the possession of administrative power. . . . The objection which I always hear there from persons who wish to restrain restrictions upon elections is this: "If you leave them to examination, Eton, Harrow, Rugby, and the other public schools will carry *everything*." I have a strong impression that the aristocracy of this country are even superior in natural gifts, on the average, to the mass: but it is plain that with their acquired advantages, their *insensible* education, irrespective of book-learning, they have an immense superiority. This applies in its degree to all of those who may be called gentlemen by birth and training; and it must be remembered that an essential part of any such plan as is now under discussion is the separation of *work*, wherever it can be made, into mechanical and intellectual, a separation which will open to the highly educated class a career and give them a command over all the higher parts of the civil service, which up to this time they have never enjoyed. (as quoted in Hughes 1949a:63)

Further pressure for finding a means to ensure accountability and uniformity of administrative behavior came from the expansion in the number of regulating and technical officials after 1832. The Emigration Act of 1833, followed by a variety of acts, such as, the Factory Law, the Ten Hours Act, the New Poor Law, required active regulation of various aspects of social life. This resulted in the creation of corps of inspectors or commissioners for whom there was no ministerial accountability since they were under the direction of autonomous boards or commissions created by Parliament (MacDonagh 1961:52–67; Clark 1973:74–75; MacLeod 1988:13–14).

While the assault on the proprietary basis of office-holding gave department heads greater control over appointments and personnel at the higher levels of administration, it also, in a persistent way, raised the question of what constituted an objective standard or sign of merit. This was true not only for appointments at the higher levels of the departmental hierarchy but also at the entry levels. Thus, a Treasury Minute of August 1833 stated that the Lords of the Treasury found it "important that all Offices under the Crown should be filled by Persons competent to perform the duties of their situations; and that strict regulations should be established for the purpose of securing that object, as far as that may be practible" (Cohen 1941:67). In 1834, the Treasury sought a "practible" means by experimenting with examinations. Melbourne, the Treasury head, introduced a system in which for each vacancy there would be three nominations. Every candidate was required to take an examination that was little more than a simple test of literacy. The candidate was merely required to write a precis and do simple arithmetic. The one performing the best—no absolute standard was created in deference to the patronage nomination—was given the job (Roseveare 1969:171). In this way, Melbourne was able to get rid of three patronage obligations where one had only been available before. Peel apparently objected to the system because he reverted to simple vacancy patronage in 1841 (Roseveare 1969:171). Other departments had also, by then, adopted simple literacy examinations. Few, however, had gone beyond this, except in a few instances, where specific duties required special knowledge, as in the case of auditors who were required to have an understanding of double-entry bookkeeping (Cohen 1941:95).

With the argument of merit employed, for the most part, to unlink junior from senior positions and thereby provide party leaders in their roles as department heads with increased patronage, incentives to find a uniform standard for the determination of merit were drastically reduced. The problem was exacerbated or helped, depending on one's point of view, by the reality that there existed no self-evident "practible" way to judge competence that would apply in a uniform fashion across any group of candidates. The absence of a uniform standard or expectation with regard to level or content of education for any group or class in the first half of the nineteenth century meant that any exam, except one testing basic literacy, would test very little. So varied was the educational structure, so varied was the understanding of what constituted appropriate education for every class, not to mention the variations in curriculum of schools dealing with students at similar ages, that it was impossible to produce people with systematic predictable behavior, skills, capabilities, and talents (Vaughan and Archer 1971:33–59; Curtis 1965:141–71, 421–60). In short, no examination system could be invoked as a solution to the problem of merit until uniform patterns of education had been established. All of this had the happy consequence for department heads of allowing them to set more or less arbitrary standards of merit and to fill vacancies at all levels pretty much as they liked.

That this problem was well understood was reflected in the attempt to develop a uniform system of education for the East India Company's civil service in the period from the turn of the century until 1858. Despite the patronage desires of the directors, the direct patronage selection process in use in the eighteenth century became overwhelming in its demands and underwhelming in its capacities. The result was the founding of Haileybury College, to which nominees of the directors were sent for a uniform and utilitarian education (Cohen 1966:87–140). This allowed the directors to continue exercising patronage but at the same provided a means for instituting a uniform pattern of training. Clearly, however, this was not an example that could be easily followed, since it hinged on the creation of a school, entrance to which depended on nomination. There existed no such system for the public service, nor would it have been easy to legitimate the creation of a public training system, entrance to which was based purely on patronage.

A different consequence of the increased resort to the idea of merit as a means of gaining control over all appointments in a department, especially at the Treasury, was the spread of the practice of requiring new appointments to serve a period of probation. Absent any but the most primitive standards by which to judge merit, department heads installed probationary periods as a means of making judgments, albeit subjective in character, about capacity. The Treasury adopted a two-year probationary period in 1831, and other departments also established probationary periods (Cohen 1941:66, 77). By 1850, most departments had come to specify periods of probation ranging from three months to a year (Cohen 1941:66, 77).

By the 1840s and 1850s, the shift from a proprietary to a contractual definition of administrative office-holding had produced in its wake a group of important changes in the administrative role. Appointment to office was now based on parliamentary rather than Crown patronage and privilege. However, patronage appointment was not at all well integrated into party organization. Indeed, it appeared that parliamentary organized patronage seemed to be both cause and effect of party weakness. Parliamentary, as distinguished from party, control of patronage provided a powerful force for continued decentralization of the appointment process.

As we have seen, the contractual definition of office had also created the problem of criteria for promotion, since possession of office no longer gave proprietary and predictable rights to office. Removing the proprietary links made promotion less predictable and thus provided some incentive for officials to pay close attention to their political superiors. At the same time, however, extending patronage to promotions raised the problem of long-term accountability since there was neither clear criteria for dismissal nor systematic retirement. In essence, the shift to contractual office-holding set the putative and incumbent officeholder loose from the moorings to which he had been safely attached under proprietary rules. He was no longer protected by actual or inferred rights of ownership of the means of administration.

The shift to contract, thus, had made Parliament, as an organization representing the state, the sole owner and possessor of rights to office. The situation was ironic. Parliament had won the long struggle to control access to administration only to have very little understanding of how to organize its power. In the first half of the nineteenth century, Parliament had no centralized organizational principles by which it might govern the allocation of patronage. In the place of such organizational rules, customary patronage rules took over and appointment came to be allocated on the basis of the MP's position in the hierarchy of parliamentary status. Those who came to be appointed as department heads, heads of commissions, or members of boards came to have the rights of patronage associated with those positions. Backbenchers, whether government or opposition, received the lowest form of patronage—the rights over field office positions in their constituencies.

Finally, the Reform Act of 1832 raised new uncertainties by expanding the franchise. Faced with the uncertainties of a new franchise, both party leaders and backbenchers sought to use whatever means were at hand—patronage, greater attention to local demands for legislative help, greater exposure in public forums—to sustain their incumbencies. Patronage became especially important to backbenchers as government party leaders successfully began to narrow their access to private bills and parliamentary debate. By the 1840s, the problem of rationalizing patronage had thus become of central importance. Without some solution to the problem, leadership uncertainty and party weakness would continue to characterize parliamentary politics.

Parliament and the Centralization of Patronage

Rationalization of office-holding vis-à-vis the Crown and Parliament did not, therefore, resolve the problem of arbitrariness in the parliamentary structure of leadership. Absent the monarch as an organizing principle, however seemingly arbitrary he or she was, the problem after 1820 increasingly became finding such a principle internal to Parliament. Kitson Clark provides a neat description of this condition as it came to fruition in the 1840s:

The House of Commons now controlled the legislation of the country, the working of government and the lives of ministries, but there was at the moment no power which could adequately control the members of the House of Commons. In the eighteenth century the members of the House of Commons had been controlled by the power of patronage and the authority of the Crown, in the late nineteenth century and in the twentieth century the Commons were to be kept under discipline by party. (Clark 1962:44–45)

No solution to the problem of parliamentary discipline, and therefore leadership uncertainty, could be arrived at so long as patronage in relation to Parliament remained decentralized. In the absence of patronage centralization, MPs could remain independent of party leadership. The core of this problem was the decentralized character of administration and the absence of central accountability. At the end of the eighteenth century there was no centralized structure of administration and as a consequence no centralized structure of patronage. In the 1780s, Burke had realized the problem facing parliamentary political leaders was not simply the absence of mediation between the legislature and the executive, but also the absence of any centralized administrative control (Roseveare 1969:121). So long as the various departments and their administrative offices retained their autonomy, it was impossible for political leaders in Parliament to gain anything like complete control over the patronage structure and use it to create predictable patterns of party activity.

The appropriation by Parliament of control over administrative appointments in the early years of the nineteenth century was in some ways a continuing exercise in irony. On the one hand, the loosely organized parties, the opposition Whigs especially, created crude forms of patronage management. Beginning in the early eighteenth century when government was organized by patronage, a senior secretary to the Treasury was created who also usually came to hold the post of government whip in the House of Commons. The whip used the Treasury's control over a number of appointments and funds in the Civil List to organize and maintain a government but not necessarily, as time went on, a party government (Aspinall 1926:396–97). With the shift in control over appointments from the monarch and his or her government to Parliament, the patronage secretary came to play a party rather than a Crown government role. His function was to try to garner from the various departments as many positions as possible for use by ministers and members of Parliament to strengthen party commitment and discipline (Gash 1953:356–57). Great difficulties lay in the way of the whip in the acquisition and allocation of patronage. First, there was the decline in the number of offices directly at the disposal of the central office of the Treasury. Burke's and subsequent attacks on sinecures had reduced the number of offices available. Thus, Arbuthnot, the Tory patronage secretary, complained to Castlereagh in 1819 that the unstable character of the ministry was due in good part to the decline in positions available: "[i]t is to be remembered that with all our sweeping reductions of patronage, I have not the tie I once had upon independent members" (Gash 1979:49). A few years later he repeated his dire warning, "[i]f the just and necessary influence of the Crown" were further reduced "it will be quite impossible for any set of men to conduct the government of the country" (Foord 1947:488).

The difficulties of the patronage secretary were compounded by the decentralized character of patronage. The independence of departments and
boards meant that a good portion of their positions were in the hands of
ministers, presidents of boards, members of commissions, or governors of
colonies. Thus, in the early decades of the nineteenth century the Treasury
Secretary had, by traditional arrangement, to share a variety of appointments. In the Excise Department, only half of the departmental appointments went to the Treasury Secretary, with the remaining half selected alter-
nately by the various departments. Appointment of excise officers were split,
with the Treasury Secretary getting fifty-five out of every hundred, the excise
commissioners getting thirty-five, and the remainder going to sons of excise
officers, which were also in the hands of the commissioners. In Customs, the
Treasury had control of all the appointments but seldom went against the
recommendations of the Customs Board (Gash 1953:348, 359).

The same was true in other departments as well. Colonial appointments,
for example, were made by governors of the colonies and were not in the
hands of the Treasury Secretary (Gash 1953:249). The problem was well-
noted as when Fremantle, the Treasury Secretary, wrote to Peel early in
1842, pointing out the anomaly of being unable to control patronage in a
large number of cases:

> Allow me to call your attention to the question of patronage vested in the
> Comsrs. of that Board [Board of Excise]. Out of every 100 officers appointed the
> Comsrs. nominate 45 [*sic*]. Much to their own inconvenience, for they have con-
> siderable correspondence connected with the appointments & much to the injury
> of the Gov. of the day, for the patronage is frequently given to persons in direct
> hostility to the Administration, on the recommendation of the opposition mem-
> bers of Parliament. Ld. Granville Somerset had this question under consideration,
> when engaged in the Comsn of Enquiry & was & is of the opinion that it is advis-
> able that this patronage like all the patronage in the Customs (excepting of course
> promotion in the service) should be vested in the Treasury. (Gash 1953:359)

The ministerial autonomy of the various departments at the beginning of
the nineteenth century strengthened the decentralized character of patronage.
Not only did departments have control over new appointments, they also had
complete control over promotions, which, as we have seen, came to be viewed
as a form of patronage. All of these were outside the direct control of the party
whip. Party leadership was, as a consequence, faced with the problem of integrating civil service offices into a centralized structure if they wished to have
sufficient patronage to impose discipline over backbenchers. Unless it did so,
party leadership would have very little leverage over the independence of backbencher MPs.

The weakness of party and party leaders in this regard was reflected in the emergence of parliamentary member courtesy during the early years of the nineteenth century. By the 1820s, patronage appointments in the lower branches of the civil service became almost completely vested in the private member whose constituency was concerned. The vesting and the courtesy occurred even when the consulting official and the private member consulted were from the party out of power (MacDonagh 1977:198). The development of this system led the Duke of Wellington to complain to Peel in 1829:

[t]he whole system of patronage of the Government is in my opinion erroneous. Certain members claim a right to dispose of everything that falls vacant within the town or county which they represent; and this is so much a matter of right that they now claim the patronage whether they support upon every occasion, or now and then, or when not required, or entirely oppose; and in fact the only question about local patronage is whether it will be given to the disposal of one gentleman or another. (Kingsley 1944:32)

By the time of the Reform Act of 1832, patronage remained decentralized and was still viewed within the framework of Parliament rather than party.

Party leaders had few strategies available to them to centralize and rationalize patronage. Since they had little or no control over nominations for parliamentary seats, party leaders did not have the means to extract control over patronage from the private member. In short, they could not control patronage through party mechanisms until they had a party mechanism in place, and as long as patronage was decentralized it was difficult to create a party mechanism. The only other strategy was to seek control of patronage by administrative and/or executive rather than party centralization. It was necessary to centralize in such a way that party leaders would have direct control and would no longer be faced with departmental or private member vested or customary rights. The easiest strategy of this kind was to use the Treasury's traditional and potentially powerful role in the collection of revenues, the regulation of their dispersal, and its control over the largest segment of local and lower-level patronage positions. Burke, as I noted earlier, was well aware that the most promising strategy for parliamentary leaders was to create effective Treasury control as the condition for effective parliamentary and party control (Roseveare 1969:121; Chester 1981:199–200).

It was this perception that led the Whigs to attack the decentralization and autonomy of monarchical patronage in the form of sinecures and fee ownership in the first place. The demand for integration of offices and control in the Treasury continued during Pitt's time. His former mentor, Lord Landsdowne (Shelburne), called for greater Treasury control over finance and administration:

[i]nstead of giving the first lord a staff . . . I would give him a knife to cut off every man's fingers that dared thrust his fingers into the public purse. . . . Every office seemed to be the lord of its own will, and every office seemed to have unlimited power over the purse of the nation, instead of their being, as the spirit of the constitution directed, under the constant check of the Treasury. It used to be the distinguishing feature of British administration that the Treasury was its heart . . . (as quoted in Roseveare 1969:129)

Landsdowne's demand for the revival of Burke's Economical Reform tactics resulted in the creation of the Select Committee on Finance in 1797. It produced thirty-six reports, all basically critical of the failure of the Treasury to control administration. It is by no means coincidental that these reports and succeeding commissions of inquiry in 1806, 1810, 1818, and 1822, were, primarily, products of Whig opposition and played a major role in maintaining cohesion within the loosely organized party which had been out of power for a generation (Roseveare 1969:130).

The major thrust of these demands for reform was Treasury control over administration and financial oversight. The classic statement of the desire for central integration and control is that made by the Select Committee on Finance of 1817:

[n]o department of large expenditure ought ever to be placed beyond the controlling superintendence of the Lords Commissioners of the Treasury. From them every other office should expect, and from them the House will require, not a judgement as to the best mode of constructing, maintaining or improving the works respectively belonging to each separate branch; but a judicious and economical allotment to every one of them, of such limited sums as can be assigned with due regard to the necessary expenses of every other service, and of the necessities as well as the resources of the country. (as quoted in Chester 1981:203)

The first major landmark in establishing the Treasury's role as the central institution of administration was recognized by Parliament when it gave the Treasury supervision and control over all pensions. The Act of 1810 provided the legal structure for Parliamentary and Treasury control over salaries and pensions. The act specifically called for an annual submission by the Commissioners of the Treasury to Parliament of every "Increase or Diminution" in the amount of salaries and pensions paid in all public offices from public funds, accompanied with full justifications (Raphael 1964:132–33). In effect, this gave the Treasury the basis for control over the creation and classification of new appointments and the power to veto any changes in salaries. Thus, while the Whigs were able to put considerable powers of sanction in the hands of the Treasury Commissioners by the late 1830s, they still had no control over appointments as such. The cabinet and the party whip were still, as a consequence, unable to centralize patronage. This despite the fact that the cabinet and whip were aided in their attempts by the unwillingness of the Tory leaders to oppose parliamentary control over administration and the Tory leaders' willingness to support any effort which would bring them greater control over independent party members.

All of this laid the groundwork for the efforts in the 1840s by Trevelyan to gain organizational control over administration for the Treasury through the creation of a uniform structure of appointments and a uniform system of financial regulation. In this Trevelyan was strongly supported by a Peelite Gladstone who was then serving as Exchequer. Trevelyan's view of this was summed up nicely by him in a letter to Gladstone in February 1854, just at the time of the submission of the Northcote-Trevelyan Report:

I am more and more confirmed in my opinion that no more first appointments of raw young men should be made to the Treasury, but that our officers should be selected from among the best men in the different departments superintended by the Treasury. This plan, properly carried out, would make the Treasury really a *supervising* Office, possessed of a firm hold of all the branches of the business which it had to deal with, would introduce a powerful principle of unity into the Public Service and would give a very beneficial stimulus to exertion in every other Department. (as quoted in Hughes 1949a:55)

This clearly suggests that the issues of recruitment, appointment, and centralization of administration were inseparable not only for Trevelyan, but that they also represented a bundle of major issues with which Gladstone would find himself comfortable in a Whig/Liberal Party. As J. R. Vincent has so admirably put it:

The flowering of the political aristocracy which constitutes the successful and memorable part of Victorian liberalism was based on the happy absence of liberal ideas. It relied instead on conduct. The creed of rectitude in government, of administrative reform, derived from notions of how a gentleman should behave (especially when in public view in a situation of some class tension), not from notions about administration. The object of administrative reform in the state was to show the English gentleman to better advantage, not to Prussianize the state or serve the gods of efficiency. This was the answer, the only conceivable, to Arnold's question, 'what was to happen when the aristocracy had gone?' The answer as most public men saw, lay in the State, reformed and moralised, acting as an independent, underived, unallied, but essentially popular and attractive social entity run by public-spirited gentlemen of the old tradition. (1976:xviii)

Parliamentary Reform and the Dilemma of Political Leadership

By the first decade of the nineteenth century, the significant group of political actors so well described above by Vincent came to view the arbitrariness of the system of representation as a major obstacle to the creation of a more rational politics. Rational politics had come increasingly to mean not just severing the executive from control or influence of the Crown but also an executive seated firmly in Parliament with unmediated control over the administration. It had become increasingly clear to many that any such centralization of power within Parliament awaited the reduction of the power of independent wealth and aristocracy to determine a great many parliamentary seats. A good number of those who held such views were independent radicals like Cochrane, Burdett, Cobden, and Cartwright. However, the appeal of a rationalized politics in the form of parliamentary reform as a complement to the reduction of Crown influence came increasingly, in the early years of the nineteenth century, to find support among the Whigs more generally. At the center of the issue stood, as in the case of Crown influence, patronage, but in a different form. Patronage in this case meant the subversion of representation by the capacity of the aristocratic purse to control the nomination process and thus command directly or indirectly parliamentary seats. From at least 1809 onward, radicals sought to attack aristocratic influence in Parliament by the demand for franchise reform (Cannon 1973:149–64; Miller 1968). It was not until after 1815 that the radicals were able to bring leverage to bear in Parliament. In 1817 they were able to produce a body of petitions attacking aristocratic influence. The effort, while prodigious, failed to make any headway in Parliament (Cannon 1973:167–74; Wright 1970:23).

The following decade saw increased attacks on the system, which now acquired ideological definition. Bentham published his *Plan for Parliamentary Reform* in 1818, followed in 1820 by Mill's virulent attack on aristocratic privilege in his *Essay on Government*. Although the Whigs firmly rejected Bentham's notion of an extensive franchise, they were willing to accept a modified version of it, something in the vein of Mill's dilution of Bentham's propositions. The 1820s saw the Whig opposition become thoroughly wedded to some form of parliamentary reform. This wedding of opposition to the idea of rationalizing parliamentary representation through franchise revealed the manner in which party would become increasingly defined over issues of publicness or public interest. The "outs," if they wished to maintain coherency as a group, would now substitute the "ins" for the Crown as the object of attack. The "ins," rather than the Crown, would increasingly be accused as the source and support of the corruption and self-interest which made it impossible for the opposition to come to power and establish proper representation.

The Reform Act of 1832, whatever the intentions of the various actors, resulted in the establishment of two principles. The foremost of these was the utilization of franchise expansion and distribution as a means of attempting to establish representation as the representation of public rather than social and private interests. By eliminating some of the worst of the close boroughs and expanding the franchise on the basis of uniform standards in counties and boroughs, the point was made by political leaders, whether they liked it or not, that representation was not inherently a function of social organization in which patron-client relations provided the means for representing interests. The second principle was that appropriate representation could not be achieved so long as patronage continued to serve as the means for recruiting either MPs or government officials. In this respect, the Reform Bill was also antiministerial in character—aimed at reducing the ability of any government in power to retain its place by purchasing or acquiring aristocratic patronage rather than seeking the support of public opinion. So long as patronage existed, it would be difficult to defend against charges of pursuing private or clique interests above those of the public (Cannon 1973:254–63; Moore 1976:225–39; Gash 1953:11–64).

By 1832, the uncertainty over political leadership and succession generated in the eighteenth century by the monarch's use of the appointment power as the organizing principle of political leadership had produced two powerful consequences. One of these was the attack on monarchical patronage and its absorption and centralization by Parliament. The second was to link patronage with private interest. The former had been accomplished by transforming the administrative or office-holding role from a proprietary one in which the officeholder virtually owned the means of administration to a contractual one in which the state was in possession of the means of administration and officeholders were employees. The latter had been accomplished by transforming the social relationship and networks of patronage from a system of social representation of interest into one of representation of private interest.

The two forms of attack on patronage between 1780 and 1832 perhaps created more difficulties for political leaders than they resolved. Indeed, the destruction of sinecures and legal tenure of office, while it eliminated the monarch from direct mediation between Parliament and administration, did not do away with patronage. While Treasury reforms gave the government leaders and the party whip greater control over the financial structure of patronage, they did not manage to separate patronage from the control of individual members. Nor did the Reform Bill eliminate the use of individual wealth as a means for determining candidacy for parliamentary seats, although it eliminated some of the most notorious nomination boroughs

(Gash 1953:203–35). Patronage, thus, in 1832 was alive and well and, unfortunately for party leaders, it continued to provide the basis for the independence of backbench MPs from direct party leadership control.

Ironically, the elimination of monarchical influence did not automatically provide a means by which political leaders could be selected in a more predictable and systematic fashion. At the basis of the attack on the monarch's or his government's patronage had been the assumption that, once diminished, there would emerge the opportunities to utilize state patronage as the basis for a new organizing principle for Parliament—one that would provide political leaders with the tools for sustaining predictable leadership and collective action.

There were three possible strategies political leaders might use to gain this end. Rotation of officials with each administration could, for example, provide the means for political leaders to reduce uncertainty about their positions, as party leaders in the United States did in the nineteenth century. Complete control of patronage in the hands of political leaders would deprive MPs of one of the most important underpinnings of their independence—the structure of local relationships which patronage helped to sustain. At the same time, the loss of local patronage would provide strong incentives for individual MPs to support specific leaders and adhere to a persistent party organization that could produce resources for reelection. Another possible strategy was the use of patronage by political leaders to sustain their positions in a social network system without the mediation of either the monarch and his or her possible arbitrariness or that of a party structure; thus, they could maintain their individual positions through the continued decentralization of patronage. A third possible strategy was one which would eliminate appointment patronage and thus make it possible for political leaders, while serving as members of the executive (the cabinet), to directly control administration and thereby eliminate one of the major sources of the independence of party backbenchers. Eliminating patronage from backbencher control would not only deprive them of the major source of electoral independence, it would drive them to increased dependence on party leaders who controlled the executive.

Each strategy had serious defects from the point of view of political leaders. As a consequence, the selected strategy of the political leaders was to try to press forward with several strategies at the same time: using patronage to sustain social network structures while simultaneously continuing to search for ways to place limits on the electoral independence of MPs. In this regard they had little choice. Prior to 1832 there was little incentive for political leaders to individually agree to hand over patronage to a party organization. In the absence of a well-defined party structure, patronage was viewed by

party leaders with ambivalence. It was viewed as a means of maintaining patron-client social networks as well as the means for creating and sustaining
government majorities, even though the tradition of localized patronage un-
dergirded the independence of the backbench MP. So long as there was no
clear differentiation between social and political party structure, office rotation could not be used, since this would simply undermine the structure of
leadership patron-client relationships as well as those of the backbenchers.
This strategy would have the effect of reducing the possibility of creating
party ties even further.

Perhaps more important in the elimination of rotation as a strategy for political leaders was the absence of specific predictable terms of office. The system
of rotation in the United States worked relatively well since everyone knew
that office-holding worked in multiples of four. One could predict that if one
was appointed to an office, it would be for a four-year term at least. In the parliamentary system, terms were not very predictable and might not last very
long. Thus, in the period between 1800 and 1832, ten different governments
with widely varying lifetimes were called into being. Furthermore, party organization patronage was, in the long run, dependent on the existence of a relatively broad franchise that provided an opportunity for the development of
more or less professional party organizers and workers.

In the absence of large-scale franchise, the work of mobilizing voters was
well within the reach of the individual candidate working with one or two
local agents. In many cases mobilization was not required at all since nomination was determined by local custom and deference or by wealth and influence: less than fifty percent of all seats were contested between 1832 and
1868 (Moore 1976:282–84). The cost of being a candidate, whether facing
opposition or not, was very high while the immediate material rewards were
inversely proportional (members of Parliament received no salaries in the
nineteenth century). The number of candidates for any seat was small
enough so that no large complex structure of party nomination was required
or called into existence. The Reform Act of 1832 did nothing in any basic
way to reduce the price of running for office. The high price served to reduce
the number of candidates for any constituency and thus served much of the
function of the party nominating machinery in the United States and less-
ened the dependence of candidates on party.

The strategy of continuing to utilize personal political patronage to
largely sustain individual political leadership and status was encouraged, as
we have seen in the case of individual MPs, by the considerable independence of the various commissions and boards. While the ones with the
most patronage in the early 1830s—the Customs, Excise, and Tax Boards
(Excise, Stamps, and Taxes were merged in 1849 to form the Board of In-

land Revenue)—were formally under the aegis of the Treasury, they were in fact able to run things in their spheres without much interference by virtue of their independent parliamentary origins (Chester 1981:225–26; Parris 1969:32). Any attempt to use systematic rotation would have undermined their portion of control over patronage and their independence and, therefore, would have been resisted accordingly.

The maintenance of personal networks, however, would be a further obstacle to the emergence of more impersonal party organizational loyalties. In a structure that emphasized organizational rather than personal loyalties, patronage was awarded for party loyalty as expressed in working to mobilize voters for specific candidates. Loss of election did not dissolve party loyalties and ties. Individuals simply sought, as in the United States, new specific objects for their party loyalty. Party or political leadership, in this situation, was a function of party organization and structure, not of personal networks of patron-client relationships. If, instead, personal patron-client networks were maintained, there was no incentive on the part of backbenchers to press for wider franchise and its greater uncertainty. Political leaders in Parliament at the end of the 1820s thus faced a real dilemma. They could not give up the traditional structure of patronage so long as they could not gain centralized control over it. It was clear by the early 1830s that they did not yet have at their disposal the means to gain centralized administrative control over patronage. The result was the continuance of the autonomy of patronage as a structural feature of the administrative role. Both department heads and backbenchers had continued strong incentives for maintaining decentralized personal structures of patronage.

The independence of the MP provided the most uncomfortable source of uncertainty for the political leaders of the 1830s and early 1840s. All the more so since the independence of the backbenchers or private members was sustained by a tradition in which the business of government was seen as purely executive. Whatever general measures of social policy were needed were properly the concern of Parliament as a whole acting as the executive and could thus be introduced by private members (MacDonagh 1977:5; G. H. L. Le May 1979:162–63). With the exception of taxation, private members had the same rights of initiation as ministers (G. H. L. Le May 1979:162–63). Thus private member bills were the normal means by which private members sought specific as well as general legislative relief for a variety of activities of their constituents. Moreover, private members had a whole range of rights, including the filibuster, which could be used to get his views or grievances a hearing. Private members, in the first decades of the nineteenth century, had not only the capacity to mediate for their constituents directly in Parliament, they also had ability to hold up ministerial action in order to force the government to give way.

The independence of the private MP was not seriously challenged by the Reform Act of 1832. Instead, the reformed franchise produced a situation in which incumbents had every reason to pay closer attention to their constituents (Gash 1979:163). While the expansion of franchise was not great in absolute terms (from about 478 thousand to 813 thousand), it was sufficient to produce, in a large number of constituencies, substantially greater numbers of voters to whom attention now had to be paid. This was especially the case since the Reform Act required voter registration lists and their publication. The process of getting supporting voters registered and issuing challenges to possible opposition supporters led to the development of the MP's local organization, headed by an agent who acted for him with the constituency (Thomas 1950; Bulmer-Thomas 1965:I, 76–78). The reform, in sum, did not have the effect of eliminating patron nominations in any complete way (Gash 1953:203–36, 438–39; Beckett 1986:430–31) nor did it produce a suffrage large enough to lead the candidates to seek the creation of extensive centralized party machinery which could get out the vote for them. Post-1832 candidates were able to construct their own local organizations, which made them, in some ways, more independent than ever (Bulmer-Thomas 1965:78–80; Stewart 1978:138). Indeed, the expansion of the franchise did little to reduce the immediate appetite for patronage. Faced with larger constituencies, MPs continued to press for patronage as a means for maintaining a constituency network that would secure their incumbency (MacDonagh 1977:199; Gash 1979:52).

The expansion of local lower-level positions, especially in the post office and customs services, provided new fields for patronage cultivation. Employment in public offices rose from 17,640 in 1797, to 21,850 in 1805, and to

Table 11.1 Employment in Revenue Departments, 1797–1829

Department	Number in 1797	Number in 1829
Customs	6,380	11,016
Excise	6,580	6,355
Stamps	521	506
Taxes	291	336
Post Office (GB)	957	1,418
Post Office (Ireland)	153	325
Totals	14,882	19,956

Source: Chester 1981, 167.

22,367 in 1829, despite cutbacks due to the ending of the Napoleonic wars (Chester 1981:167). As table 11.1 indicates, by far the greatest number of offices were in the local field services, where the Treasury patronage secretary and backbench MPs had the greatest amount of influence on appointments.

As a result of these factors, party leaders throughout the 1830s could make little headway against the uncertainties created, for the most part, by backbenchers whose ties to party and leadership were mitigated powerfully by their independence. As a result, party leaders acting as ministerial department heads continued to cling strongly to the patronage of their departments as a major means of maintaining their leadership positions, with party considerations coming in a poor second. While department heads held tightly to the patronage of their departments in the central offices, the allocation of local patronage continued to remain largely in the hands of individual backbench MPs. Furthermore, much of the local patronage continued to be decentralized; that is, it was out of the hands of the Treasury patronage secretary. Moreover, the allocation of considerable government resources continued to be, to an uncomfortable degree, in the hands of backbenchers. The tradition of determining and organizing social policy through private member bills and backbencher capacity to hold up legislation gave them considerable leverage over party leaders.

The degree to which all of these elements contributed to the lack of party discipline is reflected in the disarray that characterized the clearly identifiable but loosely organized parties during the period of 1832 to 1859. The Whigs were able to hold office for all but the Hundred Days (November 1834–April 1835) from 1831 until 1841. They did so, however, in the absence of any systematic and stable party leadership. For several years after the passage of the Reform Act, Whig leadership "seemed to envisage themselves as benevolent arbiters rather than as the nucleus of a new popular party" (Gash 1979:158). The disarray among Whig leaders over Irish church reform revealed the degree to which they were not a disciplined party. The Tories, led by Peel, now came to power for One Hundred Days by the grace of William IV, who, in the last gasp of monarchical desire to affect policy, selected first Melbourne and then Peel to lead a new government, thereby recognizing party leadership as the criterion for selection. The security of Tory leadership was no greater, since Peel, well-aware of the folly of depending too much on backbenchers, strongly believed in the Crown (the executive function) rather than party as the source of political leadership authority and legitimacy (Hanham 1969:230–33). Unable to create a majority, Peel was soon out of office.

The dominance of the Whigs/Liberals was based on a highly contingent coalition of factions—Whigs, radicals, and O'Connell's Irish followers. Gash, with his usual felicity, has described the situation best of all:

In an age when it was still conventional for candidates on the hustings to emphasize their personal independence, even the idea of a disciplined parliamentary party was novel, and to both electors and elected not always welcome. The task of party leadership was therefore considerable. If party policy attempted to reflect divisions of opinion within the party, as the *Edinburgh Review* hopefully claimed that the whig cabinet was doing in 1840, the result was ineffectiveness and drift. If party leaders attempted to impose their views on an heterogeneous following, as Peel did between 1842 and 1846, there was danger of dissension and revolt. (1979:164)

Peel's insistence on pursuing the repeal of the Corn Laws when he returned to power in 1841 produced a furious revolt among the back benches. Although victorious in battle, it cost Peel the war. The issue split the Tory/Conservatives between protectionists and Peelites, thus disabling the Conservatives for over a decade. The continued existence of the Peelites as a distinct parliamentary group, even after Peel's disappearance from the scene, with the possibility that they might form a new party or jump to either existing parties, acted further to undermine the foundations of party discipline (Cox 1987:33). On the one hand, Peelite leadership contained a number of men capable of holding ministerial posts. Any attempt to lure the Peelite vote would mean providing posts for at least several of them. But this would mean that non-Peelites with ambitions to ministerial positions would find "themselves (with good reason) wondering whether . . . their services would be rewarded once the prize of office had been attained" (Jones and Erickson 1972:222) or their hoped-for offices would go to a Peelite. Thus the Peelite faction both reflected and added to the uncertainty leaders in both parties faced (Southgate 1962:204–5). As possible leaders of a new party, Peelite leaders could be seen as an alternative source of patronage for backbenchers seeking an edge in patronage over other backbenchers. While unwilling to jump to opposition parties, they might well consider joining a Peelite party (Jones and Erickson 1972:35). Peelite leaders also offered a threat to existing leaders since, if there was a possibility of their appearing in one of the parties as leaders, backbenchers might be able to use them as leverage against their own leaders when they disagreed with them (Cox 1987:33). The period between 1832 and 1859 thus continued to produce both structural and day-to-day sources of uncertainty for political leaders.

The Attack on the Independence of the Backbencher: 1832–55

At the heart of the uncertainty over political leadership was the inability of ministers, as party leaders, and party leaders, as ministers, to overcome the obstacles blocking the way to controlling the setting of legislative priorities, specifying legislation, and controlling the implementation of legislation. Throughout the 1830s and 1840s, the inability of political leaders to forge what Bagehot was later to call the "efficient secret"—the executive (cabinet) control over policy, legislative agendas, and implementation—reflected more of the promise than the practice of party politics and discipline.[2] In response, political leaders had to increasingly depend on the idea of party. But the idea, without whip or inducement, left the dynamism of politics to backbenchers and to the opposition.

That dynamism was composed, in the first instance, of the independence (enhanced by the Reform Act) of a large number of MPs and was negative in character. It resisted ministerial encroachments while seeking at the same time to expand the area of parliamentary powers, especially in the area of social policy and the expansion of local economic development. The opposition found its dynamism in pressing for reform. Opposition party leaders found their greatest weapon for creating party discipline in this period to be the demand for reforms in the basic structure of the franchise and representation—perhaps the only issue which could raise sufficient polarization so as to put a government party on the defensive.

In response, government party leaders found themselves in pursuit of the means to constrain putative party members to act in support of ministerial and party measures even when it seemed that those measures were against the best interests of individual members. Government party leaders, regardless of party, thus had to fight what amounted to a daily battle against their own backbenchers in order to stay in power. Conflicts between government party leaders and MPs on both sides of the aisle took place over two political resources: patronage and legislation. Both of these were seen by backbenchers as rights of private members in their role as members of Parliament, regardless of party; however, party leaders, whether incumbents or hopefuls, saw these as resources necessary to provide orderly party collective decision making.

The battle over the control of legislation on a day-to-day basis was joined quite early. Beginning in 1811, during the Tory period of dominance, political leaders sought to restrict private member's independence. The so-called Order Days, which effectively allowed government precedence over private members, were introduced in 1811. This procedure led, in the years following, to ministerial encroachment on the equality of private and gov-

2. "The efficient secret of the English Constitution may be described as the close union, the nearly complete fusion, of the executive and legislative powers. . . . The connecting link is the *cabinet* . . . A cabinet is a combining committee—a *hyphen* which joins, a *buckle* which fastens, the legislative part of the State to the executive part of the State. In its origin it belongs to the one, in its functions it belongs to the other" (Bagehot 1963:64, 68).

ernment bills or Orders of the Day. Ministers claimed the press of business to establish their priority (Cox 1987:47). Over the next several decades, ministers sought to press their advantage against private members but were successful only in the sense that they achieved some degree of priority for government business. It was not until 1831 that the pressure of the government's ministers to proceed with government bills led to acknowledgment by Parliament that Mondays and Fridays would be days on which government bills would have precedence, while Wednesdays were designated as a day in which Orders of the Day would be taken up in strict rotation (Cox 1987:47). This was recognition of a distinction between government and private bills, which was to become clearer over the next several years (Fraser 1960:453). Ministers now took advantage and pressed for priority on this day as well (Cox 1987:47).

The restrictions on private member's rights was not accepted without a fight. In 1836, a backbencher bitterly complained:

[f]rom the manner in which the business before us has lately been gone through, it would appear as if none but members of the government can bring forward any measure. I have been, night after night, endeavouring to bring in a measure in which many of my constituents are deeply interested . . . but all in vain. (quoted in Cox 1987:61)

In 1838, backbenchers defeated a motion by the Liberal leader in the Commons, Lord John Russell, that another day be added in which Orders of the Day be given precedence. Another day would allow the government greater opportunity to press for its bills against Conservative/Tory MPs and a Conservative House of Lords (Cox 1987:61). The Conservatives attacked the motion. Graham (later to be head of the Home Department under Peel, 1841–46) excoriated the government's

attempt . . . at engrossing to themselves those opportunities which independent Members had hitherto enjoyed of bringing questions of importance . . . he would not wish to look at this question with reference to his own side of the House merely, but he would appeal to . . . all hon. Members on the other side, who were unconnected with the government, whether this was a fitting, proper, or even convenient course. (quoted in Cox 1987:62)

The appeal received sufficient support from the Liberal backbench so that Russell was forced to withdraw the motion (Cox 1987:62). However, by the time of Peel's second ministry in 1841, a party leadership combination of Tory/Conservative and Whig/Liberal acting over a period of thirty years had forced the backbencher out of the position of dominating the flow and substance of legislation. Private members could still pose obstacles to ministerial legislation (as Peel was to find in his repeal of the Corn Laws) through the various devices of question-asking, petitions, and even filibustering. Peel's victory over the backbenchers in the struggle to repeal the Corn Laws revealed that these were purely negative tactics. Once cabinet control was established, the tools of obstruction were to be systematically rendered harmless over the next several decades by government party leadership (G. H. L. Le May 1979:155–61). "The general result, therefore, of the reform era was to give ministers distinct advantages over other members" (Fraser 1960:454). While this pattern of development gave political leaders a distinct advantage, they did not yet possess the necessary control over the backbenchers. The conflict between party leaders and private members over patronage is in many ways wonderfully summed up by Disraeli writing to his colleague Pakington in 1858:

There is a great error on the part of some of my colleagues on the subject of patronage. They are too apt to deem the preferment at their disposal to be merely a personal privilege. In my opinion it partakes of a corporate character. No doubt the head of a department should exercise a chief and general control over the distribution of its patronage; but there should be habitual communication on this head with his colleagues . . . The spirit of the party in the country depends greatly on the distribution of patronage . . . There is nothing more ruinous to political connexion than the fear of justly rewarding your friends, and the promotion of ordinary men of opposite opinions in preference to qualified adherents. It is not becoming in any minister to decry party who has risen by party. (quoted in Parris: 1969:64–65)

Party leaders fully understood the problem, as Disraeli's letter reveals. What escaped them was a solution. The battle had been almost a daily one since patronage had become the parliamentary privilege in the first two decades of the nineteenth century. The problem seemed in some ways insurmountable. Government party leaders could hardly seize the patronage from private members on the argument of party. There was no clear way to show that patronage wielded by party leaders was for the benefit of party only. Party leaders distributing patronage would seem to be benefiting themselves just as much as party. The traditional dilemma of patronage was clearly revealed here: the inability to distinguish between private, party, and public interest.

The growth of positions in the local field services, however, was not in any way sufficient to meet the demand encouraged by the expansion of the franchise. At the same time, the demand for patronage increased as the expanded constituencies produced an increasing number of requests from voters, friends, and relatives. The inability to meet demand produced disappointed office-seekers, a situation which tended to undercut the value of patronage (Parris 1969:70–71; Chapman and Greenaway 1980:37; Mueller 1984:104–5). As demand continued to outstrip supply, patronage became an increasing burden, spreading disappointment and disaffection among incumbents' constituencies and, therefore, among the backbenchers themselves. As Sir Charles Trevelyan wrote in January 1854:

Many members of Parliament never cross the threshold of the Patronage Room and many others would gladly be released from the importunities of their Constituents and the necessity of asking for places for them and their Dependents. (quoted in Hughes 1949a:69–70)

The revolt of the backbenchers against Peel and his ministers revealed the basic weakness of party organization and discipline. Worse, the continued existence of the Peelite faction only enhanced this weakness. At the heart of the problem, as it became more and more clearly revealed in the late 1840s, was patronage. To the extent that patronage escaped party centralized control, it contributed to decentralization of power in Parliament and continued decentralization of administrative control. So long as patronage remained decentralized, there was no capacity to regulate either the status, capacity, or loyalty of such appointments. As long as decentralization continued, patronage was viewed as necessary to incumbency and to achieving leadership status. So long as patronage was viewed as essential, it became an increasing source of irritation as supporters and relatives outnumbered the available positions. But as long as these conditions existed, political leaders could not achieve integrated party organization and discipline.

Political leaders were faced with a true dilemma: if they continued to rely on patronage as the means for enforcing party discipline, then they were relying on weakness. There was little chance of enforcing anything more than limited control over backbenchers by utilizing a patronage system over which the political leaders had only partial control. To engage in this tactic was to leave them open to the uncertainties which so clearly emerged after the repeal of the Corn Laws. Political leaders could attempt to centralize patronage, but this was extraordinarily difficult since it required that party leaders (especially those in the government party) be able to overcome what was very nearly a classic prisoner's dilemma: while they would all be better off if they could agree to act together in centralizing patronage, each individual incumbent or putative minister found it difficult to abandon the advantage of continuing to use patronage as long as there was no ironclad assurance that everyone would do so as well. The role of the Peelite faction in refusing to accept party identification made it impossible for such assurances to be forthcoming. In the face of this dilemma, political leaders were forced to narrow their strategic choices vis-à-vis patronage. Basically, the only strategy left to them was to attempt to eliminate appointment patronage and thus deprive backbenchers of the basis of their independence. This strategy emerged in the form of the Northcote-Trevelyan Reports of 1853–54 and was successfully fulfilled in the Orders in Council of 1870.

The Northcote-Trevelyan Report

Much has been written concerning the importance of the Northcote-Trevelyan Report in the development of the British civil service. Since the immediate effects of the report were minimal, its significance is usually said to be that it laid down the basic principles of utilitarian administration that future political leaders would seek to follow. Close analysis, however, suggests that the report's significance is overstated. Rather, its significance lies, I would argue, in proposing a strategy for the solution of the problem of rationalizing patronage. In doing so, the report, in a masterly fashion, outlined the means by which state administration could be rendered public in character, removed from the vicissitudes and charges of private interest without, at the same time, succumbing to the creation of an autonomous structure. Northcote and Trevelyan were to propose the removal of private interest in the form of patronage from state administration by utilizing existing social institutions, such as the public school and Oxbridge, as the means for determining merit and thus access to the highest levels of state administration.

The nature of the strategy is revealed in the ostensible aim of the proposed reform and the three basic means by which it was to be achieved. The aim of the report was to create a centralized administrative structure in which the administrative role would be at once accountable primarily to the most senior political leaders while at the same time chosen on a systematic basis that would eliminate private interest in determining office-holding:

[i]t is highly necessary that the conditions which are common to all the public establishments, . . . should be carefully considered, so as to obtain full security for the public that none but qualified persons will be appointed, and that they will afterwards have every practicable inducement to the active discharge of their duties. . . . It may safely be asserted that, as matters stand, the Government of the country could not be carried on without the aid of an efficient body of permanent officers, occupying a position duly subordinate to that of the Ministers who are directly responsible to the Crown and to Parliament, yet possessing sufficient independence, character, ability, and experience to be able to advise, assist, and, to some extent, influence, those who are from time to time set over them. (Great Britain, Report on the Organization of the Permanent Civil Service 1854 [1713]: vol. XXVII, 3)

The aim was, in short, to create an administrative structure free of back-bencher rights and influence that would give the executive and the party it represented unitary, if not integrated, power over the administration.

Northcote and Trevelyan went to considerable lengths to argue that the only means for achieving this end were the following: (1) the creation of a public service characterized by what they presented as a naturally occurring hierarchical division of labor ("intellectual" as distinguished from "mechanical"); (2) recruitment to each of these levels of offices by application of an "objective" educational criteria for each level—criteria seen as arising from these hierarchies and reflected in the naturally stratified structure of education with exceptions to be made only on the basis of acquired standing or prestige in a profession; (3) the utilization of merit as the criterion for promotion and the allocation to political leaders (ministers/heads of departments) of the power to determine merit; (4) the creation of specific uniform limitations on age of entry into service related to levels of education; and (5) recommendations for specific conditions for retirement. As Northcote and Trevelyan put it:

> The general principle, then, which we advocate is, that the public service should be carried on by the admission into its lower ranks of a carefully selected body of young men, who should be employed from the first upon work suited to their capacities and their education, and should be made constantly to feel that their promotion and future prospects depend entirely on the industry and ability with which they discharge their duties, that with average abilities and reasonable application they may look forward confidently to a certain provision for their lives, that with superior powers they may rationally hope to attain to the highest prizes in the Service, while if they prove decidedly incompetent, or incurably indolent, they must expect to be removed from it. (Great Britain, Report on the Organization of the Permanent Civil Service, 1859 [1713]:vol. XXVII, 9)

Here Northcote and, especially, Trevelyan, with the very strong support of the Peelite-but-soon-to-be-Liberal Gladstone at the Exchequer, created a strategy which sought to resolve the basic problem of patronage as faced by political leadership; a problem, as we have seen, exacerbated by the role of the Peelites and the continued malorganization of political parties. That problem, as I have tried to show, was made up of several parts: (1) There was a seemingly intractable decentralization of patronage; thus, by 1850, despite (or perhaps because of) the whittling away of private MP rights, centralized party control over patronage still seemed out of the question. So long as this was the case, administrative integration also seemed out of the question. (2) There was a seemingly increased level of the privateness of patronage as it became used by incumbents and political leaders to try to stabilize their incumbencies in the period following the Reform Act of 1832; this gave rise to concern in the late 1840s over the nature of qualifications for public office (that is, the decline of gentlemanly exclusiveness) and the conflicts raised by great demand and small supply of offices. (3) Decentralization, privatization, and the decline of traditional status as the basic qualification for office all gave rise to the problem of accountability; lack of patronage centralization and the persistence of backbencher patronage privileges undermined the social basis of administrative homogeneity and accountability. This subversion of the social basis of the administrative role, in turn, threatened the capacity of political leaders to enforce uniform execution of legislation and reform. Political leaders could no longer count on a uniform understanding of gentlemanly behavior. The question of whether accountability was to be enforced by organizational rules or social homogeneity emerged as a major problem by 1850, as political leaders sought to impose systematic order on the administrative structure. Thus, Matthew Arnold's question, "what was to happen when the aristocracy was gone?" touched a tender nerve.

The Northcote-Trevelyan Report proposed a set of solutions to these problems which can be seen as clearly benefiting primarily, if not only, political leaders. The creation of a distinct administrative hierarchy, the utilization of examinations to determine recruitment to each level, and the reliance on merit to determine promotion could hardly be interpreted as benefiting the incumbents of administrative office since it undermined the predictability inherent in the use of seniority. The main argument in favor of the report's acceptance lay in its benefits for the public interest: efficiency which supposedly would result from selecting officials only on the basis of exhibited competency for specifically described levels of work. Interestingly, enough, however, the report and subsequent statements by Northcote and Trevelyan provide little in the way of evidence showing the existing levels of efficiency and what would be saved by the creation of a new system of administrative recruitment and advancement. Nowhere in the report or the subsequent *Papers Relating to the Reorganization of the Civil Service* (Great Britain 1854–55 [1870]: vol. XX) is there convincingly specific detail presented that would bear out Northcote's and Trevelyan's argument as to the efficiency of the proposed reforms. Indeed, there was considerable irritation mixed with disbelief with the argument among a large number of those asked to submit reports.[3]

On the other hand, the proposed reforms would have benefited or satis-

3. See, for example, the reports submitted by Sir Thomas Reddington, Herman Merrivale, Sir Thomas Francis Fremantle, H. U. Addington, Benjamin Hawes, H. Wassington, Sir A. Y. Spearman, and George Arbuthnot (Great Britain 1854–55 [1870]: vol. XX, 229–413).

fied political leaders, especially Whig/Liberals, in a number ways. First, placing all initial appointments under the control of an administrative body formally accountable only to Parliament but headed by a member of the executive, as the report proposed (Great Britain 1854–55 [1713]: vol. XXVII, 11) would have eliminated one of the foremost supports of backbencher independence. In the absence of local patronage rights, private members would have far fewer resources to maintain personal election machinery. They would be forced to rely, as they did more and more after 1870, on national and local party organization and party leadership to provide for the support necessary to get nominated, elected, and reelected (Hanham 1959:125–54, 347–86; Bulmer-Thomas 1965:115–32; Blake 1985:145–56).

Second, using an "objective" test for competency would have removed the criticism of private interest prevailing over public interest. As Mill approvingly commented on the Northcote-Trevelyan proposal:

It has equal claims to support from the disinterested and impartial among conservatives and reformers. For its adoption would be the best vindication which could be made of existing political institutions, by showing that the classes who under the present constitution have the greatest influence in the government, do not desire any greater share of the profits derivable from it than their merits entitle them to, but they are willing to take the chances of competition with ability in all ranks . . . (Great Britain 1854–55 [1870]: vol. XX, 92)

Third, creating a hierarchical structure of administrative responsibility (from mechanical to intellectual) resolved the problems of homogeneity in administrative leadership and thus the problem of accountability. Accountability was to be achieved by the quite brilliant maneuver of substituting a socially stratified structure of educational achievement for birth as the criterion for access to the highest levels of administrative office. By distinguishing between intellectual and mechanical labor, the authors of the report were able to argue that the simple copying skills required from the beginning-level clerks under the old arrangement were insufficient for guiding the destinies of the nation. Thus Trevelyan wrote to Gladstone on 17 January 1854:

We are apparently on the threshold of a new era pregnant with great events, and England has to maintain in concert with her allies the cause of right and liberty and truth in every quarter of the world. Our people are few compared with the Multitudes likely to be arrayed against us; & [sic] we must prepare for the trial by cultivating to the utmost the superior morality and intelligence which constitute our real strength. It is proposed to invite the flower of our youth to the aid of the public-service; to encourage the rising generation to diligence and good conduct by a more extensive system of rewards than has ever been brought to bear upon popular education, and to make a nearer approach to disinterested political action by removing one prevailing temptation from Electors and Representatives. These are the genuine elements of national power and if they are cordially adopted, their invigorating influence will be felt through every vein of the body politic. (as quoted in Hughes 1949a:70)

This strategy appears to have had two important purposes. First, it provided an alternative means by which appointments could be made in a systematic way to substitute for the existing structure of patronage. Appointment on the basis of hierarchically distinguished levels of educational achievement also had the appearance, as Trevelyan, Mill, and others had pointed out, of placing the appointment process within a public rather than private framework. Creating an examination structure for appointments to the upper civil service not only established the publicness of the process, it also fulfilled the contractarian definition of public office by removing the privilege from private considerations.

The proposed structure also had the advantage of centralizing the appointment process. By creating a committee which would oversee access to the various levels of the civil service, the private parliamentary member was not only removed from the process of appointment, but the heads of the various departments would now have almost complete control over the career structure. The report recommended that the department heads be given both the power to select from the list of successful examinees for initial appointments and complete responsibility for internal promotions (Great Britain 1854–55 [1713]: vol. XXVII, 20). This would have had the effect of removing Parliament from any direct control over the process of appointment and promotion. Administrative appointments would now be placed within the organizational structure of the executive. Moreover, by limiting access to the "superior situations" to men between the ages of 19 and 25 and to the "inferior offices" to men between the ages of 17 and 21 (Great Britain 1854–55 [1713]: vol. XXVII, 16–17), the report sought to establish more or less fully integrated career structures with specific beginning points but with all the way stations largely within the power of departments and department heads. The proposal would, thus, have the effect of transforming individual appointments and promotions, which were subject at varying times to the influence of a mixture of parliamentary influences (heads of departments, private members, heads of commissions and boards) into integrated careers subject to one parliamentary influence, that of the department head (minister/secretary of state).

The proposal to create two distinct career tracks based on levels of educational achievement was intended to be a direct response to the problem of accountability and homogeneity of the higher level of offices. The attack on patronage, however, raised doubts and opposition because it was not clear how an education in and of itself could provide individuals with a set of behavioral constraints that would make them predictable and worthy of high positions. As a large number of critics pointed out, the ability to pass an examination was no assurance that an individual adhered to the proper codes of behavior which guaranteed the public spiritedness of action. Or to put it another way, the elimination of patronage would undermine the independence of the private member of Parliament. It would also, however, open the way for breaking down the networks of social relationships and clientalism patronage sustained. But it was these relationships which provided the basis for what was thought to be the uniformly high standard of probity and absence of private advantage which so characterized the higher civil servant. Thus, Captain O'Brien wrote, echoing the opinions and concerns of a great many of his contemporaries:

If such an examination duly and fairly carried out were practicable, it would undoubtedly secure the proposed object, but there are other qualifications, perhaps more essential, which must be sought for by other means. I believe it is an acknowledged fact that as a body, the civil service in the public offices in London are remarkable for their fidelity and trustworthiness. The general prevalence of this high sense of honor among a set of men can, I believe, be ensured only by selecting them from the class of society where it exists. Mere learning effects nothing towards it; . . . Mere school learning will not do this. Who so narrow-minded as mere college men? Who so unfit to manage human affairs generally as the mere learned and scientific?

I believe therefore that the high character for moral worth enjoyed by the civil service in the principal public offices results from their having been selected generally by the high officers of State who naturally nominate the sons of their relations, friends and acquaintances. (as quoted in Hughes 1949a:72)

Both Trevelyan and Northcote penned responses:

The effect of a system of open competition will be to secure for the public offices generally and especially for the principle offices the best portion of the best educated youth.

Who are so successful in carrying off prizes at competing scholarships, fellowships, &c. as the most expensively educated young men? Almost invariably, the sons of gentlemen, or those who by force of cultivation, good training and good society have acquired the feelings and habits of gentlemen. The tendency of the measure will, I am confident, be decidedly *aristocratic* [emphasis in the original] . . . At present a mixed multitude is sent up, a large proportion of whom, owing to the operation of political and personal patronage, are of an inferior rank of society . . . *and they are, in general, the least eligible of their respective ranks.* [emphasis in the original] (as quoted in Hughes 1949a:72)

And here is Northcote again:

To this I would add that the advantages which an University training would give in the competition would almost insure the selection of a large majority from among those who have received it; & there is no kind of education, so likely to make a man a gentleman, to fit him to play his part among other gentlemen & to furnish him forth for the world, as that of an English university. (as quoted in Hughes 1949a:72–73)

And again elsewhere he wrote:

Even looking at the public service as it has been, I am convinced that an University education if turned to the right use, gives a man a great advantage in an office. I attribute my own success, such as it has been, entirely to the power of close reasoning which a course in Thucydides, Aristotle, Mathematics, &c., engenders or develops, and to the facility of composition which arises from classical studies. (as quoted in Hughes 1949a:73)

As we can see from these statements, both authors sought to equate public school and university education with the possession of gentlemanly qualities—precisely those qualities thought to be necessary for individuals to possess if they were to participate in government and not pursue private and personal advantage. This formal proposal to substitute a certain kind of education for birth and upbringing in gentlemanly or aristocratic roles and values was one whose influence was to be felt over the next several decades as political leaders sought to come to terms with the integration of administration into the executive structure of parliamentary power.

The displacement of birth by education as the means of providing not only competency but constraints on the pursuit of private desires and interests implied closely related notions of the nature and structure of education. In terms of the structure of education, the Northcote-Trevelyan proposal offered publicly for the first time a vision of what an integrated educational system ought to look like if it were to fulfill a public utility. In arguing for a distinction between intellectual and mechanical work, it is clear that the two authors equated the first with an education completely associated with the genteel classes. In effect, they were arguing, as we can see in Trevelyan's comments, that the capacity of the individual to engage in public service at the intellectual level was a function of the enhanced capacity of this class(es) to absorb and make use of this education.

This view was equally implicit in the way mechanical work was described by the report as not simply copying but the work which possessed rote and repetitive characteristics. Contemporary members of the public service had argued that the mechanical work of the early years of an individual's service provided the knowledge necessary to make appropriate decisions at a later time. The report, however, sought to make clear Trevelyan's long-held idea that mechanical work was in no way related to intellectual work. The implication was clear that the capacity for such work required a different form or level of education, the possession of which did not prepare one for movement up to intellectual work. By divvying up the white-collar work of administration between higher and lower levels of work and thus career, the reformers also sought to provide a powerful incentive for attracting a continual stream of higher-status individuals. By promising a career that would not require years and years of lower-level drudgery, Trevelyan and Northcote sought to provide an incentive for individuals who did not view "mechanical" work as appropriate to their status or ambition (Great Britain 1854–55 [1713]: vol. XXVII, 9; Hughes 1949b:213).

The implication was clear. Not only were there two forms of work and two different career tracks, but there were two different patterns of education: one suited for the genteel who could take advantage of it, and another, which presumably was suited to the nongenteel middle classes whose capacities and resources were suited to training in mechanical work. Finally, the report also appeared to envision a third educational track—one designed for the great masses of people whose capacities limited them to skilled or semiskilled work. That they had in mind this kind of stratification which matched levels and extent of education with social class is evident in Trevelyan's letter to Gladstone of 10 March 1854:

We are beginning to see our way very clearly to these Second Class examinations and much good is likely to come of it. They will apply to the great middle class, including the majority of the persons employed on the Civil Establishments who are unable to give their sons a finished university education—and the subject matter of the examination will be what used to be the Commercial School Education but *greatly improved.* . . . In another point of view, also, this is an important point because the middle class people and the majority of public officers look with great jealousy upon our Cambridge and Oxford men to whom they cannot attain—and it is, therefore, desirable to show them that the great mass of appointments will be open to be competed for by their sons who have received a really good English education. (as quoted in Mueller 1984:209–10)

In the same letter, Trevelyan went on to say that the implication of the proposed reform was the creation of a system based on "three grades of examinations: High (Oxford and Cambridge), Middle (superior *English* education), Low (or national school second-rate English studies)" (Mueller 1984:210).

Trevelyan and Northcote came to view education as a three-part structure in which the parts were conceived of as distinct educational careers not linked in any comprehensive way. In doing so, they sought to resolve the problem of providing for accountability without abandoning the social basis of political leadership—the network of class social relationships that had been the basis of patronage. By viewing education not as a means by which individuals might move from one social level to another according to their capacities but as distinct bodies of knowledge appropriate to the capacities of social class, the two authors sought to make education a mediation between class and the possession of public office. By creating a hierarchical examination system, they clearly thought they could achieve several goals: they could maintain the upper levels of public office and political leadership for members of the same classes from which political leaders were drawn; at the same time, they could claim that public office was acquired by public and not private means; and finally, by allowing department heads to select from among the examinees and to determine promotion, they could provide political leaders with greater influence while depriving private members of Parliament of one of their primary sources of independence. In effect, the examination system proposed by the report would have allowed the persistence of, and strengthened in some ways, a structure of leadership based on a system of social relationships and networks. This would be achieved by removing patronage from private members and centralizing appointments and promotions in the hands of political leaders.

Equally important, the report did not propose the "Prussianization" of the civil service. That is, it did not provide for a structure of autonomy in which the civil service would dominate the career structure of the individual. By settling on the idea of a liberal education as the best device for training the faculties of the mind for the higher intellectual levels of decision making, the authors were in a sense following the pattern of the traditional professions. Throughout much of the nineteenth century, the major liberal professions—clergy, medicine, and law—were careers which relied heavily on separating technical professional education from formal schooling. Technical training was acquired, especially in the cases of medicine and law, through forms of apprenticeships after the acquisition of the university education (Reader 1966: chapters 1 and 3; Engel 1983a:294).

Formal educational training served primarily to establish social distinctions within the professions of medicine and law. First, classical or mathematical training at Oxford or Cambridge, respectively, and then liberal university education, came to be the hallmarks of entrance into the upper levels of the these professions—the physician and barrister. The surgeon or apothecary and the solicitor, whose educations did not include public schools and Oxbridge, were relegated to a lower status (Reader 1966:44–48; Engel 1983a:293). The universities did not emerge as the site of professional training or as the site of professional definition. Indeed, Oxbridge consciously sought to distance themselves from professional training until the end of the century, when it was too late to exert any major control over qualifications (Engel 1983a:294–95).

University liberal education preceded by a public school education in the classics as prerequisites for professional status implied a specific relationship between the individual and decision making. This relationship also implied a specific kind of association between professionals and their clients and between professionals themselves. The notion of a liberal education as prerequisite to professional status, at least at its highest and most significant levels, clearly revealed the belief that such an education provided the basic elements necessary to make appropriate decisions. That is, such an education provided a paradigm or paradigms for the correct usage of technical information. It provided, in essence, a guide to appropriate selection of the technical means for resolving a particular problem. As Mill put it, the object of a university education was "not to make skillful lawyers, or physicians, or engineers, but capable and cultivated human beings . . . if you make them capable and sensible men, they will make themselves capable and sensible lawyers or physicians" (Engel 1983a:294).

Liberal education also provided, by the same token, the basis for determining the correct way in which information ought to be used. Liberal education was seen as providing an ethical sense and moral constraint on the use of knowledge so that it would not be used primarily for private purposes or self-indulgence. Thus, Benjamin Jowett of Balliol, with whom Trevelyan had consulted extensively on the reform proposal, wrote to the latter:

For the moral character of the candidates I should trust partly to the examination itself. University experience abundantly shows that in more than nineteen cases out of twenty, men of attainments are also men of character. The perseverance and self-discipline necessary for the acquirement of any considerable amount of knowledge are a great security that a young man has not led a dissolute life. (Abbot and Campbell 1899:44)

Macaulay, in defending his proposed reform for appointments to the Indian Civil Service in 1853 made the same point but with greater emphasis:

We believe that men who have been engaged, up to one or two and twenty years, in studies which have no immediate connection with the business of any profession, and of which the effect is merely to open, to invigorate, and to enrich the mind, will generally be found, in the business of every profession, superior to men who have at eighteen or nineteen, devoted themselves to the special studies of their calling. . . . He should have received the best, the most liberal, the most finished education that his native country affords. Such an education has been proved by experience to be the best preparation for every calling which requires the exercise of the high powers of the mind. . . . Indeed, early superiority in literature and science generally indicates the existence of some qualities which are securities against vice—industry, self-denial, a taste for pleasure not sensual, a laudable desire for honorable distinction, a still more laudable desire to obtain the approbation of friends and relations. We, therefore, think that the intellectual test about to be established will be found in practice to be also the best moral test that can be devised. (Mueller 1984:199–200)

In short, Macaulay, Trevelyan, and the liberal political reformers at midcentury envisioned liberal education as means by which the connection between social status and public service would be maintained. This enabled the more aristocratically inclined Whigs and their Liberal successors to abandon birth, at which much of their reform policy had been aimed, as the immediate criterion for representing the public interest. Aristocratic birth as the sole source of public-spiritedness had been shown to be corrupt, or at least successfully attacked as corrupt for almost a century. In its place Liberal/Whig/Peelite political leaders and, increasingly, Tory ones as well, sought to create an equally exclusive criterion for determining the capacity to engage in public service—a liberal education but to which only a very few had access. This idea of education, in effect, was borrowed from the higher liberal professions where the standard of exclusivity and the moral standards of self-constraint served as the basis for the professional conception of public service and monopolies over the supply of specific knowledge. Administrative service thus came to be conceived of as a profession. Like the liberal professions, it was seen as naturally divided between higher and lower forms—the distinction being one of education. It was the higher form of education that provided the ethical socialization which would enable the individual to hold the highest offices without betraying the public interest.

At the heart of this education was the idea that the individual was the focus of acquiring information and its ethical use. Indeed, the education itself served as the source of socializing the individual into the appropriate ethical standards of public service. The individual thus came to public service possessing the basic canons of ethical behavior as well as the paradigm for "sensible" decision making. These were not to be the subject of organizational rules. The gentlemanly character of the education, especially in its ethical character, would be sufficient to ensure that the public interest would be pursued sensibly and morally. In this sense, the reformers were implying that all public service, whether political or administrative, was a function of one kind of *pre*professional training and career.

The report accepted the fact that the direct link between aristocratic or upper-class birth and the right and obligation to monopolize the representation of public interest was broken. The implications of this were two-fold. From the various aspects of educational reform occurring in the first half of the century, Northcote-Trevelyan fashioned conceptions of public-interest representation and public service which distinguished between the two by career but not by career preparation, social class, or social origin. Whereas class had once been sufficient for determining access to political and administrative leadership, now education would determine access to both. But it would be an education seen as a *function* of class rather than a determinant of class. That is to say, the emergence of a class educational structure was seen as the necessary and sufficient means for preparing individuals for public leadership and service. The linkage of public school and Oxbridge education that was being forged in the first half of the nineteenth century was a response to the attacks on aristocratic privilege based on birth alone. It was seen by Northcote and Trevelyan as the only appropriate education for entering public life. Simultaneously, this education was increasingly seen as the only appropriate one for equipping individuals of this class for the station in life to which they had been called—public leadership—rather than as a ladder of social advancement open to all classes (Feuchtwanger 1985:10). In essence, it was the fact that it was the education of the upper classes that validated the superiority of the education.

Several aspects of the road to public service would not change, however, if the reforms were adopted. Social status, as reflected in access to public school and Oxbridge education, would continue to be a major determinant of recruitment to the higher reaches of public service. To the extent that access to these institutions remained highly exclusive, social networks would continue to be central to the evolution of careers in administration and politics. If entering public service required an educational career beginning with attendance at the same or similar schools from the pre- or very early teens to the early twenties, then social networks would inevitably remain a basic aspect of the professional career. Second, the utilization of the existing structure of education only reinforced the social basis of the administrative and political leadership roles. The public schools and Oxbridge were subject to very little state regulation and supervision. In effect, they were social institutions deeply rooted in a particular structure of social status. The state, in this sense, would have little to say about determining the nature of the appropriate forms of education. Rather, as Macaulay, Trevelyan, and Northcote made plain, it would be the public schools and universities that would determine the nature of education necessary for state and public service. As Trevelyan wrote in response to a question about creating a special school for civil

servants, such as the Royal Engineers enjoyed and where patronage continued to play the dominant role in appointment:

All our public schools and universities are seminaries of training and discipline
for the civil service of the State and the advantages to be obtained from some of
them exceed those which are derived from the Royal Academy. Why, therefore,
do we maintain a barrier of patronage between our public schools & universities
& public service? (as quoted in Hughes 1949a:77)

It would be this relationship between high social status and the social
autonomy of public school and Oxbridge education that would ensure the
accountability of public servants to political leaders—they would have the
same social basis to their educational experience, they would learn the same
paradigms for decision making, and possess the same moral and ethical constraints. Finally, the displacement of birth by a certain kind of educational
experience as the test of social status and access to political leadership and
public service reflects the transformation of patronage that was occurring at
midcentury. Up to the early part of the nineteenth century, patronage had
as its locus a network of social relations associated largely with high birth:
clientalism and kinship relations were the chief structural consequences of
this condition. For whatever reasons—the growth of large numbers of people with sufficient incomes to gain access to the schools of the aristocracy, or
the attack on aristocratic birth as the only criteria for leadership—attendance at public schools and then at Oxbridge became the means by which
people with somewhat lower status were able to form attachments and construct social networks which allowed them access to the patronage necessary
to enter the gentlemanly professions (Bamford 1967:20; Clark 1962:254–
59; Reader 1966:44–47). This seemed to be especially the case in the civil
service. Thus, for example, the Treasury admitted twenty-two men to its
central administrative offices between 1856 and 1870, a period in which
nomination by some patron was essential. Of these, nearly all were products
of the major public schools. The largest number, eight, had gone to public
school at Eton: "[T]he Etonian connection is one of the distinctive features
of the mid-nineteenth century Treasury" (Roseveare 1969:172–73). In effect, the Northcote-Trevelyan Report saw this transformation, in which
education was becoming a social test, as the means by which education could
serve to ensure the social homogeneity of political and administrative leadership and thus solve the problem of accountability of administration.

12

"The Efficient Secret": Administrative Rationalization and the Executive

The Consequences of the Northcote-Trevelyan Reform Proposals

The report was not universally well received. Macaulay, Trevelyan's brother-in-law, wrote in his journal,

There was open-mouthed criticism of the Report at Brooks'. Trevelyan has been too sanguine; the pear is not ripe. I always thought so. The time will come but it is not come yet. (as quoted in Hughes 1942:71)

The criticisms tended to focus on two aspects of the report. The first was the fear that examinations would allow the entry of people into the civil service about whom little was known other than they could pass an examination (Great Britain 1854–55 [1870]: vol. XX, 116, 319–37, 346–58). The second source of criticism was the fear that loss of patronage would not only make it impossible for heads of ministries and departments to extract accountability, but that it would also undermine the capacity for party discipline (Southgate 1962:205; Wright 1969:64). The opposition was sufficiently strong so that by May 1854 Gladstone was forced to admit that the report would not receive favorable action in that session (Conacher 1968:326–27). Instead, Gladstone chose to proceed on the one aspect of the report to which there was the least resistance—the creation of a centralized examining committee to provide a basic weeding out of ineligible candidates. By the time of the fall of the Aberdeen coalition cabinet in early 1855, upon which Gladstone relinquished the Exchequer to Cornewall Lewis, an Order in Council—that is, an administrative order emanating from the Queen's Privy Council, which traditionally was responsible for supervision of administration—was almost completed. Lewis, the new Exchequer, although opposed to the elimination of nomination, completed the arrangements for the issuing of the Order in Council.

The order provided for the creation of three commissioners of the Treasury whose duties were to oversee and regulate the process of admission of individuals to junior positions in the Civil Service (Great Britain, Report, Civil Service Commissioners 1856:a1). Specifically, the commissioners were given the power to examine all young men proposed for appointment to any junior position in respect to their age, health, moral character, and knowledge and ability, according to rules agreed to separately with each department (Great

363

Britain, Report, Civil Service Commissioners 1856:a1). Each individual passing such an examination would be issued a certificate of qualification without which, at least in theory, the individual could not be admitted to a required six-month probationary period of office-holding (Great Britain, Report, Civil Service Commissioners 1856:a2). Under this arrangement, a young man still had to find a patron or nominator, then take a test embodying the requirements set by the department, receive a certificate of qualification, and then serve a six-month probation period.

The creation of the commission did little, however, to advance the major objectives of the Northcote-Trevelyan Report. The commissioners had no sanctioning power, and departments could and did bypass the qualification tests (Wright 1969:71). There was no power to impose a uniform qualifying examination on all departments. The commissioners took a nonaggressive, compromising stance with regard to examinations by agreeing to support whatever examination structure a ministry employed. Examinations were not opened to everyone. For the most part, it was still necessary for individuals to have a patron to nominate them for the competition. Moreover, the competitions were limited, with only two or three individuals nominated for a position. These competitions were often undermined by the custom of nominating several people who would have no chance of passing, thus leaving qualification open for the intended nominee (Wright 1969:68).

From this vantage point, it is somewhat easier to understand why some kind of examination was established in almost every department in the late 1850s and 1860s. The examinations were, it appears, not designed to force the selection of a group of eligibles possessing a specified level of skill in something. Certainly, one aim was to establish a minimal level of literacy—and apparently quite minimal at that. Perhaps more important, closed departmental competitions placed appointments much more firmly in the hands of department heads. While others, such as backbenchers or cabinet colleagues, might recommend appointments, the department head, by nominating three people for a single appointment, had the power of determining who competed with whom. He might thus make sure to select one favorite and two others he suspected might not do nearly as well (Wright 1969:67–68).

It is not easy to understand why this commission was created. When the order was laid before Parliament, it was voted down, although this had no effect on its implementation since Orders in Council did not require parliamentary approval (Wright 1969:64). Henry Layard's motion, debated shortly afterward in June 1855, deplored the "manner in which merit and efficiency have been sacrificed, in public appointments, to party and family influences, and to a blind adherence to routine" (Chapman and Greenaway

1980:45). On coming to vote, the motion lost heavily. In July, V. Scully's motion welcoming the order and praying for an open public examination also lost (Wright 1969:65). Thus, it was clear that backbenchers were not anxious to see the implementation of even this much-weakened version of the Northcote-Trevelyan Report.

Nor could it be argued that the order was a consequence of the Crimean War disasters and the creation of the Administrative Reform Association of 1855. Just as the Northcote-Trevelyan Report was not a consequence of these events, so also the creation of the Civil Service Commission cannot be attributed to them (Anderson 1965:231–42; Wright 1969:64). The Administrative Reform Association had little patience for the kind of reforms of represented by the report or embodied in the creation of the Civil Service Commission (Anderson 1965:233, 236).

What then were the political forces that led to this rather odd outcome, which neither created an examination system nor established a two-tier career system as the Northcote-Trevelyan Report had proposed? All that emerged was a central certifying agency, which left patronage pretty much intact and seemed, on the face of it, to benefit no particular set of political interests. There are several clues that help explain this anomaly. First, the original report was voted down in the Aberdeen coalition cabinet by the Whig segment composed of Russell, Lansdowne, Clarendon, Wood, and Cranworth as against the Peelites (Hughes 1949a:84). The Whig opposition stemmed primarily from the fear that an examination system would undermine and eventually destroy the basis of political leadership—aristocratic patronage. The Whigs had long considered the highest levels of the civil service as the proper object of patronage; it had become the means by which Whig influence and parliamentary power was maintained. Thus John Romilly, a leading Whig and later Lord Romilly, was quoted on the occasion as saying:

The more the civil service is recruited from the lower classes, the less will it be sought after by the higher, until at last the aristocracy will be altogether dissociated from the permanent civil service of the country. (MacDonagh 1977:207)

For the Whigs, party power meant patronage control as against the notion of party organization (Vincent 1976:xlv). The structure of social networks from which Whig leadership was constructed, the intermarried "cousinhood," was the bulwark against the political uncertainty surrounding political leadership in the 1840s and 1850s, but at the same time it was the obstacle to the formation of party organization.

This uncertain political atmosphere was helped along very considerably by the continued factionalism of the Peelites. With their reputation for administrative ability, the Peelites sought to enhance their parliamentary position by the only means available to them—centralization of administrative control in the Treasury, where a Peelite might to continue to dominate so long as the faction controlled the swing vote in Parliament. The Peelites, small in number and without much hope of organizing anything larger, wisely chose to use the administrative structure as the base for their political power. To do so, however, required removing patronage from backbenchers while at the same time continuing to integrate administrative offices under Treasury control. To a considerable extent, all of this depended on the continued absence of systematic party mechanisms for leadership selection and succession.

This helps explain the way in which political leadership treated the Northcote-Trevelyan Report, but it does not explain why the succeeding Whig government under Palmerston allowed a ghostly version of the report to become effective. There are several clues which suggest the answer. The first of these clues is the object of the attacks by the Administrative Reform Association of 1855. The major criticism of the association was aimed at the loss of MP independence through continued aristocratic patronage and the emergence of party organization in its local forms as party clubs and party agents. As the Committee of the Association expressed it in their Official Papers:

The candidates sent down from the Clubs are chosen with the constant object of upholding, whether in or out of office, the fixed Ministerial cliques. . . . It is an essential step in administrative reform, that the Constituencies should shake off the Clubs and their Agents. (as quoted in Anderson 1965:238)

And further, the committee urged, "Let there be an end of having candidates thrust upon you either by great neighbours or great clubs, for mere personal or party ends" (as quoted in Anderson 1965:238). The second line of attack by the association was directed at the unwillingness of the government to act fully within the boundaries of contract, as in private businesses, when it came to office-holding. Thus the committee proposed an examination system: it was limited to junior clerks only; it required that there be a qualifying examination before the competitive examination that was based on pragmatic knowledge used in business offices; also, it insisted that department heads have the right to dismiss clerks for unsatisfactory performance (Anderson 1965:235).

The concern for the independence of MPs rested on the fear of a continuing expansion of ministerial power at the expense of an independent parliamentary representative system. Removal of this fear lay not in increasing the patronage for MPs so that they might be able to resist the pressures of a powerful cabinet but in the moral regeneration of electors. By changing public opinion so that electors voted not on the basis of private but public interest, ministerial power could be held in check and be held accountable (Anderson 1965:238). The selection of junior clerks by examinations stressing utilitarian knowledge would undermine the social network and class basis of patronage appointment and of examinations based on a liberal public school and university education. In short, the attacks of the Committee of the Reform Association reflected the continuation of the idea of *parliamentary* reform as the basis of administrative capacity. Once ministerial power was restricted by the dominance of independent backbenchers, policy would be made on the basis of public interest by men whose careers were not dependent on ministerial support or constituency bribery. At the entering levels of the civil service, this meant depriving ministers of a clear run at recruiting future senior civil servants from the same aristocratic or upper social classes as the ministers.

This suggests rather pointedly that the development of cabinet/ministerial power at the expense of backbenchers had not only not gone unnoticed, but that the Crimean disasters had highlighted this development. The disasters were seen as a consequence of a political evolution in which private interest suborned the public one. In this respect, the creation of the Civil Service Commission by the Whig Palmerston cabinet does, in fact, make some sense. Looked at carefully, the Order in Council sought, with some success, to satisfy three conditions faced by political leaders: (1) continued lack of centralized control over administration; (2) continued reliance on social networks as the only workable basis for selecting leadership; and (3) continued ambiguity with regard to whether political leader behavior was dominated by public or private interest.

The first of these was addressed by several aspects of the order. The fact that it was done by an Order in Council was significant in itself. The order was an instrument drawn up in the Treasury and was used increasingly in the nineteenth century as an instrument of cabinet executive power (Chester 1981:86–87). As the Treasury became the chosen means for integrating administration, the Order in Council became the instrument by which it imposed its will on recalcitrant departments (M. Wright 1972:225–26). The use of the order here was one of the first times it was used to bolster Cabinet and Treasury power by depriving the House of Commons of any direct control of the commissioners. The Northcote-Trevelyan Report had contemplated an Act of Parliament as the means for carrying out the recommendations. It was forcefully opposed by Sir James Stephen, Cornwall Lewis, and others who feared that an Act of Parliament would make it possible for Parliament to alter the arrangements on a yearly basis. Lewis pointed out that setting up the commission "would necessarily entail some expense, and however small this might be, it would necessitate an annual vote which would give the House of Commons a practical veto upon the system once in every session" (Great Britain 1854–55 [1870]: vol. XX, 124).

The commission was independent; that is, it was not accountable directly to any minister but to Parliament, even though by the Order in Council, Parliament had no direct control over the commissioners. Nevertheless, the appointment of the commissioners lay in the hands of the prime minister, and this strengthened cabinet control over administration. This can be seen in the fact that the Head of the Commission and a second member of the three-man board were associated with financial control: Sir Edward Ryan, Assistant Comptroller General of the Exchequer, and Edward Romilly, Chairman of the Board of Audit (Treasury). The third member, John G. S. Lefevre, Clerk Assistant to the House of Lords, represented Parliament (Great Britain, Report, Civil Service Commissioners 1856:a2). The commissioners thus represented the continued efforts at centralization and dominance in administration by the Cabinet and the utilization of the financial structures of control, especially the Treasury, in this process. The very act of creation of the commission thus may be viewed as another increment in the expansion of Cabinet authority over administration.

The refusal to make examinations obligatory or even uniform was clearly a consequence of the strong objections to removing the power of nomination from department heads (Hughes 1942:76). To attempt to remove this power was seen by party leaders and heads of departments in the Cabinet as undermining their capacity to maintain their status and influence. This fear was all the greater during this period of instability, in which the Peelites were seen as possible alternate sources of patronage to the major political groupings. The creation of noncompetitive examinations, in which there could now be several nominations, resolved not only the problem of maintaining patronage for department heads but also the problem of increasing demands for patronage. In the noncompetitive examination system, patrons could make more than one nomination to take the examination. At the same time,

[T]he new system made it easy for patrons to fob off clients with a minimum of offence. . . . If a client complained that his protege had failed to get in, the new system enabled the patron to shrug off responsibility on to the Civil Service Commissioners. (Parris 1969:72–73)

The absence of any regulation of promotion further sustained the patronage powers of department heads. So long as promotion was a purely departmental matter, promotions continued to offer a field for patronage awards. Much of this aspect was clothed in the rhetoric of accountability. Personal nomination by department heads, when combined with control over promotion, was said to assure that individuals would be accountable to senior officials and eventually amenable to the executive. In this fashion, account-ability continued to be part of the discourse on administrative reform and organization.

That patronage had by no means been abandoned is reflected in the num-bers that continued to obtain office without examination. In the period be-tween 1855 and 1867–68, the Civil Service Commission issued 9,826 cer-tificates of qualification for clerkships. Of these, only 28 (0.3 percent) in six departments had been awarded on the basis of open competition; 2,765 (28.1 percent) were awarded on limited competition, and 7,033 (71.5 per-cent) were awarded on nomination by department heads only (Wright 1969:75). The Order in Council thus tended not only to allow the persist-ence of patronage nominations but to centralize them in the hands of depart-ment heads.

Finally, then, the acceptance of examinations, even if they were noncom-petitive, and the creation of an independent board of commissioners must also be seen, in part, as a response to the criticisms of aristocratic and party elites in their conduct of the Crimean War. Palmerston was no great friend of the Northcote-Trevelyan Report, but he was faced with accusations of in-competency of a leadership whose selection appeared to be based on private rather than public interest. The clearest statement of this view was made by the Administrative Reform Association, whose attacks, as we have seen, were directed precisely at the private criteria by which *political* leadership was se-lected (Anderson 1965:233–39). The Order in Council of 1855 thus met the strategic considerations of political leaders by allowing political leader-ship to continue to be organized around social networks and social status through the medium of patronage. At the same time, the order continued the movement toward executive centralization of administrative authority through its association of the commission with financial regulation, and by the appropriation and use of the order by the Cabinet for its own executive power. Lastly, in the endorsement of certification by noncompetitive exami-nations for entering clerks, the Order in Council seemed to establish the pri-ority of public interest over private desires, thereby providing some response to the criticisms raised by the demands for administrative reform.

From the Order in Council of 1855 to the Order in Council of 1870

In the period from 1855 to 1870, the evolution of the civil service toward a rationalized structure was affected by three continuing developments. First, there were the continued efforts on the part of political leaders, as they came to hold executive power, to centralize and integrate the administrative struc-ture under the control of the Cabinet—*the pursuit of administrative coher-*

ence. The second of these developments was the push by political leaders to systematize a stratified structure of education that would ensure each social class would be provided with an educational experience which was deemed socially appropriate—*the pursuit of social coherence*. The third development centered on the stabilization and destabilization of political parties and leadership resulting in the Reform Act of 1867—*the pursuit of political coherence*.

The Treasury and Administrative Integration

In the years immediately following the Order in Council of 1855, the strengthening of Treasury ties to the Civil Service Commission and the control of administrative recruitment were enhanced by the department's support of the commission's limited powers. Throughout the remainder of the 1850s, and all during the decade of the 1860s, the Treasury meticulously complied with the recommendations of the commission regarding certification. This was Trevelyan and his successors seeking to make the Treasury an example to be followed by the other departments.

The Treasury's role in recruitment and appointment expanded in these years. The passage of the Superannuation Act of 1859 on 5 April had two important consequences: it provided one of the important and basic unifying elements of the civil service career, and it created a direct line of authority from the Treasury to the structure of appointment. The act confirmed the abolition of the employees contribution system by the Act of 1857 (Raphael 1964:158–59). It went on to distinguish between "established" and "unestablished" (temporary) positions by providing that qualification for a pension was reserved for those who had served continuously for at least ten years in an established capacity in the permanent civil service (Wright 1969:311).

By creating the category of an "established office," the legislation provided, for the first time, a uniform servicewide category of office-holding. Additionally, it provided those who fell within the category a right to a pension, which was the function of having performed satisfactorily (Raphael 1964:161). Performance in office over time thus came to be viewed as something beyond the purely contractual employment relationship. In establishing this right, the legislation, in effect, established the notion of a career rather than just office-holding or employment. This was reinforced by the abolition of employee contributions and their complete substitution by state contributions.

The act also provided for retirement at age sixty, thus providing for a servicewide exit point for the career. The pensions were also to be calculated in a uniform manner as they had since the 1820s (one-sixtieth of the salary at retirement for each year of service with a minimum of ten and a maximum of forty years, which meant that two-thirds of salary was the highest amount normally allowed) (M. Wright 1969:311). This arrangement served as a strong incentive for making the civil service a lifetime career, since half-salary pension would not be achieved until individuals were in their late forties or early fifties with at least ten or so years of possible salary raises yet to be seen.

The drive for the Superannuation Act of 1859 was twofold: the increased concerns of central government clerks over the consequences of the policy of promotion by merit, and the desire on the part of the executive for greater Treasury control over administration. The emphasis on merit produced concern about the role of seniority and, therefore, concern over the predictability and commensurability of salary increases. If seniority failed as the source of predictability, then career would continue to be seen as arbitrary (Raphael 1964:157–58; M. Wright 1969:356–57). These concerns, especially over pension deductions and salaries, produced the first attempts at collective action on the part of civil servants in the years from 1854 through 1859 (Raphael 1964:157–58). These activities reflected the increased attacks on the old patronage proprietary structure of office-holding. Without the protection of patrons or the concept of office as property, civil servants became increasingly uneasy about their place in the structure of office-holding. The Superannuation Act of 1859 went some direction in easing these concerns, but the continued rhetoric about merit promotion continued to cause uneasiness.

The second source of the act—the desire of the Cabinet to extend its authority over administration through the Treasury—is revealed in section 2 of the act. By virtue of this section, the Treasury was given the sole authority to determine who qualified for a pension—that is, who was a member of the permanent Civil Service. The act also included a provision, introduced by no other than Sir Stafford Northcote, which defined the officers to whom the act would apply. By this clause, which was not seen as very significant and was accepted without a division of the House, permanent civil servants were defined as those who were either appointed directly by the Crown or were "admitted into the Civil Service with a certificate from the Civil Service Commissioners" (Raphael 1964:160). Without certification by the Civil Service Commission, an individual could not now receive a pension. By fastidious enforcement of the certification rule, the Treasury became, in effect, the sole arbiter of membership in the permanent Civil Service and the commission's authority was enhanced. This was followed in 1862 by the Treasury's refusal to act as a court of appeal from other departments on the question of the commission's authority to deny certification of an appointment. This stated policy established the absolute character of the commissioners' discretion over certification (Wright 1969:75). These developments expanded the Treasury's and therefore the Cabinet's authority over the administrative structure. Although departments and their masters continued to have considerable power of nomination, they were held increasingly in rein by a Treasury with expanded powers to resist nominations if the Civil Service commissioners saw fit.

This extension of Treasury and Cabinet authority is mirrored, during the same period, by the centralization and rationalization of the Exchequer. During Gladstone's tenure as Exchequer in the years between 1859 and 1866, he created a system of financial control that significantly increased the power of the executive. By creating a permanent Select Committee on Public Accounts in 1862, and following that by the Exchequer and Audits Department Act of 1866, Gladstone created a unified process and machinery of estimate, appropriation, expenditure, and audit. The new independent comptroller and auditor-general was responsible only to the new Select Committee. The Treasury was now held accountable to these new arrangements for all its financial transactions (Roseveare 1969:139–40).

But this was all gain to the Treasury. In principle, the relationship of the Treasury to the House of Commons or its watchdog, the Public Accounts Committee, was that of servant to master. But the Treasury had also gained a powerful ally. No sanction that the Treasury might bring against the spending propensities of other departments, jealously guarding their autonomy, was more compelling than the ultimate threat of exposure before this parliamentary tribunal. (Roseveare 1969:141)

Once in place, this reform resulted in the Treasury Minute of 1868, which set forth the basic policy of Treasury control over departments. The minute admitted that it had no control over specified authorized expenditures by departments, but it set forth as policy that sanctions would be brought into effect for any expenditure not specifically authorized by parliamentary grant. The Treasury therefore called on the comptroller and auditor-general to notify the Treasury immediately if it found any such deviations (Roseveare 1969:141–42). This became the fundamental statement of modern Treasury control. Along with the Treasury control over pensions and through the Civil Service commissioners' certification powers, the Treasury and, therefore, the executive had come a very long way toward delimiting the autonomy of departments and concentrating power and influence within its own confines. Indeed, it would be difficult not to conclude that the next logical step for political leaders seeking to stabilize their position would be to continue to strengthen their positions via the Cabinet as against their positions as autonomous department heads. Certainly, they would be considerably better off if they acted as a group rather than as individuals seeking to sustain only their positions. To continue the latter would be to continue to foster the structural underpinnings of the uncertainty about their own positions. If each department head/member of the Cabinet acted only in his own best interests, the result could be, as it had been for the decade and a half since Peel left office, a continuing history of decentralized leadership and party instability.

Electoral Reform and Political Coherency

If the 1860s saw a considerable advance by political leaders in integrating and centralizing command of administration in the hands of an executive body which they controlled, it was also the 1860s which saw critical advances in the redefinition of party. The efforts of party leaders toward creating the Cabinet as the organizational basis for controlling policy-making and administration was tied to the problem of party definition. So long as administration remained decentralized and patronage continued to play a major role in determining the careers of putative political leaders, party would continue to be an ambiguous concept. Without the capacity to impose discipline, there would always remain serious questions about the capacity to govern. But basic to convincing voters that a party had the capacity to govern was not only a structural capacity to administer but also the ability to win elections in a convincing manner rather than relying on various forms of coalition politics. This was, in many ways, the central problem of English politics in the 1860s.

The ambiguity surrounding party definition is revealed in a number of ways: the continued existence of the Peelites as a faction until at least 1859, when Gladstone and a number of others finally joined the Liberals; the almost evenly balanced structure of parliamentary representation (the Peelites offering the balancing votes) until 1867–68 (see table 12.1); and the absence of any major issue dividing the parties until after Palmerston's death in 1865. Palmerston's government had been built on the maintenance of suffi-

Table 12.1 Parliamentary Representation between 1846 and 1868

Date	Conservative	Peelite	Liberal
July 1847	243	89	324
July 1852	290	45	319
March 1857	256	26	372
May 1859	306		348
July 1865	300		358
November 1868	279		379

Source: Blake 1985, 370.

cient ambiguity so as to allow a Whig/Liberal/Peelite coalition. His death released the forces desiring the sharpening of party contestation and definition
(Cowling 1967:28). Parliamentary reform emerged as the issue around
which parties could define themselves and political leaders could establish
predictable structures of leadership.

Parliamentary reform had a clear attraction as a means for the parties to
define themselves. Palmerston's informal peace on the matter so far as Parliament was concerned had dissolved with his death. Imbalances in franchise
had become increasingly, in the 1860s, an object of public and social concern—a concern reflected in the emergence of the National Reform League
and the National Reform Union in 1864. Both parties, especially their leaders Gladstone and Disraeli, saw the political possibilities of a reformed franchise. Each wanted a reform that would create stronger constituencies. Gladstone wished a reform that would expand the suffrage in Liberal centrist
fashion. That is, one that would increase Liberal representation without giving the working classes anything like a majority. The Liberal coalition strategy was to enfranchise the upper working-class elites while strengthening
Liberal county seats (Blake 1985:102).

Disraeli, of course, wanted a reform that would put an end to the Conservatives' exclusion from power. Thus, Disraeli's strategy was centered on
the crucial fact that since 1852, while the Conservatives had never held less
than 275 seats, they had never done much better. This led him to the conclusion that lowering the franchise level in some constituencies, especially
Whig-dominated ones, would result in increased penetration by the Radicals. By pushing the Liberals to the Left, the Conservatives would then become the party of the center and of stability. This, Disraeli calculated, would
drive the Liberal Right into the hands of the Conservatives (Cowling
1967:64–65; Blake 1985:104–5).

Disraeli's tactics in attacking the Liberal reform bill of 1866 emphasized
splitting off the Liberal Right—a tactic which was superbly successful. The defection of Robert Lowe and others from the Liberals to form the so-called Cave
of Adullam spelled the doom of the bill and of the Liberal government. Disraeli succeeded in both senses of the term. In creating the Reform Act of 1868,
Disraeli produced an outcome which extended the franchise to 1,120,000 new
voters, thus creating an electorate of about two and a half million (Wright
1970:81). More significantly, Disraeli had succeeded in keeping the counties
from being swamped by borough voters, thus maintaining the counties as a
balance to the increased size of the large borough constituencies (Wright
1970:81). In the long run, the expansion of the franchise and the redistribution of seats which accompanied it produced a clear division of party. The Liberals won the election of 1868 and, in the process, emerged as a coherent party.

Disraeli's turn came in 1874, when he won a resounding victory at the head of an equally coherent Conservative Party (Bulmer-Thomas 1965:115).

The expansion of the franchise, however, created a new dimension of uncertainty for the parties. No one knew quite what to expect from an electorate that had almost doubled in size. After the passage of the new law, election managers were at a loss to know how the new voters could be "approached, . . . influenced, . . . [and] won" (Moore 1976:321). Contemporary commentators on the new law declared that organization was needed as never before. This uncertainty resulted in the increasing reliance on party organization, both local and national (Hanham 1959:93, 347–68). The period following the Reform Act of 1868 saw the development of central party organization as a response to the expanded suffrage. Organizing voters now became a time-consuming task which elicited not only the emergence of professional election agents, but also of volunteer election committees as well.

Under these circumstances, candidates for Parliament were finding it increasingly difficult to organize voters on the basis of local networks in which patronage played a significant role. In an increasing number of constituencies, the number of voters had grown too large to be organized in this fashion. Candidates now had to depend on the party leadership in control of the executive to use legislation to support local candidacies to a far greater extent than before (Moore 1976:415). In this context, patronage declined as a benefit and, indeed, could become a deficit. The increased size of the electorate made patronage a difficult good to distribute without creating bitterness among one's supporters. The Reform Act, thus, undermined the importance of patronage and left it as an object of further Cabinet centralization and rationalization efforts.

Moreover, the increased size of the electorate suggested for party leaders, as it had after the Reform Act of 1832, that patronage would now be passed out to unsuitable people. Thus, Robert Lowe, the leader of the Liberal Right who opposed the expansion of the franchise and defected from his party in 1866 over the issue, saw the expanded franchise as a powerful danger to a parliamentary system in which representation, as he saw it, was based on some idea of merit. He viewed the expansion of franchise as subversive to the mediation which had for so long assured that parliamentary representation would be restrained by ideas of public rather than private or sectional interest (Sylvester 1974:28–29; Winter 1976:93). In the years immediately following the Reform Act, Lowe was to play a key role in the transformation of the Civil Service. As Chancellor of the Exchequer in Gladstone's 1868 Cabinet, Lowe was to be the major figure in the creation of the open competition system. His concern with the necessity of maintaining a mediating institution between voter and policy-making led him to be assiduous in the pursuit of the Order in Council of 1870, which established the basis of the modern civil service in Great Britain.

It is difficult to view Gladstone's selection of Lowe as Exchequer as purely coincidental or exigent. Surely, Gladstone sought to heal the wounds of 1866 and 1867 which had driven a number of Liberals, led by Lowe, to side with the Tories. Lowe and Gladstone also held many of the same views with regard to the expansion of suffrage and the necessity for strengthening an elite hold over the senior administrative structure. After all, it had been Gladstone who had instigated the Northcote-Trevelyan Report. It was also Gladstone who had made major contributions to the centralization of executive authority through his reforms of the Treasury and Exchequer. Gladstone's efforts had made the Treasury the mechanism of Cabinet control of administration and finance. Lowe had very much the same agenda, as his tenure as Exchequer would reveal (Winter 1976:247–68).

Social Coherence and Educational Reform

Central to the strategy that Gladstone had evoked in the Northcote-Trevelyan recommendations was the construction of a socially stratified educational system. Such a system was critical so long as enlarged franchises threatened to turn patronage into a channel of domination by the masses or, even worse, by backbenchers over administration. Unless backbenchers were driven from the pastures of patronage by the creation of "objective" criteria for appointment, political leaders would continue to find it difficult to gain control over Commons party discipline. As I have suggested above, party leaders sought to make high social status synonymous with profession by creating a distinct educational career which itself would transform social status so that it appeared to be a function of merit.[1]

The period between the two Orders in Council saw the reform of English educational institutions by direct intervention of the state. As one writer has put it:

When it is recalled that, in 1870, there followed an Act establishing a system of elementary schooling it becomes clear that the period 1850-70 marks a crucial moment of change in English education. During these two decades the affairs of Oxford and Cambridge and of the "public" schools were enquired into in minute detail, their shortcomings laid bare and the direction of future development determined; hundreds of small schools throughout the country were also placed under the microscope and their affairs rigorously reordered. (Simon 1960:280–81)

1. See, for example, Lowe's testimony to the Playfair Committee of 23 July 1874 (Great Britain 1875 [c.1113-I]: vol. XXIII, 124–27). Also see Winter 1976:264–65.

The energies of reform were first directed at the two ancient universities. It was the growth of internal conflict at Oxford that first attracted reform. For several decades before 1850, a struggle over the character of religious dominance, governance, and curriculum created two increasingly well-defined factions. One wished to retain the traditional Anglican orthodoxy, college dominance and control over resources, and restricted classical curriculum. Opposed to them was a faction bent on freeing the institution from orthodoxy, strengthening the university as against the colleges, introducing science into the curriculum, and freeing up the narrow college scholarships through open competition (Simon 1960:281–90; Sanderson 1975:26–33, 75–84). The reformers wanted a national university, not a training and sinecure institution for the clergy. Frustrated by the traditionalists, they sought external help or interference to undertake the reform (Faber 1957:196–98).

Their calls were answered by the creation of a parliamentary commission of inquiry in 1850. The commissioners delivered their reports in 1852. They recommended four basic types of reforms: broadening the base of university government by including the professoriat; strengthening of the university as against the colleges, primarily by building up a core of university teachers as opposed to college appointments; transforming the content of education to allow the introduction of specialization in mathematics and science; abolition of the narrow restrictions on scholarships and fellowships in favor of open competition (Simon 1960:295; Mallet 1927:III, 298–325).

In 1854, the ubiquitous Gladstone, as Exchequer and the Member from Oxford, introduced and fought through the legislation enabling the reforms to occur (the same legislation was passed for Cambridge in 1856). The legislation provided for the appointment of Executive Commissioners with statutory powers and, although not one of the recommendations, abolished the religious tests for matriculation and undergraduate degrees at Oxford and Cambridge (and the Master's at Cambridge)(Simon 1960:296). The Executive Commissioners proceeded to put into effect the basic reforms recommended by the commission of inquiry (Mallet 1927:III, 327).

The reforms did in fact break the dominance of the orthodox clerics over Oxford and Cambridge. In the process, the universities became, structurally at least, national universities. Breaking up the local scholarships and fellowships into objects of national competition, abolishing religious tests, expanding the curriculum to meet not just clerical but, in some sense, national needs—all these were aimed at restructuring the university as the instrument for preparing not only the clergy but all of the higher professions for assuming the obligations of national and public service.

The reformers and reforms were careful to leave the universities intact as primarily upper-class social institutions.[2] They were not provided with a broad array of scholarships so that a variety of social classes might be represented. Nor were the costs of university education reduced in any significant manner so as to make entry widely available to any but the well-to-do middle and upper classes. Finally, access to Oxford and Cambridge was kept very narrow by allowing only a very limited expansion of the student body over the remainder of the century. In 1861, enrollment at Oxford and Cambridge amounted to 1,200 (0.3 percent of the 18–24 age group) at each institution. In 1901, Cambridge had grown to 3,080 and Oxford to 2,800 (0.1 percent of the 18–24 age group) (Lowe 1983:45, 52). During this same period, annual admissions to these universities averaged only 0.2 percent of the relevant age group (18.5 years) for the 1850s and 1860s and 0.3 percent for the 1870s through the 1890s (Stone 1974:91–92, 103). Nor did the remainder of the university system grow much faster: in 1861, it provided for 985 students (0.2 percent) and in 1901, for 18,089 students (3.0 percent) (Lowe 1983:45, 52). It is not difficult to conclude that state policy throughout the late nineteenth and early twentieth centuries was aimed at maintaining very narrow access to higher education. To the degree that Oxbridge became the primary source for the higher professions, including the civil service, access was extraordinarily narrow.

While the universities continued to reject the concept of providing professional education until the end of the century, leaders of the reform movement like Benjamin Jowett and Oscar Browning sought to make Oxford and Cambridge education the necessary preliminary to acquiring technical professional training. This meant emphasis on developing what they felt were the mental and moral faculties required for those entering the higher professions, ones which demanded a commitment to public service and interest (Engel 1983a:293–96; Simon 1960:297). Thus, for example, only seven percent of Cambridge graduates in the period from 1850 to 1899 went into business, with the great majority of them going into the professions (Perkin 1969:213).

If the reforms of the universities were to have any bearing on the national structure of education, political leaders early recognized that reforms also had to be carried out at the preuniversity level. If no reforms were carried out, there would be considerable confusion as to the place of the "national" universities, which were viewed as essential to the training of the upper classes. But there was a welter of preuniversity schools. There were those to

2. As late as the period between 1881 and 1900, over eighty percent of the students at Oxford still came from the "gentlemanly" classes (primarily landholders, clergy, and other high professionals)(Perkin 1983:208).

which the aristocracy and gentry sent their children, the so-called "public" schools. There were those to which the middle classes sent their children, the endowed grammar schools. Then, there were a plethora of private, artisan, and religious schools that tended to serve the lower middle classes and the skilled artisans. The lines between these were not always clear, nor was their legal status. Although a good many schools were endowed and thus had a public character to them under the law, they were, for the most part, completely unregulated. The private schools were also unregulated. In effect, the distinctions between the types were a result of market forces working themselves out within a structure of social stratification (Roach 1986). Schools competed with each other for various types of clientele in the early decades of the nineteenth century, and this competition had been responsible for fashioning a variety of educations.

In this manner, these schools came to be seen, as in the case of Oxbridge, as social institutions essential to the cohesion of society. Training received at such institutions provided much of the information necessary for judging the nature and character of individuals. Just as Oxbridge came to be seen as the national institutions preparing students for entering the higher professions because of their perceived role in producing a predictable, distinctive type of individual, so too were the various types of schools seen as producing specific, predictable types of character. Thus, the Taunton Commission established in 1864 to examine the endowed grammar schools came to the conclusion that:

The wishes of the parents can best be defined in the first instance by the length of time during which they are willing to keep their children under instruction. It is found that, viewed in this way, education, as distinct from direct preparation for employment, can at present be classified as that which is to stop at 14, that which is to stop at about 16, and that which is to continue till 18 or 19; and for convenience we shall call these the Third, the Second, and the First Grade of education respectively. . . . It is obvious that these distinctions correspond roughly, but by no means exactly, to the graduations in society. (Schools Inquiry Commission, as quoted in Bamford 1967:169–70)

The commissioners went on to give their opinion that parents in the first grade comprised the aristocracy, the gentry, and the professionals and were willing to subordinate educational to social requirements, while the second and third grades corresponded to subdivisions of the middle class and tended to stress more pragmatic subjects (Bamford 1967:169–70). Thus, by 1860, the division of schools had come to be largely socially determined and part and parcel of social class culture.

If, however, the increased competition gave rise to increasing stratification and its institutionalization, it also gave rise to a welter of schools in each group, all of which made claims about the social as well as educational efficiency of their institutions. In this competitive process, some of the older public schools declined as newer schools like Wellington, Cheltenham, Marlbourough, and Lancing came into existence and offered better facilities (Bamford 1967:17–38; Roach 1986:211–27). In the unregulated context of education, decline often provided the occasion for headmasters and governing boards to stray from the original constitutions of the endowments and utilize the incomes for themselves rather than for the support of facilities and the expansion of curriculum (Simon 1960:300–302). This brought on increasing criticism, not only from parents who felt cheated or were bewildered by claims, but also by members of the upper classes, who viewed the decline as disastrous for the upper classes as education became increasingly the standard for occupying the high professions. Thus, Lord Clarendon, head of the Public Schools Commission of 1861, was painfully impressed by, as he put it, "the stick-in-the-mud" system of the public schools, which, because they were based exclusively on the classics, placed the "upper classes in a state of inferiority to the middle and lower" (Mack 1941:27).

The main political problem with regard to education in the 1860s, then, was how to establish systematic links between the social classes and socially appropriate grammar schools and between the grammar schools and the national universities. As part of this goal, political leaders came to see it as their task to separate out and ensure the continued existence of a body of "national" public schools that would provide a continuous flow of properly educated individuals to the national universities.

This goal arose, in part, as a consequence of political leaders' concern with how to make individuals accountable to a public interest while at the same time maintaining an existing body of social institutions which were highly valued because of the way in which they come to serve socially distinct groups. Or, to put it somewhat differently, the problem was how to avoid the creation of a civil service organization that had few constraining links to social institutions and therefore would be unpredictable in its social policies and relations to Cabinet and Parliament. In effect, Northcote, Trevelyan, Gladstone, Lowe, Jowett, and others wanted an educational system that would train individuals in a common set of social values, which would then govern their relations to others in a highly predictable fashion. It is no wonder that Thomas Arnold, the famous Headmaster at Rugby (1828–42), was almost apotheosized in the nineteenth century by the English upper classes. His major contribution was to view the school as the means for instilling moral and religious values and a manly spirit. Arnold sought to make the public school a guide for making decisions which would be enhanced by a liberal education (Mack 1939:236–333; Roach 1986:245–47; Bamford 1967:31–33, 40–42).

It is significant that the reform of the grammar school structure began with the so-called "national" public schools: Winchester, Eton, Westminster, Harrow, Rugby, Charterhouse, Shrewsbury, St. Paul's, and Merchant Taylor's—the latter two being endowed London schools. These schools were characterized by two aspects: preponderance of children of the upper and professional classes and recruitment to the schools from all over the nation. Between 1800 and 1850, at all the schools but St. Paul's, aristocracy and gentry accounted for about half the enrollments. Another twenty-one percent were from professional (including clergy) families; a category of "others" included gentleman's families and amounted to another twenty percent or so; only three percent came specifically from middle-class families; and less than one percent came from poor families (Bamford 1961: 224–35). St. Paul's had a more middle-class clientele, which gave way by midcentury to professional class preponderance (Bamford 1967:6).

The first object of reform, then, was not the deconstruction of the great public schools but their amendment and confirmation as schools necessary for the training of the classes responsible for the public interest. Gladstone, then Chancellor of the Exchequer and an important figure in the development of the Reform Commission, wrote to the commissioners, describing the public schools as public property, and thus required them to "lay open the whole case, and set out to the full extent of what is to be desired by way of remedy" (as quoted in Simon 1960:305).

But in Gladstone's view, . . . the public good demanded not only business efficiency in organisation and modernisation of studies, but also the maintenance of aristocratic exclusiveness—of a form of education which was markedly different from that available to other classes. . . . In the same letter he strongly advocated retention of the classics as "the paramount matter of education" for "that small proportion of the youth of any country who are to become in the fullest sense educated men" (Simon 1960:305).

The immediate occasion for the creation of the Public Schools Commission was a series of attacks in 1860–61 in several widely respected reviews. The most significant of these was by Henry Reeves, who attacked the governance and administration of the schools in the April 1861 issue of the *Edinburgh Review* (Mack 1941:12). This provided grist for the parliamentary opposition, and within a few days after the publication of Reeves' essay, Grant Duff asked in the House of Commons whether the government intended to grant an inquiry into the public schools. George Cornewall Lewis, then Home Secretary, replied that public schools were a fit subject for inquiry since they had already, in 1818, been the object of examination by the charity commissioners (Mack 1941:26).

It was the establishment of this commission, however, which made government intervention in the structure and governance of schools a standing principle (Simon 1987:89). Lewis, as Home Minister, appointed Lord Clarendon to head the commission and then chose a group of ardent supporters of public schools: Lord Lyttelton (Eton), Sir Stafford Northcote (Eton), Edward Twistleton (Winchester), Lord Devon (Westminster), Halford Vaughan (Rugby), and William Thompson (private); Lord Clarendon himself was the son of an Etonian and father of several future Harrovians (Mack 1941:28). It was clearly not a group that would undertake to democratize or substantially change the nature of the public school.

Following several years of inquiry, the commission submitted its report in 1864. Its major recommendations covered four major areas: governance, curriculum, student life, and social recruitment. On governance, the commissioners were careful to steer away from any notion of direct state control. They recommended a complete transformation that would separate the governors and the headmasters from direct financial interest in the schools. They sought to invest control in the hands of impartial trustees who had some understanding of educational affairs (Mack 1941:30–31; Simon 1960:310–11). In terms of curriculum, the commissioners reaffirmed the central place of the classics and classical learning as the basis for education. In addition, however, they went on to insist that more attention be paid to modern studies and proposed the inclusion of mathematics, foreign languages, natural science, music history, and geography. They recommended that these be included in a course of study in which the classics would be allotted just over half the total time and science about one-eighth (Simon 1960:311).

Table 12.2 Major Public Schools: Paying and Nonpaying Boys, 1861

Public School	Foundationers	
	Nonpaying	Paying
Eton	61	722
Winchester	69	128
Westminster	40	96
Harrow	33	431
Rugby	68	397
Shrewsbury	26	106
Charterhouse	45	71
Total	342 (15%)	1951 (85%)

On the problem of social exclusiveness, the commissioners confirmed what the market had created in the preceding half-century—the continuing removal of middle and lower-class representation from the public schools (Roach 1986:217; Simon 1960:312–16). The differences between paying and scholarship boys at the public schools is made clear in table 12.2 by the tabulation of the commissioners.

The commissioners made a bow toward egalitarianism by condemning the idea of schools solely for the rich. However, they did not see how the poor were to be integrated into the public school. If they were to come in numbers, they would be a drain on the foundation and thus reduce the amount of funds available for teaching. The present arrangements were equally unsatisfactory, since they thought that a separate group of poor students at a school impaired a school's unity of tone and its "atmosphere of social equality; the free and friendly competition in work and companionship in play which are among the most important advantages of public school education" (Great Britain, Parliamentary Papers 1864: vol. XX, 46ff). Furthermore, the foundation students were not getting the kind of education they needed to get on in life and, to top it all off, they were generally looked down upon (Great Britain, Parliamentary Papers 1864: vol. XX, 65, 324). The best way to solve this problem, they thought, was to eliminate the rights of the poor to the foundation funds. They recommended that entrance to the public schools be by open competitive examination. This would effectively eliminate the poor since the public schools had developed examinations that required considerable expense to prepare a student to pass them (Mack 1941:32; Honey 1987:157).

In their support of the prefect system and of athletics, the commissioners revealed their bias and that of their class. They viewed the prefect system as the major means by which students were, at one and the same time, maintained in a disciplined manner while it created and kept

alive a high and sound tone of feeling and opinion, has promoted independence and manliness of character, and has rendered possible that combination of liberty with order and discipline which is among the best characteristics of our great public schools. (Great Britain, Parliamentary Papers 1864: vol. XX, 42–44, 94)

Athletics, they felt, created health and were responsible for forming the "manly virtues" (Mack 1941:41).

Finally, although the commissioners had recognized the need for some reform, they concluded with an extraordinary encomium for the public school:

On the general results of public-school education as an instrument for the training of character, we can speak with much confidence. Like most English institutions—for it deserves to rank among English institutions—it is not framed upon a preconceived plan, but had grown up gradually. . . . The magnitude and freedom of these schools make each of them, for a boy of from 12 to 18, a little world, calculated to give his character an education of the same kind as it is destined afterwards to undergo in the world of business and society. . . . It is not easy to estimate the degree in which the English people are indebted to these schools for the qualities on which they pique themselves most—for their capacity to govern others and control themselves, their aptitude for combining freedom with order, their public spirit, their vigour and manliness of character, their strong but not slavish respect for public opinion, their love of healthy sports and exercise. These schools have been the chief nurseries of our statesmen; on them, and in schools modeled after them, men of all the various classes that make up English society, destined for every profession and career, have been brought up on a footing of social equality, and have contracted the most enduring friendships, and some of the ruling habits, of their lives; and they have had perhaps the largest share in moulding the character of an English gentlemen. (Great Britain, Parliamentary Papers 1864: vol. XX, 44, 56)

The recommendations of the commission became a battleground for the most conservative Tories, who wished no changes, and the Radicals, who wanted much greater direct state regulation and social equality. In the end, the centrists of both parties won, with the help, especially, of Gladstone. Legislation was finally completed in 1868, with the passage of the Public Schools Bill. The bill provided for an executive commission, similar to that in the Oxford and Cambridge reform bills, which had the power to implement the commission recommendations (Mack 1941:45–49, 91–92). The years during and following the debates and passage of the bill saw the institution of both voluntary and commission reforms largely along the lines outlined by the original commission. The Clarendon Commission, in the words of one historian of English education, "created an efficient and entirely segregated system of education for the governing class—one that had no parallel in any other country. The Commissioners had done what was required of them, and had done it well" (Simon 1960:318).

The Clarendon Commission was followed immediately by the creation of the Schools Inquiry Commission (Taunton Commission) in 1864, which had as its charge the examination of education for "those large classes of English society which are comprised between the humblest and the very highest," and to recommend reforms (Simon 1960:318). There had long been dissatisfaction with the endowed schools, primarily over the way in which the endowments were used. Great dissatisfaction had also arisen over the way in which subjects were taught and the claims made by schools that they provided a classical education (Bamford 1967:168–69). The state was seen as having an overriding interest because the endowments, as Parliament saw it, had been made in the nation's interest, not in that of any particular interest (Simon 1960:320). The creation of the commission was preceded by a petition from the Social Science Association asking for a Royal Commission of Inquiry to examine the educational facilities available for the middle classes (Roach 1986:280). It is not clear, however, whether this was anything other than a precipitating cause. The fact that it succeeded so closely on the heels of the Clarendon Commission suggests that political leaders were intent on constructing a system of education for the middle and upper classes that could be directly related to later life chances and careers (Simon 1987:88–93; Honey 1987:151–62). The commissioners represented a wide range of political interests, from the conservatives Northcote and Lyttleton who had served on the Clarendon Commission, to the Liberal leader W. E. Forster and the Radical Edward Baines.

After an exhaustive survey and analysis of the endowed schools, the commission published its findings and recommendations in 1868. Basically, it found that the schools, of which there were about three thousand, had been roughly stratified by an unregulated market and about which parents had very little information. They found that only 791 of these schools gave an education higher than the basic necessities usually reserved for the lower social classes. These fell into what amounted to three grades of schools:

1. Those in which the classical curriculum was taught (218)—of these, however, only 110 (including the Clarendon nine) sought to seriously prepare boys to enter Oxbridge; 152 had students in residence at the two universities in 1868; only 70 or so sent one boy a year on average to Oxford or Cambridge; and less than 50 sent 20 percent or more of their students to Oxbridge (these amounted to approximately 0.2 to 0.3 percent of the population between the ages of 8 to 15 years of age).

2. There were 183 schools which could be categorized as semi-classical; they taught some Latin and maths, modern languages, geography, and some science—these did not prepare students to enter universities (0.3 to 0.5 percent of the group between the ages of 8 to 15 years).

3. Additionally, there were 340 schools (containing 0.6 to 0.8 percent of students in the 8- to 15-years-old age group), that taught some of the subjects of the preceding group in addition to the basics of reading, writing, and arithmetic (Bamford 1967:172, 174–75; Steedman 1987:119).

The remaining 2,218 schools did not do more than teach at the level of the lower-class schools. In effect, this meant there were a very small number of schools that could be viewed as belonging to the class of public schools and a somewhat larger number that could be said to provide education for the lower middle classes.

The commissioners sought to create a three-tier system commensurate with the stratification they had observed. They recommended establishing a grading system which would indicate to parents what to expect from the schools of their choice. Furthermore, they felt strongly that the endowments which had strictly local or narrow purpose had to be eliminated if the funds were to be efficiently used. They recommended a system of open competition with some scholarships which would also be openly competitive (Simon 1960:324–26). They further recommended a structure of redistribution of resources so that there would be approximately equal access to the various levels. To achieve this, they recommended four grade-A level schools for every million of the population; one grade-B school for every 100,000, and a grade-C school for every town. These were to be administered through an administrative system working through the Charity Commission (Bamford 1967:180–81). They also recommended reforms of governance and administration similar to those of the Clarendon Commission as well as curriculum reform. The implementation of recommendations was legislated in 1869 in the Endowed Schools Act, which provided for three Endowed Schools Commissioners with wide powers and instructions to carry out the recommendations of the commission (Simon 1960:328).

With the passage in 1870 of the Education Act, the country now had an educational system the basic outlines of which would remain fundamentally the same for the next seventy-five years. The Education Act provided for the nationwide creation of elementary schools supported by national grants and a local system of school boards with the power to tax, build schools, and hire teachers. These schools were designed for the working classes and for relatively early school leaving (Simon 1960:364–66).

The three education acts of the decade between 1860 and 1870 were the greatest state intrusion on education since the Tudor endowments. Taken together with the Oxford and Cambridge University Acts, they created a stratified system of education in which social hierarchy was translated into educational hierarchy. In turn, this hierarchy came to determine access to the hierarchy of occupations and professions. Throughout this process, the state, in the form of its political leaders in Parliament, but especially in Cabinet (and very much more especially in the form of Gladstone, Lowe, and Northcote, whose hands were seemingly everywhere in this process), self-consciously created a distinctive system of education that linked specific educational experiences to the acquisition of the highest political and professional roles.

The distinctiveness of the system rested on several features. The most evident of these is the formal recognition and institutionalization of the structure of private, namely, "public schools" as social institutions. The Clarendon nine especially were apotheosized and became the defining educational institutions of the nineteenth century (Steedman 1987:113–14). These schools became the conscious object of emulation of all schools with aspirations of attracting the children of the upper and middle classes.

Perhaps equally important was the degree to which this structure of education was left to private and autonomous regulation. Although the state imposed reforms on the endowed schools, they were not incorporated into any state-dominated administrative structure. They were, thus, to a very considerable degree, left to regulate themselves through such organizations as the Headmasters Conference, organized in 1869 for just that purpose (Simon 1987:102). This attitude reinforced the idea of the public schools as institutions and not simply as educational businesses.

The social exclusiveness of the system as it emerged in 1870 is certainly one its most singular characteristics. The state legally recognized the social exclusiveness of the endowed schools and agreed to reinforce the already existing tendency to separate both schools and curriculum in terms of social class. The curriculum of these schools bore no direct relationship to the careers to which they were linked—the high professions and political leadership. Rather, the system revolved around the process of education rather than its content. This process sought to build and certify the character, safeness, and reliability of the individual (Honey 1987:161). These characteristics transformed the gentleman of birth into the gentleman of service by providing an education which internalized a body of common norms and ethics with regard to social relations.

These norms stressed the obligation of individuals to serve in the public interest. In return, they would receive the high status formerly accorded to high birth. It was a "process of character-building whose stigmata assured lifelong membership in an identifiable and mutually supportive elite" (Honey 1987:161). In short, it created a system of social accountability that eliminated the need for organizational systems of rules to enforce individual obedience to organizational norms. Moreover, it was a structure reinforced by membership in a network of "old boys" (Honey 1977:153–57). In the years that followed, the linkages created by the reforms became increasingly evident. The setting of classical examinations for entrance into the highest level of public schools geared them not only to high social and economic status but also to preparation to take the same type of classically oriented entrance examinations to Oxbridge.

Access to these schools which provided access to Oxbridge became extremely narrow. Thus, although the commissioners in 1868 had listed 152 schools as having students at Oxbridge, by 1879 the commissioners had designated only 60 endowed schools as first- or A-grade schools (Steedman

1987:119). The commissioners followed, in these years, a self-conscious policy of concentrating existing resources in a smaller number of schools which
could compete with the Clarendon nine at a reasonable cost so as to enable
middle-class children a chance at entering Oxbridge (Steedman 1987:119).
In so doing, they made possible the linkage of approximately sixty schools
plus the Clarendon nine to Oxbridge education. Thus, in 1895, access to
Oxford and Cambridge looked as shown in table 12.3.

Table 12.3 Previous Places of Education of Undergraduates
and Scholarships Awarded*—1898

	Oxford	Cambridge	Durham	Victoria (Manchester, Leeds, Liverpool)
Clarendon "7"	469/125	266/66	0/0	18/1
	24.0/21.0	14.0/10.6	0/0	2.0/0.4
Headmasters Conference	866/434	838/366	28/12	220/37
	44.0/74.0	43.5/59.0	23.7/41.4	26.3/16.0
Non HMC	313/11	391/135	33/10	403/105
	16.0/0.2	20.5/22.0	28.0/34.5	57.6/45.0
Private Tuition	292/12	354/26	52/7	71/12
	15.0/2.0	18.6/4.0	44.0/24.0	8.5/5.0
Training College	6/0	15/3	1/0	2/2
	0.3/0	0.7/0.5	0.8/0	0.2/0.8
Technical School	5/0	18/10	0/0	44/25
	0.2/0	0.9/0.16	0/0	5.3/11.0
Pupil Teacher Center	4/2	15/8	0/0	9/8
	0.2/0.3	0.8/1.3	0/0	1.0/3.5
Public Elementary School	9/3	10/6	4/0	71/43
	0.5/0.5	0.5/1.0	3.4/0	8.5/18.5

*Number of Students/Number of Scholarship and Percentages of same.
Source: Lowe 1987, 171.

Table 12.4 Harrow, Winchester, and Manchester Student Educational Careers, 1878–87

	Oxford	Cambridge	London	Red Brick	Technical	Scotland/ Ireland
Winchester	348	139	10	4	19	6
Harrow	258	356	6	2	3	12
Manchester	93	44	?	199	na	na
Total	606	495	16	6	21	18

Source: Bamford 1967, 264.

As the table indicates, the Clarendon plus fifty or so Headmasters Conference (HMC) schools accounted for 68 percent of Oxford undergraduates and 95 percent of scholarships at Oxford; for 58 percent of Cambridge undergraduates and 70 percent of scholarships; 24 percent of Durham undergrads and 41 percent of scholarships; 28 percent of Victoria undergraduates and 16 percent of scholarships. If all private schooling is pooled, it accounts for 98.8 percent of Oxford students and 97 percent of scholarships; 97 percent and 95 percent, respectively, at Cambridge; 96 percent and 100 percent respectively at Durham; and 85 percent and 66 percent respectively at Victoria. It is clear that only attendance at one of only sixty or so schools after 1870 was likely to make attendance or a scholarship at Oxbridge more than just a possibility.

This pattern is revealed rather starkly if the educational careers of students going on from Harrow and Winchester are compared with those from Manchester Grammar School for the years between 1878 and 1887 (see table 12.4). Since the higher professions continued to favor Oxbridge training as the basis for their certification processes throughout the late nineteenth and early twentieth century, the links between the public school/Oxbridge/higher professions were strengthened powerfully by the educational reforms of the period from 1855 to 1870.

Viewed in terms of civil-service rationalization, the educational reforms of the period between the Northcote-Trevelyan Report and the Order in Council of 1870 provided the basis on which the accountability of senior civil servants could rest. The individual came to possess an internalized set of norms governing behavior and relationships between equals and clients. These norms, however, did not arise out of any perception that professional knowledge required a set of ethical rules which guided behavior and decision making. There were rules which guided decisions about technical matters in medicine and law, for example, but these had no implications for guiding the individual in determining his relationships to clients, patients, colleagues, or subjects. Nor did technical knowledge provide the individual with the general reasoning faculties necessary for decision making in those vast areas where technical expertise was the equivalent of guessing. In this part of the educational system, then—that part with the highest prestige—control of the technical substance of a profession was separated from and subordinated to the social-ethical training individuals received in their career through public school and Oxbridge.

The separation of training in ethical norms and general reasoning faculties from the technical aspects of a profession allowed the former to be used and viewed as a universally valid mode of training for the higher professions. By stressing training in character and reasoning as the prerequisites to professional training, the educational system was able to postpone the emergence of opportunity costs for students. Since the public school-Oxbridge training was all but a formal requirement for entrance into all the higher professions (barrister, consulting physician, cleric, and, after 1870, civil servant), decisions about future careers could be postponed until one had taken a university degree.

This, however, was balanced against the high cost of the educational career. After the reforms of 1868–69, as noted, the entrance to public schools was based on competitive examinations which stressed the classics. This meant extensive preparation prior to entrance to a public school. The cost of the entire educational career was far more than any member of the working or lower middle classes would generally be able to afford. Thus, while opportunity costs were reduced, the investment the system required was one which created great competition for high-income, high-prestige occupations once education was completed. The creation of new professions would thus have to center on the necessity of public school-Oxbridge education plus the possibility of high prestige and income (Reader 1966:44–51).

Just as important was the point that the acquisition of these characteristics was highly limited to a narrow range of social class. So long as accountability and predictability of behavior were the functions of a narrowly accessible, socially determined educational experience, the individual's accountability and predictability would be a function of social rather than organizational life. The individual would carry with him the rules for behavior and the faculties required to make decisions, and he would share these with men who occupied the great majority of positions in the higher professions and in political leadership. State intervention in education during the mid-nineteenth century assured the social homogeneity of the higher professions and of political leadership.[3]

By 1870, the pursuit by political leaders of both parties of administrative, social, and political coherence had produced profound changes. The pursuit of administrative coherence and integration had resulted in the emergence of the Cabinet as England's "efficient secret." Through the instrument of the

---

3. This can be seen in the degree to which public school and Oxbridge came to be powerful elements of British elites in the late nineteenth and throughout much of the twentieth centuries. Thus, in 1906 over 38 percent of MPs had gone to a public school, while 36 percent had gone to Oxbridge (Guttsman 1963:90). Between 1868 and 1955, over 56 percent of cabinet ministers had gone to a public school (Guttsman 1963:99), while between 1886 and 1916, of the 101 cabinet ministers, 68 or 67 percent had gone to a public school, and in the same period over 70 percent had gone to Oxbridge (Guttsman 1963:102–3). During the period between 1868 and 1945, two-thirds of the parliamentary under-secretaries (junior ministers) had a public school education (Guttsman 1963:108).

Treasury, the Cabinet had now become, in place of a sprawling and argumentative Parliament, both the head of the executive and legislative branches of government. Surely, department heads continued to have no small degree of autonomy and sought on numerous occasions to exercise it (Mackintosh 1977:160–62). Nevertheless, their range of discretion had been narrowed greatly by the growth of Treasury control over audit and personnel. They still had powers of patronage, but these too were in the process of being narrowed by the incremental expansion of Treasury powers over the civil service. The Cabinet was increasingly less a mere collection of political or putative political leaders seeking to maintain their political networks and more a coherent organization in which individual interests were restrained.

The pursuit of political coherence had brought political leaders, especially Gladstone and Disraeli, to attempt the elimination of peripheral parliamentary forces and forge two coherent parties. In this contestation, reform became the means by which political leaders sought to define party and party leadership. Gladstone was vehement in his view of reform as the engine of politics, as Matthew has pointed out:

This [Gladstone's argument] was therefore not merely the Pitt-Peel argument that there were reforms to be done and abuses to be remedied, but a much more political argument that it was politically essential that reforms should persistently be seen to be done, for "it is rapid growth in the body politic that renders stereotyped law intolerable". "Public opinion," Gladstone argued, "is disposed to view with great favour all active and efficient government." . . . For Gladstone, therefore, big bills and big budgets represented a means of regular renewal of the legitimacy of Parliament and the political system. (1986:114)

The result was the Reform Act of 1867, which doubled the electorate and introduced large numbers of the working classes to the franchise. The politics of the reform had helped to define the parties and clarify the nature of party leadership. Uncertainties nevertheless remained. True, backbencher independence had been drastically curbed in the preceding three decades by party leaders sitting in Cabinet. Now, creation of a large new franchise produced a new element of uncertainty for parliamentary candidates. The reform had created constituencies which could no longer be easily managed by the local social networks of incumbent or hopeful MP candidates. This tended to further undermine the independence of backbenchers. They began to turn increasingly to their parliamentary leaders sitting in Cabinet to create legislation which would help their incumbency or election (Matthew 1986:173–74). All of this would seem to have strengthened the role of political party leaders and reduced uncertainty about their status.

To some degree this was true. The decline of backbencher independence certainly reduced their capacity for making mischief within a party. This was especially true of the Liberals whose fragile coalition of the late fifties and early sixties gave way to a more stable leadership by Gladstone and Russell, and then to Gladstone alone by the time of the reforms of 1867. The expansion of executive power and the franchise strengthened political leaders internally vis-à-vis backbenchers (Pugh 1982:18–19; Berrington 1968:341–43). Nevertheless, backbencher resistance to Cabinet domination continued, and governments in the 1860s and 1870s continued to suffer defeats where backbencher feelings were strong (Mackintosh 1977:178–80). Furthermore, the price for increased party Cabinet executive power was not small.

The growth of executive power and of the franchise exposed political leaders to new underlying uncertainties. If the reformed franchise drove backbenchers increasingly into the arms of party leaders cum executives, it also produced a much greater responsibility for party power on the leaders. The augmented franchise represented true uncertainty. In 1867, no one knew what the outcome of an election based on the new franchise would be. The election of 1868 revealed to both parties the necessity of finding new ways to organize voters. What these were to be was not yet clear. The Conservatives began to grope for new methods of organizing locally and to some extent nationally (Hanham 1959:356–59).

The restructuring of constituencies led to new uncertainties in local politics. These uncertainties would be met, in the 1870s and 1880s, with experimentation in local political organization (especially by the Liberals after their defeat in 1874), which would lead to the development of stronger national parties. But in 1867–68, it was not at all clear how the new constituencies should be organized to render them predictable. Thus, the Liberals were astonished at their major defeat at the hands of the Tories in 1874. The expansion of the franchise presented new and significant uncertainties for party leaders. They had to meet the challenge of providing the basis for party victories or face a loss of legitimacy with backbenchers for their claims to expanded power.

These uncertainties were heightened by the ambiguities surrounding the politics of patronage. Not yet envisioning party organization as the means of organizing voters and thus a well-disciplined parliamentary party, many party leaders and backbenchers were loath to abandon patronage. Failure to do so, however, only maintained old uncertainties. Patronage continued to be a source of friction for backbenchers. They had never had a sufficient supply to meet the demand, and now with an expanded franchise they had to meet a larger demand. Fulfillment of such demands meant a weakened central executive; weakened in the sense of being unable to exert full control over both the legislative and administrative process. An expanded franchise and continued reliance on patronage only enhanced the apprehension of political leaders about their ability to maintain the accountability of civil servants. Balanced against this was the integration of education to social status, which the educational reforms of the 1860s had accomplished so neatly. After 1870, it would be increasingly difficult to find men of high social status without the requisite prep school/public school/Oxbridge education. The only obstacle to making the civil service systematically a preserve of the new structure of education and its concomitant social status was patronage, and this was to be removed by the Orders in Council of 1870–71.

The Orders in Council of 1870–71

The Orders in Council of 4 June 1870 and of 19 August 1871 provided the basic elements of the structure of the modern English Civil Service. The two orders established the following precepts and conditions:

1. The Treasury, along with the Civil Service Commissioners, would serve as the arbiters of Civil Service regulation and superintendence. The specifics of recruitment might be set by the commissioners, but they now had to have the approval of the Treasury.

2. Any person engaged in any civil service capacity had to be examined by the Civil Service Commissioners and be granted a certificate of qualification before they could be appointed. The only exceptions to this rule were spelled out in clauses VII and VIII of the Order in Council of 1870.

3. Exceptions to the general requirement of examinations could be granted only if the knowledge and skills necessary for carrying out the functions of a specific office were professional in character or very rare and were thought to be so by both the department and the Treasury. Both the department and the Treasury had to agree that the examination was to be dispensed with in each case. The appointee also had to satisfy the commissioners as to his skills in order to receive a certificate of qualification. The minister's discretion over appointments to his department were thus narrowed very considerably over his previous capacity.

4. General exemptions were established by Order in Council or Treasury approval. Thus the Order included a Schedule [B] which listed categories exempt from regulation: appointments directly from the Crown, or those declared professional by the Treasury under the fourth clause of the Superannuation Act of 1859 dealing with the granting of pensions for those possessing professional skills; those appointments which were only slightly related to Civil Service functions, such as office cleaners, porters, and servants; appointments filled normally by promotion within departments.

5. Two distinct career routes determined by the creation of two types of examination beyond the qualifying examination in handwriting, arithmetic, English composition, and orthography were created: (a) examinations under Regulation I, which were intended to test individuals for the ability to carry out intellectual work—these included English composition; history of England; language, literature, and history of Greece, Rome, France, Germany, and Italy; mathematics; natural science; moral science; jurisprudence; and political economy, with the highest number of points going to the classical subjects and the least to the modern; and (b) examinations under regulation II were designed to test people for appointment to those positions defined as mechanical or routine—the subjects included handwriting, orthography, arithmetic, copying manuscripts, indexing and docketing, writing summaries, English composition, geography, English history, and bookkeeping. Major distinctions were made between these two categories with regard to salary.

6. A probationary period of six months was made uniform for the various departments. The conditions and passage from probation to permanent appointment were, under the Order of 1871, placed completely in the hands of the department head.

7. Appointment of temporary clerks (writers) was removed from the discretion of the department head and placed under the certification rules of the Orders of 1870 and 1871. (Great Britain, Civil Service Commissioners 1872:1–9, 12–16; Wright 1969:85–109)

These rules and precepts had two institutional thrusts. The first was the expansion of Treasury control over the civil service and its recruitment and promotion process. As a result of the reforms of the preceding fifteen years, in which Gladstone had played a major role, the Treasury had come to control the establishment of positions, and through its control of pensions, it came to have some say in appointment procedures. With the Orders of 1870–71, the Treasury came to have direct control over most of the appointment process. The consequence of this expanded influence was a decrease in the autonomy of departments and department heads. Much of the discretion once held by department heads now rested statutorily in the hands of the Treasury and, to a lesser extent, the Civil Service Commission. Although adherence to open competition by departments had been made voluntary so as to make it more palatable to the Cabinet, all the major departments, with the exception of the Home (which accepted in 1873) and Foreign Office, finally agreed to accept the principle (Winter 1976:263; Wright 1969:95–96). The Treasury and, by extension, the Cabinet gained considerably by this decline of departmental autonomy (Wright 1969:106).

While patronage was not completely wiped out by this development, only a relatively small number of positions were left to the Treasury Whips to use as incentives. What remained was mostly in the field services—the Post Office and Customs—and most of these were at the lower level (Richards 1963:56). Patronage in these departments continued until the end of the century. With the exception of some senior professional officials, such as the Examiners in the Board of Education, patronage ceased to be the means of recruitment to positions of the central ministries (Richards 1963:58–59).

The second major institutional consequence of the reforms of 1870–71 was the creation of three distinct career tracks. The establishment of two types of examination was designed to recruit individuals for two levels of official appointments with distinctively different levels of salary. Those recruited under Regulation I were viewed as having access to the highest posts within the civil establishment. Recruitment under Regulation II, on the other hand, meant, at best, that an individual would rise to only the highest level of routine administrative work. The Orders of 1870–71 did not expressly prohibit promotion of Regulation II men to positions which normally required Regulation I examinees. But this loophole was closed in 1876 as a consequence of the Playfair Commission's Report on the Civil Service of the preceding year. The Order in Council of 1876 prohibited the promotion of individuals recruited under Regulation II to positions which would normally require passage of Regulation I examinations (Richards 1963:55).

The Order of 1876 also acted on another Playfair recommendation by establishing a formal organizational link between the level of examination and specific personnel category. Those who entered the service via the Regulation II examination were from then on to make up the category labeled the Lower Division (Cohen 1941:135). This provided a basic uniform category to which individuals could be assigned, thus avoiding the problems of determining whether someone held a Regulation I or II position and should be paid and promoted accordingly. The boundaries between the Lower Division and what was later to be known as the Higher Division were reinforced by the Order's requirement that in the future any promotion from the Lower Division to the Higher depended on the recommendation of head of the department, approval of the Treasury, at least ten years of service, and a certificate of qualification from the Civil Service Commission (Richards 1963:55).

The orders, in combination with the Superannuation Act of 1859, established the basis of a third career track with significantly different features from the others. The regulations of these several orders and act carved out a professional career track in addition to the two administrative careers. This track was singular in that recruitment took place outside of any standard examination system. Rather, specific examinations for technical positions or the presentation of certification of technical education and/or experience were the means of determining eligibility. The latter were very similar to the "gathered in" examinations that were used in the early decades of the American rationalized system. This pattern of recruitment created a marked distinction between technical officers and administrative officers. The boundary between these two roles became even more difficult to breach than that between the two administrative divisions. As late as the 1960s, the organizational place of professional and technical staff continued to be viewed as completely outside the sphere of administration (Great Britain, Fulton Committee 1968: 3[2], 458–59). This meant that professional and technical staff had relatively low status and, more significantly, they had little in the way of a career structure, since promotion to policy-making positions was out of the question.

The final significant consequence of the reforms was the linkage of social status, education, and senior-level civil service appointments. The creation of the three-track career system determined by types of education, which had, by 1870, become associated with social class, produced a hierarchical profession that mirrored the structure of the other professions. Just as law had barristers and solicitors, and medicine had physicians and surgeons, the civil service, by virtue of almost identical socially stratified educational determinants, also came to have distinctions between higher and lower status. The Higher and Lower or, as they later were known, Administrative and Executive classes mirrored the status distinctions in the other professions. Oxbridge captured the upper civil service by the simple mechanism of setting an examination which fitted their graduates like a custom-made suit of clothes, thus providing almost the whole supply of students who could pass the examinations under Regulation I. In so doing, the formulators of the new structure narrowed access to the highest career roles to a very small group of people whose economic status made it possible to move through the prep school/public school/Oxbridge sequence.

By 1876, all of the basic elements of the English modern rationalized civil service career structure had come into existence. Three distinct career structures had been established. Eligibility for each had been relatively clearly defined. Entrance had been both qualitatively and quantitatively defined and thus rendered considerably more predictable in a general sense than patronage. Divisions of personnel into defined categories created relative predictability about possible movement through a series of offices. Career-leaving was well specified and rewarded in a highly predictable manner. Several other aspects of this structure are noteworthy: the absence of well-defined personnel categories within the broader administrative divisions allowed department heads continued wide discretion in promotion and thus career tracks; the relegation of technical and professional appointments to a separate category meant that administrative expertise was a function of work experience rather than specialized training; the distinction between "intellectual" and "mechanical" administration meant that civil service professionalism, like that of law and medicine, required a liberal or generalist education that emphasized social norms and values and faculties of thought.

While it is evident that the foundations of the modern civil service were put in place between 1870 and 1876, it is not immediately clear why it occurred at this juncture. There was no public outcry about the nature of patronage. There was, it is true, the usual carping about government economy and efficiency, but its effects had been muted by its constancy. Economy and efficiency had been the motto of the opposition since the late eighteenth century. There was no visible connection between economy of operation and the creation of a relatively complex hierarchical structure which now came into existence. If anything, the new structure was more costly, since its formulators intended to raise salaries of those recruited through Regulation I and seemingly did so (Winter 1976:264; M. Wright 1969:239).

To a substantial degree, the timing must be laid to the functionality of these innovations for political leaders. The new conditions regulating recruitment and appointment went a long way toward solving a number of irritating and obstructive problems. The removal of central government appointments from patronage excised the particularly difficult problem of high demand and low supply. Placing these offices outside of personal jurisdictions eliminated conflicts and discontents over the allocation of patronage. The new regulations further limited the discretion and autonomy of department heads and departments and increased the power of the Treasury and the executive significantly. At the same time, backbencher independence received further constraint, increasing once again the stability of party leaders in their positions.

Even more important, the new structure provided for limitation of access to senior civil service posts to men whose education from childhood to manhood was, by 1870, remarkably uniform and becoming even more so. This resolved the problem of accountability of civil servants whose appointments by custom, if not by contract, were for an entire career ending only with retirement and pension. If this arrangement ensured an autonomous organization relatively impermeable to outside pressures, it also reassured political leaders because it elevated to senior positions men who shared their social norms and values and whose behavior was consummately predictable. The possibility of "Prussianization"—the civil service as an autonomous caste— was reduced to the improbable by the shared socialization and internalization of public school norms.

Perhaps equally important was the way in which the integrating and centralizing aspects of civil service reform gave political leaders greater capacity to deal with the problems produced by franchise expansion. A doubling of the franchise presented political leaders with the prospect of an unpredictable electorate. Absent any coherent, disciplined body of followers who could organize voters, political leaders such as Gladstone and Disraeli saw in a powerful executive the means by which they might appeal directly to constituencies. By continually proposing a stream of major legislation that would be implemented by a well-subordinated civil service, political leaders saw the possibility of reducing the fickleness of voters.

Finally, selection and appointment on the basis of "objective" criteria— examination of the depth of knowledge—removed the last vestiges of criticism aimed at the aristocratic use of politics for private interest. The use of examinations lent credence to claims made about merit determining access to high civil service office. Merit was the key word in smoothing out the disparities of class and legitimizing the inequalities of stratification of opportunities. By creating systematic career structures governed by rules stressing merit, political leaders were able to present the civil service as a truly public institution serving the public interest. That party leaders shared the same education seemed to suggest that they too were constrained to act in the public interest despite their allegiance to party. The developments of the preceding decade had thus made 1870 a propitious time for civil service reform. The reforms in education, administration, and franchise produced by political leaders engendered both problems and opportunities. The response to these was the reformation of the civil service recruitment, appointment, and career structure; it was a response framed by its functionality for the stability of political leadership.

The degree to which this was a process framed and activated by political leadership is reflected in the very manner in which the reforms were carried through by two major political actors, Gladstone and Lowe. Gladstone had played a major role in every major reform from 1855 to 1870. He was vastly different from Palmerston, who had stayed in office largely because he avoided any legislation which would jeopardize the coalitional government and party which he led. It is safe to say that Gladstone viewed the constant generation of major legislation as the means by which party and political leaders could appeal to constituencies without depending on backbenchers. Thus, as early as 1856, writing anonymously for the *Quarterly Review* he argued that:

[w]hile the electioneering gear continues to be much in the same working order as it was, it is plain that public opinion has for many years been forming itself both broad and deep—broader in some respects and deeper too than the limits of party organisation. This public opinion is considerably adverse to speculation or constitutional changes, but it is disposed to view with favour all active and

efficient government, comparatively careless from which party such a boon to the country may proceed. . . . *That* one of the two great parties, we venture to predict, will acquire the predominance in Parliament and in the country, which succeeds in impressing the public mind with the belief that it is most deeply and earnestly impressed with the right (a right not the less real because indeterminate) of the people to what is called good government, and that it is also most largely gifted with qualities necessary to enable it to satisfy that right and the reasonable desires which attend it. (1856:567; see Matthew 1986:105fn)

Gladstone was in many respects an *étatist* who viewed Parliament, but especially the Cabinet, as the necessary source of legislation which would enhance utilitarian and commonsensical economic and social development (Matthew 1986:67, 119). As Chancellor of the Exchequer from December 1852 to February 1855, and from June 1859 to July 1866, Gladstone followed, as we have seen, a consistent and conscious policy of expanding the control of the Treasury over administration and strengthening the executive. In this Gladstone emerged as "a new kind of executive politician" (Matthew 1986:110–11, 114–17, 135).

In the face of an expanding franchise, Gladstone, without a constituency base of his own in the 1860s and lacking a party organization, prepared himself for the inevitable expansion of franchise and his political future by transforming himself into a national politician. He set out on a constant round of travel and speechmaking and created for himself a national reputation, with a national following, by which he was to maintain his leadership of the Liberal Party (Matthew 1986:128–48). Upon his accession to the premiership after the election of 1868, he was faced with a set of uncertainties: how to manage a new large enfranchised constituency that, to the surprise of many, had thrown out the party which had created the expansion; how to keep the backbenchers in line; how to proceed with the kind of legislation he thought necessary to attract the support of voters to him and to his party (Matthew 1986:171–74). Gladstone thus looked to where he might find ways to strengthen the executive and undermine backbencher independence.

He was joined in this by Robert Lowe, who became Gladstone's Chancellor of the Exchequer. Lowe had been a principal liberal opponent of franchise reform. He viewed an expanded franchise as an exercise in the destruction of parliamentary government (Winter 1976:195–241). The obverse side to Lowe's opposition to expanded franchise was a firm commitment to meritocracy.

It appears to me, that nothing can be more manifest, looking to the peculiar nature of the working classes, than in passing a Bill such as is now proposed, you take away the principal power from property and intellect, and give it to the multitude who live on weekly wages. (as quoted in Sylvester 1974:27)

Lowe's fear of how an unmanageable mass franchise might undermine government by those who merited power by force of their intellect expressed itself clearly in an address to the Philosophical Institution of Edinburgh on 1 November 1867, several months after the passage of the Reform Act (Representation of the People Act) of 1867:

I have said that I am most anxious to educate the lower classes of this country, in order to qualify them for that power that has passed, and perhaps will pass in greater degree, into their hands. I am also anxious to educate, in a manner very different from the present, the higher classes of this country, and also for a political reason. The time has gone past evidently when the higher classes can hope by any direct influence, either of property or coercion of any kind, to direct the course of public affairs. Power has passed out of their hands, and what they do must be done by the influence of superior education and superior cultivation: by the influence of mind over mind—'the sign and Signet of the Almighty to command', which never fails being recognized where ever it is truly tested. . . . The lower classes ought to be educated to discharge the duties cast upon them. They should also be educated that they may appreciate and defer to a higher cultivation when they meet it; and the higher classes ought to be educated in a very different manner, in order that they may exhibit to the lower classes that higher education to which, if it were shown to them, they would bow down and defer. (as quoted in Sylvester 1974:34–35)

Gladstone, too, was not without his belief in government through a Coleridgean clerisy. However, the elimination of patronage and reform of the civil service was not the highest item on his list of priorities in 1869. Rather it was Lowe, clearly unsettled by the uncertainties raised by franchise expansion, who sought to dissolve the voter-MP-patronage appointment link in a definitive manner. Lowe brought the matter to the Cabinet in June 1869, where it was shunted aside by sending it to an *ad hoc* Cabinet committee, most of whom opposed the whole idea of open competitive examinations (M. Wright 1969:80). Lowe refused to let go and wrote to Gladstone asking for help in pushing the matter (Winter 1976:263). Gladstone agreed, but suggested that instead of demanding the examinations be made compulsory across the board, the departments should be allowed the right to modify the scheme or withdraw from the arrangement (M. Wright 1969:81). The Cabinet accepted this formulation and gave Lowe permission to circularize the departments for their views. Lowe immediately put the Treasury on open competition and then proceeded to use the Treasury influence to get all the other departments except Home and Foreign Affairs to agree (M. Wright 1969:81–82). Following the route used for the creation of the Civil Service Commission in 1855, Lowe and his immediate colleague at the Treasury, R. R. W. Lingen, drew up the Order in Council which the Cabinet approved on 25 May 1870. In all of this, little had been heard from either public opinion or Parliament; the pressure for the reform of the Civil Service had been internal to the political process.

Completion of the Rationalized Structure: 1876–1900

The Orders in Council of the 1870s were the watershed of the rationalization of the bureaucratic structure. With the establishment of open competitive examinations for entry into both levels of the service, patronage became a negligible factor in recruitment and appointment. The accompanying expansion of Treasury authority produced a transformation that signaled a shift from the principle of parliamentary control of administration to Cabinet executive/Treasury control of administration (M. Wright 1969:349; Chester 1981:367–71; Roseveare 1969:183–85).[4] Deprived of patronage, parliamentary parties were now forced to turn to constructing party organization in order to finally subjugate the backbencher to party discipline. The development of party as a means of organizing voters in the last quarter of the century made it possible for political leaders to gain control over the nomination of candidates. The elimination of patronage thus resulted in the rationalization of party politics.

Although the reforms resolved a number of problems for political leaders, they also set in motion a number of organizational problems. For the remainder of the century, the major impetus underlying further changes in the structure of the civil service were the various problems raised by the transformation of the civil service role, especially the upper civil service. The creation of functional divisions by means of recruitment path produced several problems over the succeeding years. The examinations made it possible to create the Lower Division under the assumption that time would produce a uniformly trained class of clerks who could be easily transferred from department to department by virtue of their limitation to "mechanical" work.

This structure was seen also as providing barriers to entry into the levels of office-holding seen as requiring a different and more extensive education.

4. On 30 January 1900, the prime minister, Lord Salisbury, in House of Commons debate characterized the transformation of the Treasury in the following fashion:

"The Treasury has obtained a position in regard to the rest of the departments of the Government that the House of Commons obtained at the time of the Stuart dynasty. It has the power of the purse, and by exercising the power of the purse it claims a voice in all decisions of administrative authority and policy" (Roseveare 1969:183).

This quote is taken from a speech that was critical and far from complimentary. Salisbury had forgotten, if he ever knew, that much of the Treasury's power had come through the activities of his predecessors in office.

In part, this is reflected in the manner in which, despite the recommendations of the Ridley Commission of 1886–90, the Treasury and the Cabinet refused, until the end of the century, to specify Regulation or Class I examinees as a specific class, that is, the Higher Division (Great Britain, Fulton Committee 1968: vol. 3(2), 438). Leaving the higher examination candidates and professionals without divisional definition allowed department heads a degree of discretion in their choice of candidates for senior-level office and for promotion. Failure to provide for an all-service functional division with rules governing selection, as in the case of the Lower Division, also maintained the autonomy of departments and departmental careers.

This arrangement had several noticeable results. The establishment of a more or less uniform all-service division characterized by "mechanical" work led to the evolution of the Civil Service Supply Association, which had emerged in the late 1860s as an association of lower-division clerks that numbered three thousand by 1888 (Cohen 1941:141). The energy for association stemmed primarily from the discrepancy between functional division of careers and the allocation of duties. On the one hand, there continued to be large numbers of senior clerks who were often assigned "mechanical" work to keep them busy, while on the other hand, department heads sought to utilize less costly lower-division clerks to perform higher-level functions. These disparities led the lower-division clerks to demand more equitable pay arrangements. The year 1886 was the first year in which the promotion clause of the Order in Council of 1876 would allow promotion from the Lower Division to the Higher Division. When this was postponed by the Treasury until 1890 in view of their desire to create a new royal commission, irritation and agitation among the lower-division clerks increased. In the following year, they organized a rally and persuaded some two hundred MPs to attend (Great Britain, Fulton Committee 1968: vol. 3(2), 434). All of this activity caused enough concern for the Treasury to ask for the formation of a royal commission. On 20 September 1886, the commission was created under the chairmanship of the Conservative MP, Sir Matthew W. Ridley.

The recommendations of the Ridley Commission aimed at resolving the above problems in two ways. First, it sought to redraw the lines between the higher and lower divisions of the service by arguing that the original boundaries had been drawn too low. The commission recommended that the higher-division offices be restricted to a much smaller number of positions. By reducing the number of positions in the upper division, the problem of disparities would largely disappear. By the same token, the barriers between lower and upper offices would be raised considerably. In keeping with this direction, the commission went on to recommend that the examinations for higher-division offices be reorganized so as to allow individuals fewer options in the subjects on which they might be examined. The aim here was to make passage of the examination depend on a deeper knowledge of a few subjects rather than a thin knowledge of a great many. This seemed to be aimed at bringing the examinations closer to Oxbridge classical curricula. Finally, in regard to the upper division, the commission recommended the formal establishment of an upper division with the title of First Division. The commission also recommended a name change for the lower division, to Second Division. Higher salary ranges for the lower division were also recommended, and the commission reaffirmed the policy of promotion both within the division and between divisions on the basis of merit, thus continuing to allow department heads considerable discretion. The commission also recommended the retention of the ten-year service rule before promotion from the Second to First Divisions (Moses 1914 [1966]:162–75).

The second approach the commission sought to employ in resolving internal agitation and discontent was to recommend greater centralization of authority in the hands of the Treasury. By giving the Treasury the power to set uniform regulations for offices throughout the service and the administrative means of handling various disputes, the commission hoped to produce an integrated structure (Great Britain, MacDonnell Commission, Fourth Report 1914:17).

Two Orders in Council, 21 March and 15 August 1890, established most of the commission's recommendations. The first order dealt with the now renamed Second Division and the second order dealt with "Officers drawing salaries or placed on scales of salaries in excess of that of the Second Division" (Great Britain, MacDonnell Commission, Fourth Report 1914:18). There was, thus, no formal creation of a First Division and, as a consequence, no uniform regulation of those in the higher salary range. Access to this higher level was made more difficult by reorganization of the examinations to coincide more closely with Oxbridge degrees. In this respect, the higher division of the civil service continued to escape uniform central direction and regulation. Department heads continued to have relatively wide discretion in choice of appointments and promotion among those who passed either the Class I examinations or scrutinization of professional/technical qualifications (Great Britain, MacDonnell Commission, Fourth Report 1914:18). An administrative Consultative Committee to harmonize and integrate the departments to Treasury authority was created but over the next decade failed to achieve any significant changes. Departments continued to resist Treasury authority wherever they could (Roseveare 1969:203–4).

Indeed, from what followed in the next several decades, one can conclude that the resistance to Treasury domination and to formally defining the upper civil service was the consequence of departmental resistance to the further erosion of ministerial authority and departmental autonomy. The problems of a decentralized and ill-defined senior civil service continued to plague both the executive and departments. Especially difficult was the mixing of two career structures—those who entered via Class I examinations and those who entered by professional or technical examinations (intermediate examinations). Although informally the two were kept distinct by the failure to provide administrative promotion to professional/technical appointments, there was, nevertheless, no formal means to keep the two tracks distinct.

The disparity between formal and informal career structure created increasing discontent among the professional/technical officers (Cohen 1941:168–69). Despite this, resistance to uniform centralized regulation of the senior civil service continued. It is no coincidence that formal definition of the senior service came with the imposition of direct Treasury control. Following the hiatus of rationalization during World War I, the Cabinet agreed, in 1919, to the circularization of a Treasury minute that established the Permanent Secretary to the Treasury as the Permanent Head of the Civil Service who would advise the prime minister on civil service appointments. This was followed by another Treasury circular that established the rule that the prime minister's consent was required for the appointment or removal of permanent secretaries, deputy secretaries, principal officers, and principal financial officers (Great Britain, Fulton Committee 1968: vol. 3[2], 447). This centralized authority over the most senior departmental offices in the hands of the executive, thereby diminishing the authority of departmental ministers.

In the same year the Re-organisation [sic] Committee of the new Civil Service National Whitley Council, which contained representatives of senior departmental as well as staff interests, recommended that the civil service should have four basic functional classifications: (1) a writing assistant class for simple mechanical work; (2) a clerical class for more complex mechanical work; (3) an executive class to perform "the higher work of the supply and accounting Departments, and other executive or specialist branches of the Civil Service"; and (4) an administrative class whose work was "concerned with the formation of policy, with the coordination and improvement of Government machinery and with the general administration and control of the Departments of the Public Service" (Great Britain, Fulton Committee 1968: vol. 3[2], 449).

Once again the upper civil service was singled out as requiring such high standards of qualification that personnel should be selected by recruitment through a career pattern of examination and internal promotion (Great Britain, Fulton Committee 1968: vol. 3[2], 449). The acceptance of these recommendations closed the chapter on the institutionalization of the civil service and especially of the upper service. The establishment of the administrative class was the final conclusion of the Treasury's and of civil servant's desire for greater uniformity within the service. These changes, however, only fulfilled the logic of the basic conformation of the civil service structure created in the early 1870s. The degree to which this was the case can be seen in a variety of ways. The decade of the 1870s was clearly a dividing point with regard to educational backgrounds of those entering the upper division of the civil service. Thus, for example, the educational patterns of those who held positions at the senior administrative level (Establishment, upper division, first division clerks, and above) in the Home Office between 1848 and 1914 appear in table 12.5. In the pre-1870 period, 12 of the 13 upper civil servants who had attended school had gone to one of the Clarendon nine; while in the following period, 22 of the 40 who had attended a public or grammar school had attended one of the Clarendon nine, thus indicating the expansion of the public and endowed school structure in the period after the 1850s. With regard to university education, of the 13 who attended any university before 1870, 11 attended Oxbridge and 2 Trinity; and in the succeeding group, 43 of the 47 attended Oxbridge, Aberdeen 1, Trinity 1, and London 2 (Pellew 1982:208–13). These barebones data present clearly the effects of the educational reforms and the stratified open competition examinations.

Much the same effects are seen in Treasury recruitment. During the period from 1834 to 1870, 42 men were appointed to the equivalent of the higher division. Of these, 21 had been to university and all had attended either Oxford or Cambridge. In the period from 1870 to 1913, of the 58 men who entered the upper or higher division (primarily through open competition), 47 had attended university—44 from Oxbridge, 2 from Trinity, and 1 from London (Roseveare 1969:172–73, 179). The persistence of these patterns is revealed when we look at the kind of schools last attended by those above the rank of assistant secretary in 1929 (121) and who thus would have entered prior to World War I. Of these, 26.4 percent had attended the

Table 12.5 Educational Patterns of Senior Administrators in Home Office, 1848–1914

Year	Public School	Grammar School	No School	University	No University	Total
Pre-1870	13 (32.5)	0	27 (67.5)	13 (32.5)	27 (67.5)	40
1870 and after	37 (75)	3 (6)	9 (19)	46 (94)	4 (6)	49
Total	50	3	36	59	31	89

Source: Pellew 1982, 208–13.

top twenty public schools, while 72.7 percent had attended public schools and/or schools in the Headmaster's Conference (those schools thought to have public school status)(Kelsall 1955:127). In the same group, 73 percent had attended Oxbridge, while 11.6 had attended other schools. Of those who had entered by open competition, Oxbridge dominated to the tune of 96 percent (Kelsall 1955:138). The evidence, motley as it is, nevertheless clearly allows the conclusion that, after 1870, the stratification of education and examinations made public school/Oxbridge the primary route to the senior civil service, fulfilling the intentions of the designers of the structure.

The entry barriers to the upper service by promotion from the Lower Division and the professional technical service (barriers created in the formal regulations in the 1870s) continued to hold good through the twentieth century. The degree to which open competition came to dominate appointments is reflected in the degree to which direct appointments had almost been eliminated as a means of entry into the higher civil service. Of the 435 Higher Division and senior administrators in eleven of the main departments in 1911, not more than a dozen had entered without passing through the open competition route (Kelsall 1955:107). The promotion rate was probably higher than these data indicate, since a number of people might have entered through open competition in Class II examinations. Thus, for the period from 1892 to 1911, it is estimated by Kelsall that the promotion rate from the Second Division for the civil service (excluding the Post Office) was approximately 16 percent (Kelsall 1955:39). Of the 435 senior civil servants holding office in the main departments in 1911, 87 or 20 percent had been promoted from the Second Division. The conclusion is that entry barriers to the higher civil service were high and tied to a singular educational career which continued to exclude the vast majority of those who sought to enter through other routes.

This conclusion is underlined by the barriers placed in the way of transfers from technical/professional offices of similar salary rank. The practice of transferring specialists to administrative positions was, as Kelsall points out, never a common one (Kelsall 1955:114). Less than 10 percent of the higher civil service in 1929, 1939, and 1950 were transferees from specialist offices. The highest levels of administration were limited, as the nineteenth-century creators intended, to those whose social status and educational careers corresponded to the model of entry into the higher professions.

There is not a great deal of evidence available to provide a clear picture of just how systematic careers were after 1870. Although there was persistent resistance on the part of ministers to creating a uniform higher division that would allow easy intradepartmental transfers, there is some evidence that movement was not all that difficult. At the Treasury, of the 61 men who entered at the higher division level between 1870 and World War I, 33 (55 percent) had served in one or more departments (Roseveare 1969:178). A roughly similar pattern emerged at the Home Office. Of the 49 who entered the higher division between 1870 and 1914, 31 (63 percent) served in other departments before or after entering the Home Department (Pellew 1982:208–13). This suggests there was considerable intradivisional permeability and little concern about intradivision transfers being obstacles to career advancement where educational career and entrance mode were relatively uniform.

The emphasis on merit as opposed to seniority as the basis for promotion was, in good part, a product of the desire by department heads to retain discretion over internal appointment process. Nevertheless, there appears to have been relatively systematic patterns for promotion in which seniority played a significant role. This can be seen in table 12.6, where promotions appear to be systematically organized within the framework of seniority. These data suggest that seniority played an important role in rising to principle, assistant secretary, and permanent assistant or under-secretary, but played a lesser role as the individual moved to the next two highest ranks. Here the standard error and equivalent years in reaching these positions suggest that other forces were at work. This appears not to have changed much from two decades earlier. In 1886, the higher division officers of Principal rank numbered 20, of whom 16 (80 percent) had served 8 years; 23 of 38 (60 percent) senior clerks had served 8 years; and 24 of 39 (61 percent) established clerks had served between 25 and 30 years (Great Britain, Ridley Commission 1887:434–41). These data also suggest a systematic pattern of service in which seniority played a significant but not determinant role. This evidence suggests there was a predictable pattern of movement through offices—a pattern which stressed seniority as a basic but not singular requisite.

Table 12.6 Average Number of Years Taken by Open Competition Entrants to Reach Certain Ranks: 1909–14 Competitions

Promotion to:	Mean	Standard Error	No.
Principal	10.55	0.22	140
Assistant Secretary	19.86	0.61	115
Permanent Assistant/Under Secretary	26.73	0.49	73
Deputy Secretary	29.42	0.92	26
Secretary	28.88	1.20	17

Source: Kelsall 1955, 198.

Conclusion

It would not be stretching our credulity very much to conclude that the decade of the 1870s produced the fundamental characteristics of the rationalized bureaucratic structure. By no later, certainly, than 1880 to 1885, all the elements of the bureaucratic role were defined. There was a clearly defined career structure for upper, lower, and professional/technical officials. Entrance into each was by a narrow portal defined by distinctly different kinds, not simply levels, of educational careers. Exit was uniform and well defined, providing a widely understood and accepted completion of a career. There also existed, despite the absence of any real regulatory system, a pattern of movement through offices that was relatively predictable.

The selection of any one of these career paths depended heavily on entering, as a child, one of these paths. The defining path for the system was the preparatory/public school/Oxbridge one. Failure to enter this one excluded most individuals from gaining access to the higher professions. There were no opportunity costs for entering this path since a choice of professions awaited the individual at the time of leaving the university. Entrance to this path excluded few other opportunities. Entrance into the other paths did create opportunity costs that, for the most part, could never be recouped.

The stratification of the civil service into a functional hierarchy—intellectual, specialist, mechanical—provided the means for attracting those on whom large sums had been spent for their education. By distinguishing "intellectual" from mechanical aspects of administration, political leaders created a level of service which immediately defined a specific class of individuals as eligible for some of the highest positions available in state administration as well as the material and symbolic rewards that accompanied such positions. In doing so, they created incentives for those who passed through the public school/Oxbridge structure to enter public service.

By defining liberal education as the prerequisite for intellectual endeavors, political leaders had made higher public service a profession. In this case, like those of law and medicine, the mark of the high profession was the liberal education followed by the acquisition of skills through experience in the activities of the profession. The formulators of this career structure not only provided incentives for people who had spent large sums on education to enter public service, they had also provided an appropriate status for those individuals.

Equally important was the manner in which this professionalization of higher office resolved some of the basic problems of political leaders. The educational route and the in-service training of higher civil servants after 1870 produced a group of officials who became widely recognized as predictable and as possessing an internalized set of norms. This aspect of their training made them accountable to their seniors and political masters, who shared the same education and internalized norms. Precisely because behavior was based on internalized norms, it was unnecessary to have recourse to organizational regulation of any serious kind, just as in the cases of medicine and law.

In stressing liberal education as the essential aspect of preparation for the "intellectual" work of the civil service, its formulators conscientiously and consciously sought to subordinate the organizational structuring of information to this pre-entrance training. Organizational codification of information, either in the form of well-defined decision-making procedures or organizationally specific forms of training and administrative techniques, was largely avoided. The individual rather than the organization continued to be the center of information allocation. This made it possible for senior officials to be moved across department barriers without fear of damage to career. This stress on the individual is reflected not only in the continued emphasis laid on liberal education for the senior civil service, but also in the long persistence of specialist/professional recruitment through the presentation and evaluation of technical or professional certification. Here, too, the emphasis was on the individual's acquisition of skills and information prior to entry and the subordination of organization to individual capacities acquired elsewhere.

In the sense that the individual played an equivalent role with regard to information, the rationalization of the state bureaucracy in Britain was similar to that of the United States during the same period. The incorporation of the upper civil service role to the higher professional role meant that the bureaucratic structure would accentuate the interchangeability of bureaucratic role with other roles, such as political and managerial roles. The men who came to hold positions of power and status in British society in the late nineteenth and early twentieth centuries had ties of education and the internalized norms which that education had implanted (Guttsman 1974:22–44). More than this, however, they were members of a group who by mid-nineteenth century had come to believe that the liberal educational foundation of professional life was essential to achieving any public purpose.

The creation of this system in mid-Victorian Britain was not a consequence of public outcry. Rather, it was the consequence of the emergence of Parliament at the end of the eighteenth century as the master of British administrative fortunes but with little in the way of mechanisms to integrate the parliamentary executive and the administration. In the breach, parliamentary patronage came to substitute for monarchical patronage. But since such a system was dependent on fragile structures of personal relationships, Parliament did not produce a stable and predictable mechanism for selecting leaders and providing them with instruments of authority. In response, political leaders sought to increase the authority and stability of the executive institutions of Parliament—the Cabinet and the Treasury—and to undermine the independence of backbenchers and political leaders serving as department heads. They used the one instrument that had been hallowed by the eighteenth-century attack on monarchical power—the reform of patronage in the parliamentary franchise and, by extension and desire, at the administrative level.

These patronage reforms, although they created some stability for political leaders, also aggravated the problem of uncertainty by producing new problems in the form of voter uncertainties and continued backbencher independence. The response to these uncertainties was a further attack on backbencher and departmental autonomy. To achieve this goal, it was essential to end patronage and create a party organization that could organize voters through redistributive policies. The end of patronage would come first. But it could not be ended in any random fashion. Political leaders, especially Gladstone, recognized that the capacity of political leaders to hold a nonpatronage civil service to accountability could not be achieved without linking the administrative role to the executive in some systematic way. Fearing, as they most certainly did, the idea of an autonomous civil service, political leaders in the period from the 1850s to the 1870s saw the solution in the creation of a civil service role dependent on highly stratified educational structures; there one could assure the homogeneity of political leader and administrator socialization with a commonality of norms and values. At the same time, the stress placed on merit in the recruitment and structuring of the upper civil service career seemed to make it clear that for once and for all, public office was a function of public needs rather than private desires. In this manner, the structure of administrative roles was transformed. Its rationalization was far more political than efficient.

Conclusion

The bureaucratization of modern industrial society and state has been an important concern for at least a century. In part, this concern has been made up of what Alvin Gouldner once called "metaphysical pathos" (Gouldner 1955:498). Gouldner borrowed the idea from Arthur O. Lovejoy, who had observed that every theory had associated with it, or generated, a body of sentiments of which the subscriber to the theory was only dimly aware. This was a metaphysical pathos of ideas, a pathos which is

exemplified in any description of the nature of things, any characterization of the world to which one belongs, in terms which, like the words of a poem, evoke through their associations and through a sort of empathy which they engender, a congenial mood or tone of feelings. (Lovejoy 1948:11)

The metaphysical pathos of organizational theory, Gouldner argued, was pessimism and despair (Gouldner 1955:498). This was evoked by Weber's more or less "a plague on both your houses" conclusion about the ubiquity of bureaucratization. What would it avail anyone to persist in a socialist demand for revolution if all social organization in modern society ended in the prison or "iron cage" of bureaucratic organizational rationality? If modern social organization is condemned to converge regardless of the system of economic allocation, then fatalism becomes the hallmark of politics.

The villain of this pathos was primarily, in Weber's view, the size of organizations:

Its [bureaucracy] development, largely under capitalistic auspices, has created an urgent need for stable, strict, intensive, and calculable administration. It is this need which is so fateful to any kind of large-scale administration. Only by reversion in every field—political, religious, economic, etc.—to small-scale organization would it be possible to any considerable extent to escape its influence. (Weber 1978:I, 224)

Others, as we have seen, have stressed different aspects of social organization—complexity, uncertainty, etc. All of these, however, are functions of the scale of modernity. In effect, the seeming inevitability and the logic of modernity produced a belief in the inevitability of a bureaucratic rationality with all of the characteristics of the Weberian laundry list with which we have become so familiar.

411

Weberian pessimism was, thus, founded on the belief in the necessary evolution of rational bureaucracy. The technical superiority of rational bureaucracy meant the inevitable convergence of organizational structure in modern industrialized society. Weber's belief in convergence rested fundamentally on a functionalist view of social development and structure. Modern industrial society required specific organizational qualities. The most significant of these seemed to Weber to be organizational size. We can infer from this that Weber viewed the maximization of utility as the central feature of structural development, otherwise there would be no reason for the social preference of largeness over smallness in organizational development. Similarly, largeness was a structural quality which seemed to Weber to require the development of an internal labor market dominated by an administrative role characterized as rational-legal. In effect, Weber's calculation presented his successors with two black boxes; one that mediated between social structure and organization to produce large-scale organizations, and a second one that mediated between organizational size and the structural character of the internal labor market and its bureaucratic role. We were not told what went on inside these black boxes. Efforts have been made since Weber's analysis to unpack these boxes. One of the important consequences of this unpacking is the increasing suspicion that convergence exists more within the internal logic of Weberian thought than it does in the observable world. As a consequence, technical superiority as the source of rational bureaucracy also falls under suspicion.

Faced with the possibility that Weber's belief in the technical superiority of bureaucracy and its organizational convergence was ill-founded, this work began with the observation that state (or private, for that matter) bureaucratic rationalization did not everywhere conform to the attributes that Weber described. Nor, as time has passed, has the process of rationalization converged to produce a single type of bureaucratic role structure. The emergence, by the beginning of the twentieth century, of two distinct patterns of rationalized bureaucratic role structure which have persisted does not seem to be correlated with size or any of the other variety of determinants often suggested. Since convergence has not occurred, then the task of this analysis became the unpacking of the black box that mediated between social and organizational structure, which, in turn, should tell us something about the black box that contained the variable(s) which mediated the structure of rational bureaucracy. But, since state administration was and has always been a political matter, the mediating black box stood between the political rather than the social structure and organizational structure.

The starting point was thus the observable distinction between the two types of rationalized bureaucratic role that existed in modern political regimes. The variation, however, was not explained by Weber's speculation nor by those whose work was primarily in the area of private large-scale organizations. Rather, I have argued that the variation can be correlated with one of two possible independent variables:

1. The variation is correlated to an inverse relationship between levels of industrialization—the less industrialized states ended up with organizationally oriented bureaucratic structures, while the more industrialized states ended up with professionally oriented ones.

2. Alternatively, the variation can be correlated to historically different experiences with regard to the problem of leadership succession in the nineteenth century.

The first possibility was rejected early as a guide to this analysis. How then can we use the second possible variable as a means to explain the correlation? The answer is, I claim, that levels of industrialization are epiphenomenal to the structural conditions of uncertainty. Countries with low uncertainty, where contract governed the relations between individuals in the marketplace and, subsequently, socially as well, possessed the necessary, and perhaps sufficient, prerequisites for industrialization. Those without this contractarian substructure which sustained civil society were more open to instability and uncertainty over the conditions of capital and thus had less capacity to industrialize.

We are left with the problem of leadership and leadership succession as the significant correlation. In recounting the histories and strategies of rationalization from this viewpoint, bureaucratic rationalization does not emerge as a political process dominated by objective or exogenous conditions of economic or technical complexity. Rather, we get a picture of the rationalization process as one which was essentially political. Political leaders, embedded in their various structures of leadership sought to resolve the problems produced by the different levels of uncertainty they faced in regard to their status, power, and incumbencies. The differences in outcomes reveal that the process was not a direct, unmediated function of specific economic or social forces of nineteenth-century industrialization. If anything, they can be attributed more to the forces set in motion by the larger and grander transformation to capitalism.

The analyses of the processes of rationalization in the United States, Great Britain, Japan, and France underscore the fact that rationalization was not only a political process, but one which was without design or ideological coherence. In the nineteenth century, there was no coherent theory of administrative organization or bureaucratic role. There was no theory which prescribed a set of utilities to be derived from a particular way of constructing the bureaucratic role.[1] Office-holding was primarily seen as a function of private or social interest.

Rather than acting on the basis of a coherent ideological or utopian view of administration or bureaucratic role, political leaders engaged in a kind of Markov chain of decisions. Each decision was determined primarily by strategic considerations. Political leaders sought prompt and contingent solutions to the immediate problems facing them with regard to their continued status and power. Each solution political leaders arrived at produced new problems which evoked new strategic solutions. The process only came to an end or, rather, a fragile equilibrium when there seemed to be sufficient constraints on uncertainty imposed by the structure created by this chain of strategic decisions.

As this process proceeded, theories of bureaucratic administration emerged—theories dominated by strategic considerations as political leaders sought to outwit and outdo their opponents. Basically, two views of bureaucratic role emerged, not just the one Weber sought to elucidate. Instead, the two forms of rationalization—professional and organizational, which are described here—not only represent radically different solutions to problems of political modernity, they also represent theories of how bureaucratic rationality ought to proceed.

One path of rationalization stresses the control of information and its regulation by the individual in his role as a professional or proto-professional serving the public interest. The other stresses the control of information and its regulation by the organization in its role as a public institution. These two modes of rationalization came to be viewed as two quite different versions of theories and ideologies of what constituted the public and publicness in organizational structure.

The professional mode came to imply a notion of public that is bound irrevocably to the social. That is, bound to social institutions by individuals who carry with them from these institutions the rules regulating individual relationships—rules transformed into law by continual practice and consequently recognized by the state as the appropriate basis of organizational structure. Publicness in this context is viewed as the acquisition by individuals of a body of knowledge that is recognized and defined by practitioners themselves as scientific, and, therefore, not a function of private or personal status. To be fully within the public sphere, such information must be in the possession of individuals who profess to a code concerning its use. In this

---

1. German cameralism was a theory of sorts about administration, but it was one chiefly concerned with how to go about getting the funds to operate the state—administration as division of labor (see Small 1909 [1962]).

sense, publicness is defined by the nature of the social role around which knowledge is structured and allocated. The professional or proto-professional role is thus essential to the notion of the public and publicness. It is crucial that in this case publicness is embedded in social institutions, especially educational ones, rather than in specific political or economic organizations. It was this idea of the profession as embodying a structure of rules guiding individual acquisition and application of knowledge that became basic to one theory of bureaucratic structure and role.[2]

If Weber was wrong about the structural uniformity of bureaucratic rationalization, he was certainly right about the way in which incentives for acquiring the bureaucratic role affected the character of structure. Thus, in the professionally oriented patterns described here, incentives were directed at individuals who had borne the cost of specialized training themselves. While this provided organizations with relatively immediate and low-cost access to specialized information, it also meant less rigid hierarchies, emphasis on job descriptions, and, consequently, highly permeable organizational structures. *Social* closure is the basis of this theory of bureaucratic structure and role.

The organizational mode of rationalization may be seen to imply a concept of the public that is bound irrevocably to political institutions. That is to say, political in the sense of hierarchical organizations serving as the agents which carry with them the rules regulating the relations between individuals. Rules, that is, which are derived primarily from the construction of organizations as the predominant means for constraining individuals from opportunistic usage of skills or knowledge. Private formal, hierarchical organizations are thus strongly akin to the institutions of the state and are not so easily distinguishable. In the organizational mode, decision-making information is controlled by the organization through an explicit body of rules about its use and allocation. The formal organization is, in this sense, isomorphic to and, in many ways, a metaphor of the state. Within its domains, it possesses a monopoly over the use of coercion and authoritatively allocates values.

The degree to which the organization is an emulator as well as a recipient of the state's powers in such societies is reflected in the manner in which state institutions dominate the educational processes so as to provide formal organizations, including that of the state, with socially homogenous recruits. These recruits enter well-defined, highly predictable careers where the control of information is regulated by external organizational rather than internalized personal codes. The educational rites of passage and the well-plotted career structure, regulated by apparently objective criteria, provide the basis

2. One of the earliest explications of this relationship of the social basis of the administrative role is, interestingly enough, Tocqueville (see Mayer 1969:263–70).

for the claims to publicness. Publicness and the public character of the organization and its decisions are ensured by the objective character of the criteria utilized to regulate careers and the use of information by officials. Publicness is thus rooted in the form of the organization and its political nature rather than in the social character of the professional. *Organizational* closure is the basis of this theory of bureaucratic structure and role.

Here the structure of incentives to enter the bureaucratic role shaped the structure in the manner Weber observed. High levels of certification aimed at excluding large segments of the population rather than providing specialized bodies of information resulted in high opportunity costs for individuals. The result was the emergence of structural characteristics designed for the most part to exhibit a highly predictable career structure emphasizing seniority, hierarchy, differentiation, specialization, and career.

The consequences of the two forms of publicness these bureaucratic role structures represented were and continue to be markedly different. These two modes are related to the manner in which education and knowledge were socially structured. In one, voluntaristic social behavior and organization dominates the political through its professionally defined control over the substance of knowledge and expertise. This is illustrated in the English case by the domination of social class and its educational institutions over the political order. It takes a different form in the United States, where the political was, and to a some extent continues to be, dominated by political parties whose roots and institutional framework are social. The most visible representation of this social base is the ubiquitous professional society and its constant attempt to secure for the practitioner his and her control over the conditions of their occupations.

In the organizational mode, the formal structure, exemplified by the state, dominates the social through the substitution of organizational control of knowledge and expertise for individual and voluntary organizational control. Japan, in this regard, is an archetypical case. State institutions dominated, as they continue to do, the educational structure and, as a consequence, access to organizational leadership and power. The degree to which non-state organizations are isomorphic to the Japanese state bureaucracy in structure and rationalization is well known. France is a another case where state institutions emerged early to determine the standard of publicness. Their revolutionary roots in a preselected body, however, produced a contested form of rationalization in which political parties finally accepted the organizational and, therefore, political mode of publicness.

In these two societies, systematic information or expertise came to be allocated primarily by state mechanisms. The new political leaders of Japan and France claimed virtual monopolies over the educational process early in their post-"restoration" and postrevolutionary periods. They paid special attention to those areas of information and expertise the possession of which was viewed as conferring status and influence. The private nature of this expertise, which was characteristic of the old regimes, was now transformed. In their pursuit of publicness under circumstances of high uncertainty, political leaders sought to strip the allocation and use of information and expertise from voluntaristic social structures that might compete for power and authority. In the place of the market, political leaders substituted state organizational structures as the mechanism of allocation and certification of expertise. The public character of such expertise was displayed by the emphasis placed in explicit organizational rules regarding the appropriate use of information. To ensure that expertise was used in the public interest and not for private ends, political leaders created educational institutions to govern certification and the general allocation of expertise. The utilization of organizational structures to keep individuals from engaging in opportunistic behavior became the social model for allocating information in private organizations as well as in public ones.

The opposite was the case with the United States and Great Britain. In these two countries, the stability of civil society was based on well-understood and widely accepted rules governing individual relationships. This consensus made it possible for expertise and information to continue to be allocated by voluntaristic social structures. Indeed, in much of the nineteenth century, expertise in its professional character was dominated in both countries by market competition. The pursuit of knowledge was left to the individual, who was constrained by the courts from the most egregious forms of opportunism. As a consequence, there was a rapid and often anarchic growth of private educational systems alongside public ones in both the United States and Great Britain. In the United States, the competition between local state universities and private institutions precluded the emergence of a powerful national university system. This competition, however, led to the transformation of expertise from an almost purely market-determined structure into one regulated by the practitioners of expertise.

By the end of the nineteenth century, practitioners of varying kinds of expertise in both countries sought to reduce uncertainties created by high levels of competition between competing claims by attempting to create uniform definitions of expert training. In seeking to create practitioner control over the allocation of expertise, professionals joined forces with universities in the United States and with private training institutions in Great Britain. Expertise thus became a product of social institutions. The publicness of professionals came to be assured by transforming expertise into an individual social "calling," characterized by a powerful ethical commitment to public service. The manifestation of publicness was the socialization of individuals into a professed ethic of expertise. In effect, individuals committed themselves to a body of norms governing the use of expertise as a condition of certification. The idea of self-regulation came to be viewed as an essential characteristic of the concept of individualism. In this process, public and private organizations came to view regulation of information and expertise as the province of social institutions rather than of economic or political organizations.

I have argued that this distinction between professionally and organizationally oriented modes arose out of the universal increase in uncertainty for political leaders in the nineteenth century. For some societies, as in the cases of Japan and France, uncertainty was occasioned by transformations of leadership and the rules for leadership selection. For others, like the United States and Great Britain, uncertainty for political leaders was occasioned by the changed rules and expansion of franchise. This condition was new to the nineteenth century. Political leaders faced, as they had not done in previous times, persistent uncertainty about their incumbency. What was so different in the nineteenth century that it should produce what seems to be systemic uncertainty?

More than any other factor was the rising cost of the distinction between state and society which had emerged out of the seventeenth and eighteenth centuries. It was this distinction which provoked, in instrumental terms, a vital tear in the once relatively seamless fabric of social class, authority, and administrative power. The division between state and society and the division of labor it intimated brought into the realm of discussion and action the distinction between public and private. In this discussion, or rather argument, over what constituted the realm of the public as opposed to the private and what was the relationship between them, there emerged two basic problems. The first of these was a general one having mostly to do with the disparity between economic contractual equality, which increasingly governed relations between individuals, and political inequality, which characterized the aloofness and distinctiveness of the state. It was this problem of redefining the boundaries between social, economic, and political equality and inequality that produced powerful problems of uncertainty for political leaders in the nineteenth century. This was equally true in societies that had or had not experienced a revolutionary condition. The difference, however, was that the uncertainty was far greater in societies where the problem of equality was starkly presented by the dramatic overthrow of birth as the criterion for determining access to political leadership.

Equally difficult was the specific problem faced by political leaders in establishing the public character of the state. The history of absolutist society presented what seemed to be an object lesson in the degree to which the state could become an unregulated territory state officials were free to exploit.

The social class (and therefore private) monopoly of political power under early absolutist regimes and their attempt to separate politics from society evoked tensions of ideology and praxis in the eighteenth and early nineteenth centuries. Whether the outcomes were victories for society or the state, political leaders would have been both strategically and tactically foolish if they had not sought to establish the publicness of the state.

The necessity was not one of legitimacy in the sense of convincing society of the state's right to a monopoly of coercion and allocation of values. Rather, the necessity was one arising from the problems of uncertainty. If privacy in the state meant that the only mode of regulating the manner in which officials were appointed and carried out their duties was through personal loyalties, then one might reasonably be uncertain about the aims and purposes of official behavior. Legitimacy of any leadership is predicated to a considerable extent on the predictability of practice. Failing to provide an explicit set of rules governing the decision-making practices of officials suggests the arbitrariness of private whims.

When the two issues of equality and publicness occurred together, as they did in a number of nineteenth-century states, the problem for incumbent or putative political leaders was how to exhibit the public character of the state. The resolution to this problem was the creation of rules regarding the selection and advancement of administrative officials stressing uniformity of application across class lines. This solution required that offices no longer be proprietary and that they be filled on the basis of some "objective" criterion, such as a test of an education which was viewed as scientist or rational. Uniformity of rules, the stress on the possession of nonascriptively determined skills which could be tested, the utilitarian nature of the skills, all seemingly attested to the removal of private individual or class monopoly of office.

Beyond the publicness aspect of the bureaucratic role definition, there was no convergence of role structure. The differences which emerged in the construction of the bureaucratic role were further constrained by the way in which political leadership was organized. The significance of political leadership rests on the point that the way in which it was organized defined the manner in which bureaucratic role structures were held accountable. That is to say, political leaders sought and still seek to structure the bureaucratic role so that it presents no danger to themselves. Thus, where leadership was organized primarily on the basis of ascriptively determined social networks, as in Japan and Great Britain in mid-nineteenth century, then the varying demands for publicness transformed birth into socially segregated education as the means of gaining access to political leadership. The utilization of education as the means for exhibiting the public character of administration allowed the bureaucratic role to be integrated and held in place by the homogeneity of social networks formed through the educational experience—the old boys network worked very much the same in Japan as in England.

When, as in the case of the United States (and the former Soviet Union as well), political leadership was determined within the constraints of party organization rather than by social class networks alone, then political leaders sought ways to modify the bureaucratic role structure in ways suitable to party control. While the levels of uncertainty produced quite different consequences in defining publicness, both the United States and the Soviet Union were strangely similar in the way party organization sought to maintain its capacity to hold the bureaucracy accountable. The two-party system, seeking to avoid both an autonomous bureaucracy and a system dominated by a single party pursuing the same objective, resorted to the use of professionals and job specification. The one-party system resolved the problem of accountability by infusing the bureaucratic structure with party hierarchy— a solution that had the formal if not the real appearance of avoiding patronage since party mobility was supposedly based on merit criteria.

The structure of the bureaucratic role varied, in part, to the degree that political leaders sought to retain their discretion over decision making through direct or indirect control over the nature of information used in the decision-making process. Where, as in the United States and Great Britain, political leaders saw their discretion over decision making threatened by organizational decision making, they lent support and legitimacy to the idea of professional information. In France and Japan, where political leaders felt threatened by the possibility of a socially based structure of information, they sought to create autonomous, well-insulated structures of organizational decision making and information.

The rationalization of the administrative role also had the happy consequence of providing political leaders in both categories with a means for further reducing the uncertainty of their condition. Regardless of role orientation, the rationalized bureaucratic structure became a means by which political leaders could depoliticize a vast array of potentially explosive issues. In proclaiming the publicness of the bureaucratic role, political leaders were increasingly successful in convincing the public that their bureaucracies were essentially neutral and utilitarian in their desire to arrive at solutions that were "scientifically" determined to produce the greatest good for the greatest number. "Neutrality" became, in essence, the ideology of bureaucratic problem solving.

We might then conclude that the rationalization of the bureaucratic role was, in a sense, the mechanism by which the relationship between state and civil society achieved a new transformed equilibrium at the end of the nineteenth and beginning of the twentieth centuries. Equality, whether in its contractarian or revolutionary form, subverted the old proprietary regimes as the nineteenth century wore on. Political leaders sought to overcome the uncertainties of succession and accountability created by these forms of equality. At the same time, as the rules of equality came to dominate the relationships between individuals, there arose the problem of how to relate these norms to the explicit rules of inequality emanating from the coercive power of the state.

The choices made by political leaders to secure their places led them unwittingly to resolve many of the tensions and problems existing between state and civil society which had arisen from new concepts of equality. On the one hand, their choices resulted in the rationalization of the administrative role. On the other hand, these same choices provided a solution to the problem of conflicting values between state and civil society. The bureaucratic role, constructed as it was out of the necessity for political leaders to present an organizational representation of equality and publicness, was a new representation of the state. State authority seemed now to rest increasingly on expertise, as opposed to arbitrary authority or coercion. The pursuit of the public interest stressed the equality of merit and the neutrality of scientistic knowledge as opposed to a private interest which emphasized hierarchy and esoteric knowledge. The bonds linking state and society were strengthened and institutionalized through systems of education which seemed to ensure that merit and not private interest would be the basis of selecting decision-makers and making decisions.

It has most certainly occurred to the reader by this time that this analysis does not appear to provide an explanation for the nature of bureaucratic structure in the so-called Third World countries. The history of a large number of Latin American, African, and Southeast Asian countries seems to deny the progression of the process as it is described in the analysis. Latin America did have a revolution from Spain at the beginning of the nineteenth century, but, like most of the other countries which were also ex-colonies, they achieved their independence largely without major successions of leadership. This suggests that low uncertainty about political incumbency, combined with the powerful stress on egalitarianism inherent in independence situations, provided an environment sympathetic to the emergence of political parties.

Thus, for example, parties in nineteenth-century Latin America, as in many later Third World societies, were dominated by leaders organized on the basis of narrow social networks that were sustained by economic networks. In effect, social networks organized parties rather than the reverse. Patronage was basic to these parties whether or not there was wide franchise. Patronage served, as it continues to do, as the dominant mode by which political leaders reduced uncertainty about opposing parties or the possibility that other social networks might emerge to contest incumbents.

Essential to this narrow structure of patronage was, and continues to be, the presidential form of the executive, where the president is elected separately from the legislature. The presidential command of patronage makes it possible to maintain the social basis of party. Unfortunately, the separate election of the executive also tends to weaken parties as the executive goes his own way, claiming to represent the people directly. It is easy to speculate that patronage under these circumstances, as it did in the United States and Great Britain, became and continues to be a source of discontent and factionalism. The number of offices available can never be sufficient to fill the demand of those who make claims on the basis of loyalty. Nor can the conflict between legislative and presidential parties over patronage be completely reconciled. Rationalization of patronage is difficult, if not impossible, since there is no social group willing to challenge political party leadership by attacking patronage.

The great width and depth of patronage in these societies makes it impossible for voters to tell whether political leaders are acting in terms of individual, party, or public interest. Under these circumstances, the political opposition does not emerge as a function of party contestation in which the "outs" draw on new social criteria for political leadership. In the cases of the United States and Great Britain, bureaucratic administrative reform was generated by party and constitutional contestation in combination with the emergence of new educational standards, which came to be used to redefine political leadership. These new standards were intimately tied to the conception of publicness and public service.

In the vast majority of Third World countries over the past hundred years, new standards or criteria of leadership tended to emerge in only one institution—the armed services. As more and more countries emerged from the dissolution of colonial empires in Africa and Asia, they, too, as in Latin America, often came to experience political parties based on patronage. In many, party contestation took place but failed to produce any reform of patronage-dominated civil services. The absence of an expansive and autonomous professional class or of a social class which transformed its claim to govern from ascriptive to achievement criteria in the form of education thus seems to be critical. Their absence seems to make it impossible for new structures of civil political leadership to emerge to take advantage of contestation. The one exception to this condition is the emergence of the military as a profession with all of the earmarks of the civil public service professions. The development of the role of professional soldier almost universally came to be organized on the acquisition of a specialist or expertise education that was certified at a relatively high level. The role was organized around a career. Movement through this career was structured on the basis of explicit rules that formally emphasized merit as expressed in seniority and capacity. In short, the professional military role came to acquire the formal characteristics of publicness that made it possible for military leaders to claim that the armed services were the only institution capable of representing the public interest.

The military bureaucracy thus tended to emerge as the political opposition to parties or party in power. Encapsulated as they were in an institution almost universally organizationally oriented—limited to entry at the lowest levels and almost impermeable in terms of horizontal entry—military leaders could not serve as the source for new forms of political party leadership without abandoning the very institutional role which provided them with the status of publicness. Military leadership could only oppose political party leadership by substituting the military institution for the political one. This, however, has continually raised the problem of how to reformulate the civil bureaucratic role so that it might be held accountable by some means other than patronage and clientalism.

The problem has been an insoluble one. If the civil bureaucracy were to become incorporated into the military, that is, if all administrative posts were to be allocated on the basis of military career structure, the military institution would lose its distinctive organizational character. This might be acceptable but for the problem of determining leadership succession. The vast expansion of the military bureaucratic administration would break down the formal and informal rules by which military leadership has tended to select itself in Third World countries—seniority and service representation. Factions within each service play a role, but these are powerfully constrained by seniority and service branch.

Nor does it seem possible for military leadership to set about constructing a civil bureaucracy as a mirror image of itself. To do so would be to create another relatively autonomous institution with great powers. This would be something in the nature of a Frankenstein's monster—an institution which might come to dominate its creators. It is not surprising then that military leaders who undertake the role of political decision-makers find themselves unable to reform patronage-dominated administrations. Failing to do so results in the inability to eliminate patronage as the means for recruitment to administrative power. Once military leaders begin the process of engaging in the patronage game themselves, they become increasingly subject to demands both from civil and military society. Once giving way to this process, military leadership is bound in the end to lose the capacity to present itself as public in character. It is also bound to end by encouraging bitter factionalism within the military institution, thereby undermining the structure of career. To escape this dissolution of the public stature of their institution, military leaders must find the means for removing themselves from direct political decision making. They often do so by negotiation with civilian parties and the cycle begins over again.

It is time now to turn to what is, perhaps, the most perplexing problem raised by this analysis: did rationalization of *private* large-scale organizations in the late nineteenth and early twentieth centuries result from the same dynamic of uncertainty as in public bureaucracies or from a different one? The timing and patterns of role rationalization in the private industries and public bureaucracies of each country were much the same. Isomorphism appears to be characteristic. The problem is finding the underlying dynamics of isomorphic outcomes. One general explanation presented by DiMaggio and Powell (1983) suggests that organizations unself-consciously copy practices that have become institutionalized and legitimate. This suggests the possibility that private large-scale organizations tended to follow the lead of rationalized public bureaucracies. Private managerial hierarchies and internal labor markets were formed as a consequence of the institutionalization of rationalized role structures in public bureaucracies. The institutionalization of publicness cast an aura of legitimacy on the form itself, making it socially acceptable and something more than an instrument of private enrichment.

The problem here, however, is to understand the process by which this occurred. Did company owners or entrepreneurs simply institute these changes? It is hard to see how they might be willing to do so, since these changes might be totally against their own interests. Handing over day-to-day and long-term administration of the organization to managers could result in loss of ownership or, at least, control over financial direction. This might be offset by the admission of such rationalized organizations into the state's sphere of legitimate actors, where their managers could play some role in determining economic policy. Even here, however, we would still need to understand the process by which managers rationalized the administrative and work role as well as the incentives for the new managers's choices of strategies to reconstruct organizational administration. Indeed, in cases where there is some evidence to construct a story of how this occurred, it appears possible that uncertainty about managerial succession led to the integration of managerial and supervisory roles, especially at the foreman level, into the central administration of the organization; that varying levels of uncertainty about managerial succession and labor supply affected the manner in which this integration took place.[3] Thus, while the general structural constraint of a legitimate form for private organizations operated to delimit the

---

3. See, for example: Buttrick 1952; Stone 1974; Marglin 1974; Gordon 1988:38–80; Montgomery 1987:214–56; Pollard 1965:104–208; Noble 1977:33–49; Jacoby 1985:13–64; Gordon, Edwards, and Reich 1982:127–50; Littler 1978:189–95.

choices of entrepreneurs and managers, it was the variation in uncertainty about managerial succession and labor supply that resulted in the specific structural outcomes.

In essence, I argue, both public and private organizations came to face similar problems of uncertainty over leadership succession in the late nineteenth century and proceeded to resolve this problem in similar ways. The major difference between the types of organization was the source of uncertainty. In the case of national state bureaucracy, the varying conditions of equality produced different levels of leadership uncertainty. For private organizations, the problem of entrepreneurial and managerial succession created levels of uncertainty that were resolved by the creation of internal labor markets similar to those which existed in the state bureaucracy.

This line of argument leads to the conclusion that the rationalization of the administrative role—the creation of the norms of bureaucratic role in modern society—was the consequence of political struggles. These were struggles to redefine the structures of power and the criteria for access to them by groups of putative leaders who sought to reduce the uncertainty over their status and power and, as a consequence, their material well-being. The rationalization process was essentially a political process that redefined the nature of the modern state. It was not the product of a general social systemic process directed inevitably toward the maximizing of social utility.

The rational-legal bureaucratic role may, in fact, be technically superior to any other form of administration, as Weber wrote, but it surely was not that understanding which led to its creation by political leaders. Rather, we may generally conclude that organizational rationalization in public and private realms occurred through a process of ad hoc rational strategic responses of political and organizational leaders to persisting problems of incumbency. Each resolution constrained the nature of the resulting disequilibrium until a series of responses over time produced an equilibrium that we often call institutionalization. Once this equilibrium was reached, it became the basis for the integration of state to civil society and increasingly the basis of integrating individuals to organizational life. However, as Weber feared, in his metaphysical pathos, integration, while it produced stability, did not necessarily provide for the autonomy and fulfillment of the individual.

Bibliography

Abbott, Evelyn, and Lewis Campbell. 1897, 1899. *The Life and Letters of Benjamin Jowett, M.A., Master of Balliol College, Oxford.* 2 vols. London: John Murray.

Abouchar, Alan. 1984. *Project Decision Making in the Public Sector.* Lexington, MA: Lexington Books.

Abramovitz, Moses, and Vera F. Eliasberg. 1957. *The Growth of Public Employment in Great Britain.* Princeton: Princeton University Press.

Akita, George. 1967. *Foundations of Constitutional Government in Modern Japan: 1868–1900.* Cambridge, MA: Harvard University Press.

Alchian, Armen A., and Harold Demsetz. 1972. Production, information costs and economic organization. *American Economic Review* 62, no. 5 (December): 777–95.

Alchian, Armen A.. 1982. "Property Rights, Specialization, and the Firm," in J. F. Weston and M. E. Greenfield, eds. *Corporate Enterprise in a New Environment,* pp. 11–36. New York: KCE Publications.

Aldrich, Howard E. 1971. Organizational boundaries and interorganizational conflict. *Human Relations* 24, no. 4 (August): 279–93.

————. 1972. Technology and organizational structure: A reexamination of the findings of the Aston Group. *Administrative Science Quarterly* 17 (March): 26–43.

————. 1979. *Organizations and Environments.* Englewood Cliffs, NJ: Prentice-Hall.

Aldrich, Howard E., and Susan Mueller. 1982. The evolution of organizational forms: Technology, coordination, and control. In *Research in Organizational Behavior,* vol. 4, edited by Barry M. Staw and L. L. Cummings, pp. 33–87. Greenwich, CT: JAI Press.

Aldrich, Howard E., and Jeffrey Pfeffer. 1976. Environments of organizations. *Annual Review of Sociology* 2: 79–105.

Aldrich, Howard E., and David Whetten. 1981. Organization sets, actions sets and networks: Making the most of simplicity. In *Handbook of Organizational Design,* edited by Paul Nystrom and William Stearbuck, pp. 385–408. New York: Oxford University Press.

Allison, Graham. 1971. *Essence of Decision: Explaining the Cuban Missile Crisis.* Boston: Little, Brown & Co.

Almond, Gabriel, Scott C. Flanagan, and Robert J. Mundt. 1973. *Crisis, Choice, and Change: Historical Studies of Political Development.* Boston: Little, Brown & Co.

Almond, Gabriel, and G. Bingham Powell, Jr. 1966. *Comparative Politics: A Developmental Approach.* Boston: Little, Brown & Co.

Alt, James E. 1975. Continuity, turnover, and experience in the British Cabinet, 1868–1970. In *Cabinet Studies: A Reader,* edited by Valentine Herman and James E. Alt, pp. 33–54. New York: St. Martin's Press.

American Assembly. 1965. *The Federal Government Service.* Englewood Cliffs, NJ: Prentice-Hall.

Anderson, Olive. 1965. The Janus face of mid-nineteenth-century English radicalism: The Administrative Reform Association of 1855. *Victorian Studies* 8, no. 3: 231–42.

———. 1974. The Administrative Reform Association, 1855–57. In *Pressure from Without in Early Victorian England,* edited by Patricia Hollis, pp. 262–88. London: Arnold.

Anderson, Perry. 1979. *Lineages of the Absolutist State.* London: Verso.

Anderson, R. D. 1977. *France, 1870–1914.* London: Routledge and Kegan Paul.

Antoine, Michel, Pierre Barral, et al. 1975. *Origines et histoire des cabinets des ministres en France.* Genève: Librairie Droz.

Anty, Raymond. 1936. *Le concours: Mode de recrutement des fonctions publiques.* Paris: Librairie du Recueil Sirey.

Aoki, Masahiko. 1983. Managerialism revisited in the light of bargaining-game theory. *International Journal of Industrial Organization* 1: 1–21.

Arango, Ergasto Ramon. 1978. *The Spanish Political System: Franco's Legacy.* Boulder, CO: Westview Press.

Archer, Margaret S. 1979. *Social Origins of Education Systems.* Beverly Hills, CA: Sage Publications.

Argersinger, Peter H. 1980. 'A Place on the Ballot': Fusion politics and antifusion laws. *American Historical Review* 85, no. 2 (April): 287–306.

Argyriades, Demetrios. 1976. Neutralité ou engagement politique: L'Expérience de la fonction publique en Grande-Bretagne, 1854–1968. *Bulletin de l'Institut International d'Administration Publique,* no. 40 (Oct.–Dec.): 25–55.

Argyris, Chris. 1971. *Management and Organizational Development* New York: McGraw-Hill.

Armour, Henry Ogden, and David J. Teece. 1978. Organizational structure and economic performance: A test of the multidivisional hypothesis. *Bell Journal of Economics* 9, no. 1 (Spring): 106–22.

Armstrong, John A. 1959. *The Soviet Bureaucratic Elite: A Case Study of the Ukrainian Apparatus.* New York: Praeger.

———. 1965. Sources of Soviet administrative behavior: Some Soviet and Western European Comparisons. *American Political Science Review* 59, no. 3 (September): 643–55.

———. 1972. Tsarist and Soviet elite administrators. *Slavic Review* 31, no. 1 (March): 1–28.

———. 1973. *The European Administrative Elite.* Princeton, NJ: Princeton University Press.

Arnold, Peri. 1986. *Making the Managerial Presidency: Comprehensive Reorganization Planning, 1905–1980.* Princeton, NJ: Princeton University Press.

Aronson, Sidney H. 1964. *Status and Kinship in the Higher Civil Service.* Cambridge, MA: Harvard University Press.

Arrow, Kenneth J. 1971. The firm in general equilibrium theory. In *The Corporate Economy: Growth, Competition and Innovative Potential,* edited by Robin Marris and Adrian Woods, pp. 68–110. Cambridge, MA: Harvard University Press.

———. 1974. *The Limits of Organization.* New York: W.W. Norton & Co.

Asai, Kiyoshi. 1939 [1968]. *Meiji ishin to gunken shisō.* Tokyo: Gannandō [reprint].

Aspinall, A. 1926. English party organization in the early nineteenth century. *English Historical Review* 41, no. 163 (July): 389–411.

Astley, W. Graham. 1985. The two ecologies: Population and community perspectives on organizational evolution. *Administrative Science Quarterly* 30, no. 2 (June): 224–41.

Astley, W. Graham, and Andrew H. Van de Ven. 1983. Central perspectives and debates in organization theory. *Administrative Science Quarterly* 28 (June): 245–73.

Atiyah, P. S. 1979. *The Rise and Fall of the Freedom of Contract.* New York: Oxford University Press.

Atkinson Report. 1983. *Selection of Fast-Stream Graduate Entrants to the Home Civil Service, the Diplomatic Service and the Tax Inspectorate; & of Candidates. . .* London: Management and Personnel Service, HMS.

Aubert, Jacques, Pierre Guiral, Bernard Le Clère, et al. 1978. *Les Préfets en France.* Genève: Librairies Droz.

Aulard, Alphonse François Victor. 1913. La centralisation Napoléonienne: les préfets. In vol. 7 of *Études et leçons sur la révolution française,* edited by Alphonse François Victor Aulard, pp. 113–95. Paris: Librairie Félix Alcan.

Baecque, Francis de, et al. 1976. *Les Directeurs de ministère en France (XIXe–XXe siècles).* Genève: Librairie Droz.

Bagehot, Walter. 1963. *The English Constitution.* London: The Fontana Library/Collins.

Bailey, Jackson. 1965. The origin and nature of the genrō. In *Studies on Asia,* edited by Robert K. Sakai, pp. 129–41. Lincoln: University of Nebraska Press.

Baker, Frank, ed. 1973. *Organizational Systems: General Systems Approaches to Complex Organizations.* Homewood, IL: Dorsey Press.

Baker, R. J. S. 1972. *Administrative Theory and Public Administration.* Oxford, UK: Oxford University Press.

Bamford, T. W. 1961. Public schools and social class, 1801–1850. *British Journal of Sociology* 12, no. 3 (September): 224–35.

———. 1967. *Rise of the Public Schools: A Study of Boys' Public Boarding Schools in England and Wales from 1837 to the Present Day.* London: Nelson.

Barber, Bernard. 1963. Some problems in the sociology of professions. *Daedalus* (Fall): 669–88.

Barker, Ernest. 1944. *The Development of Public Services in Western Europe: 1660–1930.* New York: Oxford University Press.

Barnard, Chester. 1938. *The Functions of the Executive.* Cambridge, MA: Harvard University Press.

Bastid, Paul. 1954. *Les institutions politiques de la monarchie parlementaire française.* Paris: Éditions du Recueil Sirey.

Battis, Ulrich. 1980. *Bundesbeamtengesetz.* Munich: Beck.

Baumol, William J. 1967. *Welfare Economics and the Theory of the State.* 2d ed. Cambridge, MA: Harvard University Press.

————. 1970. On the discount rate for public projects. In *Public Expenditures and Policy Analysis,* edited by Robert H. Haveman and Julius Margolis, pp. 273–90. Chicago: Markham.

Baumol, William J., and Maco Stewart. 1971. On the behavioral theory of the firm. In *The Corporate Economy: Growth, Competition and Innovative Potential,* edited by Robin Marris and Adrian Woods, pp. 118–43. Cambridge, MA: Harvard University Press.

Beasley, W. G. 1972. *The Meiji Restoration.* Stanford, CA: Stanford University Press.

Beckett, J. V. 1986. *The Aristocracy in England: 1660–1914.* New York: Basil Blackwell Ltd.

Bellah, Robert N. 1957. *Tokugawa Religion.* Glencoe, IL: Free Press.

Bendix, Reinhard. 1949. *Higher Civil Servants in American Society.* Boulder, CO: University of Colorado Press.

————. 1964. *Nation-Building and Citizenship: Studies of Our Changing Social Order.* New York: Anchor Books.

Benson, J. Kenneth. 1975. The interorganizational network as a political economy. *Administrative Science Quarterly* 20: 229–49.

————. 1977. Organizations: A dialectical view. *Administrative Science Quarterly* 22 (March): 1–21.

————, ed. 1977. *Organizational Analysis: Critique and Innovation.* Beverly Hills, CA: Sage Publications.

Berdahl, Robert Oliver. 1959. *British Universities and the State.* Berkeley: University of California Press.

Berger, Morroe. 1957. *Bureaucracy and Society in Modern Egypt: A Study of the Higher Civil Service.* Princeton, NJ: Princeton University Press.

Bergeron, Louis. 1981. *France Under Napoleon.* Princeton, NJ: Princeton University Press.

Bergeron, Louis, and Guy Chaussinand-Nogaret. 1979. *Les "Masses de granit": cent mille notables du Premier Empire.* Paris: Éditions de l'École des hautes études en sciences sociales.

Berrington, Hugh. 1968. Partisanship and dissidence in the nineteenth century House of Commons. *Parliamentary Affairs* 21, no. 4 (Autumn): 338–74.

Betters, Paul V. 1931. *The Personnel Classification Board: Its History, Activities and Organization.* Washington, DC: The Brookings Institution.

Beyme, Klaus von. 1971. *Die Politische Elite in der Bundesrepublik Deutschland.* Munich: Piper.

Bialer, Seweryn. 1980. *Stalin's Successors: Leadership, Stability, and Change in the Soviet Union.* New York: Columbia University Press.

————. 1986. *The Soviet Paradox: External Expansion, Internal Decline.* New York: Knopf.

————, ed. 1989. *Politics, Society and Nationality Inside Gorbachev's Russia.* Boulder, CO: Westview Press.

Bidwell, Charles E., and John D. Kasarda. 1984. A human ecological theory of organizational structuring. In *Sociological Human Ecology: Contemporary Issues and Appli-*

cations, edited by Michael Micklin and Harvey Chodin, pp. 183–236. Boulder, CO: Westview Press.

————. 1985. *The Organization and Its Ecosystem: A Theory of Structuring Organizations.* Greenwich, CT: JAI Press.

Binder, Leonard, James Coleman, et al. 1971. *Crises and Sequences in Political Development.* Princeton, NJ: Princeton University Press.

Birnbaum, Pierre. 1982. *The Heights of Power: An Essay on the Power Elite in France.* Chicago: University of Chicago Press.

Blake, Robert. 1985. *The Conservative Party from Peel to Thatcher.* London: Methuen.

Blanc, Laurent. 1971. *Le Fonction publique.* Paris: Presses universitaires de France.

Blau, Peter M. 1963. *The Dynamics of Bureaucracy: A Study of Interpersonal Relations in Two Government Agencies.* Chicago: University of Chicago Press.

————. 1968. The hierarchy of authority in organizations. *American Journal of Sociology* 73, no. 4 (January): 453–67.

————. 1970. A formal theory of differentiation in organizations. *American Sociological Review* 35, no. 2 (April): 210–18.

Blau, Peter M., Wolf V. Heydebrand, and Robert Stauffer. 1973. The structure of small bureaucracies. In *Comparative Organizations,* edited by Wolf V. Heydebrand, pp. 516–33. Englewood Cliffs, NJ: Prentice Hall.

Blau, Peter M., and Richard A. Schoenherr. 1971. *The Structure of Organizations.* New York: Basic Books.

Bledstein, Burton. 1976. *The Culture of Professionalism: The Middle Class and the Development of Higher Education in America.* New York: W. W. Norton Co.

Bleek, Wilhelm. 1972. *Von der Kameralausbildung zum Juristenpriveleg.* Berlin: Colloquium Verlag.

Blute, Marion. 1979. Sociocultural evolutionism: An untried theory. *Behavioral Science* 24, no. 1 (January): 46–59.

Bodiguel, Jean-Luc. 1978. *Les anciens élèves de l'ENA.* Paris: Presses de la Fondation nationale des sciences politique.

Boltanski, Luc. 1982. *Les cadres: La formation d'un groupe sociale.* Paris: Les éditions minuit.

Borcherding, Thomas E. 1977. The sources of growth of public expenditures in the United States, 1902–1970. In *Budgets and Bureaucrats: The Sources of Government Growth,* edited by Thomas E. Borcherding, pp. 45–70. Durham, NC: Duke University Press.

Bottomore, T. B. 1954. Higher Civil Servants in France. *Transactions of the [second] World Congress of Sociology, University of Liege, 1953,* vol. II, pp. 143–52. London: International Sociological Association.

————. 1964. *Elites and Society.* New York: Basic Books.

Boulding, Kenneth E. 1964. A pure theory of conflict applied to organizations. In *The Frontiers of Management Psychology,* edited by George Fisk, pp. 41–49. New York: Harper & Row.

————. 1966. The economics of knowledge and the knowledge of economics. *American Economic Review* 56 (May): 1–13.

Bouloiseau, Marc. 1983. *The Jacobin Republic.* New York: Cambridge University Press.

Bourdieu, Pierre, and Jean-Claude Passeron. 1964. *Les héritiers.* Paris: Éditions de Minuit.

Bowen, Roger W. 1980. *Rebellion and Democracy in Meiji Japan: A Study of Commoners in the Popular Rights Movement.* Berkeley: University of California Press.

Braibant, Guy, et al. 1972. *Histoire de l'administration.* Paris: Édition Cujas.

Brauer, Carl. 1987. Tenure, turnover, and postgovernment employment trends of presidential appointees. In *The In-and-Outers: Presidential Appointees and Transient Government in Washington,* edited by G. Calvin Mackenzie, pp. 174–94. Baltimore: Johns Hopkins University Press.

Braverman, Harry. 1974. *Labor and Monopoly Capital.* New York: Monthly Review Press.

Brewer, John. 1989. *The Sinews of Power: War, Money and the English State, 1688–1783.* New York: Knopf.

Brewer, John, and John Styles, eds. 1980. *An Ungovernable People: The English and Their Law in the Seventeenth and Eighteenth Centuries.* New Brunswick, NJ: Rutgers University Press.

Bridges, Edward. 1950. *Portrait of a Profession: The Civil Service Tradition.* Cambridge: Cambridge University Press.

Brock, Michael. 1973. *The Great Reform Act.* London: Hutchinson University Library.

Brown, R. G. S. 1970. *The Administrative Process in Britain.* London: Methuen.

Bryman, Alan. 1986. *Leadership and Organizations.* London: Routledge and Kegan Paul.

Buchanan, James, and Gordon Tullock. 1962. *The Calculus of Consent.* Ann Arbor: University of Michigan Press.

Bulmer-Thomas, Ivor. 1965. *The Growth of the British Party System.* 2 vols. London: John Baker.

Burnham, Walter Dean. 1970. *Critical Elections and the Mainsprings of American Politics.* New York: W. W. Norton & Co.

Burns, Tom, and G. M. Stalker. 1961. *The Management of Innovation.* London: Tavistock.

Bury, J. P. T. 1973. *Gambetta and the Making of the Third Republic.* London: Longman.

Buttrick, J. 1952. The inside contracting system. *Journal of Economic History* 12 (Summer): 205–21.

Cahen-Salvador, Georges (Georges-Cahen). 1911. *Les fonctionnaires: Leur action corporative.* Paris: Librairie Armand Colin.

Cahiers chrétiens de la fonction publique. 1953–54. Vols. 14, 15.

Cahiers chrétiens de la fonction publique. 1954. "Loyauté et services publics." Vol. 22, no. 23 (January): 1–82.

Cameron, Rondo. 1961. *France and the Economic Development of Europe, 1800–1914.* Princeton, NJ: Princeton University Press.

Campbell, Colin, and George Szablowski. 1979. *The Superbureaucrats: Structure and Behavior in Central Agencies.* Toronto: Macmillan of Canada.

Campbell, D. T. 1969. Variation and selective retention in sociocultural evolution. *General Systems* 14: 69–85.

Canada. 1979. *Report of the Special Committee on the Review of Personnel Management and the Merit Principle.* Ottawa: Supplies and Services.

Cannon, John A. 1973. *Parliamentary Reform: 1640–1832.* Cambridge: Cambridge University Press.

Carchedi, G. 1977. *On the Economic Identification of Social Classes.* London: Routledge and Kegan Paul.

Carlton, Dennis W. 1979. Vertical integration in competitive markets under uncertainty. *Journal of Industrial Economics* 27 (March): 189–209.

Carr, Raymond. 1980. *Modern Spain: 1875–1980.* New York: Oxford University Press.

Carrasco Canals, Carlos. 1975. *La burocracia en la España del Siglo XIX.* Madrid: Instituto de Estudios de Administración Local.

Carroll, Glen R. 1984. Organizational ecology. *Annual Review of Sociology* 10: 71–93.

Carr-Saunders, A. M., and P. A. Wilson. 1933. *The Professions.* Oxford: Clarendon Press.

Cayer, N. Joseph. 1987. *Public Personnel Administration in the United States.* 2d ed. New York: St. Martin's.

Centre for East Asian Cultural Studies, ed. 1972. *Meiji Japan Through Contemporary Sources.* Tokyo: Center for East Asian Cultural Studies.

Chabanne, Robert. 1977. *Les Institutions de la France: de la fin de l'Ancien régime à l'Avènement de la IIIe République.* Lyon: Éditions l'Hermès.

Chambers, William Nisbet. 1975. Party development and the American mainstream. In *The American Party Systems: Stages of Political Development,* edited by William Nisbet Chambers and Walter Dean Burnham, pp. 3–32. New York: Oxford University Press.

Chambers, William Nisbet, and Walter Dean Burnham, eds. 1975. *The American Party Systems: Stages of Political Development.* New York: Oxford University Press.

Chandler, Alfred D., Jr. 1962. *Strategy and Structure: Chapters in the History of the American Industrial Enterprise.* Cambridge, MA: MIT Press.

———. 1977. *The Visible Hand: The Managerial Revolution in American Business.* Cambridge, MA: Harvard University Press.

Chandler, Alfred D., Jr., and Herman Daems. 1979. Administrative coordination, allocation and monitoring: Concepts and comparisons. In *Law and the Formation of the Big Enterprises in the 19th and early 20th Centuries,* edited by Norbert Horn and Jürgen Kocka, pp. 28–54. Göttingen: Vandenhoeck und Ruprecht.

———, eds. 1980. *Managerial Hierarchies: Comparative Perspective on the Rise of the Modern Industrial Enterprise.* Cambridge, MA: Harvard University Press.

Chapman, Brian. 1955. *The Prefects and Provincial France.* London: George Allen & Unwin, Ltd.

———. 1959. *The Profession of Government: Public Service in Europe.* London: Allen and Unwin.

Chapman, Richard A. 1970. *The Higher Civil Service in Britain.* London: Constable.

———. 1982. Civil service recruitment—Bias against external candidates. *Public Administration* 60, no. 1 (Spring): 77–84.

————. 1983. The rise and fall of the CSD. *Policy and Politics* 11, no. 1 (January): 41–61.

Chapman, Richard A., and J. R. Greenaway. 1980. *The Dynamics of Administrative Reform*. London: Croom Helm.

Chartrand, P. J., and K. L. Pond. 1969. *A Study of Executive Career Paths in the Public Service of Canada*. Chicago: Public Personnel Association.

Chase, James S. 1973. *Emergence of the Presidential Nominating Convention: 1789– 1832*. Urbana: University of Illinois Press.

Chester, Daniel Norman, Sir. 1981. *The English Administrative System: 1780–1870*. Oxford: The Clarendon Press.

Cheung, Steven. 1983. The contractual nature of the firm. *Journal of Law and Economics* 26 (April): 1–22.

Child, John. 1972a. Organization structure and strategies of control: A replication of the Aston Study. *Administrative Science Quarterly* 17 (June): 163–77.

————. 1972b. Organizational structure, environment, and performance: The role of strategic choice. *Sociology* 6, no. 1: 1–22.

————. 1973a. Predicting and understanding organization structure. *Administrative Science Quarterly* 18 (June): 168–85.

————. 1973b. Strategies of control and organizational behavior. *Administrative Science Quarterly* 18 (March): 1–17.

Choi, Jungwoon. 1985. Professionalization of American lawyers, 1870–1920. Ph.D. candidacy paper, Department of Political Science, University of Chicago, pp. 1– 61, ix.

Christie, Ian. R. 1962. *Wilkes, Wyvill and Reform*. London: Macmillan.

Church, Clive H. 1967. The social basis of the French central bureaucracy under the Directory, 1795–1799. *Past and Present*, no. 36 (April): 59–72.

————. 1970. Bureaucracy, politics, and revolution: The Evidence of the "Commission des Dix-Sept." *French Historical Studies* 6, no. 4: 492–516.

————. 1981. *Revolution and Red Tape: The French Ministerial Bureaucracy, 1770– 1850*. Oxford: Oxford University Press.

————. 1983. The process of bureaucratization in France, 1789–1799. In vol. 1 of *Die Französische Revolution—zufälliges oder notwendiges Ereignis?* edited by Ebnard von Schmitt and Rolf Reichardt, pp. 121–37. Munich: R. Oldenbourg Verlag.

Churchward, L. G. 1968. Bureaucracy—U.S.A.: U.S.S.R. *Coexistence* 5, no. 2 (July): 201–9.

Cicco, John A., and Ken Ori. 1974. *A New Perspective on the Japanese Civil Service: An Empirical Study of Its Prestige*. Tokyo: Sophia University Press.

Civil Service Commission. 1979. *Report of the Committee on the Selection Procedure for the Recruitment of Administrative Trainees*. London: Civil Service Commission.

Clark, J. C. D. 1980. A general theory of party, opposition and government, 1688– 1832. *The Historical Journal* 23, no. 2: 295–325.

Clark, Kitson George Sidney Roberts. 1962. *The Making of Victorian England*. Cambridge, MA: Harvard University Press.

————. 1973. "Statesmen in Disguise": Reflexions on the history of neutrality of the

Civil Service. In *The Victorian Revolution: Government and Society in Victoria's England,* edited by Peter Stansky, pp. 61–88. New York: New Viewpoints.

Clawson, Dan. 1980. *Bureaucracy and the Labor Process: The Transformation of U. S. Industry, 1860–1920.* New York: Monthly Review Press.

Clegg, Stewart. 1979. *The Theory of Power and Organization.* London: Routledge and Kegan Paul.

———. 1981. Organizational Control. *Administrative Science Quarterly* 26 (December): 546–62.

Clegg, Stewart, and David Dunkerley. 1980. *Organizations, Class and Control.* Boston: Routledge & Kegan Paul.

Coase, Ronald H. 1937. The nature of the firm. *Economica* NS, no. 4: 386–405.

———. 1960. The problem of social cost. *Journal of Law and Economics* 3 (October): 1–44.

———. 1972. Industrial organization: A proposal for research. In *Policy Issues and Research Opportunities in Industrial Organization,* edited by Victor R. Fuchs, pp. 59–73. New York: National Bureau of Economic Research.

———. 1984. The new institutional economics. *Journal of Institutional and Theoretical Economics* 140, no. 1 (March): 229–31.

Cobban, Alfred. 1961. *A History of Modern France. Vol. 2: 1799–1945.* Baltimore, MD: Penguin Books.

Cogan, Morris L. 1953. Toward a definition of profession. *Harvard Educational Review* 23, no. 1 (Winter): 33–50.

Cohen, Bernard S. 1966. Recruitment and training of British civil servants in India, 1600–1860. In *Asian Bureaucratic Systems Emergent from the British Imperial Tradition,* edited by Ralph Braibanti, pp. 87–140. Durham, NC: Duke University Press.

Cohen, Emmeline W. 1941. *The Growth of the British Civil Service, 1780–1939.* London: George Allen and Unwin, Ltd.

Cohen, Michael D., James G. March, and Johan P. Olsen. 1972. A garbage can model of organizational choice. *Administrative Science Quarterly* 17, no. 1 (March): 1–25.

Cole, Taylor. 1949. *The Canadian Bureaucracy: A Study of Canadian Civil Servants and Other Public Employees.* Durham, NC: Duke University Press.

Collier, David, ed. 1979. *The New Authoritarianism in Latin America.* Princeton, NJ: Princeton University Press.

Collins, D. J. 1964. Recruitment and selection for public administration: The last ten years. *Canadian Public Administration* 7, no. 2 (June): 197–204.

Collins, Randall. 1979. *The Credential Society: An Historical Sociology of Education and Stratification.* New York: Academic Press.

Combes, Émile. 1956. *Mon ministère. Mémoires 1902–1905.* Paris: Plon.

Conacher, J. B. 1968. *The Aberdeen Coalition: 1852–1855.* Cambridge: Cambridge University Press.

———. 1972. *The Peelites and the Party System: 1846–52.* Newton Abbot, Devon: David & Charles.

Contini, Bruno. 1969. A critical survey of use of cost-benefit analysis in public finance. In *Quantitative Analysis in Public Finance,* edited by Alan T. Peacock and Dieter Biehl, pp. 65–85. New York: Praeger.

Cook, Karen S. 1977. Exchange and power in networks and interorganizational relations. *Sociological Quarterly* 18 (Winter): 62–82.

Corson, John J., and R. Shale Paul. 1966. *Men Near the Top: Filling Key Posts in the Federal Service.* Baltimore: Johns Hopkins Press.

Cowling, Maurice. 1967. *1867 Disraeli, Gladstone and Revolution: The Passing of the Second Reform Bill.* Cambridge: Cambridge University Press.

Cox, Gary W. 1987. *The Efficient Secret: The Cabinet and the Development of Political Parties in Victorian England.* Cambridge: Cambridge University Press.

Crenson, Matthew A. 1975. *The Federal Machine: Beginnings of Bureaucracy in Jacksonian America.* Baltimore: Johns Hopkins University Press.

Cromwell, Valerie, et al. 1978. *Aspects of Government in Nineteenth Century Britain.* Dublin: Irish University Press.

Cromwell, Valerie, and Zara S. Steiner. 1972. The foreign office before 1914: A study in resistance. In *Studies in the Growth of Nineteenth-Century Government,* edited by Gillian Sutherland, pp. 167–94. London: Routledge and Kegan Paul.

Crozier, Michel. 1964. *The Bureaucratic Phenomenon.* Chicago: University of Chicago Press.

———. 1970. *La Société bloquée.* Paris: Éditions du Seuil.

Crozier, Michel, Samuel P. Huntington, and Joji Watanuki. 1975. *The Crisis of Democracy: Report on the Governability of Democracies to the Trilateral Commission.* New York: New York University Press.

Crunden, Robert M. 1982. *Ministers of Reform: The Progressives' Achievement in American Civilization, 1889–1920.* New York: Basic Books.

Curtis, S. J. 1965. *History of Education in Great Britain.* London: University Tutorial Press.

Cutright, Phillips. 1965. Political structure, economic development and national social security programs. *American Journal of Sociology* 70, no. 5 (March): 537–50.

Cyert, Richard M., and James G. March. 1963. *A Behavioral Theory of the Firm.* Englewood Cliffs, NJ: Prentice-Hall.

Dahl, Robert A. 1956. *A Preface to Democratic Theory.* Chicago: University of Chicago Press.

Dahl, Robert A., and Charles E. Lindblom. 1963. *Politics, Economics and Welfare: Planning and Politico-Economic Systems Resolved into Basic Social Processes.* New York: Harper and Row.

Dale, Harold E. 1942. *The Higher Civil Service in Great Britain.* Oxford: Oxford University Press.

———. 1943. *The Personnel and Problems of the Higher Civil Service.* Oxford: Oxford University Press.

Damaska, Mirjan. 1986. *The Faces of Justice and State Authority.* New Haven, CT: Yale University Press.

Dansette, Adrien. 1972. *Du 2 décembre au 4 septembre: le Second Empire.* Paris: Hachette.

Darbel, Alain, and Dominique Schnapper. 1969. *Les agents du système administratif.* Paris: Mouton.

———. 1972. *Le système administratif.* Paris: Mouton.

Davis, Richard W. 1976. Deference and aristocracy in the time of the Great Reform Act. *American Historical Review* 81, no. 3 (June): 532–39.

Dawson, R. MacGregor. 1936. The Canadian Civil Service. *Canadian Journal of Economics and Political Science* 2, no. 3 (August): 288–300.

Debbasch, Charles. 1966. *Institutions administratives.* Paris: Librairie général de droit et de jurisprudence.

———. 1969. *L'Administration au pouvoir, fonctionnaires et politiques sous la Ve République.* Paris: Calmann-Lévy.

de Calan, Pierre. 1953. Service public et bien commun. *Cahiers chrétiens de la fonction publique* 14 (October): 17–24.

Décosterd, Roger. 1959. *L'Administration Federale.* Lausanne: Centre de reserches européenes, Écoles des H. E. C., Université de Lausanne.

Delbrück, Clemens von. 1917. *Die Ausbildung für den höheren verwaltungsdienst in Preussen.* Jena: Fischer.

Delbusquet, Jules. 1843. *De l'organisation des administrations centrales des divers ministères: des droits et des devoirs des employes.* Paris: Charles Hingray.

Delfau, Albert. 1902. *Napoleon Ier et l'instruction publique.* Paris: Albert Fontemoing.

Demartial, Georges. 1906. *Le personnel des ministères.* Paris: Berger-Levrault & Cie.

———. 1909. *Le statut des fonctionnaires.* Paris: Collection de la Grande revue.

Denhardt, Richard B. 1981. Toward a critical theory of public organization. *Public Administration Review* 41 (November): 628–35.

Derry, John W. 1972. *Charles James Fox.* New York: St. Martin's Press.

Dewey, C. J. 1973. The education of a ruling caste: The Indian Civil Service in the era of competitive examination. *English Historical Review* 88, no. 347: 262–85.

DeWitt, Nicholas, ed. 1961. *Education and Professional Employment in the USSR.* Washington, DC: National Science Foundation.

Dicey, A. V. 1915 [1982]. *Introduction to the Study of the Law of the Constitution.* London: Macmillan [Liberty Classics Reprint].

Dill, William R. 1958. Environment as an influence on managerial autonomy. *Administrative Science Quarterly* 2 (March): 409–43.

DiMaggio, Paul J., and Walter W. Powell. 1983. The iron cage revisited: Institutional isomorphism and collective rationality in organizational fields. *American Sociological Review* 48, no. 2 (April): 147–60.

DiPrete, Thomas A. 1987. The professionalization of administration and equal employment opportunity in the U.S. Federal Government. *American Journal of Sociology* 93, no. 1 (July): 119–40.

DiPrete, Thomas A., and Whitman T. Soule. 1986. The organization of career lines: Equal employment opportunity and status advancement in a federal bureaucracy. *American Sociological Review* 51, no. 3 (June): 295–309.

Dobson, John M. 1972. *Politics in the Gilded Age: A New Perspective on Reform.* New York: Praeger.

Doenecke, Justus D. 1981. *The Presidencies of James A. Garfield and Chester A. Arthur.* Lawrence, KS: The Regents Press of Kansas.

Doeringer, Peter, and Michael J. Piore. 1971. *Internal Labor Markets and Manpower Analysis.* Lexington, MA: Heath.

Donajgrodzki, A. P. 1972. New roles for old: The Northcote-Trevelyan Report and the clerks of the Home Office, 1822–48. In *Studies in the Growth of Nineteenth-Century Government,* edited by Gillian Sutherland, pp. 82–109. London: Routledge and Kegan Paul.

Dore, Ronald P. 1965. *Education in Tokugawa Japan.* Berkeley: University of California Press.

———. 1983. Goodwill and the spirit of market capitalism. *British Journal of Sociology* 34 (December): 459–82.

Dorn, Walter. 1963. *Competition for Empire: 1740–1763.* New York: Harper & Row.

Downs, Anthony. 1967. *Inside Bureaucracy.* Boston: Little, Brown & Co.

Downs, George W., and Patrick D. Larkey. 1986. *The Search for Government Efficiency: From Hubris to Helplessness.* New York: Random House.

Drewry, Gavin, and Tony Butcher. 1988. *The Civil Service Today.* Cambridge, MA: Basil Blackwell.

Dreyfuss, Carl. 1938. *Occupation and Ideology of the Salaried Employee.* New York: Department of Social Science, Columbia University.

Dubois, Comte. 1859. De l'institution des auditeurs au Conseil d'État. *Revue Contemporaine* (April): 1–30.

Duncan, Otis Dudley, ed. 1964. *William F. Ogburn: On Culture and Social Change.* Chicago: University of Chicago Press.

Duncan, Otis Dudley, and Philip M. Hauser, eds. 1959. *The Study of Population: An Inventory and Appraisal.* Chicago: University of Chicago Press.

Duncan, R. 1972. Characteristics of organizational environments and perceived environmental uncertainty. *Administrative Science Quarterly* 17: 313–27.

Dunn, William N., and Bahman Fozouni. 1976. *Toward a Critical Administrative Theory.* Beverly Hills, CA: Sage Publications.

Dupuy, François, and Jean-Claude Thoenig. 1983. *Sociologie de l'administration française.* Paris: Armand Colin.

Durand, Charles. 1958. *Les auditeurs au Conseil d'État de 1803 à 1814.* Paris: La pensée universelle.

Dye, Thomas R., and John W. Pickering. 1974. Governmental and corporate elites. *Journal of Politics* 36 (November): 900–925.

Dyson, Kenneth H. F. 1977. *Party, State and Bureaucracy in West Germany.* Beverly Hills, CA: Sage Publications.

Eccles, Robert. 1981. The quasifirm in the construction industry. *Journal of Economic Behavior and Organization* 2 (December): 335–58.

École Polytechnique. 1967. *Le profil du polytechnicien de 1875–1880.* Paris: École Polytechnique, Bibliotheque Centrale.

Edwards, Richard C. 1979. *Contested Terrain: The Transformation of the Workplace in the Twentieth Century.* New York: Basic Books.

Egger, Rowland. 1949. A second view: An American administrative class? In *The Pub-*

lic Service and University Education, edited by Joseph E. McLean, pp. 205–33. Princeton, NJ: Princeton University Press.

Eisenstadt, S. N. 1969. *The Political Systems of Empires: The Rise and Fall of the Historical Bureaucratic Societies.* New York: Free Press.

Elkin, Stephen L. 1974. Political science and the analysis of public policy. *Public Policy* 22 (Summer): 399–422.

Elliot, Clifford, and David Kuhn. 1978. Professionals in bureaucracies: Some emerging areas of conflict. *University of Michigan Business Review* 30 (January): 12–16.

Ellwein, Thomas, and Ralf Zoll. 1973. *Berufsbeamtentum: Anspruch und Wirklichkeit.* Dusseldorf: Bertelsmann Universitätsverlag.

Elwitt, Sanford. 1975. *The Making of the Third Republic: Class and Politics in France, 1868–1884.* Baton Rouge: Louisiana State University Press.

Emden, C. S. 1923. *The Civil Servant in the Law and in the Constitution.* London: Stevens and Sons, Ltd.

Emery, F. E., and E. L. Trist. 1965. The causal texture of organizational environments. *Human Relations* 18: 21–32.

———. 1973. *Towards a Social Ecology.* New York: Plenum Publishing.

Engel, Arthur J. 1983a. The English universities and professional education. In *The Transformation of Higher Learning, 1860–1930,* edited by Konrad H. Jarausch, pp. 293–305. Chicago: University of Chicago Press.

———. 1983b. *From Clergyman to Don: The Rise of the Academic Profession in Nineteenth Century Oxford.* Oxford: Clarendon Press.

Engelsing, Rolf. 1968. Zur politischen Bildung der deutschen Untershichten, 1789–1863. *Historische Zeitschrift* 206, no. 2 (April): 337–69.

Evan, William M. 1960. The organization-set: Toward a theory of interorganizational relations. In *Approaches to Organizational Design,* edited by J. D. Thompson, pp. 175–91. Pittsburgh, PA: University of Pittsburgh Press.

Evans, Peter B., Dietrich Rueschmeyer, and Theda Skocpol. 1985. *Bringing the State Back In.* New York: Cambridge University Press.

Ezrahi, Yaron. 1978. Political contexts of science indicators. In *Toward a Metric of Science: The Advent of Science Indicators,* by Yehuda Elkana, Joshua Lederberg, et al., pp. 285–327. New York: John Wiley & Sons.

———. 1990. *The Descent of Icarus.* Cambridge, MA: Harvard University Press.

Faber, Geoffrey. 1957. *Jowett: A Portrait with Background.* London: Faber & Faber Ltd.

Fama, Eugene F. 1980. Agency problems and the theory of the firm. *Journal of Political Economy* 88, no. 2 (April): 288–307.

Fama, Eugene F., and Michael C. Jensen. 1983a. Agency problems and residual claims. *Journal of Law and Economics* 26 (June): 327–49.

———. 1983b. Separation of ownership and control. *Journal of Law and Economics* 26 (June): 301–26.

Farrell, Robert, ed. 1970. *Political Leadership in Eastern Europe and the Soviet Union.* Chicago: Aldine Publishing.

Federal Council for Science and Technology. 1962. *Report.* Washington, DC: Government Printing Office.

Ferrat, André. 1945. *La République à refaire.* Paris: Gallimard.

Feuchtwanger, E. J. 1985. *Democracy and Empire: Britain 1865–1914.* London: Edward Arnold.

Filler, Louis. 1976. *The Muckrakers: Crusaders for American Liberalism.* University Park: Pennsylvania State University Press.

Finer, Herman. 1975. State and nation-building in Europe: The role of the military. In *The Formation of National States in Western Europe,* edited by Charles Tilly, pp. 84–163. Princeton, NJ: Princeton University Press.

Finer, Samuel E. 1937. *The British Civil Service.* London: The Fabian Society.

Fish, Carl R. [1904] 1963. *The Civil Service and the Patronage.* New York: Russell & Russell; reprint. [1904 edition published by Harvard University Press.]

Fisher, Linda. 1987. Fifty years of presidential appointments. In *The In-and-Outers: Presidential Appointees and Transient Government in Washington,* edited by G. Calvin Mackenzie, pp. 1–29. Baltimore: Johns Hopkins University Press.

Fleron, Frederic J., Jr. 1970. Representation of career types in the Soviet political leadership. In *Political Leadership in Eastern Europe and the Soviet Union,* edited by R. Barry Farrell, pp.108–39. Chicago: Aldine Publishing Co.

Foord, Archibald S. 1947. The waning of "the influence of the Crown." *English Historical Review* 62, no. 245 (October): 484–507.

———. 1964. *His Majesty's Opposition: 1714–1830.* Oxford: Clarendon Press.

Foster, C. D. 1966. Social welfare functions in cost-benefit analysis. In *Operational Research and the Social Sciences,* edited by John R. Lawrence, pp. 305–18. London: Tavistock.

Foulke, William D. 1925. *Roosevelt and the Spoilsmen.* New York: National Civil Service Reform League.

Fox, Robert. 1984. Science, university, and the state in nineteenth-century France. In *Professions and the French State,* edited by Gerald L. Geison, pp. 68–146. Philadelphia: University of Pennsylvania Press.

Francis, Arthur. 1983. Markets and hierarchies: Efficiency or domination? In *Power, Efficiency, and Institutions,* edited by Arthur Francis, Jeremy Turk, and Paul Willmam, pp. 105–116. London: Heinemann.

Fraser, Derek. 1976. *Urban Politics in Victorian England.* Leicester: Leicester University Press.

Fraser, Peter. 1960. The growth of ministerial control in the nineteenth-century House of Commons. *English Historical Review* 74, no. 296 (July): 444–63.

Freedeman, Charles E. 1961. *The Conseil D'État in Modern France.* New York: Columbia University Press.

Freeman, John. 1982. Organizational life cycles and natural selection processes. In *Research in Organizational Behavior: Vol. 4,* edited by Barry M. Staw and L. L. Cummings, pp. 1–32. Greenwich, CT: JAI Press.

Freidson, Eliot. 1970. *Profession of Medicine: A Study of the Sociology of Applied Knowledge.* New York: Dodd, Mead and Co.

———. 1986. *Professional Powers: A Study of the Institutionalization of Formal Knowledge.* Chicago: University of Chicago Press.

Freidson, Eliot, and Buford Rhea. 1965. Knowledge and judgement in professional evaluations. *Administrative Science Quarterly* 10 (June): 107–24.

Friedman, Lawrence M. 1973. *A History of American Law.* New York: Simon and Schuster.

Friedrich, Carl J. 1939. The continental tradition of training administrators in law and jurisprudence. *Journal of Modern History* 11, no. 2 (June): 129–48.

Friedrich, Carl J., and Taylor Cole. 1932. *Responsible Bureaucracy: A Study of the Swiss Civil Service.* Cambridge, MA: Harvard University Press.

Fry, Geoffrey K. 1969. *Statesmen in Disguise: The Changing Role of the Administrative Class of the British Home Civil Service, 1853–1966.* London: Macmillan.

———. 1979. *The Growth of Government.* London: Frank Cass & Co., Ltd.

Fujii, Shinichi. 1965. *The Constitution of Japan: A Historical Survey.* Tokyo: Kokushi-kan University.

Fujino, Tamotsu. 1983. *Nihon hōkensei to bakuhan taisei.* Tokyo: Hanawa Shobō.

Fujita, Shōzō. 1966. *Tennōsei kokka no shihai genri.* Tokyo: Miraisha.

Fukai, Eigo. 1953. *Sūmitsu-in jūyō giji oboegaki.* Tokyo: Iwanami Shoten.

Garas, Félix. 1936. *La sélection des cadres administratifs à l'étude de la réforme de l'état.* Paris: Librairie Picart.

García de Enterría, Eduardo. 1961. *La administracion Española: Estudios de ciencia administrativa.* Madrid: Instituto de Estudios Politicos.

Garland, Martha McMackin. 1980. *Cambridge Before Darwin: The Ideal of a Liberal Education.* New York: Cambridge University Press.

Garrett, John. 1980. *Managing the Civil Service.* London: Heinemann.

Gash, Norman. 1953. *Politics in the Age of Peel: A Study in the Technique of Parliamentary Representation, 1830–1850.* London: Longmans, Green and Co.

———. 1979. *Aristocracy and People: Britain, 1815–1865.* Cambridge, MA: Harvard University Press.

———. 1983. The organization of the Conservative Party 1832–1846: Part II: The electoral organization. *Parliamentary History* 2: 131–52.

Geison, Gerald L., ed. 1984. *Professions and the French State, 1700–1900.* Philadelphia: University of Pennsylvania Press.

Georgin, Charles. 1911. *L'Avancement dans les fonctions publique: son organisation; ses garanties.* Paris: Librairie générale de droit & de jurisprudence.

Gerbod, Paul, Claude Goyard, et al. 1977. *Les Épurations administratives: XIXe et XXe siècles.* Genève: Librairie Droz.

Giesselmann, Werner. 1977. *Die brumairianische Elite: Kontinuität und Wandel der französischen Führungsschicht zwischen Ancien Régime und Julimonarchie.* Stuttgart: Ernst Klett Verlag.

Gill, Graeme. 1990. *The Origins of the Stalinist Political System.* New York: Cambridge University Press.

Gillis, John R. 1971. *The Prussian Bureaucracy in Crisis, 1840–1860: Origins of an Administrative Ethos.* Stanford, CA: Stanford University Press.

Girard, Louis. 1964. *Problèmes politiques et constitutionnels du Second Empire.* Paris: Centre de documentation universitaire.

———. 1968. *La 2ᵉ [Deuxième] République (1848–1851)*. Paris: Calmann-Lévy.

[William Gladstone]. 1856. The declining efficiency of Parliament. *Quarterly Review* 99 (June): 521–70.

Gluck, Carol. 1985. *Japan's Modern Myths: Ideology in the Late Meiji Period*. Princeton, NJ: Princeton University Press.

Goblot, Edmond. 1925. *La barrière et le niveau: étude sociologique sur la bourgeoisie française moderne*. Paris: F. Alcan.

Godechot, Jacques Léon. 1968. *Les Institutions de la France sous la Révolution et l'Empire*. Paris: Presses universitaires de France.

Goldman, Paul. 1973. Size and differentiation in organizations: A test of theory. *Pacific Sociological Review* 16, no. 1 (January): 89–105.

Goldman, Paul, and Donald R. Van Houten 1977. Managerial strategies and the worker: A Marxist analysis of bureaucracy. In *Organizational Analysis: Critique and Innovation*, edited by J. Kenneth Benson, pp. 110–27. Beverly Hills, CA: Sage Publications.

Goldner, Fred H., and R. R. Ritti. 1967. Professionalization as career immobility. *American Journal of Sociology* 72, no. 5 (March): 489–502.

Goode, William J. 1957. Community within a community: The professions. *American Sociological Review* 22, no. 1 (February): 194–200.

Goodlad, Sinclair, ed. 1984. *Education for the Professions: Quis custodiet . . . ?* Guildford, Surrey: Society for Research into Higher Education.

Gordon, Andrew. 1988. *The Evolution of Labor Relations in Japan: Heavy Industry, 1853–1955*. Cambridge, MA: Harvard University Press.

Gordon, David M., Richard Edwards, and Michael Reich. 1982. *Segmented Work, Divided Workers: The Historical Transformation of Labor in the United States*. New York: Cambridge University Press.

Gordon, Robert A. 1961. *Business Leadership in the Large Corporation*. 2d ed. Berkeley: University of California Press.

Gouldner, Alvin W. 1954. *Patterns of Industrial Bureaucracy*. Glencoe, IL: Free Press.

———. 1955. Metaphysical pathos and the theory of bureaucracy. *American Political Science Review* 49 (June): 496–507.

———. 1965. *Wildcat Strike: A Study in Worker-Management Relationships*. New York: Harper & Row.

Gournay, Bernard, ed. 1961. *L'Administration Française*. Paris: Fondation nationale des sciences politiques.

Goyard, Claude. 1977. La notion d'épuration administrative. In *Les Épurations administratives: XIXe et XXe siècles,* edited by Paul Gerbod, et al., pp. 1–48. Genève: Librairie Droz.

Graebner, William. 1980. Efficiency, security, community: The origins of civil service retirement. *Prologue* 12, no. 3 (Fall): 116–33.

Grandjean, Burke D. 1981. History and career in a bureaucratic labor market. *American Journal of Sociology* 86, no. 5 (March): 1,057–92.

Granick, David. 1960. *The Red Executive*. Garden City, NY: Doubleday & Co.

———. 1972. *Managerial Comparisons of Four Developed Countries: France, Britain, United States and Russia*. Cambridge, MA: MIT Press.

———. 1973. Managerial incentives in the USSR and in Western firms: Implications for behavior. *Journal of Comparative Administration* 5, no. 2 (August): 169–99.

Granovetter, Mark S. 1973. The strength of weak ties. *American Journal of Sociology* 78, no. 6 (May): 1,360–80.

———. 1979. The idea of "advancement" in theories of social evolution. *American Journal of Sociology* 85, no. 3 (Nov.): 489–515.

Great Britain. 1854–1855. *Parliamentary Papers [1870]: Papers Relating to the Reorganization of the Permanent Civil Service.* Vol. XX. London: HMSO.

———. 1854–1855. *Parliamentary Papers: Report on the Organisation of the Permanent Civil Service.* [1713] Vol. XXVII. London: HMSO.

———. 1860. *Parliamentary Papers: Report from the Select Committee on Civil Service Appointments.* London: HMSO.

———. 1875. *Parliamentary Papers: Reports from the Civil Service (Playfair) Inquiry Commission.* London: HMSO. Command paper 1113. Command paper 1226.

———. 1887–1890. *Parliamentary Papers: Reports from the Royal (Ridley) Commission on Civil Establishments.* Vols. XIX (1887), XXVII (1888), XXI (1889), XXVII (1890). London: HMSO.

———. 1912–1915. *Parliamentary Papers: Reports from the Royal (MacDonnell) Commission on the Civil Service.* Vols. XV (1912–1913), XVI (1914). London: HMSO.

———. 1920. *Civil Service National Whitley Council, Interim Report of the Joint Committee on the Organization, etc. of the Civil Service.* London: HMSO.

———. 1966–1968. *Parliamentary Papers: Report of the Committee (Fulton) on the Civil Service.* Command paper 3638. London: HMSO.

Great Britain, Civil Service Commissioners. 1856. *Report.* London: HMSO.

———. 1871. *Report.* London: H. M. Stationary Office.

———. 1979. *Report of the Committee on the Selection Procedure for the Recruitment of Administrative Trainees.* London: Civil Service Commission.

Greenwood, E. 1957. Attributes of a profession. *Social Work* 2, no. 3 (July): 45–55.

Greenwood, John R., and David J. Wilson. 1984. *Public Administration in Britain.* London: George Allen & Unwin.

Grégoire, Roger. 1943. *Le recrutement et la sélection des cadres supérieure de l'administration centrale.* Paris.

———. 1954. *La fonction publique.* Paris: A. Colin.

———. 1964. *The French Civil Service.* Brussels: International Institute of Administrative Sciences.

Grémion, Catherine. 1979. *Profession, décideurs: pouvoir des hauts fonctionnaires et reforme de l'État.* Paris: Gauthier-Villars.

Grémion, Pierre. 1976. *La pouvoir périphérique: Bureaucrates et notables dans le système politique français.* Paris: Éditions du Seuil.

Griffen, Clyde. 1970. The Progressive Ethos. In *The Development of an American Culture,* edited by Stanley Coben and Lorman Ratner, pp. 120–49. Englewood Cliffs, NJ: Prentice-Hall.

Griffith, Wyn. 1954. *The British Civil Service: 1854–1954.* London: HMSO.

Grigg, Sir James. 1949. The British Civil Service. In *The Public Service and University Education,* edited by Joseph E. McLean, pp. 147–65. Princeton: Princeton University Press.

Grossman, Sanford J., and Oliver D. Hart. 1982. Corporate financial structure and managerial incentives. In *The Economics of Information and Uncertainty,* edited by John J. McCall, pp. 107–40. Chicago: University of Chicago Press.

Grusky, Oscar. 1960. Administrative succession in formal organizations. *Social Forces* 39, no. 2 (December): 105–15.

———. 1961. Corporate size, bureaucratization, and managerial succession. *American Journal of Sociology* 67, no. 3 (November): 261–69.

———. 1964. The effects of succession: A comparative study of military and business organization. In *The New Military,* edited by Morris Janowitz, pp. 83–109. New York: Russell Sage Foundation.

Gunther, Richard. 1980. *Public Policy in a No-Party State: Spanish Planning and Budgeting in the Twilight of the Franquist Era.* Berkeley: University of California Press.

Gutmann, Amy. 1980. *Liberal Equality.* New York: Cambridge University Press.

Guttsman, W. L. 1963. *The British Political Elite.* New York: Basic Books.

———. 1974. The British political elite and the class structure. In *Elites and Power in British Society,* edited by Philip Stanworth and Anthony Giddens, pp. 22–44. New York: Cambridge University Press.

Habermas, Jurgen. 1975. *Legitimation Crisis.* Boston: Beacon Press.

———. 1989. *The Structural Transformation of the Public Sphere.* Cambridge, MA: MIT Press.

Hackett, Roger. 1968. Political modernization and the Meiji genrō. In *Political Development in Modern Japan,* edited by Robert E. Ward, pp. 65–98. Princeton: Princeton University Press.

———. 1971. *Yamagata Aritomo in the Rise of Modern Japan: 1838–1922.* Cambridge, MA: Harvard University Press.

Hage, Jerald. 1980. *Theories of Organization: Form, Process, and Transformation.* New York: John Wiley & Sons.

Halevi, Ran. 1988. La révolution constituante: les ambiguités politiques. In *The French Revolution and the Creation of Modern Political Culture. Volume 2: The Political Culture of the French Revolution,* edited by Keith Baker, François Furet, and Colin Lucas, pp. 69–85. Oxford: Pergamon Press.

Hall, Ivan Parker. 1973. *Mori Arinori.* Cambridge, MA: Harvard University Press.

Hall, John A. 1985. *Powers and Liberties: The Causes and Consequences of the Rise of the West.* Oxford: Basil Blackwell.

Hall, Peter Dobkin. 1982. *The Organization of American Culture, 1700–1900: Private Institutions, Elites, and the Origins of American Nationality.* New York: New York University Press.

Hall, Richard H. 1968. Professionalization and bureaucratization. *American Sociological Review* 33, no. 1 (February): 92–104.

———. 1982. *Organizations: Structure and Process.* Englewood Cliffs, NJ: Prentice-Hall.

Hammond, Thomas H., and Gary J. Miller. 1985. A social choice perspective on expertise and authority in bureaucracy. *American Journal of Political Science* 29, no. 1 (February): 1–28.

Hanham, H. J. 1959. *Elections and Party Management: Politics in the Time of Disraeli and Gladstone.* London: Longmans.

———, ed. 1969. *The Nineteenth-Century Constitution, 1815–1914.* Cambridge: Cambridge University Press.

Hannan, Michael T., and John Freeman. 1977. The population ecology of organizations. *American Journal of Sociology* 82, no. 5 (March): 929–64.

———. 1984. Structural inertia and organizational change. *American Sociological Review* 49, no. 2 (April): 149–64.

———. 1986. Where do organizational forms come from? *Sociological Forum* 2, no. 1: 50–72.

———. 1989. *Organizational Ecology.* Cambridge, MA: Harvard University Press.

Harden, Ian, and Norman Lewis. 1986. *The Noble Lie: The British Constitution and the Rule of Law.* London: Hutchinson.

Harootunian, Harry D. 1966. Jinsei, Jinzai, and Jitsugaku: Social values and leadership in late Tokugawa thought. In *Modern Japanese Leadership: Transition and Change,* edited by Bernard S. Silberman and Harry D. Harootunian, pp. 83–119. Tucson: University of Arizona Press.

———. 1970. *Toward Restoration: The Growth of Political Consciousness in Tokugawa Japan.* Berkeley: University of California Press.

Harris, John, and Thomas V. Garcia. 1966. The permanent secretaries: Britain's top administrators. *Public Administration Review* 26: 31–44.

Harris, Milton, and Robert M. Townsend. 1981. Resource allocation under asymmetric information. *Econometrica* 49 (January): 33–64.

Hart, Jenifer. 1972. The genesis of the Northcote-Trevelyan Report. In *Studies in the Growth of Nineteenth-Century Government,* edited by Gillian Sutherland, pp. 63–81. London: Routledge and Kegan Paul.

Hasegawa, Ryō. 1966. *Meiji ishin ni okeru hanbatsu seiji no kenkyū.* Tokyo: Hyōronsha.

Hasenfeld, Yeheskel. 1972. People processing organizations: An exchange approach. *American Sociological Review* 37, no. 3 (June): 256–63.

Haskell, Thomas. 1977. *The Emergence of Professional Social Science.* Urbana, IL: University of Illinois Press.

Hata, Ikuhiko. 1983. *Kanryō no kenkyū: Fumetsu no pawa, 1868–1983.* Tokyo: Kōdansha.

Hattenhauer, Hans. 1980. *Geschichte des Beamtentums.* Cologne: Heymann.

Hawkins, Angus. 1987. *Parliament, Party and the Art of Politics in Britain, 1855–59.* Stanford: Stanford University Press.

Hawley, Amos. 1950. *Human Ecology.* New York: Ronald Press.

———. 1968. Human ecology. In vol. 4 of *International Encyclopedia of the Social Sciences,* edited by David Sills, pp. 328–37. New York: Macmillan.

Haydu, Jeffrey. 1988. *Between Craft and Class: Skilled Workers and Factory Politics in the United States and Britain, 1890–1922.* Berkeley: University of California Press.

Hays, Samuel P. 1957. *The Response to Industrialism, 1885–1914.* Chicago: University of Chicago Press.

———. 1964. The politics of reform in municipal government in the progressive era. *Pacific Northwest Quarterly* 55, no. 4 (October): 157–69.

———. 1972. Introduction—The new organizational society. In *Building the Organizational Society,* edited by Jerry Israel, pp. 1–15. New York: The Free Press.

Hays, Steven W., and Richard C. Kearney. 1982. Examinations in the public service. In *Centenary Issues of the Pendleton Act of 1883: The Problematic Legacy of Civil Service Reform,* edited by David H. Rosenbloom and Mark A. Emmert, pp. 25–44. New York: Marcel Dekker, Inc.

Heady, Ferrel. 1966, 1979. *Public Administration: A Comparative Perspective,* 3d ed. Englewood Cliffs, NJ: Prentice-Hall. (1966, 2d ed. New York, NY: M. Dekker.)

Heclo, Hugh. 1977. *A Government of Strangers: Executive Politics in Washington.* Washington, DC: The Brookings Institution.

———. 1984. In search of a role: America's higher civil service. In *Bureaucrats and Policy Making,* edited by Ezra N. Suleiman, pp. 8–34. New York: Holmes and Meier Publishers.

———. 1987. The in-and-outer system: A critical assessment. In *The In-and-Outers: Presidential Appointees and Transient Government in Washington,* edited by G. Calvin Mackenzie, pp. 195–216. Baltimore: Johns Hopkins University Press.

Heclo, Hugh, and Aaron Wildavsky. 1974. *The Private Government of Public Money: Community and Policy inside British Politics.* Berkeley: University of California Press.

Heffter, Heinrich. 1950. *Die deutsche Selbstverwaltung im 19. Jahrhundert: Geschichte der Ideen und Institutionen.* Stuttgart: K. F. Koehler.

Henry, P. 1950. *Histoire des préfets.* Paris: Nouvelles Éditions Latines.

Hensel, H. Struve. 1949. Problems of structure and personnel. In *The Public Service and University Education,* edited by Joseph E. McLean, pp. 82–94. Princeton, NJ: Princeton University Press.

Herman, Valentine, and James E. Alt, eds. 1975. *Cabinet Studies: A Reader.* New York: St. Martin's Press.

Herzog, Don. 1985. *Without Foundations: Justification in Political Theory.* Ithaca, NY: Cornell University Press.

Heydebrand, Wolf V. 1977. Organizational contradictions in public bureaucracies: Toward a Marxian theory of organizations. *Sociological Quarterly* 18: 83–107.

———, ed. 1973. *Comparative Organizations.* Englewood Cliffs, NJ: Prentice-Hall.

Hickson, D. J., D. S. Pugh, and Diane C. Pheysey. 1969. Operations technology and organization structure: An empirical reappraisal. *Administrative Science Quarterly* 14 (September): 378–97.

Hickson, D. J., et al. 1971. A strategic contingencies theory of interorganizational power. *Administrative Science Quarterly* 16: 216–29.

Hill, Brian W. 1985. *British Parliamentary Parties, 1742–1832.* London: George Allen & Unwin.

Hintze, Otto. 1968. The state in historical perspective. In *State and Society: A Reader in Comparative Political Sociology,* edited by Reinhard Bendix, pp. 154–69. Boston: Little, Brown & Co.

———. 1975. Military organization and the organization of the state. In *The Historical Essays of Otto Hintze,* edited by Felix Gilbert, pp. 178–215. New York: Oxford University Press.

Hirano, Takashi. 1983. Sengo Nihon kanryō kikō keisei. *Rekishigaku kenkyū,* no. 516 (May): 1–18.

Hodgetts, J. E. 1955 [1956]. *Pioneer Public Service: An Administrative History of the United Canadas, 1841–1867.* Toronto: University of Toronto Press.

———. 1973. *Canadian Public Service: A Physiology of Government, 1867–1970.* Toronto: University of Toronto Press.

Hofstadter, Richard. 1955. *Social Darwinism in American Thought.* Rev. ed. Boston: Beacon Press.

Holmstrom, Bengt. 1979. Moral hazard and observability. *The Bell Journal of Economics* 10 (Spring): 74–91.

Honey, J. R. de S. 1977. *Tom Brown's Universe: The Development of the English Public School in the Nineteenth Century.* New York: Quadrangle/New York Times Book Co.

Honey, John. 1987. The sinews of society: The public schools as a system. In *The Rise of the Modern Educational System: Structural Change and Social Reproduction 1870–1920,* edited by Detlef K. Müller, Fritz Ringer, and Brian Simon, pp. 151–62. New York: Cambridge University Press.

Hoogenboom, Ari. 1961. *Outlawing the Spoils: A History of the Civil Service Reform Movement, 1865–1883.* Urbana: University of Illinois Press.

Horie, Hideichi, and Tōyama Shigeki, eds. 1959. *Jiyūminkenki no kenkyū.* Tokyo: Yūhikaku.

Horowitz, Ira. 1970. *Decision Making and the Theory of the Firm.* New York: Holt, Rhinehart and Winston.

Hough, Jerry F. 1969. *The Soviet Prefects: The Local Party Organs in Industrial Decision-Making.* Cambridge, MA: Harvard University Press.

———. 1973. The bureaucratic model and the nature of the Soviet system. *Journal of Comparative Administration* 5, no. 2 (August): 134–67.

Hough, Jerry F., and Merle Fainsod. 1979. *How the Soviet Union Is Governed.* Cambridge, MA: Harvard University Press.

Hrebiniak, Lawrence G., and William F. Joyce. 1985. Organizational adaptation: Strategic choice and environmental determinism. *Administrative Science Quarterly* 30: 336–47.

Huber, Thomas M. 1981. *The Revolutionary Origins of Modern Japan.* Stanford: Stanford University Press

Hughes, Edward. 1942. Civil service reform, 1853–55. *History* 27 (June): 51–83.

———. 1949a. Sir Charles Trevelyan and civil service reform, 1853–55; part I. *English Historical Review* 64, no. 250 (January): 53–88.

———. 1949b. Sir Charles Trevelyan and civil service reform, 1853–55; part II. *English Historical Review* 64, no. 251 (April): 206–34.

Hunt, Lynn. 1984. *Political Culture and Class in the French Revolution.* Berkeley: University of California Press.

———. 1987. The "National Assembly." In *The French Revolution and the Creation of Modern Political Culture. Volume 1: The Political Culture of the Old Regime,* edited by Keith Baker, pp. 403–15. New York: Pergamon Press.

Huntington, Samuel P. 1957. *The Soldier and the State: The Theory and Politics of Civil-Military Relations.* New York: Vintage Books.

———. 1968. *Political Order in Changing Societies.* New Haven, CT: Yale University Press.

Huntington, Samuel P., and Jorge I. Dominguez. 1975. Political development. In *Handbook of Political Science. Vol. 3. Macropolitical Theory,* edited by Fred I. Greenstein and Nelson W. Polsby, pp. 1–114. Reading, MA: Addison-Wesley.

Hurst, James Willard. 1956. *Law and the Conditions of Freedom in the Nineteenth-Century United States.* Madison: University of Wisconsin Press.

Ide, Yoshinori, et al. 1974. *Gendai gyōsei to kanryōsei.* 2 vols. Tokyo: Tōkyō Daigaku Shuppankai.

Ike, Nobutaka. 1950. *The Beginnings of Political Democracy in Japan.* Baltimore: Johns Hopkins University Press.

Inada, Masatsugu. 1960–62. *Meiji kempō seiritsu shi.* 2 vols. Tokyo: Yūhikaku.

———. 1971. *Kyōiku chokugo seiritsu katei no kenkyū.* Tokyo: Kōdansha.

Ino, K., and M. Hokuto. 1972. *Amakudari kanryō.* Tokyo: Nisshin Hodō.

Irokawa, Daikichi, Ei Hideo, and Arai Katsuhiro. 1970. *Minshūkempō no sōzō: uzumoreta kusa no ne no jinmyaku.* Tokyo: Hyōronsha.

Ishii, Ryōsuke. 1958. *Japanese Legislation in the Meiji Era,* translated by William Chambliss. Tokyo: Pan-Pacific Press.

Isomura, Eiichi, and Kuronuma Minoru. 1974. *Gendai Nihon gyōsei.* Tokyo: Teikoku chihō gyōsei gakkai.

Israel, Jerry, ed. 1972. *Building the Organizational Society: Essays on Associational Activities in Modern America.* New York: The Free Press.

Italy, Consiglio dei Ministri. 1953. *Stato dei lavori per la riforma della pubblica amministrazione, 1948–1953.* 3 vols. Rome: Instituto poligrafico Stato.

Itō, Daiichi. 1980. *Gendai Nihon kanryōsei no bunseki.* Tokyo: Tōkyō Daigaku Shuppankai.

Itō, Tasaburō. 1980. *Bakuhan taisei.* Tokyo: Shimizu Kōbundō Shobō.

Iwata, Masakazu. 1964. *Ōkubo Toshimichi, the Bismarck of Japan.* Berkeley: University of California Press.

Jackson, J. H. 1974. *A Short History of France.* 2d ed. New York: Cambridge University Press.

Jackson, P. M. 1983. *The Political Economy of Bureaucracy.* Totowa, NY: Barnes and Noble.

Jacob, Herbert. 1963. *German Administration Since Bismarck: Central Authority versus Local Autonomy.* New Haven, CT: Yale University Press.

Jacobs, David. 1974. Dependency and vulnerability: An exchange approach to the control of organizations. *Administrative Science Quarterly* 19 (March): 45–59.

Jacoby, Sanford. 1985. *Employing Bureaucracy: Managers, Unions, and the Transformation of Work in American Industry, 1900–1945.* New York: Columbia University Press.

Jacquemart, Paul. 1892. *Professions et métiers.* 2 vols. Paris: Armand Colin.

Jaguaribe, Helio. 1973. *Political Development: A General Theory and a Latin American Case Study.* New York: Harper & Row.

Japan, Naikaku Kanpō Kyoku. 1887–1945. *Hōrei zensho.* Tokyo: Naikaku Kanpō Kyoku.

Japan, Naikaku Tōkei Kyoku. 1895–1940. *Nihon teikoku tōkei tekiyō.* Tokyo: Naikaku Tōkei Kyoku.

Jarausch, Konrad H., ed. 1983. *The Transformation of Higher Learning, 1860–1930.* Chicago: University of Chicago Press.

Jenkins, Hester, and D. Caradog Jones. 1950. Social class of Cambridge University alumni of the 18th and 19th centuries. *The British Journal of Sociology* 1, no. 2 (June): 93–116.

Jensen, Michael C. 1983. Organization theory and methodology. *The Accounting Review* 58, no. 2 (April): 319–39.

Jensen, Michael C., and William H. Meckling. 1976. Theory of the firm: Managerial behavior, agency costs and ownership structure. *Journal of Financial Economics* 3 (October): 305–60.

Jensen, Richard. 1968. American election campaigns: A theoretical and historical typology. *Midwest Political Science Association.* Paper delivered at 1968 annual meeting.

Johnson, Chalmers. 1978. *Japan's Public Policy Companies.* Washington, DC: American Enterprise Institute for Public Policy Research.

———. 1982. *MITI and the Japanese Miracle: The Growth of Industrial Policy, 1925–1975.* Stanford, CA: Stanford University Press.

Johnson, Richard. 1972. Administrators in education before 1870: Patronage, social position and role. In *Studies in the Growth of Nineteenth-Century Government,* edited by Gillian Sutherland, pp. 110–38. London: Routledge and Kegan Paul.

Johnson, Terence J. 1972. *Professions and Power.* London: Macmillan.

———. 1977. What is to be known? The structural determination of classes. *Economy and Society* 6: 194–233.

Jones, Donald K. 1977. *The Making of the Education System 1851–81.* London: Routledge and Kegan Paul.

Jones, Raymond A. 1983. *The British Diplomatic Service, 1815–1914.* Waterloo, Ontario: Wilfrid Laurier University Press.

Jones, S. H. R. 1982. The organization of work: A historical dimension. *Journal of Economic Behavior and Organization* 3, nos. 2–3 (June/Sept.): 117–37.

Jones, Wilbur D., and Aryel B. Erikson. 1972. *The Peelites, 1846–57.* Columbus: Ohio State University Press.

Jordan, David M. 1971. *Roscoe Conkling of New York: Voice of the Senate.* Ithaca, NY: Cornell University Press.

Josephson, Matthew. 1938. *The Politicos: 1865–1896.* New York: Harcourt, Brace and Co.

Julien-Laferrière, François. 1970. *Les députés fonctionnaires sous la monarchie de Juillet.* Paris: Presses universitaires de France.

Juso, Raffaele. 1970. *Lo Stato e la funzione amministrativa.* Rome: M. Bulzoni.

Kaigo, Tokiomi. 1965. *Kyōiku chokugo seiritsushi no kenkyū.* Tokyo: Kotokusha.

Karl, Barry Dean. 1963. *Executive Reorganization and Reform in the New Deal, the Genesis of Administrative Management, 1900–1939.* Cambridge, MA: Harvard University Press.

Katz, Daniel L., and Robert L. Kahn. 1966. *Social Psychology of Organizations.* New York: John Wiley & Sons.

Kaufman, Herbert. 1956. Emerging conflicts in the doctrines of public administration. *American Political Science Review* 50, no. 4 (December): 1,057–73.

———. 1975. The natural history of human organizations. *Administration and Society* 7, no. 2 (August): 131–49.

———. 1977. *Red Tape, Its Origins and Abuses.* Washington, DC: The Brookings Institution.

———. 1991. *Time, Chance, and Organizations: Natural Selection in a Perilous Environment.* 2d ed. Chatham, NJ: Chatham House Publishers.

Kawanaka, Nikō. 1972. *Gendai kanryōsei.* Tokyo: Chūō Daigaku Shuppankai.

Kehr, Eckart. 1965. *Der Primat der Innenpolitik: Gesammelte Aufsätze zur Preussisch-deutschen Sozialgeschichte in 19. und 20. Jahrhundert,* edited by Hans-Ulrich Wehler. Berlin: W. de Gruyter.

Keller, Morton. 1963. *The Life Insurance Enterprise, 1885–1910: A Study in the Limits of Corporate Power.* Cambridge, MA: Belknap Press of Harvard University.

———. 1977. *Affairs of State: Public Life in Nineteenth-Century America.* Cambridge, MA: Harvard University Press.

Kellner, Peter, and Lord Crowther-Hunt. 1980. *The Civil Servants: An Inquiry Into Britain's Ruling Class.* London: Macdonald.

Kelsall, Roger K. 1955. *Higher Civil Servants in Britain from 1870 to the Present Day.* London: Routledge and Kegan Paul.

Kelsen, Hans. 1945. *General Theory of Law and State.* Cambridge, MA: Harvard University Press.

Kernaghan, Kenneth, ed. 1977. *Public Administration in Canada: Selected Readings.* Toronto: Methuen.

Kernaghan, W. D. K., ed. 1969. *Bureaucracy in Canadian Government.* Toronto: Methuen.

Kessler, Marie-Christine. 1977. Historique du système de formation et de recrutement des hauts fonctionnaires. *Revue Française D'Administration Publique* 1 (January–March): 9–52.

———. 1978. *La politique de la haute fonction publique.* Paris: Presses de la Fondation nationale sciences politiques.

Key, V. O., Jr. 1956. *American State Politics: An Introduction.* New York: Alfred A. Knopf.

Kim, Paul S. 1988. *Japan's Civil Service System.* Westport, CT: Greenwood Press.

Kingsley, J. Donald. 1944. *Representative Bureaucracy.* Yellow Springs, Ohio: Antioch Press.

Kitani, Shinichi. 1983. Sengo no Nihon ni okeru kanryōseiron. *Hō to Seiji* 34, no. 3 (November): 651–98.

Klein, Philip S. 1962. *President James Buchanan: A Biography.* University Park: Pennsylvania State University Press.

Klepner, Paul, and Stephen C. Baker. 1979. The impact of registration requirements on electoral turnout, 1900–1916. Paper presented at the American Political Science Association Conference, Washington, DC.

Knight, Frank H. 1965. *Risk, Uncertainty and Profit.* New York: Harper and Row.

Koh, B. C. 1979. Stability and change in Japan's higher civil service. *Comparative Politics* 11, no. 3 (April): 279–97.

———. 1985. The recruitment of higher civil servants in Japan. *Asian Survey* 25, no. 3 (March): 292–309.

———. 1989. *Japan's Administrative Elite.* Berkeley: University of California Press.

Koh, B. C., and Jae-On Kim. 1982. Paths to advancement in Japanese bureaucracy. *Comparative Political Studies* 15, no. 3 (October): 289–313.

Kokuritsu Kyōiku Kenkyūjo. 1974. *Nihon kindai kyōiku hyakunenshi.* 10 vols. Tokyo: Kyōiku Kenkyū Shinkokai.

Koselleck, Reinhart. 1967. *Preussen zwischen Reform und Revolution: Allgemeines Landrecht, Verwaltung und soziale Bewegung von 1791 bis 1848.* Stuttgart: Klett.

Kousser, J. Morgan. 1974. *The Shaping of Southern Politics: Suffrage Restriction and the Establishment of the One-Party South.* New Haven, CT: Yale University Press.

Kraines, Oscar. 1970. The President versus Congress: The Keep Commission, 1905–1909: First comprehensive presidential inquiry into administration. *Western Political Quarterly* 23, no. 1 (March): 5–54.

Krasner, Stephen D. 1984. Review article: Approaches to the state: Altèrnative conceptions and historical dynamics. *Comparative Politics* 16, no. 2 (January): 223–46.

Krislov, Samuel. 1974. *Representative Bureaucracy.* Englewood Cliffs, NJ: Prentice-Hall.

Krislov, Samuel, and David H. Rosenbloom. 1981. *Representative Bureaucracy and the American Political System.* New York: Praeger.

Kubota, Akira. 1969. *Higher Civil Servants in Postwar Japan: Their Social Origins, Educational Backgrounds and Career Patterns.* Princeton, NJ: Princeton University Press.

———. 1980. The political influence of the Japanese higher civil service. *Journal of Asian and African Studies* 15, nos. 3–4: 273–84.

Lalumière, Pierre. 1959. *L'inspection des finances.* Paris: Presses universitaires de France.

Lalumière, Pierre, and André Demichel. 1969. *Le Droit Publique.* Paris: Presses universitaires de France.

Lammers, Cornelis J., and David J. Hickson. 1979. A cross-national and cross-institutional typology of organizations. In *Organizations Alike and Unlike: International and Inter-Institutional Studies in the Sociology of Organizations,* edited by Cornelis J. Lammers and David J. Hickson, pp. 420–36. Boston: Routledge and Kegan Paul.

Landes, David S. 1965. Japan and Europe: Contrasts in industrialization. In *The State and Economic Development in Japan,* edited by William W. Lockwood, pp. 93–132. Princeton, NJ: Princeton University Press.

———. 1969. *The Unbound Prometheus: Technological Change and Industrial Development in Western Europe from 1750 to the Present.* Cambridge: Cambridge University Press.

Langton, John. 1984. The ecological theory of bureaucracy: The case of Josiah Wedgewood and the British pottery industry. *Administrative Science Quarterly* 29: 330–54.

Lanza, Albert. 1976. Étude sur le statut de la fonction publique au XIXe siècle. In *Études sur les rapport entre la loi et le règlement gouvernemental au XIXe siècle,* edited by Charles Durand and Albert Lanza, pp. 251–413. Aix-en-Provence: Presses universitaires d'Aix-Marseilles.

Larson, Magali Sarfatti. 1977. *The Rise of Professionalism: A Sociological Analysis.* Berkeley: University of California Press.

Laumann, Edward O., and Franz U. Pappi. 1976. *Networks of Collective Action.* New York: Academic Press.

Laumann, Edward O., Lois M. Verbrugge, and Franz U. Pappi. 1974. A causal modelling approach to the study of a community elite's influence structure. *American Sociological Review* 39, no. 2 (April): 162–74.

Lawrence, Paul R., and Jay W. Lorsch. 1967a. Differentiation and integration in complex organizations. *Administrative Science Quarterly* 12 (June): 1–47.

———. 1967b. *Organization and Environment.* Cambridge, MA: Harvard University Press.

Layard, Richard, ed. 1972. *Cost-Benefit Analysis.* Baltimore: Penguin Books.

Leatt, Peggy, and Rodney Schneck. 1982. Technology, size, environment, and structure in nursing subunits. *Organization Studies* 3, no. 3: 221–42.

Lebed, Andrei. 1965. The Soviet administrative elite: Selection and deployment procedures. *Studies on the Soviet Union* 5, no. 2: 47–55.

Lefas, Alexandre. 1913. *L'état et les fonctionnaires.* Paris: M. Giard & E. Brière.

Lefebvre, Georges. 1964a. *The French Revolution from 1793 to 1799.* New York: Columbia University Press.

———. 1964b. *The Thermidorians and the Directory.* New York: Random House.

Legendre, Pierre. 1968. *Histoire de l'administration, de 1750 à nos jours.* Paris: Presses universitaires de France.

Leibenstein, Harvey. 1966. Allocative efficiency vs. x-efficiency. *American Economic Review* 56, no. 3 (June): 392–415.

———. 1969. Allocative efficiency, x-efficiency and the measurement of welfare losses. *Economica* 30: 304–9.

———. 1973. Competition and x-efficiency: Reply. *Journal of Political Economy* 81: 765–77.

———. 1975. Aspects of the x-efficiency theory of the firm. *The Bell Journal of Economics* 6, no. 2 (Autumn): 580–606.

———. 1976. *Beyond Economic Man: A New Foundation for Microeconomics.* Cambridge, MA: Harvard University Press.

———. 1978. *General X-Efficiency Theory and Economic Development*. New York: Oxford University Press.

———. 1984. The Japanese management system: An x-efficiency-game theory analysis. In *The Economic Analysis of the Japanese Firm*, edited by Masahiko Aoki, pp. 331–58. New York: North-Holland.

———. 1987. *Inside the Firm: The Inefficiencies of Hierarchy*. Cambridge, MA: Harvard University Press.

LeMay, E. 1977. La Composition de l'Assemblée nationale constituante: Les Hommes de la continuité. *Revue d'histoire moderne et contemporaine* 24 (July–Sept.): 341–63.

Le May, G. H. L. 1979. *The Victorian Constitution: Conventions, Usages and Contingencies*. New York: St. Martin's Press.

Lenin, V. I. 1947. *The State and Revolution*. Vol. 25 of *Collected Works*. Moscow: International Publishers.

Lenöel, Émile Louis. 1865. *Des sciences politique et administratives et leur enseignement*. Paris: A. Durand.

Léonard, Jacques. 1978. *Les Médecins l'oest au XIXe siècle*. Paris: H. Champion.

Lepointe, Gabriel. 1953. *Histoire des institutions du droit public français au XIXe siècle: 1789–1914*. Paris: Éditions Domat Montchrestien.

Leroy, Maxime. 1906. *Le droit des fonctionnaires*. Paris: Ligue française pour la defense des Droits de l'homme et du citoyen.

Lhomme, Jean. 1960. *La grande bourgeoisie au pouvoir, 1830–1880*. Paris: Presses universitaires de France.

Liard, Louis. 1888–94. *L'enseignement supérieur en France, 1789–1893*. 2 vols. Paris: Armand Colin.

Lifson, Thomas B. 1979. *An Emergent Administration System: Interpersonal Networks in a Japanese General Trading Firm, Working Paper 79–55*. Cambridge, MA: Harvard University Graduate School of Business.

Ligou, Daniel. 1966. *Frédéric Desmons et la franc-maçonnerie sous la 3e République*. Paris: Gedalg.

Linz, Juan J., and Amando de Miguel. 1968. La elite funcionarial Española ante la reforma administrativa. *Sociología de la administración pública Española, Anales de moral social y economica, V. 17*, pp. 199–249. Madrid: Centro de Estudios Sociales de la Santa Cruz del Valle de los Caidos.

Lipset, Seymour Martin, Martin A. Trow, and James S. Coleman. 1956. *Union Democracy: The Internal Politics of the International Typographic Union*. Glencoe, IL: Free Press.

Littler, Craig R. 1978. Understanding Taylorism. *British Journal of Sociology* 29, no. 2 (June): 185–202.

Litwak, Eugene. 1959–60. The use of extended family groups in the achievement of social goals. *Social Problems* 7 (Winter): 184–85.

Loasby, Brian J. 1968. The decision-maker in the organization. *Journal of Management Studies* 5, no. 3 (October): 352–64.

———. 1971. Hypothesis and paradigm in the theory of the firm. *Economic Journal* 81 (December): 863–85.

454 Bibliography

———. 1976. *Choice, Complexity and Ignorance.* New York: Cambridge University Press.

Lorsch, Jay W. 1965. *Product Innovation and Organization.* New York: Macmillan.

Lotz, Albert. [1909] 1914. *Geschichte ffs deutschen Beamtentums.* Berlin: R. V. Decker's Verlag.

Lovejoy, Arthur O. 1948. *The Great Chain of Being.* Cambridge, MA: Harvard University Press.

Lowe, Roy. 1983. The expansion of higher education in England. In *The Transformation of Higher Learning, 1860–1930,* edited by Konrad H. Jarausch, pp. 37–56. Chicago: University of Chicago Press.

———. 1987. Structural change in English higher education, 1870–1920. In *The Rise of the Modern Educational System,* edited by Detlef K. Müller, Fritz Ringer, and Brian Simon, pp. 163–80. New York: Cambridge University Press.

Lowe, Rodney. 1984. Bureaucracy triumphant or denied? The expansion of the British Civil Service, 1919–1939. *Public Administration* 62, no. 3 (Autumn): 291–310.

Lowi, Theodore J. 1969. *The End of Liberalism.* New York: Norton.

Lowi, Theodore. [1967] 1975. "Party, Policy, and Constitution in America," in *The American Party Systems,* edited by William N. Nisbet and Walter D. Burnham, pp. 238–76. New York: Oxford University Press. [1967, 2d ed.; 1975, rev. 2d ed.]

———. 1978. Public policy and bureaucracy in the United States and France. In *Comparing Public Policies: New Concepts and Methods,* edited by Douglas E. Ashford, Peter Katzenstein, and T. J. Pempel, pp. 177–95. Beverly Hills: Sage Publications.

Luce, R. Duncan, and Howard Raiffa. 1957. *Games and Decisions.* New York: Wiley.

Luhmann, Niklas, and Renate Mayntz. 1973. *Personal in öffentlichen Dienst: Eintritt und Karrieren.* Baden-Baden: Nomos-Verlagsgesellschaft.

Lustig, R. Jeffrey. 1982. *Corporate Liberalism: The Origins of Modern American Political Theory: 1890–1920.* Berkeley: University of California Press.

McCormick, Richard L. 1981. *From Realignment to Reform: Political Change in New York State, 1893–1910.* Ithaca, NY: Cornell University Press.

———. 1986. *The Party Period and Public Policy: American Politics from the Age of Jackson to the Progressive Era.* New York: Oxford University Press.

McCormick, Richard P. 1966. *The Second American Party System: Party Formation in the Jackson Era.* Chapel Hill: University of North Carolina Press.

———. [1967] 1975. "Political Development and the Second Party System," in *The American Party Systems,* edited by William N. Chambers and Walter D. Burnham, pp. 90–116. New York: Oxford University Press. [1967, 2d ed.; 1975, rev. 2d ed.]

———. 1982. *The Presidential Game: The Origins of American Presidential Politics.* New York: Oxford University Press.

MacDonagh, Oliver. 1961. *A Pattern of Government Growth, 1800–1860: The Passenger Acts and Their Enforcement.* London: MacGibbon & Kee.

———. 1973. The nineteenth-century revolution in government: A reappraisal. In *The Victorian Revolution: Government and Society in Victoria's Britain,* edited by Peter Stansky, pp. 5–25. New York: New Viewpoint.

————. 1977. *Early Victorian Government: 1830–1870.* London: Weidenfeld and Nicholson.

McFarland, Gerald W. 1975. *Mugwumps, Morals and Politics, 1884–1920.* Amherst: University of Massachusetts Press.

McGerr, Michael E. 1986. *The Decline of Popular Politics: The American North, 1865–1928.* New York: Oxford University Press.

Machlup, Fritz. 1967. Theories of the firm: Marginalist, behavioral, managerial. *American Economic Review* 57, no. 1 (March): 1–33.

Mack, Edward C. 1939. *Public Schools and British Opinion: 1780–1860.* New York: Columbia University Press.

————. 1941. *Public Schools and British Opinion Since 1860.* New York: Columbia University Press.

McKelvey, Bill. 1982. *Organizational Systematics: Taxonomy, Evolution, Classification.* Berkeley: University of California Press.

McKelvey, Bill, and Howard E. Aldrich. 1983. Populations, natural selection and applied organizational science. *Administrative Science Quarterly* 28 (March): 101–82.

Mackenzie, G. Calvin, ed. 1987. *The In-and-Outers: Presidential Appointees and Transient Government in Washington.* Baltimore: Johns Hopkins University Press.

Mackintosh, John P. 1977. *The British Cabinet.* 3d ed. London: Stevens and Sons, Ltd.

McKitrick, Eric L. 1967. Party politics and the Union and Confederate war efforts. In *The American Party Systems: Stages of Political Development,* edited by William Nisbet Chambers and Walter Dean Burnham, pp. 117–51. New York: Oxford University Press.

McLaren, W. W., ed. 1914. *Japanese Government Documents. Transactions of the Asiatic Society of Japan.* First Series, Part 1.

McLean, Joseph, ed. 1949. *The Public Service and University Education.* Princeton, NJ: Princeton University Press.

MacLeod, Roy. 1988. Introduction. In *Government and Expertise: Specialists, Administrators and Professionals, 1860–1919,* edited by Roy MacLeod, pp. 1–26. New York: Cambridge University Press.

MacMahon, Arthur W., and John D. Millett. 1939. *Federal Administrators: A Biographical Approach to the Problem of Departmental Management.* New York: Columbia University Press.

Macy, J. W., Bruce Adams, J. Jackson Walters, and G. Calvin MacKenzie. 1983. *America's Unelected Government: Appointing the President's Team.* Cambridge, MA: Ballinger Publishing.

Mage, Georges. 1924. *La Division de la France en département.* Toulouse: Imprimerie Saint-Michel.

Magraw, Roger. 1986. *France, 1815–1914: The Bourgeois Century.* New York: Oxford University Press.

Maheshwari, Shriram. 1987. *The Higher Civil Service in Japan.* Ahmedabad: Allied Publishers.

Mainichi Shinbunsha kaibu, ed. 1980. *Kanryō.* Tokyo: Tairiku Shobō.

Mallet, Charles Edward. 1924–27. *A History of the University of Oxford.* 3 vols. London: Methuen & Co., Ltd.

Mansfield, Roger. 1973. Bureaucracy and centralization: An examination of organizational structure. *Administrative Science Quarterly* 18, no. 4: 477–88.

March, James G., and Johan P. Olsen. 1976. *Ambiguity and Choice in Organizations.* Bergen, Norway: Universitetsforlaget.

March, James G., and Herbert A. Simon. 1958. *Organizations.* New York: John Wiley & Sons.

Marcus, Robert D. 1971. *Grand Old Party: Political Structure in the Gilded Age, 1880–1896.* New York: Oxford University Press.

Marglin, Steven A. 1974. What do bosses do? The origins and functions of hierarchy in capitalist production. *Review of Radical Political Economics* 6, no. 2 (Summer): 60–112.

———. 1984. Knowledge and power. In *Firms, Organization and Labour: Approaches to the Economics of Work Organization,* edited by Frank A. Stephen, pp. 146–67. New York: St. Martin's Press.

Markoff, John. 1975. Governmental bureaucratization: General processes and an anomalous case. *Comparative Studies in Society and History* 17, no. 4 (October): 479–503.

Marris, Robin. 1964. *The Economic Theory of Managerial Capitalism.* London: Macmillan.

Marris, Robin, and Dennis C. Mueller. 1980. The corporation, competition, and the invisible hand. *Journal of Economic Literature* 18 (March): 32–63.

Marshall, Alfred. 1932. *Industry and Trade.* London: Macmillan.

Marshall, Lynn L. 1967. The strange stillbirth of the Whig Party. *American Historical Review* 72, no. 2 (January): 445–68.

Marshall, Thomas H. 1950. *Citizenship and Social Class.* Cambridge: Cambridge University Press.

Maruyama, Kazuo. 1983. *Bakuhansei shita no seiji to shakai.* Tokyo: Bungei Shuppan.

Marvick, Dwaine. 1954. *Career Perspectives in a Bureaucratic Setting.* Ann Arbor: University of Michigan Press.

Marx, Karl, and Friedrich Engels. 1965. *The German Ideology.* London: Lawrence and Wishart.

———. 1971. Manifesto of the Communist Party. In *On Revolution,* edited and translated by Saul K. Padover, pp. 79–107. New York: McGraw-Hill.

Massé, Daniel. 1908. *Pour choisir une carrière.* Paris: Larousse.

Masumi, Junnosuke. 1965–67. *Nihon seitōshi ron.* Vols. 1–4. Tokyo: Tōkyō Daigaku Shuppankai.

Mathias, Peter, and Michael Postan, eds. 1978. *Cambridge Economic History of Europe: The Industrial Economies: Capital, Labor and Enterprise, Part 2: The United States, Japan and Russia.* Cambridge: Cambridge University Press.

Matthew, H. C. G. 1986. *Gladstone: 1809–1874.* Oxford: Clarendon Press.

Mayers, Lewis. 1922. *The Federal Service: A Study of the System of Personnel Administration of the United States.* New York: D. Appleton and Co.

Mayeur, Jean-Marie, and Madeleine Rebérioux. 1984. *The Third Republic from Its Origins to the Great War, 1871–1914.* New York: Cambridge University Press.

Mayhew, David R. 1986. *Placing Parties in American Politics.* Princeton, NJ: Princeton University Press.

Mayntz, Renate, and Fritz W. Scharpf. 1975. *Policy-Making in the German Federal Bureaucracy.* Amsterdam: Elsevier.

Mechanic, David. 1962. Sources of power of lower participants in complex organizations. *Administrative Science Quarterly* 7, no. 4 (December): 349–64.

Medhurst, Kenneth N. 1973. *Government in Spain: The Executive at Work.* New York: Pergamon Press.

Meriam, Lewis. 1938. *Public Personnel Problems from the Standpoint of the Operating Officer.* Washington, DC: The Brookings Institution.

Meuriot, Paul. 1919. *Le baccalauréat: son évolution historique et statisque des origines (1808) à nos jours.* Nancy: Imprimerie Berger-Levrault.

Meyer, John W., and Brian Rowan. 1977. Institutionalized organizations: Formal structure as myth and ceremony. *American Journal of Sociology* 83, no. 2 (September): 440–63.

———. 1978. The structure of educational organizations. In *Environments and Organizations: Theoretical and Empirical Perspectives,* by Marshall W. Meyer et al., pp. 78–109. San Francisco: Jossey-Bass.

Meyer, Marshall W. 1968. Two authority structures of bureaucratic organizations. *Administrative Science Quarterly* 13 (September): 211–28.

———. 1975. Leadership and organizational structure. *American Journal of Sociology* 81, no. 3 (November): 514–42.

———. 1979. *Change in Public Bureaucracies.* Cambridge: Cambridge University Press.

Meyer, Marshall W., and M. Craig Brown. 1977. The process of bureaucratization. *American Journal of Sociology* 83, no. 2 (September): 364–85.

Meyer, Marshall W., et al. 1978. *Environments and Organizations: Theoretical and Empirical Perspectives.* San Francisco: Jossey-Bass.

Meyer, Marshall W., and Richard Scott. 1983. *Organizational Environments: Ritual and Rationality.* Beverly Hills: Sage Publications.

Meyer, Marshall W., William Stevenson, and Stephen Webster. 1985. *Limits to Bureaucratic Growth.* New York: Walter de Gruyter.

Meyers, Marvin. 1957. *The Jacksonian Persuasion: Politics and Belief.* Stanford: Stanford University Press.

Michel, Georges. 1925. *La loi du 14 avril 1924 et la réforme du régime des pensions de retraite.* Paris: L. Tenin.

Michels, Robert. 1966. *Political Parties.* New York: Free Press.

Miliband, Ralph. 1969. *The State in Capitalist Society.* London: Weidenfeld & Nicholson.

Miller, Gary, and Terry Moe. 1983. Bureaucrats, legislators, and the size of government. *American Political Science Review* 77, no. 2 (June): 297–322.

Miller, Naomi Churgin. 1968. John Cartwright and Radical Parliamentary Reform, 1808–1819. *English Historical Review* 83, no. 329 (October): 705–28.

Millerson, Geoffrey. 1964. *The Qualifying Associations*. New York: Humanities Press.

Minobe, Tatsukichi. 1928. *Chikujo kempōseigi*. Tokyo: Yūhikaku.

————. 1932. *Gyōseihō satsuyo*. 2 vols. Tokyo: Yūhikaku.

Mirlees, James A. 1976. The optimal structure of incentives and authority within an organization. *The Bell Journal of Economics* 7, no. 1 (Spring): 105–31.

M.I.T. Study Group. 1967. The transitional process. In *Political Modernization,* edited by Claude E. Welch, Jr., pp. 22–48. Belmont, CA: Wadsworth Publishing Co., Inc.

Moe, Terry M. 1984. The new economics of organization. *American Journal of Political Science* 28, no. 4 (November): 739–77.

Mohr, Lawrence B. 1971. Organizational technology and organizational structure. *Administrative Science Quarterly* 16, no. 4 (December): 444–59.

————1982. *Explaining Organizational Behavior: The Limits and Possibilities of Theory*. San Francisco: Jossey-Bass.

Monsen, Joseph R., Jr., and Anthony Downs. 1965. A theory of large managerial firms. *Journal of Political Economy* 73, no. 3 (June): 221–36.

Montagna, Paul D. 1973. Professionalization and bureaucratization in large professional organizations. In *Comparative Organizations,* edited by Wolf D. Heydebrand, pp. 534–42. Englewood Cliffs, NJ: Prentice-Hall.

Montgomery, David. 1987. *The Fall of the House of Labor: The Workplace, the State, and American Labor Activism, 1865–1925*. Cambridge: Cambridge University Press.

Moore, Barrington, Jr. 1965. *Soviet Politics: The Dilemma of Power*. New York: Harper & Row.

Moore, David Cresap. 1974. The matter of the missing contests: Towards a theory of the mid-19th century British political system. *Albion* 6, no. 2 (Summer): 93–119.

————. 1976. *The Politics of Deference: A Study of the Mid-Nineteenth Century English Political System*. New York: Barnes & Noble.

Moore, R. J. 1964. The abolition of patronage in the Indian Civil Service and the closure of Haileybury College. *The Historical Journal* 7, no. 2: 246–57.

Moore, Wilbert E. 1970. *The Professions: Roles and Rules*. New York: Russell Sage Foundation.

Morstein Marx, Fritz. 1957. *The Administrative State*. Chicago: University of Chicago Press.

————. 1963. The higher civil service as an action group in Western political development. In *Bureaucracy and Political Development,* edited by Joseph G. La Palombara, pp. 62–95. Princeton, NJ: Princeton University Press.

Moses, Robert. 1914 [1966]. *The Civil Service of Great Britain*. New York: Columbia University Press [reprint, AMS Press].

Mosher, Frederick C. 1978. Professions in public service. *Public Administration Review* 38, no. 2 (March–April): 144–50.

————. 1982. *Democracy and the Public Service*. 2d ed. New York: Oxford University Press.

Motoyama, Yukihiko. 1965. *Meiji zenki gakkō seiritsushi*. Tokyo: Miraisha.

Mowry, George E. 1958. *The Era of Theodore Roosevelt and the Birth of Modern America: 1900–1912.* New York: Harper & Row.

Mueller, Hans-Eberhard. 1984. *Bureaucracy, Education, and Monopoly: Civil Service Reforms in Prussia and England.* Berkeley: University of California Press.

Müller, Detlef K., Fritz Ringer, and Brian Simon, eds. 1987. *The Rise of the Modern Educational System: Structural Change and Social Reproduction 1870–1920.* New York: Cambridge University Press.

Muramatsu, Michio. 1979. Kōkyū kanryōshudan no shakaitekishusshin to kyariya. *Hōgaku Ronsō* 105, no. 2 (May): 1–46.

———. 1981. *Sengo Nihon no kanryōsei.* Tokyo: Tōkyō Keizai Shimposha.

Muramatsu, Michio, and Ellis S. Krauss. 1984. Bureaucrats and politicians in policymaking: The case of Japan. *American Political Science Review* 78, no. 1 (March): 126–46.

Murobushi, Tetsurō. 1980. Kōkyūkanryō—riken no kōzō. *Sekai* 411 (February): 54–63.

Murphy, Thomas P., Donald E. Neuchterlein, and Ronald Stupak, eds. 1978. *Inside the Bureaucracy: The View from the Assistant Secretary's Desk.* Boulder, CO: Westview Press.

Mustoe, N. E. 1932. *The Law and Organization of the British Civil Service.* London: Sir Isaac Pitman & Sons, Ltd.

Nagai, Michio. 1971. *Higher Education in Japan: Its Takeoff and Crash.* Tokyo: University of Tokyo Press.

Najita, Tetsuo. 1974. *Japan.* Englewood Cliffs, NJ: Prentice-Hall, Inc.

Nakane, Chie. 1970. *Japanese Society.* Berkeley: University of California Press.

Namier, Lewis Bernstein. 1965 [1955]. *Personalities and Powers: Selected Essays.* New York: Harper & Row [London: Hamish Hamilton].

———. 1957. *The Structure of Politics at the Accession of George III.* 2d ed. London: Macmillan.

Naramoto, Tatsuya, ed. 1967. *Ishin no shi-shi.* Tokyo: Chikuma Shobō.

Nelson, Michael. 1982. A short, ironic history of American national bureaucracy. *The Journal of Politics* 44, no. 3 (August): 747–78.

Nelson, Richard R., and Sidney G. Winter. 1982. *An Evolutionary Theory of Economic Change.* Boston: Belknap Press.

Nelson, William E. 1975. *Americanization of the Common Law: The Impact of Legal Change on Massachusetts Society, 1760–1830.* Cambridge, MA: Harvard University Press.

———. 1982. *The Roots of American Bureaucracy: 1830–1900.* Cambridge, MA: Harvard University Press.

Nettl, J. P. 1968. The state as a conceptual variable. *World Politics* 20, no. 4 (July): 559–92.

Niskanen, William A., Jr. 1971. *Bureaucracy and Representative Government.* Chicago: Aldine, Atherton.

Noble, David F. 1977. *America by Design: Science, Technology, and the Rise of Corporate Capitalism.* New York: Oxford University Press.

Norman, E. Herbert. [1940] 1975. *Japan's Emergence as a Modern State*. Westport, CT: Greenwood Press. Reprint of the edition published by the International Secretariat, Institute of Pacific Relations, NY, in I.P.R. inquiry series.

Norris, James D., and Arthur H. Shaffer, eds. 1970. *Politics and Patronage in the Gilded Age: The Correspondence of James A. Garfield and Charles E. Henry*. Madison, WI: State Historical Society of Wisconsin.

O'Donnell, Guillermo A. 1973. *Modernization and Bureaucratic Authoritarianism: Studies in South American Politics*. Berkeley: University of California Press.

O'Gorman, Frank. 1975. *The Rise of Party in England: The Rockingham Whigs 1760–82*. London: George Allen & Unwin, Ltd.

———. 1982. *The Emergence of the British Two-Party System, 1760–1832*. London: Edward Arnold.

Ohkawa, Kazushi, and Henry Rosovsky. 1973. *Japanese Economic Growth*. Stanford, CA: Stanford University Press.

Olson, Mancur, Jr. 1968. *The Logic of Collective Action*. Cambridge, MA: Harvard University Press.

Oka, Yoshitake. 1962. *Kindai Nihon seijishi*. Tokyo: Sobunsha.

Organski, A. F. K. 1967. *The Stages of Political Development*. New York: Alfred Knopf.

Osatake, Takeshi. 1938–39. *Nihon kenseishi taiko*. 2 vols. Tokyo: Nihon hyōronsha.

Osborne, Thomas R. 1974. The Recruitment of the Administrative Elite in the Third French Republic, 1870–1905: The System of the Ecole Libre des Science Politiques. Ph.D. diss., University of Connecticut, Storrs, CT.

———. 1976. Sciences Po and the concours: The recruitment of the bureaucratic elite in the early Third Republic. *Third Republic/Troisieme République*, no. 2 (Fall): 156–81.

———. 1983. *A Grand École for the Grands Corps: The Recruitment and Training of the French Administrative Elite in the Nineteenth Century*. Boulder, CO: Social Science Monographs.

Oshima, Tarō. 1981. *Kanryō kokka to chihōjichi*. Tokyo: Iraisha.

Osterman, Paul, ed. 1984. *Internal Labor Markets*. Cambridge, MA: MIT Press.

Ostrogorski, Moisei. 1902. *Democracy and the Organization of Political Parties*. 2 vols. New York: Macmillan.

Ouchi, William G. 1977. The relationship between organizational structure and organizational control. *Administrative Science Quarterly* 22 (March): 95–113.

———. 1978. The transmission of control through organizational hierarchy. *Academy of Management Journal* 21 (June): 173–92.

———. 1980. Markets, bureaucracies and clans. *Administrative Science Quarterly* 25 (March): 120–41.

Owen, J. B. 1972. Political patronage in 18th century England. In *The Triumph of Culture: 18th Century Perspectives*, edited by Paul Fritz and David Williams, pp. 369–87. Toronto: A. M. Hakkert, Ltd.

Page, Edward C. 1985a. France: From l'État to Big Government. In *Public Employment in Western Nations*, edited by Richard Rose et al., pp. 97–125. New York: Cambridge University Press.

———. 1985b. *Political Authority and Bureaucratic Power*. Brighton, Sussex: Wheatsheaf Books Ltd.

Palmer, R. R. 1985. *The Improvement of Humanity: Education and the French Revolution*. Princeton, NJ: Princeton University Press.

Palumbo, Dennis J. 1975. Organization theory and political science. In *Handbook of Political Science: Micropolitical Theory. Vol. 2*. edited by Fred I. Greenstein and Nelson W. Polsby, pp. 319–69. Reading, MA: Addison-Wesley.

Papandreou, A. G. 1952. Some basic problems in the theory of the firm. In *A Survey of Contemporary Economics,* edited by Bernard F. Haley and Howard S. Ellis, pp. 183–219. Homewood, IL: R. D. Irwin for the American Economics Association.

Pares, Richard. 1953. *King George III and the Politicians*. Oxford: Clarendon Press.

Park, Yung H. 1986. *Bureaucrats and Ministers in Contemporary Japanese Government*. Berkeley: Institute of East Asian Studies.

Parker, Harold T. 1965. Two administrative bureaus under the Directory and Napoleon. *French Historical Studies* 4, no. 2 (Fall): 150–69.

Parris, Henry. 1968. The origins of the permanent civil service, 1780–1830. *The Political Quarterly* 46 (Summer): 143–66.

———. 1969. *Constitutional Bureaucracy*. London: Allen & Unwin.

Parry, Noel, and Jose Parry. 1976. *The Rise of the Medical Profession*. London: Croom Helm.

Parry, Richard. 1985. Britain: Stable aggregates, changing composition. In *Public Employment in Western Nations,* edited by Richard Rose et al., pp. 54–96. New York: Cambridge University Press.

Parsons, Talcott. 1964. *The Social System*. New York: The Free Press of Glencoe.

Parsons, Talcott, and Edward Shils, eds. 1951. *Toward a General Theory of Action*. Cambridge, MA: Harvard University Press.

Passigli, Stefano. 1975. The ordinary and special bureaucracies in Italy. In *The Mandarins of Western Europe,* edited by Mattei Dogan, pp. 226–37. New York: Halsted Press.

Passin, Herbert. 1965. *Society and Education in Japan*. New York: Bureau of Publications, Teachers College, Columbia University.

Patrick, Alison. 1972. *The Men of the First French Republic: Political Alignments in the National Convention of 1792*. Baltimore: Johns Hopkins University Press.

Pear, R. H. 1968. United States. In *Specialists and Generalists,* edited by Frederick F. Ridley, pp. 174–87. London: George Allen and Unwin, Ltd.

Pellew, Jill. 1982. *The Home Office, 1848–1914: From Clerks to Bureaucrats*. Rutherford, NJ: Fairleigh Dickinson University Press.

Peltzman, Sam. 1980. The growth of government. *Journal of Law and Economics* 22, no. 2 (October): 209–87.

Pence, James W., Jr. 1969. Invention gone awry: The London "Times" and civil service reform in 1854. *Western Speech* (Summer): 199–204.

Perkin, Harold. 1969. *The Origins of Modern English Society 1780–1880*. London: Routledge & Kegan Paul.

———. 1983. The pattern of social transformation in England. In *The Transforma-*

tion of Higher Learning, 1860–1930, edited by Konrad H. Jarausch, pp. 207–18. Chicago: University of Chicago Press.

Perrow, Charles. 1968. The effect of technological change on the structure of business firms. In *Industrial Relations: Contemporary Issues,* edited by B. C. Roberts, pp. 205–19. London: Macmillan.

————. 1984. *Normal Accidents: Living with High-Risk Technologies.* New York: Basic Books.

————. 1986. *Complex Organizations: A Critical Essay.* 3d ed. New York: Random House.

Peters, B. Guy. 1978. *The Politics of Bureaucracy: A Comparative Perspective.* New York: Longman.

————. 1985. The United States: Absolute change and relative stability. In *Public Employment in Western Nations,* edited by Richard Rose and Edward Page, pp. 228–61. New York: Cambridge University Press.

Pfeffer, Jeffrey. 1981. *Power in Organizations.* Marshfield, MA: Pitman Publishing Co.

Pfeffer, Jeffrey, and Gerald Salancik. 1978. *The External Control of Organizations.* New York: Harper and Row.

Phillips, John A. 1982. *Electoral Behavior in Unreformed England: Plumpers, Splitters, and Straights.* Princeton, NJ: Princeton University Press.

Pinkett, Harold T. 1965. The Keep Commission, 1905–1909: A Rooseveltian effort for administrative reform. *Journal of American History* 52, no. 2 (September): 297–312.

Pittau, Joseph. 1967. *Political Thought in Early Meiji Japan, 1868–1889.* Cambridge, MA: Harvard University Press.

Plessis, Alain. 1985. *The Rise and Fall of the Second Empire, 1852–1871.* Cambridge: Cambridge University Press.

Plumb, John Harold. 1967. *The Origin of Political Stability: England, 1675–1725.* Boston: Houghton Mifflin.

Plumlee, John P. 1981. Professional training and policy dominance in the higher civil service. *Social Science Quarterly* 62, no. 3 (September): 569–75.

Poggi, Gianfranco. 1978. *The Development of the Modern State: A Sociological Introduction.* Stanford, CA: Stanford University Press.

Pollard, Sidney. 1965. *The Genesis of Modern Management: A Study of the Industrial Revolution in Great Britain.* London: Edward Arnold Ltd.

Polakoff, Keith Ian. 1973. *The Politics of Inertia: The Election of 1876 and the End of Reconstruction.* Baton Rouge: Louisiana State University Press.

Ponteil, Félix. 1966. *Histoire de l'enseignement en France, les grandes étapes, 1789–1964.* Paris: Sirey.

Porter, John A. 1968. *The Vertical Mosaic.* Toronto: University of Toronto Press.

Poulantzas, Nicos. 1978. *Political Power and Social Classes.* London: Verso Editions.

Pressman, Jeffrey L., and Aaron Wildavsky. 1979. *Implementation.* 2d ed. Berkeley: University of California Press.

Prest, A. R., and R. Turvey. 1972. Cost-benefit analysis: A survey. In *Cost-Benefit*

Analysis, edited by Richard Layard, pp. 73–100. Harmsworth, England: Penguin Books.

Presthus, Robert. 1973. *Elite Accommodation in Canadian Politics.* Toronto: Macmillan Co. of Canada.

Prince, Carl E. 1977. *The Federalists and the Origins of the U.S. Civil Service.* New York: New York University Press.

Pugh, D. S., et al. 1963. A conceptual scheme for organizational analysis. *Administrative Science Quarterly* 8 (December): 289–316.

―――. 1968. Dimensions of organizational structure. *Administrative Science Quarterly* 13 (June): 65–105.

―――. 1969a. The context of organization structures. *Administrative Science Quarterly* 14 (March): 91–114.

―――. 1969b. An empirical taxonomy of structures of work organizations. *Administrative Science Quarterly* 14 (March): 115–25.

Pugh, Martin. 1982. *The Making of Modern British Politics, 1867–1939.* New York: St. Martin's Press.

Putnam, Robert D. 1975. The political attitudes of senior civil servants in Britain, Germany and Italy. In *The Mandarins of Western Europe,* edited by Mattei Dogan, pp. 87–128. New York: Halsted Press.

Putterman, Louis. 1982. Some behavioral perspectives on the dominance of hierarchical over democratic forms of enterprise. *Journal of Economic Behavior and Organization* 3, nos. 2–3 (June–Sept.): 139–60.

Rabany, Charles. 1916. *Les pension civiles de l'État.* Paris: Berger-Levrault.

Rain, Pierre. 1963. *L'École libre des sciences politiques, 1871–1939.* Paris: Fondation nationale des sciences politiques.

Ramsey, Matthew. 1984. The politics of professional monopoly in nineteenth-century medicine: The French model and its rivals. In *Professions and the French State,* edited by Gerald L. Geison, pp. 225–306. Philadelphia: University of Pennsylvania Press.

Raphael, Marios. 1964. *Pensions and Public Servants: A Study of the Origins of the British System.* Paris: Mouton & Co.

Rawls, John. 1971. *A Theory of Justice.* Cambridge, MA: Belknap Press of Harvard University.

Reader, K. M. 1981. *The Civil Service Commission: 1855–1975.* London: HMSO.

Reader, W. J. 1966. *Professional Men: The Rise of the Professional Classes in Nineteenth-Century England.* London: Weidenfeld & Nicholson.

Reder, M. W. 1947. A reconsideration of the marginal productivity theory. *Journal of Political Economy* 55 (Feb.–Dec.): 450–58.

Reitan, E. A. 1966. The Civil List in eighteenth-century British politics: Parliamentary supremacy versus the independence of the Crown. *The Historical Journal* 9, no. 3: 318–37.

Remini, Robert V. 1981. *Andrew Jackson and the Course of American Freedom, 1822–1832.* New York: Harper & Row.

Rémond, Réne. 1965, vol 1.; 1969, vol. 2. *La vie politique en France depuis 1789.* Paris: Librairie Armand Colin. t.I, 1789–1848, and II, 1848–1879.

Reynolds, John F., and Richard L. McCormick. 1986. Outlawing 'Treachery': Split tickets and ballot laws in New York and New Jersey, 1880–1910. *Journal of American History* 72, no. 4 (March): 835–58.

Rhodes, R. A. W., ed. 1977. *Training in the Civil Service.* London: Joint University Council for Social and Public Administration.

Rice, Albert K. 1963. *The Enterprise and Its Environment.* London: Tavistock.

Richards, Peter G. 1963. *Patronage in the British Government.* London: George Allen and Unwin.

Richardson, Nicholas. 1966. *The French Prefectoral Corps: 1814–1830.* Cambridge: Cambridge University Press.

Ridley, Frederick F. 1968. France. In *Specialists and Generalists: A Comparative Study of the Professional Civil Servant at Home and Abroad,* edited by Frederick F. Ridley, pp. 92–133. London: George Allen and Unwin, Ltd.

———, ed. 1979. *Government and Administration in Western Europe.* New York: St. Martin's Press.

Ridley, Frederick F., and Jean Blondel. 1964. *Public Administration in France.* London: Routledge and Kegan Paul.

Rigby, T. H. 1970. The CPSU elite: Turnover and rejuvenation from Lenin to Kruschev. *Australian Journal of Politics and History* 16 (April): 11–23.

———. 1971. The Soviet political elite, 1917–1922. *British Journal of Political Science* 1 (October): 415–36.

———. 1972. The Soviet Politburo: A comparative profile, 1951–71. *Soviet Studies* 24 (July): 3–23.

———. 1977. *Der sowetische Ministerrat unter Kosygin.* Cologne: Bundesinstitut für Ostwissenschatliche und Internationale Studien.

Riggs, Fred W. 1964. *Administration in Developing Countries: The Theory of Prismatic Society.* Boston: Houghton Mifflin.

Ringer, Fritz K. 1979. *Education and Society in Modern Europe.* Bloomington: Indiana University Press.

Ripley, Randall B., and Grace A. Franklin. 1976. *Congress, the Bureaucracy, and Public Policy.* Homewood, IL: Dorsey Press.

Roach, John. 1986. *A History of Secondary Education in England, 1800–1870.* New York: Longman.

Robson, William A., ed. 1956. *The Civil Service in Britain and France.* London: Hogarth Press.

Roden, Donald. 1980. *Schooldays in Imperial Japan: A Study in the Culture of a Student Elite.* Berkeley: University of California Press.

Rose, Richard, and Edward Page et al. 1985. *Public Employment in Western Nations.* New York: Cambridge University Press.

Rosenbloom, David H. 1971. *Federal Service and the Constitution: The Development of the Public Employment Relationship.* Ithaca, NY: Cornell University Press.

———, ed. 1982. *Centenary Issues of the Pendleton Act of 1883.* New York: Marcel Dekker, Inc.

Roseveare, Henry. 1969. *The Treasury: The Evolution of a British Institution.* New York: Columbia University Press.

Roth, Julius A. 1974. Professionalism: The Sociologist's Decoy. *Sociology of Work and Occupations* 1, no. 1 (February): 6–23.

Rothblatt, Sheldon. 1968. *The Revolution of the Dons: Cambridge and Society in Victorian England.* London: Faber & Faber.

———. 1976. *Tradition and Change in English Liberal Education.* London: Faber and Faber.

———. 1983. The diversification of higher education in England. In *The Transformation of Higher Learning, 1860–1930,* edited by Konrad H. Jarausch, pp. 131–48. Chicago: University of Chicago Press.

Rowan, Brian. 1982. Organizational structure and the institutional environment: The case of the public schools. *Administrative Science Quarterly* 27 (June): 259–79.

Rubinger, Richard. 1982. *Private Academies of Tokugawa Japan.* Princeton, NJ: Princeton University Press.

Ruffieux, Roland. 1975. The political influence of senior civil servants in switzerland. In *Mandarins of Western Europe,* edited by Mattei Dogan, pp. 238–51. New York: Halsted Press.

Rusk, Jerrold G. 1970. The effect of the Australian ballot on split-ticket voting: 1876–1908. *American Political Science Review* 64 (December): 1,220–38.

Ryan, Alan. 1972. Utilitarianism and bureaucracy: The views of J. S. Mill. In *Studies in the Growth of Nineteenth-Century Government,* edited by Gillian Sutherland, pp. 33–62. London: Routledge and Kegan Paul.

Sack, James J. 1980. The House of Lords and parliamentary patronage in Great Britain, 1802–1832. *The Historical Journal* 23, no. 4 (December): 913–37.

Sageser, Adelbert Bower. 1935. *The First Two Decades of the Pendleton Act: A Study of Civil Service Reform.* Lincoln: University Studies of the University of Nebraska.

Sainty, J. C. 1972. *Treasury Officials: 1660–1870.* London: Athlone Press for the University of London.

———. 1974. *Officials of the Board of Trade: 1660–1870.* London: Athlone Press for the University of London.

———. 1975. *Home Office Officials, 1782–1870.* London: Athlone Press for the University of London.

———. 1976. *Colonial Office Officials.* London: University of London, Institute of Historical Research.

Sakata, Yoshio. 1960. *Meiji ishinshi.* Tokyo: Miraisha.

Sakata, Yoshio, and John W. Hall. 1956. The motivation of political leadership in the Meiji Restoration. *Journal of Asian Studies* 16: 31–50.

Sanderson, Michael. 1975. *The Universities in the Nineteenth Century.* London: Routledge & Kegan Paul.

Saurin, M. 1964–1965. L'École d'adminstration de 1848. *Politique,* nos. 25–32: 105–95.

Schiesl, Martin J. 1977. *The Politics of Efficiency: Municipal Administration and Reform in America: 1880–1920.* Berkeley: University of California Press.

Schlesinger, Joseph A. 1966. *Ambition and Politics: Political Careers in the United States.* Chicago: Rand McNally.

466 Bibliography

Schmidt, Vivien. 1990. *Democratizing France: The Political and Administrative History of Decentralization.* New York: Cambridge University Press.

Schmitt, Karl. 1984. *Political Theology: Four Chapters on the Concept of Sovereignty.* Cambridge, MA: MIT Press.

Schudson, Michael. 1978. *Discovering the News: A Social History of American Newspapers.* New York: Basic Books.

Scott, Derek J. R. 1969. *Russian Political Institutions.* London: Allen and Unwin.

Seidman, Harold. 1980. *Politics, Position, and Power: The Dynamics of Federal Organization.* 3d ed. New York: Oxford University Press.

Seifu Kankei Tokushuhōjin Rōdōkumiai Kyōgikai. 1981. *Amakudari hakusho.* Tokyo: Seifu Kankei Tokushuhōjin Rōdōkumiai Kyōgikai.

Selznick, Philip. 1949. *TVA and the Grass Roots.* Berkeley: University of California Press.

————. 1957. *Leadership in Administration.* New York: Harper & Row.

Shafritz, Jay M. 1973. *Position Classification: A Behavioral Analysis for the Public Service.* New York: Praeger.

Shapiro, Ian. 1986. *The Evolution of Rights in Liberal Theory.* New York: Cambridge University Press.

Sharp, Walter Rice. 1931. *The French Civil Service: Bureaucracy in Transition.* New York: Macmillan.

Shefter, Martin. 1978a. Party, bureaucracy, and political change in the United States. In *Political Parties, Development, and Decay,* edited by Louis Maisel and Joseph Cooper, pp. 211–65. Beverly Hills, CA: Sage Publications.

————. 1978b. Party and patronage: Germany, England and Italy: *Politics and Society* 7: 403–51.

Sheriff, Peta E. 1972. Outsiders in a closed career: The example of the British Civil Service. *Public Administration* 50, no. 4 (Winter): 397–417.

————. 1975. Careers and the organization: Locals and cosmopolitans in the higher civil service. *International Review of Administrative Sciences* 41, no. 1: 29–36.

————. 1976a. *Career Patterns in the Higher Civil Service.* London: HMSO, Civil Service Studies; no. 2.

————. 1976b. Sociology of public bureaucracies, 1965–1975. *Current Sociology* 24, no. 2: 1–175.

Shinbori, Michiya. 1969. *Gakubatsu: Kono Nihonteki narumono.* Tokyo: Fujimura Shuppan.

Shinn, Terry. 1980. *L'École polytechnique: 1794–1914.* Paris: Presses de la Fondation nationale des sciences politiques.

Shōji, Kichinosuke. 1956. Jiyūminken undō no keizaiteki haikei. In *Jiyūminken undō,* edited by Meiji shiryō kenkyū renraku kai, pp. 188–236. Tokyo: Ochanomizu Shobō.

Sibert, Marcel. 1912. *Le concours comme mode juridique de recrutement de la fonction publique.* Paris.

Silberman, Bernard S. 1964. *Ministers of Modernization: Elite Mobility in the Meiji Restoration, 1868–1873.* Tucson: University of Arizona Press.

————. 1967. Bureaucratic development and the structure of decision-making in the

Meiji period: The case of the genrō. *Journal of Asian Studies* 27: 81–94. Reprinted in *Quantitative History,* edited by R. Graham and W. Downey, Homewood, IL: Dorsey Press, 1968; reprinted in John A. Harrison, ed., *Japan,* Tucson: University of Arizona Press for The Association for Asian Studies, 1972.

———. 1970. Bureaucratic development and the structure of decision-making in Japan: 1868–1925. *Journal of Asian Studies* 29: 347–62.

———. 1973. Ringi-sei—Traditional values or organizational imperatives in the Japanese upper civil service: 1868–1945. *Journal of Asian Studies* 32: 251–64.

———. 1976. Bureaucratization of the Meiji state: The problem of succession in the Meiji Restoration, 1868–1900. *Journal of Asian Studies* 35: 421–30.

———. 1978. Bureaucratic development and bureaucratization: The case of Japan. *Social Science History,* no. 2 (Summer): 385–98.

———. 1982. The bureaucratic state in Japan: The problem of authority and legitimacy. In *Dimensions of Conflict in Modern Japan,* edited by Tetsuo Najita and J. Victor Koschmann, pp. 226–57. Princeton, NJ: Princeton University Press.

Silberman, Bernard S., and H. D. Harootunian, eds. 1966. *Modern Japanese Leadership: Transition and Change.* Tucson: University of Arizona Press.

———. 1974. *Japan in Crisis: Essays in Taisho Democracy.* Princeton, NJ: Princeton University Press.

Silbey, Joel H. 1985. *The Partisan Imperative: The Dynamics of American Politics Before the Civil War.* New York: Oxford University Press.

Silva, Edward, and Sheila A. Slaughter. 1984. *Serving Power: The Making of the Academic Social Science Expert.* Westport, CT: Greenwood Press.

Silvera, Victor, and Serge Salon. 1969. *La Fonction publique et ses problèmes actuels.* Paris: Éditions de "l'Actualité juridique."

Simon, Brian. 1960. *Studies in the History of Education, 1780–1870.* London: Lawrence & Wishart.

———. 1987. Systematisation and segmentation in education: The case of England. In *The Rise of the Modern Educational System: Structural Changes and Social Reproduction 1870–1920,* pp. 88–108. New York: Cambridge University Press.

Simon, Herbert A. 1957. *Models of Man.* New York: Wiley.

———. 1972 [1982]. Theories of bounded rationality. In *Decision and Organization,* edited by C. B. McGuire and Roy Radner, pp. 161–76. Amsterdam: North-Holland. Reprinted in Herbert A. Simon, *Models of Bounded Rationality: Behavioral Economics and Business Organization,* pp. 408–23. Cambridge, MA: MIT Press.

———. 1973. Applying information technology to organization design. *Public Administration Review* 33, no. 3: 268–78.

———. 1976. *Administrative Behavior.* 3d ed. New York: Free Press.

———. 1979. Rational decision making in business organizations. *American Economic Review* 69, no. 4 (September): 493–513.

Siwek-Pouydesseau, Jeanne. 1969a. *Le Corps préfectoral sous la Troisième et la Quatrième République.* Paris: Armand Colin.

———. 1969b. *Le Personnel de direction des ministères, cabinets ministériels et directeurs d'administrations centrales.* Paris: Armand Colin.

————. 1975. French ministerial staffs. In *The Mandarins of Western Europe,* edited by Mattei Dogan, pp. 196–209. New York: Halsted Press.

Sklar, Martin J. 1988. *The Corporate Reconstruction of American Capitalism, 1890–1916.* New York: Cambridge University Press.

Skocpol, Theda. 1979. *States and Social Revolutions: A Comparative Analysis of France, Russia and China.* New York: Cambridge University Press.

————. 1985. Bringing the state back in: Strategies of analysis in current research. In *Bringing the State Back In,* edited by Peter B. Evans, Dietrich Reuschemeyer, and Theda Skocpol, pp. 3–37. New York: Cambridge University Press.

Skowronek, Stephen. 1982. *Building a New American State: The Expansion of National Administrative Capacities, 1877–1920.* New York: Cambridge University Press.

Small, Albion W. 1909 [1962]. *The Cameralists: The Pioneers of German Social Polity.* New York: Burt Franklin. [Reprint.]

Smith, Brian C. 1982. Reform and change in British central administration. *Political Studies* 19, no. 2 (June): 213–26.

Smith, Robert J. 1982. *The École Normale Supérieure and the Third Republic.* Albany: State University of New York Press.

Snelling, R. C., and T. J. Barron. 1972. The Colonial Office and its permanent officials, 1801–1914. In *Studies in the Growth of Nineteenth-Century Government,* edited by Gillian Sutherland, pp. 139–66. London: Routledge and Kegan Paul.

Soboul, Albert. 1968. *La Première République, 1792–1804.* Paris: Calmann-Lévy.

————. 1977. *A Short History of the French Revolution: 1789–1799.* Berkeley: University of California Press.

Sontheimer, Kurt, and Wilhelm Bleek. 1973. *Abschied vom Berufbeamtentum?* Hamburg: Hoffman & Campe.

Southgate, Donald 1962. *The Passing of the Whigs, 1832–1886.* London: Macmillan.

Spaulding, Robert M., Jr. 1967. *Imperial Japan's Higher Civil Service Examinations.* Princeton, NJ: Princeton University Press.

Spence, A. M. 1975. The economics of internal organization: An introduction. *The Bell Journal of Economics* 6, no. 1: 163–72.

Spinetti, Gastone Silvano. 1964. *Parlamentarismo e burocrazia: pubblica amministrazione sotto inchiesta, parta prima: 1860–1945.* Rome: Edizioni di Solidarismo.

Spoat, John G. 1968. *The Best Men: Liberal Reformers in the Gilded Age.* New York: Oxford University Press.

Sponholtz, Lloyd L. 1973. The initiative and referendum: Direct democracy in perspective, 1898–1920. *American Studies* 14, no. 2 (Fall): 43–64.

Stack, Freida. 1969. Civil service associations and the Whitley Report of 1917. *Political Quarterly* 40, no. 3 (July–Sept.): 283–95.

Stanley, David T. 1964. *The Higher Civil Service: An Evaluation of Federal Personnel Practices.* Washington, DC: The Brookings Institution.

Stanley, David T., Dean E. Mann, and Jameson W. Doig. 1967. *Men Who Govern.* Washington, DC: The Brookings Institution.

Starbuck, William. 1981. A trip to view the elephants and rattlesnakes in the Garden of Aston. In *Perspectives on Organization Design and Behavior,* edited by Andrew H. Van de Ven and William F. Joyce, pp. 167–99. New York: Wiley.

Steedman, Hilary. 1987. Defining institutions: The endowed grammar schools and the systematisation of English secondary education. In *The Rise of the Modern Educational System: Structural Changes and Social Reproduction, 1870–1920,* edited by Detlef K. Müller, Fritz Ringer, and Brian Simon, pp. 111–34. New York: Cambridge University Press.

Steers, Richard M. 1975. Problems in the measurement of organizational effectiveness. *Administrative Science Quarterly* 20 (December): 546–58.

Steinkemper, Bärbel. 1974. *Klassische und politische Bürokraten in der Ministerialverwaltung der Bundesrepublik Deutschland.* Cologne: Carl Heymanns Verlag.

Stewart, Frank Mann. 1950. *A Half-Century of Municipal Reform: The History of the National Municipal League.* Berkeley: University of California Press.

Stewart, Robert. 1978. *The Foundation of the Conservative Party 1830–1867.* New York: Longman.

———. 1989. *Party and Politics, 1830–1852.* New York: St. Martin's Press.

Stewart, Rosemary. 1983. Managerial behaviour: How research has changed the traditional picture. In *Perspectives on Management: A Multidisciplinary Analysis,* edited by Michael J. Earl, pp. 82–98. New York: Oxford University Press.

Stiglitz, Joseph E. 1975. Incentives, risk, and information: Notes toward a theory of hierarchy. *Bell Journal of Economics* 6, no. 2 (Autumn): 552–79.

Stillman, Richard J., II. [1990] 1991. *Preface to Public Administration: A Search for Themes and Direction.* New York: St. Martin's Press.

Stinchcombe, Arthur L. 1959. Bureaucratic and craft administration of production: A comparative study. *Administrative Science Quarterly* 4 (September): 168–87.

———. 1965. Social structure and the founding of organizations. In *Handbook of Organizations,* edited by James G. March, pp. 142–93. Chicago: Rand McNally.

———. 1990. *Information and Organizations.* Berkeley: University of California Press.

Stone, Katherine. 1973. The origins of job structures in the steel industry. *Radical America* 7, no. 6 (November): 19–64.

Stone, Lawrence. 1974. The size and composition of the Oxford student body, 1580–1909. In *The University in Society,* 2 vols., *Volume I: Oxford and Cambridge from the 14th to the Early 19th Century,* edited by Lawrence Stone, pp. 3–110. Princeton, NJ: Princeton University Press.

Studienkommission für die Reform des offentlichen Dienstrechts. 1973. *Bericht der Kommission.* Baden-Baden: der Kommission.

Sule, Tibor. 1988. *Preussische Burokratietradition: zur Entwicklung von Verwaltung u. Beamtenschaft in Deutschland 1871–1918.* Göttingen: Vandenhoeck u. Ruprecht.

Suleiman, Ezra N. 1970. The French bureaucracy and its students: Toward the desanctification of the state. *World Politics* 23, no. 1 (October): 121–70.

———. 1974. *Politics, Power, and Bureaucracy in France: The French Administrative Elite.* Princeton, NJ: Princeton University Press.

———. 1978. *Elites in French Society: The Politics of Survival.* Princeton, NJ: Princeton University Press.

———. 1987. *Private Power and Centralization in France: The Notaires and the State.* Princeton, NJ: Princeton University Press.

Sutherland, Donald M. G. 1986. *France, 1789–1815: Revolution and Counterrevolution.* New York: Oxford University Press.

Sutherland, Gillian. 1972. Administrators in education after 1870: Patronage, professionalism, and expertise. In *Studies in the Growth of Nineteenth-Century Government,* edited by Gillian Sutherland, pp. 263–85. London: Routledge and Kegan Paul.

———, ed. 1972. *Studies in the Growth of Nineteenth-Century Government.* London: Routledge and Kegan Paul.

Suzuki, Yasuzō. 1944. *Dajōkansei to naikakusei.* Tokyo: Bunshōdō Shoten.

———. 1948. *Jiyūminken.* Tokyo: Sayusha.

Sydenham, M. 1961. *The Girondins.* London: University of London, Athlone Press.

Sylvester, D. W. 1974. *Robert Lowe and Education.* Cambridge: Cambridge University Press.

Szasz, Ferenc M. 1972. Protestantism and the search for stability: Liberal and Conservative quests for a Christian America, 1875–1925. In *Building the Organizational Society: Essays on Associational Activities in Modern America,* edited by Jerry Israel, pp. 88–102. New York: Free Press.

Takane, Masaaki. 1981. *The Political Elite in Japan.* Berkeley: Institute of East Asian Studies, University of California.

Taniuchi, Yuzuru, ed. 1974. *Gendai gyōsei to kanryōsei.* Tokyo: Tōkyō Daigaku Shuppankai.

Tardieu, Andre. 1937. *La profession parlementaire.* Paris: E. Flammarion.

Taylor, Henry. 1927. *The Statesman.* Cambridge: W. Heffer and Sons Limited.

Teaford, Jon C. 1984. *Unheralded Triumph: City Government in America, 1870–1900.* Baltimore: Johns Hopkins University Press.

Teece, David J. 1982. Towards an economic theory of the multiproduct firm. *Journal of Economic Behavior and Organization* 3, no. 1 (March): 39–64.

Terreberry, Shirley. 1968. The evolution of organizational environments. *Administrative Science Quarterly* 12 (March): 590–613.

Thelen, David P. 1972. *The New Citizenship: Origins of Progressivism in Wisconsin, 1885–1900.* Columbia: University of Missouri Press.

Therborn, Goran. 1978. *What Does the Ruling Class Do When It Rules?* London: New Left Books.

Thoenig, Jean Claude. 1973. *L'ère des technocrates. Le cas des ponts et chaussées.* Paris: Les Éditions d'organisation.

Thomas, J. A. 1950. The system of registration and the development of party organization, 1832–1870. *History* 35 (Feb.–June): 81–98.

Thompson, Edward P. 1975. *Whigs and Hunters: The Origins of the Black Act.* New York: Pantheon.

Thompson, James D. 1967. *Organizations in Action.* New York: McGraw-Hill.

Thompson, Margaret Susan. 1985. *The "Spider Web": Congress and Lobbying in the Age of Grant.* Ithaca, NY: Cornell University Press.

Thompson, Victor A. 1977. *Modern Organization.* 2d ed. Tuscaloosa, AL: University of Alabama Press.

Thuillier, Guy. 1980. *Bureaucratie et bureaucrates en France au IXe siècle*. Genève: Librairie Droz.

Thuillier, Guy, and Jean Tulard. 1984. *Histoire de l'administration française*. Paris: Presses universitaires de France.

Tilly, Charles. 1975. Reflections on the history of European state-making. In *The Formation of National States in Western Europe*, edited by Charles Tilly, pp. 3–83. Princeton, NJ: Princeton University Press.

———. 1990. *Coercion, Capital, and European States: A.D. 990–1990*. Cambridge, MA: Basil Blackwell.

Titus, David A. 1974. *Palace and Politics in Prewar Japan*. New York: Columbia University Press.

Tocqueville, Alexis de. 1969. *Democracy in America*, edited by J.P. Mayer. Garden City, NY: Doubleday and Co., Inc.

Todisco, Umberto. 1969. *Le personnel de la cour des comptes (1807–1830)*. Genève: Librairie Droz.

Tolbert, Pamela S., and Lynne G. Zucker. 1983. Institutional sources of change in the formal structure of organizations: The diffusion of civil service reform, 1880–1935. *Administrative Science Quarterly* 28 (March): 22–39.

Totman, Conrad. 1967. *Politics in the Tokugawa Bakufu: 1600–1843*. Cambridge, MA: Harvard University Press.

Tōyama, Shigeki. 1951 *Meiji ishin*. Tokyo: Iwanami.

———. 1968. *Meiji ishin to gendai*. Tokyo: Iwanami.

Tōyama Shigeki, Hayashi Shigeru, et al. 1956. *Jiyūminken undō*. Tokyo: Ochanomizu Shobō.

Tranchant, M. Charles. 1878. *De la préparation aux services publics en France: Améliorations dont l'enseignment politique et administratif serait susceptible sous sa forme générale*. Paris: Berger-Levrault et Cie.

Treves, Giuseppino. 1966. *L'Organizzazione Amministrativa*. Milan: Edizioni di Comunit'a.

Trimberger, Ellen Kay. 1978. *Revolution from Above: Military Bureaucrats and Development in Japan, Turkey, Egypt and Peru*. New Brunswick, NJ: Transaction Books.

Tsuji, Kiyoaki. 1952. *Nihon kanryōsei no kenkyū*. Tokyo: Kōbundō.

———. 1968. Decision-making in the Japanese Government: A study of Ringisei. In *Political Development in Modern Japan*, edited by Robert E. Ward, pp. 457–76. Princeton, NJ: Princeton University Press.

———. 1982. Public administration in Japan: History and problems. *International Review of Administrative Sciences* 47, no. 2: 119–24.

———. 1984. *Public Administration in Japan*. Tokyo: University of Tokyo Press.

———, ed. 1976. *Gyōseigaku kōza:* Vol. 2, *Gyōsei no rekishi*. Tokyo: Tōkyō Daigaku Shuppankai.

Tudesq, André-Jean. 1964. *Les grands notables en France: 1840–1849*. Paris: Presses universitaires de France.

Tudesq, André-Jean, and André Jardin. 1973. *La France des notables*. Paris: Éditions du Seuil.

Tulard, Jean. 1976. *Paris et son administration: 1800–1830*. Paris: Ville de Paris, Commission des travaux historiques.

———. 1977. Les Épurations administratives en France de 1800 à 1830. In *Les Épurations administratives: XIXe et XXe siècles*, edited by Paul Gerbod et al., pp. 49–62. Genève: Librairie Droz.

Tullock, Gordon. 1965. *The Politics of Bureaucracy*. Washington, DC: Public Affairs Press.

Udy, Stanley H., Jr. 1959. 'Bureaucracy' and 'rationality' in Weber's organization theory: An empirical study. *American Sociological Review* 24, no. 6 (December): 791–95.

Ule, Carl Hermann, ed. 1961. *Die Entwicklung des offentlichen Dienstes*. Cologne: Heymann.

Unger, Irwin, and Debi Unger. 1977. *The Vulnerable Years: The United States, 1896–1917*. Hinsdale, IL: Dryden Press.

United States, Bureau of the Census. 1960. *Historical Statistics of the United States: Colonial Times to 1957*. Washington, DC: U.S. Government Printing Office.

United States, Civil Service Commission. 1884–1931. *Annual Report, 1883–1931*. Washington, DC: U.S. Government Printing Office.

Urban, Michael E. 1982. *The Ideology of Administration: American and Soviet Cases*. Albany: State University of New York Press.

Van de Ven, Andrew, Andre Delbecq, and Richard Koenig. 1976. Determinants of coordination: Modes within organizations. *American Sociological Review* 41 (April): 332–38.

Van Riper, Paul P. 1958a. *History of the United States Civil Service*. Evanston, IL: Row, Peterson and Co.

———. 1958b. The senior civil service and the career system. *Public Administration Review* 18, no. 3 (Summer): 189–200.

Vaughan, Michalina. 1969. The Grandes Écoles. In *Governing Elites: Studies in Training and Selection*, edited by Rupert Wilkinson, pp. 74–107. New York: Oxford University Press.

Vaughan, Michalina, and Margaret Scotford Archer. 1971. *Social Conflict and Educational Change in England and France, 1789–1848*. Cambridge: Cambridge University Press.

Vidalenc, Jean. 1976. *Textes sur l'histoire de la Seine Inférieure à la epoque napoléonienne: 1800–1814*. Rouen: R.D.P.

Vincent, J. R. 1976. *The Formation of the British Liberal Party, 1857–1868*. Sussex, England: The Harvester Press, Ltd.

Vivien, Alexandre François August. 1859. *Études administratives*, 2 vols. Paris: Librairie de Guillaumin.

Vulliez, Christian. 1970. *Les grands corps de l'état*. Paris: Dunod.

Wamsley, Gary, and Mayer N. Zald. 1973. *The Political Economy of Public Organizations*. Lexington, MA: Lexington Books.

Ward, Robert E., ed. 1968. *Political Development in Modern Japan*. Princeton, NJ: Princeton University Press.

Warner, W. Lloyd, and J. O. Low. 1947. *The Social System of the Modern Factory.* New Haven, CT: Yale University Press.

Warner, W. Lloyd, P. Van Riper, N. H. Martin, O. F. Collins. 1963. *The American Federal Executive.* New Haven, CT: Yale University Press.

Weber, Max. 1947. *The Theory of Social and Economic Organizations,* translated and edited by Talcott Parsons. London: W. Hodge.

———. 1949. *The Methodology of the Social Sciences,* translated and edited by Edward Shils and Henry A. Finch. Glencoe, IL: Free Press.

———. 1958. *The Protestant Ethic and the Spirit of Capitalism.* New York: Charles Scribner's Sons.

———. 1978. *Economy and Society.* 2 vols., edited by Guenther Roth and Claus Wittich. Berkeley: University of California Press.

Weick, Karl E. 1979. *The Social Psychology of Organizing.* 2d ed. Reading, MA: Addison-Wesley.

Weisbrod, Burton. 1968. Income redistribution effects and benefit-cost analysis. In *Problems in Public Expenditure Analysis,* edited by Samuel B. Chase, Jr., pp. 177–209. Washington, DC: The Brookings Institution.

Weiss, John H. 1982. *The Making of Technological Man: The Social Origins of French Engineering Education.* Cambridge, MA: MIT Press.

———. 1984. Bridges and barriers: Narrowing access and changing structure in the French engineering profession, 1800–1850. In *Professions and the French State, 1700–1900,* edited by Gerald L. Geison, pp. 15–65. Philadelphia: University of Pennsylvania Press.

Weisz, George. 1983. *The Emergence of Modern Universities in France, 1863–1914.* Princeton, NJ: Princeton University Press.

Welch, Claude, Jr., ed. 1967. *Political Modernization.* Belmont, CA: Wadsworth Publishing Co.

Wheare, K. C. 1978. Civil service. In *Aspects of Government in Nineteenth-Century Britain,* edited by P. and G. Ford, pp. 5–40. Dublin: Irish Academic Press, Ltd.

White, Leonard D. 1954. *The Jacksonians: A Study in Administrative History, 1829–1861.* New York: Macmillan Company.

———. 1958. *The Republican Era: 1869–1901, A Study in Administrative History.* New York: Macmillan Company.

———. 1965. *The Federalists: A Study in Administrative History, 1789–1828.* New York: The Free Press.

White, Robert D. 1984. Position analysis and characterization. *Review of Public Personnel Administration* 4 (Spring): 57–67.

Wiebe, Robert H. 1967. *The Search for Order, 1877–1920.* New York: Hill and Wang.

Wildavsky, Aaron. 1968. The political economy of efficiency: Cost-benefit analysis, systems analysis, and program budgeting. In *Political Science and Public Policy,* edited by Austin Ranney, pp. 55–82. Chicago: Markham Publishing Co.

Wilensky, Harold L. 1964. The professionalization of everyone? *American Journal of Sociology* 70, no. 2 (September): 137–58.

Wilkinson, Rupert. 1964. *Gentlemanly Power: British Leadership and the Public School Tradition.* New York: Oxford University Press.

Williams, E. Neville, ed. 1960. *The Eighteenth Century Constitution: 1688–1815.* New York: Cambridge University Press.

Williams, Walter. 1971. *Social Policy Research and Analysis.* New York: American Elsevier.

Williamson, Oliver E. 1964. *The Economics of Discretionary Behavior: Managerial Objectives in a Theory of the Firm.* Englewood Cliffs, NJ: Prentice-Hall.

———. 1975. *Markets and Hierarchies: Analysis and Antitrust Implications.* New York: Free Press.

———. 1976. *The Evolution of Hierarchy: An Essay on the Organization of Work.* New York: Norton.

———. 1981. The modern corporation: Origins, evolution, attributes. *Journal of Economic Literature* 19 (December): 1,537–68.

———. 1983. Organizational innovation: The transaction cost approach. In *Entrepreneurship,* edited by Joshua Ronen, pp. 101–39. Lexington, MA: Heath Lexington.

———. 1984. The economics of governance: Framework and implications. *Journal of Theoretical Economics* 140 (March): 195–223.

———. 1985. *The Economic Institutions of Capitalism: Firms, Markets, Relational Contracting.* New York: Free Press.

Wilson, James Q. 1975. The rise of the bureaucratic state. *The Public Interest* 41 (Fall): 77–103.

Wilson, Robert. 1957. *Genesis of the Meiji Government in Japan, 1868–1871.* Berkeley: University of California Press.

Winter, James. 1976. *Robert Lowe.* Toronto: University of Toronto Press.

Wishnia, Judith. 1978. French Fonctionnaires: The development of class consciousness and unionization, 1884–1926. Ph.D. diss., State University of New York at Stony Brook.

Wolin, Sheldon. 1960. *Politics and Vision: Continuity and Innovation in Western Political Thought.* Boston: Little, Brown & Co.

Woodward, Joan. 1958. *Management and Technology.* London: HMSO.

———. 1965. *Industrial Organization: Theory and Practice.* Oxford, UK: Oxford University Press.

Wright, D. G. 1970. *Democracy and Reform.* Harlow, Essex, UK: Longman Group, Ltd.

Wright, Maurice. 1969. *Treasury Control of the Civil Service, 1854–1874.* Oxford: Clarendon Press.

———. 1972. Treasury control, 1854–1914. In *Studies in the Growth of Nineteenth-Century Government,* edited by Gillian Sutherland, pp. 195–226. London: Routledge & Kegan Paul.

Wright, Vincent. 1972. *Le Conseil d'État sous le second Empire.* Paris: Armand Colin.

———. 1976. Les Directeurs et secretaire generaux des administrations centrales sous le second empire. In *Les Directeurs de Ministère en France (XIXe–XXe siècles),* pp. 38–50. Genève: Librairie Droz.

————. 1977. Les épurations administratives de 1848 à 1895. In *Les épurations administratives: XIXe et XXe siècles,* edited by Paul Gerbod et al., pp. 69–80. Genève: Librairie Droz.

Wright, Vincent, and Bernard Le Clère. 1973. *Les Préfets du second Empire.* Paris: Armand Colin.

Yamanaka, Einosuke. 1974. *Nihon kindai kokka no keisei to kanryōsei.* Tokyo: Kōbundō.

Yamazaki, Tanshō. 1942. *Naikaku seido no kenkyū.* Tokyo: Kōzan Shoin.

Zald, Mayer N. 1970. Political economy: A framework for analysis. In *Power in Organizations,* edited by Mayer N. Zald, pp. 221–61. Nashville, TN: Vanderbilt University Press.

————, ed. 1970. *Power in Organizations.* Nashville, TN: Vanderbilt University Press.

Zeckhauser, Richard, and Elmer Schaefer. 1968. Public policy and normative economic theory. In *The Study of Policy Formation,* edited by Raymond A. Bauer and Kenneth J. Gergen, pp. 27–102. New York: Free Press.

Zeldin, Theodore. 1958. *The Political System of Napoleon III.* New York: W. W. Norton & Co.

Index

Aberdeen coalition, 365

Accountability, 5–6, 23, 69, 72, 77–79, 81–82; in France, 90; in Great Britain, 316, 328–29, 333, 352–54, 358, 363, 369, 380

Adams, John, 239

Administrative autonomy, 55–56, 77–79, 82; in France, 91–92, 106, 128, 143; in Great Britain, 314–15, 333–35, 387, 394; in the United States, 249, 281–82

Administrative hierarchy, 2, 5, 13, 21–23, 27, 39, 64, 74–75, 117; in France, 91, 107–8, 116; in Great Britain, 292–93, 296, 352–53, 396; in Japan, 180, 186; and predictability, 11; in the United States, 231, 261, 281

Administrative ideology, 58–59

Administrative Reform Association (U.K.), 294, 365–67, 369

Administrative Reform Investigation Office (Japan), 203

Administrative Reform Society (U.K.), 296

Administrative role, 4, 72, 120; and autonomy, 5, 12–13, 59, 63, 65–67; as boundaries of decision making, 57; characteristics of, 9–10; as hallmark of U.S. administrative structure, 229; in Japan, 161, 164; organization of, 11; and patterns of institutionalization, 14; predictability of, 13; structure of, 39; and subordinates, 40; transformation of, 4–6

Agency, 23

American Civil War, 249–51

American Free Trade League, 254

American Social Science Association, 253, 265

Anderson, Olive, 294

Appointment, 10, 12; in France, 97, 133; in Great Britain, 313, 337, 370, 394, 396, 398, 406; in Japan, 172; in the United States, 230, 233. See also Patronage

Armstrong, John A., 10

Arnold, Matthew, 352

Arnold, Thomas, 380

Arthur, Chester, 259, 264

Association of the Bar of the City of New York, 265

Australia, 7

Authority, 1, 21, 31, 57, 63; charismatic, 6; distinctions in, 11; in Great Britain, 344; hierarchical, 2, 24, 27; in Japan, 174–76, 178–79, 189, 195–96; legal-rational, 6, 41; organizational, 29; traditional, 6–7; in the United States, 244

Bagehot, Walter, 346

Baines, Edward, 385

Bank of the United States, 238

Bedfords, 319

Bendix, Reinhard, 288

Bentham, Jeremy, 297, 338

Boston Reform League, 254

Bounded rationality, 29, 31, 34, 49; defined, 20n; as explanation of bureaucratic rationalization, 20–24

Bourbon Monarchy, 121

Brewer, John, 30

Browning, Oscar, 378

Brumaireans, 105, 107–8, 111. See also Eighteenth Brumaire

Bryan, William Jennings, 267

Buchanan, James, 243, 248

Budgets, 77

Bureau for the Investigation of Administrative Reforms (Japan), 196

Bureaucratization, 14, 69, 411

Burke, Edmund, 299–300, 324, 333, 335–36

Butler, Benjamin, 255

Cambaceres, 108

Canada, 7, 14, 83

Capitalism, 7–8, 231–32; and accumulation, 30; structure of, 30

Career structure, 2, 10, 13, 53, 62–63, 74–75, 77; and early commitment, 10–11, 60–62; fast-tracks, 13; in France, 92, 94, 96, 117, 136, 142–45; in Great Britain,